Politics in Pacific Asia

COMPARATIVE GOVERNMENT AND POLITICS

Published

Maura Adshead and Jonathan Tonge
Politics in Ireland

Rudy Andeweg and Galen A. Irwin
Governance and Politics of the Netherlands (4th edition)

Tim Bale
European Politics: A Comparative Introduction (3rd edition)

Nigel Bowles and Robert K. McMahon
Government and Politics of the United States (3rd edition)

Paul Brooker
Non-Democratic Regimes (3rd edition)

Kris Deschouwer
The Politics of Belgium: Governing a Divided Society (2nd edition)

Robert Elgie
Political Leadership in Liberal Democracies

Rod Hague, Martin Harrop and John McCormick
*** Comparative Government and Politics: An Introduction (10th edition)**

Paul Heywood
The Government and Politics of Spain

Xiaoming Huang
Politics in Pacific Asia

B. Guy Peters
Comparative Politics: Theories and Methods
[Rights: World excluding North America]

Tony Saich
Governance and Politics of China (4th edition)

Eric Shiraev
Russian Government and Politics (2nd edition)

Anne Stevens
Government and Politics of France (3rd edition)

Ramesh Thakur
The Government and Politics of India

Forthcoming

Tim Haughton
Government and Politics of Central and Eastern Europe

Robert Leonardi
Government and Politics of Italy

Tim Bale
European Politics: A Comparative Introduction (4th edition)

* Published in North America as **Political Science: A Comparative Introduction (8th edition)**

Comparative Government and Politics
Series Standing Order
ISBN 978–0–333–71693–9 hardback
ISBN 978–0–333–69335–3 paperback
(outside North America only)

You can receive future titles in this series as they are published by placing a standing order. Please contact your bookseller for more information.

Politics in Pacific Asia

AN INTRODUCTION

2nd edition

XIAOMING HUANG

JASON YOUNG

First edition 2009 by
PALGRAVE

Second edition 2017 by
PALGRAVE

Palgrave in the UK is an imprint of Macmillan Publishers Limited, registered in England, company number 785998, of 4 Crinan Street, London, N1 9XW.

Palgrave® and Macmillan® are registered trademarks in the United States, the United Kingdom, Europe and other countries.

ISBN 978–1–137–46649–5 hardback
ISBN 978–1–137–46648–8 paperback

This book is printed on paper suitable for recycling and made from fully managed and sustained forest sources. Logging, pulping and manufacturing processes are expected to conform to the environmental regulations of the country of origin.

A catalogue record for this book is available from the British Library.

A catalog record for this book is available from the Library of Congress.

Printed and bound by CPI Group (UK) Ltd, Croydon, CR0 4YY

Contents

List of Illustrative Material

Country Profile

Pacific Asian Politics in Context

Case Study Lab

Boxes

Map

Figures

Tables

List of Abbreviations and Acronyms

ADB Asian Development Bank
ABRI Armed Forces of the Republic of Indonesia (Angkatan Bersenjata Republik Indonesia)
APEC Asia-Pacific Economic Cooperation
APT ASEAN Plus Three
ARF ASEAN Regional Forum
ASEAN Association of Southeast Asian Nations
CCYL Chinese Community Youth League (China)
CDC Community Development Council (Singapore)
CPC Communist Party of China
CPI Corruption Perception Index (Transparency International)
CPPCC Chinese People's Political Consultative Conference
CSCAP Council for Security Cooperation in the Asia-Pacific
DJP Democratic Justice Party (South Korea)
DPD Regional Representative Council (Dewan Perwakilan Daerah, Indonesia)
DPJ Democratic Party of Japan
DPP Democratic Progressive Party (Taiwan)
DPR People's Representative Council (Dewan Perwakilan Rakyat, Indonesia)
DPRK Democratic People's Republic of Korea (North Korea)
DRP Democratic Republican Party (South Korean)
DRV Democratic Republic of Vietnam (DRV)
EAEG East Asia Economic Group
EAS East Asian Summit
FPTP first-past-the-post
FTAAP Asia-Pacific Free Trade Agreement
GCI Global Competitiveness Index
GDP gross domestic product
GNI gross national income
GNP Grand National Party (South Korea)
GOLKAR Party of the Functional Groups (Partai Golongan Karya, Indonesia)
GRC Group Representation Constituency (Singapore)
HDI Human Development Index
IMF International Monetary Fund
JCP Japanese Communist Party
JSP Socialist Party of Japan
KBL New Society Movement (Kilusan Bagong Lipunan, Philippines)
KMT Nationalist Party (Kuo Min Tang, Taiwan)
LDP Liberal Democratic Party (Japan)
LPJ Liberal Party of Japan
MCA Malaysian Chinese Association
MITI Ministry of International Trade and Industry (Japan)
MMD multi-member district
MMP mixed member proportional
MNLF Moro National Liberation Front (Philippines)
MPR People's Consultative Assembly (Majelis Permusyawaratan Rakyat, Indonesia)
NATO North Atlantic Treaty Organization
NCMPs Non-Constituency Members of Parliament (NCMPs, Singapore)
NDC National Defense Commission (North Korea)
NEP New Economic Policy (Malaysia)
NGO Non-governmental organization
NMPs Nominated Members of Parliament (Singapore)
NPC National People's Congress (China)
NPM New Public Management
NTUC National Trades Union Congress (Singapore)
PA People's Association (Singapore)
PA-18 Pacific Asian 18 countries and territories covered in this text: Brunei, Cambodia, China, Hong Kong, Indonesia, Japan, South Korea, Laos, Macao, Malaysia, Mongolia, Myanmar, North Korea, Philippines, Singapore, Taiwan, Thailand and Vietnam.

PAP	People's Action Party (Singapore)
PARC	Political Affairs Research Council (LDP, Japan)
PKI	Communist Party of Indonesia
PLA	People's Liberation Army (China)
PPP	purchasing power parity
PR	proportional representation
PRC	People's Republic of China (China)
PAS	Pan-Malaysian Islamic Party
RCEP	Regional Comprehensive Economic Partnership
ROC	Republic of China (Taiwan)
SATU	Singapore Association of Trade Unions
SCAP	Supreme Commander of the Allied Powers (Occupation authorities in post-War Japan)
SCO	Shanghai Cooperation Organization
SMD	single-member district
SNTV	single non-transferable vote
SPA	Supreme People's Assembly (North Korea)
SPDC	State Peace and Development Council (Myanmar)
SRV	Socialist Republic of Vietnam
TPP	Trans-Pacific Partnership
TRT	Thais Love Thais Party (Thai Rak Thai, Thailand)
UMNO	United Malays' National Organization (Malaysia)
UNDP	United Nations Development Programme
VCP	Vietnamese Communist Party
VFF	Vietnamese Fatherland Front
WDI	World Development Indicators (World Bank)
WGI	Worldwide Governance Indicators (World Bank)
WTO	World Trade Organization

Preface to Second Edition

We write this new edition with the same original intentions behind the first edition, to make the learning of politics in Pacific Asia an enjoyable experience and an effective intellectual exercise. When we look at government and politics in the region our challenge is to respond to political crises, tensions and conflicts and to identify problems and issues in order to recommend well-informed options and solutions. Yet what we learn and indeed what we teach in politics in Pacific Asia is not always effective for making us better equipped to analyse and explain these issues or to forecast future development in the region.

This new edition reflects our thinking based on feedback from students, professors and practitioners in the public and private sector. Much has changed since the first edition. Dynamic and constant change seems to be a key feature of government and politics in Pacific Asia. In this new edition, we have thoroughly updated the content, reorganized the structure of the text and rationalized each chapter. In particular, we have tried to drive home the underlying theme that Pacific Asian government and politics function on a set of ever changing, dynamic institutions and processes. These institutions and processes are shaped by powerful political ideas of how we should organize the state and political society under modern conditions as well as the interests, capacity and influence of the political forces in play and the choices of platforms for political action. All these are working elements of the political structure that affect political order in a given society.

We also reflect on the idea that learning and teaching about Pacific Asian politics is not just about knowledge but also about skills and capacity. Students should not only gain knowledge but also acquire analytical and communicative skills that enable them to produce effective explanations and sound analysis of individual issues and problems in Pacific Asian politics. The new edition adds new content that showcases theories, approaches and methods for identifying, framing and analysing problems and issues in this subject area.

We hope this new edition provides a more effective framework and sufficient material for us to think, understand and analyse politics and government in Pacific Asia.

XMH
JY

Introduction

To write a textbook on politics and government in Pacific Asia is not an easy matter. Two things in particular make this a great challenge. First, the diversity of the region is unmatched anywhere else in the world. Since the 1950s, all the types of state and forms of government found in the world can be found in Pacific Asia. On various governance indicators, Pacific Asian countries exhibit greater differences among themselves than in comparison to other regions. As students of political science, we want to see patterns and regularities so that we can explain what happened and, if we are ambitious, ponder what might happen in the future. However, the great diversity of Pacific Asian politics defies easy generalizations.

Second, politics and government institutions have been changing constantly in Pacific Asia, much more than in any other region. As we shall demonstrate in Chapter 2, the twentieth century has been a century of change, reform and revolution for Pacific Asia. In the early 1950s, many of the new states embraced multiparty pluralist politics, while, in the 1970s, most Pacific Asian countries were under some form of non-pluralist politics. Political liberalization and democratic transition has swept across Pacific Asia since the mid-1980s. In some countries, there was a new constitution every couple of years. In others, political parties rose and fell like shares on the stock market. If a book was written about a Pacific Asian country five years ago, it is likely that it has become outdated today. Consequently, we do not have many 'classics' to refer to, as we would if studying other courses, such as political theory, and we must therefore treat the few old textbooks with caution.

This book is written with these concerns in mind. Throughout the text, diversity and change are emphasized as the underlying dynamics that shape government and politics in Pacific Asia. Identifying common themes in this diversity and using these to explain change has been a key task for the text. At the same time, the subject is treated as a coherent system of knowledge, organized with comparable concepts and frameworks in the discipline, as well as major debates on critical issues. Before we move on to explain further how this text should be used, let us define the subject matter in more detail.

What are Pacific Asian politics?

To begin our journey of inquiry into the politics of Pacific Asia, we need first to explain what people mean when they say 'Asia.' This is not simply a matter of geographical boundaries. According to a formal United Nations definition (as shown in Map 0.1), Asia is a continent of widely spread

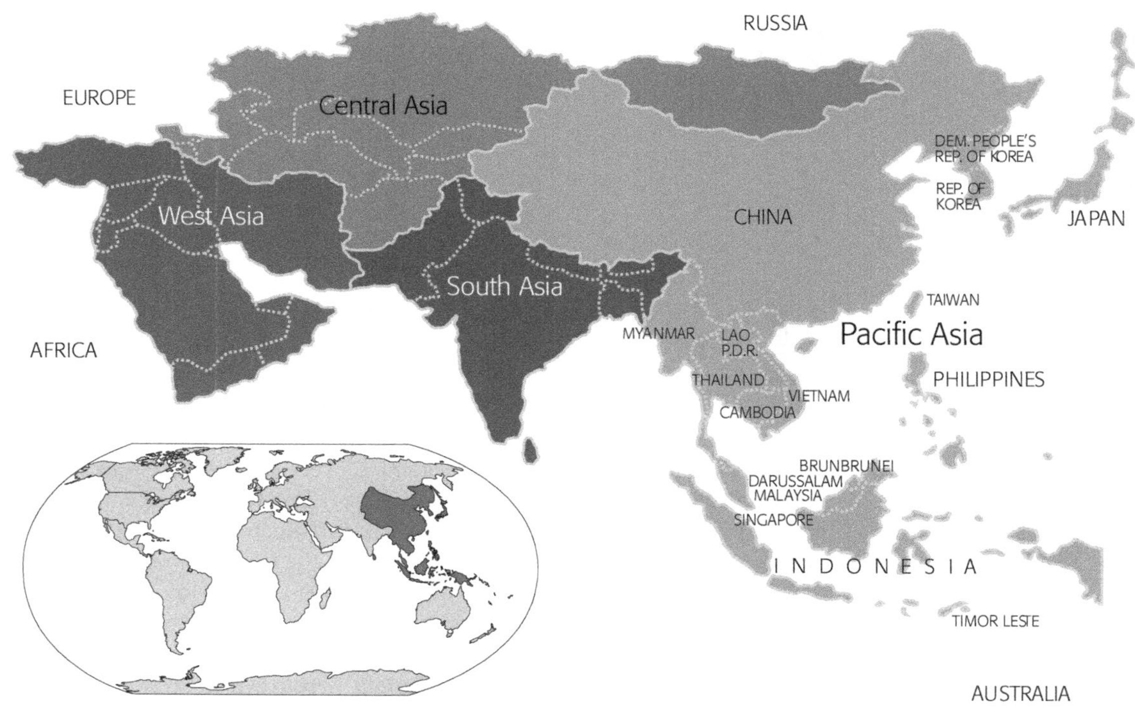

Map 0.1 Locating Pacific Asia

countries; from Turkey and Israel in the west (West Asia), to Japan and Korea in the east (East Asia); from Kazakhstan and Azerbaijan in the north (Central Asia), to India and Pakistan in the south (South Asia). And, of course, there are countries between the South and the East such as Indonesia and the Philippines (Southeast Asia). West Asia is more often referred to as 'the Middle East,' though the term is no longer useful in practice. Central Asia, on the other hand, tends to be discussed in its own right as a separate entity because of the recent history of being part of the Soviet Union.

> Diversity – geographic, cultural and political – is the overriding reality of the area we will call **Pacific Asia**, but the accompanying reality is one of interaction and mutual influence that makes a regional construct increasingly relevant and useful... This region excludes much that is traditionally embraced within the term 'Asia.' Omitted, for example, are 'South Asia' and the countries of 'Southwest Asia' ... Although Pacific Asia historically has had significant levels of interaction with these regions, its most recent cultural and economic orientations have been towards the Pacific littoral. Pacific Asia comprises *East Asia* and *Southeast Asia* ... two major sociogeographical subsets in the overarching concept of a Pacific Basin.
>
> Borthwick 2014: 7

When people talk about Asia today, in both media coverage and academic contexts, it is more likely that they are referring to a region that includes East Asia, South Asia and Southeast Asia.

This text, however, does not cover South Asia, which is nevertheless a very important part of Asia. It is not covered here not only for the reason that it is usually studied separately. Despite shared cultural and historical roots, modern developments in the region, especially since the end of the Second World War, have created a regional landscape where the interaction between Pacific Asia and South Asia has been much less than their interactions with their own sets of significant relations with Western Europe and North America.

Moreover, the rapid economic development in the second half of the twentieth century (see

Chapter 6) started in and spread primarily among Pacific Asian countries. Integrating forces of trade, investment and human movements set the region apart from South Asia (see Chapter 10 on regional integration). Finally, the Cold War geopolitical structure (Chapter 10) bore heavily upon Pacific Asian countries, shaping them into a self-sustained structure between two camps of ideological rivalry, economic competition and security conflict. This regional structure in turn produced a distinct pattern of domestic politics. There were one-party dominant states, military regimes and party-states for much of the Cold War period in many Pacific Asian countries. However, there has been a wave of transformations to pluralist politics since the late 1980s (see Chapter 2).

Pacific Asia is the part of Asia on or bordering the Pacific and includes the countries of Northeast Asia and Southeast Asia. Northeast and Southeast Asia are treated as a single region, not simply because of their geographical proximity, though that itself is a factor, but because they have together formed a unique region in world history and in the contemporary international system. Countries in the region share similar experiences in modern political development, have gone through similar processes of modern state building and face a similar set of issues and challenges in contemporary politics and governance. The region, while containing different parts such as continental East Asia and oceanic Southeast Asia that developed from various historical settings and that are structurally distinctive (Borthwick 2014: 11), is increasingly brought together by contemporary developments in regime change, geopolitical structure, security order and economic cooperation and integration.

What, then, is 'politics?' Politics can mean different things for different people. For political scientists, politics is an important area of human activities that includes those making or influencing law and policy in a governing body, those winning and holding control over such a governing body and those competing for power, influence and leadership in an organization.

Politics is an arena of human activities that make or influence law and policy in a governing body, win and hold control over such a governing body, and compete for power, influence and leadership in an organization.

Often scholars use politics and government together as a subject area of inquiry. This is also the case in this text for two reasons. First, even though not all politics is related to government, our focus here is on politics in 'the public sector,' the core of which is the government. Second, government structures, processes and institutions provide a principal platform for political activities and a focal point for political action. There are also other aspects that some people may consider as part of the definition, such as 'the total complex of relations between people living in society' (Merriam-Webster dictionary). While these aspects may have a bearing on politics, they are not politics in themselves and will be discussed here only as a background.

Patterns and dynamics of Pacific Asian politics

This book will cover a large number of countries in Pacific Asia and examine their rich political history and culture, diverse political institutions and processes and the complex interplays in these countries between politics and economy, state and society, the traditional and modern and the domestic and international. To learn about all of this is a great challenge. A key to being able to rise above the rich empirical information is to be sensitive to the underlying patterns and dynamics that give cause and meaning to what we observe. This is an intellectual habit that you will need to develop through this and other courses. But here we provide a brief introduction to the patterns and dynamics that we hope can make your navigation through the material in this book a little easier.

- *The hundred years of the making of the modern state:* The process of modern state building has not been an easy one. There have been different timeframes for different countries, with Japan starting in the late nineteenth century and most other countries after the Second World War. The process has also involved different models and different experiences. Post-Second World War political development in Pacific Asia witnessed an overall pattern of movement from multiparty pluralism in the 1950s to non-pluralist politics during the Cold War and finally to two dominant forms of polity today: pluralist and corporatist.

- *Unity in diversity:* Pacific Asian countries see significant differences in religion, ethnicity, social class, levels of economic development and historical paths of modern development within the countries as well as among them. Developing modern institutions and collective identities within this diversity involves higher levels of tension and instability in many Pacific Asian countries.
- *Institutions, culture and political structure:* Modern institutions, such as the constitution, public offices, elections, bureaucracy, branches of government and local governments, have to work in the context of the existing, or traditional, institutions, culture and values of the population, and with the underlying political structure. The existing institutions, culture and political structure may strengthen these modern institutions but, on a more fundamental level, may not necessarily be compatible with them. There has therefore been a dynamic interaction and persistent tension between the two.
- *Evolving methods of political order, change and participation:* The range of legitimate methods for politics in Pacific Asia has evolved during the twentieth century, reflecting the ascendance of modern values and institutions as well as the tension between formal institutions and informal cultural habits in political participation. Mass and violent protests, particularly those against the government, were not a preferred political method in traditional Pacific Asia, but have been practiced increasingly as a legitimate form of demand for change in government. Military intervention was a dominant method of political change in many Pacific Asian countries for much of the twentieth century, but has now largely been marginalized as a legitimate method. Increasingly, top-down political mobilization, autocratic decision-making, elite consultation and backdoor politics have been yielding to bottom-up participation, and open, transparent and institutionalized political competition. Moreover, informal institutions are now more predominant and therefore allow the underlying political structure and social relations to shape political participation.
- *State centrism:* It has been a core part of the political tradition as well as contemporary reality that the state plays a pivotal role in governing the polity, organizing the economy and managing society. Modern political, economic and social development within the country, together with globalization, have increasingly challenged state-centrism and 'eroded' state power, but the state is still central in government and politics in Pacific Asian countries.
- *Ambiguous Asia:* Relations between Pacific Asian countries and international society have been ambiguous. This has resulted partly from the diversity among the Pacific Asian countries themselves that present no unified identity to international society; partly from the double mindset that many Pacific Asian countries hold towards international society – where Asian countries view themselves as both victims of 'international society' and at the same time are eager to be accepted into and rise in such a society – and partly from the fact that many Pacific Asian countries are still developing, and the direction of their further development, their cultural and ideological identity and their future role in the international system remain unclear.

Pacific Asian politics in a comparative context

A primary reason for taking a course on politics and government in a specific region is to gain an in-depth understanding of how politics and government work in a particular cultural, historical and social environment, and therefore to enrich and enhance our knowledge of politics and government in general. International comparison is naturally a central theme for courses such as this. In this book, you will see references and discussions comparing and contrasting Pacific Asian countries with countries in other parts of the world. To guide you through this comparative aspect, some useful frameworks and questions are listed here as to why we compare, how we compare and what we expect to learn from comparative inquiry.

There can be many different reasons for wishing to compare Pacific Asian politics with politics and government in other regions of the world. We compare Pacific Asian politics with others because:

- We believe Pacific Asia is a subsystem of the international system. Therefore, such a comparison can yield knowledge as to how the general system of politics works.
- We believe that, at the fundamental level, politics in any country is essentially the same. Therefore, comparing Pacific Asian politics with others can tell us whether the fundamental elements of politics and government are manifested in different forms in Pacific Asia, and why – as well as what that means for our understanding of the fundamental nature of politics and government.
- We believe politics and government can be improved – modernized or developed. Therefore, putting Pacific Asian politics in a global context would allow us to see whether the patterns and dynamics of Pacific Asian politics are part of universal patterns, or if they represent unique paths of modern development or deviations from universal patterns.

A comprehensive comparison with all other regions would be outside the scope of this text. Here we shall identify a range of critical indicators that would allow us to ask some basic questions about politics and government across different cultures, regions and civilizations, and see how Pacific Asian politics compares with other regions on these indicators.

On Pacific Asia as a subsystem in the international system, we should ask:

- Whether politics and government in Pacific Asia are effects of the international system, or if they generate original ideas and material wealth, and set the agenda, values and institutional dynamics for the international system.
- Whether Pacific Asian politics and government are destabilizing or stabilizing forces for the international system.
- Whether political systems in Pacific Asia and the international system are compatible, whether the relationship is integrated or confrontational.

On Pacific Asian politics as instances of fundamental issues in modern politics and government, we should ask:

- How do the organizing principles of polity in Pacific Asia compare with those in other regions? What determines the organization of a political community?
- How does state capacity in Pacific Asian countries compare with countries in other regions? To what extent are they capable of managing mass society and modern society and economy?
- How do the historical experiences of modern political development in Pacific Asian countries compare with countries in other parts of the world?

Finally, on assessing Pacific Asian politics in terms of the tension between universal values and institutions and cultural and historical particularities, we should ask:

- How do the cultural and historical conditions in Pacific Asia affect the functions of modern institutions? Are such effects positive or negative for general human interests and purposes?
- Is the embedding of modern institutions in cultural and historical conditions unique only to Pacific Asian countries, or is it also found in other parts of the world?
- Can politics and government in a region share a more coherent collective identity and orientation than the extent seen in Pacific Asia?

The field of study

While politics and government have been an important part of Asian society for thousands of years, the study of Asian politics has not really matched this. There are two primary sources of early scholarly interest in Asian government and politics. One is the historical record keeping by official scholars in the Asian countries themselves. These historical accounts focused primarily on the working of the governing systems. Zizhi Tongjian (1084), or *the General Principles of Governance*, by China's Sima Guang (1019–86), is a good example. This

Box 0.1

Crossing cultural boundaries

Studies of social phenomena beyond our own cultural community can be a challenge. It is not always clear whether and how much of what we make of things in other countries is only a reflection of our own experience: what we believe things should be, or the way we do things as a habit. Consequently, there are some issues in cross-cultural scholarly inquiries that students of Pacific Asian politics should be aware of.

Orientalism is a term coined by Edward Said (1935–2003), an influential American social theorist. Said warns of the often false assumptions by Western academics about Asia, which in turn limit their efforts to understand Asia and distort their knowledge about it.

Cultural relativism is an argument that social phenomena cannot be generalized across different cultures. Political communities develop their own ways of organizing their government and regulating politics that can only be relevant and meaningful to their own community. Attempts to develop universally applicable models, theories or standards can only lead to cultural insensitivity, lack of empirical substance in academic research and distortions of the truth.

Those who believe in **scientific universalism**, however, disagree. For them, politics in any country involves the same set of basic human interests and relationships, as well as issues and problems. It is therefore entirely possible and perhaps even desirable to generalize local experiences into *the* system of knowledge, built around the core political logic, explanatory concepts and analytical frameworks.

294-volume work examines the rise and fall of the political systems in China from 403 BC to 959 AD, focusing on how politics and government operated. Because of the huge size of the book, like many other similar works in many Asian countries, it is not available in English.

The other source is Western interest in Asian governments and politics. Early Western knowledge was advanced by the work of missionaries from Western Europe and North America in Asia. One of the earliest works on Asian governments and politics is *Missions and Politics in Asia* (1898) by Robert E. Speer (1867–1947), who, like many others of his time, tried to describe and explain Pacific Asian politics from an outsider's point of view, and perhaps more pointedly, from a Christian one. Indeed, early efforts like this led to the dominance of a scholarly tradition in Asian studies later on, which Edward Said labelled as *orientalism* (Said, 2003).

Since the end of the Second World War, we have seen a growing number of studies by political scientists on Pacific Asian government and politics. With the rise of the field of comparative politics, concepts, theories and methods from mainstream political science are being used to explain Pacific Asian politics. Two approaches have emerged to dominate the field. The first approach, represented in the works of Samuel P. Huntington and Lucian W. Pye, shows a great interest in the original contents of Pacific Asian politics and makes good efforts to incorporate them into mainstream political science. Huntington's work focuses on the conditions and institutional requirements for political order in countries of late development (Huntington, 1968). Pye's work explores the Confucian models of authority in East Asian countries (Pye, 1985). These works, and many others taking the same approach, have greatly enriched comparative politics in general and the study of Pacific Asian politics in particular.

The other stream of studies is informed primarily by the prevailing ideologies, values and political concerns of the times. They range from those in the 1950s to 1970s, centred on the problems of communism and modernization in non-Western countries, to those since the 1980s, that are concerned primarily with the problems of democratic transition and political liberalization, as well as human rights and civil standards in Pacific Asian countries. Studies in this category have been an important part of the external pressures for fundamental social and political change in Pacific Asia, and, together with those of the first approach, have formed the backbone of the field.

Unlike the situation during colonial times, when Pacific Asian studies were conducted predominantly by Western scholars, based on their casual observations and personal experiences, the post-war period saw a large number of scholars from Pacific Asian countries who were trained in West Europe and North America and then returned to universities in their own countries. While this has helped to build a bridge between mainstream theories, concepts and methods on the one hand, and local content on the

Case Study Lab 0.1

Approaching Pacific Asian politics: what to research and how to analyse it

Studying Pacific Asian politics is often a great challenge for students because of the great diversity, huge amount of material, rich historical experience, cultural and civilizational differences and the political nature of the subject matter. Below is an example of how scholars identify issues and develop a perspective for their analysis and explanation. This can help guide you through getting a handle on particular aspects and perspectives in studying and inquiring about politics in the region.

In laying out his framework for 'interpreting Southeast Asian politics,' Richard Robinson lists three big questions that guide their enquiry about Pacific Asian politics in terms of what to research and how to analyse it:

- Why liberal politics has proven so fragile across the region and why various forms of authoritarianism or electoral politics based on one-party rule or money politics have been so pervasive.
- Why various forms of interventionist state and predatory systems of governance have survived and flourished despite the embrace of market capitalism.
- Whether recent patterns of decentralization of authority, the spread of democratic reforms and the participation of social movements and local actors in the political arena signal the long-awaited rise of a progressive and self-reliant civil society or the consolidation of new social and economic oligarchies and mechanisms for control on the part of the state.

Robinson further identifies three dominant scholarly traditions in the study of Pacific Asian politics, which can lead to different analyses and explanations of these issues:

- American political science, in both its pluralist and behavioural aspects and its structural functional dimensions, especially as this is constructed with modernization theory, and a new pluralist political sociology and cultural politics emphasizing the critical importance of civil society, social movements and the politics of culture and identity in the transformation of political systems.
- Political economy in the British and European tradition, especially as this is influenced by Marxist ideas about the relationship of capitalism, state power and class interest, and a more recent shift from mainstream ideas about class and state in the 1970s and 1980s in the form of dependency theory, to an emphasis on the primacy of global relations of exploitation and dependence in shaping the dynamics of politics and power in developing countries.
- Public choice/rational choice political economy and new institutional economics, focusing on transformative possibilities of institutions and markets and the possibilities of agency, and a new trend that recognizes the transformative capacity of institutions and the pathway of possibilities they establish for political and economic reform.

Robinson 2012: 5–6

other, the whole picture of 'we study you' has not changed a great deal.

Exacerbating this problem perhaps is that the field has come to be dominated not just by scholars in the West, but also primarily by those in English-speaking parts of the West. The influence of the scholarly works on Pacific Asian politics in non-English languages are confined to their own language communities and become largely inaccessible beyond them. At the same time, translation, debate and critique of works of English origins have become a principal form of scholarly activity in the field in non-English-speaking countries. There is clearly an asymmetry in professional communication 'between researchers residing in different and separate political jurisdictions' and between '"production" and "consumption" of theories, ideas, concepts, and methods and data' (Holsti, 1985: 102). It would be unrealistic to expect this asymmetry to change any time soon, if at all, given the nature and structure of the international scholarly community. What is important for us is to understand the limits such an asymmetry might impose upon us, and the nature of the knowledge that we acquire in this scholarly environment.

Even within mainstream political science and international relations, scholars of Pacific Asian politics, while having a great influence in the field itself, are largely on the margins of the discipline in their own countries. In the United States and Great Britain, for example, politics and government in developing countries tend to be approached as cultural variations of the established models and systems. Scholars of Pacific Asian politics often face a difficult task. On the one hand, they need to keep abreast of the dominant scholarly interests and discourses, and the legitimate and effective methods of their discipline. On the other hand, they need to be sensitive and receptive to the rich and challenging content and phenomena from Pacific Asian countries.

All these issues in the study of Pacific Asian politics have no doubt complicated the development of the field as a subject in political science and as an international community of scholarship. These issues make the problems of orientalism, cultural relativism and the dominance of 'American social science' (Hoffmann, 1977) more acute in this field.

How to use this text

How do we go about using this text? Let us start with the chapters.

Overview of chapters

We begin with a chapter on the traditional political institutions and structure in Pacific Asian countries and how politics and government were organized before modern times. This is important for us to understand the roots of the patterns and dynamics of contemporary politics and government in Pacific Asia and the underlying causes for the unique trajectory of political development and change in Pacific Asia and the unique character of the emergent political institutions, structure and political order.

Chapter 2 focuses on the profound experiences of political development and change in Pacific Asia in the twentieth century. Revolutions, reforms as well as war and violence, inspired by competing ideals of the modern state, have played their part in these mostly newly independent nation states to shape political institutions and order.

Chapter 2 looks at four key ideologies, their political economic models and the political forces they represent: communism, democracy, capitalism and Confucianism. It also looks at how these ideas and forces drove efforts to reform, revolutionize or conserve the state institutions and forms and platforms of politics in Pacific Asia. It demonstrates the century-long historical experience of political development and change and identifies key areas of tension and conflict in the shaping of the modern state.

The next four chapters explain state structure and constitution, government institutions and their roles, relations and functions. Chapter 3 examines the organization of the state in its broad sense, that is, the constitution of the polity, legitimacy and institutions of state authority and the problem of state dominance. Chapter 4 explains the organization of government and the problem of executive dominance. Chapter 5 deals with the changing role of the bureaucracy. Chapter 6 discusses one of the key functions that many Pacific Asian governments perform: the organization and management of the national economy.

The following two chapters look at Pacific Asian politics and government from the bottom up: the structure and organization of political society and how political forces, individual or collective, participate and influence government and politics. Chapter 7 outlines the development and functions of modern political parties and electoral systems and their role as a primary form of political participation, contestation and mobilization in the shaping of political order. Chapter 8 introduces the development of political society and illustrates how individuals and social groups participate, influence and even control politics and government as well as the different forms and methods this influence takes. We shall look at the predominant methods of political participation, influence and change, and how they differ from those we see in our own countries.

One key aspect of modern state building in Pacific Asian countries is the very existence and legitimacy of the state itself. This involves the problem of fostering the national basis for the state and shaping state institutions for the unique ethnic, religious and cultural configuration of the nation. This includes questions of how the nation state is accepted, integrated and legitimized in the international system of nation states. The last two chapters, therefore, look at issues and developments in building the nation state in Pacific Asian countries internally and externally. Chapter 9 focuses on the unique challenges arising from the very unique set of ethnic, religious and cultural foundations Pacific Asian countries have in building the nation state and the different models or practices of how the ethnic, religious and cultural relations or identities are managed in building 'the nation,' and the state itself, and hence the nation state.

Chapter 10 deals with the consolidation and development of Pacific Asian nation states in the regional and international system and the role of politics and government of Pacific Asian countries in the shaping of the region's international system, the international system and the global political economy. It explains how Pacific Asian politics is shaped and to some extent dictated by forces, interests and ideas from outside and discusses the growing impact and influence of Pacific Asian countries on the international system.

As you will see, the text is organized around the idea that when we study Pacific Asian politics, we are interested in the institutions, actors and their actions as integral parts of the political system, and how their interplay leads to political outcomes (Easton, 1953). We explain political action and behaviour, institutions and process, and political structure and order, and their change. It is this idea of a political system that provides a framework for us to understand politics across these countries with diverse conditions and constant change.

Organization of illustrative material

To assist learning with this text, each chapter includes **Highlighted Areas** for easy access to definitions of key concepts, a list of which is included at the end of the chapter. **Boxes** expand on concepts, issues, theories and debates as well as comparative materials where these are considered to be useful.

Box 0.2

Overview of issues and debates covered in Boxes

***Boxes** cover some of the most important debates presented in each chapter, including:*

- *Chapter 1: state formation in Northeast and Southeast Asia, Confucianism and its interpretation, colonialism and independence, the premodern interstate system and early attempts at political modernization.*
- *Chapter 2: political modernization, the decline of communism, non-pluralist politics, democratization, Asian democracy, human rights, the military and the Asian values debate.*
- *Chapter 3: state dominance, types of state, legitimacy, models of Chinese politics, grand political alliances, central–local relations, the vertical administrative control model and local government autonomy.*
- *Chapter 4: organizing principles and forms of government, the head of state, parliament and cabinet in Japan, the legislature, law making, parliaments and political change, the rule of law, opposition tactics, constitutions and the role of courts.*
- *Chapter 5: models of bureaucratic evolution, the role of bureaucrats, the political executive–bureaucracy relationship, corruption, the decline of bureaucratic power, the civil service, public sector reform and good governance.*
- *Chapter 6: developmental state theory and debate, regimes and economic growth, state versus the market, economic planning, law and economic development, explaining the 'East Asian miracle' and economic transition.*
- *Chapter 7: debates around political parties in Pacific Asia, single-party dominance, personalistic rule, political party systems and their organization, change and democratization, the cadre system, factionalism, regionalism, party funding, electoral systems, electoral culture, political-party reform, parties, elections and the overall political order and partisanship.*
- *Chapter 8: state–society relations state corporatism, continuous politics, citizenship and suffrage, political participation, gender equality, becoming a politician, civil society groups, power relations, political movements, income inequality and the role of the media and public opinion.*
- *Chapter 9: nationalism, the monarchy, paths to independence, religion, Islamization, multination states, ethnic politics, national identity claims and ethnic nationalism.*
- *Chapter 10: the interstate system, domestic sources of security policy, the flying geese pattern, regional order, trade liberalization, regional institutions, Pacific Asia and the world, the standard of civilization, globalization, voting rights in the IMF and the rise of Asia debate.*

Each chapter also includes **Case Study Labs** which showcase the use of analytical frameworks and methodological tools in analysing and explaining unique research problems in Pacific Asian politics. These case studies are related to the content covered in the chapter. A list of Case Study Labs is provided in the List of Illustrative Material at the beginning of this text. Further illustration of facts and issues in government and politics of Pacific Asia is assisted of course with standard **Figures**, **Tables** and **Country Profiles**. You will find a list of them also under the List of Illustrative Material.

At the end of each chapter, there is a **Chapter Summary** covering the chapter's main points, a list of **Study questions** on major issues in the chapter, a list of **Key terms** and an annotated bibliography directing you to further reading on particular issues and aspects.

Because of the rich diversity and the rapid pace of change discussed earlier, and indeed, because issues in Pacific Asian politics have always been contentious – and emotionally as well as ideologically charged – this text should not be considered to impose an authoritative view on matters. Rather, textbooks, including this one, should be seen as a starting point leading to further information and materials elsewhere, as a framework to organize information and knowledge that has been accumulated from various sources and as a point of reference to locate facts, events, concepts, issues and theories in the field. We challenge you to raise questions while using this text. You might stand up in class and say I disagree on this and on that. We believe this is what university learning and teaching is all about. In the end, what you learn here is not just information, or even knowledge, which is monopolized by a few specialists with their textbooks, but rather the skills and intellectual confidence in studying the governance and politics of Pacific Asia.

Further reading

Some further reading to help you think about the fundamental nature and the structure and dynamics of Pacific Asian politics:

- Gilley, Bruce (2014) *The Nature of Asian Politics* (Cambridge: Cambridge University Press).
- Slater, Dan (2010) *Ordering Power: Contentious Politics and Authoritarian Leviathans in Southeast Asia* (Cambridge: Cambridge University Press).
- Shinoda, Tomohito (2013) *Contemporary Japanese Politics: Institutional Changes and Power Shifts* (New York: Columbia University Press).
- Borthwick, Mark (2014) *Pacific Century: The Emergence of Modern Pacific Asia* (Boulder: Westview).
- Pye, Lucian W. (1985) *Asian Power and Politics: The Cultural Dimensions of Authority* (Cambridge: Belknap Press).
- Huntington, Samuel P. (1968) *Political Order in Changing Societies* (New Haven: Yale University Press).

Chapter 1
Political traditions in Pacific Asia

Politics and government in Pacific Asia can appear very foreign to students of comparative politics with little experience of the region. This chapter aims to provide tools for organizing the study of early Pacific Asian states and a context from which to understand contemporary events, structures and institutions. The chapter is important, especially for those students unfamiliar with the complicated history of the region, because the remainder of the text presumes some knowledge of the traditional practices and structures in the region.

Early politics in Pacific Asia provides students and researchers with key examples of state formation and early forms of politics and government. The region exhibits a variety of patterns of state formation, varying structures of governance and differing patterns of political behaviour. This is evident across different geographical areas and over different historical periods. These rich empirical cases are therefore ideal material from which to approach comparative questions of state formation and premodern politics and governance that sit at the heart of comparative politics.

Pacific Asia has produced some of the world's most impressive early states and some of the most sophisticated early systems of politics and state organization. The Chinese bureaucracy, its vast governing structure and the system of scholar-officials that not only governed but also acted as scholars and social elites are some of the most sophisticated examples of governance anywhere in the premodern world. China not only marvelled at early travellers like Marco Polo or the scholars that read their works, but also served as inspiration for European renaissance and enlightenment thinkers putting together the ideal features of the modern state (see Hobson, 2004).

Likewise, in Japan, the honour code of *bushido* was a highly respected moral code that guided the actions of samurai loyal to their regional daimyo or feudal lord. This code helped organize local politics in early Japan through a highly developed system of political ethics and loyalty (see Nitobé 1905). In Southeast Asia, kingdoms wedged between major empires evolved systems of statecraft that produced stories as tragic and inspiring as those of early Greece while the trade routes through the region rivalled those of the Mediterranean in complexity, activity and importance to regional prosperity.

One of the great puzzles of the early modern era, then, is how Europe and its offshoots expanded to dominate politics in the region and became a model for Pacific Asian nations seeking to become wealthy and powerful. Early states and kingdoms in Pacific Asia were highly advanced systems of politics and governance but were universally supplanted by systems developed in the European context. The chapter therefore asks the reader to consider the strengths and weaknesses of the premodern state system in Pacific

Asia and to ask how and why these states experienced such turmoil during the early modern era.

Similarly, the regional order that loosely governed relations among nations in Pacific Asia did not survive into the modern era. Contact with foreign traders, missionaries and government envoys, as well as military and ideational incursions, threw Pacific Asian order into question and replaced it with a Eurocentric treaty-port system that gradually evolved into a branch of the liberal international order built upon Westphalian notions of the sovereignty and equality of nations. How the premodern regional order functioned and why it collapsed remain important questions for scholars of comparative politics and international relations.

As the chapter hopes to illustrate, while the traditional order fell as it came into contact with modern systems of governance, economics, science and technology, traditional organization of power and authority continue to shape governance and politics and remain an important part of understanding and explaining contemporary Pacific Asian politics. The text encourages the reader to question how scholars have sought to distinguish the forces shaping the early modern state and draw links between traditional forms of politics and governance in Pacific Asia and those of the contemporary era.

In this chapter, we categorize some principal forms of government and politics in premodern Pacific Asia and introduce a traditional world order that loosely governed interactions between states, kingdoms and empires in the region. The introduction is brief, as a thorough analysis of the traditional political systems in Pacific Asia would require a complete text covering the various historical epochs and regional differences. As this is a political science textbook, we shall not dwell too much on historical detail, such as identifying the long list of historical figures or presenting the major historical events that shaped political development in each country. Instead, we put forward a sketch of the evolution of significant political structures and government institutions, and discuss the tensions and issues the process has brought to bear on contemporary government and politics.

We focus on the structure and institutions of the state and the historical forms of government and politics. We seek an understanding of how these structures and institutions interacted to form models of governance that varied considerably across the region. We aim to illustrate the underlying political logic that drove early state formation in Pacific Asia and to encourage students to ask what, if anything, of this order remains. We identify three models of early state formation and demonstrate how these models responded in the early modern era to colonialism and the challenge presented by the early modern state.

The chapter also explores the premodern 'world order' in Pacific Asia as a way of illustrating how diplomacy was organized before the Westphalian system of nation-states came to dominate interactions between nations globally. Primarily by way of illustrating the premodern Chinese world order, we seek to impress upon the reader the magnitude of the changes that occurred in the early modern era.

A **government** is the governing authority of a political unit. A polity is such an organized political unit. The state can mean either government (for example, in state–society relations) or polity (for example, interstate relations) or both (for example, modern-state building).

The chapter concludes in an era of great transformation and turmoil as colonial and indigenous regimes experiment with different forms of government and politics and where social and economic structures in Pacific Asia are turned upon their head. The chapter demonstrates how far politics and governance in the region shifted during this era and alludes to many of the contemporary puzzles scholars face when studying politics and governance in the region today. These puzzles form the focus of chapters to come. Here, we ask the reader to pay attention to how Pacific Asia's traditional states differed from the modern ideal and to consider in what ways and to what degree they have changed with the coming of the early modern era.

Early states and state formation

Early history shows two very different experiences of state formation developed in two areas of Pacific Asia. In the North, state formation led to more centralized and bureaucratic states that were more similar to today's modern state. In the South, a series of kingdoms with loosely defined boundaries and governance structures developed. A third model of state formation occurred in the maritime nation of Japan where the centralized model evolved into a highly fragmented and localized system of governance. In many ways the historical division of Northeast and Southeast Asia remains important for understanding some of the salient differences of contemporary politics and governance in the region.

In the early period of Northeast Asia, the Chinese imperial system dominated. This system was established following a tumultuous period of Chinese history, the Warring States Period (475 to 221 BC), when the Kingdom of Qin defeated rival states in today's China to establish the first Chinese Empire in 221 BC. The King of Qin proclaimed himself the First Emperor of China and went on to build a centralized imperial state that lasted about 2,000 years. This centralized imperial system survived regular changes in ruling dynasties and even foreign invasions until it was overthrown in 1911 and the Republic of China was proclaimed.

A unified state also formed in today's Korea in 668 following the end of the warring Three Kingdom period (37 BC–AD 668). The Silla kingdom had a centralized government similar to the governing systems that emerged from China. Around the same time, across the strait in Japan, the Yamato state established its supremacy over competing clans, unified the country and reorganized the government following the Chinese model of a centralized state. However, Japan's centralized state soon evolved into a system where power was far more dispersed than that of early China.

State formation is the establishment of the structure and processes of a political community, the institutions and functions of its governing body, and the sovereignty of the polity within the international system. State formation can be distinguished from state building, as the former does not necessarily imply an institutional design and intentional attempts driven by such a design to construct a particular type of state. The issue of state formation is important as it helps us to understand how and why a state is configured as it is and the historical context in which the state emerged.

Scholars of pre-Meiji political order in Japan largely agree that from the twelfth to the nineteenth century, the Japanese state was a feudal system where a regional daimyo exercised much of the powers of the national government over the region they controlled. The regional daimyo had the power to control taxation and the armed forces and to administer land titles and other important acts of government. Fighting among warlords, clans and the court often determined the fate of the national government: the winning warlord set up the national government, which sometimes had little control over the regions.

At various points in Japan's premodern history, national unity was attempted through the establishment of centralized state institutions. The Bakufu system is an example of one such attempt to centralize power (Oishi, 1990; Hane, 1992: 6–83). However, even when strong leaders such as Tokugawa Ieyasu managed to crush his opponents in 1600 at the Battle of Sekigahara and gain the ear of the emperor, the overall centripetal force remained weak.

Japan was not highly centralized between the twelfth century and nineteenth century. Prior to the twelfth century, the state structure was modelled on the Chinese centralized state. From the late nineteenth century a strong central government emerged with the Meiji Restoration. But in between, the state is characterized by weak, fragile and unstable central control over the regions. Nevertheless, the territorial boundaries of the Japanese premodern empire remained relatively similar over each period and while not always centralized there was a clear notion of the Japanese state among the vying regional Daimyo.

In contrast, the emergence of states in Southeast Asia was slow and more complicated. Donald G. McCloud (1995) discusses the three main forces shaping the early formation of territorial states in Southeast Asia:

- International commercial trade that led to the rise of 'maritime or commercial kingdoms' along the coastal areas of today's Indochinese Peninsula;
- Agricultural activities that led to the rise of 'land-based agricultural kingdoms', such as Angkor in Khmer (600–1432), and Sailendra and Mataram (600–1049) in Java, today's Indonesia;

- European colonial economic and political activities starting around the 1500s that made a lasting impact on state systems in the region.

As can be seen above, the forces shaping early state formation in Southeast Asia are diverse and do not apply equally across all of the region. This has led scholars to interpret the formation of traditional states in a diverse number of ways. Premodern Southeast Asian states have been conceptualized as a 'galactic polity' (Tambiah, 1976), a 'mandala' (Wolters, 1982), a 'solar polity' (Lieberman, 2003) or even a court-village dual-sphere structure (McCloud, 1995). The common theme that ties all these concepts together is that they all depict a loosely connected network of concentric zones with the capital/court at the centre.

However, there are two further conventional ways to categorize traditional states in Southeast Asia. The first is on the basis of geographical conditions and the consequent patterns of political and economic activities that are shaped by geographical conditions. Using this criteria, scholars have identified three types of 'early Southeast Asian states' (McCloud, 1995: 22–32; also Hassall and Saunders, 2002: 14):

- Maritime or commercial kingdoms in the archipelago of Southeast Asia;
- Land-based agricultural kingdoms in lower Indochina;
- Confucian bureaucratic kingdoms in upper Indochina.

The second conventional way to categorize traditional states in Southeast Asia is on the basis of the patterns of power structure influenced by the two predominant Asian civilizations: Indian Buddhism and Chinese Confucianism (Kingsbury, 2005a: 14). Southeast Asia is geographically located as the maritime link between these two large and influential civilizations. Early states in Southeast Asia were highly influenced by both civilizations but each was generally influenced more by one than the other. For example, Vietnam was strongly influenced by premodern Chinese philosophy, governance and religion. Based on this categorization, we can identify two types of early state in Southeast Asia:

- Indianized states;
- Sinicized states.

Given the differences across Southeast and Northeast Asia, scholars have often treated them as separate regions. This theme will be returned to in the following chapters through exploration of a variety of issues that show regional differences across Northeast and Southeast Asia. Notably, however, there are also other ways to subdivide the Pacific Asian region, such as type of state and form of government or maritime and continental. The complexity and diversity of the region over and above the traditional Southeast-Northeast categories will become apparent in the following chapters. For now, it is worth clearly stating the similarities and differences in early state formation between Northeast and Southeast Asia to help summarize some of the main characteristics of early states in the region:

By the mid-nineteenth century three significant types of political system dominated Pacific Asia:

- The centralized state, such as those in China and Korea, under a unitary state authority and the rule of aristocracy and bureaucracy at various levels;
- The fragmented state, such as in Japan at that time, where the political arena was divided into several regional centres, each of which had their own arms, governing authority and taxation powers; and
- The 'galactic polity' (Tambiah, 1976: 102–31) in much of today's Southeast Asia, where village settlements and other satellite communities were loosely connected to the court through patrimonial and contingent arrangements.

The following three sections go into more detail about each of the three major premodern political systems in Pacific Asia. Here we ask the reader to identify the major features of each system and to ask why they emerged. You should be able to link each to a real historical example and to understand why each system differs as it does. We encourage you to build your own case study by listing some of the major historical events and key people in one of the premodern Pacific Asian nations and by identifying which model it fits by way of analysis of the major political institutions and actors. In a subsequent part of the chapter we explore how these models evolved when brought into contact with increasingly dominant European powers. We therefore encourage you

Box 1.1

Comparing early state formations in Northeast and Southeast Asia

- The concept of god and its embeddedness in the king or emperor developed and became an important institution in the early kingdoms. This seems to be true in both Northeast and Southeast Asia.
- Hinduism, Buddhism and Islam all took root in Southeast Asia, while in Northeast Asia, only Buddhism prevailed. As a consequence, Southeast Asia has experienced a complexity of religious influences not matched in Northeast Asia.
- Unlike their counterparts in Northeast Asia, early kingdoms in Southeast Asia, while also based heavily on irrigation systems, did not evolve into a centralized, unitary state system, as would be expected from Karl A. Wittfogel's much admired model of 'oriental despotism' (Wittfogel, 1957). Instead, these early kingdoms were dominated by very autonomous village settlements. The court had much weaker administrative and bureaucratic functions and capabilities.
- States in Northeast Asia evolved a power structure heavily influenced by Chinese civilization and Confucianism but not all in Southeast Asia were influenced to the same degree with some more strongly influenced by Indian Buddhism (Kingsbury, 2005a: 14).

to consider the strengths and weaknesses of these premodern systems as you read through the following sections.

The centralized state model

The concept of a centralized state is often used in connection with that of 'autocracy', but these terms do not refer to the same thing. An autocracy is defined by personalized rule of the state, while a centralized state refers to the structure of state authority. Autocracy is the opposite of democracy, while the centralized state is a contrasting model to a federal state or state with a high degree of local autonomy. While an autocracy will have a high degree of centralization, a centralized state could be either an autocracy or a democracy.

> The **centralized state model** refers to a type of political system in which the polity's governing capacity and power is concentrated at the national level, most commonly in the hands of the executive, and where the state has great control over domestic and international interaction.

The centralized state model is most common in the contemporary era but some states employed this model in the premodern era. China is one of the most important examples of the centralization of power and authority as an integral part of its early state formation (see Fukuyama, 2011; Figure 1.1). The centralized state model rose with the large new state that was built over the conquered warring states over 200 years before the Common Era (221 BC). Measures were taken to gain effective control over the vast new territories and prevent possible rebellions. These measures centralized the

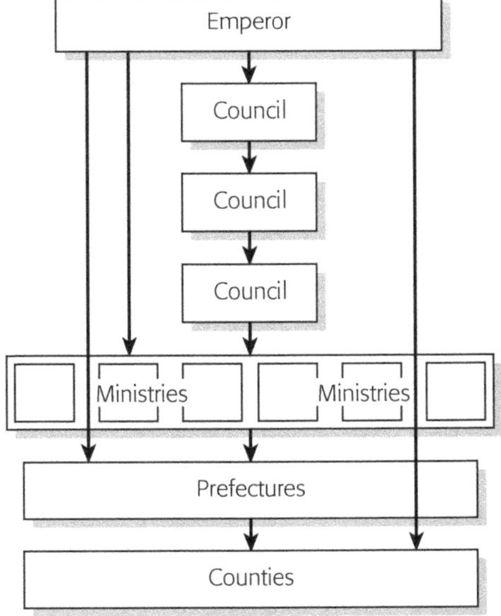

Figure 1.1 The traditional Chinese centralized state model (221 BC onwards)

functions and authority of the state in a system where accountability, legitimacy and process were closely linked to the authority of the court and centralized imperial system.

The centralized state system experienced several major reforms over the long span of imperial China. During this time, until it gradually evolved into the autocratic state that we see in the later dynasties. The centralized state model (see Box 1.2) that China employed contained a unitary political structure. All aspects of the polity were integrated into the whole with sovereignty resting at the national level. The model contained both hierarchical and vertical control structures that integrated each section of government with the overall control and authority situated at the centre of the structure. Governments at local levels were usually the extended branches of the central government, from which their mandate came.

While the Chinese imperial system developed the centralized state model it did so in a way quite different to the majority of centralized states today. The system had a singular government structure similar to contemporary centralized states but modern concepts such as 'separation of powers', 'checks and balances' and 'local autonomy' were largely irrelevant. The Chinese centralized state was built on economic and social necessity. It strove for effective and efficient management of premodern society rather than for modern concepts of rights, legitimacy or constitutional government.

Early scholarship on state formation in Northeast Asia identified a link between the degree of centralization of state power and authority and the social and economic requirements of premodern Pacific Asian communities. For example, Karl A. Wittfogel argued that there was a causal link between the mode of economic and social management of the time and the traditional highly centralized state model in his well-known theory of Oriental despotism. In Wittfogel's model, control of natural, human and financial resources were in the hands of the central government.

Oriental despotism or hydraulic despotism is a theory that links the rise of the centralized, despotic, bureaucratic state in traditional 'Oriental' societies such as China or India to their large-scale irrigation works. The need to manage large-scale water resources led to the rise of forced labour, social hierarchy, centralized state control and bureaucratic power. The theory is best known through the work of German historian and Sinologist, Karl A. Wittfogel, on the rise of strong states in hydraulic societies in Asia (Wittfogel, 1957).

Along with Buddhism and Chinese culture, this model of state and government also spread to neighbouring countries, most significantly, Korea and Japan to the east and Vietnam to the south. The centralized state model became the prevailing system of government in premodern Northeast Asia.

There are a number of reasons why scholarship on the centralized state model remains significant for Pacific Asian politics. First, it has been the dominant model of state organization in much of Northeast Asia in both premodern and contemporary times. While, the centralized state is not only a Pacific Asian phenomenon as clearly many European countries developed a similar centralized state in the sixteenth and seventeenth centuries, it has been more dominant throughout the history of Northeast Asian politics. The fact that this model has survived and remains dominant in Pacific Asia is certainly an interesting issue for scholars of comparative politics.

Secondly, the relationship between the centralized state of premodern Northeast Asia and the modern

Box 1.2

Basic features of the centralized state model

- A unitary state with a single source of legitimacy and authority.
- Appointment of local government officials by the central government.
- Local governments are the extension of the central government, with delegated authority from above.
- Sophisticated central government bureaucracy with a broad range of functions.
- Nation-wide flows of materials, products and labour.
- Central control and management of natural, human and financial resources.
- A hierarchical political order.

COUNTRY PROFILE

JAPAN

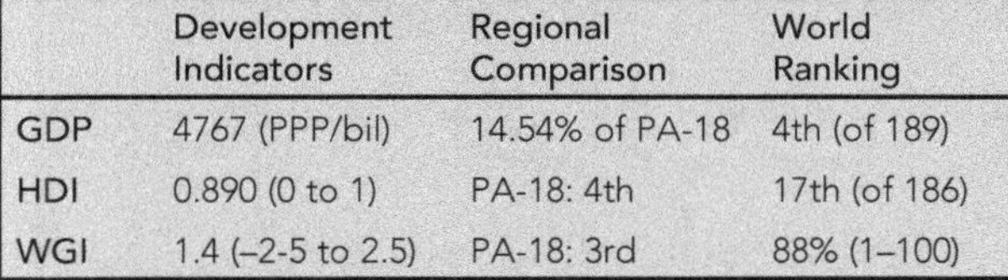

	Development Indicators	Regional Comparison	World Ranking
GDP	4767 (PPP/bil)	14.54% of PA-18	4th (of 189)
HDI	0.890 (0 to 1)	PA-18: 4th	17th (of 186)
WGI	1.4 (–2-5 to 2.5)	PA-18: 3rd	88% (1–100)

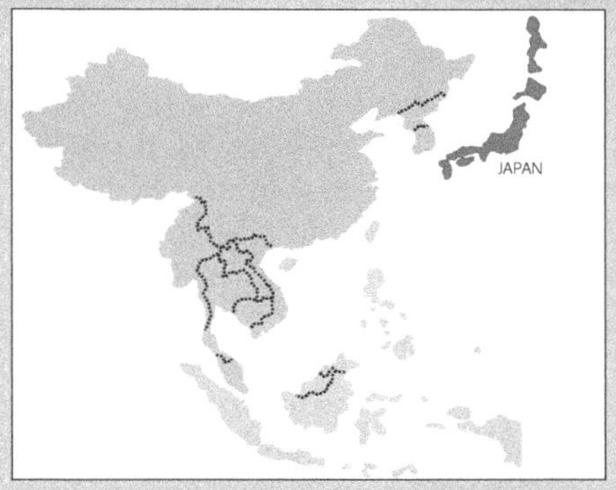

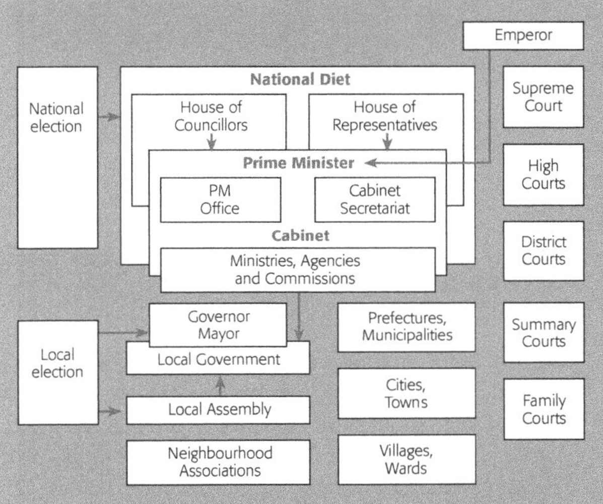

Key political facts

Electoral system for National Legislature
Mixed Member Regional Proportional Representation

Political cycles
General election for House of Representatives, every four years unless earlier dissolution.
Local elections every four years.
Annual budget enacted by the Diet in March.

Further reading

Hayes, 2009; Gaunder, 2011; Shinoda, 2013.

Timeline of modern political development

1868	1868 Meiji Restoration restores the power of the emperor, transforms the feudal state into a centralized state, and builds modern state *institutions*.
1882	Parliamentary system introduced.
1920s	Taisho democracy, with a two-party system; liberal elites controlling government; and a more tolerant political environment.
1925	Universal male suffrage.
1930s	The militarized state, with the military and right-wing extremists controlling the government and pursuing an imperial expansionist policy.
1947	New constitution grants a genuine constitutional monarchy with a parliamentary system; universal suffrage.
1947	Laws of government organization, civil service and local autonomy define the basic structure and functions of government.
1955	Two major parties emerge to dominate the political system, with the LDP and its conservative alliance starting its 38-year control of government – known as the '1955 system'.
Late 1960s and early 1970s	Administrative reform to downsize government.
Early 1980s	New round of administrative reform, including privatization of major public corporations.
1993	LDP loses the Lower House elections and its long hold on government; reforms of the electoral system, political funding mechanisms and political ethical rules.
1994	Reforms change the electoral system from SNTV to MMP.
1996	Administrative programme for comprehensive government reform.
2004	Political reforms: reform of political party, election and political funding laws.
2007	Referendum Law passed, preparing for constitutional amendments in the future.
2009	Opposition party wins general election, ending more than 50 years of LDP control of government.
2012	Abenomics to revitalize the economy.
2015	New Security Law passes, providing legal basis for Japan's international role as a normal state.

state in Pacific Asia and elsewhere remains unclear. In some ways they overlap but in others they do not. Understanding how and why they differ remains central for understanding Northeast Asia's political evolution.

Finally, the study of the centralized state model in premodern Pacific Asia provides an interesting comparative case of modern state formation that raises important questions about the nature of the modern state and the transition from premodern to modern governance structures. In particular, does the modern state necessarily require centralized bureaucratic control and management? Does centralization precede the modern state or can a highly decentralized state evolve modern structures of government like democracy, citizenship and constitutionalism? As the model below shows, however, even Northeast Asia experienced periods of decentralization as part of its early state formation. How this experience shaped later state building also remains an important consideration for scholars of Pacific Asian politics and government.

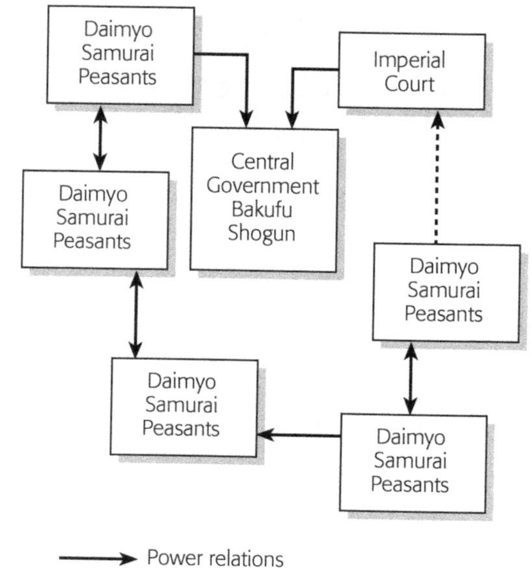

Figure 1.2 The Japanese fragmented state model (twelfth to nineteenth centuries)

The fragmented state model

Our second model of early state formation is the fragmented state model. This model points to cases in Northeast and Southeast Asia during different historical epochs when the governing structure was not effectively centralized and competing or complementary centres of power and authority existed. The key case for this model is the Japanese state from the twelfth to the nineteenth centuries.

> The **daimyo** were regional rulers or warlords in feudal Japan (twelfth to nineteenth century). They were similar to the feudal lords of medieval Europe. Usually, the strongest daimyo exercised the powers of the shogunate (government). A samurai was a warrior who served and was ultimately loyal to a daimyo.

The precise nature of the Japanese feudal system aside, what distinguished the Japanese fragmented state model from the centralized state model is the fragmentation of state authority. As Figure 1.2 shows, from the twelfth to the nineteenth century, the Japanese state was organized in a way that saw the dispersion of state power across daimyo-controlled regions. There was no effective hierarchical or vertical control from the centre. Regional daimyo held political authority, exercised state powers and performed national government functions largely independent of the centre.

The fragmented state is a unique political structure that is neither a federal state, as it reflects merely the weakening of central state authority and not a breaking down of a unitary state; nor is it a feudal state in the pre-modern European sense, as beyond the regional domains there was a central government, along with the institutional framework of the state.

This model should also not be confused with controlled decentralization since the end of the Cold War common in many contemporary states in Pacific Asia (see Chapter 3). The fragmentation of state power and authority in premodern Japan was not institutionally designed by a central court and involved intense competition between regions. The distribution of state power in premodern Japan was contingent on the balance of power among regional warlords, clans and the court. It reflected the inability of the court to uphold central state control rather than a preference of the court to decentralize government power and authority.

The **fragmented state model** refers to a structure of polity where state authority is often contested and government powers are dispersed among rival regional forces. The distribution of state functions and capacity tends to be non-hierarchical.

The fragmented state model can be viewed as a specific phase in the historical cycles of polities with a long history. Such polities often witness the rise and fall of centralized state authority as part of the competition between central and regional powers. History shows a persistent pattern in polities with a long history. There is always a tension between the process of fragmentation and centralization in Northeast Asian polities. The fragmented state model in Japan was sandwiched between the classical centralized state from the sixth to twelfth century and the modern centralized Meiji state from the late nineteenth century.

Even in China, where the centralized state was clearly dominant in the premodern era, the state usually became 'fragmented' near the end of a dynasty and before a new unitary state authority was restored. In fact, the original model of the centralized Chinese state, the Qin Dynasty (221–206 BC) was followed by the Han Dynasty (206 BC–220 CE), which dissolved into a period of fragmented authority. The Three Kingdoms era (220–265 CE) that followed involved three major regions that vied for central authority and legitimacy with each controlling their own regions. The epic battles, strategies and tragedy of the era formed the basis for one of China's most memorable early novels, Romance of the Three Kingdoms. The period of fragmentation ended with the establishment of effective central authority under the Jin Dynasty (265–420 CE).

Another example is evident in the period of warlordism in the early years of China's Republican era (1911–49). After the collapse of the last imperial government, the Qing Dynasty (1644–1911), the country was dominated by warlords and witnessed the fragmentation of centralized state authority. The warlords controlled their own regions with little effective centralized control. The warlord who controlled Beijing exercised authority in the name of national government but did not have effective control over the other regions of early modern China.

These examples therefore show the fragmented state model can be a transitional model, with the possibility of either further fragmentation into independent states, or recentralization and restoration of authority, powers and functions of the national government. For Northeast Asia, fragmentation was generally followed eventually by recentralization and the continuation of the centralized state model. Japan's half millennium of fragmentation was no exception.

The Meiji Restoration (1868–1912) represents the end of Japan's fragmented state model and the beginning of a centralized modern state. Increasing tensions and conflicts among warring factions led to the eventual overthrow of the Tokugawa shogunate government and the restoration of the rule of the emperor. The campaign was actually aimed at a narrow agenda, and indeed was initiated by a group of marginalized warlords rebelling against the ruling shogun. However, subsequent institutional changes, reforms and the recentralization of power in the hands of the central government and the emperor constituted a fundamental transformation of Japanese governance. Among other things, land titles were returned to the central government, taxation power was taken back from regional daimyo and a national conscription system was established. The reconstitution of these and other 'national' institutions signal the recentralization of state authority and power and the beginning of Japan's modern state building. We will return to this important period of Japanese history at the end of this chapter and at the beginning of Chapter 2.

The court-village structure

The galactic polity is different again from the two models above. Figure 1.3 presents Stanley Tambiah's depiction of the structure of the seventeenth century Ayutthayan polity in what is today's Thailand. Stanley Tambiah coined the term 'galactic polity' for the unique type of state structure in Southeast Asia. The polity is galactic because the capital region is 'surrounded by differentiated satellites which are more or less "autonomous" entities held in orbit and within the sphere of influence of the centre ... It is only after appreciating the decentralized locational disposition of the traditional polity and its replication of like entities on a decreasing scale – which constitute a galactic constellation rather than a bureaucratic

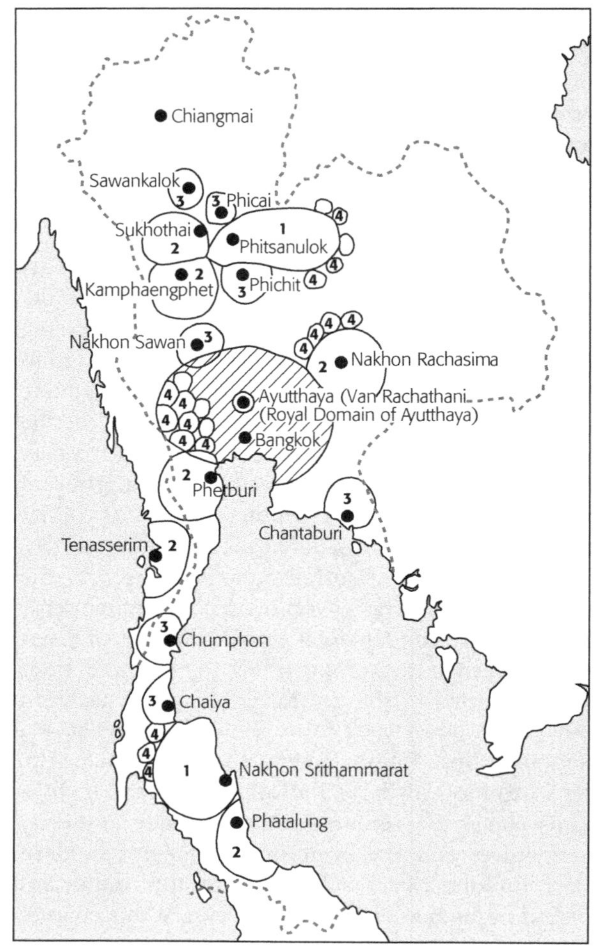

Figure 1.3 The Ayutthayan polity in the seventeenth century
Source: Tambiah, 1976: 137

Box 1.3

Comparing early state formations in Northeast and Southeast Asia (II): imperium versus mandala

An **imperium** can be defined as an area of dominion over which imperial rule or control is exercised. This was the type of polity often found in Northeast Asia, where Confucianism and Chinese imperial influence dominated. The imperium, or 'Sinicised state' (Kingsbury, 2005a: 14), usually had clear boundaries of imperial control, with a hereditary head of state through dynastic succession. More importantly, state authority reached out to all levels through government bureaucracy and state institutions.

A **galactic polity**, Mandala, or 'Indianized state', in contrast, was a polity with regions loosely connected to the court, and influenced and controlled by the court to varying degrees. It usually has no clearly defined boundaries of state control, and power resides with the monarchy, radiates outwards, and recedes as it travels towards the peripheries. The monarchy maintains power relations with regional and local chiefs 'through patronage, as opposed to bureaucracy or feudal obligations' (Kingsbury, 2005a: 14–16). This was a dominant state type in much of traditional Southeast Asia.

hierarchy – that we can move on to a consideration of the polity's centripetal aspects, and of how the centre attempts to hold the remainder' (Tambiah, 1976: 113–14).

Tambiah's galactic polity reflects the influence of Indian Buddhism. This was also stressed in Damien Kingsbury's discussion of the dichotomy of the 'Indianized state' and the 'Sinicised state' (Kingsbury, 2005a: 14–16; see also Box 1.3). Also underlying the galactic polity were the unique dynamics of political economy and political organization. These dynamics are important for understanding early state formation in Southeast Asia and the impact of colonialism and the process of colonial rule in the early modern era.

As McCloud's (1995) study shows, the principal relationship in the polity of many of the early Southeast Asian states was the one between the court and the village settlements. Unlike the centralized state model, where the state had substantial responsibility and functions in organizing economic and social life as well as maintaining security and order at all levels, the court in Southeast Asia usually had limited substantive bureaucratic and administrative functions. Rather, the village was the primary unit of economic and social activity. In fact, the village tended to have a well-followed framework of governance. The court's relationship with the village was more ceremonial, spiritual and patrimonial than hierarchical, authoritative or functional.

The extent to which the court was involved in village affairs varied over different cases in Southeast

Asia but overall there is a general pattern of weak centralized functional control and strong village governance. Also, at times, such as in Vietnam, a highly centralized model was introduced. However, as in the case of the fragmented state in Japan, the central authorities would often lose control over direct governance over time. The court-village structure is not, however, the same as a fragmented state model. The relationship among villages was not competitive and there was no desire for them to seek or challenge the power of the court.

The court-village structure has had a profound impact on political development in contemporary Southeast Asia. It is the historical basis of village-based consensus decision-making and the fragile link between grassroots communities and the state. This fragile link shaped Southeast Asia's experience of colonial rule in the early modern era and continues to present a challenge to modern state building in the postcolonial era.

The Confucian structure of political power and authority

While the early states were largely structured in these models, there was also an underlying political tradition that developed over a thousand years. This political tradition informed how traditional political society is organized, authority is legitimated and power is exercised. While a political tradition seemed to prevail universally in most premodern societies around the world, the Confucian structure of political power and authority systemically developed in mainland Pacific Asia. In China, Confucianism was thoroughly debated as a key philosophy for society and the state. It provided legitimacy and ideological and institutional support for political power and authority that was hierarchical, centralized and heavenly mandated. The Confucian structure also spread to and influenced political structure and institutions in political societies in the wider Pacific Asia, through the expansion of Chinese influence, firstly in the crescent area around mainland East Asia, then further to Southeast Asia. The Confucian political tradition has continued to be an influential force in the shaping of the modern state in many Pacific Asian countries in the twentieth century and beyond, and a key framework for explaining and debating Pacific Asian politics and government.

Confucianism and a moral political order

Any discussion of Confucianism and political traditions in Pacific Asia has to start with the concept of Confucianism itself, not necessarily to arrive at agreement on the meaning, but to help the reader understand what is being discussed. One difficulty with the concept concerns the question of whether Confucianism is a religion. Traditionally, Confucianism was treated as a religion. This is understandable. The dominant role of Confucianism in politics, state institutions and social life in the traditional societies of many Pacific Asian countries led scholars of Western presumptions in search of the role of religion in these societies to view Confucianism as a religion. For many, the question of whether Confucianism is a religion is linked to the question of what religion is. As Julian Ching argues, 'My definition of religion ... focuses on a consciousness of a transcendent dimension, and I perceive it as present in Confucianism from the very beginning' (Ching, 1993: 89).

Increasingly, however, scholars have begun to analyse Confucianism as something different to a religion. Even though some still 'conveniently' put it in the category of religion, many now recognize that, as a belief system, Confucianism is not especially otherworldly or transcendental in character, and therefore should be seen not as a religion but rather as an ethical system (Costopoulos, 2005: xiv). Confucianism has no god, no church or temple, no Koran or Bible. Rather, Confucius' Analects were about how to become a noble person and how to perform one's social role.

Confucianism is a set of moral standards and social values that developed from the teachings of Chinese ancient thinker Confucius (551–479 BC). It advocates a social order based on the ideal behaviour of individuals as expected from their role in society and their ascriptive relations with others. Confucianism has been widespread in Japan, Korea, Vietnam and Taiwan, as well as in Confucius's home country, China.

More pointedly, by rejecting the religious nature of Confucianism, many have come to view Confucianism as a moral guideline for social order.

Confucianism is a tradition of moral standards and social values intended for a social order sustained on mutually supportive social relations, largely on what Parsons calls an 'ascriptive' basis (Parsons, 1951). Relations between individuals are ascribed by the teachings of Confucius as based on gender, age, social status and so on. Some go so far as to argue that Confucianism represents a moral approach to political order, in contrast to the legalist and naturalist approaches within the Chinese tradition, and to the natural order (via Hobbes), utilitarian (via Bentham), religious (via Aquinas) and modern institutional approaches in the broader international context of human history (Huang, 2002: 227).

Indeed, it is argued that the tradition of Confucianism as a moral solution to political order has survived in contemporary modern state building. In a study examining the fundamental nature of state-making in China since the Qing Dynasty (1644–1911), Patricia M. Thornton finds 'a profoundly normative and normalizing process, which seeks not only to impose a particular moral order within which the state can claim primacy but also to make the presence of the state at the centre of that totalizing vision appear both natural and necessary' (Thornton, 2007: 4).

Moving beyond Confucianism as a moral framework, Lucian W. Pye also sees Confucianism as a model of authority structure (see Box 3.2). Pye's influential work on Asian authority and culture (Pye, 1985) is one of the first systematic investigations of the relationship between traditional culture and political structure in what he called 'Confucian states'. Pye went to extra lengths to discuss the differences between alternative national models of the Confucian authority structure and to demonstrate the institutional quality of this structure.

The impact of Confucianism on political development in Pacific Asia is also noted in the widely read works of W. Theodore de Bary. However, de Bary distances the family-morality-centred Confucianism from the legalistic tradition of imperial China (de Bary, 1998) and explores the ambivalence of Confucianism in relation to contemporary modern liberal values and institutions (de Bary, 1991).

What makes Confucianism a more critical issue in Pacific Asian politics and government is that, traditionally, as Costopoulos observes, 'it was almost completely identified with East Asia's imperial and monarchical regimes' (Costopoulos, 2005: xiv). Contemporary debates about the cultural foundations of the Asian economic miracle and the authoritarian and corporatist political order in Pacific Asia all point to the transformation and influence of Confucianism and a political order and social structure governed by Confucian principles.

Given the conservative nature of Confucianism and its close association with the traditional political order of hierarchy and authority, questions have naturally arisen as to whether Confucianism and its associated political structure and social relations would have to be overcome for modern institutions and values to develop in these societies. In actual political development, the rise of the modern state and capitalist economy in Japan since the Meiji Restoration has diminished much of the influence of Confucianism as a model of political order.

In China, such efforts in transforming the political order and social structure away from Confucianism were equally significant, but less successful. The New

Box 1.4

Confucianism and political order and development

There are competing views on how Confucianism is related to political order and development. Below are four representative approaches:

- Confucianism as a moral approach to political order. This emphasizes the ideal human behaviour and moral discipline of individuals as the foundation for political and social order.
- Confucianism as a model of authority structure. It is the underlying structural relations in Confucian states that define political order and stability of hierarchy, ascriptive roles and structural coherence.
- Confucianism as a primary obstacle to modern political and social development. Confucianism is fundamentally incompatible with modern institutions and values, and liberal democratic ones in particular.
- Confucianism as a distinct set of modern institutions and values. Confucianism is compatible, complementary or even remedial to liberal modern institutions and values.

Box 1.5

Confucian concepts of power and authority

In discussing the Confucian concepts of power and authority in four Confucian countries, Lucian Pye summarizes their fundamental elements:

- Morality: power was supposed to flow inexorably from the morally superior.
- Hierarchy: power was seen as emerging out of the relationships between superiors and inferiors.
- Legitimacy: treating formal government as the sole legitimate basis for power.
- Role model: those in power should use their own exemplary conduct as a means for influencing the behaviour of others.

These basic features of the Confucian model underlie the political structure of dependency, hierarchy, moral legitimacy and ethical propriety, found in many Pacific Asian countries.

Pye, 1985: 86–9

Culture Movement in the early decades of the twentieth century targeted Confucianism as the primary obstacle to modern political and social development in China. However, this type of elite-led cultural movement, and later political campaigns by Mao to eradicate Confucianism, such as the Cultural Revolution, did not succeed. Subsequent debates inspired by the New Culture Movement are still going on in today's China. Whether the development of the market economy and the consequent social transformation will mean the real end of Confucianism as a model of political order and social structure is yet to be seen.

Singapore's case is perhaps the most complicated. On the one hand, Singapore's modern political and economic development since the 1960s, and in particular its new political and social system that relies heavily on legal institutions rather than Confucianist moral appeal, have clearly moved Singapore away from its Confucian roots. On the other hand, the political order, at least under former Prime Minister Lee Kuan Yew, was very much operating on the principles of Confucianism (see final section for the Asian values debate promoted by Lee Kuan Yew).

Within the scholarly community, the relationship between Confucianism and democracy has also been a key issue of debate. Given the general discourses of both Confucianism and democracy, it is not difficult for scholars to argue that Confucianism and democracy are incompatible and contradictory to each other. Samuel P. Huntington, for one, claims that 'almost no scholarly disagreement exists regarding the proposition that traditional Confucianism was either undemocratic or antidemocratic'. According to Huntington, Confucianism is fundamentally incompatible with democracy (Huntington, 1991: 24) because:

- Confucian societies emphasized the group over the individual, authority over liberty, and responsibilities over rights:
- Confucian societies lacked a tradition of rights against the state; to the extent that individual rights did exist, they were created by the state:
- Harmony and cooperation were preferred over disagreement and competition. The maintenance of order and respect for hierarchy were central values. The conflict of ideas, groups and parties was viewed as dangerous and illegitimate:
- Confucianism merged society and the state and provided no legitimacy for autonomous social institutions at the national level.

There are, however, 'scholarly disagreements' over Huntington's proposition. Francis Fukuyama, for example, believes that Huntington overstates 'the obstacles that Confucianism poses to the spread of a political system'. In Fukuyama's view, there are many ways in which Confucianism and democracy can be compatible (Fukuyama, 1995: 24–6):

- The traditional Confucian examination system was a meritocratic institution with potentially egalitarian implications;
- Confucianism is the personal ethic that regulates attitudes towards family, work, education and other elements of daily life that account for the success of capitalist economies in Confucian societies;
- Confucianism was never political Confucianism, which legitimates a hierarchical political system culminating in the emperor, but rather an intense familism that took precedence over all other social relations;

- Confucianism builds a well-ordered society from the group up rather than the top down, stressing the moral obligations of family life as the basic building block of society.

Fukuyama's view that Confucianism is in many ways compatible with modern values and institutions is shared by W. Theodore de Bary. Confucianism, and what de Bary calls Western values and institutions, share fundamental 'humanistic concerns'. They differ mainly with regard to 'the primacy of the morally responsible self and the social norms' of Confucianism and the 'coupling of individual rights and legal protection' in the West (de Bary, 1998: 24).

Fukuyama and de Bary see areas of compatibility between Confucianism and modern institutions and values – democracy in particular – Daniel Bell and Chaibong Hahm go a step further. They wanted to revive Confucianism for the modern world 'by bringing about a creative synthesis between the two' (Bell and Hahm, 2003: 26). For them, the matter is not just whether Confucianism is compatible with democracy, but rather that Confucianism represents a distinct set of 'values and practices that could shape modern political, economic, and legal institutions in desirable ways, mitigating some of their more obvious excesses' (Bell and Hahm, 2003: 28) – a synthesis they call 'Confucian democracy' (ibid.: 5). Essays in their collection examine the relationship of Confucianism and the modern state in three key areas: democracy, capitalism and rule of law, and argue that Confucianism is not only relevant, but also desirable for the modern state.

If, how and to what degree Confucianism remains relevant to political order in Pacific Asian countries remains a major debate in the field. At the very least, it is possible to show how Confucian values in society still resonate and have supported elements of the developmental process. For example, Confucian teachings about self-cultivation have resulted in a strong emphasis on education in the region. These social values appear to coexist with values, such as those underpinning capitalism, suggesting a melding of the social structures. As a political ethic underpinning government, however, it is far harder to demonstrate the role of Confucianism in the development of modern institutions. As later chapters show, however, the informal functioning of these institutions does, at times, resemble traditional Confucian practices and concepts of power and authority.

The family as a model of governance

Among the key institutions of Confucianism, the family is a primary institution and model of broader relationships in traditional Confucian society. For example, relations between emperor and subject were modelled on relations between an ideal father and son relationship. Sons and subjects were to be

Case Study Lab 1.1

Interpreting Confucianism

Daniel Bell comments on the branch-root problem when studying the implications of political traditions in China and uses that perspective to explain how Confucian political institutions, social structure and civility manifest in contemporary China:

- China specialists in the West often focus their energies on a study of the "branches" (such as democracy, civil society, property rights) that seem to own their origin to Western "roots." As a result, they often misconstrue or miss altogether the contemporary branches that arise from China's own roots and show little capacity for predicting what new branches might sprout from its powerful and venereal traditions.
- On the other hand, specialists in Chinese thought often spend their time on historical interpretations of texts. They sometimes gesture at implications for modern society, but rarely spell them out in any detail.
- Any sound understanding of China needs to explore both the roots and the branches ... to uncover and explore distinctive and deep aspects of Chinese culture and point to contemporary manifestations ... and to sort out the good from the bad, and to suggest how traditional values and practices can be adapted and made defensible in contemporary Chinese society and perhaps beyond.

Bell, 2008: xiv

filial, loyal and devoted while fathers and emperors had a duty to provide and protect the interests of those in their care. In the Confucian system the family was the most important unit of society.

In traditional society, the relationship between those in positions of public authority was with the family unit and mediated through the head of the household who spoke for the entire family unit. This had both positive and negative implications. For example, the status of one member of the family would have a positive influence on the activities of all the family members. Alternatively, if, for example, one of the family members committed a crime, the entire family or even the local neighbourhood could receive punishment.

The traditional Confucian relationship between rulers and the family bears heavily on the state's efforts to develop a direct relationship with the individual, a hallmark of the modern state. On the one hand, regulations on family matters, including marriage or the rights of women, are an important form of 'the expression of state power' (Glosser, 2003, xiii). On the other hand, the state's vision and capacity often depends as much on family behaviour as on public law. This is especially the case for the Northeast Asian countries, for two main reasons. First, the family has been promoted in state ideology, namely Confucianism, as a cornerstone of social order and as an integral part of the centralized state system.

Second, the family has evolved to become a primary unit of human association and activity. In both the public and private spheres, the family is seen as a primary value, a preferred form of human relations and association, and a legitimate platform for social interaction and representation. The family was an important form of public authority in premodern society, and modernization in a sense means the removal of the function of the family, and, in the case of Pacific Asian countries, the denial of patriarchal authority. The tension between the existing family system and modern values has created a profound dilemma for the state in promoting modern values.

There is a widespread view that the success of industrialization and rapid economic growth, and the persistence of non-pluralist politics and government in parts of Pacific Asia, are all related to the role of the family. The family is seen by many as an important cultural factor behind the success of industrialization and rapid economic growth in Pacific Asia. For example, family-based firms and conglomerates in Korea and Taiwan are considered to have played an important role in the early phase of rapid growth (Fields, 1995). Family relations and the model they create for broader relations in society, have also been blamed for the crony capitalism and advent of non-pluralist politics in a long list of Pacific Asian countries (Okochi and Yasuoka, 1984; Tai, 1989; Hamilton and Gao, 1990; Kim, 1998).

Clearly, then, there are different conceptions involved in the discussion of the role of the family in Pacific Asia. Indeed, 'familism' can refer to:

- Family values of an individual and the individual's family-centred attitude and behaviour.
- Preferences for business to be run by family members.
- Family authority structures as a model for business and polity.

Familism in the Pacific Asian tradition, therefore, played an important role as a model of governance and as a primary unit of society. There is also evidence that the family remains important in contemporary times. Only recently has universal suffrage been achieved, there is still evidence of business relations being structured along family lines and, as future chapters will illustrate, scholars have pointed to informal state practices such as informal bargaining and coalition building, as evidence that the polity is still organized along the model of the traditional family. As such, there are several issues in Pacific Asia with the role of the family in modern state building:

- First, the inevitable tension between the Confucian model of social relations, where individuals' rights are shaped by their ascriptive roles in family relations, and the essential requirement of equal citizenship for everyone in an ideal modern state.
- Second, a level of competition between the family as the basic unit that manages family members' political, economic and moral life in traditional society and the state that intends to build direct relationships with individual citizens in the modern state.
- Third, a level of incompatibility between the structure of polities and governments modelled after the traditional family structure and those of the modern state.

There is also much evidence that the traditional family and family–state relations have changed in the process of modern state building. This can be illustrated through a review of the issue of gender inequality and the problem of the family acting as the intermediate layer between the state and the individual thereby regulating family matters on behalf of the state.

Take Japan as an example. Modern reforms of the relations between state, family and the individual began with the Meiji Restoration, but significant progress was not made until after the Second World War. The Constitution of 1947 and in particular Article 24, as well as the Family Law of 1947, removed the power and authority heads of families held through the household-centred registration system and confirmed the principles of individual freedom and gender equality. Reforms eliminated previous restrictions placed on women to marry or gain access to state resources directly with the state. Marriage became contractual and the sole basis for the family and all siblings gained an equal share of inherited family property. On the basis of these post-war reforms, Japan completed the transformation from the traditional family system to the modern 'institutional family' (Sano, 1973: 71).

A similar process of reform took place in South Korea a few decades later. The principle of equality between men and women was not recognized until the Civil Code of 1968. However, the dependence of women upon the male household head – that is, family interference in women's direct relationships with the state – was not eliminated completely until 1989 when a new set of amendments were made to the Civil Code against the backdrop of the historic political transition of 1987.

In China, modern reforms began early in the twentieth century, in particular on two key fronts. First, the state, under both the nationalist and communist governments, has largely removed the family as a form of public authority. Second, gender equality was legally established from the early years of communist rule. Unlike the situation in Japan and Korea, the reform of family–state relations in China took place within the larger context of excessive state power. Accompanying the retreat of the family's institutional power, however, has been the state's 'highly intrusive and coercive role' over family matters (Davis and Harrell, 1993: 3; see also Diamant, 2000: 329). Moreover, institutions such as the household registration system still play an undue role tying individuals' access to state provisions and public goods via the family (see Wang, 2005, Young, 2013), with many restrictions on the ability of individuals to change this status.

Confucianism as a social ethic remains an important part of the fabric of society in Pacific Asia. This has led scholars to try to understand how Confucianism relates to the function of government and to the process of modern state building in the region. The above review, however, shows that while Confucianism remains an important part of the ethic systems in Pacific Asia and the family remains a basic building block of society, the general trend has been towards institutionalizing regulations and systems that marginalize their role as a form of public authority. As outlined below, the marginalization of Confucianism began when Europeans entered the region on mass from the eighteenth and nineteenth centuries. Many Pacific Asian states lost their right to govern independently as early European exploration and trade was extended to colonial governance over the majority of the region.

Models of colonial governance

Europeans began to arrive in Pacific Asia from the sixteenth century onwards. The presence of traders, soldiers, missionaries, philosophers and diplomats reshaped political order in a way that challenged local control of resources and the traditional way of organizing politics, economy and society. Their activities had a major and lasting impact on the structures of government in the region.

No state, however powerful, remained untouched by the organizational and industrial power that European traders and diplomats wielded. The very real threat of direct control by a foreign power led to even the most advanced states capitulating to European demands for open trade and to conduct diplomacy and international relations on terms developed in Europe.

Colonization, or semi-colonization as was the case for China, Japan and Siam (today's Thailand), generally involved military defeat of the traditional power and authority, the establishment of trade on preferential terms that gave European traders access to resources and opened Pacific Asian markets for exports of European products, and finally, either the direct or indirect establishment of governing structures that mirrored the ideals and interests of the colonizing power.

Such changes, coupled with the introduction of enlightenment thinking and Christianity and new organizing principles underlying state and social organization, such as universal education, changed not only the state structures of Pacific Asian states but infused society with new values and ideals that underpinned a series of major social, political and economic revolutions in the region that continue to play out to this day. The introduction of constitutionalism, the rule of law, representation and popular legitimacy for example, still reverberate through popular movements towards functioning democracies in the region.

There were, however, different systems, methods or models by which different colonial powers established their presence and 'governed' the territory to the extent they did. We can therefore classify different models of colonial governance, based on the extent to which colonial rulers managed to impose a different system of politics and governance on the local polity. The three models are direct rule, self-government and indirect rule.

France established a long-standing presence in the region from the mid-nineteenth century through their Indochina colony in present-day Vietnam, Laos and Cambodia. This was achieved through military victory over local and Chinese forces and through the systematic introduction of a series of institutions that supported direct rule. These included legal, general administrative and communal institutions that gave French authorities direct power and authority over the local population. Colonial authorities then controlled major sectors of the economy, the military and police and the civil service.

In the Philippines colonial rule by the United States (previously Spain) was less direct. By adopting 'self-government' they introduced a very different model of colonial governance to that of the French in Indochina. The United States ruled from afar largely through the establishment of model institutions. The constitutional design for the Philippines was based largely on the American presidential system. However, this system coexisted in a society that remained dominated by landed elites and the legacy of Spanish rule. Self-governance in the Philippines therefore allowed much of the existing local structure to undermine the function of the intended state institutions, thereby further complicating political development in the region.

Between these two colonial governments was the vast archipelago and peninsula of Southeast Asia, where British and Dutch influences dominated. In both cases, new institutions serving the economic interests of the colonial administration, such as taxation and cultivation systems, altered the traditional structure significantly. They brought village-centred economic activities under the exclusive control of the 'state', and in doing so strengthened the function of the state. These institutions were, however, far less intrusive than the institutions of direct rule by the French. This is not to say British and Dutch rule did not channel resources away from the locals, but that this was achieved for most in an indirect manner by enlisting the support of certain local elites.

For example, Robert Cribb's study of the Dutch East Indies (originally established by the Dutch East

Box 1.6

The formation of colonial governance

Once it become apparent that Europeans had entered a region in force and with intent to stay, traditional leaders negotiated with them the terms of their unequal relationship. As noted, colonial authorities were quite prepared to co-opt local rulers where possible, as a means of gaining wider control over the population. Thus, while formal power accrued to the new regime, administrative powers were often delegated to this co-opted class. Matters of personal status were generally left in the realm of customary law, although individual rights and freedoms were considerably restrained by legal regimes designed to control and monitor rather than liberate and foster. Different laws applied to the indigenous population and the Europeans, and the unequal nature of these relationships planted the seeds of aspiration for autonomy and national independence.

Hassall and Saunders, 2007: 27

India Company in present-day Indonesia) explains the administrative structure of Dutch colonial rule in Indonesia:

> At the core of the Indies administration stood a relatively straightforward administrative hierarchy headed by a governor general and a Council of the Indies and staffed by a few hundred European men appointed for their general administrative skills. In each region of the colony this European hierarchy interacted variously with one or more indigenous political institutions. In many places, specially outside Java, the local polities thus enmeshed were so-called native states – once independent entities that, by treaty or conquest, had fallen under Dutch control ... In managing the affairs of their own subjects, the rulers of most states enjoyed a fairly high degree of autonomy, so long as they did not attract the attention of the colonial authorities by hindering European economic interests. (Cribb, 1999: 10)

Models of colonial rule also changed over time and even within the colonial region. For example, British rule in Malay combined direct and indirect forms of

Case Study Lab 1.2

Analysing colonial legacy

The impact of colonialism and colonization on modern political development in Pacific Asia is always an issue causing great controversy. It is controversial because not only are there contending interpretations and contradictory evidence of the nature and extent of colonial legacies in different countries, but also because the nationalist view has been dominant in the discourse, which tends to make an objective assessment difficult. At the core of the debate is the question of whether colonialism was a positive or a negative force for the emergence of the modern state. More specifically, whether colonialism has helped to shape modern forms of government; whether colonialism prepared economic, social and cultural conditions for modern institutions to emerge; and whether colonial government itself practiced and promoted the rule of law, civil liberty and actively advanced modern values. (For a related debate, see Barlow, 1997; and Shin and Robinson, 1999.)

Those who argue that colonialism and colonization were destructive to local society and political order, and disruptive to the normal process of political development, tend to come from three different academic traditions.

Nationalists emphasize the harsh rule colonial governments imposed on the indigenous population and the exploitative and suppressive systems they relied on for running the colony.

Culturalists argue that, first, each society has its own unique cultural and historical conditions that support the function of local institutions. European colonialism broke down these conditions, which led to the dislocation, disconnection and delay in development and progress in these societies. Second, because of the different historical 'trajectories' of different countries, modernity can develop in various forms. Modernities as a historical phenomenon can and should be plural. The idea that European colonialism brought modern development to Pacific Asia carries a discriminatory view against other forms of modernity.

Structuralists draw on Wallerstein's core-peripheral framework (Wallerstein, 1974), and argue that the ultimate effect of European colonialism is the integration of those colonized societies into the world capitalist system, and thus the perpetuation of their position in the periphery of the system.

Institutionalists look at the form and institutions of colonial governance and how they affect the shaping of the state, state institutions and political structure in contemporary political development. Hassall and Saunders, for example, argue that 'colonization has left much of the Asia Pacific a paradoxical legacy of both a strong executive and a reliance on the Westminster model of parliamentary democracy. The result has been a failure of parliaments to function well, often having their role diminished by a president or prime minister, or even by the armed forces'. Moreover, the unequal relationship between colonial authorities and local rulers, and different laws applied to them 'planted the seeds of aspirations towards autonomy, national and independence'. (2007: 8, 27) rule, with direct governance over certain cities and indirect rule through the patronage of sultans in federated states. Governance over plantations, particularly the highly lucrative rubber plantations, was also more hands on. After losing effective control of the colony to the Japanese during World War II, British colonial forces returned at the end of the war and 'quickly re-established the colonial state after regaining control, and direct rule expanded even further in the last decade of colonialism'. The communist and anticolonial insurgency that followed from 1948, known as 'the Emergency', 'forced the territorial and administrative expansion of the state' (Lange, 2009: 184-186).

There are, however, increasing numbers of scholars, dubbed revisionists, starting to recognize the contributions of colonialism to modern development in colonial societies. Colonial rule was harsh by today's standards, but colonial economy, governance, and social policy advanced the local economy, and prepared the infrastructure for modern development. Institutional developments during the colonial era became the foundations for government and society of many newly independent states. There is an underlying continuity from colonial development to contemporary government and politics.

The consequent state structure featured a European-controlled government; collaborative local elites; a 'state'-led economy that integrated local economic and social activities; and the use of all necessary means by the 'state' to secure and maintain these arrangements. These elements formed an important part of the institutional foundation for the new states in post-independent Southeast Asia.

There seems to be no question that colonialism has left a significant impact on contemporary government and politics in Pacific Asian countries (see Case Study Lab 1.2 for debates on this). For one thing, the particular forms of government in many Pacific Asian countries have been influenced significantly by their colonial history (Kingsbury, 2005a: 35–6). The parliamentary systems in Singapore and Malaysia, for example, clearly have their roots in the British system. The presidential system in the Philippines is an institutional consequence of American colonial rule. However, one has to recognize that colonial rule was established and maintained through trade, diplomacy, political deals and coercion and force. In most cases, there was little local participation. Governance by elites, corrupt governments, and the use of coercion and violence as political methods of control by colonial authorities was not rare, and left a significant impact.

Box 1.7

Pacific Asia: gaining independence in the twentieth century

Country	*Status In 1910*	*Year became Independent*
Brunei	British rule	1984
Cambodia	French rule	1953
China	Independent state	
East Timor	Portuguese rule	2002
Indonesia	Dutch rule	1945
Japan	Independent state	
Korea	Japanese rule	1945
Laos	French rule	1945
Malaysia	British rule	1957
Myanmar	British rule	1948
Philippines	American rule	1946
Singapore	British rule	1965
Taiwan	Japanese rule	
Thailand	Independent state	
Vietnam	French rule	1945

Empire and the early interstate system

Of the three models of early state formation in Pacific Asia the centralized state model provided the most effective means of harnessing the resources of the state. The Chinese state had established itself as the preeminent premodern empire in Pacific Asia through its technological prowess and complex systems of governance, military and economy. China, with its large population and prosperous resources, grew powerful and enlarged its borders in the years between 221 BC and the colonial era (Cohen, 2007). Chinese governance, political philosophy and military prowess therefore exerted a significant impact on how early states in the region organized relations with each other. The Chinese empire dominated the East Asian mainland and exerted influence on all surrounding kingdoms in what has come to be known as the Chinese world order.

The Chinese world order was a system of interstate relations based on a set of organizing principles that stressed hierarchy, inequality and tribute. The 'Son of Heaven' (*tianzi*) sat at the centre of this order and ruled on the premise that virtuous conduct (*de*), proper ceremonial forms (*li*), right principles (*li*) and regulations (*fa*) conferred upon him the authority and prestige to govern (Fairbank 1968). This order spread outwards through conquest (Cohen, 2007) and expansion of cultural influence. As it grew it developed a 'sense of all-embracing unity and cultural entity' consuming the lands of today's China and establishing outposts in Korea, North Vietnam and Central Asia (Fairbank, 1968: 5). Unequal relations with vassal states required them to follow Chinese norms and respect the values of the Chinese world order to gain trade rights, knowledge and protection.

According to John Fairbank, the Chinese world order consisted of three concentric zones: the Sinic Zone; the Inner Asia Zone; the Outer Zone (see Figure 1.4). The Sinic Zone included the closest and most culturally similar tributaries of Korea, Vietnam, and Ryukyu/Liuqiu (today's Okinawa in Japan). The Inner Asian Zone included the tributary tribes and states of the nomadic or semi-nomadic peoples of today's Central Asia. The Outer Zone included the outer 'barbarians' further from China either over land or sea, namely, Japan, the remainder of Southeast Asia, South Asia and Europe (Fairbank, 1968: 2).

Organizing principles differed considerably to the nation-state system that governs interstate relations in contemporary Pacific Asia and the world. Today's interstate relations are founded on key principles that originated in the Peace of Westphalia (1648) between the major European powers in the seventeenth century:

- *Sovereignty.* The state has the highest authority over matters within its internationally recognized territories. Other states should respect such authority and refrain from intervening in matters under the territorial jurisdiction of other states.
- *Equality.* All states are equal in terms of territorial rights and jurisdiction.
- *Treaty and diplomacy.* Matters between equal states should be settled through diplomacy and formal treaties.

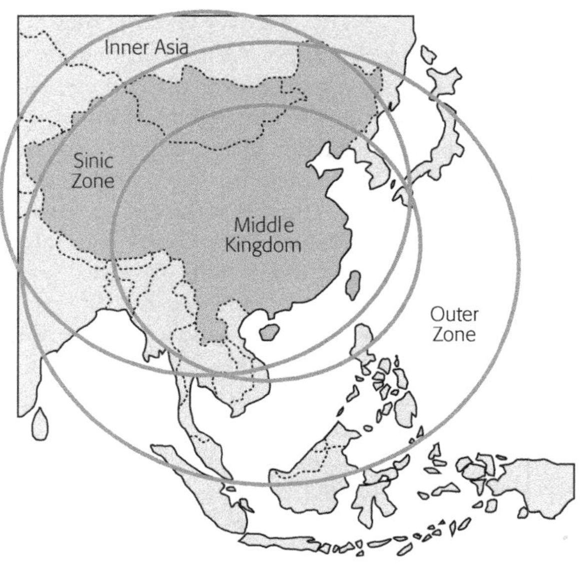

Figure 1.4 Fairbank's Chinese World Order in seventeenth century

The Chinese World Order, in comparison, operated on a system of hierarchy and inequality and was institutionalized through a complex pattern of tributary relations:

- Hierarchy and inequality. 'The Chinese tended to think of their foreign relations as giving expression externally to the same principles of social and political order that were manifested internally within the Chinese state and society. China's foreign relations were accordingly hierarchic and nonegalitarian' (Fairbank, 1968: 2). Countries within the Chinese world order were positioned in concentric zones with China at the centre.

Case Study Lab 1.3

Identifying the pre-modern East Asian international system

Inquiries into early East Asian international relations focus on three key questions:

- Was there an international system in East Asia before the European international system expanded there?
- What did the early East Asian international system look like? What was the underlying structure, the organizing principles and the rules of operation? How did the system transform and evolve?
- How does it relate to the broader international system and its modern transformation?

David Kang (2012) focuses on the tributary system in East Asia from the fourteenth to the nineteenth century, illustrating how China and its principal neighbours, Korea, Vietnam and Japan, were at the core of an East Asian international system with a formal hierarchy and its own history and character.

Barry Busan, Yongjin Zhang (2014) and a team of international scholars extend the work of the English School to examine the existence of distinctive international social structures as the basis for an East Asian international society. Yongjin Zhang places the tributary system, or what he calls 'universalist empire', in the broader context of the historical evolution of the East Asian international system and argues there have been 'three historically varying forms of international order' in East Asia: a multistate system in Ancient China; a unified and universalist empire and a world order associated with it; and the empire and world order transforming into a state among states under the Westphalian order (Zhang 2001: 45).

The idea of empire and the tributary system as different forms of international order led Joseph MacKay (2015) to argue that there are more subtle institutions and structures that define the grey area between empire and an international system.

- Tributary relations. The conduct of China's relations was institutionalized through tributary relations whereby other countries paid tribute to China on a regular basis as a way of recognizing special relations with China and respect for Chinese power and influence. In return, China accepted other countries in its world order, provided protection and legitimacy for the governing regime and retained the right to intervene in their domestic affairs.

The tributary system in particular formed a key part of the Chinese world order. It operated as a 'boundary mechanism' between the 'barbarian' world and Confucian China. According to Mancall (1984), the tributary system functioned to 'intermesh rather than to integrate the Central, East, and Southeast Asian societies' with China. The intermeshing of one or more societies or cultures with China involved, broadly speaking, patterns of behaviour and institutions through which material goods, political positions, and ideological statements were communicated between otherwise discrete societies, that is, societies between which the system functioned to maintain a prescribed and optimal distance.

This intermeshing was more than mere contact because it was highly institutionalized and simultaneously took place along several dimensions, such as the economic, the political, and the cultural. The existence at any given moment of a wide variety of mechanisms for intermeshing allowed participants in the East Asian international society a choice of means to achieve their ends (Mancall, 1984: 15).

China's interstate system therefore served a set of functions very different from the modern international system. This 'world order' did not follow the same principles as the 'world order' that evolved in Europe and eventually came to underpin the nation-state system the world over. Some scholars, most notably Fairbank, have argued the Chinese world order was particularly difficult to square with the European order because it contained:

> a set of institutionalized attitudes and historical precedents not easily conformable to the

> European tradition of international relations among equally sovereign nation-states. Modern China's difficulty of adjustment to the international order of nation-states in the nineteenth and twentieth centuries has come partly from the tributary tradition of the Chinese world order. (Fairbank, 1968: 4)

These differences meant that when the Chinese world order came into contact and entered competition with a view of world order promoted by European traders, diplomats and missionaries, the two could not coexist.

Towards modern state building in Pacific Asia

Politics and government in Pacific Asia in the nineteenth and early twentieth centuries witnessed major, and in many ways ongoing, transition from traditional forms of political, economic and social organization, to systems more recognizable today. The diversity of the early Pacific Asian states in the region, in particular the differing degree of centralization of power and authority and level of bureaucratic sophistication between Southeast and Northeast Asia, played out in these states responses to the direct and indirect challenges of European incursions and how these states entered their transition to modern systems of governance and politics.

While Europeans established their presence, developed their economic and social interests, and established new forms and institutions of social and political organization in Southeast Asia, it was far more difficult for them to do the same in Northeast Asia. This was partly because in Northeast Asia, there was a well-established and highly centralized social and political system that had existed and functioned for hundreds and thousands of years.

This system had evolved and developed on traditional ideas and conditions similar to the ones the Europeans had managed to change and reform in Europe in the early modern time. Francis Fukuyama identifies the strong and highly centralized system of governance that developed in China very early on as a key feature of the origins of political order in the region (2009). The system that evolved had a strong legacy of tradition and organizational capacity. Even when faced with an increasing inability to sustain the political, economic and social order as European incursions challenged this legitimacy, political order could not change overnight.

The period is highly significant for political development in the region. Traditional practices were challenged, questioned and even usurped by systems and processes developed largely in a European context. New ideas, reforms and competing power groups challenged the existing political order culminating in a period of reform and even revolution. It was this cross-civilizational encounter and interaction, more intensified from the nineteenth century that pressed East Asian countries to consider change and act to reform and modernize their political systems.

When the Emperor of Japan, Meiji, looked around the region in 1868 and proclaimed Japan's first modern constitution and the first in Pacific Asia, he would have been acutely aware of the challenges traditional systems in Pacific Asia were facing in the early modern era. The dominant system, the Chinese empire built upon a centralized state model, was facing a significant challenge to sustain itself with European powers controlling important Chinese ports and establishing a strong presence within the previously closed country. Much of Southeast Asia had come under the influence of European colonial powers and its traditional village-court system was being incorporated into the emergent forms and institutions of colonial governance. Overall, the traditional forms of politics and government, and the established institutions of political organization of society, were increasingly facing the problem of legitimacy and effectiveness, with the underlying social and economic dynamics rapidly shifting.

Large-scale interactions with incoming Europeans exposed the region's elites to the power of technology, money and ideas. Gunboat diplomacy forced kings, emperors and sultans to the negotiation table. 'East India' companies penetrated and reorganized local economies. European arts, Christianity and the notion of civilization went almost hand in hand with science and modern institutions. The prevailing sentiment was to 'become European'.

Japan's Yukichi Fukuzawa (1834–1901) was one of the first in the late nineteenth century to advocate nation-state building in Japan after the European models. The strong contrast between European powers on the one hand and China's decay and turmoil on the other reinforced the idea that Japan ought to become a nation like those in Europe.

Indeed, the same sentiment was also found among Chinese intellectual and political elites. Sun Yat-san was a leading figure in the early twentieth century. There was a strong sense of admiration in Sun of European models and institutions. But for Sun, Manchu's rule of China was a primary cause for China's lagging behind Europe. Moreover, like many elites in China at the time, Sun's admiration of Europe was mixed with some suspicion and distrust.

For Sun, the solution to the Asian problem – that is, inferiority to European power and global influence – was national sovereignty and a Pan-Asian unity, rather than trying to 'become European'. Both Japan and China were looking for ways to re-energize or revitalize themselves, and to become a 'rich country with a strong army'. One can already see clearly here the roots of the fundamental differences between Japan and China in approaching the task (for more discussion on this, see Yoda, 1996).

The exposure of European power, institutions and culture through their advance, penetration and settlement in Pacific Asia also led local elites to take a hard look at the systems and culture in their own countries. Constitutionalism, democracy, elected government, political parties and a national army, along with science, modern education, economic organization and institutions became widely accepted as necessary for remedying systematic problems and building a modern country.

Ideological debates, political reforms, and mass revolutions became popular forms for expressing these sentiments and dominated the political landscape in the early twentieth century. Notable among the early attempts at reform were the Meiji Restoration (1868–89) in Japan, the Hundred Day Reformation (1898) in China, the Kabo Reforms in Korea (1894–6) and the Chulalongkorn reforms (1880s) in Thailand (see Box 1.8).

Of these nominally independent states in the nineteenth century, reforms in China, Korea and Thailand had limited impact on their efforts to

Box 1.8

Early attempts at political modernization in Pacific Asia: what happened, and how successful were they?

Country	*Time*	*Programme*	*Content in area of government*	*Form*	*Outcome*
China	1898	'Hundred-Days' Reformation	Modernization of government and administration	Decrees by conservative Court upon advice of progressive scholars	Failed; advocates executed
Japan	1868–1889	Meiji Restoration	From absolute to constitutional monarchy, from fragmented state to modern centralized state	Regional daimyos allied with emperor to overcome the shogunate	Successful
Korea	1894–1896	Kabo Reforms	Reform of government, military modernization, new judicial system	Government decrees with conservatives; the backing of the Japanese	Unpopular; Pretext to further reform under Japan's colonial rule
Thailand	1880s	Chulalongkorn Reforms	Government and admin reforms	King's own efforts	Carried out

institutionalize modern systems of government. The imperial system limped on in China before the country descended into warlord states supported by vying European powers and ultimately a long and bloody civil war between the Nationalists and Communists. Reforms in Korea, with the support of Japan, acted as a pretext for further Japanese incursions on the peninsula and ultimately the full colonization of Korea by Japan. The Chulalongkorn reforms in Thailand made some significant improvements in Thai governance, abolishing slavery and introducing salaries for Thai officials as well as centralizing provincial governance and introducing new but limited forms of education based on European schooling and building new infrastructure such as railways. Like China however, the pace of reforms was significantly curtailed due to popular or stakeholder opposition.

Of those colonized states, predominantly in Southeast Asia, reform came in the form of institutions imposed by the colonial power. Indigenous efforts at modern state building had to wait until the more urgent task of consolidating sovereignty and territorial integrity could be achieved, often at a high cost, to the local populace. This is not to argue modern state building did not occur under colonial rule but that political development was significantly interrupted and complicated by colonialism and the struggle for independence.

Only Japan is considered to have fully succeeded at meeting the challenge of modern state building in terms of creating a modern centralized state with a parliamentary system and modern systems of education, bureaucracy, military, and political economy. However, by the 1930s even Japan was descending into a military led state underlying the long-term challenge modern state building presents states in Pacific Asia in the post-war era.

Irrespective of whether Pacific Asian states in the late nineteenth century were under colonial rule, trying to maintain a dynastic system or introducing radical reforms, all states were faced with responding to, adapting to and ultimately incorporating the influx of enlightenment thinking, science and technology, foreign religions and ideologies as well as technology that radically changed how society was organized and the relationship between government and society.

As shown in the next chapter, this challenge is ongoing. The chapter will therefore explore the factors that have complicated modern state building in the region, some of which have their origins in the traditional order of politics and government described here.

Chapter summary

- There are three models of governance in traditional Pacific Asia: the centralized state model, mainly in Northeast Asia; the fragmented state model in some historical periods of Japan and China; and the galactic polity, largely in Southeast Asia.
- Confucianism is a moral approach to political order and a distinct model of power and authority. It informed how traditional political society in much of Pacific Asia was organized, how authority was legitimated and how power was exercised.
- Different forms of colonial governance operated in Pacific Asia and are largely distinguished by the degree to which the colonial power intervened directly or indirectly in the day-to-day governing of the colony.
- There is a major debate in comparative politics about the lasting impact of colonial rule on modern state building in the region with nationalists, culturalists and structuralists pointing to the negative impact of colonial rule while some revisionist scholars point to a partially positive legacy in the form of institutional development.
- By the late nineteenth century no state in Pacific Asia, whether colonized or not, remained untouched by incursions of European trade, religion and ideas and new forms of science

and technology and political organization. The intermingling of these civilizations created a dynamic and at times an explosive social and political environment where a number of reforms were attempted with varying outcomes.

- The Chinese world order was the dominant interstate system in Pacific Asia before the nineteenth century and was organized on a system of tribute and hierarchy and inequality between states.
- Of all the states in Pacific Asia in the nineteenth century, Japan emerged the strongest in the early reform era through a radical and well-implemented system of reforms. This rise, however, ended tragically through military rule and aggressive expansion in the region followed by Japanese defeat in World War II.
- The process of modern state building remains a significant challenge for many states in Pacific Asia.

Further reading

On the general history of political development in Pacific Asian countries, see Borthwick (2014). On traditional forms of government and politics, see Huntington (1968) on political order in changing societies; Pye (1985) and Keyes et al. (1994) on Asian conceptions of authority; and McCloud (1999) and Gesick (1983) on traditional state structures in Southeast Asia. On the role of colonial rule in political development, see Barlow (1997), and Shin and Robinson (1999). On twentieth-century nationalism in Pacific Asia, see Leifer (2000).

There is a substantively large volume of literature on modern political development in individual Pacific Asian countries. Some of them are recommended in the country profile in each chapter.

Study questions

1 What conditions affected early state formation in Pacific Asia?

2 Was colonial rule a positive or negative force for modern political development in post-colonial Pacific Asia?

3 How did the incursion of European powers in the region change the dynamics of the regional order? What has been the lasting impact of this on regional order and political development in Pacific Asia?

4 Using examples from Northeast and Southeast Asia, explain why the experience of Japan in the late nineteenth century was so different to that of China and the colonized states in Southeast Asia. How could European powers come to dominate the region?

5 What, if any, has been the lasting impact of early state formation and state building in Pacific Asia on the contemporary process of modern state building in the region?

6 Do you think Confucianism is a religion? Does it make a difference for our understanding of the role of traditional values and institutions in modern state building in Pacific Asia whether it is or not?

Key terms

State formation (11); Centralized state model (15); Oriental despotism (15); Fragmented state model (18); Colonial governance (26); Court-village structure (19); Confucian structure of authority (21); Indianized and Sinicized states (14); Galactic polity (15); Imperium (20); Chinese empire and world order (12); Meiji Restoration (13).

Chapter 2
Building the modern state

From the mid-nineteenth century, Pacific Asian countries experienced a series of efforts to reform and change the political system in their countries. These efforts aimed to transform existing institutions and establish new institutions according to modern ideas, principles and values. For more than a century following the beginning of these efforts, incremental reform, revolution and mass political movements have supplanted the traditional political order of Pacific Asia.

The considerable challenges Pacific Asian states have experienced building the modern state over this period can be partly explained by the massive social, economic and political changes that took place as elites and social groups pushed for reform and revolution but also by the vulnerability this transitional period created for the new states. As noted in Chapter 1, in the early modern era, states in Pacific Asia faced major challenges maintaining sovereignty and integrating into international society as states of equal standing.

Prior to World War II (WWII), most of Southeast Asia was under some form of colonial rule. Japan introduced a successful modernization programme but descended into military imperialism from the 1930s, laying the seeds of its military defeat in WWII. China, the largest of the East Asian powers, became the 'sick man of Asia' as provincial warlords jockeyed for power and patronage from rival great powers and a devastating civil war and Japanese invasion further weakened the state. Poverty was rife across the entire region.

Reforms in the early era, therefore, sought to harness 'modern' ideas of how to organize politics and economy in order to first and foremost build a 'rich country with a strong army'. Over the long run, the ideas introduced from the nineteenth century have been harnessed in various forms to meet this challenge. Various groups and actors have also sought to reform the institutions of government to create modern systems of representation and governance.

The forces driving development and modern state building in Pacific Asia are complex and diverse. On the one hand, reformers had the benefit of models of modern state building developed elsewhere. Thorstein Veblen (1915) described this as the 'advantage of backwardness'. Veblen had analysed Germany's efforts to catch up economically to the United Kingdom in the nineteenth century and argued being able to quickly and efficiently incorporate innovations from the UK created a significant developmental advantage. Similarly, then, Pacific Asian countries in the nineteenth century had a ready blueprint of modern state building from the social, economic and political transformations of Europe and the Americas that provided them with a considerable developmental advantage.

On the other hand, however, modern state building unleashes contestation between different political actors and interest groups over how the modern state will support differing ideals and values. There has been no single blueprint for modern state building in the region. The ideas that underpin it range from communism to socialism, nationalism to imperialism, republicanism to democracy and socialism to capitalism. Each spread rapidly from Europe to Pacific Asia in the early colonial era where the contestation between different models and modes of modernity that originated with the early modernizers was fiercely replicated. However, differing from earlier modern state building, Pacific Asia's development was further complicated by traditional forms of public authority and a legacy of foreign control.

W. Macmahon Ball observed that three forces in particular dominated the region: a nationalist revolt against foreign political control, colonialism and imperialism; a social and economic revolt against poverty and inequality; and a racial revolt against the West (Ball, 1956: 1). Those groups that could harness these forces could forward their cause for reform or revolution. This process often repeated itself over the tumultuous nineteenth and twentieth centuries before the newly formed modern states found stability and predictability in the later twentieth century.

Japan, for example, witnessed the rapid spread of the teachings of Marxism, communism and socialism, republicanism, constitutionalism and democracy, nationalism and self-determination. Early Meiji era reformers, such as Itō Hirobumi, the principal author of the Meiji Constitution, successfully adopted and incorporated ideas and institutions from abroad. Moreover, the political parties and social movements that mushroomed in Japan in the 1920s owe much to ideals advocated in a variety of modern ideologies. The dominance of imperialism, nationalism and militarism from the 1930s ultimately forced Japan to return to a more pluralistic tradition of adopting modern ideas for modern state building in the post-war years.

Similarly, science and democracy, nationalism and republicanism, communism and revolution gained great popularity in China. Nationalism and republicanism, as well as communism and revolution, quickly resulted in significant changes in the political landscape, supporting two major revolutions and a long and protracted civil war. Principal reformers like Kang Youwei and Sun Yat-sen were strongly influenced by ideas such as nationalism and constitutionalism. This pattern reoccurred following the failure of early reforms to create a strong country capable of repelling Japanese aggression and an affluent country capable of providing the basic necessities of life. This time, however, revolution was undertaken in the name of communism. Communist revolutionaries, such as Mao Zedong in China and Ho Chi Minh in Vietnam, successfully harnessed nationalist sentiments to establish a strong and independent state and to improve social outcomes.

As Pacific Asian states worked to wrestle control of their own political destiny the region became a battleground for the world's competing ideologies. By the 1950s, competition between the political systems of communism and liberal democracy and the economic systems of socialism and capitalism had come to dominate modern state building in the region. This further delayed the already slow introduction of democracy on both sides of the Cold War divide.

The end of the Cold War in Asia provided the opportunity for reformers to push a new wave of reform and revolution. By the 1980s the most radical of the communist-led experiments in soviet-style planning were coming to an end. State-led economic development under the socialist model gradually gave way to region-wide success in industrialization and economic development under the 'Asian model' (see Chapter 6). Economic success was widely viewed as vindication of the power of the market economy further supporting the adaptation of Asia's political economy towards a liberal market.

Moreover, strong authoritarian, single-party and military dominated states experienced political liberalization and democratic transition from the 1980s and communist states introduced limited reform and opening. Liberal democracy and capitalism have therefore become the dominant political ideologies of Pacific Asian countries, signalling a consolidation of ideas introduced more than a century ago.

This chapter looks at the forces shaping political development and modern state building in Pacific Asia. It employs the concept of the modern state as an overarching framework for analysing and interpreting political change. The chapter identifies three major ideas that have shaped the evolution of states in the region – communism, democracy and capitalism – and explores the role of the emergent political forces in the process of modern state building. These ideas and movements, more than any other, have shaped how people approach the issue of development, the struggle to institutionalize a centralized state and the call for modern democratic institutions.

The century of political development and change: ideas, ideals and driving forces

The concept of the modern state is a difficult one, not only because of the competing definitions of the concept (Pye, 1966b) but also because of the different perspectives on the subject (Held, 1989; see also Cudworth et al., 2007). One way to define the modern state is to look to theories and ideologies that emerged with the modern state. Erika Cudworth, Tim Hall and John McGovern, for example, identify ten theories and ideologies of the modern state, ranging from liberalism to Marxism, social democracy, feminism, anarchism and fundamentalism. David Held, in a similar project, puts forward four threads of political analysis on the problem of the modern state (Held, 1989: 12):

- Liberalism, which became focused on the question of sovereignty and citizenship.
- Liberal democracy, which developed liberalism's concerns while focusing on the problem of establishing political accountability.
- Marxism, which rejected the terms of reference of both liberalism and liberal democracy and concentrated on class structure and the forces of political coercion.
- Political sociology, which has elaborated concerns with both the institutional mechanisms of the state and the system of nation-states more generally.

The concept of the modern state is generally traced back to Max Weber (Weber, 1947, 1968). Weber argued that in the transformation of traditional society into a modern state, there was an inevitable process of centralization of power in the hands of the state, to meet the challenge of organizing mass economic and social life under modern conditions. The centralization of power often led to sovereign and exclusive authority of the state in an increasingly broad array of political, economic, social and even cultural and religious domains.

A modern state, in its narrow sense, is therefore about the capacity and functionality of public authority in providing order in a mass society (Pye, 1966b: 45–7; see also Box 2.1). 'The capacity of a political system' (Pye, 1966b: 46) is measured by its outputs and the degree to which it can affect society and the economy; its effectiveness and efficiency in the execution of public policy; and the rationality of its administration. Functionality concerns the structures and institutions of government offices and agencies, how different functions are differentiated and ultimately what functions the state performs. A modern state is also ultimately about the equality of its citizens. Only when citizens have access to a neutral public authority that treats citizens with impartiality and according to a universal set of rules can an equality of membership be achieved.

Box 2.1

The concept of political modernization

Lucian W. Pye identifies three fundamental themes in the various definitions of political modernization:

- Equality: mass participation and popular involvement in political activities; laws should be of a universalistic nature, applicable to all and more or less impersonal in their operation; the recruitment to political office should reflect achievement standards of performance and not the ascriptive considerations of a traditional social system;
- Capacity: the sheer magnitude, scope and scale of political and government performance; effectiveness and efficiency in the execution of public policy; rationality in administration and a secular orientation towards policy;
- Functionality: differentiation and specialization of structures, increased functional specificity of the various political roles within the system, and the integration of complex structures and processes.

Pye, 1966b: 45–8

This two-tiered definition of the modern state – a public authority with the necessary capacity and functionality for governing mass society, and a polity governed by the principle of equal membership – provides a useful and informative conceptual framework for understanding the problem of modern state building in Pacific Asia. It is useful because it brings together core concerns of the theories, ideologies and ideas that have shaped how scholars and political actors have viewed the modern state in the region.

This broad definition of the modern state allows us to consider how states in Pacific Asia have approached modern state building. Here the concept of political modernization is relevant. Political modernization is the process whereby state institutions gain capacity and functionality to meet the challenge of organizing mass economic and social life under modern conditions and whereby political life within the polity is increasingly governed by modern values such as equality and fairness. Political modernization is therefore political progress towards the 'modern state' in which government is capable of organizing social and economic life for a society with a mass population and large-scale economic activity; where individuals have direct and fair access to state services and public goods that are conferred with equal rights and obligations; and where the political community has decent living standards and humanitarian values.

The **modern state** is a polity with equal citizenship and a public authority capable of effective and efficient governance of mass society on behalf of its citizens.

The process of modern state building requires both the introduction of new institutions to meet the challenge of modern conditions and modern values and ideas, such as a parliament or congress to provide central authority, representation and legitimacy, as well as the adaptation and integration of existing institutions, such as the family or military, into the state framework. Understandably then, the process of modern state building represents a challenging transformation for any country.

Moreover, ideas and ideology play an important role in the transformation towards a modern state. They provide the rationale that allows political actors to harness political forces and direct them towards a particular set of goals in the process of modern state building. As the following sections show, communism, democracy and capitalism have each left an indelible mark on political development and modern state building in the region.

Red star over Asia

Of all the ideas to come to Pacific Asia, few have cut so deep as communism. This section illustrates how the spread of communism in Asia impacted modern state building in both communist and non-communist states. It argues communism was an effective ideal for organizing political forces towards revolution and independence movements but that the institutions of socialism failed to live up to the ideals espoused by the early revolutionaries and severely hampered modern state building in the region. Moreover, the threat of revolutionary communism created regional instability and the centralization of power within non-communist countries. The section concludes by illustrating how states have more recently moved away from radical communism but that the legacy of socialist institutions remains strong in the region.

In 1936, American journalist Edgar Snow visited the Chinese Communist Party's headquarters in Yan'an, a remote region in Central Western China. At that time, few could predict the Chinese Communist Party, established only in 1921, would go on to establish a people's republic (1949), overthrowing the republican government and radically transforming the political order in China and the region. Snow's book, *Red Star Over China*, was the first authentic introduction to the world of a Party that would introduce radical and revolutionary changes in the region and became a journalistic sensation.

The roots of communism in Pacific Asia go back to Karl Marx in nineteenth-century Europe. Socialist ideas of continental Europe influenced intellectual elites in late nineteenth century Japan, Korea and China, where economic backwardness, political chaos and social decay in these countries forced elites to seek alternative ways of organizing society. But it was through the Bolshevik Revolution of 1917 in Russia that the idea of communism came to Pacific Asia and spread quickly across the region (see Table 2.1). Mao Zedong, the Communist leader of China for much of the twentieth century, once proclaimed, 'The salvoes of the October Revolution brought us Marxism–Leninism'.

COUNTRY PROFILE

THAILAND

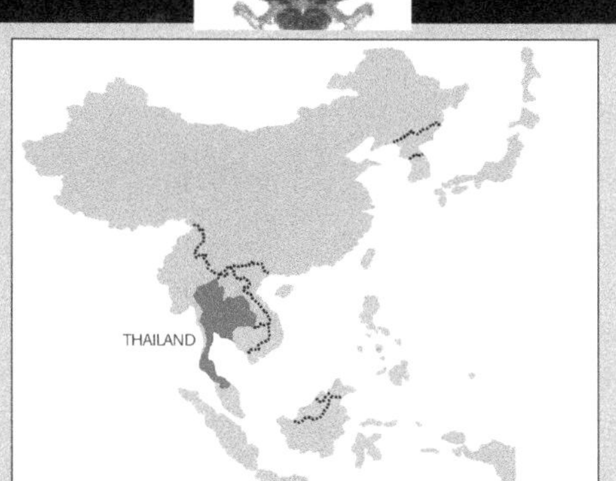

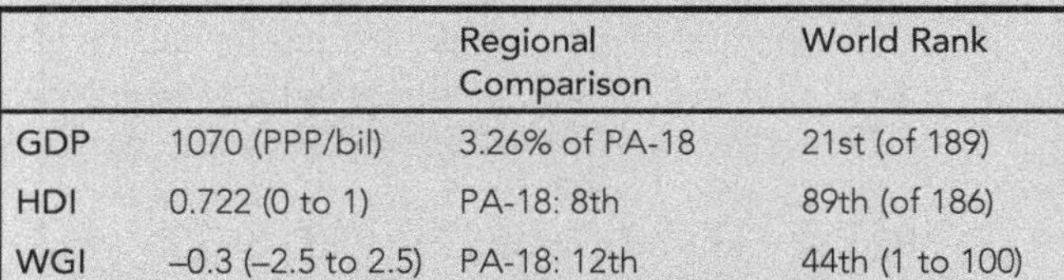

		Regional Comparison	World Rank
GDP	1070 (PPP/bil)	3.26% of PA-18	21st (of 189)
HDI	0.722 (0 to 1)	PA-18: 8th	89th (of 186)
WGI	–0.3 (–2.5 to 2.5)	PA-18: 12th	44th (1 to 100)

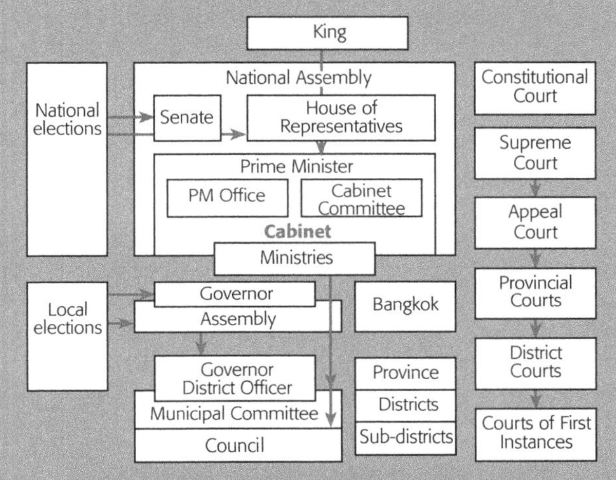

Key political facts

Electoral system for national legislature
Multimember districts and mixed member proportional representation.

Political cycles
Frequent military coups as a decisive factor in change of government.
General elections for House of Representatives, every 4 years. Elections for the Senate, every 6 years.
Annual National Budget to be presented to National Assembly in May for approval by September.

Further reading

Terwiel, 2011; Ferrara, 2015

Timeline of modern political development

1932 Military coup overthrows monarchy. A new constitution for constitutional monarchy with a parliamentary form of government.
1947 Militant coup and new government under Phibun. Search for political models.
1950 Bhumibol is crowned king.
1957 Sarit coup.
1958 Sarit starts strongman rule and popular reforms, revitalization of the monarchy and economic development.
1973 Student riots and the fall of the military government. Free elections.
1976 Military government.
1980 General Prem takes over power.
1983 Prem elected prime minister, 'Premocracy'.
1991 Military coup. 1992 King's intervention leads to a civilian government.
1990s Political reforms: the rise of parliamentary democracy and political–business alliance, and fine-tuning of the relations between the political executive, parliamentarians and bureaucrats.
1997 People's constitution: wide public participation, both houses of legislature elected.
1998 Thaik Rak Thai is established and party politics set in.
2005 Thaksin and his Thaik Rak Thai win landslide victory in general election for a second term.
2006 Constitutional Court declares election invalid, military coup installs interim government with interim constitution.
2007 Constitutional Court bans Thaik Rak Thai and its key members from participating in politics.
2008–2014 Continual tension and conflict between Thaksin supporters and anti-Thaksin forces through elections and street demonstrations and protests, leading to prolonged political instability.
2014 Military takes over government, with an interim government and an interim constitution.

Table 2.1 Communist parties in Pacific Asia

Country	*Year Established*	*Current Status*
Cambodia	1951	Dissolved 1981
China	1921	Ruling party
Indonesia	1914	Banned 1965
Japan	1922	Active
N. Korea	1945	Ruling party
S. Korea	1925	Banned 1946
Laos	1930	Ruling party
Malaysia	1930	Outlawed
Myanmar	1939	Illegal
Singapore	1925	Dissolved 1930
Taiwan	1928	Suppressed 1931
Thailand	1942	Banned, inactive 1990s
Philippines	1968	Banned
Vietnam	1930	Ruling party

A key difference between the factions of international communism was not so much the ultimate goal of socialism and communism, but the path towards that goal. Evolutionary socialists believed they could pursue their socialist and communist ideals through existing institutions, seeking to moderate the worst excesses of capitalism, redistribute wealth through progressive taxation and increase state provision of social services like health, education, housing and even employment.

Communism and socialism appealed to Pacific Asian peoples because of the deep-rooted social inequalities and poverty found across the region. The class-based framework gave intellectual elites in these countries a very effective tool to explain their social ideals and to mobilize society for revolutionary change. Of the two different factions within the Communist International (or Comintern) at the time – moderate, reformist evolutionary socialism on the right and radical, revolutionary socialism on the left – radical, revolutionary socialism as developed by Lenin dominated the popular spread of communism in Pacific Asia. This brand of communism called for the complete overthrow of existing regimes, the abolishment of private property and the establishment of a Leninist one-party state. This was attempted, and in select cases achieved, through armed revolutionary struggle.

Revolutionary socialists, however, were convinced that the socialist and communist cause could succeed only by destroying the existing capitalist economic and political institutions as had occurred in Russia. It was this aspect of Leninism that left a great impact on the fate of communism in Pacific Asia and, because of this, marked the political development of Pacific Asian countries in three main ways.

First, communist movements in Pacific Asia took very radical forms. Communist parties were set up, led by armed radical revolutionaries, with the primary aim of overthrowing existing political and economic systems and establishing a people's republic ruled exclusively by the communist party. By the mid-1950s, communist parties had succeeded in seizing political power in most Northeast Asian countries (China and Korea), had almost succeeded in Indonesia and posed a significant threat to the ruling regimes in most Southeast Asian countries (see Figure 2.1).

Second, those states where the communist party took power adopted very radical economic, social and political programmes. These programmes were in stark contrast to even the comparatively moderate socialist programmes introduced in the Soviet Union and Eastern Europe during the same period.

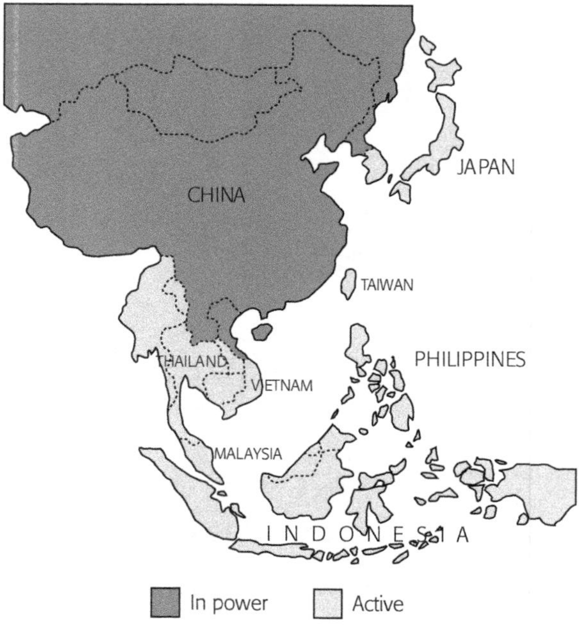

Figure 2.1 Communists in Pacific Asia, 1955

For China, this was more a demonstration by Mao of his own ideological authority and autonomy from the Soviet Union than what was called for by the conditions in China (Schwartz, 1968). For example, the Great Leap Forward in the late 1950s and early 1960s that was followed by tens of millions of people dying from famine and the Cultural Revolution in the 1960s and 1970s that led to the effectual shutdown of most state functions, were far more radical than programmes in the Soviet Union.

The radical economic, social and political programmes in China featured nationalization of the urban economy and communization of the rural economy within a short period of time, as well as the elimination of private property and establishment of the state's absolute authority over the economy, social organization and individual life; and military-style campaigns for industrialization, urban and rural development and political rectification.

The Cultural Revolution was an ideological and political campaign by Mao and his radical associates to impose his radical socialist values and ideas on the life of the Chinese people and to eradicate any political enemies that opposed it. Through a cult of personality, Mao enlisted the support of the masses, particularly millions of young students, the so-called Red Guards (*hongweibing*), which led to severe factionalism and outright conflict within state and society.

In Cambodia, Pol Pot and the Khmer Rouge emptied the cities and sought to return Cambodia to 'year zero' through hard labour in rural areas and the elimination of all political opposition and educated people through highly brutal methods. In North Korea, following the Korean War (1950–53), Kim Il-sung introduced a policy of *juche* or self-reliance, closing the North to the outside world and monopolizing political power and authority in the intergenerational hands of the Kim family and the military.

Third, communist movements in Pacific Asia were a regional phenomenon. While communist parties and communist states in Northeast Asia were influenced by Leninist theory and practice from the Soviet Union, the Chinese communist model, and Mao's ideas and concepts of communist revolution, became the primary source of widespread communist movements in Southeast Asia. Armed rebellious forces and communist parties and factions under the Maoist influence were active in the 1960s, 1970s and even 1980s in Indonesia, the Philippines, Malaya (Malaysia), Thailand and Burma (Myanmar). Their activities, including guerrilla warfare, forced emergency orders in these countries aimed at eliminating the communist threat to their regime.

The radical communist states and aggressive communist movements and activities in neighbouring states led to the fear of a domino effect, where Southeast Asian countries might fall into the hands of the communist forces one after the other. Indonesia was the first country to take violent action by the military to suppress the Communist Party of Indonesia (PKI) in 1965. America's intervention in Indochina and the consequent Vietnam War was also aimed at preventing the further spread of communist influence in Southeast Asia. Indeed, much of the Cold War in Pacific Asia was driven by the 'spectre of communism' (Marx and Engels, 2002: 1).

Notably, then, the idea of communism not only created radical experiments in modern state building in those states where the communist party came to power, but it also led to conservative and at times militant crackdowns in non-communist countries. As discussed in the next section, this severely hampered the spread of democratic intuitions, checks and balances and government accountability throughout the region. Militant and authoritarian regimes in South Korea, Vietnam and Taiwan are examples of non-communist states that cracked down on progressive forces and political freedom during this period.

After China's public falling out and split from the Soviet Union in the 1970s and 1980s, Chinese radical communism became the centre of the radical wing of world communist movements. Communist parties around the world were split between factions loyal to the Soviet Union and factions following the Chinese. Those following the Chinese usually labelled themselves as 'Marxist-Leninist'. China became the champion of national liberalization movements around the world, particularly in Africa, Latin America and Asia. Communist forces in these countries adopted Maoist guerrilla warfare as China and Vietnam had done.

The failure and legacy of radical communism

Experiments in socialist governance in Pacific Asia in the second half of the twentieth century, like those in other parts of the world, were a failure and a tragedy. By the 1980s, more moderate forces had taken control in China, Vietnam and Cambodia. Open-ended reforms, including opening to the world and restructuring governance and the economy in China and Vietnam, undid the radical programmes of the earlier decades. Communist movements in Southeast Asia, without the support of the North, gradually wound down, and laid down their arms.

The experiences of communism and socialism reveal a great deal about the role of communism as an ideology in Pacific Asian countries. First, ideology can be a very effective means of mass mobilization by political and intellectual elites. As Benjamin Schwartz and others have found, ideologies such as communism or socialism can take root even in a society where the necessary social conditions for its popularity do not exist. The type of communism that spread in Pacific Asia was a product of the interaction between a foreign theoretical ideal of a classless society with full equality and the reality of poverty, inequality and foreign control. This ideal was therefore interpreted and manipulated by political and intellectual elites in order to mobilize the populace towards their revolutionary ideals.

Second, because of the gap between theory and reality, the institutions and processes required to support the ideology were more politically imposed than demanded socially. Extreme and ultimately tragic idealism was evidenced in China's Great Leap Forward and Cultural Revolution as well as in Pol Pot's short and disastrous reign where more than 1.5 million people perished. There was therefore an inherent tension between economic, social and political institutions on the one hand, and conditions, structures and forces that these institutions were supposed to command.

Third, the exit paths from the socialist system, those of China and Vietnam in particular, offer a model of gradual, piecemeal and controlled institutional change, in contrast to the radical, systematic and revolutionary model of institutional change as seen in Eastern Europe and the Soviet Union (Shirk, 1993; Naughton, 1995; Walder, 1995; Misra, 1998).

Box 2.2

Decline of the socialist and communist movements in Pacific Asia

The socialist and communist movements had their greatest influence during the nationalist struggle from the 1930s and following the Second World War. In these struggles, coalitions of workers, peasants and nationalists became indispensable elements of the anti-colonial movements. In particular, the communists often provided organization strength to the independence movements. While there were both links and divisions between the left and other nationalist parties with, for example, the largest communist party in Asia in Indonesia, for a time the prospects for socialism in Southeast Asia seemed promising. However, ... despite taking power in Vietnam, Cambodia and Laos in 1974–75, the political influence of communist and socialist movements and ideas of egalitarianism have declined across the region. To a degree, the political gap left by this decline has been filled by a bourgeois, often liberal, opposition seen in the social democratic forces ...

Hewison and Rodan, 2012: 25–26

In late 1978, China introduced reforms that would later become known as 'reform and opening' (*gaige kaifang*), signalling to the Chinese people and the world the failure of radical socialism and a desire to move towards economic liberalization and political institutionalization. These reforms took place without the guidance of an overarching ideology under the influence of competing ideologies. Some elites held a vision of China as a social democratic state while others pursued new authoritarianism (Chen, 1995: 202–10). Similarly, in Vietnam, the ruling communist party introduced its own reform agenda in 1986 and as of 2016 remains firmly in control.

Doi Moi, or economic renovation, was the reform programme adopted by the Vietnamese Communist Party in 1986 'to turn the country from a "bureaucratic centralized state subsidy system" to a regulated market economy'. (Litvack and Rondinelli, 1999: 21). Doi Moi marked the beginning of Vietnam's post-socialist reform and transition.

Today, the 'gap' between fundamental communist ideology as proclaimed in party constitutions in the region and the market economy practiced in communist states allows room for ideological transformation. However, while the institutions of political economy have moved towards the ideals of a liberal market economy, deciphering political reform in communist states remains far from simple. In North Korea, the communist one-party system remains with a closed-door economic policy, extensive state control and autarkic foreign policy. North Korea remains ruled by descendants of Kim Il-sung and the military, resembling in many ways a modern-day oligarchy.

In China, political reform has not kept pace with economic reform. The Leninist party state remains controlled by a single party that has maintained strict control over political, economic and even social forces in the country. Moreover, China maintained three decades of rapid growth from the 1980s to the early 2010s. This period propelled it from a very low income to an upper middle-income country. With a population close to 1.4 billion, China is now the world's first or second largest economy with considerable economic, diplomatic and even military clout. The 'rise of China' under continued communist party rule questions some of the assumptions political scientists have made based on historical development in the now advanced economies and led many to look more closely at China's modern state building in order to explain the evolution of communism there.

The legacy of communism in China, and similarly in Vietnam and Laos, therefore remains strong, with the communist party still ruling through what appears to be a highly resilient authoritarian model. This poses a stark contrast to the fall of communism in the former Soviet Union and Eastern Europe where almost overnight communist parties were expelled and political regimes transformed towards multiparty democracies. Just how communism has evolved and why it has remained resilient in Pacific Asia is of particular importance for comparative politics. In Pacific Asia, the idea of communism and socialist governance, however, adapted through development and modernization, remains significant for shaping political development and modern state building in the region. Around 30 per cent of the world's population is found in Pacific Asia of which well over half, or one fifth of the world population, continue to live under communist regimes.

'Mr D and Mr S'

Democracy, like the idea of communism, is one of the major political ideas introduced into Asia in the nineteenth century. It has had a major impact on modern state building in the region by acting as a catalyst for reform and revolution from the early days of the modern era. Transforming democratic ideals into effective democratic practices, however, has been far more challenging for Pacific Asian states. Only recently have democratic institutions become the predominant mode of organizing politics in Pacific Asia.

Many of the core concepts of modern politics, economy and society came to East Asian countries via Japan. The spread of democratic ideas in Pacific Asia owes much to early Japanese reforms. Democratic institutions began to be set up from the early Meiji era (Ike, 1950) and included a constitution, a parliament, a political party system, elections and so on, along with other modern economic and legal institutions. While many of the democratic institutions were compromised in the early twentieth century as Japan lurched towards WWII, over the long run democracy has constituted a principal rallying point for those wishing to build a modern state.

Democracy represents a view of human equality and rights against the state. Like science, democracy is founded upon a rational, this worldly view of society that emerged out of the Enlightenment movement in Europe. Both concepts, however, clashed with the old order in Pacific Asia that based political legitimacy on moral order, class and transcendental power. For Japan, the focus on rationality and science and technology in their early modernization drive helped create a fertile ground for the introduction of the ideals of democracy. Political institutions were developed with the capacity to harness and direct Japan's modern state building that removed traditional forces of public authority. The success of Japan's modernization drive in the late nineteenth and early twentieth centuries helped these ideas take root in the wider region.

In China, reformers such as Kang Youwei employed democratic ideals in his promotion of a constitutional monarchy as a way to reform the decaying Qing Dynasty. Sun Yat-sen, the Father of Modern China (*guofu*), promoted revolution and republicanism and put forward his Three

Principles of the People – nationalism, democracy and people's livelihood. Both, however, sought a gradualist introduction of democratic institutions in China believing the centralization and rationalization of state authority as well as the cultivation of civics was a prerequisite for a functioning Chinese democracy.

After the fall of the last Chinese dynasty in 1911, democracy and science became a rallying call for reformers unhappy with ongoing concessions to foreign powers and a real lack of progress in building a modern state. This call was repeated several times over the next century (see Mitter, 2004).

In particular, the May Fourth Movement erupted in 1919 as students protested, among other things, the decision of the Paris Peace Conference (1919) to award German Concessions in China to Japan. One of the leading intellectuals behind the movement and the first Secretary General of the Chinese Communist Party proclaimed that 'Now we determined that only *De Xiansheng* (Mr Democracy) and *Sai Xiansheng* (Mr Science) can rescue China from all the darkness in politics, morality, scholarship and thoughts and ideas' (Chen, 1919).

Even in the early years of modern state building in the region, then, democracy was an idea that rallied people together and incited political activity. However, much of the first half of the twentieth century saw little movement towards the institutional reality of democracy. The region was engaged with more urgent issues of colonialism and imperialism, particularly in Southeast Asia, as well as the emergence of communist forces seeking radical change. Japan was an important exception to this rule, though even there democratic institutions were superseded by the military in the 1930s before a constitutional monarchy was fully established under American Occupation in the post-war years.

Beyond Japan, the early enthusiasm for democracy in Pacific Asia was closely associated with popular sovereignty, the idea that people are the masters of the state. The notions of republicanism and democracy were therefore mixed. Consequently, the idea of democracy was largely embedded within the independence movement against colonial rule, and social revolutions against the ruling elites. In China, decades after the Xinhai Revolution (1911) that ended the Chinese Dynastic system, and the May Fourth Movement (1919), political elites were still fighting amongst themselves as to who could bring democracy to China, rather than building functioning democratic institutions. The Chinese Civil War between the Communists and Nationalists then dominated much of the first half of the twentieth century with a detrimental impact of the establishment of democratic institutions.

This foreshadowed a pattern for the whole region for much of the Cold War era: communist and non-communist forces on both sides of the political spectrum claimed they could bring real democracy to the country, but neither actually delivered. Not only did the communist states twist the meaning of democracy in their political practice, but the non-communist states also failed to deliver genuine democracy. Instead, democracy took a backseat to more pressing concerns:

- Tension between communist and anti-communist forces and the Cold War geopolitical structure;
- Struggles for independence and sovereignty and the urgent challenge of consolidation of newly established nation-states;
- A focus on rapid industrialization and economic development to alleviate extreme poverty and national weakness.

Such concerns subordinated much of the democratic aspirations of the region for much of the century. Perhaps because of this, democracy emerged as a primary political idea in the late Cold War period and provided much of the political dynamism for change. As the Cold War structure collapsed the problem of communism was largely gone. At the same time, there was great progress in industrialization and economic and social development and a wave of democratic transitions took place around the world. The idea of democracy enjoyed its most popular time in Pacific Asia.

Democratization is the prevailing of democratic institutions and processes in a polity. The collapse of non-democratic systems often precedes and is an integral part of the process. The consolidation of democratic institutions requires the development a civic culture that supports the working of democratic institutions.

A century after its initial introduction to Pacific Asia, the idea of democracy has emerged as a dominant ideology. It has generated large-scale mass political movements across Pacific Asian countries and shaped and reshaped the political landscape and the way of political life. In the last few decades of the twentieth century, the social movements democracy generated went beyond the idea of popular sovereignty. More attention was paid to concrete steps taken to promote the building and consolidation of democratic institutions and the cultivation and development of the 'civic culture' required to support and sustain the functioning of formal democratic institutions.

As with other political ideologies, the process of transforming the idea of democracy into political institutions and practice, or democratization, led to the restructuring of the political order, the redefining of relations among key political forces and the redistribution of political resources. On one level, democratization opened up political space for institutionalized political participation and popular checks and balances on government, while at another level, democratic transition shifted political power from the bureaucracy to the elected officials, from political elites to interest groups, and from central government to local constituencies.

In the setup of democratic institutions in early Meiji Japan, for example, a power struggle occurred between the military factions that controlled the Meiji government and the professional politicians who gained power and influence through the new democratic institutions of party politics and elections. This was not completely resolved until the end of the First World War but returned in the decade prior to Japan's expansion in WWII.

Similarly, the democratic constitution of 1997 in Thailand shifted the balance of power from the state bureaucrats who had dominated the Thai bureaucratic polity to elected MPs and political elites, who rose in power and influence through the new institutions. The 2006 coup and the following political developments suggested that the power struggle between the two dominant political forces was far from over. The 2014 coup, under a caretaker government and following six months of political crisis, reaffirmed the failing of democratic institutions in Thailand.

Because of the different political forces in Pacific Asian states, the strategies for democratic transition have also varied. In some countries, such as the Philippines, Indonesia, Thailand and South Korea, mass movements and revolutions were required to shift the power balance towards democratic forces. In other cases, notably the democratic transition in Taiwan, it was more an elite-led process of political manoeuvring, bargaining, coalition building and, when necessary, threats of mass movement and revolution. As shown below, it has taken many decades since the introduction of democratic ideas for democratic institutions to become the dominant form of political organization in Pacific Asia.

Box 2.3

The early post-war movement, from pluralist to non-pluralist politics

Country	*Pluralist, multiparty politics*	*Non-pluralist, single party/force/person dominance*
China		Mao/CPC (1949–)
Indonesia	1950–65	Suharto/GOLKAR (1965–98)
Japan	1945–55	LDP (1955–93)
Korea	1953–62	Park/Military (1962–87)
Malaysia	1957–69	UMNO/Mahathir (1969–2003)
Myanmar	1948–62	Ne Win/Military (1962–)
Philippines	1946–65	Marcos/Military (1966–86)
Singapore	1959–65	Lee/PAP (1965–90)
Taiwan		Chiangs/KMT (1945–86)
Thailand		Military (1948–97)

The failure of pluralist politics in early post-war Pacific Asia

The early post-war era was an exciting time for Pacific Asia. The war was over, and many countries had achieved their long sought after independence. Almost universally, modern and liberal constitutions were proclaimed across the region and elections established. Political parties quickly organized themselves and became a principal platform for political representation, mobilization and participation. Almost all countries, old and new, began the post-war period with some form of multiparty, pluralist politics.

As Box 2.3 shows, of the ten stable self-governed states at the time, all experienced a brief period of pluralist politics in the late 1940s and 1950s. In China a civil war had torn the country apart and the communist party had ruled since 1949. In Taiwan martial law had been in place since the Nationalist retreat from China in 1949. In Thailand, the military had controlled the government from 1948. Those countries experiencing pluralist politics had just come out of civil war and/or colonial rule. No single political force was able to dominate, but all were aggressively seeking dominance in the very fluid new political environment. Social, religious and political forces organized themselves into political parties and campaigned actively for state power and for the direction of the new state. All countries, however, soon experienced the rise of a conservative political force or an alliance of such forces that dominated government and politics for decades to come.

Conservatism means different things at different times in different countries. In Japan in the early 1950s, it represented the interests of industrial capital, pro-Western intellectuals and ruling bureaucrats, as well as traditional Japanese values. They were conservative in relation to the Japanese Socialist Party (JSP) and the Japanese Communist Party (JCP). The latter represented the interests of labour unions, leftist social movements, Marxist sympathizers, and liberal, progressive social values. They were conservative also in relation to the discredited extreme nationalists, imperialists, the military, and other social and political forces associated with the wartime regime.

Let us look at some of the cases in detail. In pre-war Japan, during the relatively tolerant period of Taisho democracy in the 1920s, various political thoughts and ideas, and the social and political forces they represented, competed for political power and public attention. Military and right-wing extremists came to dominate, however, and eventually to control the government in the 1930s. After Japan's surrender at the end of the Second World War, there was an expectation that the political pendulum would swing back to the left.

The initial intention of the American occupation authorities in the early years of occupation was very much to encourage such a shift away from the extreme right. A new liberal constitution was drafted by the Americans and proclaimed in 1947. The military was dismantled and the financial, business and industrial conglomerates of Imperial Japan, the zaibatsu, were outlawed. New labour laws were passed and land reforms carried out. In national politics, dozens of new political parties emerged, representing diverse social and political interests, with four major parties at the front: the Liberal Party of Japan (LPJ); the Democrat Party of Japan (DPJ); the Socialist Party of Japan (JSP); and, the Japanese Communist Party (JCP). The overall political environment was liberal, pluralist and perhaps slightly tilted towards the left.

However, the international environment changed quickly in the late 1940s and early 1950s as the communist party came to power in China through peasant rebellion and military victory. The outbreak of the Korean War (1950–53) signalled the onset of the Cold War in Asia (see Jervis, 1980). The United States soon changed its mind about post-war Japan. Many of the liberal reforms and policies were 'reversed'.

Following this, the major political parties merged into two large political camps in 1955: the Democratic Party and the Liberal Party merging into the Liberal Democratic Party (LDP) on the conservative side, and the JSP and JCP on the progressive side. The new LDP, with the support of the state bureaucrats, social elites, reformed industrial capital and the US-led Western world, formed a formidable conservative alliance that controlled the government for the next thirty-eight years, keeping the liberal JSP as a permanent opposition. Pluralist politics thus ran for about ten years, from 1945 to 1955, before LDP dominance set in.

A new political structure emerged in Japan in 1955. The dominance of the LDP and its conservative alliance in a largely two-party system, and its pro-business, pro-American policy and programmes, is often referred to as the **1955 system**. The system collapsed when the LDP lost its 38-year control of government in 1993.

Indonesia is another country where pluralist politics existed for a brief period before a single political force dominated. Present-day Indonesia had been colonized for around 450 years first by Portugal, then Spain, followed by the Netherlands, briefly the British and then the Dutch again. The new republic finally gained recognition of its independence in 1949, following Japanese wartime occupation (1942–45) and a brief post-war period when the Dutch did not recognize the new republic. After independence, there were several key forces pulling the country in different directions: the nationalists under the leader of the independence movement, Sukarno; the communists under the Indonesia Communist Party (PKI); Muslim groups; and the military.

Sukarno led the nationalists, but leant increasingly towards the communists. Each of these groups had a different vision about the new state. The communists wanted a Marxist or socialist state. The Muslim groups wanted a state based on Islamic teachings. The nationalists wanted what Sukarno called 'guided democracy'.

Guided democracy was the political order in Indonesia from the late 1950s to 1965, under Sukarno, the first President of Indonesia. Over the years, Sukarno began to restrict parliamentary politics and dictate national politics with a single ideology and to designate political parties and organized representation through functional groups. Guided democracy experienced one crisis after another until it was replaced by the New Order of Suharto in 1966.

In his speech in 1956, titled 'Let us bury the parties', Sukarno declared, 'the democracy I crave for Indonesia is not a liberal democracy such as exists for Western Europe. No! What I want for Indonesia is a guided democracy, a democracy with leadership' (Feith and Castles, 1970: 82). Believing that Western democracy was unsuitable for Indonesia, Sukarno called for 'democracy with guidance' in order to adopt a political system based on cultural traditions such as consensus decision-making at the village level. Under guided democracy, the president

> set up a National Council (Musyawarah Nasional), led by himself, and supposedly modeled on the traditional Indonesian village council. Decisions would be reached through masyawarah (deliberation) in order to achieve mufakat (consensus), and not through voting. The National Council would consist of representatives of so-called functional groups (golongan karya). In contrast to the ideologically based political parties, functional groups were based on the roles that different groups played in society, generally defined by their main occupation, such as workers, peasants, students, artists, intellectuals and the military. This essentially corporatist organization of political representation, characterized by non-competitive functional groups rather than antagonistic, class-based or ideology-based organizations, sat very comfortably with the family principle and its vision of a harmonious and naturally integrated society. (Eklöf, 2004: 36)

While agreeing with the president on the need for a more restricted political system, the military was increasingly uneasy about the growing strength of the communists. On 30 September 1965, in a complicated sequence of events, the army, under General Suharto, took action and put down an alleged communist-supported coup by a group of junior army officers. In the following weeks and months, they eliminated the entire communist force in Indonesia. Indonesia entered a new political era of military dominance under Suharto's 'New Order' for the next thirty-four years.

A third case is South Korea. The newly independent Korea was initially under separate occupation by the Soviet Union in the north, and by the United States in the south. At the end of the occupation, in 1948, the Republic of Korea, or South Korea, was set up with Dr Syngman Rhee as the president backed by the United States. In the meantime, the Democratic People's Republic of Korea, or North Korea, was established with the support of the Soviet Union and China and led by the Communist leader, Kim Il-sung.

South Korea was a nation born of political expediency. Like many other new states, liberal democracy was also adopted there. A constitution was proclaimed in 1948 stipulating that the new republic was committed to 'a democratic system of government'. The constitution set out the principle of popular sovereignty, as well as the basic values of liberty, equality, freedoms, rule of law, citizenship and political rights (Oh, 1999: 28–30). In addition to a new liberal constitution, the American occupation authorities allowed elections as the primary mechanism in the determination of state affairs, for the first time in Korean history. Dr Rhee was elected the first president of the Republic and ruled with a functioning National Assembly.

However, the young democracy also had a dark side. A looming threat from the north allowed some repressive elements in the political system to develop that only intensified as the Korean War ripped Korea apart. The Constitution itself stipulated that 'laws imposing restrictions upon the liberties and rights of citizens shall be enacted only when necessary for the maintenance of public order or the welfare of the community'. An emergency clause, however, allowed the president 'the power to issue orders having the effect of law' (Oh, 1999: 29). The notorious National Security Law was passed in 1948, giving further powers to the state to 'protect the state from its enemy'. With these powers, the government crushed the Cheju rebellion of 1948 and tried to silence the student uprising of 1960.

Moreover, the president himself became increasingly 'autocratic'. He declared himself the head of state, head of the executive branch, and the chief legislator (Yang, 1994: 467). The economy was in a very bad shape, the government was largely corrupt, and the president wanted unlimited terms for his presidency. The Constitution provided a presidential system, and the president concentrated political power in his own hands. The student uprising in 1960 led to the ousting of the president and the Constitution was amended in light of this experience. The Second Republic adopted a parliamentary system with the prime minister as the head of government. The National Assembly was split into two houses. The prime minister was nominated by the nominal president, but confirmed by the Lower House. The cabinet was headed by the prime minister and responsible to the Lower House.

The restructuring of state institutions, however, created a different problem. The new National Assembly soon turned to 'gridlock' between two principal factions and little legislatorial progress was made on any important national issues. In the meantime, the economy continued to slide and government corruption remained. Ten years after the Korean War, and eighteen years after independence, the government was still not able to meet the people's long-held expectations.

On 16 May 1961, Major General Park Chung-hee launched a military coup, overthrowing the civilian government. A governing body, the Supreme Council for National Reconstruction, led by General Park, was established. The military takeover was welcomed by the public and accepted by the United States. In 1963, a civilian government under military watch was restored and Park was elected president (1963–79), thus ushering in the Third Republic. President Park was re-elected in 1967, 1972 and 1978.

A similar pattern is evident in the Philippines. Ferdinand Marcos had neither a military background nor powerful family connections, both of which were important in Philippine politics. He was elected president in 1965 (1965–81) on a middle-class, social progressive platform: the idea of a New Society, law and order, as well as land reform. The implementation of these programmes brought initial economic recovery and growth, but seriously affected the interests of the landed elites. The tradition of weak state institutions, political challenges to his presidency and social programmes, particularly from the landed elites, and the growing discontent among the public over widespread corruption and the troubled economy, led Marcos to turn to the military to strengthen and secure his presidency.

In 1972, Marcos declared martial law, and with the support of the military, ran an increasingly authoritarian and corrupt government. The military provided critical support for the president. Other than the military, however, Marcos had a very small support base. Consequently, the space for political liberty and pluralist politics was very narrow.

The movement towards non-pluralist politics also happened in Myanmar, where General Ne Win took over the government via a military coup in 1962; in South Vietnam, where President Diem was executed in a military coup in 1963 and the country came under the rule of a military junta; and in Malaysia and Singapore where single-party dominance developed fully in the 1960s and 1970s. Lee Kuan Yew, prime minister of Singapore from 1959 to 1990, and his People's Action Party (PAP), for example, came to power through a landslide victory in a multiparty competitive election in 1959. The single-party dominance that emerged turned Singapore into a unique single-party-dominant state. As Diane Mauzy and R. S. Milne observed, 'the longer the PAP remains in power, the harder it becomes to distinguish between' the party and the state (Mauzy and Milne, 2002b: 25).

The breakdown of democratic regimes in Pacific Asia is a well-researched subject (Linz, 1978; Przeworski et al., 1996; Diamond and Plattner, 1998). A variety of different views on the causes underlying the failure of pluralist politics in the early post-war period have been put forward (see Case Study Lab 2.1).

The period from the 1960s to the 1980s was a dark one in the history of modern political development in Pacific Asia. Most countries were under some form of non-pluralist politics, and collectively they survived under the heavy shadow of the Cold War. The urgent tasks of consolidating newly found independence, building state institutions and developing the economy, as well as threats from the other side of the Cold War, closed the space for plurality and dampened prospects for the realization of functioning democratic institutions and civic culture. The idea of democracy in Pacific Asia was forced into hiatus until the early 1980s when a wave of democratic reforms and political liberalization swept the region.

Case Study Lab 2.1

The failure of pluralist politics in early post-war Pacific Asia

While the problem of pluralist politics in early post-war Pacific Asian countries has often escaped much-needed scholarly attention, there are various theories put forward that explain it either directly or indirectly:

Domino theory: There is a popular suggestion that these countries moved to non-pluralist politics one after another in anticipation of the so-called domino effect in the region. The theory argues that because pro-communist leftist forces instigated most popular movements, the weak, internally chaotic new states would inevitably fall to communist expansion and subversion. Non-competitive politics, therefore, developed with the support of the Western alliance as a reaction to the threat from communism.

Democratic experiment theory: Minxin Pei rejects the domino effect theory and argues that the failure of 'the initial experiments with democracy' in Pacific Asia had more to do with internal conditions. According to Pei, circumstances leading directly to the collapse of 'democratic experiments' differed from country to country but there were 'similar structural and institutional causes'. Pei puts forward five. First, the weakness of political institutions expected to organize and mediate interests and moderate conflicts in these societies. Second, the original institutional framework of the new states. Third, unfavourable structural socioeconomic conditions, such as low levels of socioeconomic development, high levels of economic inequality and deep structural cleavages. Fourth, the collapse of grand coalitions. Fifth, the legacy of the revolutionary past (Pei, 1998: 62–4).

Changing society theory: Beyond these country-specific 'internal factors', there were some more general conditions across these countries that affected their institutional choices. One of these conditions is discussed in Samuel P. Huntington's seminal work on changing societies (Huntington, 1968; Huntington and Moore, 1970). Changing societies are those in the early stages of modernization. This theory argues that societal and institutional conditions in the early stages are unique and there is a general inability of institutions to cope with rapid social and economic change coupled with a weak government that 'lacks authority and fails to perform its function' (Huntington, 1968: 28). For these new societies, then, the 'degree of government' seems to be more important than the 'form of government' (Huntington, 1968:1) making the centralization of state authority for more government effectiveness an almost inevitable scenario.

Cultural theory: Confucian models of authority are often seen by many as the cultural background of non-pluralist politics in Cold War Pacific Asia (see, for example, Roy, 1994). Lucian Pye (1985) explains how Confucian concepts of authority underlay the various Confucian models of political order in Asia. While Pye may not necessarily argue for Confucian models, his theory does help us understand why a non-pluralist political order would prevail in 'Confucian' societies (see the next section for more discussion of this theory and the debate on Asian values).

Transformation of the Cold War regimes

The causes of political liberalization and democratic transition in Pacific Asia since the mid-1980s have engendered considerable scholarly debate (Pei, 1998a: 66–71). A long list of possible explanations for the wave of political change has been put forward ranging from developmental and societal changes to being swept up in the latest recurring wave of global democratization (see Case Study Lab 2.2). As this section shows, politics and governance in the region has been transformed from predominantly non-pluralist to one where liberal democratic institutions are now embedded within most, but not all, Pacific Asian countries.

The first major crack in the non-pluralist politics of the Cold War came in 1986 when a 'people power' revolution in the Philippines overthrew the government and forced Marcos to flee the country. Within a decade, Pacific Asia had experienced a large-scale movement towards pluralist politics (see Case Study Lab 2.2). In most cases, this movement led to the overthrow or collapse of the ruling political alliance. However, there are some important exceptions.

First, in China, political liberalization and the democracy movement in the 1980s failed to break up the party-state, and ended with a bloody crackdown on the student movement by the government. Another exception is Thailand. After the 1997 constitution, there was a widely held belief that stable democracy had been firmly established (ADB, 1999: 5; also Alagappa, 2001). However, the 2006 and 2014 military coups have made many rethink the fundamental nature of political change in Thailand in the 1990s.

The transformation of the Cold War regimes took different forms in different countries (see Box 2.5). In countries such as the Philippines in 1986, Indonesia in 1998, Korea in 1987, China (unsuccessfully)

Box 2.4

A decade of political liberalization and democratic transition (1986–98)

Philippines	1986	Fall of Marcos
S. Korea	1987	Constitution
	1992	Founding elections
Taiwan	1987	End of martial law
		Restoration of Constitution
	1996	First direct election of president
Japan	1993	End of the 1955 system
Thailand	1992	Civilian government
	1997	Constitution
Indonesia	1998	Fall of Suharto

Case Study Lab 2.2

Explaining the wave of political liberalization and democratic transition

Development-to-democracy thesis: Economic development leads to demands for democracy (see the following section).

Middle class theory: The general orientation of the middle class in favour of pluralist politics (see the section on illiberal democracy).

Third wave democratization theory: According to Samuel Huntington's well-received observation (Huntington, 1993), the surge in the number of countries experiencing democratic transition in the 1970s and 1980s in Latin America and Asia is the third time this has happened in recent world history. The first wave was the hundred years from the 1820s to the 1920s. The second wave ran for twenty years before and after the Second World War. Democratization in Pacific Asia occurred during the third wave of global democratization in the 1980s and 1990s. Huntington does not necessarily endorse external factor explanations. His research mainly summarizes the factors leading to the third wave. The third wave theory asks us to consider the wave of political liberalization and democratic transitions as a recurring pattern in world history rather than explaining them through the historical and institutional logic of political development in these countries themselves.

Box 2.5

Forms of post-Cold War political liberalization and democratic transition in Pacific Asia

Model I	Popular revolution Challenging existing system	Indonesia, Korea, Philippines, Thailand, China (1989)
Model II	Opposition movement and elite-led reform Challenging/reforming existing system	Taiwan
Model III	Elite-led, political bargaining Reforming existing system	Japan
Model IV	Gradual, elite-led, incremental reform Reforming existing system	China (after 1989), Vietnam

in 1989, and Thailand in 1992, the ruling elites were determined to keep themselves in power and defend the regime by all means. The democratic movement turned into violent confrontation between the political regime and the population. Except in the case of China, the resulting people power revolutions overthrew the ruling government, restored constitutional order, legalized political parties and ushered in genuine democratic elections.

Scholars have argued that revolutions, or poplar uprisings, are inevitable in democratic transition. In a survey of democratic revolutions, Mark Thompson makes the point that democracy fighters not only have to rebel but also need the ability to do so (Thompson, 2004: 113). From this perspective, mass revolutions, violent confrontations and collapse of the ruling regimes in Pacific Asia were no accident. They were the logical consequence of the history of tensions built up among key societal forces of different political interests, visions and agendas during the post-war decades.

That political liberalization and democratic transition took a revolutionary and violent form in these countries suggests that the tensions and conflicts between the ruling regime and the majority of the population, and indeed between dominant and opposing political forces, could not be solved within the existing constitutional framework. It also says that the interests of the ruling elites, and the political processes and procedures promoting and securing these interests, were so closely intertwined that there was little room for political compromise or incremental change. The final breakdown of the ruling regime had to be part of the larger shift in the balance of power in society (see Chapter 8) so that the power and capacity of the ruling regime could be overcome. China in 1989, where the protest movement was overcome by the regime, was not able to reach this point.

Democratic transition in Taiwan presents a different and scholarly significant model. Here democratization combined an opposition-led mass movement, unique leadership and self-transformation of the ruling party (Dickson, 1997). The role of the KMT's leadership at the time was critical and unique – resembling in some ways the role Mikhail Gorbachev played in his 'political change from within' in the Soviet Union.

From 1987, when President Lee took over the KMT leadership, to 2000 when the KMT fell from power after fifty years of rule in Taiwan, political transformation took shape in three stages: first, consolidation of Lee's power within the KMT; second, constitutional amendments and the promotion of Taiwan's national identity and international status; third, Lee's break away from the KMT conservatives and the building of his leadership at the national level.

Taiwan's phased-in, elite-led popularly based movement towards pluralist politics represents a distinct model of political change. The process was largely controlled by the ruling party and was advanced under the existing but evolving political arrangements. At the core of the democratic transition was the ending of the KMT's authoritarian rule and the party-state system. The lessons from Taiwan's transition to pluralist politics are rich, saying a lot about how a process of transition from non-pluralist politics is shaped or even manipulated by the ruling party. It speaks of the possibility of alternative patterns, if not models, of political liberalization and democratic transition.

Democratic transition in Myanmar may be following this model. After 50 years of military rule, important constitutional changes in 2014 and the incremental relaxation of curbs on political, economic and social freedoms are positive signs that Myanmar is following the general trend in the region towards an institutionalized democracy. Many challenges remain, however, including the urgent task of developing the economy and institutionalizing transparent and fair representation and fair laws for all Burmese citizens. The landslide victory for Aung San Suu Kyi's National League for Democracy (NLD) in November 2015 means a civilian government should now control parliament, choose the president and control the military that have monopolized Burmese politics since the 1960s.

It is perhaps too early to ascertain what model of democratization Myanmar's transition will follow. On the one hand, there has clearly been a high level of popular pressure, protest and opposition activities pushing the reform agenda. On the other hand, the military government was not pushed from power but institutionalized constitutional reforms while still in power. This suggests Myanmar's transition is more likely following the second model of reform.

Japan falls into a third model with two distinct but related elements. First, there were fundamental economic, social and political changes in the country, which led to the weakening of the support base for LDP dominance. In his work examining the regime shift in post-war Japan, T. J. Pempel (1998) argues that the Japan of the 1990s was drastically different from the Japan of the 1960s. The conservative political alliance, the primary support base for the LDP, had largely been transformed, if not broken down. The political and economic institutions nurturing LDP leadership also underwent significant change. By the early 1990s, the LDP faced a stagnated economy, unruly conservative forces, confusing and ineffective government policy, and growing political challenges to LDP dominance. The LDP finally failed to win a majority in the Lower House elections in 1993 and thus lost the government they had held since 1955.

Whether single-party dominance finally ended in 1993 is certainly an issue of different opinions and requires further observation. Given that the LDP regained control of government during Prime Minister Koizumi's years, some question whether the 1990s was a brief interruption of the LDP's rule or a new era of more competitive and pluralist politics in Japan. With the victory of the Democratic Party of Japan in 2009, scholars such as Krauss and Pekkanen (2010) have argued for a significant shift towards consolidated multiparty democracy. The quick return of the LDP in 2012, however, suggests LDP dominance remains strong. Together with the coup in Thailand, and village democracy in China, these cases defy linear thinking and simplistic generalizations.

Since LDP dominance was not imposed on society with force or coercion, but rather nurtured through very well-tailored institutional arrangements, institutional reforms were critical and inevitable, to solve the growing tensions between the new political and economic reality and the old institutional frameworks. In 1994, the ruling coalition finally passed laws that changed the electoral system and placed strict regulations on party financing – efforts that were expected to remove the institutional basis for LDP dominance (see Chapter 7).

The Japanese model is therefore a political bargaining process, in which institutions adjusted to the changing reality and where the rules of the game were renegotiated. This occurred when the ruling political force no longer commanded sufficient power, capacity and support to impose, direct or resist. All parties, however, respected the fundamental constitutional order of Japan and political change occurred within this order.

Signs of similar institutional adjustment have been observed in countries such as Singapore and Malaysia. In Malaysia, for example, even the ruling party itself began to discuss the problems associated with the government's Malay privileged New Economic Policy (see Chapter 9). In Singapore, bringing 'the Chinese' back has also become an important part of the government's new thinking. With the departure of charismatic and strong leaders in both Singapore and Malaysia, one can expect to see a more relaxed, open, tolerant and perhaps more pluralist political environment.

Given the Japanese experience, political development in these countries concern, first, the nature of social stratification after half a century of successful economic and social development and how and to what extent this will translate into a form of pluralist politics (see the next section); second, how the existing political and economic institutions respond to the shift in social and political alliances.

The final model of post-Cold War political liberalization is the one emerging in those people's republics such as China and Vietnam. A significant number of studies have been carried out on gradualism in economic reform in China since the 1970s (for example, Naughton, 1995; Larus, 2005) and the fact that the emergent market economy has coexisted with a lingering non-pluralist politics. Scholars have therefore sought to understand and explain the nature of political change in Pacific Asia's communist countries in the post-Cold War era.

Cheng Li, for example, looks to the 'transformation of China from an all-powerful strongman-dominated political system to its current structure of collective leadership' and points out the significance of 'new institutional rules and norms in elite politics' and the introduction of 'intra-party democracy' (Li, 2012: 23). Scholars have also looked to the advent of grassroots democracy through open competitive elections at the village level, China's so called 'village democracy' (see Perry and Goldman, 2007). In Vietnam, steps in political liberalization have been much bolder, and the pace of the move towards pluralist politics much faster (see Luong, 2003; McCargo, 2004).

Village democracy is a political development in China since the late 1990s where open and competitive elections for council and party branch chiefs are being held at the basic administrative level in rural China – the village. This has happened while the overall political system has remained non-competitive and non-pluralist. Village democracy can be seen as part of a controlled experiment in political reform in the same style in which China's much celebrated economic reform took place.

Optimists, therefore, argue the same gradualism that shifted the economy towards a market and improved the institutional environment for economic development (Yang, 2004), may well become the working model for political liberalization in years to come. This would be a piecemeal, accumulative process, to control its potential impact on existing and evolving interests. Such political change may lead to transparency, accountability and efficiency in functional areas, and eventually to more fundamental institutional change and structural reform in government structure and the overall political system. These optimists point to recent developments in village democracy, intraparty democracy and the party's new idea of 'three representatives', and the fact that elections are already open and competitive on a much larger scale in Vietnam, as signs of the unfolding of this political logic.

Pessimists (for example, Pei, 2006), however, point to the impasse that China's social and economic development has reached, and argue that without fundamental change in the core of the system, that is, the party-state, further development will be difficult if not impossible. Moreover, such rapid economic expansion can be dangerous under a party-state system that lacks the institutions to manage new interest groups and social forces.

Both optimists and pessimists have pointed to the significance of economic and social changes that have occurred in these countries and the region as a force for political change and democratization. Many Pacific Asian countries, including China, have experienced rapid growth and development, making them excellent cases for the debate on how economic development and social change relates to democratization in the process of modern state building.

'Adam Smith in Beijing'

The introduction and slow adoption of the principles of capitalism and the market economy has had a profound impact on society and politics in Pacific Asian nations. Differing significantly to the principles espoused in traditional social systems in the region and encountering significant obstacles from nationalism, independence movements and radical communism, capitalism and the market economy has emerged as the primary means of economic organization in the region.

The significance of this should not be understated. At one level, the emergence of capitalism as the primary means of organizing economic life represents a major shift in the social and political arrangements of Pacific Asian countries and the rejection of communist models of economic planning and state control. At another level, the successes of East Asian economies in particular, coupled with their large industrious populations, has ushered in a major transformation of the region. Their integration into the global economy has reshaped the distribution of worldwide economic activity. Pacific Asia is now home to two of the world's largest national economies, as measured in GDP (China and Japan), and some of the world's largest consumer markets and industrial centres.

The introduction of capitalism, or "Adam Smith in Beijing" as Giovanni Arrighi describes and explains as its latest instance with China (Arrighi 2007), has therefore had a profound impact on the process of modern state building in the region. Where communism had introduced economic planning, command economics and state control over the means of production to predominantly agrarian societies through revolution and radical transformation of the political order, capitalism was introduced slowly to Pacific Asia. After some gestation, capitalism and the market economy have evolved to the point where it is now the primary means of organizing economic activity in the region.

Debate remains, however, over the diversity of Pacific Asian capitalism, with some scholars going so far as to suggest that markets may exist but that the function and governance of markets in the region does not follow the standard principles of capitalism. Whatever the precise nature of markets in Pacific Asian countries, the evolution and institutionalization of capitalism in the region is shifting the balance of economic and financial power back to Asia (see Arrighi, 2007). This section explores the role of the idea of capitalism in Pacific Asian state building, from its early inception and gradual introduction to the current significance of the return of Pacific Asian economies.

The spread of capitalism and market economy

Unlike the expansion of socialism and communism that headed the spread of Western ideologies in Pacific Asia in the early twentieth century, the introduction, acceptance and eventual dominance of capitalism in Pacific Asia has been more gradual. Indeed, capitalism as an idea was never positively promoted or received in Pacific Asian societies. This was related partly to the traditional values and structures of Pacific Asian societies, and those of Confucian societies in particular. Traders and craftspeople were considered the lowest within the Confucian hierarchic social structure, lower than the large agricultural class. The fundamental but gradual change in social values and preferences in the twentieth century (and for most Pacific Asian countries in the second half of the twentieth century) and the success of the market economy were crucial for the ideals and values of capitalism to take root.

Capitalism is not just economic activities using modern technologies for mass production. It is also a set of social relations between employers and employees, a type of economic activity aimed at making a profit through commodity exchange and a set of national institutions that ensure the working of social relations and economic activities. At a more fundamental level, it is a civic culture regarding the purposes and preferences of life, and values and norms of society.

The spread of capitalism in Pacific Asia therefore presents a complicated picture of an ideology that was not as popular as communism or nationalism in the early modern era. In fact, for much of Pacific Asia capitalism was only a practical matter of business expansion, industrial development and international trade. Not until the late twentieth century did capitalism become the ideology of choice for organizing economic and social relations in the region. Two examples help illustrate the critical role of capitalism in Pacific Asia's political development and modern state building.

The first was the transformation of the samurai into capitalist entrepreneurs and labour towards the end of the Tokugawa era and early Meiji era, when modern capitalism started to take shape in Japan. Samurai were a unique class of warriors-turned-social-scholars, bureaucrats and administrators who served under regional daimyo. Under the ideal of Confucianism, pure moral self-cultivation was essential for samurai.

New initiatives by the young Meiji government in the 1870s, however, had a significant effect on the samurai. As W. G. Beasley observed, 'at the end of 1871 samurai had been given permission to enter farming, commerce and other occupations' (Beasley,

1963: 110). The government encouraged them – and later made it 'compulsory' for them – to commute their stipends in government bonds at half the rates for daimyo, 'a great deal less than they could live on' (Beasley, 1963: 110). This made it necessary for samurai to enter new professions. A study by Johannes Hirschmeier documents 'the rush of the samurai to found banks' and invest in new enterprises out of 'necessity to avoid starvation' and the considerable support by the government for these activities (Hirschmeier, 1964: 56–64).

Government initiatives not only provided 'former daimyo with substantial capital sums' (Beasley, 1963: 110), but also 'forced the samurai into new entrepreneurial activities such as craftsmen, merchants, bankers, company managers, property owners, or traders, and gradually formed a new entrepreneurial class that prepared for the rise of modern capitalism in Japan' (Huang, 2005: 150). More importantly, as Huang argues, behind the social change the samurai experienced 'the undermining of the core Confucian values that were an important part of traditional Japanese society… [but] no longer considered sufficient, or even appropriate' in the modern era (Huang, 2005: 150–1).

Secondly, a similar change in social values and attitudes towards business, profit-making, private property and individual entrepreneurship took place in a very different historical context, almost 100 years later in China. Like Japan, the traditional Chinese social system had placed little value on craftsman, merchants or entrepreneurs and not until the early modern period did social values begin to slowly shift and to accept and value business activities as a feature of the developing modern state. However, unlike Japan, the communist revolution of 1949 rebelled against this transformation and established a socialist planned economy with a largely autarkic model of international trade.

The communist economic model was placed in stark relief when by the end of the 1970s, Japan, South Korea, Taiwan, Singapore and Hong Kong had all experienced some kind of 'economic miracle' while China remained largely poor and underindustrialized. A second shift then occurred as China slowly introduced institutions to support the development of a market economy from the late 1970s and signalled a new government view of the market economy.

At the end of the 1970s, socialist values and ideals, particularly the Maoist-style socialist institutions, were deeply entrenched in the mindset of the Chinese people. When China's reformist leader of the time, Deng Xiaoping, proclaimed, 'to get rich is glorious', he was running against a society that still firmly believed in collective well-being and public ownership. It took over three decades of constant government propaganda and mass media, rapid expansion of the private economy and a gradual unfolding of the benefits of an alternative form of economic activity for people to gradually accept capitalist ideas and values as well as their associated institutions and social relations. This shift occurred in a very different manner to how economic planning had been introduced to China and the region.

Barry Naughton contrasted the Chinese model of post-socialist economic reform with models of reform in Eastern Europe in the 1960s and the 'big bang' reforms of the 1990s. Naughton argues the Chinese reform experience constitutes a distinct model of economic reform in the socialist command economies due to a series of unique features (Naughton, 1995: 9–13). China's experience of institutional change towards a market economy without an ex ante blueprint but with 'substantial ex post coherence' (Naughton, 1995: 13) presents a fundamentally different approach to institutional change and the shift towards a market economy.

> '**Growing out of the plan**' is a crucial feature of the Chinese transition. Economic growth is concentrated on the market track. Given the obvious fact that the market economy was growing rapidly, this implied that the plan would become proportionately less and less important until the economy gradually grew out of the planned economy.
>
> Naughton, 1995: 9

In short, the history of capitalism, the market economy (more discussion of this in Chapter 7) and globalization in Pacific Asia (further analysis on this in Chapter 10) illustrates the importance of viewing the impact of ideas over a long timeframe. Moreover, the spread of capitalism denies simplistic understandings of the role of ideas in modern state building that look only to major historical events such as revolutions or mass movements as markers of change. While communism and democracy both made their mark on modern state building through mass popular movements and revolutions, the influence and gradual acceptance of capitalism has come about over time and largely in the absence of clearly observable historical markers. Moreover, even when capitalist ideas appeared to be sidelined or strongly opposed, such as during the communist and state-led development era during the Cold War, they still existed and reappeared to become the dominant ideology for organizing society and the economy.

The relationship between capitalism and modern state building in Pacific Asia is therefore highly complex. Capitalism is a foundation of the modern state but differing from communism the role it has played shaping the direction of state building has been subtler. Only in recent decades have elites and intellectuals outwardly advocated the deepening of the market economy, promoted the norms and values of capitalism in society and pushed reforms to protect the rights and privileges of workers, businesspeople and companies, foreign and local, within the evolving regulatory systems of Pacific Asian countries. The success of economic growth and development in parts of the region, particularly in Northeast Asia, has strengthened elite and stakeholder support for capitalism and globalization in the new century and led to the emergence of a highly dynamic and competitive centre of global growth.

In short, after a long and gradualist process, capitalism has become the dominant value system and institutional framework for organizing the economy in Pacific Asian countries. It has shaped the development of the modern state in Pacific Asia by providing both the material basis for prosperity, though this remains challenging in many parts of China and Southeast Asia, and by supporting the spread of modern values of efficiency and the rule of law. As noted below, this has significantly changed the way Pacific Asian countries engage with the global economy.

The dynamics of political change

These major political ideas and forces have swept Pacific Asia in the twentieth century, generating significant political movements, revolutions, wars and conflicts. They have been the basis for elite reform efforts and led to profound change in state institutions, the way political society is organized and the processes and procedures in politics. This has created tension with existing, traditional or Asian institutions and processes. In this section, we provide some examples of the dynamic interaction between traditional and modern, local and imported, and conservative and progressive forces. We illustrate the dynamics of political change and development and show the consequences of institutional development.

The problem of Asian democracy

Democracy has emerged as the foundation for politics and governance in Pacific Asia. As illustrated earlier, democratic ideals have moved far beyond providing a rallying point for movements of self-determination and sovereignty. Democratic institutions and a democratic civic culture are now either consolidated, as in Japan, Taiwan, South Korea and Indonesia, or a central part of the functioning and ideals of the modern state. However, as noted above, the context in which these transformations have occurred differs considerably to other parts of the world. This has led some scholars to put forward the idea that democracy in Pacific Asia functions with observable and significant differences to democracy in other regions; that democracy in Pacific Asia is Asian democracy.

Asian democracy is a unique set of political institutions and values found in Pacific Asian countries resulting from the shaping of democratic institutions and values by the traditional structures and values as well as contemporary conditions of political economy in these countries.

However, we should be cautious on this line of argument. The observance of democratic variations in Pacific Asia at a certain point in their political development does not necessarily present evidence of an Asian variant of democracy. The process of consolidating democratic institutions is long and forces that once had a strong role on the functioning of the state, such as social views on the role of women and non-dominant ethnic groups in politics, can and do change over time. For example, full universal suffrage for men, women and all ethnic groups was not achieved in the United States until 1965. Just as

Box 2.6

Interpreting 'Asian democracy'

The issue of the precise nature of Asian democracy and its relationship to liberal democracy invites scholarly debate and competing views.

Form–substance argument: Asian democracy is democracy in form (formal institutions and declared values), but Asian (that is, non-democratic) in substance (effective structure and actual practices).

Democracy works thesis: Asian democracy is the function of democracy. It is the people who decide what political party they want in government and for how long.

Alternative-way theory: Asian democracy is a challenge or even an alternative to liberal democracy.

Traditional–modern tension explanation: Asian democracy is the adaptation of modern institutions and values to local conditions, or a compromise between the modern and the traditional (local, cultural).

it would be wrong to judge Western democracy on how it functioned in the early sixties before the civil rights movement and to conclude this represented a unique model of American democracy, we should be careful about viewing current democratic practices in Asia as representing a unique form of Asian governance.

Scholars in the second group do not necessarily think modern values and institutions are problematic, but believe there are different types of modern institutions and values, such as liberal, communitarian and others. They argue that modern values and institutions, as well as other values and institutions, are needed for a more balanced political and social order. Beng-Huat Chua, like many others, sees the prevalent model of democracy as a liberal variant. He argues that the non-liberal communitarian democracy, as found in Singapore, shares similar 'requisite conditions' with those of a liberal democracy. But the 'philosophical grounds' for their justification are different for a liberal democracy and the PAP version of communitarian democracy (Chua, 1995: 201).

One also needs to be aware that even on the very concept of the 'modern state', different people may take it to mean different things. Max Weber's original conception (Weber 1947, 1968) focuses on the role of the rational and centralized bureaucracy to provide effective and efficient management of mass society and the secularization of politics that legitimize state power on a 'this-worldly' basis. However, as David Held (1989) has shown, different theories and practices of modern state have developed that range from the Marxist to social democratic to developmental to liberal democratic. Increasingly, the ascendance of liberal democratic theories and practices in the post-war period has led to debates as to whether the modern state is, or should be, synonymous with the liberal democratic state (Huntington, 1996).

It is within this wider scholarly context that we discuss how the traditional forces and social ethics affect modern values and institutions in Pacific Asia. The tension between traditional values and institutions and the modern state in Pacific Asia are felt most acutely in the way they have shaped democratic institutions in these countries. Traditional values and institutions affect whether democracy works and how it works, in several ways.

First, the persistent dominance of traditional forms of public authority prevented democracy from developing in many countries. Constant military intervention in politics, and prolonged control of the state by the military, for example, leave little room for democratic institutions to develop.

Second, the prevalence of traditional social structures and values can delay the rise of democratic institutions. These structures and values are often closely associated with the early stage of development in these countries where the focus was squarely on achieving a strong state and a prosperous economy. Thus, development has often come before democracy in Pacific Asia. Moreover, even with significant progress in economic development in many countries, democracy has still not universally arrived as expected by many.

Third, for those with democratic institutions in place, the underlying social structure governed by the ascriptive values of traditional forces can make the political system democratic only on the surface. Behind the democratic institutions, elections, party systems, constitutional order, citizenship and so on, there is clearly a hierarchical, elitist political order and a top-down and corporatist political processes.

A description of the Malaysian political system by Harold Crouch typically illustrates this point:

> The constitutional framework of the Malaysian political system is essentially democratic. Elections have been held regularly, the government is responsible to an elected parliament, and the judiciary is constitutionally independent. But the democratic framework is accompanied by a wide range of authoritarian controls that greatly limit the scope for effective political opposition and make it very difficult to envisage the defeat of the ruling party at the polls. (Crouch, 1996: 5).

Deliberative democracy is critical of existing liberal democratic arrangements because the latter do not sufficiently address the problems of pluralism, inequality and complexity that are characteristic of modern (Western) societies. Unlike liberal democracy, deliberative democracy does not just rely upon the aggregation of preferences and majority voting. By giving priority to reasoned argument and discussion, deliberative democracy enables 'interests' to be recognized, but does not permit them to dominate proceedings. Unlike republican democracy, deliberative democracy is sceptical about whether a single shared vision of the common good could ever be attained or be effective in motivating citizens. Deliberative democracy still allows for the formation of provisional notions of the common good by deliberation.

Stokes 2006: 53–54

Fourth, in many Pacific Asian democracies, old or new, there is a lack of 'civic culture' (Almond and Verba, 1963) that can sustain the functioning of democratic institutions. State institutions are not always the embodiment of democratic values. Public office can be corrupt. Votes can be purchased. Elections are not about issues or policies, but more about personal relations. In these cases, the institutions of a democracy are present but due to a lack of civic culture do not function as would be expected.

There are three distinctive features of **illiberal democracy** that have developed in Pacific Asia since 1945:

A non-neutral understanding of the state that governments may justifiably intervene in most if not all aspects of social life in order to promote an officially predetermined conception of the public good;

The evolution of a rationalistic and legalistic technocracy that manages the developing state as a corporate enterprise;

The development of a managed rather than a critical public space and civil society.

Jones et al., 1995: 163–4

All these are important aspects of what has been described as 'Asian democracy'. The problem of Asian democracy can manifest in the form of 'deliberative democracy' (Stokes 2006, Leib and He, 2006), 'illiberal democracy' (Brown and Jones, 1995; Bell and Jayasuriya, 1995; Bell et al., 1995; Zakari, 1997), 'paternalistic states' and 'soft-authoritarianism' (Scalapino, 1989; Fukuyama, 1992; Roy, 1994; Means, 1996), 'democracy without competition' (Scheiner, 2005), 'uncommon democracies' (Pempel, 1990),

Box 2.7

Debating human rights in Pacific Asia

There are two key issues in the debate:

- Whether human rights are universal, or if they are only specific to individual countries:

Cultural relativists: Human rights are country, cultural and historically specific;

Universalists: A minimum set of human rights is universally applicable.

- Whether economic and social rights can be separated from political and civil rights:

Economic rights first argument: Different historical priority allows economic rights first.

Linked rights thesis: Economic and political rights cannot be separated. One cannot do without the other.

and the politics of human rights. Often, an Asian democracy can have all the institutions of democracy: elections, multiparty institutions, rule of law and so on. But the institutions are often subject to the broad economic and social agenda as claimed by the dominant political forces, which typically emphasize stability, order and development. The consequent political order is therefore anything but a liberal democracy.

Development and democracy

The relationship between democracy and development, and the debate over experiences in Pacific Asian countries are significant for our understanding of political modernization in the region. There are several issues involved. The first is whether democratic institutions are necessary for economic development. Second, can economic development be sustained without democracy? Third, how do political institutions change as economy and society develop? These questions are part of the long-running debate on the nature of the link between democracy and development (Lipset, 1959, and see Box 2.7; Olson, 1993; Neher and Marlay, 1995; Leftwich, 1996; Laothamatas, 1997; Przeworski et al., 2000).

Scholars trace those who see a positive link between economic development and democracy back to the modernization theory of the 1950s and 1960s. Modernization theory, however, is seen to have originated from the teachings of Karl Marx and Max Weber. It was Karl Marx who believed that 'capitalist development gave rise to the bourgeoisie, who in turn, found that the pre-existing monarchical regime stood in the way of their achieving economic power. The bourgeoisie thus turned to democracy as the alternative regime' (Laothamatas, 1997: 2).

Prominent among modernization theory in the 1950s and 1960s is S. M. Lipset (1959), who pioneered a scholarly tradition that employed quantitative methods to prove a positive link between economic development and democracy (see Box 2.7). In the view of modern liberalism, therefore, modern development has both an economic and a political aspect. They are intertwined, mutually supportive and one is indispensable to the other.

Depending on the actual equation in mind and the time of the debate, studies advocating this theory have different sets of arguments. In the early stages of post-war rapid economic development in Pacific Asia, the debate usually centred on whether democratic institutions are necessary conditions for modern economic development. The argument in modern liberalism is usually that:

- Democratic institutions are necessary for economic development because non-democratic regimes tend to be corrupt and concerned with accumulation of wealth for themselves rather than for the people and society.
- Non-democratic regimes are not able to properly represent a vast range of societal interests in their decision-making process and thus are ill equipped to organize economic development on a mass scale.
- Non-democratic regimes have limited space for civil liberty and individual freedom, and do not respect individual property rights. Such regimes therefore are incompatible with the market economy, which is centred on private

Box 2.8

The Lipset thesis and the positive link between democracy and development

Anek Laothamatas summarizes the two defining elements of the scholarly tradition pioneered by S. M. Lipset's 1959 essay as follows:

Political efficacy: Economic development brings about better political communication and education among the citizens, a more mobile way of life (geographically and socially), and a career system of rewarding people by the work they do and how well they do it, rather than who they are. All these spill over into the political culture and political behaviour of a 'modernized' people, resulting in their clamouring for a substantial role in politics and public affairs.

Pluralist dynamics: Meanwhile, economic progress turns a relatively passive and functionally homogeneous society into a wide range of socioeconomic groups vying for the attention of the state and, thus, necessitating a new political system which is more accountable to society and simultaneously capable of reconciling conflicting aspirations of societal groups in a fair and free manner.

Laothamatas, 1997: 3

> ownership and individual entrepreneurship. In short, 'getting the institutions right' (for more on this, see Clague, 1997) is crucial for economic development.

The failure of non-pluralist politics across the region from the 1960s to the 1980s was correlated with poverty, inequality and corruption in many countries. However, non-pluralist politics did not prevent some countries, such as Japan, Taiwan and Korea, successfully moving from low-income to middle or upper-middle income economies through rapid economic growth (see Chapter 6). In these countries, democratic institutions were only partial during the early rapid growth period and developed as the economy and society evolved. This has reignited a third debate about how economic and social changes support democratization. As the four Asian tigers, Hong Kong, Singapore, South Korea and Taiwan, experienced rapid development and society transformed, the push for the development of functioning democratic institutions such as the rule of law, government accountability and predictability, is clearly evident. South Korea and Taiwan provide particularly strong evidence that development supports the transition and consolidation of democracy in the process of modern state building.

Other countries in the region, however, are developing but have yet to transition. Thailand, for example, has experienced many coups. China in particular has emerged as an upper-middle income country with significant economic capacity, a majority urban population and well-educated populace but has not transitioned to a multiparty liberal democracy. Similarly, Vietnam has entered a rapid early growth period and shows encouraging signs of political liberalization. These cases, however, raise more questions than provide answers. There is abundant evidence to suggest there is a link between development and democracy but that the level of economic development and social change has yet to reach a level to propel democratic transition. On the other hand, some scholars have suggested a potentially different model of governance is evolving in response to the social and economic changes (see Bell: 2015).

While the largest or second largest economy in the world, China remains a developing country with many social, economic and political hurdles to overcome in its drive towards modernization. The current policy of 'economics first' follows the well-trodden path of earlier developing countries in the region but has some way left to run. It remains too early to make concrete statements on the link between development and democracy in the Chinese case.

In summary, political liberalization and democratic transition occurred under different circumstances and took different forms but the overall pattern is clear. After decades of rapid industrialization, economic growth and social development, as well as non-pluralist politics in various forms, most countries have returned, restored or established pluralist politics, with the exception of China and Vietnam on the one hand, and North Korea and Laos on the other. But even in Vietnam and China, a level of political institutionalization, if not liberalization, is clearly visible.

Today, democracy is seen as the most desirable solution to fundamental political and social problems in Pacific Asia and the most effective and fairest way of governance and political participation. Democracy has emerged as a foundational principle for organizing political life in modern Pacific Asian society and is therefore one of the most important analytical frameworks for understanding and explaining the political structure and dynamics of the region.

The Soldier and the State

Samuel Huntington discussed in length the problem of civil-military relations in his 1957 book *The Soldier and the State*. While his focus was largely on the challenge of Western civilian governments achieving and maintaining effective control over the military in the process of modern state building, his analysis is particularly relevant for post-WWII Pacific Asia.

The armed forces have been an important part of the state in Pacific Asia. The ruling forces in most newly independent nations post WWII, be they the communist or nationalist, had come to power through political violence and war as had traditionally been the case in the region. As Huntington pointed out, in many early modern states the military was one of the most, if not *the* most, well-trained and effective organizations. This makes their role in the newly formed modern state very significant.

For example, when the Meiji Emperor set in motion reforms in early modern Japan, it was the military that ultimately dominated the government and ensured they were effectively carried out. Similarly, Mao and the Chinese Communist Party relied heavily on the People's Liberation Army (PLA) in their protracted civil war with the Nationalists and again post-1949 in their efforts to build a 'new China'. Mao famously proclaimed, 'Political power grows out of the barrel of a gun'.

A large group of countries in Pacific Asia fell under direct or indirect military rule after the initial pluralist period in the early post-war period (see earlier sections). These ranged from South Korea and Myanmar where the military removed a weak and ineffectual government to install military governance to the Philippines where Ferdinand Marcos resided as President from 1965 to 1986 largely through support of the military. Thailand in particular has a long and recurring history of the military removing the government and revising the constitution. As illustrated in the 2014 military coup, when the government was dissolved and the country placed under direct military rule, an active role for the military has not been effectively removed.

The post-war years have witnessed a long journey for Pacific Asian countries to depoliticize the role of the military. Military-state relations vary in different Pacific Asian countries, ranging from civilian rule, to military state institutions or even military as the ultimate source of political authority. A clear expectation of the modern state is for the military not to be a legitimate agent in government and politics. However, in many states the military has sought a political role, to act as a guardian of the state independent of civilian control or to intervene in the functioning of government. As such, the role of the military as a traditional form of public authority remains a significant challenge for some Pacific Asian states.

One of the essential features of the modern state, according to Max Weber, is its monopoly on the legitimate use of force (Weber, 1965). As the military is principally an instrument of force, tension between it and the modern state is inevitable. Political modernization requires de-politicization of the military: the military accepts civilian control and becomes politically neutral – a principle that Huntington has called 'military professionalism' (Huntington, 1957). The use of force by the military can only be legitimatized by the state.

Military professionalism is the pursuit of modern standards and principles in the organization of the armed forces as a profession, in particular, the principle of political neutrality and civilian control.

Huntington's thesis is challenged by others (see Janowitz, 1964; Abrahamsson, 1972; Perlmutter, 1977) who question 'Huntington's linkage between professionalism and political neutrality' (Godwin, 1978: 220), particularly in 'new' or 'developing' countries. Amos Perlmutter, for example, argues that the concept of corporatism should be 'extracted' from the concept of professionalism. The military can be professional but still politically active. It is the corporateness, that is, the military's group consciousness and its relations to the state, that determines the military's political behaviour and level of political intervention by the military (Perlmutter 1977: xvi).

Consequently, Perlmutter rejects the deterministic dichotomy between 'civil' and 'military' and advances a thesis of three types of military-political relations in modern times (see Box 2.8). The *classical professional military* emerges when a civilian coalition gains supremacy with electoral support and establishes political authority over the military. The *praetorian military* is, potentially or actually, interventionist; its disposition to intervene is permanent and it has the power to bring about constitutional change. The *revolutionary military* becomes an instrument of mobilization for the revolutionary party but its tendency towards political intervention is never totally eliminated.

The three-types model is useful as it exposes a wide range of different types of military–state relations, and different kinds of political roles the military has assumed in new or developing countries. Perlmutter's three types cover most military–state relations in Pacific Asian countries. Many Pacific Asian countries experienced a transition from praetorian to professional military–state relations, generally along the progressive line of political modernization. All the revolutionary militaries have been stable in their partnership with the party-state.

Among the different types of military–state relations, those in Thailand and China are worthy of further discussion. Thailand is a typical example of a praetorian military. Under Perlmutter's

Box 2.9

The military and politics in modern times

Three general types of military organization have arisen in the modern nation-state as a response to the different types of institutionalized civilian authority.

The ***classical professional military*** emerges when a civilian coalition gains supremacy with electoral support and establishes political authority over the military. The solider, with his professional knowledge and expertise, becomes the single and supreme protector of the state in its military function. The military establishment, which is a corporate unit, is careful to maintain this relationship.

The ***praetorian military*** arrives within political control systems often in the wake of a failed social, political or modernizing revolution. Praetorians emerge in largely agrarian, transitional or ideologically divided societies. The military is, potentially or actually, interventionist; its disposition to intervene is permanent and it has the power to bring about constitutional change. The nature of military clientship shifts when the military 'decides' who represents the nation and political order. The locus of authority can also shift from the central government level to regional, tribal or ethnic levels.

The ***revolutionary military*** manifests a strong propensity to succumb to political influence, especially before and during a 'revolutionary war'. As the revolution becomes institutionalized, the past movement becomes the supreme authority in the state. It then opposes the surrogate role of the military in politics and accepts the rational officer (professional) type of military organization. However, it rejects the premises of military corporatism and the right to intervene in politics. Thus, in the initial stages of the revolution, the military loses its autonomy and modifies some of its professional characteristics in favour of the party or the movement and becomes an instrument of mobilization for the revolutionary party. In most cases, however, the revolutionary military's tendency towards political intervention is never totally eliminated and it continues to have at least a latent political role despite its professional orientation.

Perlmutter 1977: 9–14

model, the Thai military's disposition to intervene is permanent. In 1932 Thailand's absolute monarchy was abolished in a bloodless coup and a constitutional monarchy was established. Since that time there have been 19 military coups, the most recent in 2014 and 2006. Of the eighty-two years of this period, fifty-nine years were under a government headed by the military. Judged by the different enemies the military interventions were aimed at in each period and the mission the military assigned to itself (Ockey, 2001: 190), one can see that the military regarded the Thai polity as an unsettled one, constantly under threat from both internal and external dangers. The military's mindset (Huntington, 1957; Perlmutter, 1977) is characterized by the military seeing themselves as the guardians of the state, with the right to intervene being inherent in such a guardianship role (see Box 2.9).

In contrast, while the military in China is political by definition, such a political role is not independent of the party-state, but rather defined by it. It is political because it is defined as the political instrument of the party-state. The People's Liberation Army (PLA) has been promoted as the legitimate tool of the Communist Party, and soldiers portrayed as model citizens. The PLA was used politically during the Cultural Revolution (1966–76) and the Tiananmen Movement (1989). On the other hand, the PLA is tightly controlled by the Communist Party, with Party branches being set up at all levels of its governance. As with other political, economic and social organizations in China, the Party is heavily integrated into the PLA. The role of the PLA in society and its relations with the state, as established under Mao, matches what Perlmutter calls the 'revolutionary military' model, in which the military sees itself as the primary defender of

Box 2.10

Why the military intervenes

Among the numerous explanations that have been advanced to explain the politicization of the military and military intervention or non-intervention in politics, those focused on the nature of the military profession, the military mission and roles, the weakness of political institutions and the government's performance have been influential.

Military professionalism:

- Professional military are apolitical and do not intervene in politics;
- Professionalization breeds corporate interest, the preservation of which leads to civil–military conflict and military intrusion in politics;
- The 'new professionalism' of the military in developing countries encourages political intervention.

Military mission and roles:

- The continual threat of war blurs the civil–military distinction and leads to the political ascendance of the military;
- The specific mission of a nation's military has a major impact on civil–military relations;
- Mobilization for war has an impact on civil–military relations.

Weakness of political institutions:

- The propensity to intervene is related to the level of political culture;
- Military intervention is a function of unbalanced institutional development;
- The military intervenes to protect and advance the interests of a specific class or ethnic/religious group.

Government's performance:

- Performance failures on the part of civilian governments provide the impetus for military intervention;
- A coup is a function of underdevelopment.

Alagappa, 2001: 42–50

a revolutionary cause. In terms of modern state building, therefore, there have never been any efforts to marginalize the military from state affairs. Rather the party-state has incorporated the PLA, and formed a 'symbiosis' (Bickford, 2001: 31; see also Shambaugh, 1991) with it.

While this critical aspect of the Chinese state has changed somewhat since the 1980s, the PLA remains unable to stand on its own and break down this party-state–military symbiosis. Since the reform period began in the late 1970s, China has moved to modernize its military, including institutionalizing its role in the state and professionalizing its ranks. On the back of three decades of rapid growth, the PLA has grown to represent a formidable force in the region. As such, countries in the region pay particular attention to Party-PLA-state relations in China.

The different types of military–state relations indicate the different extents to which the military is still active as a form of public authority. The problem is most significant with the praetorian military, which is politically active, independent of the state and interventionist as a self-proclaimed public authority ensuring political order.

If the military were politically active because of an inability of the state to provide political order, the political role of the military would decline as the capacity of the state enhanced. Scholars have put forward a variety of views on this. In explaining the determinants of the military's political behaviour and level of political intervention by the military, Perlmutter argues that corporatism and ideology are more important than state capacity. In other words, the propensity of the military for political intervention is shaped by the military organizational structure and its mindset.

Offering an alternative view and explaining the recent decline of the military's political role, Muthiah Alagappa proposes that the political power and influence of the military goes with the 'weight of coercion in governance'. The weight of coercion is 'inversely proportional to the legitimacy of the nation-state and political system and the capacity of the non-coercive institutions of the state', and 'declines with increasing levels of economic development' (Alagappa, 2001: 4–5). Clearly, the rise and fall of the military's political role is seen here to be closely related to the overall political economy of the country rather than to the military's own institutions, organization and ideology. This is perhaps the basis upon which Alagappa and his associates declared that the political role of the military in Pacific Asia is declining.

This is evident in the vast majority of Pacific Asian countries. Japan, for example, once had an interventionist military that at its height controlled government and pushed Japan towards the horrors of the Pacific War from the mid-1930s. In the post-war years, the military was severely restricted from taking any sort of political role and constitutionally designated as having a defensive role only. The removal of the military's role in politics and its increasing professionalism and modernization has gone hand in hand with economic and political development to the point where today Japan has one of the most professional militaries in the world.

Efforts in 2015 to reinterpret the constitutional constraints on the deployment of Japanese forces did not touch on provisions that remove the Japan Self-Defence Force from any role in the political process. The historical memory of the Pacific War means countries in the region will pay particular attention to this important civilian-military relationship.

In summary, traditional forms of public authority have shaped the process of building the modern state in Pacific Asia. This is evident in the analysis of the relationship between the military and the state and through exploration of the role of social and moral ethics in contemporary society. The next section focuses on the Asian values debate that posits social ethics and values as an explanatory factor for understanding politics and governance in the region.

The Asian values debate

As early as the 1970s, the issue of the relationship between Asian values and modernization was raised (Seah, 1977) in a collaborative research effort by a team of scholars in Singapore just ten years after the birth of the new republic. At this time, modernization for countries such as Singapore meant 'rationality, equality of economic and social opportunities, comprehensive planning, attitudinal transformation, and nationalism and national consciousness' (Seah, 1977: xi). One of the authors in the research group argued that some Asian values are incompatible with modernization, and as such questioned whether modernization was in fact good for mankind in general (Ho, 1977).

In the 1990s, the same issue emerged to become a major debate on a larger scale. There was a series of high-profile exchanges of statements and commentaries by politicians, political commentators, policymakers and scholars over the role of Asian values in government, politics, economic development, and social order in Pacific Asia. The exchange started with high-profile pronouncements by politicians, policymakers and political commentators in Singapore, Malaysia and Japan over the importance of Asian values as an alternative to Western liberalism (Lee, 1994; Mahathir and Ishihara, 1995; Mahbubani, 1995).

> The **Singapore school** refers to a group of scholars, politicians and media commentators featured in the Asian values debate in the 1990s who generally proclaimed the primacy of Asian values. As some key figures in the group and the most high-profile advocates of these ideas – such as former prime minister of Singapore, Lee Kuan Yew; retired diplomat, Tommy Koh; and former diplomat and then Dean of the Lee Kuan Yew School of Public Policy at the National University of Singapore, Kishore Mahbubani – are related in some way to Singapore, these advocates of Asian values are often conveniently referred to as the Singapore school.

In an interview with Lee Kuan Yew in Foreign Affairs in 1994, Lee summarized the essential argument of the so-called Singapore school and stated how he saw the fundamental differences between Asian values and Western liberalism:

> The expansion of the right of the individual to behave or misbehave as he pleases has come at the expense of orderly society. In the East the main objective is to have a well-ordered society so that everybody can have maximum enjoyment of his freedom. This freedom can only exist in an ordered state and not in a natural state of contention and anarchy (Lee, 1994: 111).

Lee's comment underlies much of the subsequent scholarly discourse about communitarianism (Chua,

1995; de Bary, 1998). The views of the Singapore school can be summarized as follows:

- There are unique cultural traits in Asian countries that are responsible for their economic development, social harmony and political stability;
- These so-called Asian values are family-centred, order-orientated, community-privileged, and have their roots in Asian cultural traditions such as Confucianism; and
- Societies built upon Asian values can better meet the challenge of organizing modern society and the social and political model built upon Asian values can provide an effective alternative to Western individualism and utilitarianism.

These high-profile views were not accepted without a challenge. The debate focused on four related issues (see Box 2.10). First, is there a coherent set of values that can be called 'Asian'? If so, what are these values? Challengers argue that the diversity of cultural traditions in Pacific Asia makes it hard to find one shared cultural tradition. Judged on the various lists of the Asian values proposed (Seah, 1977; Dupont, 1996; Milner, 2000), they are clearly related to Confucian values and ethics. Even Lee Kwan Yew conceded that when he says Asian societies, he means 'Korea, Japan, China, and Vietnam, as distinct from Southeast Asia' (Lee, 1994: 113).

Second, are these values responsible for the economic prosperity and social development in Pacific Asia? The advocates of Asian values believe that Asian values were the reasons for the economic renaissance of Pacific Asia. Not everyone agreed. As Eric Jones charged, 'what happened to them will have been transient and historically contingent, not the working out of some indefeasible Sinitic trait' (Jones, 1994: 21).

Third, are these values universal or uniquely Asian? It is clear from the claim by the Singapore school that Asian values are considered to be unique and better than those in Western liberalism. For many others, so-called Asian values, such as family values, hard work and so on, are universal values that are not especially Asian. Chris Patten, the last British governor of Hong Kong, stated, 'Asia's growth has been driven by values, but the values doing the driving are not uniquely Asian. They are universal, and if allowed to, they will work as effectively in Europe, in North America or anywhere else' (Patten, 1996: 12). The same view was shared by Kim Dae Jung, former president of South Korea (Kim, 1994) in his response to Lee and important essay on the struggle for liberal democracy in Korea.

Finally, do these values constitute a credible challenge or a positive alternative to Western liberalism? In recent years, some media commentators in the West have viewed the political economy in Northeast Asia and once again drawn a link between a notion that Asian values were responsible for a well-ordered and prosperous society relative to the global financial crisis that emerged in Western nations.

Scholars also look to surveys on satisfaction in government, such as those conducted by the Pew Research Center, and note the high levels of satisfaction in government in those Northeast Asian countries maintaining good levels of growth and development, China included. However, the overall trend in the academic literature is to analyse the broader development of political values in Pacific Asia that point to increasingly liberal values over much of the region and the strong support for individual rights, liberties and democracy (see Chu, Diamond, Nathan and Shin, 2008).

Box 2.11

Four issues in the Asian values debate

- Is there a coherent set of values that can be called Asian values?
- Are these values responsible for the economic prosperity and social development in Pacific Asia?
- Are these values universal or uniquely Asian?
- Do these values constitute a credible challenge to Western liberalism?

Chapter summary

- A modern state is about the capacity and functionality of a public authority in providing order in a mass society and is measured by its ability to provide capable, effective and functionally differentiated governance and to protect the equality of its citizens.
- Political modernization is the process whereby state institutions gain capacity and functionality to meet the challenge of organizing mass economic and social life under modern conditions and whereby political life within the polity is increasingly governed by modern values such as equality and fairness.
- Three ideas, communism, democracy and capitalism, more than any others have shaped modern state building and political development in Pacific Asia but each has left its mark on the modern state in different ways.
- Communism appealed to the subjugated and poor of the region and was spread through armed revolutions that overthrew the state and introduced radical socialist systems.
- Socialism in Pacific Asia introduced radical and damaging developmental programmes that sought to abolish private property and enterprise and communize agriculture. Communism failed in the region due to a mismatch between ideology and developmental requirements.
- The legacy of communism remains strong with well over half of the people in Pacific Asia living under a one-party state governed by a ruling communist party. How communist governments are evolving following the introduction of market forces remains a key debate in the study of Pacific Asian politics.
- Democracy has been employed by forces looking first to secure sovereignty and independence from foreign control and later by groups in the region looking to establish functioning democratic institutions.
- Pluralist politics failed in the early post-war era due to a wide range of factors. From the 1980s, a wave of democratic transitions occurred following different models of democratization. Socialist states have made limited progress by institutionalizing governing systems and leadership transition and by introducing local elections and limited reform of national elections.
- Capitalism was introduced slowly in the region and needed to overcome strong nationalist sentiment, traditional social values and norms and the obstacle of socialist models of economy.
- The East Asian 'miracle' led to capitalism and the market economy becoming the dominant model of organizing national economies and transforming social values and relationships in the region.
- Political modernization in Pacific Asian countries is not a simple, straightforward process of maximization of efficiency and equality. It is a process complicated by the traditional values, institutions and structure of these countries, their colonial past and the contemporary interaction between East and West.
- Democracy has emerged as the foundation for politics and governance in Pacific Asia but variations in democratic practices, such as the persistence of single party dominance, has raised questions about how to interpret Asian democracy.
- The emergence of an illiberal middle class questions liberal theories of modernization and social change.

- The politics of human rights in Pacific Asia has focused on two key questions: whether human rights are universal and whether political and civil rights can be separated from political rights in the process of development.
- The political role of the military has largely declined since the 1940s. However, in many countries, military government and military intervention in government is still seen.
- Proponents of the Asian values debate argue Asia is family-centred, order-orientated and community-privileged, and that these values have their roots in Asian cultural traditions such as Confucianism. They argue Asian values are responsible for their economic development, social harmony and political stability and a superior alternative to Western liberalism.

Further reading

For the concepts of the modern state and political modernization, and its Weberian origins, see Pye (1966b), Held (1989, 1992) and Pierson (2004).

For an overview of the problem of modern state and traditional values and institutions, see Huang (2002). For religion and the modern state, see Keyes et al. (1994), Smith (1971, 1974) and Haynes (2006). On Confucianism and the modern state, see Fukuyama (1995), Tamney and Chiang (2002) and Bell and Hahm (2003). For Chinese culture, Confucianism and East Asian cultural identities, see Pye (1985), de Bary (1988) and Huang (2002). For traditional views of family and state, see Glosser (2003).

Studies on communism in Asia are largely outdated. However, works on the political system and history, as well as post-socialist reforms in China and Vietnam can be a good starting point: see Nee and Stark (1989), Porter (1993), William and Selden (1993) Chen (1995), Lieberthal (2004), Pei (1994), Litvack and Rondinelli (1999), Blecher (2003), and Lin (2006) For capitalism and democracy in Asian societies, see Bell and Hahm (2003) and Dalton and Shin (2006).

For military–state relations, see Huntington (1957), Perlmutter (1977) and, in Pacific Asia in particular, Alagappa (2001), Tang (1994), Christie and Roy (2001) and Eldridge (2002) provide a survey of the issues, main approaches, and the debate over human rights in Pacific Asia. For debate on Asian democracy, see Bell et al. (1995) and Diamond and Plattner (1998). For the democracy–development thesis, see Neher and Marlay (1995), Leftwich (1996) and Laothamatas (1997). For the Asian values debate, see Dupont (1996) and Milner (2000).

Study questions

1. Discuss some of the unique characteristics of the experiences of political modernization in Pacific Asia.
2. Why did communism and socialism appeal to Pacific Asian societies in the twentieth century while capitalism and democracy took much longer to take root?
3. Why did pluralist politics fail in Pacific Asia in the early post-war years?
4. Given the historical experiences of the spread of democracy in Pacific Asia, why has it exercised a much greater power and influence from the 1980s?

5 Is capitalism in Pacific Asia 'real' capitalism?

6 Are the optimists, the pessimists or neither correct in their views on the progress towards democratization and liberalization in communist states? What about in illiberal or Asian democracies?

7 Is culture destiny?

8 What is the Asian values debate? Why did the debate occur? If you were to participate in the debate, how would you answer the key questions raised?

Key terms

Modern state (37); Political modernization (39); Political development (38); Communism and socialism (42); Communist movements (42); Cultural Revolution (43); Doi Moi (44); Democracy (38), democratization (46); democratic transition (38); Political liberalization (51); 1955 system (52); Guided democracy (49); Asian values (51); Village democracy (54); Capitalism and market economy (56); Economic reform (4); Growing out of the plan (57); Transitional economy (63); Asian democracy (58); The Singapore school (66); The Lipset thesis of development and democracy (61); Pluralist politics (47); Non-democratic regimes (61); Deliberative democracy (60); Illiberal democracy (60); Professional, praetorian and revolutionary military (63).

Chapter 3

Types of states in Pacific Asia

In this chapter, we shall take a close look at the constitution of the state, and the structure and legitimacy of state authority and explain the phenomenon of state dominance (see Box 3.1). More specifically, this chapter will cover four main issues in the constitution of the state and structure of state authority:

- Types of state and the distribution of state power.
- Constitution of the state and the problem of constitutional legitimacy.
- A particular phenomenon in Pacific Asian politics: the institutionalized political alliance among ruling political forces as an integral part of state structure.
- Relationships between the central and local governments in a multi-level polity, in particular, why federalism is weak in Pacific Asia and the recent reforms across Pacific Asian countries to decentralize state authority and functions.

But before we move on to these issues, let us look at some of the reasons why the state is paramount in Pacific Asian countries.

The institutional and cultural foundations of state dominance

If the President of the United States addresses his nation, the speech will usually involve words like, 'my administration ...'. However, when the President of China addresses his country, he would probably start with a line like this: 'On behalf of the Party Centre, the State Council, and the Central Military Commission ...'. Often, what he claims to be 'on behalf of' is simply referred to as 'the Centre ...' (*zhongyang*). Even though it appears in various guises in many Pacific Asian countries, the phenomenon of the 'centre' is important for us to understand state dominance. It reflects a unique structure in the organization of state institutions, as well as informal practices that define state authority and government power in a way not usually shown in the formal state organizational chart (Saich, 2004: 122).

The **Centre** is often the actual location of state authority and the operational core of the state. In China, it is the leadership of the Communist Party and the central government. In Japan, it has been an alliance among the LDP through its Public Affairs Research Committee, the state through its bureaucracy and the business community through its interest groups. In Indonesia, it was Suharto and his inner ruling circle during the country's New Order. It is mainly in China, however, that the core of the party-state is referred to as 'the Centre' (*zhongyang*) in both formal and informal political communication.

The centralization of state authority is not a unique Pacific Asian phenomenon, nor exclusively a phenomenon of modern times (see the discussion of the traditional centralized state structure in Chapter 1), but it became a wider phenomenon in post-war Pacific Asia. This can be explained to a great extent by the economic, political and security conditions of the time and the functions of state institutions in response to these conditions. Theories of oriental despotism and modern state building discussed earlier fit this category of explanation.

Moreover, there are unique institutional and cultural conditions that are seen as contributing to state dominance. At the formal institutional level, there are many factors that account for state dominance. Chief among them are the types of state, forms of government and models of domestic and international interaction.

Box 3.1

State dominance: how do we measure it

State dominance refers here to the predominance of state institutions in the governance of a polity, and a high concentration of state power in the hands of the central government, particularly, its executive branch.

As Kenji Hayao suggests, there are three different ways in which the centralization of state authority can be observed and measured: (i) The division of authority between the central government and local governments; (ii) the effective authority of the executive within the central government; and (iii) the degree of centralization within the executive (Hayao, 1993: 30).

State types can mean different things in different contexts. The term is used here to mean regime types. However, the concept of state types is broader than that of regime types, as 'regime' is often used in a narrow, negative sense. Categorizing states on the basis of their governing ideological principles is a widely accepted practice in political science. We often speak of a state as a liberal democracy, an oligarchy, of authoritarianism, Asian democracy, military regimes, traditional states, modern states, communist states and so on.

Different types of states have different effects on the distribution of power and authority among state institutions and different levels of the political system, and thus contribute to the different extent of state dominance. In Chapters 1 and 2 we discussed the overall historical patterns of politics in Pacific Asia. A majority of the countries were non-pluralist states during the Cold War (military authoritarian regimes, one-party dominant states, communist party-states). There has been a dominant trend of these different state types transforming into pluralist and democratic states since the 1980s.

A **regime** in its general sense is a government associated with a particular individual or ideology, for example, the Kim Jong-un regime. In its purely academic use, the term does not have to be negative. When we discuss whether 'regime types' matter for economic development, for example, this term is used in a neutral sense as it naturally includes different regime types, such as liberal democracy and authoritarian state. However, in its popular use, 'regime' is often used for a government, particularly a foreign government, that is disliked.

However, in comparison with other parts of the world, the presence of non-pluralist politics in Pacific Asia is still significant. In Pacific Asia in Context 3.1, we compare Pacific Asia with the rest of Asia (South Asia, West Asia and Central Asia), as well as with Europe, North America and Australasia, in terms of different types of state in these areas. The table shows that, of the sixteen countries in Pacific Asia, two are under extra-constitutional regimes (12.5 per cent). Four are of the people's republic type, with a strong communist background (25 per cent).

Pacific Asia in Context 3.1

Types of state

Pacific Asia (16)	Federal (1)	Unitary (15)	%
Constitutional monarchy (4)	Malaysia	Cambodia, Japan, Thailand	25
Republic (6)		Indonesia, Singapore, South Korea, Taiwan, Philippines, East Timor	37.5
People's republic (4)		China, North Korea, Laos, Vietnam	25
Extra-constitutional (2)		Myanmar, Brunei	12.5
Percentage of total	6.25	93.75	100
Europe, North America, Australasia (45)	**Federal (9)**	**Unitary (36)**	**%**
Constitutional monarchy (7)	1	6	15.5
Commonwealth realm (4)	2	2	8.9
Republic (34)	6	28	75.6
Percentage of total	20.0	80.0	100
Other Asia (29)	**Federal (5)**	**Unitary (24)**	**%**
Republic (17)	3	14	58.6
Islamic republic (4)	1	3	13.8
Constitutional monarchy (6)	1	5	20.7
Monarchy (2)		2	6.9
Percentage of total	17.2	82.8	100

These two types of non-pluralist state together constitute 37.5 per cent of the total. In contrast, there is no 'extra-constitutional' state, nor any people's republics in the other two groups. There are, however, a larger number of constitutional monarchic states. In other parts of Asia, 20 per cent of countries are constitutional monarchies. In Europe, North America and Australasia, 25 per cent are constitutional monarchic states and Commonwealth realms. There is also a dominance of republics in the other two groups. In other parts of Asia, 75.6 per cent of countries are republics while the rate is 58.6 per cent in Europe, North America and Australasia.

Non-pluralist states tend to have state power concentrated in the hands of the governing party, the executive branch, the ruling junta/clique or even the individual 'strongman/woman'. There is clearly a close relationship between non-pluralist politics and state dominance in Pacific Asian countries.

In some single-party dominant states, state dominance and party dominance are mutually reinforcing. As Lee Kuan Yew once declared, 'I make no apologies that the PAP is the government and the government is the PAP' (Mauzy and Milne, 2002: 26). Consequently, efforts by the ruling party to build dominance through its party system constitute a very important part of the institutional support for state dominance. Chan Heng Chee's study on the dynamics of party dominance in Singapore details 'how the PAP succeeds in consolidating and maintaining its dominance and in mobilizing support to achieve its social, economic, and political goals' from the level of the constituency (Chan, 1976: 11).

There is a particular type of state in Pacific Asia that does not fit into the standard categorizations of state types, but relates directly to state dominance in many countries. Chalmers Johnson (Johnson, 1982) found that the state in Japan is different. At its core is a small but powerful elite bureaucracy. The political system gives the bureaucracy sufficient power to take initiatives and operate effectively. The state has a development-centred agenda. A pilot

Case Study Lab 3.1

Explaining Pacific Asian states

There are various ways of approaching the problem of Pacific Asian states: what types of states they are; how they are constituted, organized and structured; how they differ from states in other parts of the region. Richard Boyd, Tak-wing Ngo and their team challenge the vast studies in this area in the development paradigm that 'takes the state as explanation', and brings political economy into the state itself. By problematizing the state and 'taking the state as explanation', they shift the object of analysis, the dependent variable and the things to be explained. Their political economy approach centres around three sets of questions:

- **State tradition, the idea of the state and the state apparatus**: How far do state traditions shape political debates, underpin, bind and potentiate regime goals? How far do they influence institutional reforms and state making? How far do they facilitate or inhibit the development of an activist conception of executive power?
- **The international construction of the Asian state:** To what extent and in what ways and means are Asian states constructed in response to external agents? How far and in what ways have the goals and practices of the USA, Japan and the World Bank and IMF had an impact upon state institutions, state projects and regime imperatives in Asia? How far have external pressures had an impact upon the domestic political economy?
- **State-making projects**: How variable are the problems and imperatives that drove the state-making projects of modern Asian states? What kind of state apparatus emerged in the process? How and why do these differ? What are the consequences? How have different colonial heritages shaped the emergent state and with what contemporary consequences?

Boyd and Ngo, 2005: 15–16

organization, the Ministry of International Trade and Industry (MITI), leads and coordinates the process of policy formulation and implementation (Johnson, 1982: 305–24). With these key elements of support, the state develops an extensive capacity to dominate public policymaking and the organization of national economic activities. This 'developmental state' is also found in many other Pacific Asian countries (Wade, 1990; Woo-Cumings, 1999; Amsden, 2001. See further discussion in Chapter 6).

The second institutional factor affecting the extent of state dominance is the form of government. Forms of government are types of institutional settings for the distribution of government power and functions among different state institutions and different levels of government. These are usually stipulated in the constitution, but are also shaped in actual practices of government (see Chapter 4). Generally, the presidential system and the unitary state tend to have a higher level of concentration of state power and authority. As shown in Chapter 4, the majority of the countries in Europe, North America and Australasia have a parliamentary system (77.8 per cent), while in Pacific Asia there are more countries with a presidential or a semi-presidential system (50 per cent). Even in those parliamentary systems, it is the cabinet – that is, the executive – rather than the parliament, that dominates.

In addition to the structures of state–society relations, the relationships between the central and local governments also matter. We are talking here about the distribution of state power among different levels of government and how it affects the extent of state dominance. Discussion later in this chapter will demonstrate that state dominance has been well served by the models of central–local relations in Pacific Asia.

The third institutional factor contributing to state dominance is the model of domestic and international interaction. Most Pacific Asian countries have experienced colonial rule, mainly by European powers. The newly independent states faced various challenges in the international system. For many, their survival as an independent state was under threat for many decades. This had a great impact on the internal organization of the polity, leading to a strong state to provide defence for the country, protection

Case Study Lab 3.2

State dominance in Pacific Asia

Types of state and forms of government: Certain state types and forms of government tend to have a higher concentration of state power than others.

Domestic and international interaction: State authority and government power are stronger in countries with greater needs for control of domestic and international interaction.

State–society relations: Societal interests are incorporated into the state, which provides a coherent social basis for the state to exercise its power and advance its agenda.

Confucian concepts and practices: Culture matters. Centralization of power in the hands of government has been essential in the political and cultural traditions of many Pacific Asian countries.

for the people and security for society (Tilly, 1985, 1990). For these new postcolonial states, national sovereignty is a particularly important concept, but one that often lacked sufficient support from the political economy, was hampered by poor national integration or a lack of international respect. Consequently, the concentration of power in the hands of the state provided some remedy to this.

Moreover, the new states came to exist with the high expectations of delivering rapid industrialization and modernization. Most countries developed a model of state-led economic development where there was a separation of domestic and international markets, and the state had strong and effective control over interaction across national borders (Haggard, 1990; Amsden, 2001; Huang, 2005).

The explanations of state dominance (see Case Study Lab 3.2), using standard concepts and categories of state types, forms of government and models of domestic and international interaction, have laid out the general institutional conditions for state dominance in Pacific Asian countries. However, the formal institutional factors can explain state dominance only to some extent. Beyond formal state institutions, the type of state–society relations also contribute to state dominance (see Chapter 8).

State corporatist control of social groups, for example, enhanced state dominance. According to Jonathan Unger and Anita Chan, 'Japan, Taiwan, and South Korea each erected strongly authoritarian corporatist structures during periods of intensive development and amidst perceived threats from abroad' (Unger and Chan 1995: 32). China is very much following suit by organizing societal groups such as the national trade union, the national women's federation, the national youth federation and so on, into peripheral organizations around the Communist Party. State corporatist control of social groups has been an important part of the party-state organization. Such functional groups are also seen in the formal process of political representation in Indonesia and Singapore.

Beyond formal institutional arrangements and social structure, there are deeper cultural traditions and historical practices that significantly shape the structure of state authority. The cultural dimensions of authority are not normally defined in the constitution or laws of state institutions, but they are effective and often more so than formal institutions. Lucian W. Pye, for example, investigates how the traditional concepts of power can help us to understand contemporary political structures in Pacific Asia (Pye, 1985). In particular, we can see from his analysis that many aspects of state-centred authority structures have their roots in the Confucian model of power and authority. In more practical terms, the Singapore state under former Prime Minister Lee Kuan Yew is a good example of the significant impact of the Confucian model of paternalistic authority on the contemporary political structure (see the related discussion on the paternalistic state later in this chapter, and a broader examination of the debate on Asian values in Chapter 2).

Another example of the impact of the Confucian model is the phenomenon of 'the centre' that we discussed earlier. The notion of the centre reflects the hierarchical and top-down nature of the Confucian authority structure. The notion of the centre is not limited to states of the Confucian political tradition. In explaining the obsession of the political leadership in contemporary Indonesia with the importance of national unity and the centre, Benedict Anderson also finds a connection between the concept of power in traditional Javanese polity and state dominance in contemporary Indonesian politics. In the Javanese tradition, according to Anderson, power is concrete, homogeneous, constant and naturally legitimate. The homogenizing and unifying dynamics of power are the underlying cultural base for the concentration of power in the centre, of which Suharto often saw himself as the embodiment (Anderson, 1990: 23, 36).

In the following sections we shall examine in more detail how state dominance is ensured in the organization of the state.

The distribution of state power and types of states

We first discuss different types of states according to how the state is constituted and state authority is structured. The types of states in Pacific Asia at the time of writing can be divided roughly into four general categories: constitutional monarchies; republics; people's republics; and extra-constitutional regimes (see Box 3.2).

There are five countries in Pacific Asia with a system of constitutional monarchy (see Box 3.3): Brunei, Cambodia, Japan, Malaysia and Thailand. Of the five, a sultan heads both Brunei and Malaysia. But Brunei's monarch is the strongest of the five, as its sultan is both the chief of state and the head of government. The nature of Brunei's monarchy is therefore highly controversial. In theory, Brunei is a constitutional monarchy as it has had a constitution since 1959. But, in reality, Brunei is an absolute monarchy (Kershaw, 2001: 11). For this reason, Brunei will also be discussed later, in the category of extra-constitutional states. Malaysia's Paramount Ruler is politically the weakest of the five, as the monarch is not hereditary, but rather elected for a five-year term by the sultans of nine states, out of the total of thirteen states, according to the constitutional arrangements.

The role of the monarchy in the other three countries has undergone significant change over the past century. Constitutionally, the monarch in these countries is the symbolic head of state, and has only a nominal role in the overall political system. This is the case in Cambodia. Constitutional monarchy returned to Cambodia in 1993 after decades of civil war, international conflict, foreign invasions and communist rule. The constitution still defines the king as the head of state, the supreme commander of the armed forces, and chairman of the Supreme Council for National Defence, and all major policy and political decisions must be made by royal decree. While this may cause concern for some (Funston, 2001: 42), in reality, the prime minister exercises the real powers of government.

The beginning of Japan's modern constitutional monarchy dates back to the Meiji Restoration. Unlike the cases, seen mainly in European history, where constitutional monarchy was designed to constrain the power of the absolute monarch, the power of the emperor, insignificant in pre-Meiji Japan, expanded drastically from the Meiji period (1868–1912) through to the end of the Second World War in 1945. The emperor had 'absolute power', with the assistance of the military-dominated government.

After the Second World War, the monarchy was retained, but the monarch was stripped of all real political power. Given the historical role of the emperor, and the circumstances of his marginalization after the war, there has been an ongoing debate among the Japanese over the emperor's role. At the core of the debate is the issue of state–religion relations. Some believe that the principle

Box 3.2

Types of state (I): constitutional orders

- *Constitutional monarchy*
  Cambodia, Japan, Malaysia, Thailand
- *Republic*
  East Timor, Indonesia, South Korea, Philippines, Singapore, Taiwan
- *People's republic*
  China, North Korea, Laos, Vietnam
- *Other*
  Brunei, Myanmar, Thailand

COUNTRY PROFILE

INDONESIA

		Regional Comparison	World Rank
GDP	2686 PPP/bil)	8.19% of PA-18	8th (of 189)
HDI	0.684 (0 to 1)	PA-18: 11th	108th (of 186)
WGI	–0.2 (–2.5 to 2.5)	PA-18: 11th	44th (1–100)

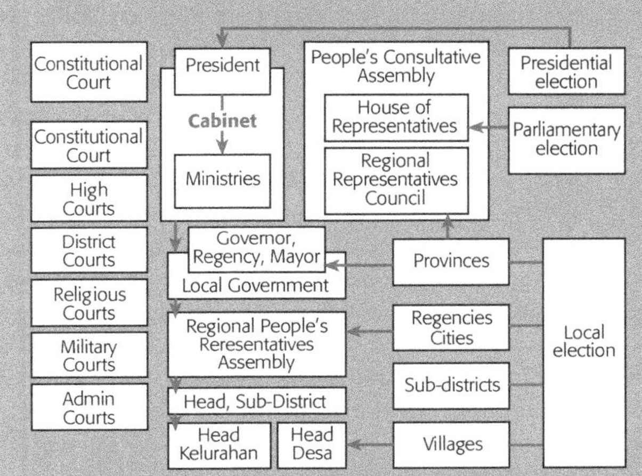

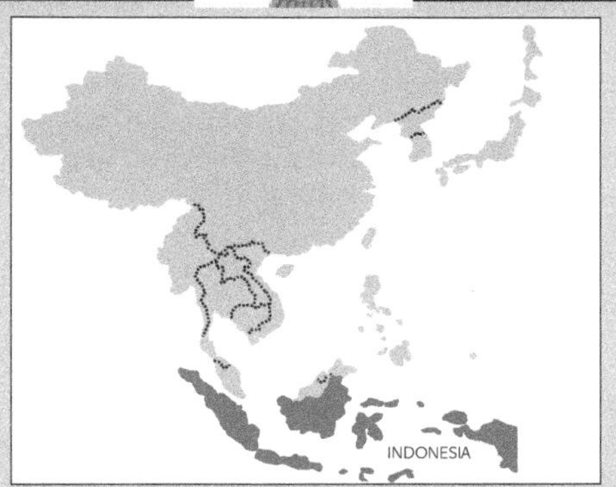

Key political facts

Electoral system for National Legislature

Proportional representation in multi-member districts.

Political cycles

Elections for president and People's Representative Council every five years.

Session of House of Representatives at least once a year.

President introduces budget bill to parliament in early January.

Further reading

Kingsbury, 2005b; Vatikiotis, 1998.

Timeline of modern political development

1945	Independence declared, constitution proclaimed with a presidential system and the Pancasila as the organizing principles of the new state.
1945–9	War against the Dutch.
1950–9	Provisional constitution with a parliamentary system.
1959	Restores 1945 constitution for 'a presidential system with parliamentary characteristics'.
1959–65	Sukarno's Guided Democracy.
1963–5	War with Malaysia.
1965	Military coup and suppression of communists.
1966–98	Suharto's New Order.
1975	Invasion of East Timor.
1985	Referendum law for constitutional change.
1998	Reform movement, protests, riots, Suharto resigns.
1999	East Timor referendum.
1999	Local Government Law for greater local autonomy and decentralization.
1999–2002	Four rounds of constitutional amendments to restrict the power of the president; expand the power of the Supreme Court; add clauses on human rights; and establish a Constitutional Court and Judicial Commission.
2003	Constitution Court established.
2004	Susilo Bambang Yudhoyono elected president with first direct popular vote.
2005	Heads of local government elected through direct popular elections.
2005	Peace agreement with Aceh.
2006	Law on the Governing of Aceh, giving greater autonomy to Aceh, allows partial practice of Islamic laws.
2006	First direct election in Aceh province.
2007	Ongoing crackdown on Islamic radicals and militants.
2012	Dutch government publicly apologizes for summary executions by the Dutch army in 1947.

> **Box 3.3**
>
> ### 'Reign but not rule'
>
> Constitutional monarchy is a system where the constitution vests the monarch with sovereign power, but the monarch exercises the power only within the limits defined by the constitution, usually in a ceremonial fashion. Japan, Cambodia and Malaysia are examples of this. Usually monarchs 'reign but not rule', but in some cases the monarch reigns and also rules, either subtly (Thailand), or not so subtly (Brunei).

of state–religion separation is good. The emperor should remain as a historical, cultural symbol and continue to be separated from state affairs. Others argue that the monarch is an important part of the nation's life, providing national unity and identity for the country, and thus is an important part of the state institutions.

Constitutional monarchy came to Thailand through the 1932 revolution. But from the beginning, a military government controlled the country, with the king largely marginalized in national politics until the 1970s. Over the years, the king, the world's longest-serving monarch (since 1946), gradually rebuilt the credibility of the monarchy, and transformed it from being a minor competitor to the military rule to an institution above the military. The monarchy rebuilt its relationship with the Thai people and established itself as one of the three pillars of the state, along with the nation and religion.

After more than eighty years since the birth of the constitutional monarchy, a real constitutional monarchy with the substantial influence and power of the king is finally in place. However, Kevin Hewison observes that

> in his approach to politics, the King is inherently conservative, and from this position he has attempted to define a conservative polity. Such a polity would preserve and further extend the power of the monarchy. To do this, the King has had to become increasingly involved in politics. Far from being "above politics", this King is intimately involved. His involvement means he is an "activist monarch", quite an innovation when it is considered that most other constitutional monarchies have increasingly been withdrawn from direct political activity over the last century. (Hewison, 1997: 74)

With the exception of Brunei and Thailand, the constitutional monarchies in Pacific Asia follow more or less a similar pattern around the world: the monarch is primarily a symbol of the country and does not hold any significant political power.

A third of the countries in Pacific Asia are republics: Indonesia, Singapore, South Korea, Taiwan, Philippines and East Timor being the newest. With the exception of East Timor, all these republics were new states and gained their independence from colonial rule at the end of the Second World War. Like their counterparts in other parts of the world, these republics usually have an effective constitution, a multiparty political system and an electoral system that regulates the elections for public offices, including the head of state, to ensure that the people rather than the monarch have the ultimate power to decide state affairs. Historically, the emergence of a republic represents an important part of their modern state building. Almost all these countries were under a monarchy before they were under colonial rule. Most of them chose to be republics after independence.

If a republic is defined narrowly as a non-monarchic type of state, then being a republic does not necessarily mean it is a liberal democracy. In fact, most of the countries in this category were non-democratic during the Cold War. The people's republics are also republics, but they are certainly not liberal democracies. Moreover, being a republic does not necessarily tell us much about the extent of state dominance. For example, Indonesia had a high degree of state dominance under Suharto before liberalizing in the new century. In both periods Indonesia has constitutionally been a republic.

The third type of state is people's republics, namely: China, Vietnam, Laos and North Korea. These countries practiced radical communism during the Cold War (see Chapter 2). The political system then was designed for a grand transformation towards a communist society where there would be no private ownership and economic activity would be centrally planned, organized and managed by the state.

Democratic centralism is the claimed organizing principle of state institutions in people's republics. Article 3 of the Chinese Constitution states, for example, 'The state organs of the People's Republic of China apply the principle of democratic centralism.' Other states that have a similar clause in their constitution include Vietnam (Article 6, 1992), Laos (Article 3, 1991) and North Korea (Article 5, 1998). The idea is that, while policy issues are open for discussion and comment, usually in a controlled fashion, the final authority of decision-making rests with 'the unified leadership of the central authorities' (Article 3, Chinese constitution).

However, the term 'communist' was problematic for these countries even then. Unlike their counterparts in Eastern Europe, there was little industrial, economic or social basis in these countries for a 'communist' society, even according to Karl Marx's own proposals. Without the support of these economic and social conditions, much of the idealist values and associated institutions would have to be imposed and sustained through political force and coercion. The party-state that emerged in these countries was very much an institutional setting for the exercise of such political force and coercion. Much of what these 'communist' states did, therefore, was for the survival of the economic model, the party-state that protected and promoted such an economic model, and indeed the survival of the communist party itself. The term 'communist' was used primarily because these countries were ruled by a self-proclaimed communist party, and were related closely to the communist Soviet Union.

Things have changed significantly in these countries, particularly in Vietnam and China. Communism is no longer a purpose, ideology or value for the state, much less for society. The idea and practices of an economy built solely on public ownership and state planning have long gone. The institutions and culture associated with the failed economic model and political movement have undergone significant change. Many aspects of these institutions and culture are still lingering on, but overall the clear trend is that emergent economic, social, and political forces are marginalizing them.

The term 'people's republic' is therefore more useful for this category of countries. First, this is the name they themselves use, with some variations. Second, the term suggests that these states are not liberal democracies, nor the communist states of the 1970s. Third, the term allows for significant variation among these states. At one end of the spectrum, Vietnam has a more advanced level of political reform and liberalization than China, but at the other, North Korea has just started what China did in the 1970s on a very small scale.

The states labelled as people's republics generally feature a lingering rule of the Communist Party with pragmatic economic ideas and programmes, a corporatist model of social management and a narrow political agenda. Some form of democratic centralism is stipulated in their constitution as the fundamental principle of governance. Much of the setting of the party-state remains effective, and the communist party has no intention of dismantling itself. However, the emergent economic, social and political forces, such as industrial capital, techno-bureaucrats, and social opinion makers and shapers, are increasingly coming into play. This is building pluralist dynamics into the system and reshaping the ruling party's platform, ideological basis, governing principles and the make-up of its general membership and elite circles.

State dominance in people's republics has largely been preserved, partly because the core institutions of the party-state have survived the years of economic transformation and political turmoil and partly because they have gained new functions providing breaks and controls in the loosening up of the old economic system and management of the state-led market economy. With a high degree of state dominance and little stated interest in moving towards liberal democracy, the evolution of the party-state in Pacific Asia remains a key analytical concern for scholars of Pacific Asian politics.

Finally, Myanmar and Brunei are currently under some form of extra-constitutional order. Myanmar has been under military rule since 1962 and even with the introduction of a new constitution in 2008 and national elections in 2015, the military still holds veto power over the civilian government. In this model, state dominance has few institutional constraints; all state power is ultimately defined and exercised by the military. In terms of the military's role in politics, we also have to mention Thailand, where the military coups in 2006 and then 2014 overthrew the civilian government, terminated the constitution, and restarted the political process.

There is, however, a significant difference between Myanmar and Thailand in this regard. In Myanmar, the military is the highest de facto authority in the country holding veto power over the civilian government and controlling the state institutions. Traditionally, the Burmese (Myanmar) military has organized itself in government without a due constitutional process, though this may be changing through its democratic transition (see Chapter 2), but in Thailand the military is not necessarily the highest authority. The king is an equally important, or perhaps more important, part of the state. The military's action in 2014 clearly had the consent of, if not instructions from, the king. The fact that the king and the military jointly have the final claim on state power and legitimacy is undeniable.

As for Brunei, there are different views on what type of state Brunei is. On the one hand, the country has had a constitution since 1959, which established the authority of the sultan as the head of state. In reality, however, the sultan has run the country as an absolute monarchy. The country has had no elected parliament since 1962. The sultan has full executive authority as the head of state and head of government. Indeed, parts of the constitution have been suspended since 1962. For all these reasons, one can argue that Brunei is in reality an absolute monarchy.

Constitution of the state and the problem of legitimacy

This leads us to the question of the role of constitutions in Pacific Asia. More specifically, what is the role of formal constitutions in the organization of states? And, how are the various types of state in Pacific Asia legitimized? A constitution is the foundation of a political community. It defines a political community and its organizing principles and establishes institutions, relationships and procedures as well as values and purposes for its governance in general terms. A constitution is not just a phenomenon of modern times. The first written constitution in Pacific Asia is arguably the Seventeen Article Constitution adopted in Japan in 604 AD by Prince Shotoku of the Yamato state. The Yamato Constitution reflects some of the fundamental principles that have underlain the traditional political order in Pacific Asia for centuries. Key among them are:

- A three-layer political community: Heaven, the Imperial Court and Society, where the emperor represents the will of Heaven to Society;
- The ultimate value of such a political order – harmony among different layers of the polity;
- The importance of the moral standards exhibited in the behaviour and activities of those in government.

The Yamato Constitution was adopted at a time when government institutions and organizing principles based on Confucianism were spreading rapidly in Northeast Asia. It shows how the source and legitimacy of political authority, and the relationships within a political community, were perceived in a typical traditional society in Pacific Asia. It defines a political order based on the 'Mandate of Heaven'. The state – in most cases, the monarch – is claimed to be the only embodiment of the supernatural, divine force and rules the country on its behalf, and thus has the natural 'right to rule'.

Such a claim for legitimacy can be seen as one of the four 'key elements of legitimacy' as identified by Muthiah Alagappa: that is, shared norms and values, including ideology. 'Shared norms and values can be interpreted as normative regulation of society on the

Box 3.4

Popular claims of legitimacy for state authority and government power in Pacific Asia

Popular will: Government exercises power on behalf of the people.

Paternalistic state: Government exercises power because it provides public good.

Military as guardian of the state: Military exercises state power because it safeguards the security and protects the interest of the state.

Mandate of Heaven: The state exercises power on behalf of a higher supernatural force.

basis of universal consensus.' 'They determine the type of political system and hence the structure of domination' (Alagappa, 1995: 15).

> The **Mandate of Heaven** is a popular claim of legitimacy for public authority in traditional society in Pacific Asia. It is an important foundation for most monarchies. It claims public authority through a mixture of national myths, legends and religion. The phrase itself has its origins in imperial China. In this depiction of the political world, the emperor is the sole embodiment of the supernatural force (Heaven), which gives him the mission and authority to rule the real world. For a political scientist, such a claim represents a theory of the origins and foundation of state authority that are not found in the world over which the state authority is exercised, but rather outside and above this real world.

However, political practices based on the claim have long been challenged in Europe in their modern transformation, and in post-war Pacific Asia. The Mandate of Heaven is no longer accepted as the foundation for public authority and political legitimacy. This has created problems for Pacific Asian countries, especially in their early post-war years, when the new states tried to build their legitimacy primarily on the procedural rules, against competing ideological and political persuasions. As Alagappa observes in his survey of the post-war experiences of legitimacy in Pacific Asian countries:

> in the absence of an established normative order, the procedural element cannot be the primary basis on which political authority is claimed, acknowledged, or resisted. Other rationales (normative goals, performance, personal authority, a politically defining moment, and international support) will be more important in the legitimation of government. Legitimation on the basis of these rationales, however, is highly contingent and subject to periodical erosion and crisis. (Alagappa, 1995: 293)

There are two such 'other rationales' that have been particularly noticeable in Pacific Asia. One often cited is based on the delivery premise that if the government can deliver a good life for its citizens, it fulfils the expectations of the people and therefore satisfies their mandate. This whole claim sees the political community as a family and the state as the head of family, hence the concept of a paternalistic state. The primary mandate for the state, as for the head of family, is to provide the common good.

Under this conceptual framework, the government takes on state responsibilities just as a father takes on the responsibilities for the family. It holds undisputable authority, as, like a father, the government 'naturally' knows and works for the needs of the family members. The relationship among members of the polity is hierarchical and unequal, depending on the role each has in the community. The state and society are mutually dependent; and the government is the 'exemplar centre' (Geertz, 1980: 11) for the moral standards of society.

For many, the term 'patrimonialism' is used almost interchangeably with 'paternalism'. In this use, patrimonialism is about the type of government where the ruler takes government as a personal matter and 'the ruler's authority is personal-familial, and the mechanics of the household are the model for political administration' (Adams, 2005: 238).

> A **paternalistic state** is a type of state practiced and/or perceived to be practiced on the organizing principles of the father-dominant family.

Paternalistic elements can be found in government practices in many Pacific Asian countries, partly because of the impact of similar cultural roots. In William de Bary's view, for example, there are Asian ideals of leadership and the notion of the common good in Confucianism. These ideals shape the purpose and function of government in these countries (de Bary, 2004). Stepan Eklöf, as another example, traces the founding ideology of Indonesia, and thus the basis for the Indonesia state, Pancasila, to 'the family principle and the ideal of consensual decision making' in the traditional political culture of Indonesia (Eklöf, 2004: 30; see also Anderson, 1990: 17–78). The notion of paternalistic state was closely associated with a dominant political order in Pacific Asia during the Cold War, often vaguely dubbed 'Asian democracy' (Neher, 1994; Neher and Marlay, 1995: 13–28; see also Chapter 2).

Many scholars find countries such as Singapore, Indonesia and Malaysia to be good examples of the paternalistic state. The Singapore state under its first prime minister, Lee Kuan Yew, is often referred to as a paternalist state. According to another former prime minister of Singapore, Goh Chok Tong, who once described the Singapore political system as a 'trustee model of democracy':

> The government acts more like a trustee. As a custodian of the people's welfare, it exercises independent judgment on what is in the long-term economic interests of the people and acts on that basis (cited in Kausikan, 1998: 20).

Clearly, such a paternalistic state assumes full responsibility for making decisions for people, and therefore an exclusive legitimate authority. Increasingly, people's republic states are using this line of argument to seek legitimacy for the party-state under changing circumstances and justification for the market economy within a non-pluralist political order.

For example, Dingxin Zhao argues historically and today, the Chinese state bases its right to rule on a form of performance legitimacy. In traditional times, the peasants were right to overthrow a dynasty that was not performing and therefore had lost the mandate of Heaven. In contemporary times, Zhao argues the Chinese Communist Party has moved away from the ideological legitimacy claims of the Mao era to claim a legitimate right to rule based on its performance to oversee economic and social development. According to Zhao, however, 'performance legitimacy is intrinsically unstable because it carries concrete promises and therefore will trigger immediate political crisis when the promises are unfulfilled' (Zhao, 2009: 416).

Another widely used claim for state authority and legitimacy is related to the military. Seeing itself as the guardian of the state, the military reserves extra-constitutional powers for itself as the final authority of the state. It changes the government as it sees fit, runs a government as necessary, rewrites the constitution and incorporates the military into the new constitutional order. Unlike the model of paternalistic state, which operates within the constitutional framework, the military-sanctioned political process operates beyond and above the constitutional framework. Consequently, legitimacy in its modern sense is always a serious problem for such a political order. For example, military general Park Chung-hee overthrew the Second Republic of South Korea in 1961 and ruled through support of the military until his death by assassination in 1979.

Finally, popular will as the foundation of government became a major principle in political debates and practices in Pacific Asian countries throughout the twentieth century. In particular, political liberalization and democratic transition towards the end of the twentieth century has turned the ideal of government founded on a social contract and popular will into a political reality in an increasing number of Pacific Asian countries.

Along with the rise and consolidation of popular-will-based constitutional order is the fact that traditional claims of legitimacy have gradually lost their relevance. Modern constitutionalism has prevailed, though often with some variants. However, one should not underestimate the residual power and capacity of those traditional forms to complicate and compromise modern political institutions and process (see a more in-depth examination of this problem in Chapter 2).

Leninist party-states, military regimes and single-party dominant states

Non-pluralist politics during the Cold War took various forms in Pacific Asia. Falling into the first category were obviously those people's republics – what we often refer to as communist states. These include China (the People's Republic of China, or PRC, as distinct from the Republic of China, which is today's Taiwan), North Korea (the Democratic People's Republic of Korea, DPRK), and Vietnam (the Democratic Republic of Vietnam, DRV). All of them were in Northeast Asia and part of the communist world during the Cold War.

Communism is an ambiguous term to describe the political systems in these countries (see more on this in Chapter 2). What existed in reality was what is often called the Leninist party-state (Dickson, 1997: 37–108). In this party-state, each state institution or social organization performs a unique role or function for the Communist Party, which is designated constitutionally as the 'governing core' of the state. For example, the court is a people's court, and its primary function is to defend the party and the state on judicial matters. The military, for another example, is the people's army, and more precisely, the Party's army. Its main function is to do the job the Party instructs it to do. The national workers' union, as yet another example, is to reach out to the working class for the party and serve as the 'transmission belt' (Unger and Chan, 1996: 96) between the party-state and the working masses.

This party-state is Leninist because of the early experience of the young Soviet state under Lenin in the 1920s, where this model first developed. This was followed by Communist China, Korea and Vietnam after the Second World War. At the core of the Leninist party-state was a revolutionary communist party with the state machinery under its total control, strict membership and internal party discipline, complete devotion and loyalty of the members, a highly centralized decision-making structure; and often secrecy in its operation.

Because of historical and institutional reasons – not so much ideological ones – the political regime under Chiang Kai-shek and then his son Chiang Ching-kuo in Taiwan from 1949 to 1986 resembled much of the Leninist Party-state, a regime scholars call a 'quasi-Leninist regime' (Cheng, 1989. See also Tien, 1989; Chao and Myers, 1998: 40–2). The two Chiangs had absolute control over the Nationalist Party (KMT). The KMT then controlled the state machinery, the military and the police, and much of the national economy. The Chiang family and the KMT ruled Taiwan for thirty-five years. In fact, during these years, politicians and the public often referred to the government literally as the 'party-state'. According to the Constitution, state powers were to be exercised by the five branches of government. But in reality, they were firmly in the hands of four unique institutions: the president, the KMT party centre, the Executive Yuan and the National Security Council (Tien, 1989: 109).

The **Leninist party-state** features a tight control of the state by the ruling Communist party and its military arm. This political trinity turned the state, the Party and the military into an interlocked, integrated ruling machine – 'the party-state' – that incorporates every aspect of society into the system.

In the second category are the military regimes or military dominant governments. This type of regime was different from those in the first category in that the military, rather than a political party, much less a communist party, controlled the state. In a familiar scenario, the military came to control the government through a military coup, overthrowing the civilian government. In some cases, such as in Thailand (from 1947 to 1973, and on and off from 1973 to the time of writing) and Myanmar (from 1962 to 2015), the military stayed on to operate directly as the government. This is called a military regime or a military government. Prior to the national elections in Myanmar 2015, the cabinet consisted of ministers appointed by the State Peace and Development Commission (SPDC), formerly the State Law and Order Restoration Council (SLORC). Nearly two-thirds of ministries had 'senior military officers (colonel and above) as ministers, the majority of the remainder are manned by retired military officers' (Than, 2001: 218). Than summarizes some of the key features of the cabinet (Than, 2001: 214–20) in the first decade of the century:

- With no effective constitution and legislature, the SPDC exercises 'absolute power and authority';
- The head of state, chairman of the SPDC, 'is not a titular position but a position of ultimate authority in the public domain'; and,
- The highest executive authority rests with the military junta. The cabinet of ministers 'is subordinate to the junta and is entrusted with the day-to-day conduct of governing Myanmar'.

In other cases, such as South Korea and Indonesia, the military restored a civilian government a short time after the initial coup, turning themselves into civilians, and organizing a political party of some kind, running elections and controlling the civilian government following constitutional and electoral procedures, often designed by themselves. The government remained dominated by the military up until the democratization movements from the 1980s. As noted above, the military regime in Myanmar has also recently re-established constitutional order and allowed civilian elections at the national level. The military still held legislative veto power as of early 2016 suggesting Myanmar is also shifting towards a military dominated regime with potential to shift further towards liberal democracy and civilian control of the state.

Case Study Lab 3.3

Models for analysing Chinese politics

There is great interest in the type of the state and political system in China due to its uniqueness, the importance of China in the world and its profound experience in modern political development. This has led to various different scholarly approaches or frameworks to explain how the Chinese state functions and operates. June Dreyer, in her influential work on China's political system, summarizes some key theoretical models of Chinese politics and government. These models have been popular among scholars at different times during China's post-war political development: the early PRC period, the Cultural Revolution and the post-Mao years:

- Totalitarian model: focuses on the institutions and organization of the communist system.
- Generational school: focuses on leadership and change positing a common generational viewpoint based on a shared personal and political experience of its leaders.
- Strategic interaction school: argues the crucial issue motivating Chinese politics is a struggle for great power status and points out the present-day importance of China's 'century of humiliation' at the hands of foreign powers in the nineteenth century.
- China is China is China school: focuses on the economic landscape, psychological mind set and bureaucratic processes that are basically the same as those of imperial China.
- Factional model: Factions are based on clientelist ties. These are cultivated essentially through constant exchange of goods and favours and result in relationships that involve unwritten but nonetheless well-understood rights and obligations among faction members.
- Central regional school: focuses on central-local tensions and localism as a driving force influencing the working of the political system.
- Political cultural school: China's struggle to accumulate Western technology without destroying its own cultural traditions.
- Bureaucratic politics model: focuses on which part of the PRC bureaucratic organization has decisive power over the directions and scope of social and political change.
- Palace politics school: focuses almost exclusively on the issue of who will succeed to the top position within the Chinese leadership.
- Pluralist paradigm: points out that political competition begins when a totalitarian state is established.
- Neo-traditionalism: focuses on competition and conflict within the state and argues distinct communist institutions make organized control possible and that these forms of organization shape patterns of association and political behaviour in distinctive ways.
- Fragmented authoritarianism: maps policymaking and the protracted bargaining between the top leaders and their bureaucracy, particularly in the provinces.

Dreyer 2014: 10–19

A **military regime** is a government that is claimed, organized and imposed by the military. Myanmar's State Peace and Development Council (SPDC) is an example. A **military-dominant government** is a government significantly influenced or controlled by the military. South Korea from the 1960s to the 1980s, Indonesia under Suharto, and the Philippines under Marcos fall into this category. There is also the **military state**, where the military not only takes over the government, but also militarizes the whole polity in terms of its internal organization and overall governing principles and programmes. Japan in the 1930s was such a military state.

The case of the Philippines was unique. Marcos came to power through the constitutional process, but increasingly had to rely on the military to keep his government running. He declared martial law with the support of the military. The military was a critical power holder, but did not take over the government. So Marcos's regime was a military dominant government only to a certain extent. More precisely, his government was a military supported government. As Gretchen Casper describes, the military was 'a partner with the civilian ruler' during the martial law period after 1972 (Casper, 1995: 92).

The forms of non-pluralist politics in the third category were subtler. Included in this group were Japan, Singapore and Malaysia. There were neither military coups nor communist parties but there was a single political party that controlled the government, and a single alliance of political interests dominated the state. The Liberal Democracy Party (LDP) controlled the government in Japan from 1955 to 1993. The People's Action Party (PAP) has controlled the government in Singapore since 1959. The UMNO-dominated Alliance and the Barisan Nasional after 1969 has controlled the government in Malaysia since 1957.

The longevity of a political party in government is not a necessary indicator of non-pluralist politics. It can simply be a reflection of the unusually satisfactory performance of the government led by the party. In fact, electoral competitions have been normal in these countries. In many cases, particularly Japan and Singapore, the government has delivered impressive economic growth and social development as well as security and order.

Politics in these countries during the long reign of a single political party were non-pluralist, for three main reasons. First, the government's policy and programmes reflected the interests and power of particular societal forces. This was clear in the case of Malaysia after the ethnic riots in 1969 and for much of its NEP era (New Economic Policy, 1970–90). The government 'adopted much more frankly the character of a primarily Malay government of a primarily Malay nation' (Church, 1995: 79) in a country where the Chinese, Indians and other non-Malay groups constituted half of the population. It was the opposite in Singapore where the strong PAP government made efforts to 'impose' a neutral identity (Singaporean) and culture (English language) over the Chinese-dominated country in the early decades of the new republic.

In Japan, under the 1955 system and the Yoshida doctrine – a principal policy framework for Japan during the Cold War – Japan focused primarily on its economic recovery and development, while its security alliance with the USA took care of its security and defence needs. The interests of the growth alliance dominated the LDP government.

A **one-party state**, such as the Leninist party-states, is a political system in which there is only one political party – the ruling party – that is legally recognized and allowed to function fully, and indeed its dominance is constitutionally and institutionally ensured. In the one-party state, therefore, there are no party politics, and no multiparty competition. A **single-party dominant state** is also dominated by a single party, but other political parties also exist and are fully functional. In the single-party dominant state, other political parties are not able to post an effective electoral challenge to the dominant party.

Second, great restrictions were placed on contending voices and forces, however, which became excluded or marginalized from the mainstream political process. Early restrictions in Singapore were targeted mainly at the Chinese – the Chinese language and the Chinese community. Such restrictions, marginalization and exclusion were significantly increased in Malaysia after 1969 against the Chinese and the Indians. In Japan, the battles by the ruling conservative alliance against the labour movements, leftist and progressive social forces took place mainly in the 1960s, starting with the confrontations in 1960 over the renewal of the security treaty with the United States, labour strikes and student protests.

Third, the institutional setting, such as the electoral system and the party system, favoured the ruling party's continual control of government. The electoral system in Japan before 1993, for example, was based on a 'medium-sized, multi-seat' district system. This, combined with the faction-centred party system and party financing mechanisms, gave great advantage to candidates of the ruling party and thus contributed to the prolonged rule of the LDP (see more discussion on this in Chapter 7).

All these different forms of non-pluralist politics varied in their actual institutional manifestation; in the extent to which the political system was open, transparent, and competitive; and in their ideological underpinnings. However, there were some critical features shared across the board. First, there was a prolonged reign of a single political force/party or an alliance of political forces/parties. Second, there tended to be a strong and very intrusive and interventionist state, except in the case of the Philippines.

Third, there was an element of corporatism in state–society relations. This was certainly more so in Northeast Asian countries than in Southeast Asia. Fourth, non-pluralist politics and a strong state in the people's republics existed with a deteriorating national economy to the point of a complete collapse. In contrast, most non-communist countries saw a thirty-year period of rapid industrialization and economic growth, the so-called 'East Asian economic miracle' (World Bank, 1993).

Grand political alliances: the fourth branch of government?

Attentive observers note that in many Pacific Asian countries, the most important state institution is not the supreme court, nor even the legislature. Rather, it is the grand political alliance engineered by the ruling political party. This was particularly true during the period of non-pluralist politics of the Cold War. We see such a political alliance in China (Chinese People's Political Consultative Conference), Indonesia (People's Consultative Assembly), Japan (growth alliance, iron triangle, or ruling triad), Vietnam (Vietnamese Fatherland Front) and Malaysia (Alliance/Barisan Nasional on ethnic bargaining).

> **Consociationalism** refers to a managed representation of key groups in government as a way of forming political consensus and cooperation in a politically divided society. The concept was first developed by Arend Lijphart (1977: vii, 25). Lijphart lists some key features of consociationalism as: grand coalitions, mutual veto, proportionality and segmental autonomy.

If state corporatism (see Chapter 8) is more about the state's control, management and mobilization of societal forces, a grand political alliance is more about shared interests between the state and various elite forces in society. Political alliances arose because of diverse interests among major political forces, and the fact that the formal institutional processes were not able to channel, coordinate, reconcile and represent these interests.

Ethnic bargaining, or what Alasdair Bowie calls the 'communal settlement' in postcolonial Malaysia, for example, reflected a trade-off between the interests of the Chinese elites and Malay elites, with the primary interests of the Chinese being the security and prosperity of their businesses; and those of the Malay elites being their status within the political and economic system and society at large. In this ethnic bargaining, there was

> a series of compromises over controversial communal issues; essentially, Chinese and Indian leaders accepted Malay political and cultural dominance, and the inclusion of special rights and privileges for Malays in the Constitution, in return for Malay recognition of Chinese and Indian rights to full citizenship and to a voice in the government of independent Malaya. (Bowie, 1991: 73)

More specifically, 'the Malays would dominate government with the support of the immigrant communities, in return for a Malay commitment to accord the Chinese and Indians full citizenship rights and not to challenge (or interfere with) Chinese and Indian commercial freedom' (Bowie, 1991: 29).

> **Ethnic bargaining** was the distribution of political and economic powers among three leading ethnic groups in postcolonial Malaysia, to provide a political foundation for a new multi-ethnic state and the support base for new economic and political programmes.

Ethnic bargaining, brokered by the ruling UMNO (United Malays National Organization), allowed a satisfaction of the interests of both the Malay and Chinese elites, and thus led to the formation of a grand coalition among three major ethnic groups: UMNO, MCA (Malaysian Chinese Association) and MIC (Malaysian Indian Congress) in 1973. The Barisan Nasional coalition and its smaller predecessor has provided the necessary political foundation for the control of government by UMNO and its coalition partners since its independence in 1957.

Scholars call this consociationalism. John Funston uses this term to comment on the practice of a grand coalition in Malaysia as a framework that incorporates different communal interests represented by different political parties when it is not possible to accommodate them through existing constitutional and institutional frameworks. Their coalition in turn provides a stable political basis for government that

Box 3.5

Formal and informal grand political alliances

While political alliances performed similar functions in supporting the government's agenda and programmes, some of them survived the initial political bargaining and became a permanent branch of government. This has complicated the development of the ideal model of three-branch government in these countries. The People's Consultative Assembly (MPR) in Indonesia became the highest body of state power that was to 'determine the Constitution and the guidelines of state policy' (1945 Constitution). This situation applied until very recently. In the Chinese case, the People's Political Consultative Conference was replaced by the National People's Congress as the highest body of state power, but it retained its function of pre-legislative consultation. In both cases, the institutional form of the original political alliance has survived. While political consultation soon lost its substance, the institution has been recognized formally and treated as a separate institution.

The conservative alliance in Japan is the least institutionalized. It is not part of the formal government structure, and has no formal organizational structure for its existence and functions.

Between Japan's informal conservative alliance on the one hand and the formal grand political alliances in Indonesia and China is semi-institutionalized ethnic bargaining in Malaysia. It is semi-institutionalized because, on the one hand, the political alliance has no formally recognized institutional presence in government structure. On the other hand, on the basis of this alliance the political coalition has been able to control the government since Malaysia's self-governance in 1957.

otherwise might be troubled by ethnic tensions and conflicts (Funston, 2001: 198).

In Suharto's Indonesia, the People's Consultative Assembly (MPR) was also such a political alliance that provided broad political support for the New Order. Indonesia's legislature at the time, the House of Representatives (DPR), 'had no effective legislative function until 1999' (Kingsbury, 2005b: 359). The MPR had 1,000 members (the number changed over time), with a mixture of presidential appointees, elected members and representatives of the functional groups (see Chapter 8), such as the bureaucracy, the military (ABRI) and religious groups – the core support groups for Suharto's New Order. Since the MPR was treated as the highest body of state power, Suharto relied on this political coalition for his legitimacy. At the same time, because of the way the MPR was organized, Suharto and his party GOLKAR had complete control of the MPR.

The Chinese People's Political Consultative Conference (CPPCC) also served to provide broad political support and legitimacy for the Communist state – at least in the early years of the PRC. The CPPCC emerged from negotiations among major political parties and functional groups to produce a provincial Constitution in the early 1950s. Like its counterpart in Indonesia, the CPPCC also has functional group representation and performs a non-binding advisory role on broad principles of government programmes and policies.

Finally, the conservative alliance in Japan during the Cold War is a more subtle case of a political alliance. The 1955 system (see Chapter 2) was made possible by the convergence of the interests of the bureaucracy, the LDP and industrial capital. This political alliance provided the general policy guidelines for the LDP government, enabled the LDP regime to survive the radical and progressive political environment in Japan in the 1950s and 1960s, and allowed the country to focus on rapid economic growth. Like ruling political alliances in other countries, the conservative alliance in Japan was essential for the stability of the 1955 system (see Chapter 7).

After twenty years of political liberalization, there has been a convergence in the types of societal interests and their relations that dominate society and dictate the state's interests in promoting and defending them. In this emergent model of political alliance across Pacific Asian countries, there are interlocked interests, expectations and demands among the state bureaucracy, the ruling political party and the business community that underlie various state systems and transcend patterns of state and executive dominance.

However, the political, economic and social conditions today are significantly different from the situation in the Cold War era, which greatly affected the makeup and roles of political alliances. Pempel's thesis of regime shift (Pempel, 1998) is a case in point. One can apply the same thesis to Indonesia, South Korea, Taiwan, Thailand, the Philippines and, to a lesser extent, Malaysia, Singapore, China and Vietnam.

A key consequence of regime shift is that the formal institutions of government, such as the legislature, are gaining increasing prominence and political significance. Grand political alliances outside the formal institutions of government have become increasingly unnecessary and ineffective. In fact, much of the activities in political bargaining and coalition building have shifted inside the legislature. In Indonesia, for example, the People's Consultative Assembly (MPR) has been retained since the fall of Suharto, but its function has been transformed into a federal assembly that consists of members of the legislature (DPR) and members of the Regional Representative Council (DPD). Functional group representation and GOLKAR dominance are no longer guaranteed. Instead, the DPR now actively exercises legislative power.

China's CPPCC has long lost its original rationale for genuine political bargaining and political support for the ruling CPC. With the increased significance attached to the People's Congress, the role of the CPPCC has become ambiguous. In some way, the CPPCC may follow the way of MPR in Indonesia and transform itself into some form of an upper house or federal assembly that takes care of regional as well as ideological interests.

In Japan, informal political alliances are still important. However, because of the fundamental change in the underlying political, economic and social conditions, and, more importantly, the changes to the electoral and party systems (see Chapter 7), coalition building is seen more in the Diet itself.

Not much has changed in the grand political alliance in Malaysia – the Barisan National – in terms of its rationale and organizational form. This is no surprise. The Barisan National has never been made a formal part of the government structure, as appeared to be the case in countries such as Indonesia and China. It gained its dominance in government through electoral processes and it continues to be an important political basis for the ruling UMNO.

Grand political alliances are a significant aspect of Pacific Asian politics, particularly during the Cold War years and in rapid growth and development phases. They provide a platform for an alliance of interests to dominate the state. However, as noted above, this function is slowly being replaced by bargaining within the formal institutions of government. As shown below, changes in the organizational structure of central relations have also weakened the high degree of state dominance by providing local areas with more power, authority and autonomy over the last few decades.

Central-local relations: federalism, local autonomy and decentralization

The high concentration of state authority is also reflected in the relationship between the central government and local governments. There are two standard types of central–local relations – depending on how the local government is constituted and related to the central government: the system of federalism and the system of a unitary state. However, in Pacific Asia, under the system of unitary state, there is also a further two different models: the unitary state with vertical administrative control and the unitary state with local autonomy (see Box 3.6).

In comparison with Other Asia and Europe, North America and Australasia, there are much higher proportions of federal states in the other two groups, 17.2 per cent of states in Other Asia are federal. 20.0 per cent of Europe, North America and Australasian states are federal. Pacific Asia has only one federal state, with its powers concentrated heavily at the federal level.

Box 3.6

Types of states (II): central–local relations

Federal: Malaysia

Federalism attempted: Indonesia, Myanmar;

Unitary: Brunei, East Timor, Cambodia, China, Japan, North Korea, South Korea, Laos, Philippines, Singapore, Taiwan, Thailand, Vietnam

This section illustrates how central-local relations in Pacific Asia have concentrated power and authority in the hands of the central authorities. This is particularly prevalent during the Cold War period. Following the general trend of democratization and liberalization from the 1980s, Pacific Asian governments introduced a series of reforms that decentralized and devolved power and authority to local areas.

Federal states without federalism

Federalism in Pacific Asia reflects the ethnic and religious diversity of the new political units, and is a result of a political compromise between the need for political unity and the reality of competing political forces and interests within the political unit. A federal system allows a constitutionally defined separation of power and authority, and shared sovereignty between the federal government and constituent states. While Pacific Asia and Europe both have federal and unitary states, the actual distribution of state power between the federal government and local governments is very different.

At the time of writing, Malaysia is the only constitutional federal state in Pacific Asia. Myanmar remains problematic due to its ongoing political transformation. Many consider Malaysia to be a 'quasi-federation because the center, the federal government, holds too much power and dominates the political system to such a degree that it can decide the survival of individual state governments' (Chin, 2001: 28; see also Shafruddin, 1987).

Malaysia's federal system reflects the political reality at the time of its independence. The birth of the Federation was a response to the troubled Malayan Union (1946–8) the British initially planned for the region. The Malayan Union gave universal citizenship to all residents and did not reflect the unique status of the Malays, and particularly the sultans of the Malay states. The Federation of Malaysia consequently has allowed different rights, privileges and sovereign powers to different states in the union. This recognized the role of sultans, the Islamic religion and the Malay language in the constitution. This type of federalism with 'one or several states having more autonomy than others' has been described as 'asymmetric federalism' (United Nations 2005: 8).

Post-independence political development in Malaysia, however, saw a concentration of power in the hands of the central government in relation to the Paramount Ruler and the member states. In one important aspect of federal–state relations,

> the constitution provided for a pattern of Centre–State financial relations which is dominated by the Central Government because it controls most of the richest and most productive revenue sources as well as most areas of expenditures. Thus, large-scale Central transfers to the State Government were and still are inevitable and necessary to fulfill the latter's expenditure commitments. (Shafruddin, 1987: 99)

Asymmetric federalism involves one or several states having more autonomy than others. Malaysia has given the states of Sabah and Sarawak powers that normally fall under federal jurisdiction. These Bornean states have considerably more autonomy than the eleven other states in areas such as taxation (in particular, customs and excise), immigration and citizenship, trade, transportation and communication, fisheries and several social affairs sectors. The aim of this approach is to protect the distinctive characteristics of the two states and their interests.

United Nations 2005: 8

Graham Hassall and Cheryl Saunders point out that:

> the federal principle was for a strong central government that could hold together states of considerable ethnic diversity which desired considerable regional autonomy. The federal government has power to legislate for external affairs, defense, internal security, civil and criminal law, administration of justice, finance, trade, commerce and industry, education, labor, and social security ... The states can make laws on matters not reserved for federal parliament or not included in the joint list; that is, they can legislate for Muslim law, land, agriculture and forestry, and local government. Subjects on the concurrent list, concerning which both the federal and state governments have power to legislate, are social welfare, town and country planning and

> public health. The federal government is the main taxing authority and controls the borrowing powers of states, so that, apart from land revenue, states enjoy no significant sources of income. (Hassall and Saunders, 2002: 224–5)

It is apparent, therefore, that the notion of federalism in Malaysia has little substance. Local governments in many of today's unitary states have much higher levels of local autonomy than in Malaysia.

The political nature of the attempts at federalism can be seen more clearly in the de facto failure of federalism in Myanmar, and an even more short-lived experience in Indonesia (1949–50). Myanmar set up a federal system in the 1947 Constitution that included seven divisions (Burmese) and seven states (ethnic minorities). The constitution defined the powers, rights and obligations of the union government and individual states, mostly in the north.

But the military coup in 1962 and the consequent military rule complicated the working of the federal arrangements. The new constitution in 1974 removed these specific stipulations, except for stating that the system of the country is 'local autonomy under central leadership'. In 1988, the constitution was suspended completely, and the country was placed under extra-constitutional military rule.

A **unitary state** is a polity organized under a single public authority and indivisible sovereignty. The relationship between governments at different levels is a relationship between the central government on the one hand, and local governments on the other. The authority and power of the former is primary, and that of the latter is secondary, extended from the central government.

However, federalism has revived somewhat – though not necessarily intended by the military government. The military government has had difficult challenges from minority groups in the north in search of autonomy and independence. The government has reached cease-fire agreements with various rebel armed forces. These agreements essentially allow various levels of autonomy or even semi-independence in areas controlled by these groups. 'The resulting cease-fire arrangements amount to a federalist structure for all intents and purposes' (Rajah, 1998: 144).

This troubled fate of federalism leads to a larger phenomenon in Pacific Asia. Many countries did not adopt Federalism as an option even when the conditions favoured a federal system. China is one of these countries. The People's Republic of China (PRC) covers a vast area that includes both China proper of the Han people, and vast 'frontier areas' of non-Han ethnic populations. At the beginning of the PRC, there was a debate over whether the new China should have a federal or a unitary state. Mao Zedong, leader of the Communist Party and president of the new China, opted for a unitary state with twenty-three provinces for predominantly Han Chinese and five autonomous regions for Tibetans, Uygur, Mongol, Zhuang and Hui. The resultant model is 'a unitary system, but a strong federalist character derives from the arrangement of the administrative system as a nested hierarchy' (ADB, 2004: 25; see also Chapter 10).

The unitary state also prevailed in Indonesia after a nine-month trial of a federation in 1949/50. With concentrations of various ethnic populations of different religions, languages and cultures, a federal system was a natural option. But the issue soon came to be framed in a debate of nationalism versus colonialism as the federation designed by the Dutch was considered to be a colonial tactic of 'divide and rule' (Hassall and Saunders, 2002: 223).

The fact that federalism has not been a favoured form of government in Pacific Asia may be related to a general perception of the modern state by Pacific Asian countries at the time when the new states were set up. Universal citizenship and an effective centralized government were more appreciated than regional diversity and institutional sensitivity.

Faces of unitary states

Most countries around the world today are unitary states, and Pacific Asia is no exception. Of the sixteen countries in Pacific Asia, fifteen are currently unitary states. A unitary state tends to have a concentration of state power in the hands of the central government, precisely because of the political philosophy and tradition behind the system. The modern idea of sovereignty, dating back to Jean Bodin (1530–96), is that a government should be able to exercise effective authority over its entire jurisdiction. Sovereignty is therefore absolute, and non-divisible.

Unitary states existed in Pacific Asia perhaps as early as the Qin Dynasty of China (221–206 BC). After Qin conquered six other states and established

Box 3.7

Indicators of the level of centralization of state authority

- Appointment of chiefs of local governments.
- Reporting lines of local government.
- Legislative powers of local government.
- Functional division between local and central governments.
- Sources of budget and revenue in local governments.
- Civic participation in local government.

Box 3.8

Levels of subnational government

Cambodia 2:	Provinces/municipalities; Communes/sangkat
China 4:	Provinces/regions/large cities; Prefectures/cities; Counties; Townships
Indonesia 3:	Provinces/regions/capital; Cities/districts; Villages
Philippines 4:	Provinces; Cities; Municipalities; Village
Thailand 4:	Provinces; Districts/municipalities; Subdistricts; Village
Vietnam 3:	Provinces; Districts; Communes

Smoke, 2005:27.

the first imperial state in Chinese history, it adopted a prefecture-county system rather than a feudal vassal system. Qin divided China into thirty-six prefectures over the conquered states, and established the first emperor, who symbolized the new centralized state authority. The head of each prefecture was appointed directly by the emperor. The Qin state imposed a new national conscription; standardized the language, legal code, currency, measurements and bureaucratic system across the empire; as well as built nation-wide roads and irrigation systems and organized social and economic activity in an almost military style. Many of the institutions for the new unitary state have been inherited through thousands of years of dynasties to become a defining core of the traditional Chinese political system. The system also served as a model for traditional state-building in Japan and Korea.

After the Second World War, most new states in Pacific Asia opted for a unitary state. As explained earlier, at the core of the differences between a federal state and a unitary state is whether a country's constitutional power is shared and can be exercised separately by the union and its member states.

A unitary state does not allow the splitting of sovereignty and constitutional power. That alone, however, does not provide sufficient information for the actual distribution of state authority between governments at different levels. The extent of the central government's power in unitary states can vary significantly. Key indicators (see Box 3.7) include whether office holders in local governments are elected by local constituencies or appointed by central government; whether the local governments are responsible or accountable primarily to the central government or to the local legislature; the extent to which local governments have their own legislative powers; how much a local government has control over its own resources and revenues; and is responsible for its own budget requirements; and whether citizens have direct participation in local and national political processes.

Two issues are important in defining the central–local relationship: one is the distribution of state authority and power, and the other concerns the assignment of revenues and expenditure, and the allocation of functions and service delivery between central and local governments. As one can see, these two issues are related as one very much affects the other.

Unitary states in Pacific Asia mainly followed a highly centralized state model before decentralization in the 1990s. Decentralization since that time has focused on restoring local government autonomy, devolving government functions and services, and developing some form of fiscal federalism. Today, more countries have various levels of local autonomy (see Box 3.8). Given this overall pattern, we shall first explain the predominant model of central–local relations during the Cold War and then examine the reforms in the past decade and how they have changed the dominance of the central government in the relationship.

The vertical administrative control model

Across the different types of state, Pacific Asian countries developed a highly centralized model of central–local relations during the Cold War. Most states had a new constitution and relevant laws that provided some form of local government. However, few countries saw the real development of subnational governments. In a study on decentralization and democracy in Indonesia, for example, Edward Aspinall and Greg Fealy found that the structure of centre–region relations in Indonesia,

> changed little between the late 1950s and the late 1990s. Sukarno's Guided Democracy and Suharto's New Order were centralized, authoritarian regimes in which the authorities saw regionalism as a major threat to Indonesia's survival as a unitary state. The New Order in particular built an extensive edifice of state surveillance and control to ensure that central government policies and directions were enforced right down to the village level. Uniform administrative structures and procedures were imposed across the nation, often replacing long established and effective local forms of community leadership and dispute settlement. Power relations during this period were essentially pyramidal ... for four decades, the regions had neither influence over national government policies nor the power to control their own affairs. Local politics and power constellations reflected the interests of the centre rather than those of the regions. Communities had scant opportunity to participate in local politics, while provincial and district legislatures and governments seldom dared to voice concern at national decisions that they viewed as inimical to local interests. (Aspinall and Fealy, 2003: 2)

The model of central–local relations described here was widely practiced in Pacific Asian countries at the time. Considering the 'galactic nature' of the state structure in Indonesia before that, we can imagine the extent of institutional restructuring involved in reshaping state authority in the newly independent Indonesia towards the centre. In many other countries, the highly centralized model was simply an essential part of their political traditions. Clay G. Wescott observes that, for example, 'Thailand is a unitary state that has traditionally employed a highly centralized form of government. Historically, subnational governments have comprised only about 5 per cent of total civil service employment' (Wescott, 2001: 39). Their share of total government expenditure is almost 10 per cent, in contrast to about 70 per cent in China (see Box 3.9).

There are scholars who argue that local governments during the Cold War were active and had a real impact on central government policy. Michio Muramatsu, for example, finds that the role of local governments in Japan was assertive and significant. The 'bottom up political competition of local government in fact determines central–local relations' (Muramatsu, 1997: xx).

But even Muramatsu recognizes that Japan's central–local relations exhibited a model of relations described as a 'vertical administrative control model' (Muramatsu, 1997: 28–30. See Box 3.10). This model reflects some of the key characteristics of central–local relations in many Pacific Asian countries.

There are some similar elements found in both the vertical administrative control model on the one hand, and the authoritarian state structure on the other. Authoritarian states in post-war Pacific Asia tended to have a highly centralized form of government. At the same time, the highly centralized

Box 3.9

Subnational expenditure as a share of total public spending (percentages)

Cambodia	17
Philippines	26
China	69
Indonesia	32
Thailand	10
Vietnam	48

White and Smoke, 2005:2.

Box 3.10

Features of the vertical administrative control model

- Local governments acted as agents of the central government and performed responsibilities delegated from the centre.
- Local governments had high level of financial dependence on the central government.
- Central control and management of administrative personnel.
- Centralized planning, decision-making and implementation processes in which the central government had exclusive legislative powers and were able to enforce national laws 'uniformly'.

Muramatsu 1997: 28–30

control model provided conditions for political corruption and a lack of accountability, transparency and responsiveness – traits often associated with an authoritarian state.

However, in political science, they are two different concepts and are concerned with different issues. The notion of authoritarianism concerns the constitutional legitimacy and democratic nature of the state, and is more about the problem of state type.

The vertical administrative control model deals primarily with the distribution of government powers and responsibilities, as well as the assignment of functions and services between different levels of government, a subject matter that sits better in the field of public administration.

This distinction is useful for understating Pacific Asian politics. There have been three significant political developments since the 1980s. First, there was a movement towards political liberalization and democratic transition in a large number of countries in the 1980s and 1990s (see Chapter 2).

Second, there are interesting and significant issues in the working of democracy in these new democratized states. The idea that democracy in Pacific Asia tends to be 'illiberal' (Bell et al., 1995; Zakaria, 1997; see Chapter 2) suggests that installing democratic institutions – a constitution, party politics and elections – may not be sufficient. Corruption, lack of civic participation, transparency and accountability, and more importantly, prevalence of non-liberal values and attitudes are still significant problems.

Third, almost every country in the region, regardless of its level of commitment to political liberalization and democratic transition, has been promoting the idea of decentralization and has experienced some form of institutional and administrative reform aimed at the government structure and functions, particularly central–local relations.

Together, these three political developments suggest that building the modern state on modern values and institutions is a long-term project, going beyond the initial excitement of democratic transition and requiring deeper institutional reform and change. Political liberalization and democratic transition are issues relevant to many Pacific Asian countries. But the problem of the vertical administrative control model is an issue of no less significance, and is an important part of the challenge of modern state-building.

Decentralization and devolution

Many forces drove the movement of decentralization in the 1990s in Pacific Asia. The World Bank study by Roland White and Paul Smoke (White and Smoke, 2005) singles out two primary sets of factors (ibid.: 4):

- Structural factors that 'have created an environment conducive to decentralization'; and
- Political factors that 'have been the more proximate and powerful drivers of the process'.

The structural factors White and Smoke refer to are the structural changes brought about by 'significant and continuous periods of economic growth and urbanization', which led to 'growing pressure to provide services to rapidly expanding and increasingly concentrated populations'. They note that 'in most East Asian countries, decentralization has been preceded by such periods' (ibid.: 4).

The political factors, on the other hand, include the movement towards political liberalization and democratic transition. In many countries, such as Indonesia, the Philippines, Thailand and South Korea, decentralization programmes were adopted as a consequence of the democratic transition. The political factors were not only 'an important trigger' to the process, but also 'shaped the nature of decentralization arrangements' (ibid.: 4). Much of the devolution of state authority to city and district governments in Indonesia after the fall of Suharto, for example, reflected the concerns of the national political elite that, with the collapse of Suharto's strong government, there could be an increase in regional rivalries to state power.

In addition to these two sets of factors, there are others providing momentum for the decentralization movement (Pranab and Mookherjee, 2006: 15). One particular factor is that the institutional setting responsible for rapid industrialization and economic development during the Cold War has become increasingly ineffective. At the core of this institutional setting is the highly centralized government coordination structure. A number of significant problems are associated with this form of economic development (see more on this in Chapter 6) that led to further pressure on decentralization.

Finally, the global wave of political and economic liberalization of the 1990s was also responsible for the movement. The backbone of the global wave of reform came from the 'Thatcher revolution' of the 1980s led by Prime Minister Margaret Thatcher in the United Kingdom, and 'Reaganomics' led by President Ronald Reagan, in the United States. More profoundly, neoliberalism became the guiding ideology behind these political and economic programmes. Because of the unique nature of the dominant political and economic systems in Pacific Asia that were seen as largely incompatible with many neoliberal values, much of the international pressure for liberalization centred on Pacific Asian countries who correspondingly sought to demonstrate their commitment to the new international norms and values through devolution and decentralization.

Generally speaking, the decentralization process in Pacific Asia has been aimed at three key objectives:

- Restoring local government;
- More effective and efficient service delivery;
- Good governance and increased civil society and civic participation.

Given the fact that local governments were very much suppressed or marginalized under the vertical administrative control model, the restoration of local governments and local autonomy was a natural step in the decentralization process for most Pacific Asian countries. Great attention was paid to the role of local governments, with hopes that better rationalized intergovernmental relations would lead to more effective and efficient delivery of government services in education, health, local infrastructure and welfare; and to good governance, with active civic participation at all levels of government.

The background for decentralization differs from one country to another. In some countries, such as the Philippines, Indonesia, South Korea, Thailand and Taiwan, decentralization in the 1990s was part of the wider process of political liberalization and democratic transition. In the people's republics, decentralization was part of post-socialist reform. In some other countries, such as Japan, there was no comparable political and ideological shift as seen in the other Pacific Asian countries. Decentralization has been at the centre of national politics since the 1990s, when the national economy dragged its feet for a decade and much of the problem was found to be in the existing government structure.

Given the diverse backgrounds, approaches to decentralization and the aims of the decentralization programmes were also different across Pacific

Pacific Asia in Context 3.2

International comparison of decentralization programmes

The world-wide movement of decentralization in developing countries in the 1980s and 1990s can be classified into three types:

Type A: Comprehensive big-bang political-cum-economic devolution (Bolivia, Indonesia, post-1994 South Africa).

Type B: Comprehensive political devolution and partial and uneven economic devolution (Brazil and India).

Type C: Limited political devolution with more significant administrative and economic devolution (China, Pakistan, Uganda and pre-1994 South Africa).

Bardhan and Mookherjee, 2006: 36

Asia. Of the three types of decentralization summarized in Bardhan and Mookherjee's study (2006: 36), for example, Type A (comprehensive, big-bang and political and economic devolution) and Type C (limited political devolution with more significant administrative and economic devolution) dominated the decentralization processes in the region.

Decentralization in Type A countries took place with the mandate of a new constitution or constitutional amendments, as part of the rebuilding of constitutional order. Decentralization in Indonesia, for example, was based on Laws 22 and 25 of 1999 after the fall of Suharto in 1998. Law 22 established local authority and restored the power of local governments, while Law 25 provided a form of financial federalism in which 'regions would gain a far larger share of the revenue generated within their borders' (Aspinall and Fealy, 2003: 3).

This district-centred decentralization resulted in a new central–regional relationship in which

> the central government is required to cede authority to regional governments in all fields except foreign policy, defense and security, monetary policy, the legal system and religious affairs. It also retains control of a number of specific functions such as national planning and the setting and supervision of technical standards. These district governments, whose powers had previously been strictly circumscribed, were now to take on full responsibility for such important areas as education, health, the environment, labor, public works, and natural resource management. Local parliaments gained the power to elect and dismiss district heads of government (that is, buptapi and mayors) and to determine budgets and the organizational structure of the bureaucracy. (ibid.: 3–4)

Type C countries are mainly people's republics. In these states, decentralization proceeded with no clear overall plan, strategy or timetable. Often it is not 'officially documented policy. Instead, it is anchored in historical realities and broader political and economic reforms' (World Bank, 2005: 6).

Japan can be seen as a third type, where it took five years to prepare the political and legal foundations of its decentralization programme. The preparation began with the Promoting Decentralization Act of 1995 – which set up a committee to produce a decentralization plan – to the passing of the decentralization package in the Diet, Japan's parliament, in 2000. In contrast to the other two types, decentralization in Japan has been a well-debated public process, leading to a comprehensive programme of administrative reforms. It has a clearly stipulated legal foundation, programmes and policy content, and a clear strategy and timetable for implementation.

These variations in the motivation and design of decentralization also affected the actual content of decentralization in these countries. In terms of the three broad objectives (that is, local autonomy; devolution of services and functions; and civic participation), the focus and preferences of the decentralization programmes varied from one country to another. In terms of local autonomy, many countries, particularly the Type A countries, gave local governments independent constitutional or statutory authority for elections, functions and responsibilities, as well as the control of their resources. Local governments gained legislative authority in a wide range of responsibilities. This is the case in Indonesia, Korea, Taiwan, Thailand, the Philippines and Japan.

In the people's republics, the political autonomy of local governments is still very limited. Chief executives of local governments in China, for example, are still appointed by the central government. At the time of writing, direct elections are held primarily at the basic administrative levels.

Local autonomy has been enhanced across these countries with the establishment or strengthening of some form of fiscal federalism, where the

Box 3.11

Functional allocation among levels of government

(Education, health, social welfare)

Cambodia	Provincial
China	Local
Indonesia	Local
Philippines	Central, provincial, local
Thailand	Central, provincial
Vietnam	Provincial, local

While and Smoke, 2005: 10

central and local governments have separate authorities and responsibilities over revenue, resources and expenditure. However, decentralization is not always a one-way process as shown by the fiscal reforms in central-local relations in China. Prior to 1994, provincial governments in China could negotiate with the central government on the proportion of tax that the centre would take. In 1994, as part of broader economic reforms, Premier Zhu Rongji consolidated the tax take from local governments and removed a major source of income for local governments by privatizing, centralizing or 'letting go' locally governed state owned enterprises. At the same time he increased the economic autonomy of local governments to coordinate economic activities in their region.

This consolidated the centre's commanding role in economic governance and increased local governance patronage of Beijing in some areas. However, it also led to some unintended consequences, such as the rapid expansion of heavy industry and pollution and the conversion of arable land to construction and residential land as local government began encouraging these industries and activities in their regions in order to increase their tax take. This led some scholars in China to call for a further recentralization to reign in local autonomy and to deal with increasing imbalances in economic activity. In 2013, President Xi Jinping's administration further announced a new round of fiscal decentralization and institutionalization in their Third Plenum Decision.

Related to fiscal federalism is the second objective of decentralization: reassignment of government functions and services. Many of them used to be in the hands of the central government, but have now become the responsibility of local governments (see Boxes 3.9 and 3.11). Box 3.9 shows a high proportion of public spending is taken up by local governments, particularly in Northeast Asian countries. Box 3.11 shows the varying functions and services that local governments are responsible for providing. These can range from education, health, social security and welfare to local infrastructure projects and maintenance.

Finally, with regard to the third broad objective, again, Type A countries have seen a substantive increase in the level of civic participation (see

Box 3.12

Level of local government autonomy

Cambodia: Subnational representative bodies elected through universal suffrage only at the commune level; commune governments have their own budgets, whereas provincial budgets are linked to the national budget; strong central civil service control.

China: People's Congresses in China exist at all levels of government, but only the village level is directly elected; subnational governments have their own budgets but are hierarchically integrated with higher levels and subject to central civil service regulations; control is weaker in practice and off-budget activity is considerable.

Indonesia: Regional People's Assemblies elected at local and provincial levels; subnational governments initially had complete budget autonomy, with the next-higher level having legal review, and national civil service regulations allowed a reasonable degree of subnational discretion; Law 32 of 2004 significantly expanded control by the next higher level over budgeting and the civil service.

Philippines: Directly elected bodies exist at all subnational levels of government; subnational governments prepare budgets with legal review by the next-higher level; national civil service regulations allow subnational discretion.

Thailand: Different types of subnational governments have directly elected councils of different sizes; local governments prepare budgets subject to certain central mandates and follow civil service regulations.

Vietnam: People's councils at all levels of government are directly elected and ratified by the immediately superior council; subnational governments have their own budgets, but these are hierarchically integrated and approved by higher levels; major cities have been permitted to experiment with greater autonomy.

Adapted from Smoke, 2005: 33, 34

Box 3.12). This increase is related partly to the restoration of local autonomy and self-governing mechanisms in these countries. Genuinely open, competitive elections for members as well as chief executives of local governing bodies (with actual legislative powers and resources) lead citizens to be more interested in participating in elections, policy-making processes and public debates.

Moreover, many countries, such as China, Indonesia and the Philippines, have no formal mechanisms for civic participation. Others, such as Thailand, Vietnam and Cambodia, have some mechanisms in place, but they are either very weak in practice, or too new to be effective (World Bank, 2005: 36). For Japan, Korea and Taiwan, constitutional and legal frameworks for civic participation are very well developed or have been restored recently, and are practiced effectively.

Beyond formal mechanisms, the level of civic participation also increased in some countries where the legal basis for these activities is still ambiguous. In China, for example, rights support groups usually led by lawyers, direct appeals to the higher levels of government by citizens, investigative reporting by journalists for alleged wrongs at local levels, and public policy hearings at local governments have emerged as popular forms of civic participation (see Chapter 8).

Decentralization in Pacific Asia has been a significant phenomenon. In many countries, it has restored the independent role of local governments in the overall government structure; brought about a fairer balance in authority, responsibilities, functions and services between the central and local governments; and promoted the development of civic participation and civil society. However, there are significant variations in the extent and nature of the decentralization programmes and their outcomes. In some cases, whether decentralization has really solved the problems as was intended is not clear (Aspinall and Fealy, 2003).

In terms of the organization of state authority, decentralization has transformed the highly centralized forms of government to various extents in favour of local governments. However, such decentralization has not diminished the dominant role of the central government, much less the dominance of state institutions.

Rationalizing state power: political liberalization, decentralization and legitimization

The tradition of state dominance in Pacific Asia has experienced significant challenges during much of the last few decades. In the post-war years, state dominance was reinforced in one way or another by the overarching Cold War structure. Three forces, however, have reduced state dominance in Pacific Asia from the 1980s.

Box 3.13

Ending of the three-decade rule of the centralized state in Indonesia

After the fall of President Suharto, the relationship between the centre and regions changed fundamentally through a series of institutional reforms that promoted decentralization and local autonomy:

Law 22/1999, administrative decentralization, with actual transfer of extensive formal administrative and political authority to lower levels of government.

- Elected parliaments in provinces, districts and municipalities would choose their own administrator and decide their own budgets.
- The central government was only responsible for national security and defence, foreign policy, fiscal and monetary matters, macroeconomic policy, justice and religion. Districts and municipalities were responsible for infrastructure, healthcare and trade, agriculture, industry, investment, environmental and land issues, education and culture.
- New autonomy located at the district level. The power of provinces was dismantled.
- National not regional political parties.

Revenue Sharing Law 256/1999 fiscal decentralization

- 25 per cent of the net domestic revenues channelled to the region. Regions are allowed to raise their own income in special taxation. Budgets of districts and municipalities consisted of a lump sum.

Nordholt, 2012: 229

Firstly, democratic transition and political liberalization has created formal checks and balances on the central authorities and introduced transparency that has increased the state's accountability and responsiveness to the public. We will discuss this more in the following chapter.

Secondly, local autonomy and decentralization has shifted aspects of decision-making and governance away from the centre and increased the discretion local authorities have to govern in accordance with local conditions. As shown above, the vertical administrative control model that operated in Pacific Asia during the Cold War period has largely been dismantled but elements of this model remain problematic in many countries. While the bureaucracy is no longer fully insulated from the demands of the public and executive delegation is more attuned to local conditions the tension between local autonomy and central fiat remains common. This is found in fiscal policy but most acutely in the area of institutionalizing civil society and civic participation in local decision-making.

These three forces have achieved to a great extent the rationalizing and legitimatization of state institutions and the authority structures in Pacific Asian countries. They provide evidence of authority structure and shift in power and capacity of government from central to local. Institutional reform and change in these countries has not only brought in a more legitimate constitution for organizing and structuring of state power but also a more balanced government structure for effective and efficient delivery of public services and performing public sector functions.

We began this chapter by overviewing the institutional and cultural foundations of state dominance in Pacific Asian states. We overviewed the types of states, forms of government and domestic and international interaction as institutional factors that contributed to a high degree of state dominance in the region. We also overviewed those studies that attribute Pacific Asia's high concentration of power and authority at the centre vis-à-vis other Asian and Euro-American states to cultural factors and traditional understandings of power and authority. Throughout the discussion, we have also highlighted an overall trend of the erosion of state dominance. As the next chapter shows, one reason for this erosion is the ongoing institutionalization and growing primacy of formal institutions of government as the desired means of pursuing politics in the region.

Chapter summary

- There are very different types of states in Pacific Asia, a region that is more diverse than any other in the world. Different types of state reflect different historical traditions, contrasting experiences in modern political development and different contemporary conditions.
- Across these different types of states, there has been a broad pattern of state dominance.
- At the heart of state dominance is the dominance of the executive branch of government.
- There are both institutional and cultural foundations for state dominance in the region.
- There is a very weak tradition of federalism in Pacific Asia.
- State dominance has been largely weakened because of political liberalization and democratic transition since the 1980s, social and economic development, and the consequent strengthening of civil society, as well as the forces of globalization.
- There are two different models of central–local relations among the unitary states: the vertical administrative control model during the Cold War and the one with more local autonomy and participation as a consequence of devolution and decentralization since the 1990s.
- Decentralization has resulted in some level of reduction in state dominance, but has not diminished its overall structure.

Further reading

The quality of the literature on the organization of state institutions and government organizations of Pacific Asian countries varies from country to country. For state types, Hassall and Saunders (2002) give a good sketch. There are a series of studies, such as the Country Governance Assessment Report (ADB, 1999–2005) and the Public Administration Country Profile by the United Nations (United Nations, 2004–07), that provide a good overview of state institutions mainly on individual countries. In addition, Wang (1994) is more a comparative study of government on a range of Asian countries, and Funston (2001) is a collection of excellent introductions on each individual country in Southeast Asia. As an example of the functions and organization of the executive branch, Hayao (1993) has a good and detailed explanation of how Japan's cabinet and prime ministerial system work. Saich (2015) has a good overview of how the centre in Chinese politics functions. On federalism, local government and decentralization reforms, books can be found in libraries that cover individual countries. For example, Aspinall and Fealy (2003) on Indonesia, and Muramatsu (1997) on Japan. The World Bank (2005) and Bardhan and Mookherjee (2006) are systematic studies on a range of Pacific Asian countries.

Study questions

1 Why has state dominance been an important feature of government and politics in Pacific Asia? Illustrate your answer with examples from a variety of countries in the region.

2 In comparison with other regions of the world, what are some of the unique characteristics of the types of states in Pacific Asia?

3 How did cultural traditions in Pacific Asian counties shape the structure of state power?

4 Is state dominance a unique Pacific Asian phenomenon? Or it is a wider phenomenon around the world?

5 Do central–local relations matter for good governance, and if they do, in what way(s)?

6 Why has federalism been in decline and local autonomy on the rise in Pacific Asia?

Key terms

Types of state (71); State dominance (72); 'Centre'; Political regime (83); Democratic centralism (79); Mandate of heaven (80); Constitutional order and legitimacy (80); Paternalistic state (75); Patrimonialism (81); Leninist party-state (82); Military regime (83); One-party state (85); Single-party dominant state (85); Grand political alliance (86); Consociationalism (86); Ethnic bargaining (86); Asymmetric federalism (89); Vertical administrative control (88); Decentralization and local autonomy (88); Unitary state (88).

Chapter 4
Organization of government

This chapter examines how government is organized. We look into different forms of government, where heads of government are located in different parts of the state structure and how different branches of government support government purpose and functions. In Chapter 3, we discussed the problem of state dominance in terms of the organization and structure of the polity. In this chapter, we shall further discuss the dominance of state power and perhaps, more precisely, executive dominance, in terms of the relationships among principal branches of government. Let us start with the various models of how government is organized.

Forms of government

In today's Western democracies, there are two dominant models of government structure: one based on the system of separation of powers among branches of government, best exemplified by the American three-branch model; and the other based on the system of fusion of powers, particularly between the executive and the legislature, best represented by the British Westminster system.

Both systems have had a significant impact on Pacific Asian countries. For example, the American model has significantly influenced the Philippines and to a lesser extent South Korea. Likewise, the British system heavily influenced Singapore, Malaysia and Japan. However, as we shall see in this chapter, the 'transplantation' (Hassall and Saunders, 2002: 77) has not always gone as planned, or resulted in exact copies of the British and American models. Consequently, there are significant ambiguities in the models of government structure in Pacific Asia.

More importantly, there seems to be a residual impact of the traditional state models in Pacific Asian countries that adds to the complexity and diversity of their structures of government. The notion, and indeed the historical practice of the unity of state power, represents a conception of state authority and government power that is different from those of separation of powers and fusion of powers.

A **form of government** is the structural setup of government based on a particular organizing principle. It defines the relationship among key branches of government. In most Western democracies, these different branches often come down to three distinctive areas of state functions: legislative, administrative and justice. However, in Pacific Asian countries, state institutions are not always structured as such and the relationship among them is much more ambiguous. Even in those with the three branches of government, these branches do not always have the same constitutional weight and institutional power.

These three concepts and institutional practices explain to a large extent the various forms of government in Pacific Asia. It is not rare that one single country can exhibit elements of more than one of the organizing principles. J. A. Stockwin's research on the government structure of Japan, for example, points out: 'The Meiji Constitution was strongly German in inspiration ... At the same time the constitutional relationship between emperor, prime minister, cabinet, parliament and the bureaucracy are highly reminiscent of British arrangements, while the structure and role of parliamentary committees are American-inspired' (Stockwin, 1999: 113). The 'German inspiration' here may well be the influence of the political tradition of unity of powers, while the 'British arrangements' are clearly of the tradition of fusion of powers.

The form of government refers to the way a government is organized. On the basis of the organizing principles (see Box 4.1), we can define three main forms of government in Pacific Asia: presidential, parliamentary and semi-presidential. While state types have a significant impact on the distribution of state power, as already discussed in Chapter 3, the form of government also shapes the distribution of state power. As seen in the comparison with Europe, North America and Australasia (see Pacific Asia in Context 4.1), more countries in Pacific Asia are found with a form of government that favours the concentration of power in the central government and in the hands of the executive branch. Of the sixteen Pacific Asian countries, there are five with a parliamentary system (31.3 per cent), while of the twenty-seven countries in the European Union; twenty-four have a parliamentary system (88.9 per cent). Pacific Asia has eight countries (50 per cent) with a presidential system (18.7 per cent) or a semi-presidential system leaning strongly towards a presidential system (31.3 per cent), while the European Union has only three (11.1 per cent). There is an overwhelming dominance of the presidential system in Pacific Asia.

For Pacific Asian countries, the issue of forms of government has a unique significance. Many of these countries were newly independent countries that had their political history interrupted by war and dictatorship. This gave them a unique opportunity to face the question of 'which system?' at independence or the restoration of pluralist politics. Cambodia was such an example. After years of war and the Khmer Rouge's rule of terror, a

Box 4.1

Organizing principles of government in Pacific Asia

Separation of powers is an organizing principle of government where the government is divided into separate branches, with each serving as a checker and balancer against one another. The three branches are constitutionally equal. This system is associated mainly with the presidential systems. It was the belief of the framers of the US Constitution that this is the best way to prevent government, particularly its executive branch, from becoming a 'tyranny'.

Fusion of powers refers to a model of government organization where there is a close intertwinedness between the executive and the legislature, and a lack of clear separation of powers among the branches of government. This fusion of powers is seen mainly in parliamentary systems. The idea is that parliament is the highest state power, and the cabinet is its executive arm. By design, government power is not distributed equally among the branches of government.

The idea of **unity of powers** does not recognize the divisibility of government power. It rejects the idea that government branches should be made antagonistic to one another, sees state institutions as being functionally dependent on one another and argues that they ought to support each other and collaborate for overall state purposes. The idea has strongly influenced the organization of government in traditional states, contemporary people's republic states and non-pluralist states during the Cold War in Pacific Asia.

Pacific Asia in Context 4.1

Forms of government

Pacific Asia (16)	Parliamentary (5)	Presidential (3)	Semi- presidential (5)	Other (3)	Percentage of total
Constitutional monarchy (4)	Cambodia, Japan, Malaysia, Thailand				25
Republic (6)	Singapore	Indonesia, South Korea, Philippines	Taiwan, East Timor		37.5
People's republic (4)			China, Laos, Vietnam	North Korea	25
Other (2)				Brunei, Myanmar	12.5
Percentage of total	31.3	18.7	31.3	18.7	100
Europe, North America, Australasia (45)	**Parliamentary (35)**	**Presidential (3)**	**Semi- presidential (6)**	**Other (1)**	**Percentage of total**
Constitutional monarchy (7)	7				15.6
Commonwealth realm (4)	4				8.9
Republic (34)	24	3	6	1	75.6
Percentage of total	77.8	6.7	13.3	2.2	100
Other Asia (29)	**Parliamentary (11)**	**Presidential (9)**	**Semi- presidential (5)**	**Other (4)**	**Percentage of total**
Republic (17)	6	7	4		58.6
Islamic republic (4)	1	1	1	1	13.8
Constitutional monarchy (6)	4	1		1	20.7
Monarchy (2)				2	6.9
Percentage of total	37.9	31.0	17.2	13.8	100

UN-introduced parliamentary system was established in the new Cambodia. However, there is still a significant debate (Peou, 2001: 67–70) among those who support the parliamentary system, those in favour of monarchical rule and those who want a presidential system.

Let us now examine each of these three forms of government in more detail – keeping in mind the key question of how the organization of government relates to the general characteristics of the political system in these countries.

Presidential systems

A substantial number of countries in Pacific Asia have a presidential system. Indonesia, South Korea and the Philippines are all in this category. In these three countries, the president is elected through a direct popular vote and is both the head of state and the head of government as well as has control of the executive powers. All of them had the experience of a military, authoritarian rule in some form during the Cold War, followed by a democratic transition in the 1980s and 1990s. Consequently, there is significant antipathy towards a strong presidency. Because of this, the new constitutions, or constitutional amendments, have placed various constraints on the power of the president.

In South Korea, for example, under the current constitution (1987), the president is allowed only one term in office of five years. This rule is designed to prevent the repetition of early post-war experiences when presidents sought unlimited terms in office while building up their autocratic and authoritarian rule. Moreover, the president appoints the prime minister, and this needs the consent of the National Assembly. Indeed, the National Assembly is given 'momentous powers' to restrict presidential authority (Oh, 1999: 104). The National Assembly is given powers to 'inspect affairs of the state', to impeach the president and other government officials, and to call the prime minister and other ministers to the National Assembly for questioning.

A **presidential system** is a form of government in which the president is both the head of state and the head of government. The president is usually, though not always, elected through a popular vote, and the executive and legislative branches are separated. The president represents the state and controls executive powers.

All these have a significant bearing on the working of the political system in Korea. For example, the president was impeached for breaking electoral laws in 2006, but survived. The five-year fixed term has become an issue of debate in Korea. In January 2007, President Roh proposed a constitutional revision to adopt a system of two consecutive four-year terms for the president. However, this did not come about.

The presidential system in the Philippines is very much a copy of the American model (Wurfel, 1988: 76, 83–4; Kingsbury, 2005a: 296; see Pacific Asia in Context 5.2). But since the Marcos era, the president has mainly been weak. The president is limited to only one term of six years by the current constitution (1987) for the same reason as in South Korea.

There are different views over the extent of the power of the president in the Philippines (see Box 4.2). An Asian Development Bank study, for example, finds that:

Pacific Asia in Context 4.2

Comparing Philippine and American models of government

Similarities: Separation of powers between three branches of government, structure and power of Congress (two houses and the committee system), local government as a municipal corporation.

Differences: The Philippines is a unitary, not a federal state, with a stronger Senate based on national constituencies, and a bureaucracy that is politically loyal and not neutral.

> whoever gets elected or assumes power as the president exerts tremendous influence on the alignment of political forces in Congress, as well as on the process and outcome of choosing the leadership of both chambers. Legislators tend to affiliate themselves with the political party of the incumbent President ... This pattern of influence of the president over the leadership and the alignment of political forces in both houses has raised questions on the independence of Congress as a separate branch of the Government. The president's virtual control of the leadership of both houses and the majority of their members, places him or her in a position to dictate the legislative agenda and control both houses. (ADB, 2005: 50–1)

Challenging the view that presidents in the Philippines have tended to be strong dictators, Alex B. Brillantes finds that the 'notion of a historically dominant president may be mistaken' (Brillantes, 1988: 129). His survey finds only four presidents 'actually tried to dominate the office'. A weak president in the Philippines is part of the problem of the weak state, which most scholars would attribute to the dominance of the landed elite.

In Indonesia, after the fall of Suharto in 1998, a series of constitutional amendments were passed between 1999 and 2002, stipulating that the president be elected through a direct popular vote (for the first time in 2004) for a maximum of two five-year terms.

While presidents are more constrained with the new democratic system, the presidential system still

Box 4.2

Role of the head of state

Ceremonial: Singapore (president), Japan (emperor), Cambodia (king), Malaysia (paramount leader).

Substantial: China (president), Vietnam (president), Taiwan (president), Thailand (king).

Also head of government: Indonesia (president), Philippines (president), South Korea (president), Myanmar (president), Brunei (sultan).

renders a relatively strong executive in these countries, particularly in South Korea and Indonesia. In all three countries, the president is the chief of state, the head of government and the chief of the armed forces, elected through a direct popular vote that gives the president a stronger political basis in relation to the legislature.

Parliamentary systems

It is interesting to note that most countries in Pacific Asia with a parliamentary system are in Southeast Asia. This is perhaps the legacy of European colonial rule. The institutional roots of parliamentary government go back to European history. Along with constitutional rule, the parliamentary system was designed to place constraints on the power of the monarchy. As Graham Hassall and Cheryl Saunders explain:

> a key presumption in the Westminster system of parliament is that the best 'check and balance' on the allocation and use of public power is to place executive power in the hands of those who constitute 'the majority' of the elected members of parliament, and to make this executive responsible to the whole parliament. (Hassall and Saunders, 2002: 78)

Of course, when you put executive power in the hands of the legislature, the relationship can be very ambiguous, to say the least. In many Pacific Asian countries with a parliamentary system, the original intention to confine the power of the monarchy has largely been lost. Instead, the parliamentary system would allow dominant societal forces to control both the legislature and the executive through the ruling party and build a one-party dominant state. This to a large extent explains the long reign of a single political party during the Cold War in countries such as Japan, Singapore and Malaysia.

Japan established its parliamentary system during the Meiji Restoration, but subsequent developments saw the expansion of the power of the emperor and the military. A genuine parliamentary system was restored after the Second World War with a substantial reduction of the powers of the emperor. The parliamentary system in Malaysia and Singapore were set up at independence following their colonial ruler's model.

A **parliamentary system** is a form of government where the executive branch is formed on the basis of a majority in parliament. There is consequently a substantial overlap between the executive branch (cabinet) and the legislative branch (parliament). Parliament is considered to be the highest body of state power. The executive branch depends on the legislative branch for support. Government policies and programmes are required to be debated thoroughly and approved in parliament.

Most parliamentary systems in Pacific Asian countries have a heavier 'fusion of powers' between the legislature and the executive because of the nature of the parliamentary system. This is exacerbated by the political tradition of unitary state power. As Sorpong Peou observes in the case of Cambodia: 'Cambodia's parliamentary system is based on the principle of a "fusion of powers". All powers are fundamentally concentrated in the parliament rather than separated, as is generally the case in a presidential system' (Peou, 2001: 41).

Alongside the fusion of powers is usually the concept of parliament supremacy, where the executive is embedded in and therefore institutionally constrained by parliament. This is because the mandate of the executive comes from parliament. In this sense, Cambodia's legislature is

> a crystal-clear case of parliamentary supremacy. The executive does not exercise its authority apart from within the legislature. The head of the executive, namely the Prime Minister, must come

COUNTRY PROFILE

CHINA

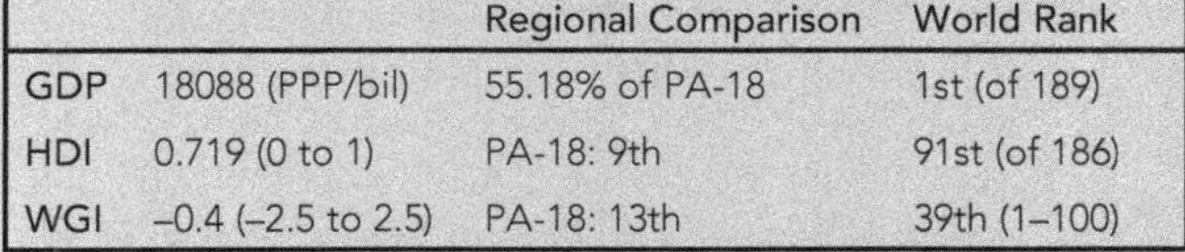

		Regional Comparison	World Rank
GDP	18088 (PPP/bil)	55.18% of PA-18	1st (of 189)
HDI	0.719 (0 to 1)	PA-18: 9th	91st (of 186)
WGI	–0.4 (–2.5 to 2.5)	PA-18: 13th	39th (1–100)

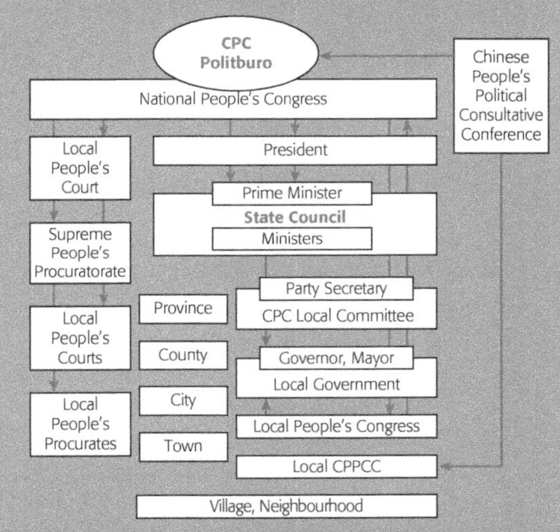

Key political facts

Electoral system for national legislature
People's republic electoral system

Political cycles
Annual meeting of the CPC Central Committee in October; CPC National Convention every five years.
Annual sessions of NPC and CPPCC in early March. NPC and CPPCC are constituted every five years.

Further reading

Saich, 2015; Lieberthal, 2004; Dreyer, 2005.

Timeline of modern political development

1911 The 1911 Revolution overthrows the imperial system and establishes the first Republic in Pacific Asia.
1916–27 Warlords control a fragmented state, with no effective central government.
1928 Chiang Kai Shek establishes a united central government.
1945–9 Civil War between the Nationalists and the Communists.
1947 New Constitution, with a five-branch government.
1949 Mao establishes the PRC, and government under the Communist Party.
1954 The first PRC Constitution, outlining 'people's democratic dictatorship'.
1966–76 The Cultural Revolution, with no effective government at any level. Revolutionary Committees functioned as the government.
1975 A new constitution with the CPC as the 'core leading force' of China and outlining the CPC's control of the military.
1982 Another new constitution to restore the pre-Cultural Revolution state institutions and government structure.
1989 Popular movement to challenge the political system failed. The party-state survived.
2004 Constitutional amendment recognizing private ownership and mixed economy.
2007 Property law passed, providing equal protection for public and private properties. New labour law passes with new standards for labour rights and conditions.
2011 China takes over Japan as world's second largest economy.
2012 Xi is confirmed the new leader of the Party and Sate under the established system of transfer of power in Party and state leadership.
2014 Hong Kong protests against Beijing's plan for methods of election of Chief Executive in 2017.
2015 One-child policy formally ends.
2015 Chinese President and Taiwanese President held official meeting in Singapore for the first time.

> from the Assembly, and both he and his government require a two-thirds vote of approval before they can take office. After that the Assembly may at any time bring down the executive with a vote of no confidence if it can muster a two-thirds majority. This is sometimes called an 'elective dictatorship'. (Peou, 2001: 47)

However, this is only the relationship in theory. In Pacific Asian parliamentary systems, the fusion of powers does not necessarily mean the supremacy of parliament. It is often more the dominance of the executive over parliament. This is the case from Japan to Singapore and Cambodia to Malaysia. In political reality, the cabinet tends to dominate in Pacific Asian countries. Except in the case of Thailand, the prime minister is the real power-holder in relation to parliament and the head of state. This, in the case of Japan, leads some scholars to call Japan's parliamentary government a 'cabinet government', or even a 'prime ministerial government' (Hayao, 1993: 33, 43). 'The cabinet's dominance of the legislature' in the case of Japan, according to Hayao, is shaped by the very parliamentary system itself (ibid.: 33, see Box 4.3).

There is also a general pattern in Pacific Asia that a constitutional monarchy goes with a parliamentary system. Singapore is an exception, in that it has an elected president as the head of state. Cambodia, Japan, Malaysia and Thailand are all constitutional monarchies. Thailand is an interesting case in terms of its parliamentary system. The question is whether the king or the military is above the constitution. Because of the political influence of both the king and the military, the parliament can be irrelevant, and in fact this has been the case for much of its post-1932 history. If the military was the real power-holder in the early days, the current pattern of national politics now suggests a much stronger influence of the king.

If this pattern holds, Thailand can be seen in reality as an active monarchy where the king holds the highest state power and parliament produces a government with the direct or indirect consent of the king and the military.

Overall, the extent of executive dominance in those countries with a parliamentary system is no less than in those with a presidential system. A combination of parliamentary majority and executive privilege often leads to strong executive dominance. Japan under the LDP, Singapore under the PAP and Malaysia under the UMNO are all good examples of this.

Box 4.3

How does Japan's parliamentary system differ from others?

Japan's parliamentary system is often compared to the Westminster model, in contrast to the continental European model or the Congress model of the United States. However, such a comparison is always troublesome. Hayes sees the following distinctive features of Japan's parliamentary system (Hayes, 2005: 48, 52–5) that seem to defy conventional categorizations:

- Diet members do not see themselves collectively as the supreme power of the state, as is typical in parliamentary systems – the British Parliament in particular.
- The Diet does not have the kind of independence that characterizes many legislatures, especially the US Congress. The system of 'checks and balances' does not exist in Japan.
- Power is shared among the legislature, the cabinet and the bureaucracy.
- The Diet does not play a decisive role in the initiation and refinement of public policy.
- What is important to legislation is not committee deliberations, as in the US Congress, or floor debates, as in the British Parliament, but rather the influence of the LDP, and its Public Affairs Research Council (PARC).

Semi-presidential systems

Beyond the presidential and parliament systems, there is also a semi-presidential system, or mixed, dual executive system. In this form of government, executive power is shared, if not contested, between the executive and legislative branches and there are elements of both the presidential and parliamentary systems. The term 'semi-presidential' is preferable for those in Pacific Asia because, in reality, these mixed systems lean heavily towards the presidential system.

There are two groups of semi-presidential systems in Pacific Asia. The first group includes Taiwan and East Timor. Taiwan's 'dual executive' system has its origins in the constitutional design of the state institutions. The original constitution (1947) set up five branches of government where the National Assembly, the highest body of state power, elects the president and the president reports to the National Assembly. The Executive Yuan (cabinet) is the highest administrative body of the state and the Legislative Yuan is the highest legislative body. In recent rounds of constitutional amendments, the National Assembly was abolished and the president is now elected directly by popular vote. With the National Assembly abolished, the current constitution specifies no highest body of state power. With both elected directly by the people, the president and the Legislative Yuan are in competition to be the highest body of state power.

As an indicator of a presidential system, the president neither reports nor is accountable to the Legislative Yuan, as the president is elected directly by the people in a separate process. The president appoints the prime minister and the cabinet and has many of the powers the president in a presidential system would normally have. As indicators of a parliamentary system, however, the president is the head of state, but not the head of government. The prime minister is the head of government and reports and is accountable to the Legislative Yuan. The mixed system in Taiwan creates a 'two-executive' government system where both the president and the prime minister share executive power and responsibilities.

Party-State system

Another group of countries that have a mixed system are the people's republics: China, Laos and Vietnam. There are two unique features to their systems. First, their form of government is 'a hybrid of classic cabinet and presidential models' (Wescott, 2001: 55) – a mixture of the presidential and parliamentary systems. In all cases, the president and the prime minister are nominated by the Communist Party and 'confirmed' by the National People's Congress/ National Assembly.

Their system is a mixed one because the president is the head of state and shares substantive executive powers with the prime minister, who is the head of government. All the constitutions of these countries stipulate that the Communist Party is at the core of the state. All state institutions are organized and state powers are integrated under the Communist Party. There is an extremely high concentration of state authority, not so much because of the president or the executive branch, but because of the Communist Party.

Second, unlike a normal presidential system where the executive and the legislative branches are separate, with each having a separate electoral mandate, the National People's Congress (China), or National Assembly (Vietnam and Laos), is designated as the highest body of state power with legislative powers. In theory, the National Congress/Assembly elects the president and the prime minister is nominated by the president but confirmed by the National Congress. The prime minister reports to the National Congress on behalf of the government. In theory, therefore, the mandate of the president comes from the National Congress/Assembly. The president performs assigned functions 'in pursuance of decisions of the National Congress' (China's constitution, 1982, Article 82). This bears all the signs of a classic parliamentary system.

The semi-presidential systems in these people's republics therefore render a very strong executive branch on behalf of the Communist Party. Moreover, there are substantial checks on the president and the executive branch under the overall watch of the Communist Party.

Other forms of government

There are three countries whose governments are neither presidential, nor parliamentary, nor semi-presidential: North Korea, Myanmar and Brunei. North Korea is a slightly different case from its fellow people's republics. The general government structure of North Korea is very similar to that of China. The Supreme People's Assembly (SPA) is the highest body of state power and other state institutions are functional arms of the state. But the actual structure of state authority since the early 1990s has been rather different. Since the death of the first President, Kim Il-sung in 1994, there has been no successor to the office of president. In fact, the current constitution (1998) has reserved the office of the president permanently for the deceased former president. The president of the SPA presidium – an executive committee that exercises the powers of the SPA when it is not in session – represents the state. The real leader, Kim Jong-un, has inherited powers from his father, Kim Jong-il, but officially only holds the office of chairman of the National Defence Commission – 'the nation's highest administrative authority' (United Nations, 2006 North Korea: 6) and is Supreme Commander of the Korean People's Army. This form of government is very much the same as the system China had under Mao and Deng Xiaoping, where the political power resides exclusively in the hands of one individual, regardless of the formal institutions of government.

Extra-constitutional powers also complicate the functioning and organization of government in Myanmar where the military maintains veto rights over the civilian-elected government (see Chapter 3). As for Brunei, constitutionally it is a parliamentary system. But the sultan is in fact above the constitution and his extra-constitutional rule requires no assistance from parliament. The sultan has an absolute control of state authority.

This survey of the current forms of government in Pacific Asia has shown that Pacific Asia has a relatively high number of countries with a presidential or semi-presidential system. In both systems, and even in those parliamentary systems, there is a greater concentration of state power in the hands of the executive branch. Moreover, the state institutions tend to be less competitive with each other. The influence of the traditional and communist political order is still felt, particularly in the people's republics and single-party dominant states. State institutions are therefore largely the functional arms of the state, controlled by the ruling party. Under such an overall structure, state authority is more integrated and centralized than it would otherwise be.

Having examined the overall patterns of the organization of government, we now turn to the other individual branches of government. Let us start with the executive.

Organization of the executive branch

The above discussion of the different forms of government in Pacific Asia gives us a useful context in which to understand the position of the executive in the overall state structure and government system.

The word 'government' often refers to the executive branch in its narrow sense. It is also used to refer to state institutions as a whole in a broader sense. The latter usage would include all branches of government. Here, we use 'government' in its narrow sense. In particular, we are interested in the headship of state, headship of government and organization of the executive branch.

In terms of headship, there are three types:

- First, the head of state is also head of government, possibly with a prime minister assisting the president. South Korea, the Philippines, Brunei, Myanmar and Indonesia currently have this type of headship.
- Except for Brunei, the president is usually elected through a direct popular election, but is accountable to the legislature or national assembly in its capacity as the head of government. The president appoints cabinet ministers.
- In the case of South Korea, where the president is both the head of state and head of government, the prime minister is not head of government, but rather the 'principal administrative assistant to the President' (United Nations, 2006: 6).
- Second, the head of state and head of government are two separate positions, with the prime minister as the head of government that controls executive power. The head of state is usually a ceremonial figure. Japan, Singapore, Malaysia, Cambodia and Thailand currently have this type of headship.
- Often, the prime minister is chosen from the majority party or party coalition in parliament and appointed by the head of state. The prime minister is generally accountable to parliament. The prime minister appoints cabinet ministers.
- Third, the head of state and head of government are two separate positions, with executive power shared between the two: people's republics such as China, Vietnam and Laos are in this category, as well as those with semi-presidential or dual headship systems, such as Taiwan and East Timor.

In China and Vietnam, the National People's Congress/National Assembly elects the head of state. In turn, the president appoints the prime minister with the consent of the National People's Congress (NPC), and the prime minister reports to the NPC. The prime minister appoints cabinet ministers with the consent of the NPC.

As shown above, the high prevalence of presidential and semi-presidential systems renders a relatively strong executive and in particular, a powerful presidency where one elected official can shape the direction of government and implementation of government policy. Likewise, the organization of government has a large impact on the distribution of power and authority and how the executive operates on a day-to-day level.

There are standard mechanisms and institutions for organizing the government. For example, in most countries where genuine elections are held regularly, senior ministerial appointments are political appointments that come and go with the ruling political party. Below that, there is a strong, professional bureaucracy (see Chapter 5). Across different types of states in Pacific Asia, however, there are exceptional features of organizing the executive that are worthy of special discussion.

In China, the Communist Party of China (CPC) dominates the state institutions through a variety of methods. First, in theory the appointment of senior ministers, including the president and the prime minister, are the privileges of the National People's Congress. In reality, however, all the senior ministerial appointments are made on recommendation of the CPC Centre. This is part of a political tradition that originated with the introduction of the nomenklatura system (see Chapter 5) from the Soviet Union during the Communist era. This system was widely replicated and diligently applied in the people's republics.

Second, as in any administrative unit in China, there will be a CPC committee at each ministry and each level of government. Generally, the minister and deputy ministers would be the members of the committee, but the minister may not necessarily head the committee. All significant policy or personnel decisions are discussed and decided on first in the CPC committee. Indeed, the CPC committee takes political responsibility for the work of the ministry.

Third, major government policies and programmes are first discussed and approved at Politburo meetings (the central leadership of the CPC). Once the CPC Centre makes a decision, this is transferred to the state institutions and the government will take over its implementation. In many cases, the people who make the decision in the CPC committee or CPC Politburo are the same people who are responsible for introducing and implementing the decision in the formal institutions of government.

Finally, there are several different forms in which a decision can be implemented. In addition to those that require legislation, which the State Council will introduce to the National People's Congress (see next section), the government can issue directives, documents, regulations or announcements. In China, government policy includes all government decisions, regulations and directives that have no legislative basis but have equally binding power on the intended parties.

A second feature of the organization of government in Pacific Asia is factional politics in the working of Japan's cabinet. Since the late 1940s, apart from brief periods between 1993 and 1994 and between 2009 and 2012, the LDP has controlled the government. But that is only part of the story. The real battle for portfolio allocation takes place among dominant factions within the LDP before and after the confirmation by the prime minister (see Box 4.4). Often, the make-up of the cabinet, and the government policy and programmes, would reflect the balance of power and results of political bargaining among LDP factions.

Box 4.4

Formation of the cabinet in Japan

1. Key factions agree to form a coalition to support a particular candidate to be president of the LDP.
2. The candidate gains the support of the LDP legislators and LDP regional branches to become president through a competitive, open presidential election.
3. Under the parliamentary system, the leader of the majority party or party coalition in the Diet becomes prime minister. If the LDP or its coalition has a majority of seats in the Diet, the new president becomes prime minister.
4. Once confirmed by the Diet, the prime minister will consult with faction leaders for cabinet ministerial appointments. News reports of the appointments would often come with detailed information about the faction background of the appointees and the deals among factions behind these appointments.

A third feature of the organization of government in Pacific Asia is the role of the military junta in government. This was a phenomenon more widely seen during the Cold War (see Chapter 2) but continues to be the case in some countries. It is useful therefore to explain briefly how the military junta organizes its 'government'. Let us use the example of Myanmar.

Before Senior General Than Shwe signed a decree that officially dissolved the State Peace and Development Council (SPDC) in 2011, it was the highest body of state authority. It consisted of the chiefs of the defence services and regional (state and division) military commanders. The chairman of the SPDC was also the prime minister, the defence minister, and commander-in-chief of the defence services. There are also Peace and Development Councils at the state, district, township and village levels. These controlled the institutions of government at every level and facilitated a tight link between the military and the state. With the dissolving of the SPDC the military have slowly transferred much of the day-to-day operations of government to civilian-based institutions but at the same time they have maintained effective links to ensure their ongoing role in government. As Min Zin argues:

> There are provisions included in the Constitution for the purposes of ensuring the military's continued role in determining the pace of reforms. They include the reservation of 25 per cent of parliamentary seats for military appointees, the military's control of key ministries and even the military's right to seize power again. (Zin 2015: 311)

These exceptional features of executive governance in Pacific Asian countries suggest their ongoing dominance over other branches of government. As shown below, however, the legislature and the judiciary are increasingly acting as a check and balance on executive dominance. The evolution of an effective system of checking executive dominance is evolving slowly with democratization and liberalization in some countries and efforts to institutionalize the governing structure and shift political bargaining and decision-making into the formal organs of the state in all countries.

Parliaments, congresses and people's congresses

In discussing the changes that the Occupation authorities brought to Japan's parliamentary system in the early post-war years, a report by the Supreme Commander of the Allied Powers (SCAP) commented that, because of the introduction of the American-style standing committee system in a largely British-style parliament:

> whether the Diet becomes 'the highest organ of state power and the sole law-making body', or continues to pursue its historic role as a mere organ of discussion will depend, in the last analysis, upon the degree to which the standing committee use the powers conferred upon them and the skill with which they employ the legislative aids and devices provided in the Diet law. (SCAP, 1949: 164)

It turned out, as the report admits, and perhaps it has continued to be the case, that the emergent parliamentary system resembles neither an American Congress nor a British Parliament. At the heart of the 'structural problems' is that:

> American Congressional practice – at least in theory – rests on the Constitutional doctrine of the separation of powers. Its theoretical foundation is the sharing of political power on a basis of equality and distinction. By contrast ... Japanese parliamentary theory and practice rests on a different premise, namely, that there is a fusion of power between the executive and the legislature, with the Cabinet in effect acting as the Diet's executive committee (Baerwald, 1974: 89).

As we shall demonstrate below, there are also aspects of Japan's traditional political culture and practice in the shaping of its parliamentary system.

Box 4.5

Structures of legislature

Bicameral: Japan, Cambodia, Indonesia, Malaysia, Philippines and Thailand.

Unicameral: China, North Korea, South Korea, Laos, Singapore, Taiwan and Vietnam.

In this section, we discuss different types of legislature in Pacific Asian countries, and the unique features of each. Not including the extra-constitutional regimes such as those currently in Myanmar and Brunei, the legislatures as a branch of government are of three different types:

- Parliamentary systems, as found in Singapore, Malaysia, Cambodia and Japan;
- People's congress systems, as found in China, Vietnam, North Korea and Laos;
- Congress systems, as found in the Philippines and to a lesser extent in South Korea.

However, in the actual operation of these legislatures, some unique features are found across these categorizations.

The floor or committee room?

One key factor that separates the parliamentary system from the Congress system is the centre of legislative activity: the Congress system sees the importance of the committee system, while the Westminster model puts more emphasis on floor debate. The parliamentary systems in Singapore, Malaysia and Japan are often seen as following the Westminster model. Louis D. Hayes, for example, suggests that the Japanese model 'is a parliamentary system in the pattern of the Westminster model of Britain' (Hayes, 2005: 53; see also Stockwin, 1999: 95; Patapan et al., 2005, especially chapters 5 and 6).

The actual function of these parliaments reveals a more complicated picture. For a Westminster-style parliament, one would expect 'a more adversarial style of debate', more importance placed on plenary sessions than committee meetings, and 'a greater separation of powers among branches of government' than in the German model. Instead, in all three countries, floor debate and plenary sessions are less important and less significant for legislation. All have more concentration of power in the hands of the executive and thus less separation of powers between parliament and the executive. In the case of Japan, the committees are more important than the floor debate and substantive policy decisions on legislations are generally 'formulated outside the Diet' (Hayes, 2005: 55).

One particular detail may give you some idea of how legislatures operate in Pacific Asia. Those familiar with the US Congress and the UK Parliament may think legislatures in Pacific Asia would spend most of their time debating issues, making laws and questioning ministers. However, this is not necessarily always the case. There are basically two types of sessions in these countries: in the first type, the legislature meets only once a year for a very short period of time. This type includes most people's republics. In the Chinese case, for example, the National People's Congress meets for only a few days each year, in early March. Sessions tend to be ceremonial and an elite standing committee of the legislature manages day-to-day legislative matters. There is a second type legislative session in other countries like Japan, Taiwan and Thailand. In these countries, the normal session usually runs for several months, and extensions, extraordinary sessions and special sessions can be added.

To help in understanding the role of the legislature in the overall political system, and in particular, in their relationship with the executive, let us examine a typical process of legislation in two countries: China and Japan. Each represents a different model of political system, type of state and form of government.

The making of law

In China (see Figure 4.1), a major legislative initiative would generally pass through three stages to become a law:

- Drafting: a political decision by the Centre; that is, the CPC Politburo, to initiate a process of legislation on a particular issue. Often, a special group will be set up under the NPC to produce an initial draft, or it will be commissioned from an external research institution.
- Comment and revision: the draft will be distributed to specialists and professionals for comment. Comments will be collected for consideration and revision by the Centre.
- NPC plenary session.

The well-publicized case of the controversial Property Law that the NPC passed in March 2007 is a good illustration of this general pattern. The initiative came from the plan of the Centre in 1998 to legislate a Civil Code in three phases. In 2001, the Commission on Legal Development under the

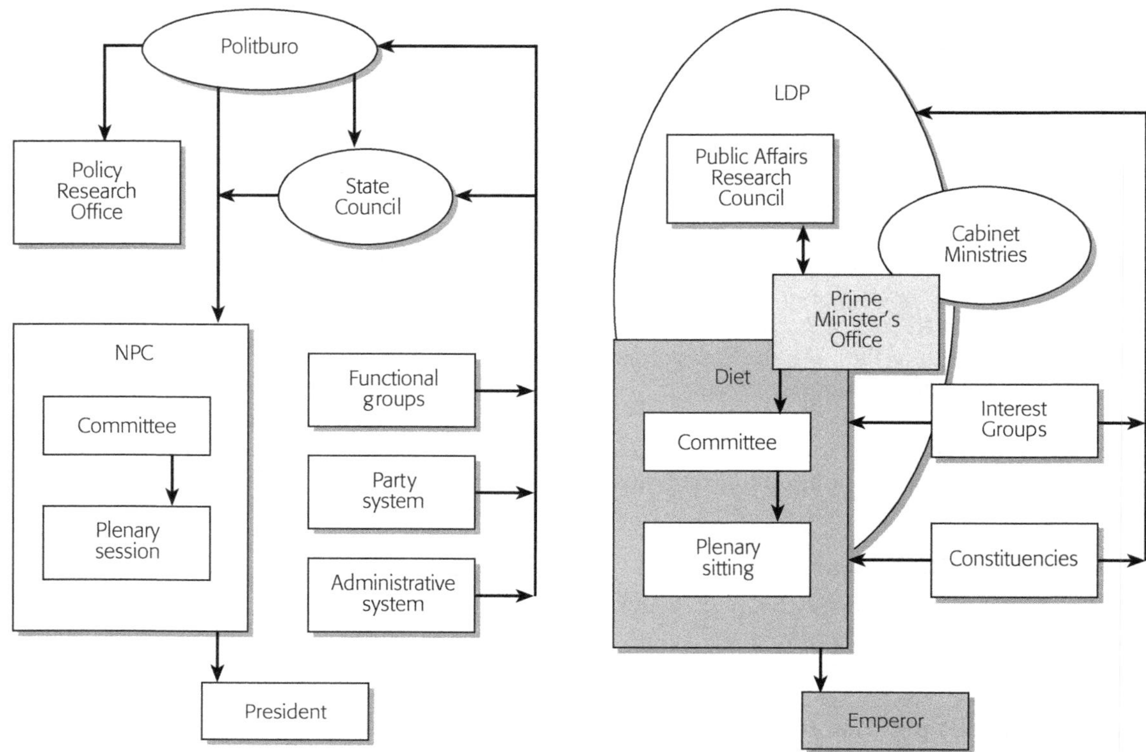

Figure 4.1 A typical process of law making in China's NPC

Figure 4.2 A typical process of law making in Japan's Diet

NPC produced a draft based on two commissioned papers by scholars at the Chinese Academy of Social Sciences and Renmin University, and distributed it to the courts at various levels for comment. From 2002 to 2007, the bill was tabled seven times at NPC plenary sessions, with each leading to a series of revisions before it was finally passed in 2007. At one point, the bill was suspended for a time because of the tensions it had created among interest groups and very strong ideologically charged oppositions.

This model of legislation is a managed process, where the Centre, through its presence at the NPC controls the initiation, content and final passage of a bill and manages its interaction with the interested public and pressure groups (see ADB, 2004: 12 for more discussion on legislation and policy processes). But unlike the old model under Mao, where law making was exclusively in the hands of the party-state, legislation in some issue areas, such as economic and social matters, is now open to organized public input. There is more involvement by the interested public, scholars and groups with a special interest in legislation in these areas.

In other issues areas, such as the Anti-Secession Law in 2006, it is still a closed process with little public input. Here, law making is very much an internal exercise. The draft will most probably come from the centre's internal research department. The way that the NPC operates, such as the session schedule discussed earlier, also facilities central control of the agenda and process.

In the case of Japan (see Figure 4.2), every member of the House has the right to introduce a bill, though the prime minister and his cabinet submit most bills. Adding to this executive heavy-handedness is the critical role played by the Policy Affairs Research Council (PARC) of the LDP, a core policy design and deliberation body. This Council has seventeen subcommittees on specific policy issues (defence, agriculture and so on) and thirty commissions on broader and long-term issues. It is the principal decision-making body of the LDP, where the interests and activities of the elite LDP legislators, government bureaucrats and interest groups, known as the 'iron triangle' (Stockwin, 1999: 96), converge. Given that most bills introduced in the Diet are from the cabinet, and that the LDP has long had control of the government, the PARC plays a pivotal role in ensuring the executive branch's dominance over the legislative process.

Let us demonstrate this process using the case of the Post Privatization Law of 2006. Privatization of Japan's postal services was Prime Minister Junichiro Koizumi's campaign pledge in 2001. The reform plan had strong opponents, however, even within the LDP itself. The key issue here was to master enough support in the Diet for the bill to be passed. In 2004, Koizumi won cabinet approval for the reform. The prime minister submitted the bill prepared by the PARC in April 2005. The bill was voted down by the Upper House, with the LDP almost splitting, and Koizumi dissolved the Lower House. His landslide victory in September paved the way for the bill to be passed in October.

This case indicates that more genuine policy debates are found in Japan's Diet than in China's NPC. Competitive party and electoral systems and institutions of accountability and transparency support genuine policy debates in the Japanese system. There are important similarities, however, between the two models. For example, the committees are a more significant platform for bill deliberation and debate than are plenary meetings. Plenary voting is almost ceremonial. More importantly, in both cases, the executive branch has clear dominance over the legislature.

Membership in the legislature

The question of membership in the legislature concerns eligibility criteria for members. In a modern democracy, this is usually not an issue, as its legislature would be broadly based, with no particular restrictions on property, religion, race or other such criteria. However, in many democracies, the upper houses still have eligibility criteria or, if by appointment, selection criteria.

Legislatures in the majority of Pacific Asian countries have no restrictions on membership. But there are two issues related to membership in the legislature. First, the overall pattern of the backgrounds of legislators can be different from what we normally see in the US Congress. Unlike the case of the US Congress, where a large number of members are either lawyers before becoming legislators, or have formal legal training, in Japan's Diet, 'the experience of most members, outside politics, has been in the world of business. Following at a considerable distance in terms of numbers are representatives formerly employed by the bureaucracy' (Hayes, 2005: 49; see also Table 4.1).

Case Study Lab 4.1

The role of parliaments in political change

Studies of Pacific Asian politics have not focused as much on parliaments as there is a widely held view that parliaments in Pacific Asian states can be just 'rubber stamps' that are largely irrelevant to the political process. Ruland, Jurgenmeyer, Nelson and Ziegenhain use an institutional approach to investigate the role of parliaments in political change. They take parliaments as a collective actor in a model of 'interrelationships between social structure, actors and institutions'. They analyse their role in politics in three critical areas:

- Whether legislatures under different forms of government are 'more conducive to the consolidation of democracy'. This involves the classic debate of presidentialism versus parliamentalism.
- Whether parliaments are more inclusive in 'integrating diverse and heterogeneous societal forces' and hence enhance the legitimacy and efficiency of state authority and institutions. This dimension of investigation is framed in the majoritarian versus consensus democracy debate.
- Different roles and contributions of parliament in different stages of political transition, in 'bringing down authoritarian regimes, in democratization and in the consolidation of democracy', using the sequential model of transition theory.

Ruland, Jurgenmeyer, Nelson and Ziegenhain, 2005: 1–12

Table 4.1 Profile of members of the Japanese Diet, 1945–90

Prime occupation	%
Business/Banking	18.5
Politics	17.3
Government	15.9
Law	7.5
Education	7.4
White collar	6.7
Journalism	6.6
Agriculture	5.4
Labour/Soc	5.1
Medicine	2.7
Blue collar	2.4
Higher education	2.1
Writing	0.7
Soka Gakkai	0.5
Religion	0.4
Women's organizations	3.0
Military	0.2
Other/None	0.2

Source: Adapted from Ramsdell, 1992: 26

Table 4.2 Allocation of delegates to the Chinese NPC

(Official Guidelines for Election of Delegates to 11th NPC, 2008)

Maximum total	3000
Hong Kong, Taiwan, Macau	2.0 (%)
PLA	8.8 (%)
Ethnic minorities	12 (%)
Returned overseas Chinese	1.2 (%)
Women	22 (%)
Workers and farmers	some

Chinese NPC

Profile of delegates to 9th NPC	1998
Government and Party officials	33.1 (%)
Military personnel	9.0 (%)
Intellectuals	21.1 (%)
Workers and peasants	18.9 (%)
Party members	70 (%)
Ethnic minorities	15.4 (%)
Women	21.8 (%)

ADB, 2004: 6

In China's NPC (see Table 4.2), the primary function of membership is a showcase of the wide representation of the population. The membership quota is therefore distributed according to government guidelines among various social sectors, such as workers, farmers and soldiers during Mao's time, and increasingly intellectuals and entrepreneurs in recent years. Table 4.2 shows the government guidelines on delegate allocation among key sectors in society for the 11th NPC in 2008 and the profile of actual delegates elected for the 9th NPC in 1998.

In Singapore's case, Chan Heng Chee notes that there is 'a predominance of the well educated as well as people with administrative and managerial backgrounds. Singapore parliamentarians are selected because they can fit into one of the four dominant roles defined as supporting the functioning of the dominant one-party system. They are either technocrats, mobilizers, Malay-vote getters or Chinese educated intellectuals' (Chan, 1987: 85–6).

There are also several unique membership requirements in some Pacific Asian countries that are of interest. These requirements are not necessarily restrictive. Many of them are to promote specific purposes or broad political agendas and social values. One category of such requirements is the representation of functional groups (see Chapter 7). Thus a percentage of the seats in the legislature are reserved for socially or politically significant groups.

Rule of law and rule by law

The role of the legislature in Pacific Asian countries needs to be understood within the larger context of the role of law. The issue here is the perceived or practiced relationship between government authority on the one hand and laws and legal procedures on the other. The problem of rule of law in Pacific Asian countries involves another concept – rule by law – that connotes a very different political science phenomenon. In the latter case, there is a utilitarian attitude towards the law on the part of government. Like economic policy, social policy or political propaganda, law becomes an instrument through which government can achieve its governing agenda.

> **Rule of law** refers to a political environment where government authority is exercised according to law. Here, law is above government authority. **Rule by law**, however, refers to a political environment where law is used by the government as a governing instrument. In this sense, government authority tends to be above the law.

As Table 4.3 shows, the level of rule of law in Pacific Asian countries varies widely, ranging from Singapore with the highest level to North Korea at a very low level. There are, however, different types of rule-of-law problems in Pacific Asian countries in relation to politics and government. First, rule of law has long been an issue in China. It is not that China does not have laws – this is very much a misperception by some China watchers. The question is whether laws apply to government authority. The debate between those of the Legalist School and those of the Confucian School in traditional Chinese political thought centred on the question of which way, moral or legal, is more effective in ensuring social order and discipline. While the legalists favoured the use of law for political and social order, law was conceived to be an instrument of government. As such, China has little traditional precedence for the law to be applied as a means to constrain government authority and a lingering issue of the state applying law to meet government agendas.

The case of Singapore is also relevant here, as Singapore is known for its wide-ranging and strident laws. One can argue that Singapore is a country of rule of law. The question is whether government authority is also subject to the law. Singapore scores incredibly highly on the rule of law indicator but some have also argued that there is an element of rule by law adherent in the system. Since the post-war years, there has been a notion that law and order was necessary for the city-state to survive in a harsh environment. In the past, this allowed the government to pass various laws to serve its political and policy agenda: whether economic development, social harmony or state security.

Table 4.3 Measuring the rule of law

	Rule of law*
Singapore	95
Japan	89
Taiwan	86
South Korea	81
Malaysia	75
Brunei	70
Thailand	51
Vietnam	45
China	43
Philippines	43
Indonesia	42
Lao PDR	27
Cambodia	17
Timor-Leste	9
Myanmar	9
North Korea	2

Note: *Units are percentile rank 0–100, with 100 as the highest
World Bank 2015

The PAP's rule has never seriously been contested and the government has been able to pass laws as it sees fit. It is therefore hard to see whether the government subjects itself to the established laws and procedures. Adding to this was the particular style of the first-generation politicians. Lee Kuan Yew's paternalist style of management left his legalist approach difficult to categorize. Lee is seen as the founding father of the country and he and his PAP were privileged in defining the boundaries of law – for the good or ill of the country. This led him and his PAP often to be seen as above the law. With the passing of the first generation, the younger generation of politicians no longer has the stature or power to secure such privileges.

A third type of rule-of-law problem is that in some countries there are prominent forces in society that see themselves as being above the law, and perhaps even above the constitution. The military is certainly one such force. For them, there is something that transcends both the law and the constitution and provides the ultimate guarantee for political order and justice.

Things have been changing in China and many other Pacific Asian countries in recent decades. The overall trend is that, with political liberalization, and democratic transition and economic development, the rule of law becomes increasingly possible and necessary because of ever more competitive and pluralist politics. Whether the greater importance of law in society leads to rule of law or rule by law will depend on the particular circumstances of each country.

Legal pluralism

In many parts of Pacific Asian countries, for religious and political reasons, different sets of law apply under different types of courts for a particular group of population, particularly on religious, personal and family matters. This is mostly seen in countries with a Muslim population such as Malaysia, Indonesia, the Philippines and even Singapore, for which Islamic law is considered appropriate for religion-related matters.

Sources of legal pluralism, where different sets of law, administered by different courts, apply to different groups of the population within the state, come also from the political process of state building where state authority has to compromise with political authority at the regional or local level where different religious political groups are not fully integrated with the national system or some form of federalism or autonomy is put in place after the political settlement. Philippine's Mindanao and Indonesia's Ache are examples of this.

Legal pluralism is also advanced in the revival of legal traditions that prevailed before modern laws were imposed after independence, or before the arrival of European colonial power with their legal system. Community and groups use these traditional legal traditions as basis to reclaim rights over properties, land in particular, and the way for regulation and governance. The revival of *adat* in Indonesia is a good example of this (Davidson and Henley, 2007).

Legal pluralism is a unique phenomenon in Pacific Asia. It reflects the political nature of the development of state institutions where different legal traditions claim their legitimacy and efficacy. At the same time, it raises a quite interesting question on a fundamental principle of the modern state and citizenship that all are equal before the law, an issue that underlies much of the political, ethnic and religious tensions in today's world that we will return to in Chapter 9.

Box 4.6

Three dimensions of legal pluralism in Indonesia

Legal pluralism is used in many contexts but actually has its origins in the historiography of Dutch colonial law. There were three dimensions to this plurality of legal systems:

- Vertical dimension: Native Indonesians were not subject to European law.
- Within the native category, different ethnic groups and communities were supposed to be governed according to their own diverse laws and customs.
- Islamic law, based on internationally authoritative interpretations of the Koran and Hadith, also received institutional support from the colonial state for inheritance and family law purposes in some predominantly Muslim regions.

Davidson and Henley, 2007: 19

Legislative powers over the executive

In Chapter 3 we discussed at length the challenge of state dominance in Pacific Asia and exceptional executive dominance over society and other branches of government. The above overview of legislatures and rule of law shows, however, that the legislature is developing as an important branch of government. As such, we can explore the degree to which the legislature can act as a check and balance of the power of the executive.

In an official document, Japan's Diet lists four principal mechanisms in its 'control of the executive' (House of Representatives, Japan, 2007):

- Election of the prime minister;
- Vote of no-confidence;
- Questions to the cabinet;
- Investigation of government.

As can be seen, however, the Diet is very respectful towards 'its executive arm'. These are obviously only the minimum number of legislative powers that are possible over the executive in a parliamentary system. Some of the important functions which are in fact not listed include:

- *The power of the purse.* One key mechanism in legislative powers over the executive is the authority to approve the government budget. Almost universally, the legislature controls the government budget, though in some countries, such as the people's republics, the approval of the budget by the legislature is only ceremonial.
- *The power of legislation.* Of course, the legislature's primary job is to make laws. Without necessary legislation, the executive's action will have no legal basis. While the government will largely get what it wants, the passing of a piece of legislation always comes with the executive's accommodation of the legislators' interests.
- *Sharing of executive power.* The legislature also enjoys some executive powers: for example, approval of international treaties, declaration of war, and consent to appointments of senior government ministers.

The powers that the legislature has over the executive can be very significant as often be seen in the US system. However, in Pacific Asia, the exercise of these powers may not be so straightforward. For example, surveys show the executive introduces the most important bills that are passed in the legislature (see, for example, Hayes, 2005: 47–57; Hayao, 1993: 33). Because of the unique alliance of the ruling party, bureaucracy and interest groups that often outmanoeuvre the legislators, the executive dominates the legislative process.

As Chapter 2 illustrated, the long period of single-party dominance in Pacific Asian countries has led to an almost permanent opposition. In this type of scenario, the opposition has resorted to unusual tactics to have their position heard or to obstruct the executive's dominance of the legislative process (see Box 4.7). However, as Baerwald (1974) points out, tactical devices are minimal in number. It is, for example, difficult to frustrate the will of a determined majority in the Diet. An old-fashioned American Senate-style filibuster cannot be mounted.

Moreover, as the period of single-party dominance ended with democratization and liberalization in the 1980s and 1990s, a series of new democracies began to experiment and develop their own relations between the legislature and executive.

In many new democracies, including Japanese democracy in the early post-war years, the competitive nature of the democratic system spurred unintended confrontations within the legislature as opposition party(s) sought to restrain the forces that controlled the executive from dominating the legislative agenda. Baerwald's study of the Japanese Diet in the 1950s provides some insight into the reasons behind these confrontations (see Box 4.8).

The consolidation of democracy in many parts of Pacific Asia has meant a peaceful transfer of power from the ruling coalition or party to another. At the same time, debates within the legislature have become formalized and physical confrontations have been reduced as they did in Japan following the 1950s.

Box 4.7

Ox walk: obstructive tactics by weak oppositions

In a legislature dominated by the executive and its ruling party, which is often the case in Pacific Asian countries, weak oppositions have to find ways to get their opposition heard. Louis D. Hayes discusses some of the tactics that Japanese oppositions use in the LDP-dominated Diet (Baerwald, 1974: 108; Hayes, 2005: 58):

- They talk or debate at length to tie up legislative business.
- They can engage in an 'ox walk', or 'snail's pace tactic', a procedure where members take an inordinate amount of time to walk a short distance to cast their ballot, as there is no time limit for taking a formal ballot.
- The conduct of business can be interrupted by members blocking the doors, the podium or the corridors of the Diet.
- Motions of no confidence.
- Although only one-third of the members are needed for a quorum (the minimum number of members required for legal proceeding of parliamentary business), a boycott of the proceedings by the opposition has been known to be effective.

Box 4.8

Confrontations inside the parliament chamber

We are familiar with scenes of legislators fighting each other inside the parliament chamber in the newly established democracies in Pacific Asia, notably in Taiwan and South Korea. Hans H. Baerwald's explanation of why 'extraordinary, similar scenes of confrontation have taken place' in Japan's Diet in the 1950s and 1960s may help us to understand the reasons behind this (Baerwald, 1974: 104):

- The ideological factor: 'the deep schism between the majority LDP and its fractured Opposition'. We can certainly see this in twenty-first-century politics in Taiwan on the issue of national identity and in Korea between conservative and progressive forces on national and foreign policy issues.
- The structural factor: internal organizational structure of the LDP and those of its Opposition parties where factionalism within a party gives little flexibility for legislators to 'trifle' with the party's positions in the Diet.
- The value factor: high value placed on loyalty and thus less willingness to compromise with opponents.
- The time factor: confrontations slow down legislation processes and are therefore used as tactics to achieve a legislative agenda.
- The electoral factor: individual legislators in Japan in the 1950s and Taiwan and South Korea at the turn of the century can use parliamentary confrontations for personal publicity and voter mobilization.

With the embedding of elections, contestation for control of government is conducted through electoral campaigns and appeals to popular opinion. While heated critique and opposition to controversial legislation remains, the consolidation of elections has provided a check on excessive executive control by one coalition of political forces. The following section rounds out the debate on the organization of government by exploring the role of the judiciary in Pacific Asian governments.

Judicial power

Supreme courts and constitutional courts

The diversity in the legislature's relationship with the executive and the underlying historical patterns of executive dominance are also found in judiciary–executive relations.

There are three types of arrangement of judicial power in Pacific Asian countries, in terms of whether they have a constitutional court, and where the constitutional court and the supreme court are located in the overall structure of government (see Box 4.9). The simple model is where the supreme court is the highest body of a multilevel court system. Japan, Singapore, the Philippines and Thailand all belong to this category. The supreme court in Japan is, for example, the highest court, and under the supreme court are the high courts, district courts, family courts and summary courts. There is no constitutional court.

In a more complex model, the supreme court is only one of the bodies of judicial power, along with the constitutional court. Indonesia, South Korea, Taiwan and Cambodia are in this category. In Taiwan, for example, under the Judicial Yuan, there is the constitutional court (Council of Grand Justices), the supreme court and other subordinate courts. The constitutional court is not necessarily the highest body of judicial power. It is a conference of grand justices that 'exercises the authority of constitutional review' (Tien, 1989: 140).

A **constitutional court** is usually a court that hears and rules cases concerning the interpretation of the constitution. In many Pacific Asian countries, there is no constitutional court. For those countries with a constitutional court, the power and influence of the court can be limited.

An **administrative court** is a court that hears and rules on cases involving the actions of the administration, usually including both the executive and the civil service of the whole government. The existence and active function of administrative courts is significant as it symbolizes a check on the executive.

The same can be said about Indonesia, where the constitutional court was set up as recently as 2003. Since it was set up to look after constitutional matters

Box 4.9

The different roles of the supreme court

Simple model:	The supreme court is the highest body of judicial power.	Japan, Singapore, Philippines, Thailand
Complex model:	The supreme court is one of the bodies of judicial power along with possibly the constitutional court	Indonesia, S. Korea, Taiwan, Cambodia
People's republic model:	The supreme court is the highest body of judicial power but accountable to the National Congress/Assembly.	China, Vietnam, Laos

that used to be under the jurisdiction of the supreme court, it is not clear whether the constitutional court is higher than the supreme court. It is only in South Korea that the constitutional court is seen as being the highest level of the four-level judicial system, with the supreme court at the second level.

A third model is the people's republic model in countries such as China, Vietnam, Laos and to some extent Cambodia. Key features of this model are:

- There is no constitutional court. Constitutional matters are under the jurisdiction of the People's Congress.
- The supreme court is the highest body of the judiciary.
- However, the supreme court is not an independent body of state power. It is accountable to the People's Congress.
- The People's Prosecuratorate is a separate branch of the judicial system.

This summary suggests that the supreme court is not necessarily the highest judicial body, as it is in the American system. In many cases, the supreme court shares the judicial power with other bodies of the judicial branch, and there is the constitutional court alongside or above the supreme court. Moreover, there are various institutional arrangements that effectively subject the judiciary to the rule of the executive. In some countries, the judiciary is not independent, but accountable to the legislature. For example, Law 14/1970 in Indonesia provides that 'each branch of the judiciary is subject in organization, administration, and finance of the ministry in which its jurisdiction is primarily concerned' (United Nations, 2005: 7). This law has been changed only recently, after the fall of Suharto.

Judicial review and judicial activism

The different roles of the supreme court lead to two important concepts in the judiciary's relationship with the other branches of government: judicial review and judicial activism.

Judicial review is a system where the court has the power and perhaps also the responsibility to make sure that laws passed by the legislature are constitutional (constitutional review) and actions by the executive are lawful (administrative review).

Judicial activism is a pattern of activity by the courts, particularly the constitutional court and supreme court, to influence the political, social and moral agenda of society through its interpretations of the constitution and fundamental principles of justice.

For a country with the system and practice of judicial review, a court will have constitutionally delegated power to do so. For various reasons, judicial review as a system has not been well institutionalized in Pacific Asian countries. This is not a problem limited only to these countries, however: Parliamentary systems generally do not provide for judicial review.

In Pacific Asia, only five out of eleven countries have a constitutional court, and four have a separate administrative court. China passed its Administrative Procedure Law in 1989 with no separate administrative court. Malaysia used to have judicial powers, even within its Westminster system, but a constitutional amendment in 1988 removed such powers. In many countries, there has been an institutional tradition that the administration of justice is under the jurisdiction of the Justice Department of the executive branch.

For constitutional review, many countries do not have a separate constitutional court. In the case of Japan, courts at all levels are empowered to review constitutional matters. Consequently, there can be conflicting rulings on constitutional matters. One high court, for example, ruled that Prime Minister Koizumi's visit to the Yasukuni Shrine was unconstitutional, while another high court found that Koizumi broke no law. This seriously compromises the power of constitutional review. For most people's congress systems, constitutional review is buried within the people's congress itself, and judicial independence does not exist.

Related to the issue of judicial review is the practice of judicial activism. If the power of judicial review is limited in Pacific Asian countries, the level of judicial activism is even more so. The concept of judicial activism is closely related to the Supreme Court of the United States in that its rulings have significant impact on both society and government. In one way, the term can imply a sense of disapproval that the court oversteps its boundary and inserts its own political or social agenda in constitutional interpretation.

In Pacific Asian countries, this is hardly an issue. In most countries, the problem is not so much that the judiciary overstretches its powers, but rather that it is still constrained within a structure of state institutions overwhelmingly dominated by the executive. As Itoh and Hayao observe in the case of Japan, the Supreme Court is 'self-restrained' from challenging the policies and actions of the LDP-dominated government (Itoh, 1989: 196; Hayao, 1993: 37).

Many studies report that the courts 'rarely showed interest in reinterpreting the law in ways that might restrict the prerogatives of the government and its bureaucracy' (Crouch, 1996: 138 on Malaysia; see also Yang, 1994: 470 on South Korea). A lack of judicial review and judicial activism, combined with a lack of judicial independence in the people's republics, means the role of the judicial branch of government in Pacific Asia as a check and balance on executive and legislature powers remains underdeveloped.

One state with three branches?

Political liberalization and democratic transition has led to a renewed interest in the independent roles and functions of the legislature and the judiciary as an ideal model for modern governance in Pacific Asia. Legislatures and judiciaries are reclaiming their roles as primary bodies of state power. The model of three independent branches of government and their checks and balances on one another appears to be a principal option for remodelling or reforming state institutions in the region.

Caution, however, is needed here in assessing the overall pattern of recent political developments. There are two aspects in Pacific Asian politics that complicate the spread of the competitive model of government structure. The first is that Pacific Asian politics has deep roots in traditional political thought, that can be traced back to pre-modern times in both Pacific Asia and Europe, and which sees the state as a coherent, integral or even 'organic' whole.

The theory of the organic state has been a controversial one, as it can be seen as subjecting individuals to the collective interests of the state (see Popper, 1963; Goggans, 2004). Some believe the concept can be traced back to the eighteenth-century political philosopher Jean-Jacques Rousseau, to seventeenth-century Thomas Hobbes, or even to Plato in ancient Greece (Conroy, 1979; Goggans, 2004).

Organic state theory sees the state as a unified and organic whole, where individuals and sectors of society are integral parts of the state. It envisages a mutually dependent relationship between state and society; central and local governments; and among branches of government.

Grand political alliance is a formal or informal framework among principal political forces for national political bargaining and consultation. It provides political support for the ruling party and its government.

The idea also has its deep roots in Pacific Asian political culture, particularly in societies where Confucian concepts of power and authority had an influence. For many in Pacific Asia, state power is unitary and non-divisible (see Chapter 3). Branches of government are instruments of state power, rather than a partial representation of the state.

Moreover, the concept underlies the relationships not only between state and society, where the controversy is usually focused, but also between the central government and local governments, and among the branches of government. On central–local relations, such a concept supports the vertical administrative control model (see Chapter 3).

With regard to the inter-branch relationship, the concept seems to be behind the original parliamentary systems, and national assembly systems and today's people's congress systems, where state power is exercised as a unified whole, symbolized and overseen by the highest body of state power, either the parliament, the national assembly or the national people's congress.

Given this strong tradition of unified state power, we shall probably continue to see less clear boundaries but more mutual dependence among branches of government in Pacific Asian countries. By definition then, this complicates the emergence of the competitive three-branch model of government.

The second aspect is the generally low level of confidence in formal institutions among politicians in Pacific Asian countries. Formal institutions here imply a binding commitment to formal rules and procedures. Informal institutions, however, usually give politicians greater room for political manoeuvre, to maximize gain with minimum risk.

The three branches of government are primary examples of formal institutions. The phenomenon of a grand political alliance (discussed in Chapter 3), is one where political forces form an alliance of interests outside the formal institutions of government. Such an alliance, such as that of the iron triangle (LDP, bureaucracy and industrial capital) allow political forces to bypass state institutions in a way that negatively impacts the ability of the legislature and judiciary to check and balance executive power.

In many ways, the role of communist parties in the people's republics is similar. They co-opt the interests of social and economic forces into the overall structure of the communist party where all major decisions and policy recommendations are formed. Until the aversion political forces have to using the formal institutions of government ends, the judiciary and legislature branches of government will not be able to act as an effective check on executive power.

Limits of executive dominance

In this chapter, we have explored the different models of the organization of government. In doing so, we have discussed the problem of executive dominance, and how it is manifested as well as constrained within the overall government structure. It is evident from the discussion that we cannot assume simplistically that the other branches of government – that is, the legislature and the judiciary – act as checks and balances on the executive. There are huge variations here. In many countries, the system of separation of power, and checks and balances are well established, but in many others they are not. To the extent that there are checks and balances, they come mainly from the legislature and not so much from the judiciary.

It should be noted that, with the political liberalization and democratic transition since the end of the Cold War (see Chapter 2), the legislature and judiciary are increasingly claiming their roles as independent bodies of state power, and there has been a growing sense of constitutional obligation on the part of the other branches of government to serve as a check on executive dominance.

Furthermore, with the restoration of competitive party and electoral systems, the legislature has emerged as a key platform for political contest, bargaining and in opposition to the ruling party. The checks and balances on the executive branch have thus gained real substance. There seems to be a clear movement towards the competitive, three-branch model of government in Pacific Asian countries. Many countries, such as Cambodia and South Korea, declare specifically in their new post-Cold War constitutions that the separation of powers among the three branches is their fundamental organizing principle for government.

However, there are some structural factors and unique institutional arrangements that have complicated such a movement, and will perhaps continue to do so. First, in a large number of Pacific Asian countries, the government is not structured into three branches, each with an equal constitutional standing. In the typical American model, all three branches are equal under the constitution. There is no single state institution considered to be, or accepted as, the highest body of state power.

In most systems in Pacific Asia, there is one state institution representing the highest state power. In parliamentary systems, for example, the parliament is often considered the highest body of state power. In the people's congress systems, the people's congress is the highest body of state power. The highest body of state power is more than a legislature. It has both constitutional and legislative powers. It appoints the heads of state and government branches.

Even in those countries that have the three branches, however, they may not play the same role. In some countries, the supreme court is merely one component of the judiciary, with no power of judicial review. In other countries, particularly in those with parliamentary systems, there is a substantial overlap between the legislature and the executive and thus genuine checks and balances on the cabinet can hardly be expected. In both cases, the legislature and the judiciary would find it hard to develop a collective identity of their own and see their definable institutional interests clearly in relation to the executive branch.

Second, there are other institutional tools that the executive can use to go around the standard branches of state power. The grand political alliance discussed above is just one such method. Aided by the party and electoral systems (see Chapter 7), this type of system allows the state to organize major political and functional interests into a non-constraining political coalition supportive of the state and its ruling ideology and platform.

Third, the roles and functions of government institutions need to be understood within the larger political structure. In the people's republics, for example, the dominance of the party-state makes any independent challenge by the legislature or judiciary impossible. In fact, the legislature and the judiciary are very much internalized as part of the party-state. They are assigned a very different set of roles and functions in support of the overall political structure and the party-state itself.

Fourth, the political culture that sees government as a unified, organic and moral whole does have an impact on the institutional make-up of government. Surveys in new democracies such as Taiwan, South Korea and Thailand show that the public dislikes partisan politics and impasses between government branches.

On balance, these factors point to the prospect that the competitive three-branch model will continue to expand its influence in Pacific Asia as the primary institutional framework for government organization. The predominance of the market economy and the new society that has emerged through Pacific Asian development provide a strong basis for the evolution of government institutions in that direction. At the same time, other organizing principles will still have a presence for various historical, structural, institutional and cultural reasons.

Chapter summary

- There are three main organizing principles of government in Pacific Asia: separation of powers, fusion of powers and unity of powers.
- The model of separation of powers and checks and balances has not been an important part of the political tradition in Pacific Asian countries.
- The strong tradition of unity of powers and executive dominance has led to a greater number of presidential and semi-presidential governments in Pacific Asia.
- Many of the parliamentary systems in Pacific Asian countries are inherited from their colonial era, but the actual practice has turned the fusion of powers largely in favour of the executive branch.
- The people's republic governments have the highest power concentration and executive dominance, and are shaped by the party-state framework as well as the political tradition of unitary state power.
- There are also a number of countries where the form of government is not based on a constitution, and the government operates very much outside the constitutional framework.

- While the legislature is traditionally weak in Pacific Asian governments, the judiciary is even more so. In many of the Pacific Asian countries, the judicial powers to check on the other branches of government are almost non-existent.
- Besides the three branches of government, ruling elites in Pacific Asian countries have developed many alternative mechanisms or institutions of governance. The grand political alliance is one such alternative mechanism.
- Political liberalization and democratic transition since the 1980s have brought change to the functioning of the three-branch model of government. Executive dominance has been weakened to some extent. The separation of powers model has gained prominence.

Further reading

On forms of government in Pacific Asian countries: Hassall and Saunders (2002), UN Public Administration Country Profiles (United Nations, 2005–2007) and ADB Country Governance Assessment Reports (1999–2005) are good introductions on most countries in Pacific Asia; see Wescott (2001) on Cambodia, Laos, Thailand and Vietnam and Bowornwathana and Wescott (2008) on Thailand, Hong Kong, Indonesia, China, Taiwan, South Korea, Japan and for general introductions to the World Bank governance indicators in the region. Wanna and Weller (2005) discuss the Westminster model in Pacific Asian countries. Baerwald (1974) gives a more critical examination of Japan's Diet.

On the problem of rule of law in Pacific Asia, Peerenboom's volume (2004) gives a country-by-country investigation of the problem, as well as an overview of the debate in a broader international context and perhaps within the framework of the liberal tradition. With the same comparative appeal, Jayasuriya's volume (1999) presents a more sophisticated view exploring the relationship of legal institutions with the broader economic, social and political conditions. Turner (2015) provides a case study on the rule of law in China.

For comparative constitutional law in Asia see Dixon and Ginsburg (2014). Finally, Rosett et al. (2002) explore the broad issue of the tension between universal legal concepts and practices, cultural traditions and institutions in Pacific Asia.

Study questions

1. Why has the system of checks and balances been generally weak in Pacific Asian governments?
2. How useful and effective are those concepts such as separation of powers, and checks and balances for analysing the organization of government in Pacific Asian countries?
3. How have traditional political structures and practices affected the organization of government in Pacific Asian countries?
4. What is the difference between 'rule of law' and 'rule by law'? Can the different approaches to law help to explain government structures in Pacific Asia?
5. Has the separation of power model gained predominance as a primary principle for organizing government in Pacific Asia?
6. Does organic state theory provide a useful analytical tool for understanding the organization of government in Pacific Asian countries?

Key terms

Form of government (101); Organizing principles of government (101); Presidential system (102); Parliamentary system (104); Party-state system (107); People's congress (105); Rule of law (114); Rule by law (114); Legal pluralism (116); Constitutional court (118); Administrative court (118); Judicial review (119); Judicial activism (119); Organic state theory (120); Grand political alliance (120).

Chapter 5
In the name of the state: bureaucracy and public service

Pacific Asian countries have a long tradition of sophisticated bureaucratic systems. The bureaucracy plays a great role in administering government, formulating public policy and managing the overall political system, to the extent that some countries in the region are referred to as bureaucratic states.

At the same time, during much of the Cold War the political executive overwhelmingly dominated the bureaucracy. The overall political environment meant political power was highly concentrated in the hands of the political elite who employed the bureaucracy as an 'organizational weapon' of the state. This compromised the professionalism and accountability of the bureaucracy and the responsiveness of public policy to the interests and demands of the public.

As in other parts of the world, there have been substantive efforts in Pacific Asia to reform the public sector. The global 'good governance' movement, political liberalization and democratization and development have created pressure for administrative reform. Questions remain, however, as to how successfully these reforms have enhanced the efficiency, effectiveness and responsiveness of the bureaucracy and reshaped the problematic bureaucracy–politics relationship common in the Cold War era.

Bureaucrats are those permanently employed to carry out government functions. **Bureaucracy** is the system in which bureaucrats are organized and bureaucratic functions are performed in the formulation, implementation and enforcement of public policy and regulations and the delivery of public services.

Let us first clarify some of the key concepts used in this chapter. There are several related terms in discussions of bureaucracy: public administration, public service, civil service and public sector. These terms refer more or less to the same parts of the political system and the same group of people in society – though their boundaries may vary and the contexts in which these terms are used may be slightly different. 'Bureaucratic arena', as Goran Hyden, Julius Court and Ken Mease put it, 'refers to all state organizations engaged in formulating and implementing policy as well as in regulating and delivering services' (Hyden et al., 2003: 2).

The word 'public' is used in the context of modern society where the public – the arena of government – and the private – the arena of private citizens – replaces the monolithic royal framework. 'Civil' here also implies the bifurcation of the public and the private. Civil service is the service provided by government for citizens in the private sector. In essence, public service and civil service are two terms that mean the same thing.

Bureaucrats are those permanently employed to carry out government functions, and the bureaucracy is the system in which the bureaucrats are organized and bureaucratic functions are performed. As we shall see in this chapter, what makes the problem of bureaucracy more challenging in Pacific Asia is not only those generic issues that affect bureaucracy in any country, but also the specific issues associated with the traditional structure, the challenge of industrialization and modernization and ongoing political development in Pacific Asian countries.

In this chapter, we locate the bureaucracy in the overall political system and discuss the range of roles it performs. We review the politician-bureaucrat relationship during the Cold War and analyse the post-Cold War public sector reforms. Finally, we compare measures of good governance across a range of Pacific Asian countries.

In the name of the state

The bureaucratic tradition in Pacific Asia, particularly in Northeast Asia, is long and sophisticated. The extraordinary *Travels of Marco Polo*, the first populist European account of life in China, India and Japan in the thirteenth century, attests to the complexity of the governing structure and in particular, the splendour of the Chinese court. This and the following works of translators and Jesuit missions from the seventeenth century onwards had a great influence on the thinking of scholars and officials in the formation of the early European state system (Jones, 2001). They described a unified empire with a large population and sophisticated systems of organizing, administering and governing a highly diverse population. As we shall see in this chapter, however, the bureaucratic systems that evolved in the Pacific Asian tradition, while not dissimilar to those of Europe, have certain unique emphasis, such as a focus on maintaining a moral political order.

Here we discuss the role of working for government in Pacific Asia by first outlining the traditional bureaucratic structure and discussing how it evolved in the process of modern state building. This is followed by a discussion of the position of bureaucrats in contemporary Pacific Asian society that shows the social status of public servants is comparatively high due to the social value placed on working for government.

From emperors' servants to public servants

In their examination of the historical evolution of bureaucracy, Jos C. N. Raadschelders and Mark R. Rutgers divided the development of modern bureaucracy into chronological periods in the rise of the modern state (see Box 5.1). The premodern roots of the modern bureaucracy were similar: bureaucrats were originally servants of the emperor.

This was more so in Northeast Asia than Southeast Asia because of the stronger imperial system that developed in Northeast Asia (see Chapter 1). Bureaucrats turned from being the servants of the emperor to being the servants of the state, according to Raadschelders and Rutgers, around the seventeenth century in Europe. In Northeast Asia, key elements of the modern European state, such as population, territory, government, army, organized political community, and economic, social and legal institutions, existed long before they arose in Europe. The bureaucrats were therefore the servants to both the emperor and the state for quite some time.

Consequently, the development of a modern bureaucracy in Pacific Asia features a prolonged dominance over state institutions by bureaucratic

Box 5.1

Raadschelders–Rutgers model of bureaucratic evolution

- Origins in the Catholic Church during the Middle Ages (11th and 12th centuries).
- Bureaucrats as personal servants to emperors and kings (13th century).
- Bureaucrats as state servants with the rise of nation-states (17th century).
- Bureaucrats as public servants with demarcation between public and private, and between the political and administrative (late 18th century).
- Bureaucracy as a protected service with job security from political interference or arbitrary dismissal (mid-19th century).
- Bureaucracy as a professional service with recruitment, training and specialization (20th century).

Raadschelders and Rutgers, 1996: 71–88

elites in collaboration with the ruling political elites. There are diverse experiences in the development of a modern bureaucracy and its relationship with other institutions and forces. But these experiences revolved around some key issues in modern political development, namely:

- The relationship between the ruling political regime and the bureaucracy.
- The role of the bureaucracy in government, politics and policy.
- The qualities of modern bureaucracy in terms of its capacity, efficiency and professionalism.

At the heart of these issues is the bureaucracy's relationship with the political executive and the question to whom the bureaucracy is accountable.

Raadschelders and Rutgers' categorization is clearly a reflection of the European experience. They recognize their discussions 'pertain to developments in the West' and challenge us to 'compare Western developments with those elsewhere in order to verify the contingencies and universalities of the development of civil service systems' (1996: 90). The picture of how bureaucratic relationships developed in Pacific Asian countries is more complicated. There are several reasons for the different paths (see Box 5.2) the modern bureaucracy has taken to evolve in Pacific Asia:

- Strong statist tradition in Pacific Asia retained the bureaucrats primarily as servants to the state.
- Colonial rule in much of Pacific Asia tied the bureaucracy to the system rather than to the public.
- The national drive for industrialization and modernization firmly turned the bureaucracy into the 'organizational weapon' of the state (Selznick, 1952).

The process of modern state building in Pacific Asia (see Chapter 2) has complicated the transformation of bureaucrats from servants of the emperor to public servants. In particular, the non-pluralist states that emerged with the failure of pluralist politics in the post-war years created a bureaucracy that was tightly aligned with the interests of the ruling coalition of conservative forces.

Scholar-officialdom is a system of scholars becoming government officials through a competitive examination system and performing both roles of scholarly adviser and government official in China.

As Box 5.2 shows, by the 1960s in all states in the region the bureaucracy was no longer a servant of the royal family, court, king or emperor. At the same time, nor were they public servants according to

Box 5.2

Bureaucrats as servants: the paths of Pacific Asia

	1910	*1960*	*1990s*
China	Emperor/State	Party/State	Transitional
Indonesia	Colonial	Party/State	State/Public
Japan	Emperor/State/Professional	State/Party/Professional	Public
Korea	Colonial	State	Public
Malaysia	Colonial/Party/State	State	State/Public
Singapore	Colonial	Party/State/Professional	State/Public
Taiwan	Colonial	Party/State	Public
Thailand	King	State	Public
Philippines	Colonial	State/Public	Public
Vietnam	Colonial	Transitional	Party/State

Raadschelders and Rutgers' definition. The demarcation between public and private and between politicians and bureaucrats was not yet fully developed and these officials lacked independence from political forces. In many cases, such as in Singapore and Japan, the bureaucracy first developed as a professional service with strict training and specialization. This process is akin to the rise of China's 'technocrats' today (see Lee, 1991). However, China's bureaucracy went through a highly tumultuous period before becoming the technical arm of the state-led industrialization, reform and opening programmes.

In a critique of China's Mao era bureaucracy (1949–1976), Eddy U (2007) argues Marxist-Leninist regimes, in particular China, failed to establish modern bureaucratic administrations. Instead, both Lenin and Mao favoured concepts of bureaucracy clearly antagonistic to the modern form of bureaucracy as espoused by Max Weber. China developed an administration that represented 'the mirror image of the rational bureaucracy'. This form of bureaucracy was neither modern nor traditional in the Weberian sense and 'was the principal reason for the decline of Soviet-type societies'. For U, Mao era administration represented a case of 'counter-bureaucracy', the antithesis of a modern Weberian bureaucracy which proved ultimately 'counter-productive to the welfare of Soviet-type societies' (U, 2007: xi, 9–10).

By the 1990s, only Japan, Korea, Taiwan, Thailand and the Philippines had made the transition to a bureaucracy that served the public. In the other states, the bureaucracy remained a servant of the state, servant to a particular political party or in a transitional state. Bureaucratic evolution in Pacific Asia, like the overall evolution of the state and form of government, has therefore been complicated by traditional practices and competing ideologies, in particular communism and Confucianism, and the tension between a focus on economic development and order on the one hand, and equality and public interest on the other.

The best and the brightest: bureaucracy as a social class

Civil servants traditionally enjoyed great social prestige and to a large extent, this is still the case in Pacific Asia. There are several reasons for their prestigious position in society: first, the traditional system of scholar-officialdom rendered bureaucrats more than simply desk clerks implementing policy made by the political executive. They were the core of state institutions. Those in the scholar-officialdom system performed functions that would be allocated to the political executive, bureaucrats, scholars and think tanks, public educators, and social and moral elites in a modern state. Institutionally, this scholar-officialdom system has long broken down as modern institutions have developed in these counties. But socially and culturally, those working in government are still expected to live up to these traditional roles.

Meritocracy is an idea and a principle of government and society that bureaucratic recruitment, appointment and promotion, and a person's advance in society in general, should be based on the person's ability, performance and contributions, rather than the person's race, gender, religion, age or popularity (see Young, 1958).

The second reason for the bureaucracy's prestigious position in society is related to the scholar-officialdom system, namely, the examination system that recruited the best and the brightest from society to work in government. This examination system was generally open to everyone and, in the traditional hierarchical society with a highly centralized and exclusive political and policy process, ensured a level of competent bureaucrat recruitment. This examination system has been largely inherited in Pacific Asian countries, notably in Singapore, Japan and now in China. In countries like Singapore, a more robust merit-based system of government recruitment, appointments and promotion has developed. This is often called the system of meritocracy.

Meritocracy is not new or unique to Pacific Asia (Young, 1958; McNamee and Miller, 2004), but several factors make the practice in Singapore unique. Singapore's adoption of meritocracy occurred with the historical context of its troubled relationship with Malaysia, where privileging of Malays emerged as a constitutional principle, and Chinese-dominated Singapore felt marginalized in the union. There was therefore a political element to the adoption of meritocracy in the newly independent Singapore. This then became a key element in Singapore's model of state-ethnic group relations (see Chapter 9).

Singapore has also long been seen as a country with weak pluralist politics. Meritocracy is often perceived in the debate as something in contrary to or in lieu of democracy.

COUNTRY PROFILE

SINGAPORE

		Regional Comparison	World Rank
GDP	454 (ppp/bil)	1.39% of PA-18	40th (of 189)
HDI	0.901 (0 to 1)	PA-18: 1st	9th (of 186)
WGI	1.6 (–2.5 to 2.5)	PA-18: 2nd	88 (%)

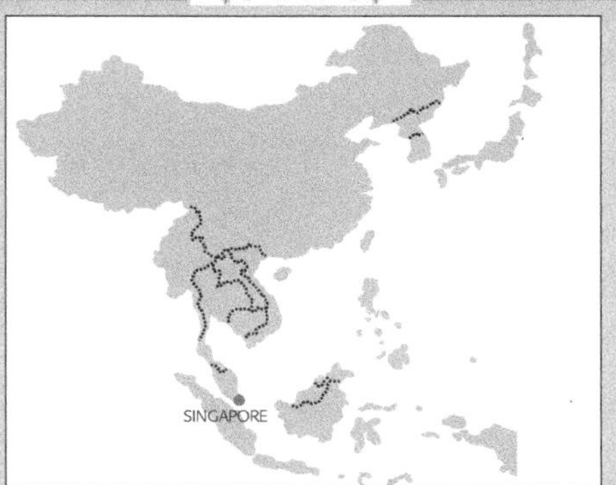

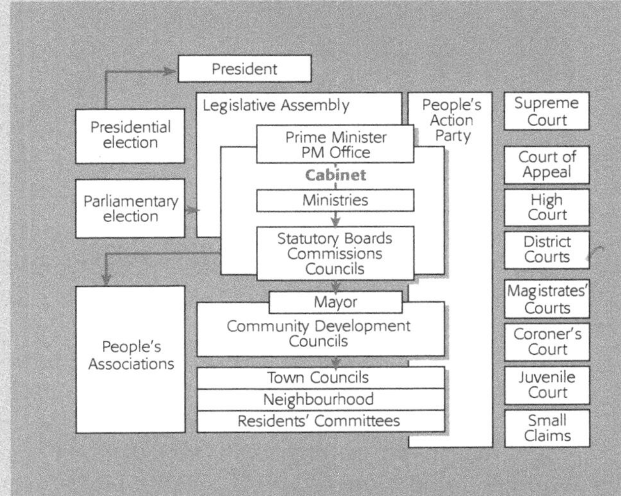

Key political facts

Electoral system for National Legislature

First-past-the-post for single-member districts and multi-member blocks, and arrangements for special seats;

Voting is compulsory.

Political cycles

Parliamentary elections every five years;

Presidential elections every six years;

Annual budget to be enacted by Parliament in March.

Further reading

Low and Vadaketh, 2014; Hass, et al., 2014; Barr, 2008.

Timeline of modern political development

1955 Rendel Constitution for limited self-government; Legislative Assembly established.
1958 State of Singapore Act and Constitutional Agreement establish Singapore.
1959 Singapore Order-in-Council establishes self-government; PAP election victory.
1961 Economic Development Board and Housing Development Board established.
1963 Forms Malaysia with Malaya.
1965 Separates from Malaysia and becomes an independent republic.
1967 National Service introduced.
1968 Central Provident Fund established.
1970 Presidential Council for Minority Rights established.
1984 Non-constituency Members of Parliament (NCMP) introduced; first time opposition parties elected to parliament.
1988 Electoral reform: Group Representation Constituencies (GRCs) introduced.
1990 Nominated Members of Parliament (NMPs) introduced.
1990 Lee Kuan Yew steps down after 31 years as prime minister.
1991 Constitutional amendment to provide for a popularly elected president.
2004 Lee Hsien Loong, Lee Kuan Yew's son, becomes prime minister.
2007 Petition to repeal the Victorian law that criminalizes homosexuality.
2013 Riot of foreign workers over the death of an Indian migrant worker.
2013 Huge demonstrations against government plan to boost population.
2015 Government introduces stronger measures against corruption.
2015 The ruling party, People's Action Party, wins general election after the nation's founding father, Lee Kuan Yew passes away. The PAP has been the ruling party since 1959, the longest in Pacific Asia.

Box 5.3

Becoming a civil servant in Japan

- Open and equal access: no education or other requirements.
- Examinations

Comprehensive		Competitive
Stage I:	general culture and special knowledge on the chosen field	2–10 per cent pass rate
Stage II:	essays or problem-solving questions	
Stage III:	Physical examination and background investigation	Success rate: 36:1 (1980, A-level)

- Actual hiring: by individual ministry or agency. Hiring rate: 50 per cent (higher levels)

Koh, 1985

For a country with few natural resources and complex racial relations that often tend to complicate efforts in industrialization and modern state building, meritocracy is believed to be a major contributor to Singapore's success story.

> 'To study and excel, and to serve in government'
> *Xue er you ze shi.*
> *Analects of Confucius*: Zi Zhang

In countries where pluralist politics is restricted and corruption rampant, an examination system can ensure the quality of bureaucratic recruitment.

Table 5.1 Government employees as a percentage of the total labour force

Country	*Year*	*%*
China	2000	32.08
Japan	1998	0.8
South Korea	1999	4.08
Malaysia	1998	7.7
Philippines	1998	4.52
Singapore	1999	33.9
Taiwan	2000	10.06
Thailand	2000	8.1

Cheung and Scott, 2003: 288–309.

Some use this to explain the success in social and economic development in Pacific Asian countries where democratic development lags behind economic development.

A third reason for the high status of the bureaucrats in society is related to the material benefits that their position brings. Civil servants are well paid and their positions come with various benefits and privileges. In Singapore, high salaries for civil servants are a deliberate policy to attract the best and the brightest. In Taiwan, one strange policy associated with the old KMT regime allowed civil servants to have an 18 per cent interest rate on their pension savings. In China, government officials have long been a special class, with job security, social status, material benefits in housing, medical care, pensions and job subsidies, as well as access to political power and resources that can increasingly be turned into material benefits. To be selected for the public service, therefore, is an indication of personal success and family glory.

Not only do civil servants enjoy relatively good job security, but their public service also allows them to take lucrative positions in the private sector after they retire from or opt out of public service. Because of the knowledge, personal relations and contacts they have accumulated in their bureaucratic positions, they are highly sought after in the private sector. In Japan, this phenomenon is called 'descent from heaven'.

'Descent from heaven' is 'the Japanese term for the practice whereby senior civil servants, having reached their terminal government position around age 45 to 55, become 'counsellors' to big companies' (Drucker, 1998: 69). This practice indicates the privileged position of civil servants and the close link between the government bureaucracy and the business community.

Indeed, civil servants in Pacific Asia form a unique social class in their own right – a tradition found in the roots of imperial China, traditional Korea, and feudal Japan.

Bureaucracy and the political executive

The diverse experiences in the shaping of the bureaucracy's relationship with the political executive, the public and society at large have led to three dominant types of bureaucracy-political executive relations in Pacific Asia during the Cold War era (see Box 5.4). At one end of the spectrum, the Chinese bureaucratic system inherited much of the essential elements of its imperial system (Herson, 1957; Frederickson, 2002). It features:

- Strong centralized political control of the bureaucracy;
- Sophisticated checks and balances among various sectors and levels of the bureaucratic system;
- A heavy reliance of the political executive on the advice and expertise of the bureaucrats in decision-making and implementation;
- The moral justification of the bureaucracy's role and functions.

The revolutionary ideology, socialist command economy and the party-centred political apparatus during Mao's rule in the early decades of the People's Republic of China only served to reinforce the traditional bureaucratic system. In particular, a unique system of cadre recruitment, deployment and promotion developed, a system often referred to as the 'nomenklatura system' (Burns, 1987) where the bureaucracy became primarily the tool of the party-state.

The nomenklatura is a select class of political elite who occupy senior political and administrative positions in central and local government, bureaucracy, the military, courts, social organizations, universities and all other institutions and organizations of political significance. The nomenklatura system is a system of selection, training, appointment, promotion and removal of the nomenklatura to those senior positions by the Communist Party's personnel department. This system has been a core part of the party-state in the former communist countries.

This is the standard interpretation of China's bureaucracy. However, scholars such as U (2007) have questioned the applicability of this interpretation to the Chinese bureaucracy during the Mao era. U argues that under the Maoist government, in particular during the Cultural Revolution, China's most pressing problem was a lack of bureaucratic capacity. U argues a 'counter-bureaucracy' severely impaired the ability of the state to formulate and implement government policy and was a major factor in the failure of the socialist planned economy.

The **nomenklatura system** 'consists of lists of leading positions over which party committees exercise the power of appointment, lists of reserve cadre for the available positions, and the institutions and processes for making the appropriate personnel changes. The system is arguably the major instrument of Communist Party control over contemporary China's political, economic, social and cultural institutions. Through nomenklatura, a variant of which is employed by all communist parties in power, authorities ensure that leading institutions throughout the country will exercise only the autonomy granted to them by the party.'

Burns, 1987: 36

At the other end of the spectrum is what is often referred to as the bureaucratic polity, as Fred W. Riggs found in Thailand in the 1960s (Riggs, 1966). In contrast to the Chinese bureaucratic model, under this model there was no effective political control of the bureaucracy in Thailand. Because of the frequent changes of political regime and control of government by the military elite for much of the period after 1932, the political executive – that is the prime minister – that usually exercised control over the bureaucracy tended to be very weak. The military

Box 5.4

Models of the political executive–bureaucracy relationship before recent reforms

Bureaucracy under the	*Relation to political executive*	*Role in politics and policy process*
Chinese bureaucratic model	Controlled by	Neutral and isolated
Thai bureaucratic polity	Dominant over	Dominant
Japanese bureaucratic state	Alliance with	Competitive and isolated

elites relied heavily on the bureaucratic elites for governance. 'Pariah entrepreneurs' (Ockey, 2004: 144) and society at large depended on the bureaucratic elites for access to policy processes. Consequently, there was dominance by the bureaucratic elites not only over the state, but also over society.

Bureaucratic polity is a term used by Fred W. Riggs to describe the political system in Thailand in the 1960s where the bureaucratic elites dominated the state, economy and society.

While the Riggs model dominated views of the bureaucracy in Thailand and the nature of the Thai political system from the 1930s to the 1990s, scholars are questioning whether, or to what extent, the bureaucratic elites enjoyed exclusive dominance. For some, the bureaucratic elites were not a self-interested entity, but part of the state apparatus or government alliance that shared political dominance (Ockey, 2004: 146).

Between these two models is the bureaucratic state of Japan. The modern and national bureaucracy began to emerge around the time of the Meiji Restoration, designed, according to T. J. Pempel, to serve as an instrument for modernization and industrialization. Laws provided the necessary legal basis for its functions and activities. The bureaucrats, recruited through open competition based on knowledge and training, saw themselves as the servants of the emperor and as an integral part of the state. However, they stayed neutral and outside of politics (Pempel, 1992). One key element in the early development of the modern bureaucracy was the 'differentiation' of politicians and bureaucrats (Inoguchi, 2005: 92). The bureaucracy was seen as the primary policymakers and implementers, while politicians and political parties were marginalized.

The US occupation and the MacArthur Revolution introduced politics into state matters and thus reduced the influence of the bureaucracy (Pempel, 1992: 20). In fact, it forced an alliance between state bureaucrats and elected officials. Their further collaboration with the industrial capital formed the 'iron triangle' (see Chapters 6 and 8) that underlay the post-war Japanese political system.

The bureaucratic state in Japan therefore features a close collaboration between the political executive and bureaucratic elites. Political and bureaucratic elites performed different functions in the name of the state. In this model, there is no overwhelming dominance of one over the other as seen in the Chinese bureaucratic model or the Thai model of bureaucratic polity. But in all the three cases, the state institutions are strong and effective.

It is worth pointing out that these fixed models are summaries of the politics–bureaucratic relationships during the Cold War. Political changes and bureaucratic reforms since the 1990s have transformed much of the bureaucratic system in these countries, which we shall turn to later in this chapter.

Bureaucracy as an 'organizational weapon of the state'

Philip Selznick invented the concept of bureaucracy as the organizational weapon of the state (Selznick, 1952). His work was mainly an investigation of how the Soviet party-state worked and how the cadre system in the Soviet Union was designed to serve as an instrument of the state. The bureaucracy as an organizational weapon of the state in Pacific Asia

Case Study Lab 5.1

The close relations between the political executive and bureaucracy in Thailand

There is a close relationship and mutual dependency between the cabinet and the bureaucracy in Thailand. The bureaucracy plays a significant role in government and policy. Thak Chaloemtiarana uses the power structure in the Thai political system to explain:

- The lack of power centres or policymaking groups outside of the bureaucracy;
- Why political parties and parliament have always played secondary roles to the executive branch of government, which has manipulated or represented them according to their needs and circumstances;
- How periodic coups and attempted coups by military and civilian groups have helped make the solid institutionalization of party and parliamentary system very difficult;
- How the lack of any organized countervailing forces means the 'government lite' has usually become the spokesmen for and instruments of the bureaucracy;
- How the political elite has acted in the interests of the bureaucracy by providing job security, status and privileges, and how the bureaucracy in turn has carried out the programmes of the elite. Without the bureaucracy's support, the regime in power has been helpless to implement its policies.

Chaloemtiaranba 2007: 182

goes beyond the communist framework back to the pre-modern history of Japan, Korea, Taiwan and China. This is evident in the post-war industrialization and rapid economic development of communist and non-communist states.

While the conditions controlling exactly how the bureaucracy performed its role as the weapon of the state were different from country to country, two overall mechanisms were widely found in these countries. These permitted:

- Maximum authority of the political executive to ensure an uncontested political environment that favoured the growth of industrial capital.
- Maximum freedom of the bureaucracy to exercise technical and managerial power to ensure the support of the economic and financial institutions and effective implementation of policies and programmes.

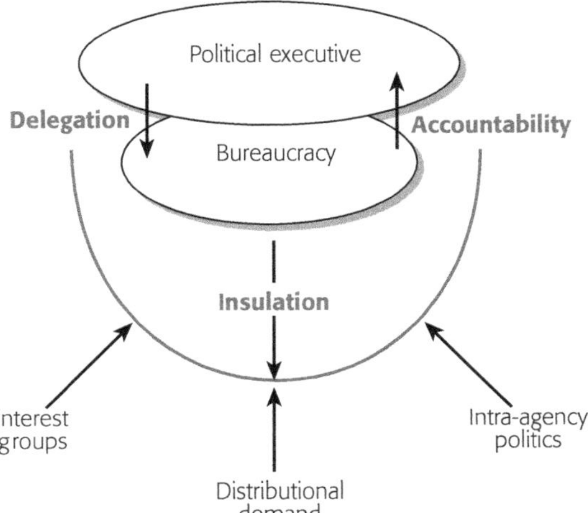

Figure 5.1 Authority delegation and bureaucratic insulation

Authority delegation is a practice of government where the political executive delegates decision-making powers to its loyal, dedicated bureaucratic elites. **Bureaucratic insulation**, on the other hand, is a practice in which the political executive exercises political power and authority to fend off popular and distributional demands from the public and from special interest groups regarding the bureaucracy's decision-making and policy implementation, and to take political responsibility for what bureaucrats do. In both cases, it requires upward accountability from the bureaucracy to the political executive.

The first mechanism is called bureaucratic insulation and the second, authority delegation. Authority delegation and bureaucratic insulation were found in most Pacific Asian countries, particularly during the Cold War, when highly concentrated authority in one form or another dominated (see Figure 5.1).

But authority delegation and bureaucratic insulation were not simply a division of labour between the political executive and bureaucratic elites. Instead, it was more a solution to the fundamental problem of economic development under this type of political environment.

In a non-pluralist political environment, there is what Tun-Jen Cheng, Stephan Haggard and David Kang call 'the authoritarian's dilemma' (Cheng et al., 1998: 87). On the one hand, the political executive had to convince bureaucrats of 'the security of property rights and the stability of a given strategy', which was essential for the type of economy they were developing. But on the other hand, it was the very nature of an authoritarian system that the political executive could 'change policy at will' and was not subject to laws and regulations that could curb their power to intervene in the private sector. A solution was to 'grant decision making powers to relatively insulated technocratic agencies' (ibid., 1998: 87). The study by Cheng et al. details the bureaucratic reforms in Korea and Taiwan in the 1960s, and how the reformed bureaucracy effectively supported the broader policy projects of the political executive.

Moreover, in many countries, the military (as in South Korea, Thailand and Indonesia) or revolutionary soldiers (as in China) were in fact the political executive. They had neither the expertise nor the experience of running a government or managing the country and had to rely on bureaucratic elites for ambitious projects of state building, economic growth and social development.

Typically, the political executive would delegate authority to a powerful intra-departmental agency in a particular policy area (see Box 6.3 in Chapter 6). In the area of industrialization and economic development, which was the primary government project for most Pacific Asian countries during the Cold War, there was almost universally some form of economic decision-making board that planned, coordinated and implemented economic growth and development at the highest level. Such a board would have the full trust of the political executive; political and personal loyalty to the political executive; and absolute authority in economic decision-making and implementation. This board was accountable only to the political executive.

Case Study Lab 5.2

Strong bureaucratic tradition in Japan

Takashi Inoguchi uses a historical institutionalist and political economy approach to explain the strong bureaucratic tradition in Japan. He traces the tradition to the Tokugawa era in the sixteenth and seventeenth centuries where the bureaucratic ideology developed among Japanese elite to reorganize the state and build a strong state to meet the military and economic threat from the West:

- The basis of the Japanese bureaucracy is meritocratic rather than partisan. The warriors transformed into bureaucrats over farmers, artisans and merchants, as they seem more capable of performing modern bureaucratic functions.
- The emergent national aspiration to be a 'rich nation' with a 'strong military' fostered a bureaucratic ideology that turned the bureaucracy as the primary instrument in mobilizing national resources, organizing state capacity, coordinating national programmes and activities in the name of the state.
- The emergent Meiji State was based on the emperor system, the bureaucracy and the military. The bureaucracy played an important role as the servant of the Emperor, in legislation, in decision-making and implementation for public policy.
- The bureaucracy's role was further augmented by the necessity for war mobilization in the 1930s and the weakening of other political groups after Japan's defeat in 1945.

Inoguchi, 2005: 4–12

The level of delegation from the political executive to bureaucrats varies. In some countries, such as Taiwan, the political executive left much of the economic management and decision-making to the bureaucratic elites. In other cases, such as South Korea, the political executive took a hands-on approach to economic matters. Charles Wolf observed in 1962 that 'in assigning the task of plan formulation to the [Economic and Planning] Board the SNCR [Supreme Council for National Reconstruction] provided it with a basic plan framework which specified the broad strategy and overall objectives of the new plan, including an average annual growth rate and national targets for the principal economic variables, as well as for the principal sectors' (Wolf, 1962: 24). President Park Chung-hee reportedly often personally sat on the export promotion board meetings.

The Weberian ideal and Pacific Asian practices: patrimonialism and corruption

Bureaucratic power, whether growing out of the strong statist tradition or because of the challenge of managing mass society and economy, is not unique to Pacific Asian countries. But Pacific Asian countries have faced unique challenges in developing state institutions and a modern bureaucracy. Max Weber is the main intellectual force behind the concept of modern bureaucracy (Weber 1947, 1968). In his original conception, there are at least three key qualities defining a modern bureaucracy. A modern bureaucracy would:

- Have clearly specified official duties and jurisdiction;
- Be regulated by impersonal rules;
- Be staffed by full-time, life-long professionals on a fixed salary and recruited on the basis of their technical qualifications and professional training.

Each of these is important for the modern bureaucracy, but points 2 and 3 are especially significant for Pacific Asia. Impersonal rules are the foundation of modern institutions. Only when the power of rules is not dependent on any particular person or group and when these rules can be applied universally to everyone, can the rules be effective and bureaucratic functions efficient.

In Max Weber's original conception, **patrimonial bureaucracy** refers to a type of bureaucratic system where a bureaucrat's official jurisdiction and his personal properties and interests are not effectively separated.

In many Pacific Asian countries, where personal relations are crucial and the loyalty and trust between the political executive and bureaucratic elites discussed above can be very personal, this has always been a problem. Bureaucrats can act and apply rules very differently depending on with whom they are dealing. The effectiveness of rules can vary significantly depending on who uses the rules, for what purposes and how.

The essence of point 3 is about the relationship between bureaucrats and their office and jurisdiction. In the modern bureaucracy as envisaged by Weber there is a clear distinction between the interests of the public office that a bureaucrat occupies and the bureaucrat's private interests. A fixed salary and job security separate the bureaucrat's jurisdiction from his/her personal well-being. This, according to Weber, ensures the efficiency of bureaucratic responsibilities is not comprised by personal interest. It is 'patrimonial', according to Weber, when bureaucrats mix their official jurisdiction with their personal interests.

The concept of patrimonialism builds on Weber's original idea to connote a (deliberate) practice by politicians and bureaucrats of mixing public offices and private interests, and pursuing personal interests with official jurisdiction in a broad governmental setting.

Patrimonialism is prevalent in Pacific Asia. Mixing of public jurisdiction and personal interests provides much of the institutional foundation for corruption, cronyism and nepotism in Pacific Asian government and politics, particularly in its bureaucracy. According to Transparency International's 2016 Corruption Perceptions Index (CPI), a widely used index on perceptions of public sector corruption in 168 countries and territories based on a range of surveys, Pacific Asian country rankings are spread evenly across the index (see Table 5.2), with Singapore and Japan being the cleanest and Myanmar, Cambodia and North Korea the most corrupt. Moreover, Northeast Asian countries are generally found in the better part of the ranking, with the

Table 5.2 World ranking of Pacific Asian countries on the Corruption Perceptions Index (CPI)

	World rank	*Score*
Singapore	8	85
Japan	18	75
Taiwan	30	62
South Korea	37	56
Malaysia	54	50
Thailand	76	38
China	83	37
Indonesia	88	36
Philippines	95	35
Vietnam	112	31
East Timor	123	28
Laos	139	25
Myanmar	147	22
Cambodia	150	21
North Korea	167	8

Note: 100 = very clean; 0 = most corrupt.
Transparency International, 2016

notable exception of North Korea, while Southeast Asian countries are generally in the middle to worst half of the ranking. In terms of scores, the average of the Pacific Asian countries listed above is 41.5, close to the world average score (43).

There is a debate about what corruption is, and why it is widespread in Pacific Asia (see Box 5.5). The problem of corruption in Pacific Asia is often associated with the rapid economic growth in these countries and in particular with the close government–business alliance in promoting such growth (see Chapter 6).

Consequently, there is no clear distinction between corruption in government bureaucracy and corruption in the business community, which is the private sector. Indeed, much of the corruption happens between government officials and the business community. For many, corruption is more an issue of business ethics (Kidd and Richter, 2003). For others, it is the whole 'Nation, Inc.' that is corrupt (Hutchcroft, 1991; Bello and Rosenfeld, 1992; Clifford, 1994; Lingle, 1998).

Box 5.5

Why corruption and what to do about it

- **Political development explanation:** A problem associated with underdevelopment; modernization is required.
- **Cultural explanation:** Integral part of the social relations and cultural tradition; a matter of perception and context.
- **Institutional explanation:** Reflecting problems in the institutional setting. Institutional reform is needed.

When discussing corruption one should therefore keep in mind the intellectual roots of this concept. Max Weber warned the modern bureaucracy may fail to perform its functions efficiently and effectively because of patrimonial arrangements and practices that allow bureaucrats to use their official jurisdiction for private gain. Corruption in this sense is a failure of public institutions to live up to their official purposes and values because of the complications of bureaucrats' abuse of their jurisdiction and compromising of their official duties.

One should also note the extended use of this term in Pacific Asian government and politics. It not only means the corruption of the bureaucracy, but also the business community, and even the entire polity.

Scholars not only debate what corruption is, but also why it occurs, particularly in Pacific Asia. For Max Weber, patrimonialism is a matter of traditional society. It is precisely through the idea of the modern bureaucracy that patrimonialism can be eliminated in a new ideal institutional setting. The problem of corruption in Pacific Asia is, therefore, first and foremost seen as a problem of political development. The political system in many Pacific Asian countries is very traditional in the Weberian sense and includes:

- The dominance of personal relations and rules.
- A lack of division between public and private.
- A hierarchy based on unclearly specified relations, roles and responsibilities.

The perspective of political development and modernization allows some level of optimism that, as political development and modernization proceeds, modern institutions will take their shape and corruption should be reduced.

For those who believe corruption may be related to the culture and people in Pacific Asia, however, the view is more pessimistic. The cultural explanation sees corruption as part of the social behaviour dictated by the prevalent culture (Kidd and Richter, 2003; Lindsey, 2002). It is part of the way things function or operate in these countries. Personal relations and rules, a hierarchical organization, and the blurring of the public and private are at the core of their cultural tradition. If culture is a permanent quality of a population, then one cannot really expect corruption to be eliminated.

There are also scholars, mainly institutionalist political economists associated closely with the IMF and the World Bank, who use a different framework to look at the problem of corruption. For them, corruption is not simply a problem of ethics but a matter of costs and benefits to the economy and society (Tanzi and Davoodi, 1998; Mauro, 1997). In their analysis, corruption can be either good or bad for economic growth. In a study on corruption in Korea and the Philippines, David Kang, for example, argued that in 'a situation of "mutual hostages" among a small and stable number of government and business actors, cronyism can actually reduce transaction costs and minimize deadweight losses' (Kang, 2003: 439) and thus does not impede economic growth.

Moreover, the prevalence of cultural behaviour driven by informal rules and personal relations suggests that there is a lack of trust in formal institutions and public office. Corruption in this sense is seen as an alternative strategy in promoting one's interests under such an institutional environment. As such, an institutionalist response to the problem of corruption in Pacific Asia would be to strengthen the institutions of government to give public and private actors confidence that their interests are best met using the formal institutions of government.

How political liberalization reduces the power of the bureaucracy

Whether in the Chinese model of political executive dominance, the Thai model of bureaucratic polity or the Japanese model of alliance between the political executive and bureaucratic elites, bureaucratic elites play a pivotal role in government and politics in Pacific Asia. Their unique role, as discussed above, has been reinforced by the challenge of industrialization and modern development, and the particular circumstances of the large political environment in these countries at the time.

Economic development will continue to be a priority for the state and bureaucracy in these countries, and therefore will continue to support the strong role of the bureaucracy in the overall political system. On the other hand, in most of these countries the larger political environment has undergone significant change and there is evidence that this has affected the position of the bureaucracy in the political system (see Box 5.6).

Bureaucratic dominance in Pacific Asia has been reduced significantly through several significant key developments in recent decades. Evidence of the impact of political change on the bureaucracy is seen most clearly in the case of Thailand. Bureaucratic dominance in Thailand was built on the suppression of civilian politicians by the military. As Martin Painter has observed, the democratic movement in the 1990s put civilian politicians back on the political stage.

Box 5.6

The decline of bureaucratic power

- Political liberalization and democratic transition has increased the role of politicians at the expense of bureaucrats.
- Administrative reforms and restructuring, mainly in the 1990s, have redistributed bureaucratic powers, decentralized state authority and functions and increased transparency, accountability and legislative oversight in bureaucratic functions and activities.
- The end of prolonged single-party dominance has made the political support for bureaucratic power uncertain and insecure.
- Changes in the overall social environment have provided more alternative career options to professional bureaucrats and thus reduced the quality and influence of the bureaucracy.

Subsequent administrative reforms sought 'to take political control of resources formally locked up in bureaucratic processes and structure', and Painter argued that these administrative reform initiatives were 'deployed in order to redistribute bureaucratic power to the political executive and, in particular, to the prime minister and his political circle' (Painter, 2006: 28).

The same weakening of bureaucratic power following political liberalization and democratic transition is also seen in Taiwan. Qingshan Tan provides a comprehensive analysis of the changes (Tan, 2000), which can serve as a general framework for understanding political change and bureaucratic power in Pacific Asia. Tan argues that following radical political liberalization and democratic transition in Taiwan, many new actors 'have either gained new access or dramatically increased their power to influence government decision-making processes'. Moreover, 'the bureaucracy is now held accountable to elected officials, especially at the local level' (ibid.: 60). The bureaucracy, exercising great power through bureaucratic insulation in the old days, now faces 'increasingly legislative oversight and influence', 'mounting interest group pressure', 'claims of autonomy by local government' and changing dynamics in the 'bureaucratic examination and recruitment system'. All these, Tan argues, have reduced significantly the level of discretion the bureaucracy enjoyed in the past 'in terms of macro-management and the formulation of developmental policies' (ibid.: 61).

The decline of bureaucratic power not only occurred in countries that experienced political liberalization and democratic transition, but also in countries such as China, where political liberalization is controlled and the party-state is still very dominant. There are different views on the nature of changes that have taken place in China since the 1980s. On the one hand, there is a pessimistic view (Pei, 2006) that, without fundamental political change – that is, change in the party-state system and democratic transition – these changes are insignificant. Indeed, the party-state system is the ultimate source of the problems that the country is facing.

On the other hand, scholars are noticing increasingly that economic reforms since the 1980s have not only raised the living standards for millions of people, but more importantly, have brought significant changes to how the government bureaucracy operates in China (see Yang 2004). The bureaucracy is now more exposed to the demands of the private sector and the interests of the public. Bureaucrats are increasingly under pressure from various directions besides the party-state's direction and control.

Case Study Lab 5.3

Explaining the power shift from bureaucrats to politicians in Japan

The impact of the 1990s political liberalization and reform of state institutions and the consequences of this reform on the political structure and order can be clearly seen in the power shift between bureaucrats and politicians as key movers and shakers of politics and policy. Tomohito Shinoda uses an institutional framework to capture such shifts and hence explain how political institutions and change shape political structure and order.

- Culturists use Japanese political culture and tradition to explain the strong bureaucracy until the 1990s.
- The pluralist model of structural change in the power shift between the bureaucracy and politicians, leading to a decentralized LDP, and weak cabinet and prime minister in the 1990s.
- The institutionalist framework looks at how institutions are designed to address this shift and strengthen the leadership of the political executive in the political and policy process.
- Institutional reforms included the 1994 electoral reform, the 1999 government reform and the 2001 administration reform. The electoral reform created a more centralized and cohesive party and the government and administrative reforms strengthened the cabinet and created a top-down decision-making council to carry out a series of major economic reforms.
- Institutions do not produce leadership; they only enable it. This raises the question of how and when institutions matter.

Shinoda, 2013: 1–7

The bureaucracy is increasingly seen not just as the organizational weapon of the party-state but a public service to the people, particularly at the local level. Indeed, bureaucrats are no longer one of the only privileged social classes, as they were up to the 1970s.

The case of Taiwan clearly demonstrates the critical impact of democratic regime change on the bureaucratic system. The Chinese case, on the other hand, may provide a scenario where bureaucratic power is increasingly constrained by the expansion of the market economy and the institutions and relations associated with it. It also suggests that the transformation of the bureaucracy may lead to the further weakening of the institutional basis of the party-state.

Government that governs and government that serves

Since the 1990s, there has been an international movement of good governance and growing pressure on Pacific Asian countries to reform their bureaucratic systems. The forces pushing Pacific Asian countries to reform are many.

First, our discussion above illustrated the dependency of the bureaucracy on the political executive. The bureaucracy enjoyed great power over its policy constituencies and was protected by the political executive. The bureaucracy, however, had little autonomy in relation to the political executive in carrying out policy decisions and providing public services. The bureaucracy's function was effective in so far as it was in line with the agenda and priority of the political executive. It was not only part of the state machinery but the organizational weapon of the state for state designated tasks and functions. Bureaucrats' performance was judged by how much it satisfied the quota and targets set by the political executive rather than how much it performs according to professional standards and how well it delivers services to the public. There was a lack of transparency, responsiveness and accountability at various levels.

Second, most Pacific Asian countries allowed little time to develop state institutions following

Case Study Lab 5.4

Analysing the civil service system in Pacific Asia

- Heady's five-dimension model (Heady 1996) focuses on variations in institutional settings and functions to explain whether the civil service systems are ruler trustworthy, party controlled, policy receptive and collaborative:
  - Relation to the political regim
  - Socioeconomic context
  - Personnel management
  - Qualification requirements
  - Sense of mission: values of civil servants integral to the system
- Morgan's two-core dimension model (1996) aims to capture political change and explain political development in developing countries. It seeks to explain how the system develops from one type to another positing pragmatic, patrimonial, positivist, absolutist change as the state-society relations change and civil services become more professional.
  - State-society relations

    Degree of institutionalization of the nation-state measured by its degree of cohesiveness and shared commitment to basic procedures and practices.

    Aggregated public attitudes to the state.
  - Key characteristics

    Relative values placed on process or outcomes.

    Degree to which the civil service is politicized or managed with professionalism.

Burns and Bowornwathana, 2001b: 18–20

their independence after the Second World War. After thirty years of special institutional settings for rapid economic growth and increasingly significant cultural complications in the working of the state institutions there was an urgent need to examine the bureaucratic systems and bring them up to date with contemporary conditions and challenges, and to incorporate new values and purposes.

Third, the liberal model of political economy in the United States and the United Kingdom steadily expanded its influence and became a global movement in the 1990s. In the public sector in particular, the New Public Management movement also turned into a global phenomenon. With this movement came pressure for Pacific Asian countries to initiate institutional reform and restructuring and to adopt more market-orientated government institutions and functions.

Fourth, there was a financial crisis in the region in 1997–8. There is a dominant view, led by major international donor agencies such as the World Bank, the International Monetary Fund (IMF), the United Nations Development Program (UNDP) and the Asian Development Bank (ADB), that the crisis occurred because of problems in the governing and economic institutions. Along with the rescue packages of the international donor agencies came conditions that recipient countries would fundamentally reform and restructure their governing and economic institutions.

Finally, there was a drastic change in the political environment in Pacific Asian countries. The majority of countries experienced a transition from non-pluralist politics to pluralist politics in the 1990s. This change put further pressure on the bureaucratic system to reform itself as new voices and interest groups found representation in government and a stronger recourse to the law.

Public sector reforms: 'paradigm shifts or business as usual?'

In their volume assessing public sector reforms in Asia, Anthony Cheung and Ian Scott discussed the 'paradox in reform' (Cheung and Scott, 2003: 17) in Pacific Asian countries. The paradox they referred to was that reforms could not proceed effectively without the 'strong and sustainable support from domestic "reform" elites' but such reforms would eventually impinge upon the 'vested interests of those elites'. Moreover, reforms cannot go ahead effectively without 'regime stability and authority' but it is the regime itself at which the reforms are targeted. This paradox creates ambiguity in the nature of the reform programmes and the extent to which progress can be made.

Bureaucratic reforms of the 1990s in Pacific Asian countries, also known as administrative reforms in Japan, institutional reforms in China or public administration reforms in many other Pacific Asian countries, were intertwined with political liberalization and democratic transition, as well as post-socialist transformation in these countries. They were clearly influenced by what is called the New Public Management movement in the UK and the reinvention movement in the USA (Halligan, 1996; Hood, 1991). The international context of the reforms was the global movement of neoliberal political economy during the 1980s and 1990s.

Of course, bureaucratic reforms did not start in the 1990s. For most Pacific Asian countries, adjustment and reform in their bureaucratic system has been a constant challenge since the early post-Second World War years. Cheng et al. (1998) detail how Taiwan and South Korea restructured their bureaucratic system in the 1960s and 1970s to meet the challenge of rapid industrialization and economic development. Painter traces the roots of the bureaucratic reform in the 1990s in Malaysia, Singapore, Taiwan and Thailand back to the 1950s and 1960s (Painter 2004). John P. Burns' examination of China's bureaucratic reforms for 'a rational and efficient bureaucracy' in the late 1970s and early 1980s demonstrates that the reforms were only part of a long series of bureaucratic reforms in PRC history:

> the 'crack troops and simple administration' campaigns of 1941 to 1943; concerted drives to eliminate 'bureaucratism, corruption, and waste' during the Three-Anti's Campaign in 1952; an attempt to simplify administrative organizations in 1955; mobilization to eliminate corruption among rural cadres during the Four Clean-Ups Campaign from 1963 to 1965; and drastic simplification of the state machine during the Cultural Revolution from 1967 to 1969. (Burns, 1983: 692)

Even more recently a constant process of reform is evident in China. Under President Xi Jinping, a major focus of his early presidency has been his anti-corruption and anti-graft campaigns to fight the 'tigers' (powerful leaders) and 'flies' (lowly bureaucrats) in the Chinese system.

For Japan, Pempel sees two major 'conscious historical reformulations' of Japan's bureaucratic system: 'the explicit imitation of the Prussian model' during the Meiji Restoration and the systematic reformulation by US Occupation Authority (Pempel, 1992: 21). The latter administrative reforms of the 1990s were first conceived in the 1960s, thoroughly debated, and carefully prepared over the following years.

The reforms that took place in Pacific Asia in the 1990s were large in scale and conceived as a set of philosophical beliefs and institutional values. At the heart of the reforms were the changing purposes and functions of the bureaucracy. The reforms were therefore aimed at making the bureaucracy 'smaller, more efficient, performance oriented, customer driven, accountable and open' (Burns and Bowornwathana, 2001: 13). These 'managerially inspired' reform programmes (Painter, 2006) treat the political executive as the CEO and the bureaucrats as its managers. The CEO manages the bureaucracy through a 'service delivery agreement', and performance management through measurable indicators.

Generally, these reforms involved the decentralization of government authority and functions (see Chapter 3), a reduction in government size and the number of bureaucratic organizations, more transparency in bureaucratic processes and procedures, more legislative and public oversight and provision of quality service to the public.

The bureaucratic reforms are important for Pacific Asian politics. The dominant political and bureaucratic models during the Cold War stand for one of the two competing models of bureaucratic efficiency and performance. The Cold War models generated efficiency and ensured performance through a tightly controlled and highly personalized alliance between the political executive and the bureaucrat elite.

Box 5.7

Public sector reforms in Pacific Asia: experiencing new public management

There was a 'considerable shift' in the nature and mode of the bureaucracy towards a 'market-cantered approach' in the 1990s. As Shamsul Haque observes, 'in line with the current state policies such as deregulation, privatization, and liberalization, there have been adjustments in the objectives, priorities, roles, institutions, norms, attitudes, and beneficiaries of bureaucratic reforms in these countries'. More specifically:

- Objectives and priorities of the bureaucracy: From traditional focus on overall nation-building and socioeconomic progress to more specific economic concerns such as economic growth and productivity.
- Role of the bureaucracy: Recent reforms have highlighted a supportive role rather than an active involvement of state bureaucracy in socioeconomic activities while encouraging the private sector to play a greater role in such activities.
- Institutional or organizational measures: A new set of market-orientated organizations and techniques in the public sector – including privatization committees, public–private partnership programmes and quality control mechanisms.
- Performance requirements: More emphasis on market norms such as competition, profit, efficiency and productivity.
- Managerial structures, attitudes and commitments: From a centralized to a decentralized structure, from an impersonal to an informal attitude, from a people-orientated to a customer-orientated outlook.
- Target groups or beneficiaries: Emphasis on the needs and demands of so-called 'customers' rather than citizens.

Haque, 1998: 99–108

The New Public Management model emphasizes the constraints of market forces and public interests on bureaucratic organization and performance. Moreover, the Cold War models were very much an exclusive process, with internal and upward accountability and little public participation. The bureaucratic reforms in the 1990s brought liberal values into the bureaucratic processes and intended to bring the bureaucracy in line with the changing political environment.

The assessment of the administrative reforms in the 1990s has been mixed. There is clearly a view that the reforms have not achieved what they were intended to do. Indeed, if one compares the 2007 governance indicators used in Pacific Asia in Context 5.1 for each of these countries with the same indicators in 1996 when administrative reforms were launched, there has not been much positive movement over the ten-year period. In many cases, the ranking has actually decreased.

Burns and Bowornwathana have noted the 'failure' of administrative reform in many Pacific Asian countries because of the lack of political will and an unwillingness of powerful bureaucrats to sacrifice their position' (2001: 13–14). Moreover, it is also related to the dominant model of public sector reform. In a major assessment of the public-sector reforms, Anthony Cheung and Ian Scott argue that:

> the fundamental inadequacies of a NPM paradigm of reform for Asian countries lie in the misfit between its logic and the socio-political reality of Asia. NPM emphasizes the market rather than the state as the locomotive of governance and public sector reforms. Indeed, the whole logic of NPM is to downsize the public sector in favour of the 'private' market and for public sector organizations to emulate business practices and the management ethos of the private sector and to introduce market measures which would presumably carry the virtues of the private sector. Such a paradigm does not fit in well with the East and Southeast Asian experience where state institutions have always dominated the scene and where the market for practical purposes has seldom been independent of state power, but on the contrary, has been dependent on it for patronage and support. (Cheung and Scott, 2003: 12)

Overall, the bureaucratic reforms of the 1990s in Pacific Asia were not only affected by political liberalization and democratic transition within these countries but also influenced by the global movement of neoliberal political economy and the 'good governance' movement instigated by such international organizations as the World Bank and the International Monetary Fund.

Different visions and theories and a different set of values about the role, purpose and function of the bureaucracy in modern society drive the reforms. This makes for a stark contrast to many of the traditional ideas and practices of bureaucracy in Pacific Asia and to the ideas and values of the modernization drive in the early decades of post-independent Pacific Asia.

Let us now take a look at the general quality indicators of the bureaucracy in Pacific Asian countries and see where they stand among the nations of the world.

How Pacific Asia measures up in good governance

The notion of good governance has gained currency in recent years. There have been various efforts to define and measure good governance. Given the historical context in which modern bureaucracy has developed in Pacific Asian countries, and the recent programmes of public sector reform and restructuring, it is interesting to see how Pacific Asian countries measure up in terms of good governance.

The Asian Development Bank (ADB) lists four core values of good governance (see Box 5.8). The World Bank Institute has over the years developed a framework, a set of indicators and annual data for measuring governance. The Governance Indicators it produces every year provide a comprehensive measure of governance levels worldwide. There are six standard categories of indicator used (Kaufmann et al., 2008: 7; The World Bank, 2015):

- **Voice and accountability:** 'The extent to which a country's citizens are able to participate in selecting their government, as well as freedom of expression, freedom of association and a free media';

- **Political stability and absence of violence/ terrorism:** 'The likelihood that the government will be destabilized or overthrown by unconstitutional or violent means, including politically-motivated violence and terrorism';
- **Government effectiveness:** 'The quality of public services, the quality of the civil service and the degree of its independence from political pressures, the quality of policy formulation and implementation, and the credibility of the government's commitment to such policies';
- **Regulatory quality:** 'The ability of the government to formulate and implement sound policies and regulations that permit and promote private sector development';
- **Rule of law:** 'The extent to which agents have confidence in and abide by the rules of society, and in particular the quality of contract enforcement, property rights, the police, and the courts, as well as the likelihood of crime and violence';
- **Control of corruption:** 'The extent to which public power is exercised for private gain, including both petty and grand forms of corruption, as well as "capture" of the state by elites and private interests.'

We provide the data from the World Bank on the six categories for Pacific Asian countries in its entirety to give a full measure of governance in the region (see Table 5.3). Clearly, there is a diverse range of scores both across the region and in individual countries over different measures. The overall governance levels of individual Pacific Asian countries range from 1.59 for Singapore to –1.66 for North Korea, on a scale of –2.5 to 2.5. They can generally be seen in four groups. Singapore and Japan are in the first group in the range of 1.00 to 2.00 on most indicators. Singapore scores above 2.0 on measures of government effectiveness, regulatory effectiveness and control of corruption. However, the measure of voice and accountability remains negative. Japan's overall score is slightly below Singapore but more consistent over all measures, including voice and accountability.

Taiwan, South Korea, Brunei and Malaysia are in the second group. Their average governance score falls in the range of 0 to 1.0. Taiwan and South Korea have the most consistent scores in this group. Brunei and Malaysia, like Singapore, fall short on the measure of voice and accountability. This is followed by a third group of countries that include the Philippines, Indonesia, Thailand, China, Vietnam, Laos,

Box 5.8

Values of good governance

Accountability: Public officials must be accountable or answerable for their actions and responsive to the entity from which their authority is derived. Government must be able to build capacity to undertake economic reforms, implement reforms successfully and provide citizens with an acceptable level of public services. Evaluation criteria and oversight mechanisms are necessary to measure the performance of public officials and to make sure standards are met.

Participation: Participation refers to the involvement of citizens in the development process. Beneficiaries and groups affected by projects or other development interventions need to participate so that the government can make informed choices with respect to their needs and social groups can protect their rights.

Predictability: A country's legal environment must be conducive to development. A government must be able to regulate itself via laws, regulations and policies that encompass well-defined rights and duties, mechanisms for their enforcement, and impartial settlement of disputes. Predictability is about the fair and consistent application of these laws and the implementation of government policies.

Transparency: Transparency refers to the availability of information to the general public and clarity about government rules, regulations and decisions. It can be strengthened through the citizens' right to information with a degree of legal enforceability. Transparency and disclosure in government decision-making and public policy implementation reduces uncertainty and can help to inhibit corruption among public officials.

Table 5.3 Quality of governance

	Voice and accountability	*Political stability*	*Government effectiveness*	*Regulatory quality*	*Rule of law*	*Control of corruption*	*Overall*	
Brunei	−0.66	1.27	1.08	0.97	0.50	0.63	Singapore	1.59
Cambodia	−1.08	−0.04	−0.68	−0.40	−0.93	−1.08	Hong Kong	1.50
China	−1.54	-0.46	0.34	−0.27	−0.33	−0.33	Japan	1.39
Hong Kong	0.50	1.13	1.84	2.05	1.85	1.64	Taiwan	1.07
Indonesia	0.13	−0.37	−0.01	−0.10	−0.35	−0.58	Macao	0.96
Japan	1.04	1.02	1.82	1.14	1.60	1.73	S. Korea	0.77
N. Korea	−2.13	−1.09	−1.65	−2.20	−1.54	−1.34	Brunei	0.63
S. Korea	0.68	0.19	1.18	1.11	0.98	0.49	Malaysia	0.52
Laos	−1.65	0.46	−0.39	−0.85	−0.71	−0.76	Mongolia	−0.07
Macao	−0.36	1.21	1.45	1.68	0.93	0.86	Philippines	−0.19
Malaysia	−0.33	0.34	1.14	0.84	0.64	0.48	Indonesia	−0.21
Mongolia	0.23	0.87	−0.41	−0.25	−0.35	−0.47	Thailand	−0.28
Myanmar	−1.39	−1.06	−1.28	−1.39	−1.17	−0.92	China	−0.43
Philippines	0.13	−0.70	0.19	−0.01	−0.33	−0.44	Vietnam	−0.47
Singapore	−0.11	1.23	2.19	2.23	1.89	2.12	Lao PDR	−0.65
Taiwan	0.88	0.80	1.37	1.30	1.20	0.84	Cambodia	−0.70
Thailand	−0.85	−0.91	0.34	0.27	−0.15	−0.41	Myanmar	−1.20
Vietnam	−1.34	0.00	−0.06	−0.59	−0.31	−0.50	N. Korea	−1.66

Notes: units – estimate measured on a scale –2.5, weak governance performance, to 2.5, strong governance performance.
Kaufmann et al., 2015.

East Timor and Cambodia. The overall scores here are in the negative range from 0 to −1. Even though all score poorly on each measure, the major issue for these countries differs slightly. China, Thailand and Vietnam struggle with issues of voice and accountability. Others, such as the Philippines and Indonesia, generally score poorly on measures of regulatory quality, rule of law and government effectiveness. East Timor, Laos and Cambodia score poorly on most measures. The final group of countries has the worst scores, falling in the range −1 to −2. These countries score poorly in terms of all measures of good governance.

Pacific Asian countries as a whole, in comparison with other world regions, are generally low on voice and accountability, reflecting the types of states and forms of government in the region, but high on government effectiveness (see Pacific Asia in Context 5.1). However, their governance scores are better than those of South Asia (India, Pakistan, etc.), which are all in the negative territory and those of the former Soviet Union, including Russia, which are further down the scale towards the worst. There are clearly gaps between Pacific Asia and Western Europe, North America and Australasia (Australia and New Zealand), particularly on those measures of voice and accountability and political stability.

This review of the bureaucracy in Pacific Asia reflects general trends in political development in the region. The ongoing influence of the traditional order in the region as well as the lingering impact of non-pluralist politics from the Cold War era, is clearly still felt and complicating the development of a public service that is independent of the political executive and can provide effective and efficient services in the public interest.

Pacific Asia in Context 5.1

Quality of governance

	Voice and accountability	Political stability	Government effectiveness	Regulatory quality	Rule of law	Control of corruption	Overall
Pacific Asia	–0.44	0.21	0.47	0.31	0.19	0.11	0.14
South Asia	–0.46	–0.96	–0.51	–0.74	–0.51	–0.45	–0.60
Europe, North America, Australasia	0.92	0.68	0.96	1.02	1.00	0.87	0.91
Eurasia	–1.19	–0.35	–0.48	–0.74	–0.77	–0.85	–0.73
Latin America	0.35	0.22	–0.12	–0.05	–0.16	–0.05	0.03
Africa	–0.49	–0.51	–0.57	–0.48	–0.49	–0.46	–0.50

Notes: units – estimate measured on a scale –2.5 to 2.5. Higher values correspond to better governance.

Kaufmann et al., 2015.

The public sector reforms of the 1980s and 1990s have gone some way towards remedying these issues with varying results. Measures of good governance in the region have improved on most measures in most countries over the last few years. This is an encouraging sign. However, certain issues appear resilient. In particular, low scores on voice and accountability, while not universally poor in the region, have plagued Singapore, China, Vietnam and North Korea, as well as those parts of Southeast Asia in the early stages of economic development. This suggests an effective, efficient and responsive public service is not only related to the overall level of socioeconomic development in a polity but also to the overarching political environment it operates within.

Chapter summary

- There are similar issues with regard to the role of the bureaucracy in relation to other political institutions such as the political executive, the state and the public. But the evolution of the relations in Pacific Asia has been less clear than depicted in the Raadschelders–Rutgers model.
- Bureaucrats in Pacific Asia are generally selected through competitive recruitment processes and enjoy much higher social status, respect and privileges. Because of the way they are recruited, they tend to serve as a bridge between the state and the social elite, interest groups and the public in general.
- The relationship between the political executive on the one hand and the bureaucracy on the other is quite complicated in Pacific Asian countries, but can generally be seen in three distinct models most evident during the Cold War era: the Chinese model of the dominance of the political executive over the bureaucracy; the Thai model of the dominance of bureaucratic elites; and the Japanese model of collaboration and alliance between the political executive and the bureaucratic elites.
- Modernization of the bureaucracy has long been a challenge for Pacific Asian countries, but the level of development achieved varies in these countries. Pacific Asian countries spread across the range of governance indicators. There are still debates over the nature of the gap

between the Weberian ideal and Pacific Asian practices, and whether the causes of such a gap are fundamentally cultural, historical or institutional.

- Political liberalization and democratic transition has led to the reduction of bureaucratic power and reforms in bureaucratic organization and functions in some countries. In other countries, such as the former socialist counties, reforms in bureaucratic organization and functions happened first and appeared to gradually weaken the institutional basis of the party-state.
- Bureaucratic reforms in the 1990s reflect a shift in our view about the role, purpose and function of bureaucracy in modern society, from the traditional ideas and practices of bureaucracy in Pacific Asia, and ideas and values of the modernization drive in the early decades of post-independent Pacific Asia, to the good government movement, New Public Management and social network theory in the 1990s.
- Measures of good governance are very diverse in the region reflecting both the varying levels of socioeconomic development and the overarching political environment.

Further reading

For general discussions of bureaucratic systems in Pacific Asia, see Burns and Bowornwathana (2001) and Perry and Toonen (1996). Burns and Bowornwathana (2001) provide an in-depth look at the individual bureaucratic systems of major Pacific Asian countries. The theoretical frameworks in Bekke et al. (1996) allow us to understand the bureaucratic systems in Pacific Asian countries in a broader international comparison. Harding (1981) on the Chinese bureaucracy, Riggs (1966) on the Thai bureaucracy and Johnson (1982) on the Japanese bureaucracy are the three classics on the models of bureaucracy–political executive relations. On the recent reforms of bureaucratic systems, see Burns (2015), Cheung and Scott (2003) and Painter (2004). In particular, John Halligan's (1996) chapter discusses the impact of civil service reforms and their reform concepts and models of the West.

Study questions

1. Why did the transformation of bureaucrats into servants of the public come much later in Pacific Asia?
2. What is meritocracy? What role does it play in the working of the bureaucracy in Pacific Asia? What role does it play in their overall political systems?
3. How do Pacific Asian countries match up with the Weberian ideal type of bureaucracy?
4. What is patrimonialism? How does the concept help us to understand bureaucratic systems in Pacific Asia?
5. Using the measures of good governance provided, identify patterns in the results over different countries and measures. What do you think best explains these patterns?
6. Discuss the public-sector reforms in Pacific Asia in the 1990s. Why did they go ahead? What were they expected to achieve? How successful were the reforms?

Key terms

Bureaucrats as servants (127); Modern bureaucracy (126); Scholar-officialdom (127); Raadschelders–Rutgers model of bureaucratic evolution (126); Meritocracy (128); 'Descent from heaven' (131); Nomenklatura system (131); Bureaucratic polity (131); Authority delegation (133); Corruption (135); Bureaucratic insulation (133); Patrimonial bureaucracy (135); Public sector reform (142); New public management movement (140); Good governance (139).

Chapter 6
The state and the economy

Given the central importance of industrialization and economic development in Pacific Asian countries in recent decades and the intense debate that Pacific Asian practices have caused over the role and function of the state in development, this chapter is devoted to this critical aspect of Pacific Asian government and politics.

The chapter illustrates the organization of the polity for the purpose of national economic growth and development, the core institutions defining state–business relations that have supported and sustained the 'Nation Inc.' and the primary instruments for the state to ensure growth-centred economic activities of private citizens and groups, as well as those for the private sector to influence government policy and decision-making.

This chapter is therefore not about economic miracles in Pacific Asia. Rather, as part of an introductory textbook on Pacific Asian government and politics, it is about how the state sees its core functions, and how it associates itself with national economic activities. It concerns the fundamental debate in the discipline about the role and function of the state in modern society.

The chapter explains the concept of economic activism, defines the boundaries of public and private and provides examples of how governments have actually 'governed' the market in Pacific Asia. We shall examine some of the principle instruments the state uses to ensure its growth agenda and activities and look at the key 'institutions of high-speed growth' (Johnson, 1982: xi). We also broaden the analysis to explore the role of other actors important to growth and development in the region. We discuss growth participants and growth alliances between government, the private sector and bureaucracy and cover the debate on the role of law in development. We discuss the concept of the developmental state in full and ask if there is an Asian model of economic growth.

The chapter ends with a survey of the strategies and scenarios in the transformation of Pacific Asian countries, coverage of the development model debate and an overview of the paradigm shifts that are fundamentally changing the relationship between the public and private sector in the region.

The rise of the developmental state in Pacific Asia

In his classic 1982 study on the institutions of high-speed growth in Japan, Chalmers Johnson explored the puzzle of how the Japanese economy developed so rapidly in the post-war years while arguably 'flagrantly flouting all received principles of capitalist rationality' (Dore, 1986: 18 cited in Johnson 1999: 33). Johnson drew our attention to the differences between what he termed the 'Japanese developmental state' and the 'American regulatory state' (Johnson, 1982: 10) and argued the Japanese state played a crucial role in this 'economic miracle':

> The two models of the state represent two different orientations toward private economic activities, the regulatory orientation and the developmental orientation, and two different kinds of government–business relationships. The United States is a good example of a state in which the regulatory orientation predominates, where Japan is a good example of a state in which the developmental orientation predominates. (Johnson, 1982: 19)

Since then, many other studies have followed and demonstrated that the Japanese developmental state is not an isolated phenomenon (see Wade, 1990 on Taiwan; Amsden, 1989 on South Korea; Bowie, 1991 on Malaysia; Hill, 1996 on Indonesia; Huff, 1995 on Singapore; Muscat, 1994 on Thailand; Öniş, 1991 and Castells, 1992 for region-wide reviews; and Johnson 1995 for further thoughts on Japan). These studies suggest there is a wide practice of state intervention during rapid periods of growth in Pacific Asian countries. These studies have unleashed a great debate in comparative political economy that has revisited one of the fundamental questions of political science: the role of the state in economic development and whether governments govern the market. Let us first explore the idea of economic activism before turning more directly to the debate with reference to East Asia's rapid economic development.

> A **regulatory** or market rational **state** concerns itself with the forms and procedures – the rules, if you will – of economic competition, but it does not concern itself with substantive matters. The **developmental** or plan-rational **state**, in contrast, has as its dominant feature precisely the setting of such substantive social and economic goals.
>
> Johnson 1982: 19

The developmental state literature has evolved over the decades since Chalmers Johnson's original conceptualization of the developmental state in Japan. In particular, the replication of patterns of state-economy relations across the Pacific Asian region have led some to argue the developmental state is the basis for an Asian model of economic development, an issue we will return to later in the chapter.

The developmental state

Let us begin by summarizing the main tenants of the developmental state literature. The concept of the developmental state is closely related to the concept of the regulatory state. Their differences can be imagined as in a competitive game. In a regulatory state, the state is only the referee, ensuring that all players behave in accordance with the previously agreed rules of the game. If they do not, the referee

Case Study Lab 6.1

Johnson's puzzle and the developmental state theory

In explaining 'the Japanese miracle' of high speed economic growth in the 1920s and 1970s, Chalmers Johnson explores whether the Japanese state, and in particular its capable and effective bureaucracy, played a decisive role in organizing economic activities that delivered the economic miracle. Johnson therefore went beyond popular understandings that emphasized 'national character-basic value-consensus', 'no miracle occurred', 'unique structural features' or 'free ride' explanations. Johnson's work on the role of MITI, the state's industrial policy, and how the state coordinates industrial development with 'clients' in the growth process led him to suspect that the particular type of state, the developmental state, was unique in effecting the miracle. This led to the development of a whole research paradigm in explaining East Asian political economy over the next several decades.

Johnson 1982: 325

Box 6.1

Political regimes and rapid economic growth

	Rapid growth	*Political regime*
China	late 1970s	Party-state
Indonesia	Mid-1960s–1990s	GOLKAR government
Japan	1950s–1970s	LDP government
S. Korea	1960s–1990s	Military government
Malaysia	1970s–1990s	UMNO government
Singapore	Mid-1960s–1990s	PAP government
Taiwan	1960s–1990s	KMT government
Thailand	1960s–1990s	Military government
Vietnam	Late 1980s	Party-state

has the power to censure or punish players for their indiscretion. In a developmental state, however, the state is referee and player, if not *the* most important player.

A developmental state, therefore, is not easy to imagine in theory and much more complicated in reality. As Hal Hill commented on Indonesia's industrial transformation, 'the state has always been closely involved in manufacturing, as a direct investor and as a regulator' (Hill, 1997: 6). It is this complicated role the state takes on in Pacific Asian countries that has caused much scholarly attention and academic debate (Deyo, 1987; Öniş, 1991; Woo-Cumings, 1999).

A developmental state can usually be recognized by the following characteristics:

- A determined and unified political executive with a self-proclaimed mandate for growth and economic development and a rule of government not regularly interrupted.
- An effective bureaucracy that provides operational plans and implementation guidance for a growth agenda and is accountable primarily to the political executive.
- A set of peripheral organizations that serve as an institutional linkage between the state and their respective sectors and industries.
- A series of policy instruments at the disposal of the state to influence the economic activities of growth participants and the state's ability to 'pick and choose' winners and losers.
- The ability of the state to carry through their economic programmes and policies – however politically unpopular they might be – and to fend off rent-seeking activities of growth participants.

Clearly, such a developmental state cannot be a pluralist or democratic state. Indeed, if one looks at the political regime at the time of the rapid economic growth in Pacific Asian countries, most of them had either a single-party dominant state or a military government or a communist party-state (see Box 6.2).

Here, the question is not so much about a possible 'causal link' between regime types and economic performance. At issue is the political nature of the developmental state and the institutional and political requirements for the developmental state to operate. The key feature of these institutional arrangements is the ability for the state to intervene in the economy, to cross the boundary between public and private and to coordinate activities in the private sector. This can, and did, occur under a military government, such as in South Korea, and in a democratic setting dominated by one political party, such as in Japan. In each case, however, the state had the capacity to coordinate the activities of the private sector and to shape the growth agenda.

Box 6.2

The developmental state debate

Following Chalmers Johnson's (1982) seminal work on this concept, studies of the theory and practices of the developmental state in Pacific Asia have centred on a series of key questions. Three of them feature most often in this debate.

- Was the developmental state really the primary cause of rapid industrialization and economic development?

  Yes — Major studies have confirmed this.

  No — It was the market economy that worked.
  The developmental state cannot be singled out: it is part of society and a network of actors.

- Has the developmental state impeded the development of political liberty and legal institutions in Pacific Asia?

  Yes — The developmental state is essentially a form of controlled politics that limits the political liberty of the individual and the private sector in particular.
  The developmental state is an efficiency-driven policy process that was achieved at the expense of other political, legal and social values.

  No — One cannot satisfy all values at the same time. For late development, the developmental state is most capable of ensuring priorities and effectiveness among competing values and interests, which in the long run provides the best chance of securing these values.

- Is the developmental model transferable?

  Yes — If it is to deal with similar historical (late development), institutional (demand exceeds resources) and developmental (economic development as a priority) challenges.

  No — Many of the conditions and requirements for the developmental state were unique to the cultural and historical conditions at the time.

Even if it is desirable for given conditions and values, it may not be possible, as institutional and cultural conditions in other countries may not tolerate the institutions and values associated with the model and/or cannot provide the institutional and political support required for the model to be effective.

Economic activism

At the heart of the state's economic activism, as Andrew MacIntyre points out in explaining government–business relations in Indonesia (MacIntyre, 1990: 6–7), are the interests of the state itself. A developmental state is a self-serving entity, pursuing its perceived self-interest at the expense of other diverse interests in society. This differs radically to the Marxist view that the state is 'a tool of the capital class or the liberal view that the state represents the interests of the voters'.

Economic activism refers here to a wide practice in Pacific Asian countries where the state is actively involved in the management, guidance and promotion of national economic activities, through national economic planning, coordination and at times intervention.

The developmental state literature asserts there was a wide pattern of economic activism during the rapid periods of economic growth in the region leading scholars to attribute that growth to economic activism. A more orthodox view argues economic activism may have occurred in these countries during this period; however, such activism presented more of a hindrance to the market and private sector, which was ultimately the source of economic growth.

The issue here relates to the different schools of economic thought. In political economy we can distinguish between market oriented and non-market-oriented approaches to governing the economy. For Pacific Asia, there is a history of economic planning under the communist states. Economic activism, however, should not be confused with economic planning as seen in command economies, such as China, during the 1950s, 1960s and 1970s. Under these command economies, the state abolished private property and took control of pricing, distribution and allocation of resources. Supply and demand forces did not operate and next to no market existed.

In those Pacific Asia states that did not abolish the market and that allowed market forces to operate with some degree of security of property rights, more often than not economic activism is evident. Under these market conditions, economic activism describes the degree to which the state was active in managing, shaping or governing market forces. The term is therefore relevant to most countries in Pacific Asia, including the now former socialist states, at one time or another.

Case Study Lab 6.2

State versus market: explaining the role of government in Pacific Asian industrialization and economic development

Robert Wade summarizes three principal theories of the role of government in Pacific Asian economic success, with the governed market theory, favoured by himself:

- Free market theory: According to this theory, Pacific Asia does better than other newly industrializing countries because Pacific Asian states interfere hardly at all in the working of the market. Economic growth results from 'the actions and efforts of private individuals and enterprises responding to the opportunities provided in quite free markets for commodities and labor' (Patrick, 1977: 239). 'What the state provided is simply a suitable environment for the entrepreneurs to perform their functions' (Chen, 1979: 185).
- Simulated free market theory: Governments of Pacific Asia did more than just liberalize markets and reduce distortions. They also intervened more positively to offset other distortions. The 'active interventionist attitude of the State has been aimed at applying moderate incentives which are very close to the relative prices of products and factors that would prevail in a situation of free trade … It is as though the government were "simulating" a free market' (Berber, 1979: 64).
- Governed market theory:

At the **first level**, the superiority of East Asian economic performance is the result in large measure of a combination of:

- Very high levels of productive investment, making for faster transfer of newer techniques into actual production;
- More investment in certain key industries than would have occurred in the absence of government intervention; and
- Exposure of many industries to international competition, in foreign markets if not at home.

At the **second level**, the above are themselves the result, in important degree, of a set of government economic policies. Using incentives, controls and mechanisms to spread risk, these policies enabled the government to guide or govern market processes of resource allocation to produce different production and investment outcomes than would have occurred with either free market or simulated free market policies.

At the **third level**, policies have been permitted or supported by a certain kind of organization of the state and the private sector that includes a hard or soft authoritarian state that develops corporatist relations with the private sector and is able to confer enough autonomy on a centralized bureaucracy for it to influence resource allocation in line with a long-term national interest.

The free market and simulated market theories emphasize efficient resource allocation as the principal force for growth and therefore interpret superior Pacific Asian performance to efficient resource allocation. More efficient resource allocation comes from more freely functioning markets…. Hence these countries show the virtues of 'getting the prices right'…The governed market theory, on the other hand, emphasizes capital accumulation as the principal general force for growth. Government policies deliberately got some prices 'wrong' so as to change the signals to which decentralized market agents responded and also used non-price means to alter the behaviour of market agents.

Wade, 1990: 22–9

One can also find economic activism in a variety of different political systems around the world. Arguably, the economic policies of Alexander Hamilton in the eighteenth century contained a healthy dose of economic activism as the US sought to develop the industrial capacity of the new nation (Chang, 2003). Moreover, Franklin D. Roosevelt's 'New Deal' of the 1930s provides another example of economic activism, whereby large government programmes and projects were initiated to re-energize a US economy in deep recession. There remains considerable debate over whether bailouts following the Global Financial Crisis can be termed economic activism or fit more closely with the regulatory state framework.

Often, economic activism stands on one end of two dominant government orientations in Western democracies. It is often associated with the view that sees government as the solution to economic and social problems, a view espoused by economists such John Maynard Keynes and echoed in the more contemporary works of economists like Joseph Stiglitz and Paul Krugman.

On the other hand, economic minimalism is the philosophy behind conservative thinking and policy, which sees government as a source of social and economic problems. This is the general orientation of mainstream economists, including Friedrich Hayek and Milton Friedman, for example, and fits with the mainstream economic view that promotes free trade, privatization, minimal government intervention in the private sector and reduced public expenditure. As such, economic activism in the late twentieth and early twenty-first century, as seen in many countries in Pacific Asia, was politically unpopular and heavily criticized at the time.

The emergence of economic activism in post-war Pacific Asia, however, was less an academic debate and more a response to the political and economic reality facing these countries at the time. Prior to the advance of the developmental state in the 1960s, there was a brief period of pluralist politics (see Chapter 2) and economic laissez-faire policy. However, due to many factors, including a weak industrial base, an underdeveloped economy, poor finances, weak institutions and growing security risks, this period ended in large-scale economic chaos and downturn. It was against this background that the state started to take an active role in guiding the economy.

A few key elements of economic activism in Pacific Asian countries stand in contrast to economic activism as practiced in most Western countries. First, economic activism, at least in the rapid growth period during the Cold War, was a more systematic, long-term effort than that seen in other parts of the world. As such, it was not simply an exercise of fiscal, monetary and taxation policy to redirect economic activity to address short-term economic challenges. In fact, fiscal and monetary policies were the least favoured policy instruments. Economic activism in Pacific Asia involved a combination of normal economic instruments and central and long-term planning, including developing corporatist arrangements with a variety of public and private 'growth participants' and intervening in parts of the economy to 'kick-start' activity there.

Second, economic activism in Pacific Asia generally occurred under non-pluralist circumstances. The government was not elected on the back of high popular support, such as Roosevelt was on his 'new deal' campaign, but rather dominated the political system and often suppressed or marginalized the opposition to the regime and their economic development programme. Box 6.1 shows the regime in power in Pacific Asian countries during their rapid economic growth and at the height of their economic activism. A single party or political force dominated all countries during this period.

Thirdly, economic activism in Pacific Asia serves a developmental purpose. In the developmental state, the state takes a greater interest in which actors and parts of the economy do well, while in a regulatory state, the state has no direct interest in this. In the developmental state, therefore, there is a built-in bias towards certain actors and industries. This bias can favour a developmental agenda. As W. G. Huff sees in the case of Singapore, 'government autonomy itself creates incentives which push the government to act "developmentally". Often the incentives appear to be related to the fact that the government has become the dominant interest group and requires economic development to legitimize and perpetuate itself' (Huff, 1995: 1435).

State-market balance: across the boundaries

Economic activism actively crossed the boundaries of public and private and between actors in the private sector. In practical terms, the first boundary

Table 6.1 Economic freedom

Country	1970		2012	
	EFW Index	World rank	EFW Index	World rank
China	3.64*	96*	6.39	115
Hong Kong	8.34	1	7.30	50
Indonesia	4.56	47	6.89	80
Japan	7.68	7	7.60	23
S. Korea	6.00	30	7.45	33
Malaysia	6.38	26	7.00	74
Myanmar	3.86*	91*	5.28	143
Philippines	5.43	36	7.29	51
Singapore	7.08	13	8.54	2
Taiwan	6.43	25	7.71	18
Thailand	6.20	27	6.62	102
Vietnam	5.67**	115**	6.42	114

Gwartney et al., 2014. *1980, **2003

that the state crosses is the one between the private and the public.

As in the earlier discussion on Weber's ideal type of bureaucracy (see Chapter 5), the demarcation between public and private is considered to be a cornerstone of the modern state and indeed the institutional foundation of the regulatory state. Douglass C. North and Robert P. Thomas have effectively demonstrated (North and Thomas, 1973) that the conception and protection of private property rights was essential for the development of modern capitalism in seventeenth-century England and for the rise of the West.

The index of economic freedom indicates the level of economic freedom in each country measured by size of government, legal structure and security of property rights, access to sound money, freedom to trade internationally and regulation. A higher level of economic freedom suggests a lower level of state involvement and thus a smaller role of the developmental state. Indicators here compare Pacific Asian countries in 2012 to the earliest year of data availability. In the index above, 10 is the highest possible score and zero (0) is the lowest. A higher score indicates a greater degree of economic freedom and thus less state intervention and control.

In Pacific Asia, there was no clear-cut dismissal of the traditional conception of the polity that sees the political community as an organic whole (see Chapter 3) and, more importantly, that gives the state the overwhelming responsibility for the well-being of the community.

The persistence of the traditional idea of polity and associated political and social practices was only exacerbated by the urgent challenge of survival and rapid catch-up in industrial and economic development.

For many observers, the state's active involvement in private economic activities is an encroachment on the private sector by the state. For many growth participants, though, the mutual embeddedness of public and private interests not only resulted in blurred boundaries between the private and the public but also blurred boundaries between actors in the private sector.

The state's economic activism not only crossed boundaries 'vertically' between the public and the private, but also 'horizontally', promoting collaboration, coordination and even integration among independent economic agents.

Companies and corporations in the regulatory state are the basic economic unit, and their relations by definition are competitive. For the developmental state to be effective, however, the relations among companies, corporations or industries were restructured to allow more collaborative relationships and integrative arrangements to accommodate the state-led growth agenda.

A consequence of the blurring of these boundaries was what Kanishka Jayasuriya called 'political capitalism' (Jayasuriya, 1999: 7) where 'networks of non-market relationships' operate 'horizontally between economic agents and vertically between economic agents and state actors'. The market is no longer a 'pure market'.

It is in this institutional and philosophical setting, where the state is economically active and crosses the boundaries between public and private and between independent economic actors that we can understand many of the approaches that Pacific Asian states have taken to guiding economic growth and development. With these points in mind, let us now turn to a review of scholars work on Pacific Asian states' approaches to governing the market.

COUNTRY PROFILE

SOUTH KOREA

		Regional Comparison	World Rank
GDP	1783 (ppp/bil)	5.44% of PA-18	13th (of 189)
HDI	0.891 (0 to 1)	PA-18: 3rd	15th (of 186)
WGI	0.77 (–2.5 to 2.5)	PA-18: 6th	74 (%)

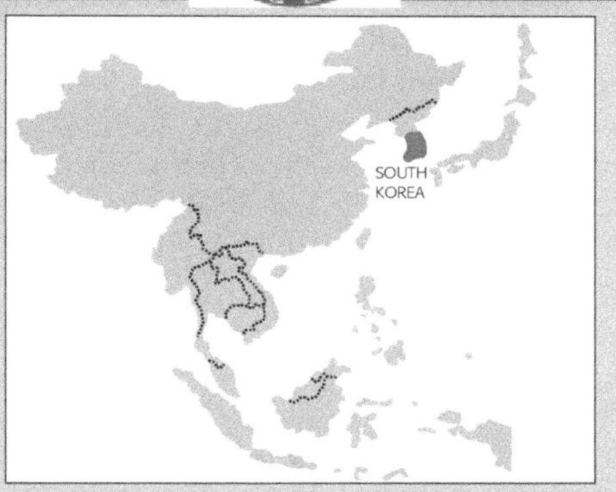

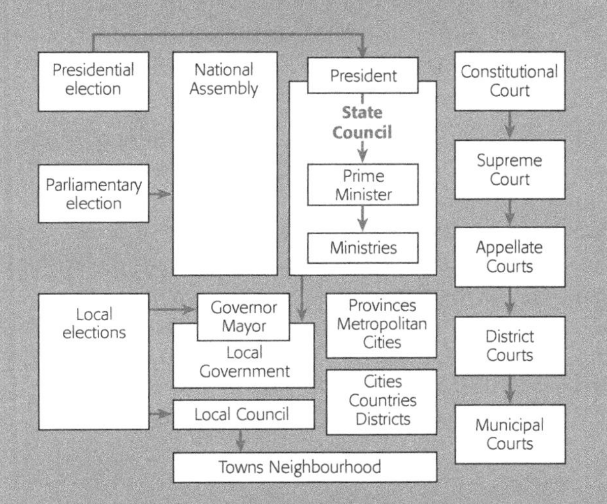

Key political facts

Electoral system for national legislature
Mixed member proportional representation (MMP).

Political cycles
Presidential elections every 5 years;
Parliamentary elections every 4 years;
Local elections every 4 years;
Annual national budget to be approved by the National Assembly in December.

Further reading

Lee, 2007; Kihl, 2005; Kim HM. 2011

Timeline of modern political development

1945 Independence declared.
1948 Republic of Korea established. First constitution with a presidential system and a unicameral legislature.
1950 Korean War breaks out.
1952 Constitutional amendments to allow direct presidential elections and a bicameral legislature.
1960 Student protests, President Syngman Rhee resigns. New constitution to provide for a bicameral parliamentary system.
1961 General Park Chung Hee leads a military coup and takes over government.
1963 The Third Republic begins with a new constitution and returns to a presidential system. Park elected president.
1972 The Yonsin Constitution with an unlimited term and more powers for the president.
1980 The Fifth Republic. A new constitution with a mixed form of government.
1987 Pro-democracy protests. The Sixth Republic. A new constitution provides for a popularly elected president and a presidential system.
1988 First free parliamentary elections.
1995 Political reforms on electoral law, political funding and local autonomy.
1996 Local autonomy restored.
2000 Summit between the North's Kim Jong Il and the South's Kim Dae Jung.
2004 Parliament impeachment of President Roh Moo Hyun.
2007 Proposals to allow more than one term for the president and return to a parliamentary system.
2007 Summit meetings between leaders of North and South Korea and their prime minister for the first time.
2012 Park Geun-hye is elected first female president of South Korea.
2014 Constitutional Court bans left-wing Unified Progressive Party, for being pro-North Korean.
2015 Constitutional Court revokes a 1953 law criminalizing adultery.
2015 Mass labour demonstrations against government labour policy.

The 'economic general staff'

A key assertion of the literature on economic development in Pacific Asia is that the state is economically active, crossing the orthodox boundaries of government-market relations and driving a developmental agenda. This section focuses on what governments actually do in 'governing the market' (Wade, 1990). Their involvement in national economic activities can be divided into four general areas: planning; coordination; promotion; and intervention.

Central and long-term economic planning is a crucial feature of state–economic relations. As Box 6.3 shows, in Pacific Asian countries experiencing rapid economic growth, there is generally a central decision-making body in government that is responsible for the overall planning of the national economy. During the rapid growth period from the 1960s to 1990s, these planning agencies had great powers. They provided short-term (one year), medium-term (three to five years) and long-term (ten years) goals of economic growth, and specific industrial targets and frameworks of control and promotion in various areas of economic and social development.

Often these central bodies had power over normal government ministries and departments. To form a coherent national growth plan these central bodies took on the responsibility of coordinating programmes and policies among government ministries and departments on matters of national economic and growth. Over the years, this function of interagency coordination has given the central planning body tremendous power.

A third area of involvement in national economic activities is to promote state economic ideas and agendas with respect to the overall economic plan, industrial priorities and particular policy directions at the time. Industrial promotion was deemed necessary for three main reasons:

- Late development: Late development often means that conditions and resources for 'natural' economic growth no longer exist. Limited resources and market accesses would need to be allocated according to development priorities.
- International competition: Pacific Asia's rapid growth and economic development after the Second World War depended heavily on international markets. Given the technological and

Box 6.3

The organization of central and long-term planning

Country	*Agency*	*Period*	*Responsible to*
South Korea	Economic Planning Board	1961–94	President
Singapore	Economic Development Board	1961–present	Prime minister
Malaysia	Economic Planning Unit	1961–present	Prime minister
Thailand	National Economic and Social Development Board	1950–present	Prime minister
Taiwan	Council for Economic Planning and Development	1963–present	Prime minister
Japan	Economic Planning Agency	1954–2001	Prime minister
China	State Development Planning Commission and National Development and Reform Commission	1952–Present	Prime minister

Note: Agencies may have functioned under different names over the years.

capital advantage of those mainly Western companies that already controlled these markets, the expansion of market share of Pacific Asian countries required industrial concentration and nationally coordinated export campaigns.
- Regional dynamics among Pacific Asian countries: There were waves of industrialization and rapid economic development in post-war Pacific Asia: from Japan in the 1950s and 1960s to South Korea, Singapore, Taiwan and Hong Kong in the 1960s and 1970s and to Southeast Asia and China in the 1980s and 1990s. The 'waves' of rapid industrialization and economic development required the leading economies to upgrade products and move to technology and capital intensive industries to avoid competition from the newcomers at low industrial levels. This allowed a level of complementariness between the economies at different development stages.

All these required promotion of a particular set of products and industries at a given time, and moving up to a new set of products and industries after a period of time. This is where much of the debate about the role of government in the economy in Pacific Asian countries concentrates: whether the state should pick winners or losers and the whole range of practices of industrial policy (see below).

Finally, as in other parts of the world, governments in Pacific Asian countries would have to intervene in response to unfavourable economic downturns, fluctuations or crises. Pacific Asian governments, however, tend to combine short-term stabilizing measures with long-term industrial restructuring and economic reform programmes in their response. Anne Booth, for example, explains how the Indonesian government responded to the slowdown in the 1980s after the oil boom (1968–81) with a lively debate about the country's economic performance, which in turn has led to the adoption and implementation of a series of measures designed to increase the efficiency of resource use in the domestic economy, remove disincentives to production for export, and improve resource mobilization for investment in both the public and the private sectors (Booth, 1992: 2).

The government interventions in the Asian financial crisis of 1997–8 and responses to the Global Financial Crisis (2007-8) are further examples of governments in the region responding to unfavourable economic downturns through a variety of institutional reforms and restructuring programmes.

Industrial policy

One aspect of 'how governments govern the market' in Pacific Asia has received great attention thanks to the early interest in the technical mechanisms of the Japanese developmental state (Johnson, 1982; Okimoto, 1989). Industrial policy has almost become synonymous with government intervention and state-led industrialization in Pacific Asia.

The original notion of industrial policy, however, is much narrower. Both Daniel I. Okimoto and Robert Wade, for example, separate industrial policy, which deals with individual industries and sectors, from macroeconomic policies that affect the economy as a whole (Okimoto, 1989: 8–9, Wade, 1990: 29–33). Wade further distinguishes industrial policy from public goods policy intended for issues such as physical infrastructure and distributional policies aimed at income and asset distributions.

Industrial policy has a unique significance in the rapid industrial and economic development in Pacific Asia. At the core of the issue is the competitiveness of national industries in international markets. Most Pacific Asian countries faced 'initial conditions' (Huang, 2005: 48–79) in their take-off period that compelled them to rely on international markets for rapid industrialization and economic growth. To do so, their products and industries needed to be competitive in cost and quality in international markets against well-established global competitors. Control of competition among domestic enterprises and the concentration of limited resources and capacities on key industries were seen by many Pacific Asian countries as the key to raising industrial productivity.

Industrial policy involves the government's use of its authority and resources to administer policies that address the needs of specific sectors and industries (and, if necessary, those of individual companies) with the aim of raising the productivity of factor inputs.

Okimoto, 1989: 8

Often, this industrial rationalization involves a restructuring of industries that optimizes deployment of human resources, capital and material resources across different industries and enterprises that would make them internationally competitive. As Chalmers Johnson explains in his work on the rise of industrial policy in Japan, even before the Second World War, 'rationalization came increasingly to emphasize that competition among enterprises should be replaced by cooperation, and that the purpose of business activities should be the attempt to lower costs, not make profits' (Johnson, 1982: 108).

More specifically, industrial policy often involves government activities in three areas:

- The government usually has industry-specific short, medium and long-term plans for industrial structure and development. This becomes an important guide for economic decisions in private sectors. This is particularly useful when industrial upgrading is the goal.
- The government publishes, or has unpublished, rules and regulations, as well as powers to issue licenses and permits for controlled activities and access that directly affects the economic activities of the private sector.
- The government intervenes to influence market and corporate activities, for example, to broker corporate merging, during periods when general guidance and regulatory powers are not effective in generating desired industrial movements.

A key consequence of industrial policy in rapid industrialization and economic growth in Pacific Asian countries has been the expansion of industrial groups in size, capacity and influence under government promotion schemes. Japan and Korea are two examples of this. Major industrial groups, known as keiretsu in Japan and chaebol in Korea, transformed themselves into giant international corporations that have dominated one or several industries, not only within the national economy but also globally. These industrial groups are the cornerstone of the growth alliance led by the government, particularly in the early stages of rapid industrialization and economic development.

'Japan Inc.', 'China Inc.', 'Nation Inc.'

Studies of the patterns of economic growth and development in Pacific Asia have, as above, put a strong emphasis on the role of the state. In fact, developmental state theory is largely predicated on the assertion that the state played an indispensable role in that growth. Any analysis of economic growth in the region, however, must also take into account the other actors in the growth process.

However, the state not only simply issues policies that growth participants would follow. Economic growth is also 'a social movement' where various groups of growth participants are 'incorporated' into the national project of economic development. In this sense, we can think of economic growth, industrialization and socioeconomic development as a national project with growth participants clearly oriented towards developmental goals.

A clear sense of national solidarity and orientation has led pundits to describe Pacific Asian countries, starting with Japan, using the 'Nation Inc.' rubric. This is in reference to the clear strategic goal to develop and associated activities from growth participants. Just as any corporation has a clear strategic goal and all participants within the company work towards the realization of that goal, rapid growth in Pacific Asia exhibits the pattern of a coordinated national project.

Japan Inc. is a popular term used to describe the powerful economic and political system that delivered Japan's transformation to an industrial power. It is a metaphor for an economy propelled forward by a system in which interests of big business, the Liberal Democratic Party (LDP) and the bureaucracy were aligned in the pursuit of national economic goals and all the apparatus of the state, and institutions that helped define corporate Japan, such as lifetime employment, cross-shareholding and keiretsu enterprise groupings, was brought to bear on that end.

It conveys some sense of distinctive features of the Japanese political economy that were present to a lesser degree in other market-oriented economies. It suggests more cooperative rather than contentious relations between government and industry, a blurring between the public and private sphere, and a less than transparent policy-making process.

Amyx and Drysdale, 2003: 1–2

This section broadens the analysis to explore the patterns of development within Pacific Asian states and to identify the role of growth participants in that development. It presents studies of how these participants interacted with government and other parts of society and economy, how their activities were shaped by and also shaped government policy and what role the law played in securing long-term economic growth in the region.

Growth alliance

Scholars may then have overstated the role of government in economic development. Indeed, in many Pacific Asian countries, rapid industrialization and economic development has been a 'social movement' (Huang, 2005: 148) that required more than just the governing of the market by governments. The effectiveness of a government's economic plans, programmes and policies required the broad support of the growth participants, from the state bureaucracy to the ruling political parties, from the business community to labour forces, from the military to dominant ethnic groups.

These groups have different interests in the growth process and often find their interests cannot be secured without the support of the other groups. Together they form a political alliance, or what is called a 'growth alliance' (Rowen, 1998: 51), that incorporates key growth stakeholders into the growth process and provides the core political arrangements for the overall incorporation of the polity.

To some extent, a growth alliance overlaps with the grand political alliance that was discussed in Chapter 4. This is particularly true of the informal grand political alliances. This should not be a surprise, given the close link between the political and economic dynamics of a modern state. What is emphasized in the discussion here is the institutional arrangement for the type of economic development in Pacific Asia and conversely the institutional consequences of such development.

Growth alliance is a collaborative relationship that emerged among key stakeholders in pursuit of a national growth agenda and the broad supporting political environment it required: a phenomenon often seen in Pacific Asian countries during their rapid industrialization and economic development after the Second World War. This growth alliance is often the political basis for the governing political structure and its power and influence often transcend the boundaries of formal state institutions.

Growth alliances can work for public interests, such as economic growth. They can also provide an overall political environment in which private gains become the primary purpose of the growth participants. There are often trade-offs among these stakeholders in terms of what they can get from the growth process and why they should support it.

Iron triangle refers to the close collaborative and mutually beneficial relationship among LDP legislators, state bureaucrats and business elites in Japan in support of the country's post-war rapid economic growth. The term is extended to mean a political alliance of mutual interest among major societal forces, the military included, in Pacific Asian countries, in support of their common political, economic and social agenda.

There are several forms of such growth alliances in Pacific Asian countries: The first type is the so-called iron triangle in Japan. This reflects the close intertwining of the interests of three key elite groups: LDP legislators, the state bureaucracy and the business community. These three groups formed a close collaboration in pursuit of national economic growth and development. Consequently, this collaboration allowed the concentration of political power and policy influence in their hands.

In this growth alliance, the business elites want to get their interests into the state policy process and cultivate deep relations with politicians and bureaucrats. LDP legislators often need substantial financial support to survive, to move up in the party apparatus and to function in government when in office. The business community is the primary source of such financial support. State bureaucrats develop their relations with the business community while in government and go to work in the private sector after early retirement from government. Such an alliance helped keep the LDP in power and created a working economic policy in favour of the business community and economic growth. This became the shared interests of the growth participants.

The second type of growth alliance is ethnic bargaining, which we discussed in Chapter 3 with reference to Malaysia as the basis of a grand political alliance. The political alliance built on this ethnic bargaining resulted in the Alliance, and later the Barisan National, which has dominated Malaysian politics and controlled government since 1957. It provided the broader political environment for rapid economic growth to take place under. Different participants benefited from the growth process. Harold Crouch goes further and describes the political basis for state dominance in Malaysia:

> UMNO's dominance of the political system was backed by the Malay elite's domination of the institutional pillars of the state: the bureaucracy, the armed forces and the police, the judiciary, and, at the symbolic peak, the monarchy. While UMNO, the bureaucracy, the military and the judiciary each had its own functions and interests, these elites were all part of a common Malay elite. They often came from the same family backgrounds and had gone to the same types of schools and it was not uncommon for them to be related through blood or marriage. (Crouch, 1996: 130)

More significantly, in Malaysia's case, the specific growth alliance has also shaped Malaysia's development strategy. As Alasdair Bowie's study shows, communal alliances produce compromised arrangements 'that govern relations between potential antagonistic ethnic, religious, or linguistic groups. Communal alliances or coalitions also influence the course of a country's economic and industrial development'. This 'intercommunal settlement' leads 'to different levels of constraint on the state actors in economic policymaking and subsequently to markedly different approaches to industrial development strategy in succeeding decades' (Bowie, 1991: 67, 29).

The third type of growth alliance is the military orchestrated political coalition, with a primary focus on industrialization and economic growth, as seen in South Korea, Indonesia and Thailand. While initiating political takeover on its own, the military would need some form of political basis for its political survival and continual rule. At the core of this type of growth alliance is the mutual dependence of the military and the business community. Speedy delivery of industrialization and economic growth is essential for the military's legitimacy and industrial capital is critical for the military's political and economic agenda. On the other hand, the business community cannot operate without access and political protection provided by the military.

The fourth type of growth alliance is to be found in countries such as China and Singapore, Taiwan during the Chiangs' years and Indonesia of the Suharto era. In these countries there was a single dominant political party that controlled the state machinery and utilized strong, penetrating corporatist arrangements to institutionalize the discipline, compliance and mobilization of various growth participants.

Beyond the specific characteristics of each type, growth alliances in Pacific Asian countries generally provided an informal but more effective governing structure than formal state institutions at the time. As such, these growth alliances led to corporatist governance in various guises and a very coherent social structure. Scholars have described this sort of polities as 'Japan Inc.', 'China Inc.', 'Singapore Inc.', and so on, or simply as the 'Nation Inc.'. This refers to the way key forces in society were 'incorporated' to form something akin to a national 'corporation' led by the state.

Rent deployment and rent seeking

It might be misleading to assume that, since the government is able to forge growth alliances and promote national incorporation in support of its growth agenda, it is the will of the state that determines the nature of the state-market, or government–business relationship. However, this is, in many cases, only half of the picture. A growth alliance, particularly those in a market economy, would need to be a setting from which not only the state but also various other participants could benefit. The concept of rent seeking explains how private capital and distributional groups endeavour to benefit from close government–business relations.

Let us start by comparing the socialist centrally planned economy and the Asian governed market economy. In both cases, there is a monopoly on resources. In the centrally planned economy, there is no international trade as such. Internal distribution and exchange are all controlled by the state. In the governed market economy, international flows of product, capital and labour are also tightly controlled by the state.

The effect of this monopoly is, however, different in these two types of economy – depending on whether there are market forces at play or not. In the governed market economy, as most Pacific Asian countries were when they experienced rapid industrialization and economic growth, the government uses its monopoly power to direct economic activities in the private sector. It is here that the concept of rent seeking arises. Moreover, such an arrangement also points to the debate about corruption in East Asian development due to close government–business relations.

When the government has a monopoly over necessary economic resources under a protected political and administrative environment, two things can happen, and indeed did happen in Pacific Asian countries. First, it can use its monopoly to shape the industrial structure and affect economic movements, by creating privileges for growth participants (traders, bankers, investors, manufacturers, distributors and so on), and by engaging in certain types of economic activities rather than others. A privilege, through licenses, export and import quotas, contracts or permits, is a comparative advantage that a growth participant enjoys over his/her competitors.

Rent-seeking activities are those by growth participants who, under competitive market conditions and state monopoly of economic resources and opportunities, seek favourable government treatment and gain a competitive edge over their fellow competitors in the growth area.

Rent deployment occurs when the government strategically targets its provision of privileges and preferential treatment to certain growth participants, to influence their economic activities and thus direct industrial and economic movement.

A privilege that the government issues to a particular participant is called rent, a term borrowed from economics with a slightly different meaning. Rent deployment therefore is the government giving privileges or special treatment to target growth participants in their particular industries and types of economic activities, in order to direct industrial and economic movement in desired directions.

Second, growth participants under competitive market conditions seek preferential treatment from the government and gain a competitive edge over their fellow competitors in the same industries. Efforts by growth participants to seek such privileges are called rent-seeking activities. Rent-seeking activities themselves are nothing unusual. The problem arises when they use illegal ways of gaining these privileges. If government officials are party to such illegal exchange, corruption occurs (see Chapter 5).

Corruption therefore tends to occur more systematically when the following four conditions are found simultaneously:

- The government has significant control of resources and access to resources.
- There is market competition under conditions of limited resources.
- There is a protected political and administrative environment.
- There are more incentives than constraints for public officials to be involved in rent exchange.

Pacific Asian countries saw these conditions to various degrees and in various combinations during their period of rapid industrialization and economic growth, which led to different levels of corruption (see Table 5.2 in Chapter 5). Singapore, for example, had the first three conditions, but for the fourth, the country has been different from the majority of Pacific Asian countries. Constraints placed on bureaucrats in the form of government discipline, a well-structured and effective legal system and strong political will to create a highly efficient and clean bureaucracy were complemented by the incentives of following the law and maintaining a lucrative government post.

Constraints on state power

The above section argued Pacific Asian states were capable of controlling and governing the market to implement its growth agenda during their rapid period of economic growth. For many, especially those critical of the developmental state theory, however, this is not the whole picture. Indeed, the state does not operate in a political vacuum.

The state's ability, strategy and policy in pursuit of rapid industrialization and economic development are shaped significantly by various factors and forces, some of which are unique to Pacific Asian countries. These constraints not only affect the state's capacity but also the direction of its policies and programmes.

In addition to other social and political constraints (see Chapter 8), industrial capital and domestic political structure are clearly two important constraints on how a state makes its decisions and to what extent it can put its growth agenda into action. Let us look at two unique cases illustrating this point. Alasdair Bowie, for example, discussing Malaysia, lists all the possible forces and factors that might have had a constraining impact on the state's industrial and economic policy: preferences for growth participants and their 'intermediate association', the structure of the polity and the economy, the character of policymakers, national political culture, the international system and others (Bowie, 1991: 1–8). But he argues that what best explains change in the economic development strategy in Malaysia is 'the changing nature of a communal settlement that has prevailed … since 1957' (ibid.: 9). Critical here, in Bowie's view, is the level of constraint that the communal settlement 'imposes on state autonomous decision making' (ibid., 1991: 21).

According to Bowie, the first phase after independence (1957–69) saw a mixture of market-led strategy in some sectors and extensive state intervention in others. This development strategy was clearly the effects of the intercommunal settlement that required the state to be active in 'improving the economic conditions of rural Malays', but placed 'severe constraints on the extent to which the state could intervene in the Chinese and Indian dominated modern commercial and industrial sector'.

The 1970–80 period saw 'increasing intrusive state policies designed to benefit Malays while limiting the entrepreneurial freedom of non-Malay business' in commerce and industry. This reflected a new agreement in ethnic bargaining to 'enlarge the Malay role in commerce and industry'. Finally, a state-centred industrial development strategy began to dominate from 1980, with large-scale state-controlled industries being set up to expand and consolidate a Malay presence in traditionally non-Malay sectors. This strategy began to dominate because the intercommunal settlement failed to address Malay interests (Bowie, 1991: 29–30).

A similar argument is put forward by Jeffrey A. Winters in his work on Indonesia. However, Winters focused on the structural power of industrial capital on the state. Observing a similar pattern of change of development strategy from market-led to state-led and back to market-led, Winters explores the structural power of 'capital controllers' and the limits they impose on government policy and strategy. At the core of the issue is industrial capital's 'decisive capacity to constrain decision makers' (Winters, 1996: 193). In Winters' view, different capital controllers (investors, financers, manufacturers and others) with different levels of mobility of resources that they commanded would have different demands on government's industrial policy and development strategy. 'Investors who were more mobile tended to favour the markets, whereas capital controllers who were less mobile tended to favour intervention by officials' (ibid.: 42). The question for Indonesia was how much structural power mobile capital had over the state, and how much that in turn affected the general orientation of the state's industrial choice and development strategy.

The first period, from 1965 to 1973, witnessed a bankrupt state in 'desperate need of financial and investment resources to stabilize the economy and society'. Economic policy during this period was consequently 'highly responsive to the demands and interests of the most mobile investors' (ibid.: xii) and thus more market-friendly. The oil boom from 1973 to the mid-1980s allowed the state access to abundant capital resources and thus diminished the leverage of capital controllers over the state. Consequently, the state was able to pursue a strong state-centric economic policy. The country's economic policies 'underwent a clear shift back to more market-based access and opportunity' after the oil boom, 'when the responsiveness of the state to those controlling private capital increased sharply' (ibid.: xiii).

Andrew MacIntyre interpreted this in more general terms. There is, according to MacIntyre, a 'strong consensus' among scholars of Indonesia 'that influence over policy is largely limited to the state, with societal groups being almost wholly excluded from participation on any systematic basis' (MacIntyre, 1990: 245). However, in MacIntyre's view, 'business groups can turn a restrictive corporatist institution to serve their own purposes, rather than those of the state's political strategists' (ibid.: 246).

Does law matter for economic development?

In considering the constraints on the state's hand to dictate the patterns of industrialization and economic activity, we have explored the role, interests and activities of non-state actors. Here we can also highlight the role of the law in the shaping of overall economic activity. In fact, the Pacific Asian case fits closely in a major debate in comparative politics about the role of legal institutions in industrialization and growth.

The question here is slightly different from that of the rule of law discussed earlier (see Chapter 4). The debate here centres around some key issues: Does law matter for economic development? What types of legal institutions matter? How do legal institutions affect economic development?

The debate can be traced back to the law and development movement in the 1960s in the United States, a movement associated closely with modernization theory and its promotion in developing countries. Law professors, in alliance with leading development aid agencies and donor organizations, saw themselves as generators of economic development and social change in developing countries. Consequently, early attempts to link law and economic development tended to be broad and progressive in vision and prescription.

The idea of 'social engineering through law' (Merryman, 1977: 465) put legal institutions at the centre of economic development and social change. More specifically, the law and development movement believed, as World Bank reports summarized a few decades later, that law is central to the development process, and law was an instrument that could be used to reform society.

As the laws they spoke of were formal institutions sanctioned by the state, the state should therefore 'initiate and promote economic development'. Moreover, law reform could lead to social change, and the law itself was an engine of change. Consequently, lawyers and judges could serve as social engineers (World Bank, 2008). As the broad modernization theory and its promotion in developing countries became increasingly problematic in the 1960s and 1970s, the law and development movement quickly declined. Among the reasons cited for the failure was the 'naive belief' that American legal institutions can be transferred easily to developing countries (World Bank, 2008a; Ginsburg, 2000: 829).

The revival of the law and development movement in the 1990s took a very narrow focus in a very different global environment (see Box 6.4). The role of law in economic development became a principal research issue and policy agenda for the World Bank and the International Monetary Fund (IMF). The World Bank initiated a focus on the role of law and economic development (World Bank, 2008a), and the IMF, together with the World Bank, organized a major conference on 'second generation reforms' that dealt with the broad issue of institutions and economic growth (IMF, 1999).

Box 6.4

Law and economic development: evolution of a view

Law and Development Movement of the 1960s

- Formal institutions provide the overall framework.
- Law and legal reform lead to economic development and social change.
- The state plays a critical role in initiating and promoting legal reform, and therefore economic development.

Neoliberalism of the 1990s

- Legal institutions ensure the working of the essential elements of a market economy.
- Informal institutions, that is, social capital, can make a difference to how formal institutions work.
- The role of the state should be kept to a minimum.

Unlike the early law and development movement, the debate in the 1990s on law and economic development was more precise on the question of how exactly law can affect economic development. Here, law is perceived as 'facilitating market transactions by defining property rights, guaranteeing the enforcement of contracts, and maintaining law and order' (World Bank, 2008a). The underlying rationale for the argument seemed to come not from lawyers and law professors, as in the 1960s, but from economists such as Douglass North. North saw that formal legal institutions, particularly those regarding property rights, were essential for the rise of modern capitalism in the West (North and Thomas, 1968, 1973). In his 1990 work, North extends this to a general theory (North, 1990).

While the new advocates share a broad belief with the law and development movement of the 1960s that institutions matter, there are sceptics even among the new advocates. Their challenges focus on three broad categories of issues, as Matthew Stephenson summarizes (Stephenson, 2008):

- Why institutions affect economic development: Legal institutions vary in their capacity 'to protect property rights, reduce transaction costs, and prevent coercion', and therefore, do not necessarily all lead to economic development.
- How institutions affect economic development: It is difficult to assess institutional quality in practice: it depends on context and is not easily observable. At times of crisis, institutions may hinder a government's ability to respond; and finally, correlation does not equal causation.
- How we measure institutional quality: Competing approaches and national conditions make a scientific way of measurement difficult.

A more substantive challenge to the law and development thesis however came from Pacific Asia. As Tom Ginsburg observes, 'there is clearly a tension between the centrality of law in theories of development and existing evidence from Asia' (Ginsburg, 2000: 830). Rapid economic growth took place in many Pacific Asian countries with no 'sound legal institutions' in place.

In a multi-year study by the Harvard Institute of International Development and the Asian Development Bank (ADB) on the relationship between law and economic development in India, Japan, China, Korea, Taiwan and Malaysia, Katharina Pistor and Philip A. Wellons found 'a relatively high level of state involvement was compatible, and perhaps even conducive to, economic growth' (Pistor and Wellons, 1999: 10). Legal reform became an issue only after the rapid economic growth period. In Ginsburg's words, the study shows that 'formal legal rules were not sufficient to generate rapid growth initially, but growth resulted from specific (statist) policies. Only when the policy shifted to reliance on market mechanisms did legal change begin to have an important impact' (Ginsburg, 2000: 839).

The Pacific Asian challenge is not merely empirical. At the theoretical level, the debate focuses on the two questions that have been at the centre of the law and development movement, namely, whether and how law matters for economic growth in Asia. The most serious challenge to the law and development thesis is a study by Kanishka Jayasuriya and his associates that directly questions the law and development thesis and argues that there is no 'necessary causal connections between markets, liberal politics and the rule of law', and the absence of these causal connections suggests the existence of a rather different set of institutional arrangements, or an 'institutional package', in Pacific Asia (Jayasuriya, 1999: 1).

Among these unique institutional arrangements is the fact that formal legal institutions were generally weak or even missing in many Pacific Asian countries during their rapid growth period. Economic activities relied on informal institutions for effectiveness, and certainly for protection. Moreover, instead of being constrained by law, the state is empowered in such an institutional environment. Those challenging the law and development thesis therefore suggest that there might be two possible ways of ordering private economic activities, either by law or by state policy. State policy seemed to be the dominant mode in Pacific Asia, particularly during their period of rapid economic growth, where law mattered much less.

However, we should note carefully the second of Ginsburg's conclusions that points out the important role of the law in maintaining growth and development in Pacific Asia when the economy has shifted towards a market economy. As the next section highlights, putting North Korea to one side, all countries in the region either have transitioned to a functioning market economy or are well on their way towards this goal.

Even China, once the largest planned economy in the world and a one-party state, has made significant reforms towards the market system. Since the 1980s, a series of regulatory reforms have moved China in this direction. These range from land reform to state-owned enterprise reform, from the protection of private ownership to the introduction of financial institutions and stock exchanges. In 2013, China's rulers further pledged a 'decisive' role for markets in the economy by 2020 suggesting further reform in state-owned enterprises and a shifting of the state approach towards the economy away from intervention towards regulation.

How then can we conceptualize the patterns of state-involvement in the economy in Pacific Asia?

The development model debate

The above 'unorthodox' patterns of political economy have engendered a major debate on how economic growth and development occurred in Pacific Asia. Referring back to Johnson's original puzzle, the task of explaining the underlying patterns and dynamics of development in the region requires making sense of what has occurred. Adding to the complexity, however, is the fact that Pacific Asia remains a highly dynamic region, with the patterns of state-economy relations of 1960s Japan, for example, differing significantly from even the 1990s. Moreover, due to historical contingency, patterns across the region also differ significantly.

In Jayasuriya's critique of the liberal model of law and development, he suggested an alternative model built on two pillars (Jayasuriya, 1999: 2):

- A common set of normative understandings of the purpose and function of state power and governance.
- A form of managed and negotiated capitalism.

Indeed, there has been a long-lasting debate among scholars and political commentators as to whether there is an Asian model of economic development. Sceptics cite vast differences among Pacific Asian countries in development level, economic structure and regime type, as well as cultural and social conditions. This makes a generalization of Pacific Asian experiences difficult. Despite the differences, many see the argument that there is an Asian model of economic development as being valid. Some build their model on a single, but most critical, aspect of the way that rapid economic growth is generated across Pacific Asian countries.

This first of such models is the developmental state model discussed above (see Johnson, 1982). A second emphasizes cultural factors, usually either Confucian ethics or Asian values (see Chapter 2). This model is represented in the work by Hung-chao Tai (1989). The Confucian work ethic, corporate relations and family structure constitute what Tai calls an 'oriental alternative' to the Western rational economic model.

A third popular model is the export-led development model (Chow and Kellman, 1993). This argues a great expansion and great reliance on exports is found almost universally among Pacific Asian countries during their rapid growth period. Peter C. Y. Chow and Mitchell H. Kellman, for example, find there is a causal relationship 'between the growth of exports and their concurrent and subsequent economic growth' (ibid., 1993: 7).

Finally, a well-received World Bank study (World Bank, 1993) attributed the 'East Asian miracle' to sound, unorthodox public policy that includes factors from macroeconomic management to savings policy, and from fair income distribution to export promotion.

There are other factors that have been singled out. For example, a key puzzle for scholars studying economic development in Pacific Asia is squaring the observation that states have played a big role in the economy, especially during the early rapid growth period, with measures of economic freedom that have increased over the long-term (see Table 6.1).

Some scholars have interpreted the increase in economic freedom as evidence that removing barriers, impediments and interference in the market economy was responsible for economic growth, not state planning as the developmental state literature asserts. This has led to a major debate, especially since the 1990s, over how to interpret the growth of the market economy and the retreat of the state in Pacific Asia.

Case Study Lab 6.3

Single factor explanations of the 'East Asian miracle'

There are theories attempting to explain why Pacific Asian countries have been able to achieve remarkable rapid industrialization and economic development, on the basis of a single, most critical enabling factor. Below are some of the typical arguments:

Developmental state:	The type of state that was capable of bringing all societal forces to bear positively on the national growth agenda.
Oriental alternative	The type of society with unique state–society relations and cultural habits.
Export-led growth	The type of growth strategy that took advantage of the domestic and international conditions of the time.
Public policy	Sound and unorthodox public policy that worked.

At one end of the debate, scholars have critiqued any discussion of an 'Asian model' of economic growth and placed that growth in the long historical pattern of global growth. Paul Krugman, for example, argued that growth in Asia was due to mobilization of resources and not to increases in efficiency, thereby strongly refuting the view that 'Asian successes demonstrate the superiority of economies with fewer civil liberties and more planning than we in the West have been willing to accept' (Krugman, 1994):

> the realities of East Asian growth suggest that we may have to unlearn some popular lessons. It has become common to assert that East Asian economic success demonstrates the fallacy of our traditional laissez-faire approach to economic policy and that the growth of these economies shows the effectiveness of sophisticated industrial policies and selective protectionism. Authors such as James Fallows have asserted that the nations of that region have evolved a common 'Asian system,' whose lessons we ignore at our peril. The extremely diverse institutions and policies of the various newly industrialized Asian countries, let alone Japan, cannot really be called a common system. But in any case, if Asian success reflects the benefits of strategic trade and industrial policies, those benefits should surely be manifested in an unusual and impressive rate of growth in the efficiency of the economy. And there is no sign of such exceptional efficiency growth. (Krugman, 1994)

Many are sceptical of single-factor explanations. In fact, these factors in isolation may not be unique to those Pacific Asian countries experiencing rapid economic growth, nor were they only found in their rapid growth period. But put together they may be unique to these countries during their rapid growth period.

Therefore, a list of factors is also a popular way of building a model for Pacific Asian economic development. Paul W. Kuznets, for example, lists five shared characteristics that seem significant in the contemporary economic development of Japan, Taiwan and Korea, as well as being key components of the East Asian model. These include 'high investment ratios, small public sectors, competitive labour markets, export expansion, and government intervention in the economy' (Kuznets, 1988: S38–9).

The problem with listing factors, however, is that there is no clear internal relationship specified among those factors within the 'model'. These factors therefore may not constitute a coherent, logical model of economic development.

In his growth system model, Xiaoming Huang identifies five principal elements of the growth system (Huang, 2005: 248):

- A growth-at-any-cost mentality;
- A core economic decision-making structure;
- A national growth unit;
- An economy based upon strategic product(s) and their constant upgrading;
- A centripetally dynamic society.

In this growth system, the initial conditions at the take-off led to:

- An export-centred development regime;
- A series of government policies and institutional arrangements to support and sustain the growth pattern;
- A reorganization of production and consumption that breaks the conventional boundaries over property, accounting and territories;
- A centripetal society with the social, structural and cultural attitude that can sustain such an interventionist state and a corporatist industrial organization.

In Huang's view, rapid economic growth in Pacific Asia was more than the effect of economic transactions. It was also part of a social movement. A model of this explanation should therefore be able to account for the broad institutional transformation generating and sustaining the rapid economic growth.

These models ask the reader to consider carefully how we should classify the 'unorthodox' development strategies in Pacific Asia. They each identify aspects of the patterns of development across the region and suggest that, put together, these elements present a model of development. Such an assertion is not to say a model could be replicated in different geographical locations and in different historical periods but rather that put together the patterns of development in Pacific Asia during rapid growth show a certain similarity across the majority of cases. However, as shown below, even accepting a model of economic development in Pacific Asia during the rapid growth period, there is increasing evidence that a paradigm shift has occurred since then.

Paradigm shift

In his investigation of the causes for Japan's lost decade in the 1990s, T. J. Pempel called our attention to the profound shifts in the political economic structure of Japanese society, and the institutions built upon such structure, and consequently the inability of the Japanese system to continue to deliver economic growth (Pempel, 1998). Such an analysis captured the beginning of the ending of the development pattern in Pacific Asia, and explores the institutional causes of such development.

Growing out of the model

The 1997–8 Asian financial crisis was a significant event for Pacific Asia. As with almost every aspect of the rapid economic growth in Pacific Asia, there are vastly different views on what the financial crisis signifies (see Box 6.5). Many see this as evidence of what is fundamentally wrong with the model (Clifford and Engardio, 1999; Richter, 2000). The financial crisis was a confirmation of their long-held view that there was no economic miracle, and that the problems inherent in Asian state's approaches to growth are not curable.

Another view puts the blame on the inadequacy of the global and regional financial architecture (Noble and Ravenhill, 2000; Lee and Bohm, 2002; Sharma, 2003). The financial crisis came about because the international financial system was not able to manage the increasingly rapid and more complicated global movement of capital and products.

A third view, led by leading international financial organizations such as the World Bank and the IMF, found the root causes of the crisis in the economic institutions within Pacific Asian countries (Agenor et al., 1999; Hunter et al., 1999; Stiglitz and Yusuf, 2001; Woo et al., 2000; World Bank, 2000). The problems in capital markets, banking institutions, asset management, monetary and fiscal policy, currency systems, corporate governance, social policy, exchange rates, trade policies and regulatory capability required further and deeper reform and restructuring for the economic miracle to continue.

Finally, there is a view that the Asian financial crisis is an indication of the end of the rapid economic growth (Huang, 2005) in the region. The system generating and sustaining rapid economic growth has over the years lost its effectiveness. The financial crisis was a form of hard landing for countries such as Korea, Thailand and Indonesia, where the conditions for the growth system to work were no longer present, but a transition away from the growth model had not been properly prepared.

Box 6.5

How the financial crisis affected Asian political economy

The Asian financial crisis in 1997–98 had significant impact on Asian political economy. Andrew MaCintyre and T. J. Pempel and their team see the crisis affected the way Asian political economy is organized, and indeed the very model of developmental state, and served as a catalyst for reform and change:

- The crisis has a profound effect on pre-existing patterns of political economy, in practices and policies regarding banking, corporate regulation, ownership in manufacturing and services, social protection as well as national links to regionalization, globalization and internationalization.
- The commitment to 'growth with equity' was more reasserted than abandoned.
- The crisis stimulated new perspectives among political and business elites on some of the underpinnings of East Asian success, as often debated between liberals on 'get the prices right' and developmentalists on 'close government business relations' as they are seen to have caused the crisis.
- The crisis has also led to a profound change in the region in the vital areas of finance, including the introduction of currency swaps, Asian bond markets and enhanced accumulation of foreign reserves, creating new regional institutions: ASEAN plus 3, East Asian submit, negotiation of bilateral FTAs and enhanced commitment to state directed social welfare system. Cumulatively these changes have left East Asia as a more institutionalized and more 'Asian' region than before.

MaCintyer and Pempel, 2008: 2–3

As well as the hard landings of rapid economic growth during the Asian financial crisis, there were other forms of exit from the model. China, Singapore and Malaysia managed to survive the financial crisis. At the same time, serious reforms were introduced and new growth strategies were pursued. Breaking away from the normal practice under the Asian model of economic growth, these countries sought to:

- Reduce the direct involvement of the state in the economy;
- Expand their domestic consumer demands;
- Attract international capital to invest in these countries;
- Move to new areas of global competitiveness;
- Bring down barriers between domestic and international markets;
- Forge closer integration with the international economic system.

Today, the economies of Pacific Asian countries are much transformed. Barry Naughton wrote in 1995 that Chinese economic reform was to promote economic growth within the existing socialist, centrally planned system, rather than to replace the system with a new one (as in the post-Soviet reform in Russia in the 1990s). The old system faded away as the new market economy grew rapidly along with new economic institutions and relationships. The new economic system is now established and the old model marginalized as the new economy becomes dominant. This 'growing-out-of-the-model' phenomenon can also be observed in many Pacific Asian countries in their economic transition from the Asian model of economic development.

Most important among all the changes taking place in Pacific Asian countries in their reform and transformation is the role of the state in economic development, and the relationship between state and market. More specifically, how much has the developmental state changed, adjusted or reformed? It is certain that the role of the state has been much reduced, if not eliminated. Robert H. Wade, for example, explains how new international regulations limit the authority of national governments to take many of the industrial policies proven to be instrumental for economic success under the developmental state model. Yun Tae Kim also questions whether it is still 'the era of the developmental state?' (Kim, 1999: 450). He argues that:

Case Study Lab 6.4

Analysing interaction between political institutions and policy preferences in political economic transition

In explaining why countries responded to the financial crisis differently, Peter Gourevitch looks at how political institutions, mechanisms of interest aggregation and influence responded to the financial crisis and in particular the policy changes in corporate governance:

- The Asian financial crisis unleashed pressures to change policy towards corporate governance:
  - Some pressure from interest groups within each country,
  - Some from international investors, and
  - Some from international policy institutions such as the IMF.
- How these preferences actually influenced policy was influenced by the mechanisms of interest aggregation, that is, the political institutions. Because these variables differed within each country before the crisis, the county responses varied.
  - Korea: change in political institutions was substantial and had strong effects on economic policy towards corporate governance. Significant democratization altered the power relations among groups in Korean society. This led to strong shareholder protections and efforts to limit the authority of the oligarchs.
  - Singapore, Malaysia and China: political institutions remain the same but interest group pressures led to some modification of governance policy and practices.
  - Thailand, Philippines and Taiwan: somewhere in between. Partial institutional change, some interest group pressures. Modest policy shifts.

Gourevitch, 2008: 73

> the state has become a less internally cohesive actor … the post-democratization process has made the state more responsive to popular demands and has subsequently led to the politicization of the economic policymaking process … the liberalization of economic relationships has considerably eroded the capability and possibility for the state to direct a whole range of macroeconomic policies. (ibid.: 458)

More specifically, using the case of Korea, Kim shows that the state–business relationship has been transformed. There has been a decline in the number and effectiveness of government policy instruments controlling the private sector, and therefore a 'reduced dependence of big business on the state'; financial control is becoming a less effective method of controlling the chaebol as they turn to direct financing in domestic and foreign financial markets (ibid.: 452).

For many, while the developmental state is adapting itself to the changing environment, some of its features may survive (Weiss, 1998; Polidano, 2001). In Charles Polidano's view, if autonomy – the ability of states to act independently of the wishes of non-state actors – is at the heart of the developmental state, features of the developmental state will continue to exist, as it is simply 'a component of state capacity' (Polidano, 2001: 524). From a different perspective, Linda Weiss argues that the Asian financial crisis is 'not a vindication, but a contradiction of the proposition that the developmental state model is ill-suited to a "global" economy'. Moreover, the viability of the developmental state is required by the fundamental logic of global capitalist diversity (Weiss, 1998: 25, 37).

Shifts in the institutional foundation of the model

The shift away from the classic developmental state or the Asian model of economic development has highlighted major changes in the institutional foundations of Asian growth. A number of important studies are now exploring how and why Pacific Asian states are evolving the institutional foundations of the Asian model.

Studies have outlined the fundamental economic, social and political changes that have occurred in the region and linked them to changes in the institutional foundations of the Asian growth model. Dali Yang's study, for example, presented a detailed study of the relationship between a more market driven and competitive economy and institutional change in China. Yang concluded:

> governance reforms, ranging from the streamlining of government and the simplification and rationalization of administrative approvals, to the divesture of military business, the reforms of government financial management, and the utilization of competitive mechanisms for government procurements and land allocation, and others, have already helped enhance the efficiency, transparency, and fairness of the administrative state, strengthen the regulatory apparatuses, remove various institutional incentives and loopholes for corrupt practices, and improve the environment for business. (Yang, 2004: 290–1)

In Japan, studies flowing from the 'lost decade' (Hayashi et al., 2002) of Japanese growth in the 1990s began to take seriously the notion that the institutional foundations of the developmental state have shifted or are shifting significantly. For example, commenting on the impact of the economic crisis, globalization and and liberalization on the institutions of Japanese political economy, Streeck and Thelen note:

> Despite the strains of prolonged economic crisis, traditional Japanese political-economic institutions have exhibited remarkable staying power. Much remains of the institutions that support and sustain Japan's version of a 'coordinated' market economy… [but] stability should not obscure change, particularly in the way in which old institutions and policies are being used in the service of new ends. Among other things, the corporate ties that are often seen as defining a distinctively 'coordinated' as opposed to a 'liberal' model of capitalism are being tapped as mechanisms through which to accomplish corporate downsizing and a move towards more liberalized labor markets. Liberalization in Japan, that is to say, has unfolded above all by traditional institutions being deployed in novel and, indeed over the long run, transformative ways. (Streeck and Thelen, 2005: 17)

The Japanese case, on which the developmental state theory was originally built, shows that many elements of the Asian economic model, such as growth alliances, industrial policy and state coordination of economic activity, are falling by the wayside. At the same time the institutions of political economy, as in the Chinese case, remain resilient but adaptive to the new economic realities of a more mature and competitive market economy. Political liberalization and democratization has further reshaped the institutional foundations of the Asian model of economic growth as have international pressures in the realm of good governance and secure regulatory practices.

Finally, globalization has reduced the ability of the state to intervene in trade and economic relations between Pacific Asian states and the developed consumer markets of the world's advanced economies. Pacific Asian states are major destinations for foreign direct investment. The multinational companies attracted to the region expect the regulatory system to treat all businesses without favouritism and to create a level playing field.

Southeast Asia, arguably, has experienced this type of dependency on the global economy far longer than the Northeast Asian states. As Beesen argues, with a long history of colonial dependence followed by strong economic relations with Japan (and now also China), 'for much of the region the idea that governments enjoyed economic autonomy and the capacity to determine national policy either independently or in pursuit of some exclusively national sovereign interest was always a myth' (Beeson, 2003: 767).

Hill advances a set of factors driving politico-economic reform in Southeast Asia, pointing out in particular how:

> major negative exogenous shocks, economic crises, the imminent cessation of external support, and a dawning realization that 'the system is broken' have all played a role. The first (a sharp terms-of-trade decline) was the trigger

Box 6.6

Reforming Japan Inc.: transparency, openness and competition

There are competitive perspectives on the consequence of the regime shifts in Japanese political economy:

- The 1990s breakdown of Japan Inc. led to economic stagnation and policy malaise, a lost decade or two, and weak and incapable government and state institutions.
- Profound change took place in response to the regime shift, to reform the system to be transparent, open and competitive in meeting the challenge of industrial and demographic maturation.
- Institutional and structural reform in a series of new laws to bring transparency, opening and competition in the system:
  - Administrative Procedure Act (1994). Makes it mandatory for government agencies to have a legal basis for administrative guidance and to document the guidance in writing when requested.
  - Public Comments Procedure (1999). Requires ministries and agencies to solicit comment from the public at the midpoint of deliberations over setting, changing or abolishing regulations or their interpretation.
  - National Ethnics Law for Central Government Public Servants (2000). Defines acceptable behaviour for central government bureaucrats versus the individuals and companies they deal with in an official capacity. Prohibits the type of wining and dining that went on between regulators and those they regulated in the past in an attempt to eradicate collusive relationships between central government bureaucrats, industries and external government organizations.
  - Information Disclosure Law (2001). Forces government agencies to make more information available to the general public about its interaction with regulatory constituencies and its financial expenditures.
  - Major political, bureaucratic and administrative reforms also bring openness, transparency and competition to government institutions and shift policymaking power and initiatives from the bureaucracy to the political level, as well as from LDP factions to a strong political executive.

Amyx and Drysdale, 2003: 3–10

> for Indonesia's major reforms in the 1980s. The third and fourth were the key factors in Viet Nam's doi moi, and they were of some relevance in the Philippine reforms of the 1990s. The second resulted in substantial macro and financial sector reforms in the economies affected by the 1997–1998 Asian financial crisis. (Hill, 2013: 124)

Overall, then, we can conclude that while Pacific Asian states still play an active role in the development and growth of the domestic economy, as in many parts of the world, the methods they use to achieve this have changed significantly since the heyday of governing the market last century. In more contemporary times, a paradigm shift has occurred as these economies integrate with the global economy and mature as market economies. At the same time, significant changes within the overall political system have created a much more dynamic and pluralistic environment that has meant institutions of the state have retreated from outwardly interventionist policies to take on more regulatory roles.

In lieu of a definitive conclusion on the political economy of growth and development in Pacific Asia, some important observations must suffice. First, the state has played an active role in the economy. Second, economic liberalization has progressed along with industrialization and development. Third, while the state has arguably played an important role, it is clearly not the only actor responsible for Pacific Asia's impressive economic growth, a raft of social and economic actors have played a part.

Fourth, since the 1990s, economic reform in Pacific Asia has changed the very institutions that supported the developmental state in the early stage of economic growth and development and supported the evolution of the market as the primary means of economic exchange.

Finally, we observe ongoing changes in the role of the state in economic growth and development in the region suggesting Pacific Asia's era of transition is far from over. This is evident not only in the former communist planned economies, such as China and Vietnam, but also in Japan and a number of Southeast Asian nations at varying stages of development. We hope this chapter has provided some insight into these debates to help you classify and understand this transition as it unfolds in one of if not the largest and most dynamic parts of the world.

Chapter summary

- The developmental state features a market economy governed by the state that takes the organization of the national economy as its central purpose and function.
- The state governs the market through industrial policy and a growth alliance with industrial capital, incorporating key societal forces into the growth process.
- Industrial capital and other societal forces also seek privileged relations with the state and pose primary constraints on state power.
- There have been great debates over the role of law in economic development. The Pacific Asian experiences provide challenging evidence to the theoretical foundations of the old and new law and development movements.
- The unique state–business relationship constitutes a key component of the patterns in the organization and promotion of rapid economic growth in Pacific Asian countries in the second half of the twentieth century. Whether this, together with other features of rapid economic growth, amounts to an Asian model of economic development is a matter of intense debate.
- The strategies and scenarios of transformation of Pacific Asian countries from their pattern of rapid economic growth have varied. In particular, while the role of the state has clearly been reduced, views differ on the future of the state–business relationship in Pacific Asian countries and indeed on the fate of the developmental state.

Further reading

Woo-Cumings (1999) is a good starting point for an overview of the concept of the developmental state, the debates surrounding the concept and the evolution of the research paradigm centred on this concept. For the actual working of the developmental state in Pacific Asian countries, refer to individual studies from which the concept and the whole research programme has emerged (Johnson, 1982; Deyo, 1987; Amsden, 1989; Wade, 1990). Öniş (1991) and Castells (1992) provide good summaries of these studies and the main issues on the topic. For the large problem of the role of the state in economic development, Linda Weiss and John M. Hobson's volume (1995) provides a good comparative historical analysis of the East Asian and European experiences and a good summary of the related theories, concepts and debates. Wade (1990) provides a good overview of the literature on the role of government in East Asian industrialization. For the role of industrial policy and its critics, see Johnson (1982) and Okimoto (1989). David Kang's work (2002) is good reading on the whole issue of rent seeking, corruption and what difference it can make to economic development. For constraints on state power, see Winters (1996), MacIntyre (1990), Bowie (1991) and Haggard (1990). For discussions on an Asian model of economic development, see World Bank (1993) and Huang (2005).

Study questions

1. Discuss the institutional and political foundations of the developmental state.
2. Can the developmental state be market friendly? If so, how?
3. Does the state have its own interests in national economic activities? If so, what are these interests? If not, what motivates the state in its economic activism?
4. Explain the consequences of industrial policy.
5. Do you think there is an Asian model of economic development? If so, why?
6. Why has Pacific Asia arguably experienced a 'paradigm shift' in the state's orientation towards economic growth and development?

Key terms

Regulatory state (149); Developmental state (149); Johnson's puzzle (149); State-economy relations (149); Free, simulated and governed market (152); Economic activism (151); Industrial policy (157); Economic planning (151); Government-business relations (168); Government intervention (152); Export-led development (165); Law and development movement (163); Neoliberalism (163); Economic freedom (154); Japan Inc. (158); Growth alliance (158); Iron triangle (159); Rent seeking (160); Rent deployment (160); Asian capitalism (161); Asian model of economic development (165); Economic reform and structuring (167).

Chapter 7

Political parties, elections and political order

Political parties and elections play a significant role in modern politics. They are the core practices of democratic politics. Without the freedom of assembly and open and fair elections, there is no genuine democracy. Moreover, different parties and electoral systems affect the way that interests are represented and how political power is distributed in a political system. Indeed, the differentiation in the development of modern political systems can partially be explained by the differences in party and electoral systems. The problem of political parties and elections is more acute in Pacific Asia because of the different roles they play in governance and politics, and their close association with the rise and fall of different political regimes in post-war political development.

This chapter discusses, in the first part, the role of political parties in Pacific Asian politics, party politics in different political systems and the organization of political parties; and, in the second, the electoral systems in Pacific Asia, how they affect politics and governance, and key issues in recent electoral system reforms. The focus of this chapter is on the institutional arrangements in the party and electoral systems, and how they shape the patterns of political mobilization and participation, as well as the overall political structure.

The rise of modern political parties in Pacific Asia

Multiparty party politics came late to Pacific Asia for a number of reasons. First, the traditional order was maintained in many countries into the twentieth century and generally had little tolerance for allowing the organization of political forces against the state. In China, for example, the saying *jiedang yingsi* expresses traditional disdain for forming a group or 'ganging up' to pursue 'selfish' private interests. The character *dang* refers here to a gang, a clan and now also to a political party. The saying itself conveys the logic of the overall political order in premodern Northeast Asia. Loyalty to the dynasty was seen as non-divisible. Early attempts to create parties along interest or ideological lines were therefore going against the traditional political logic.

A second reason is the historical pattern of colonialism in the region. More often than not, political parties emerged out of armed struggles against colonial powers or foreign invasion such as the Vietnamese Communist

Party's struggle against French Colonial forces in Indochina. As with the Indonesian National Party formed by Sukarno in 1927, colonial authorities, in this case the Dutch, made every effort to dissolve the party and arrest and imprison the leaders.

A third reason lies in the breakdown of pluralist politics in the early post-war years. As previous chapters have explored, the consolidation of conservative alliances left very little space for multiparty politics. In some cases, such as in South Korea, the military took over the role of political parties. In other cases, such as China, one political party, the Communist Party of China, emerged victorious in a bloody civil war against the Nationalist Party and made every effort to remove their opposition. Such a consolidation of conservative forces in the military or one-party system hampered the evolution of multiparty politics.

Japan was the first state to introduce political parties into the overall political order. Parties began forming as early as the 1870s. In 1890, the Japanese Empire successfully undertook its first general election for the House of Representatives becoming the first country in Asia to popularly elect its national assembly. While most countries in the region were under some form of colonial rule, or struggling to adapt to the new international conditions and reform challenges, Japan constituted a national assembly made up of three major political parties, one small party and a number of independents. At this time, however, Japan was a monarchy shifting towards constitutionalism and much political power remained in the hands of the Emperor, the military and the elites.

Following World War II (WWII), political parties became the key institution for political advocacy and mobilization. With liberalization and democratization in the 1980s and 1990s, political parties and elections have taken on a new significance in the region and are now the primary, legitimate platform for gaining political power, for representing divergent interests and ideologies and for constituting the government through national popular vote.

The significance of the development of political parties lies in the relationship they have with the overall political order. Combined with the functioning of the electoral system, they are some of the key institutions for determining how political forces will compete for power, how interest groups are represented and even how decisions are made. Understanding party and electoral systems, therefore, provides insight into the overall functioning of the political order in Pacific Asian countries. Moreover, as the chapter will demonstrate, electoral rules, party politics and political order interact and are closely intertwined. To what extent each can affect the other depends on the overall political environment and the organization of the polity in each case.

The following sections conceptualize the patterns of party organization in Pacific Asia and illustrate some of the challenging dynamics across the region. This is followed by an overview of the electoral system and a discussion of their role in the overall political system.

Political parties and party systems

In 1966, political scientist and Asia scholar Lucian Pye observed, 'Asian politics are caught in a profound dilemma: they can neither get along well without political parties nor work well with them' (Pye, 1966a: 369). Even in 1985, in a comparative survey of political party systems in Pacific Asia, Haruhiro Fukui concluded that the Asia and Pacific area had so far proved to be 'a generally inhospitable terrain for the development of Western-style political parties and party politics' (Fukui, 1985: 10).

More than forty years since Pye's observation, the patterns of development of political parties in Pacific Asia are much clearer. As in most countries in the West, political parties are primarily a platform for elections in an increasing number of Pacific Asian countries. They are fast becoming what Otto Kirchheimer called 'catch-all parties' or what Angelo Panebianco calls 'electoral-professional parties' (Kirchheimer, 1966; Panebianco, 1988: 262).

However, the transformation of political parties into predominantly electoral-professional parties happened much later in Pacific Asia than in Western countries. Maurice Duverger, Otto Kirchheimer and Leond D. Epstein (Duverger, 1954; Kirchheimer, 1966; Epstein, 1967) placed this transformation in Western democracies in the early part of the twentieth century. In Pacific Asia, the transformation has been closely related to the movement of political liberalization and democratic transition from the mid-1980s, and the establishment of electoral systems thereafter.

Box 7.1

Pacific Asian political parties in comparison to those in a Western democracy

Political parties in Pacific Asia, particularly those catch-all parties, are different in many ways from political parties in a Western democracy:

- Lack of pre-existing social cleavages and patterns of elite politics.
- More pragmatic than programmatic, with low institutionalized programmatic electoral competition.
- Traditional left–right economic cleavage or similar broad ideological frameworks appear underdeveloped.
- Extent of party system institutionalization varies.
- Most parties are recent creations, with a lifespan shorter than 20 years except Japan's LDP and Taiwan's KMT.
- Depend more on the popularity of their charismatic leaders than voters' partisan attachment.
- Thin in organizational structure and mass member support with a party administrative elite.

Dalton, Shin and Chu, 2008: 2–3

The **Leninist Party** is a type of political party modelled after the Soviet Communist Party during its formative Lenin era (late 1910s to early 1920s). This type of party features communist ideology, secrecy, strict discipline, closed membership, party loyalty and complete devotion. The Leninist Party was the model for Mao's Chinese Communist Party, Kim's Workers' Party of Korea, Ho's Vietnamese Communist Party and Chiang's KMT.

For much of the twentieth century, political parties in Pacific Asian countries took a rocky road to establishing themselves as a standard part of modern institutions. The first part of the twentieth century was an age of 'class, ideology, and revolution'. Nascent political parties were soon turned into a useful platform for societal representation, political advocacy and mass mobilization.

There are several factors that shaped the early development of modern political parties. First, the idea of modern political parties as the principal framework and platform for interest articulation and representation met strong resistance from the political reality of the traditional power structure and political practices. The battle between politicians and military generals in the Meiji (1868–1912), Taisho (1912–26) and early Showa (1926–89) eras in Japan ended with the military generals marginalizing politicians and hijacking the political party system.

The phenomenon of the military generals marginalizing politicians and delaying the development of modern political party institutions was also seen in Thailand during much of its post-1932 modern political history.

A second factor was the influence of the world communist movement and, in particular, the Soviet model of a political party – what is called the Leninist party. The communist revolution in Russia brought communist ideology to Pacific Asia. Advocating a society with no private property or classes, communism appealed a great deal to Pacific Asian populations who had long been under the siege of a suppressive social hierarchy, as well as enduring class division and tensions (see Chapter 2). The Soviet revolution brought a unique type of political party, the Leninist Party, to Pacific Asia. The Leninist Party model had a great impact on communist parties in Pacific Asia, both in those countries the communist party eventually took power – China, Vietnam and North Korea – and those where the communists were active in seeking political power – Indonesia, Thailand, the Philippines and Malaysia. Communist parties were set up to mobilize and organize mass revolutionary movements.

A third factor was the effect of nationalist movements across Pacific Asia seeking independence from colonial rule (see Chapter 1). While, in some cases, independence was achieved through negotiation with colonial rulers, in the majority of the countries, independence was fought for and hard earned with armed struggle against colonial rule. In the former cases, such as Singapore, Malaysia and the Philippines, political parties were set up as organized interests and a platform for negotiation with the colonial government. In the latter cases, notably Indonesia, Korea and Vietnam, and to a large extent China, political parties emerged as the institutional core of the political movement, military operation and social management.

COUNTRY PROFILE

MALAYSIA

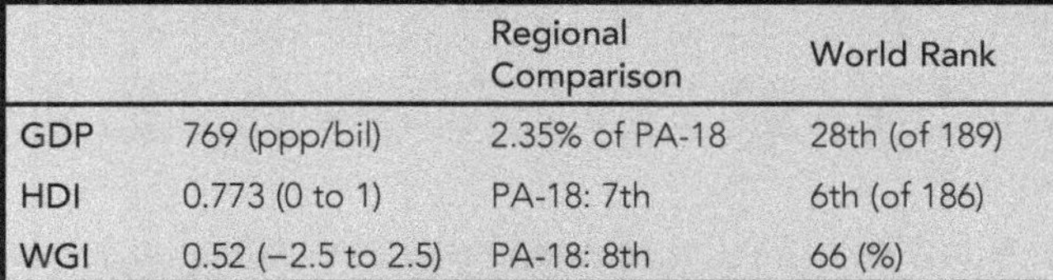

		Regional Comparison	World Rank
GDP	769 (ppp/bil)	2.35% of PA-18	28th (of 189)
HDI	0.773 (0 to 1)	PA-18: 7th	6th (of 186)
WGI	0.52 (–2.5 to 2.5)	PA-18: 8th	66 (%)

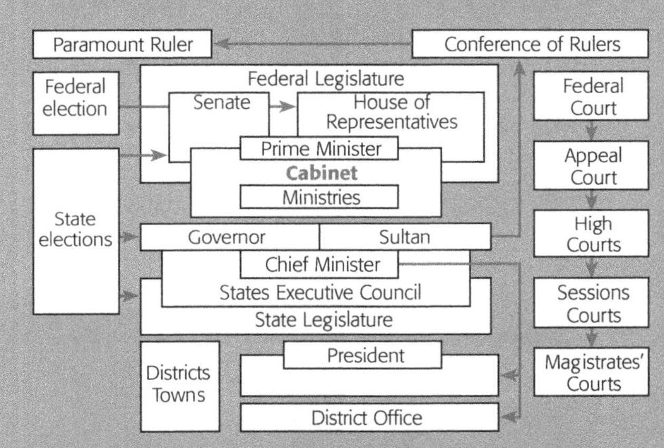

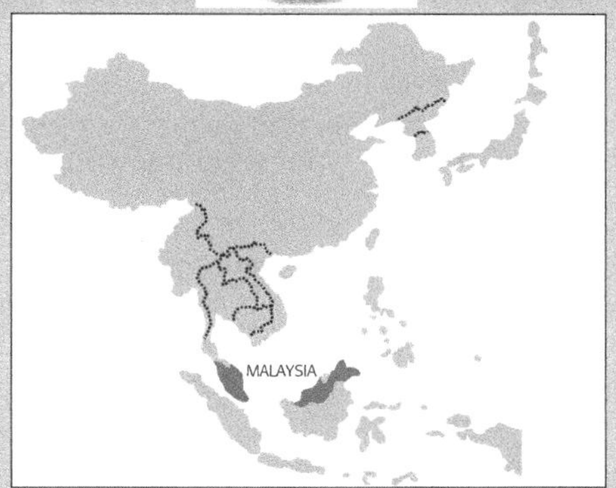

Key political facts

Electoral system for national legislature
First-past-the-post in single-member districts.

Political cycles
General and, in usual cases, state elections, every 5 years.
Government to table annual budget at Parliament for approval in September.

Further reading

Saw and Kesavapany, 2006; Gomez, 2004.

Timeline of modern political development

1957	Independence from Britain. Constitution establishes Federation of Malaya with a federal state model and a parliamentary system. The Alliance has been the ruling political coalition ever since.
1962–6	Conflict with Indonesia over the formation of Malaysia.
1963	Forms the Federation of Malaysia with Singapore, Sabah and Sarawak.
1965	Singapore separates from Malaysia.
1969	Ethnic riots and suspension of parliament.
1970	Barisan Nasional succeeds the Alliance.
1971–90	New Economy Policy (NEP) promotes economic, social and political status of Malays through special rights and privileges.
Early 1970s	Dakwab (Islamic revivalism) movement.
1981	Mahathir Mohamad becomes prime minister.
1980s	Islamization of UMNO.
1987–8	UMNO leadership and judicial crisis.
1991	Mahathir's Vision 2020 speech for a modern, Islamic Malaysia. National Development Policy replaces.
1993	Constitutional amendment removes sultans' legal privileges.
1999	Reformasi movement for Islam Madani with a more liberal interpretation of Islam.
2001	Mahathir's 9.29 declaration of Malaysia as an Islamic state.
2003	Mahathir steps down after 22 years as prime minister.
2007	Court of Appeal establishes that separation of powers is part of the Constitution under Malaysia's Westminster System.
2010	Court decision to apply the Islamic law to punish women for extra material sex amid religious tension.
2013	Court rules against use by non-Muslim to use the word Allah to refer to God.
2014	Government bans Comango civil rights coalition.
2015	Opposition Pan-Malaysian Islamic Party (PAS) seeks parliament's approval to expand hudud laws, a very strict Islamic legal code, in the northeastern state of Kelantan.

Case Study Lab 7.1

Understanding political parties in Pacific Asian countries

There are various different questions regarding political parties in Pacific Asia: their historical origins and contemporary development, social and political bases of party organization, role of political parties in political order, change and development, and how they different from Western democracies where modern political parties grew. Dalton, Shin and Chu, with their research team, focus on the level of institutionalization of political parties as an organizing framework for their inquiry into these issues.

- Better understand the structure of party systems in Pacific Asia, sources of party preferences, and consequences of partisanship on citizen behaviour.
- Political parties connect citizens to democratic process; levels of institutionalization of political parties reflect how this is generally effected.
- Role of political parties, different from other forms of political representation, interest articulation, and citizen participation and from those in Western democracies, varies among Pacific Asian countries. Level of institutionalization is a key indicator of how voters make choice, how party preferences shape, the impact of participation and social cleavage, level of party identification and attachment.

Dalton, Shin and Chu, 2008: 2–5

In the first half of the twentieth century, therefore, political parties became an important platform for ideological advocacy, mass mobilization, social revolution and nationalist movements. To a great extent, they formed similar functions as those 'mass-based' political parties in the West before their transformation to 'electoral professional' parties.

This type of political party usually had broad grassroots support, loyal membership and represented the interests of certain sectors of society. They formed a bridge between the elites with various ideas and programmes for social change, political reform and revolution on the one hand, and the mass population hoping for a better life, a fair society and good government on the other. Through political parties, elites mobilized the masses in support of their political and social agenda and integrated them into national politics.

The post-Second World War era saw the emergence of different political party systems in Pacific Asian countries (see Box 7.2). In countries where the Communist Party came to power (China, North Korea, North Vietnam), the communist one-party system emerged. Most political parties were either incorporated by the Communist Party into some form of a 'united front', an umbrella organization for various collaborative political forces, in support of the Communist Party's rule, or eliminated or marginalized. The Communist Party became the only active, effective political party. The Communist Party itself, once in power, incorporated state institutions and turned the ruling political structure into a party-state (see Chapter 2).

Box 7.2

Political party systems in Pacific Asia, 1980

Communist one-party system:	China, Vietnam, North Korea, Laos, Cambodia
Single-party dominant system	Japan (LDP), Singapore (PAP), Taiwan (KMT), Malaysia (UMNO), Indonesia (GOLKAR), Philippines (KBL)

Of the three main functions that Otto Kirchheimer considers that a 'mass-based' political party performs – namely, mass integration, policy determination and officeholder nomination (Kirchheimer, 1966: 188–9) – the communist parties were strong in one of them: mass integration. Indeed, the primary function of the communist parties and their collaborative political parties in the communist countries was to serve as 'transmission belts' that integrate the mass population and various political and social forces into the political order envisaged by the communist ruling elite.

Like many other mass-based political parties, the communist parties were also heavily bureaucratized. Bureaucratization was even more of a significant phenomenon with communist parties than with non-communist ones, because the communists took on themselves not only the task of managing the party's large organization but also the challenge of running the country.

The **communist one-party system** is based on the communist ideology that the Communist Party is the sole representative of the working classes. The Communist Party is constitutionally the core leadership party. While there are other legal political parties under the system, they are mainly consultative, a legacy of the past political history, and a showcase of the party's wide support. These parties have little substance in competitive politics. The core leadership party governs the political system with the aid of the state institutions.

The communist parties also obtained some features that were only to be seen in the professional electoral parties in Western countries, and later in Pacific Asian countries themselves: elite-centred party organization. There was a shift of power from the mass to the elite after a communist revolution. Increasingly, the ruling elites were more interested in retaining power than in representing the interests of the mass population. There was little room for members to participate in real decision-making. The personality of the leadership became important for the party's ruling basis.

In a similar fashion, though without the communist ideology, there were 'mass-bureaucratic' parties. These were seen in a wide range of countries, from Indonesia to Malaysia, and from Singapore to Japan. Like their counterparts in the communist countries, these political parties became a primary vehicle for ruling elites to mobilize the mass population to carry out their programmes of economic and social development as well as nation-state building. The ruling party that emerged from the early stage of competitive multiparty politics was chosen to represent the interests of industrial capital and other dominant social interests.

The ruling political party became a key player in the national policy decision-making apparatus (that is, the iron triangle, see Chapter 6) and a principal platform for interest representation. The ruling political party, like their communist counterparts, was also a channel for government policy implementation and political communication with various constituencies. It was a key part in the chain of the state-dominated corporatist management of society. Electoral rules (see sections on 'electoral systems in Pacific Asia' in this chapter) and other institutional arrangements helped to prolong the ruling party's stay in power. All these constituted a single-party dominant system.

T. J. Pempel, in a study of ten cases of single-party dominance around the world, defines single-party dominance as a political system in which the dominant party dominates 'the electorate, other political parties, the formation of governments, and the public policy agenda' (Pempel, 1990: 4). These aspects are interrelated; and together, according to Pempel, they create a virtuous cycle of dominance (see Box 7.3).

There is the unique case of Indonesia during the Suharto years. While there was no communist ideology, its party system resembled more closely the communist one-party system than the single-party dominant system in its neighbouring Southeast Asian countries. Suharto replaced the old political parties with 'a nonparty electoral alternative' – GOLKAR (Weatherbee, 2002: 259).

GOLKAR was designed to unite all organizations and interest groups for the common goals of stability and development. GOLKAR became the quinquennial electoral machine of the Suharto regime. Backed by ABRI, the organizational cement of GOLKAR was the government bureaucracy. In an increasingly

Box 7.3

The virtuous cycle of single-party dominance

A dominant party must gain at least an electoral plurality, which means dominance in socioeconomic mobilization. It must also enjoy or create a bargaining advantage vis-à-vis other political parties so that it remains at the core of any coalitions that are formed. Then it must remain in office long enough to implement its historical agenda. Finally, while in office it must be able to implement its historical programme and use the instruments of state so as to isolate its opposition and strengthen its own electoral position. Dominance thus involves an interrelated set of mutually reinforcing processes that have the potential to beget even more dominance.

Pempel, 1990: 16

corporate state framework, all functional groups were to be brought under the GOLKAR umbrella (Weatherbee, 2002: 259).

There was a third category of political parties in countries with extra-constitutional rule by either the military or autocrats: South Korea from the mid-1960s to the mid-1980s; Thailand on and off since 1932; Myanmar since 1962 until the second decade of the new century; and the Philippines during the Marcos years in the 1970s and 1980s. In these cases, the ruling political parties, if there were any, were largely nominal. They had no real functions apart from legitimizing the ruling group. In some cases, political parties were completely banned. In others, they were allowed to exist under significant restrictions.

Catch-all parties and corporatist parties

Since the end of the Cold War, there have been two significant trends in the development of political parties in Pacific Asia. The first is the transformation of mass-bureaucratic parties into electoral-professional parties (Panebianco, 1988), or what Otto Kirchheimer called 'catch-all parties' (Kirchheimer, 1966).

The rise of catch-all parties in Pacific Asia was for much the same reasons as their rise in the West in the early twentieth century. Political liberalization and democratic transition in South Korea, Taiwan, Indonesia, the Philippines and Thailand came with the establishment of institutions for open, competitive elections. Regular elections are accepted as the only legitimate process of the distribution of power and resources.

On the other hand, it is practically impossible for one dominant ideology to appeal to the majority of voters in a pluralist society. So to win elections beyond a party's traditional ideological and organizational basis, the party had to broaden its political appeal to wider constituencies. Ideology has increasingly become a barrier to the efforts of political parties to broaden their electoral appeal.

> A **catch-all party** is a political party that works to catch all categories of voters beyond its traditional class and ideological bases, or at least catch more voters in all those categories whose interests do not adamantly conflict.
>
> Kirchheimer, 1966: 186

The transformation of the Nationalist Party (KMT) in Taiwan is a good example. The KMT was for a long time built along the lines of the Leninist Party – with Sun Yat-san's Three Principles of the People ideology, bureaucratic party organization with mass membership, party loyalty and discipline, and grass-roots organizations. After fifty years in power, the KMT lost the presidential election in 2000 and again in 2004. With twenty years of political liberalization and democratic transition, the KMT had to reform itself to survive in the new political and electoral environment.

To this end, the party has restructured itself. The party adjusted its stand on China, on national identity, on the ideological foundations of the party and on its party organization and operation. No longer the ruling arm of the party-state, the KMT has become an election-centred political organization. In 2008, the KMT was successful in the parliamentary and presidential elections. A similar transformation was also seen with GOLKAR in Indonesia.

In South Korea and Thailand, political parties had a much less significant role because of military suppression in the past. Catch-all parties were very much born to the new political electoral environment. As for Japan, 1993 was a turning point for the LDP, when it transformed itself from a corporatist single dominant party to a catch-all party.

While mass-bureaucratic parties are increasingly becoming catch-all parties in newly restored or established democratic systems, the Leninist parties in the former communist countries are

Box 7.4

Why are Pacific Asian political parties more personalistic or patronistic?

- Not the same developmental trajectory as political parties in Western democracies.
- Social group basis: pre-existing social cleavages and patterns of elite politics.
- A firm social group base can provide a foundation for party ideology and identity, without such group connections, parties may be more personalist or patronistic organization.

Dalton, Shin and Chu, 2008: 2

experiencing their own transformation. Ideology is no longer the foundation of the party. Indeed, with economic reform and social change, much of the ideological claims in the original party constitution are no longer relevant. New economic and social conditions have also brought change in party membership and basic constituencies. The party can hardly claim that it still represents the interests of the working classes.

Changes are also seen in the selection of party officials and decision-making processes. The party has increasingly become a platform for a trade-off of interests among the various social groups represented. However, the function of the Communist Party as a primary vehicle for political control and social management has survived. The basic organizing principles of the party, such as 'democratic centralism', grassroots membership and branches, the nomenklatura system (see Chapter 5), and the party's dominant role in the political system, have not changed greatly.

A **corporatist party** is a long-established political party that takes mass integration as its primary function, without either the ideological undertones (as in the case of a Leninist party) or any significant electoral challenge (as in the case of a catch-all party). Mass integration is defined by Otto Kirchheimer as a situation where parties function 'as channels of integrating individuals and groups into the existing political order' (1966: 189). A corporatist party usually has a cadre system, an extended party bureaucracy and extensive grassroots networks and organizations, either of its own or embedded in state institutions.

Singapore's PAP, particularly under Lee Kuan Yew, can also be seen as a corporatist party. For many, it is difficult to characterize the PAP: is it a personalized party (because of Lee Kuan Yew) or an institutionalized party? Is it a catch-all party, or a corporatist party? Raj Vasil argues that the PAP has little direct influence on government, has no grassroots-level institutions, does not give any special attention to routine organizational functions and does not feel the need to create effective organizations of its own for students, young people, women and so on to mobilize support from these sections of the population (Vasil, 2000: 35).

A **dominant party** holds power for more than two or three decades through the ballot box. It is dominant in the number of seats in parliament and the level of political support, the length of time in office, and policymaking reflects the preference of the party. It is controversial whether the dominant party also shapes the norms and values of the country.

A **one-party dominant system** comprises a perennial party-in-power and is distinct from and should not be confused with a one-party state. In the former, the dominant party must compete against opposition parties in periodic elections but it invariably wins. In the latter, the one-party state does not permit any challenges from other political parties for the reins of power through the electoral process.

Lam 2011: 136

However, Diane K. Mauzy points out that the organization of the PAP and its corporatist substance has been shaped by its early history, where the PAP built up its corporatist institutions and mechanisms in a wide range of grassroots organizations, such as the People's Associations, Citizens' Consultative Committees, Community Centres and Resident Committees. As these have also evolved as state institutions, funded by the government, 'many of the roles one would expect a major party to perform are in fact conducted by government organizations, and the line between party and government has been substantially blurred' (Mauzy, 2002: 248).

Essential to a corporatist party is the party's primary function. Because they have often been in power for a considerably long period of time and are expected to continue to do so, it becomes their primary function to integrate the masses into the existing political order centred around the party through various corporatist arrangements.

Pacific Asia today is therefore dominated by two types of political parties: catch-all parties and corporatist parties (See Box 7.5). Ideological undertones and electoral cleavages that are dominant in Western countries between left and right, conservative and liberal are universally weak in Pacific Asia (Sachsenroder, 1998: 2). Caution is needed here, though, as political parties are still evolving and the boundaries between the two are not always clear in Pacific Asian politics. The catch-all parties

Box 7.5

Political party systems in Pacific Asia, 2008

Leninist Party		*Corporatist party*		*Catch-all party*
Examples				
N Korea	Singapore China Japan,	Taiwan, Thailand,	S. Korea, Indonesia	Philippines
Role of ideology				
Dominant	Weak	No	No	No
Mass integration				
Yes	Yes	No	No	No
Role of political parties in the overall political system				
Fundamental	Fundamental	Significant	Useful	Irrelevant
Election platform				
No	Limited	Yes	Yes	Yes
Number of parties				
One party	One party or Single dominant party	Single dominant party or Two dominant parties	Multiparties	Multiparties

Case Study Lab 7.2

Forecast directions of change in political party systems and democratization

There has been significant change in political party systems in Pacific Asian countries. Whether such change will lead to convergence of the party systems into modern, effective multiparty systems remains an important research question. Liang Foo Lye, Wilhelm Hofmeister and their research team use a framework of different types of political systems to explore and capture the potential directions of further development of political party systems in Pacific Asia and show how this relates to the overall trend of political liberalization and change:

- A framework of types of political party systems: One party system; dominant party system; and multiparty system.
- Whether these different party systems will converge into multiparty systems in the overall political change and liberalization.
- How these different parties evolve, adapt and respond to changing structural and political economic conditions that support the particular party system.

Lye and Wilhelm Hofmeister, 2011: 1–15

see themselves primarily as a platform for voter mobilization. Party activities are organized to win elections.

Corporatist parties, on the other hand, take the challenge of social management and political control to be their primary function. They are the party in power and work with state institutions to incorporate societal forces into the political order. Party organization itself serves as the institutional fabric for state-led corporatism.

Case Study Lab 7.3

Understanding change in political party systems: the party-oriented model and legislator-oriented model

The party structure provides a unique perspective to observe change in the political party system in Pacific Asia. Much of the political party models focus on how political parties connect with the masses, voters and general public, and neglect how they connect with legislators. The power shift between the bureaucracy and politicians has been a consequence of political liberalization in Pacific Asia since the 1990s and a dimension of political change and development. Sunghack Lim uses a two-model framework to capture political party system change in the case of South Korea:

- The party-oriented model posits the centre of politics as the political party. The key political functions, such as interest articulation and aggregation, election campaign, fund raising or political donation, political recruitment, policy initiatives, and so on, are performed by the political party.... A party's base usually refers to the mass public motivated by the party's cause and ideology. Party members actively participate in party running and decision-making processes. Each legislator depends on the party and finds it almost impossible to cross-vote and establish his/her own voice in the parliament due to strong party discipline.
- The legislator-oriented model focuses more on the activities of legislators. Political parties perform an overall administrative role and surrender the responsibility of basic political activities to the legislator or candidate. The legislator or candidate sets the basic guidelines for party members and designs the grand strategy of election campaigns. They are also responsible for fundraising, policy proposals and maintenance of office, and so on. Due to weak party discipline and self-autonomy, cross voting in the national legislature is tolerated.
- The 2004 political reforms on political funding, party law and election law in South Korea, brought elements of both models into Korea's party system.

Lim, 2011: 227–228

Party structures

The differences between the catch-all party and the corporatist party are reflected first and foremost in the organization of the party. As illustrated in Figures 7.1 and 7.2, one of the key differences is that, as a catch-all party, the LDP is what Ronald J. Hrebenar has called an 'elite-cadre party', with all its organizational strength on the national level (Hrebenar, 1992: 26).

The party leadership consists of the president (that is, the prime minister when the LDP is in power): the LDP's legislative caucus, the party's policy core, the Policy Affairs Research Council (PARC), and heads of factions. The party's central bureaucracy is limited. The structure of the LDP therefore shows the elitist nature of the catch-all party: the party is controlled and resolves around professional politicians, mainly MPs, faction leaders and PARC old hands.

As a corporatist party, on the other hand, the organization of the Chinese Communist Party (CPC) is much more comprehensive, and more institutionalized (see Box 7.6). The overall structure consists of the party leadership, a large bureaucracy, party committees, and branches across various sectors of society, from the national all the way down to the village level, and millions of permanently loyal members. Because of the party's corporatist function in social management and political control, its bureaucracy (that is, the various functional departments) is enormous in both size and influence. It not only serves the party leadership, but also manages the huge party machinery, implementing the party's programmes and forming the organizational core for vertical and horizontal mass integration.

A second difference is the party's presence at the local and grassroots levels. The LDP's presence at local and grassroots levels is very weak. It relies on local personal support groups of individual MPs to provide grassroots support and voter mobilization. Consequently, the party's political base is the voter, and this can change from election to election.

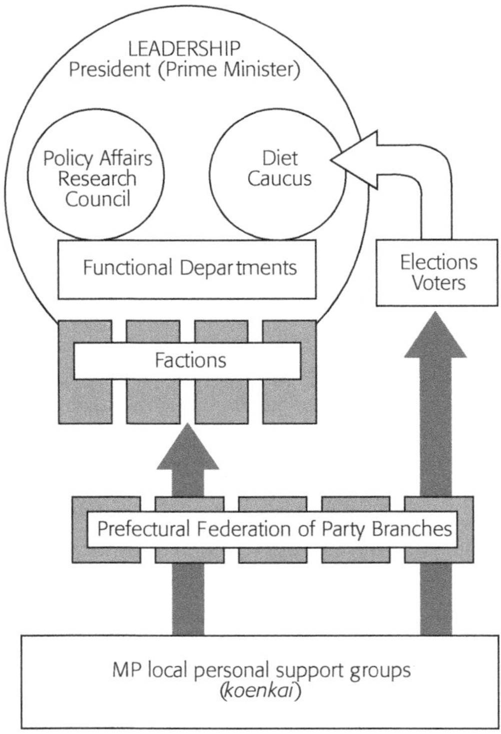

Figure 7.1 Organization of a catch-all party: Japan's Liberal Democratic Party

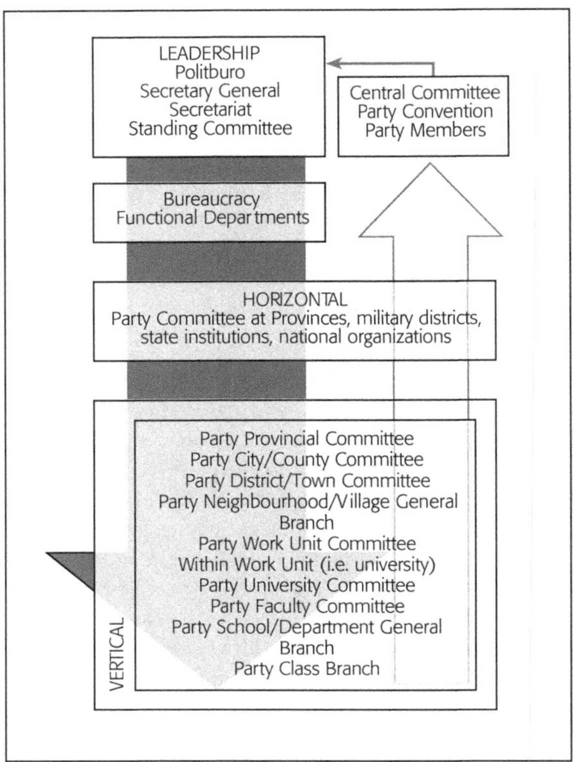

Figure 7.2 Organization of a corporatist party: the Chinese Communist Party

The CPC, however, has a penetrating presence at all levels of the polity, from subnational and regional, to local and grassroots levels. This vertical integration is an important part of the corporatist function of the party. The party committees and branches at these levels are both the instrument for the party's corporatist efforts and part of the corporatist arrangements between the party elites and the masses.

A third difference is the political support base of the party. For the catch-all party, voters are the political base. The LDP relies on the support of its voters to survive. Its activities centre on getting the maximum number of votes and sending their MPs to the Diet. The party has very little function as a vehicle for top-down social management. For the CPC, it is the millions of permanently loyal party members that form the political base of the party. However, the voters and the members perform different roles in these two different types of political parties. In the catch-all party, the voters can determine the fate of the party or its general policies and programmes. For the corporatist party, the members do not have such decisive power.

Finally, there is a different set of political and structural constraints on the two different types of parties. The leadership of the CPC is more a self-contained elite group subject to less open political pressures than a catch-all political party. In theory, its mandate comes from the members through the party convention and Central Committee. In reality, this is more of a negotiated process led by the leadership. The LDP is more constrained by its voter-centred platform and factional politics.

Candidate selection procedures

One of the key functions of a political party is to nominate its candidates for public offices. This applies more to the catch-all parties than the corporatist ones, as winning elections is essential for

Box 7.6

Party organization in Pacific Asia

	Corporatist party	*Catch-all party*
Leadership	Institutionalized	Personalized
Bureaucratization	High	Low
Structure	Hierarchic	Elitist
Membership	Controlled	Open
Support basis	Membership	Voters
Grassroots	Organized branches	Local factions and personal support groups

catch-all parties. For the corporatist parties, the issue of candidate selection is confined to the party's internal posts, as these are more important than public posts in their political system.

For catch-all parties, candidate selection is an important intra-party mechanism for resource and power distribution, trading on interests among key players within the party, and the shaping of the party's identity and electoral image. Traditionally, candidate selection for public office was done mainly through negotiation among party leadership and factions behind a closed door. Increasingly, selection processes are more open, transparent and institutionalized. However, primaries are not always the first choice or the only way through which candidates are chosen.

Box 7.7 shows a range of different methods through which party candidates for the highest public offices are decided. Japan has a long history of its president being decided through primaries. Currently, three-fifths of the vote in the primary is from LDP Diet members and two-fifths from designated party members from regional charters. Primaries are also established in political parties in South Korea but the history of democratic institutions is very short and political parties notoriously unstable. Parties are organized mainly around star politicians. Presidential hopefuls can easily walk out on the party and form their own new parties. For this reason, the rules of the primary are less effective for these parties.

Between those parties with primaries and those parties where candidates can evade the disciplinary power of the primary system by organizing a new party are the political parties in Taiwan. The compromise formula for selecting presidential candidates in both the KMT and the DPP in 2008 was 30 per cent from the votes of the party members and

Box 7.7

Primary methods of party candidate selection for highest public offices

Primary	*Primary and poll*	*Party recommendation party/coalition*	*Candidate breaks to form a new party*
Japan	Taiwan	China	Philippines Thailand
South Korea		Singapore Malaysia Vietnam	

Box 7.8

How political parties select their candidates in Thailand

Political parties rely on such methods as nomination, application, invitation and utilizing monetary payment. As far as nomination is concerned, every party usually allows its members to nominate themselves or some other members to run for an election. As for the second method, parties with a good chance of winning a majority of seats in the election usually attract a lot of applications from both veteran politicians and newcomers ... as a last resort, the invitation, method or monetary payment methods, or both, are employed. For the former, popular or influential politicians and highly educated academics and technocrats are invited to join the parties, sometimes with an offer of high-ranking positions in the parties ... For the latter, some politicians with high potential are bought from other parties.

Limmanee, 1998: 425

Box 7.9

Rise to the top: Chinese Communist Party Secretary General and President of China, Xi Jinping

Rise to the top: Xi Jinping

1969	Village Party Branch secretary
1975	College student, chemical engineering, Tsinghua University
1979	Secretary, Central Military Commission
1983	County Party Committee Secretary, Hebei Province
1988	Region Party Committee Secretary, Fujian Province
1990	Fuzhou City Party Committee Secretary, Fujian Province
2000	Governor, Fujian Province
2002	Provincial Party Committee Secretary, Zhejiang Province
2007	Party Committee Secretary, Shanghai
2007	Member, Politbureau Standing Committee
2008	Vice President, PRC
2010	Vice Chairman, Central Military Commission
2012	Party Secretary General, Chairman, Central Military Commission
2013	President, PRC

70 per cent from public polls. This compromise formula reflects the transitional nature of the party system in Taiwan, moving from selection through party elite consultation to open and formal primaries.

For the corporatist parties, decisions on party candidates for public office are entirely the matter of the party leadership, as well as party committees and branches at local levels. Given the dominance of the party within the political system and its nomenklatura system (see Chapter 5), the party's nominations to public offices amount to actual appointment.

However, there have been gradual but significant changes since the mid-1990s in these corporatist parties. In Vietnam, for example, there have been 'substantial changes in the Politburo, the Central Committee and its secretariat' within the Vietnamese Communist Party. Reforms were aimed at 'renovating the party organization and elements of the governing structure, notably the National Assembly, relaxing controls over the media and promoting more open comment and discussion' (Dixon, 2004: 20). More pointedly, in the election of senior party and state officials since the 1990s, open and multi-candidate competition has been introduced (see Vu, 2014: 136).

In China, the CPC is more cautious with changes in party organization and procedures. The primary concern since the 1980s has been transparency and accountability in intra-party politics, and institutionalization and stabilization of the system of party official selection as well as changes in senior leadership. Over the years, the CPC has developed a unique system of selection, training, probation and promotion of its senior officials, as well as a system of succession of the party leadership (see: Zeng, 2016: 1–28; Fewsmith, 2013 particularly Chapter 3; Zheng, 2014: 162). Within the CPC, an organization department exists at all levels of its structure for selection and appointment of senior officials to internal party posts at each of these levels. Candidates are selected and reviewed for

> **Box 7.10**
>
> ## Party selection of candidates to high offices: Singapore's PAP
>
> Michael D. Barr details the process of how the PAP searches for candidates to stand for Parliament and potential candidates for cabinet positions in Singapore. A selection committee of senior MPs is formed to identify and recruit potential MPs, a large proportion of which are for 'the explicit purpose of short-term elevation into the cabinet' (Barr 2014: 86). The process usually includes going through identifying candidates across all sectors of society, invitation to the party with members of the cabinet and psychological tests of the candidate.
>
> Barr, 2014: 86–87

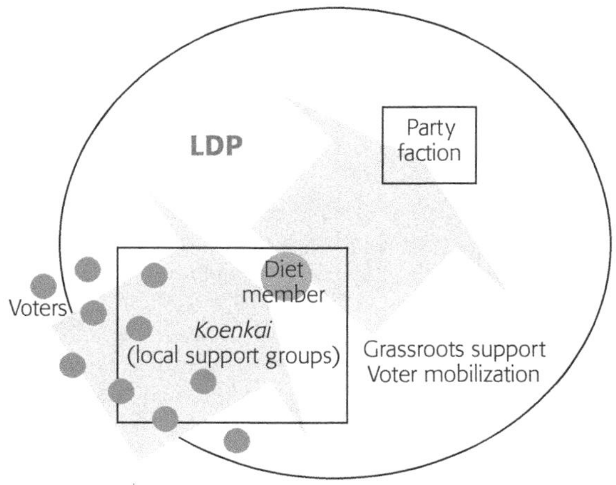

Figure 7.3 From voters to party: Japan's LDP

political confidence by the organization department. The party committee at a higher level makes decisions of appointment.

As for the process for selection of candidates and their appointment to the highest posts in the party and the state, this takes decades from the initial selection to finally taking up the posts. In the case of Party Secretary Xi Jinping (see Box 7.9), for example, the first ten years was a period of observation, testing and building up governing experiences in various areas of state affairs. The second ten years was mainly a period of on-the-job training and fitting into the political apparatus.

Membership, recruitment and grassroots organization

The two types of political parties are vastly different in how they recruit their members. The corporatist parties have kept, to a large extent, this aspect of the Leninist party: very strict party membership requirements, tightly controlled procedures for the entry of new members, and significant political and social privileges as well as responsibilities for party members.

Unlike the Leninist parties, where it was possible for members to join the party purely for its revolutionary cause and communist future, the corporatist parties attract members implicitly with significant political and social privileges. These include members having a higher social and political status within the workplace than non-members; access to resources, information and opportunities coming through the party channels; a higher level of trust enjoyed within the political system; and meeting the basic requirements for promotion to high party and government posts.

Given the privileges, the party also imposes heavy demands on members: party members need to be role models for society; they have to keep strictly in line with the party politically; they explain and defend party policy and programmes to the public; they are the 'frontline soldiers' for the party's corporatist efforts.

> **Vote chiefs** are local operators for the catch-all parties. They organize campaign events and functions at the grassroots level for the party and factions and pursue voters to vote for the party and specific candidates. They are usually heads of personal support groups for the party's MPs or faction. In countries where vote-buying is an issue, campaign funding of the party, factions, and individual candidates reach voters through these vote chiefs.

To become a member of the party is a very competitive process among politically active citizens, a process that is controlled by party branch committees in the workplace. To become a party member, an applicant would need to be sponsored by two current party members. Following an inspection and review by the party organization department and

> **Box 7.11**
>
> ### How the cadre system works in Singapore
>
> Political parties in Singapore are organized on the cadre system. This means there are at least two types of party membership. Only selected members (cadres) can vote for or be elected into the Central Executive Committee (CEC). These cadre members have to be approved by the CEC. In other words, in a circular manner, the CEC is elected by selected members that the CEC must have approved prior.
>
> Ooi, 1998: 363

consultation within and beyond the party branch, the party branch committee can make acceptance on the condition of a one-year probation. The process gives the party branch committee enormous political and social power and the capacity to impose the party's corporatist agenda. The millions of party branches and its governing committees are the party's primary organizational and functional units at the grassroots level.

Grassroots organization by corporatist parties is also seen in Singapore and Malaysia. As Sachsenroder points out, 'the penetration of the provinces by a closely knit UMNO network ... has created a lot of civic engagement; consequently, the political weight of the party divisions on the ground seems to be higher and more developed in Malaysia than elsewhere in the region' (Sachsenroder, 1998: 18). In Singapore (see Box 7.11), the PAP's unique grassroots organizations are intertwined with the state administrative institutions at the grassroots level, giving the PAP effective organizational support for its corporatist functions (ibid.; Mauzy, 2002: 248).

In contrast, the membership of the catch-all parties is very limited, consisting mainly of a handful of party loyalists at regional and local levels, and professional politicians at the national level (see Figure 7.2 as an illustration of Japan's LDP). As winning elections is the primary function of the party, voters are the most important constituency of the party. For the same reason, party branches at the grassroots level either do not exist, or exist primarily for voter mobilization.

A vote chief system exists in various guises in many catch-all parties for this purpose. The vote chiefs are the primary link between voters and their candidate, faction and party. This system is a key mechanism for party grassroots operation and voter mobilization.

Factionalism and regionalism

There are two distinct features of political party systems in Pacific Asia that are worth special discussion. The first is factionalism within political parties. A faction, according to Raphael Zariski, is

> any intra-party combination, clique, or grouping whose members share a sense of common identity and common purpose and are organized to act collectively as a distinct bloc within the party to achieve their goals. These goals include patronage (control of party and government office by members of the faction), the fulfillment of local, regional, or group interests, influence on party strategy, influence on party and governmental policy, and the promotion of a discrete set of values to which members of the faction subscribe. (Zariski, 1960:33)

Pacific Asian countries fall into three categories in terms of the level of factionalism in the party (see Box 7.12). In Japan's LDP and Taiwan's DPP, factions are open, legitimate and institutionalized as an integral part of party organization, though efforts have been made in recent years in both parties to eliminate factions. Japan's LDP is known for the dominance of factions over the party. Factions emerged as a legitimate form of party organization and decision-making.

On the other hand, the political party organization structure, funding system and electoral rules (more on this later) made intra-party politics more competitive, not so much on ideology and policy but more on the basis of personnel, funding and distribution of resources and opportunities. Competition in these areas and the fact that it is not viable to break away from the party over differences on these issues led to the rise of factions. Operating through factions is the most effective way to gain political security and career advancement.

Zariski categorizes factions into four types (Zariski, 1960: 36):

- Factions of shared values;
- Strategic conceptions;
- Common material interests, origins or functions;
- Personal or local cliques.

The LDP's factions can be seen as the third and fourth types. However, the dominance of factionalism in the LDP is also related to the party's funding model and the electoral rules.

A **faction** is an organized interest group within a political party. **Factionalism** is a phenomenon in many political parties in Pacific Asia where factions are a primary form of intra-party organization, activity and decision-making.

Factional dominance is also seen in Taiwan's Democratic Progressive Party (DPP), though the DPP's factions are more of the first and second types than the third and fourth types. The DPP's factions arose from the shared origins of their members in the democratic movement in the 1970s and 1980s, or a shared view about the party's platform, strategy, and policy. They are less personalized than those in Japan's LDP.

In the second group are those corporatist parties, including China's CPC, where factions are prohibited, at least in theory. In general, a corporatist party tolerates little factionalism. China's CPC had a long history of factional politics, most notably under Mao (Huang, 2000).

Policy debate and personal politics can still be seen in intra-party politics at the time of writing. But with Mao being long gone, a higher level of consensus among party senior leaders over the party's direction and programmes, and a greater extent of institutionalization in party politics, factional politics is now much less significant.

Taiwan's KMT under the two Chiangs used to be a party where factions were not tolerated. The same tradition forced those of different views and interests to break away from the party under Chairman Lee Teng Hui in the 1990s, which resulted in two major splits of the party.

The KMT model of the 1990s is in fact more widely seen among political parties in Pacific Asia: factions are not a practical or effective mechanism for the settlement of intra-party differences and conflict. Given a more pluralist political environment in these countries, the changing pattern of political parties (transforming to catch-all parties), and new rules for electing representatives, breaking away from the party to form a new party has appeared to be a more appealing option. This is the case in South Korea, Taiwan, the Philippines, Indonesia and Thailand.

Coalition building among ever-changing new parties is increasingly overtaking intra-party factionalism. A significant consequence of this is the instability of political parties, a growing number of political parties, and increasingly personalized political parties – all reinforcing key elements of the catch-all party. Parties can form or break easily. In South Korea, for example, senior politicians have broken away from their party and formed a new party – primarily for electoral reasons – so often voters are more likely to recognize candidates than their parties. In the 2004 parliamentary election in Indonesia, twenty-four parties participated and seventeen held seats in parliament after the election.

Thailand is a unique case. Inter-party coalitions have been the rule of civilian government in

Box 7.12

Factionalism in political parties

Japan's LDP Taiwan's DPP Legitimate, open, dominant	China's CPC Singapore's PAP Prohibited, underground, informal	South Korea, Thailand Indonesia, Philippines Less relevant, more inter-party coalition than intra-party factionalism

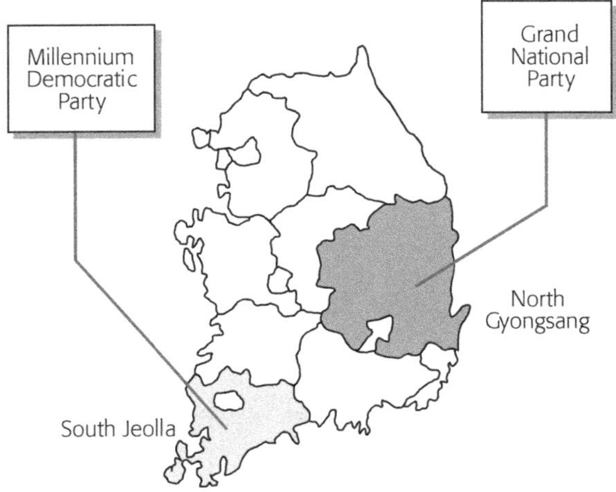

Figure 7.4 Regional basis of political parties: South Korea

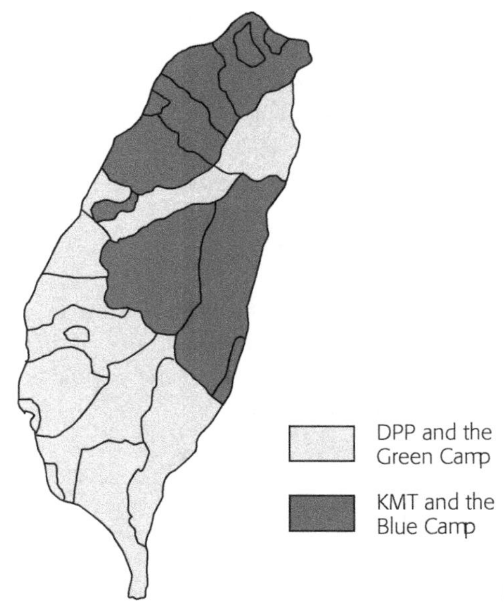

Figure 7.5 Regional basis of political parties: Taiwan 2004 presidential election

Thailand apart from during the only single-party majority government of Thaksin, in 2005–6. The Thais Love Thais Party (TRT) was founded on many pre-existing parties and factions. Therefore factions were dominant in the TRT.

> **Regionalism** refers to a phenomenon in political parties where the organization, structure and intra-party and inter-party politics are decisively effected by the geographical background of the party leadership and their supporters.

Another distinct feature in the Pacific Asian political party system is regionalism. Regionalism here goes beyond the fact that a party's policy and programmes appeal especially to voters of certain demographic areas. In one sense of regionalism, Japan's LDP traditionally appealed more to rural voters, while the JSP appealed more to Tokyo metropolitan voters; and Thaksin's TRT in Thailand appealed more to rural voters in the regions and the Democratic Party was more popular with voters in Bangkok and southern Thailand. Even before Thaksin, there was an indication of regionalization of political parties in the 1990s (Surin, 1992: 45–6, 2002: 192).

At a more profound structural level, however, regionalism is of a more institutionalized kind. Voters can vote for their candidate simply because the candidate is 'one of them' from the same region, province or town. This aspect of regionalism is supported by the often very personalized system. On the other hand, senior party leaders are more willing to recruit party supporters, promote party officials, and have more trust in fellow politicians from their own region.

This more institutionalized regionalism is nowhere more predominant than in South Korea. The Grand National Party (and its predecessor the Democratic Justice Party) is heavily connected with the eastern region, the Gyeongsang region. All the presidents from this party – Park Chung-hee, Chun Doo-hwan, Roh Tae-woo, and Lee Myung-bak – came from the northern Gyeongsang region. The region, with a concentration of industrial activities, gives the party a more conservative base.

Support for more liberal parties, particularly Kim Dae-jung's Millennium Democratic Party, came from southwestern, less-developed Jeolla, particularly the southern Jeolla area. Kim's election victory drew strong voter support from there, and Kim's administration was staffed overwhelmingly by people from the region (see Figure 7.5).

Table 7.1 Electoral systems for national legislatures (primary house)

Country	*Name*	*Seats/ Delegates*	*Electoral system*	*Term*	*Electoral reform*	*Electoral System before reform*
Cambodia	National Assembly	122	PR	5	1993	Absolute majority by block vote
China	National People's Congress	Max 3,000	Indirectly elected with absolute majority by block vote	5		
Indonesia	People's Representative Council	550	PR in multi-member districts	5	1999, 2003	PR in multi-member districts with reserved seats for the army, limited competitiveness
Japan	Diet	500	Mixed: 300 by FPTP; 200 by PR	4	1993	SNTV in multi-member districts
N. Korea	Supreme People's Assembly	687	Absolute majority in single-member district with a single candidate	5		
S. Korea	National Assembly	299	Mixed: 253 by FPTP, 46 by PR	4	1987	Various different systems
Laos	National Assembly	99	Block	5		
Malaysia	House of Representatives	192	FPTP	5		
Philippines	House of Representatives	221	Mixed: 80% by FPTP, 20% by PR	3	1987	FPTP in SMDs
Singapore	Parliament	At least 84	84 by FPTP/ block; Up to 15 appointed	5		
Taiwan	Legislative Yuan	113	Mixed: 73 by FPTP 6 for aboriginals 34 by PR	4	2004	Mixed: 168 by FPTP and SNTV; 8 for aboriginals; 41 for PR; 8 for overseas Chinese
Thailand	House of Representatives	480	Mixed: 400 in 157 Districts: 80 by PR	4	2007	Block vote in multi-member districts
Vietnam	National Assembly	450	Absolute majority by block vote	5		

Hsieh and Newman, 2002: 4; Nohlen et al., 2001: various chapters, with latest updates.

Regionalism is also a major feature of party politics in Taiwan. The DPP is traditionally dominant in southern Taiwan, while the KMT is dominant in urban, northern Taiwan, particularly the greater Taipei area. The 2000 presidential election (see Figure 7.4) shows the political support of the DPP and its green camp concentrated in southern Taiwan, while the support of the KMT and its blue camp is located in northern Taiwan. There was an overlap in central Taiwan.

Regionalism is an effective and useful mechanism for political parties to mobilize voters. In Pacific Asian countries, this is particularly significant because of the cultural tradition that a shared regional background can be an important bond between people. However, the fact that voter decisions can be motivated primarily by regional identity reduces the space for policy debate in election campaigns.

Elections and electoral systems

As our discussion of the party systems above has shown, party structure and organization, funding models, factionalism, money politics and regionalism have a great deal to do with the electoral system in the country. Indeed, some see political parties as 'an important part of the electoral process' (Hsieh and Newman, 2002: 8). Scholars agree, for example, that the medium-sized multi-member district model from 1947–93 shaped the political structure, party system and party politics in Japan significantly (Krauss and Pekkanen, 2004). Similarly, electoral rules in China are also designed to support the political system in general, and the party system in particular.

Arend Lijphart once commented, 'among the most important constitutional choices that have to

Table 7.2 Electoral systems for presidential elections

Country	*Electoral system*	*Term*	*Electoral reform*	*Electoral system before reform*
China	Indirect election with absolute majority by NPC with a single candidate	Two 5-year terms	1982	Life-long rule by Mao
Indonesia	Direct popular vote, simple majority	One 6-year term	2003	Indirect election by MPR
S. Korea	Direct popular vote	One 5-year term	1987	Frequent changes, but mainly indirect election
Laos	Indirect election by national assembly	5 years		
Malaysia	Indirect election by Council of the Rulers, rotational	5 years		
Philippines	Direct popular vote	One 6-year term	1987	
Singapore	Direct popular vote	6 years	1991	Indirect election by parliament with a single candidate
Taiwan	Direct popular vote	Two 4-year terms	1995	Indirect election by national assembly, with a single candidate
Vietnam	Indirect election by national assembly	5 years		

Nohlen et al., 2001 various chapters, with latest updates.

Box 7.13

Models of electoral system: majority system versus proportional representation

The plurality rule produce a one-party majority government and easily guarantee accountability while the proportional representation rule produces fair and responsible representation. The choice between plurality and proportional representation rules engenders a trade-off between accountability and representation (Lim 2011: 226).

- Majority systems overwhelmingly dominate in Pacific Asian countries, partly explaining why there is one-party dominance and long holds on power.
- There is a sign of change in electoral systems in Pacific Asia as countries adopt proportional representation (PR) in their newly reformed electoral systems (Taiwan, Japan, Korea).
- There is a good level of debate as to whether the change in the electoral systems brought significant shifts in the political party system and the structure of the political system or if the latter are forces that drive change in electoral systems.

be made in democracies is the choice of the electoral system, especially majoritarian election methods versus proportional representation' (Lijphart, 1994: 202).

The choice of electoral systems, however, is not only important for democratic, pluralist polities but also for non-pluralist, corporatist and even communist political systems. 'Even rigged elections or manipulated electoral provisions in non-democratic regimes testify at least to the importance that autocratic rulers ascribed to elections as a powerful instrument of political legitimation and (alleged) contestation' (Nohlen et al., 2001: 25). A survey of the electoral systems in Pacific Asia (see Table 7.1) suggests that a political order is clearly supported by a unique type of electoral system. The LDP's prolonged rule in post-war Japan, for example, and indeed the single-party dominance in many Pacific Asian countries such as South Korea and Taiwan at the time, was attributable to the single-non-transferable vote (SNTV) system to various degrees (see Grofman et al., 1999).

Like the political party systems, the electoral systems in Pacific Asia also experienced significant reform and change in recent years (Hsieh and Newman, 2002). We shall first provide an overview of the electoral systems and their post-war evolution. After that, some of the defining electoral rules will be discussed in more detail.

An examination of efforts in electoral reform in recent years and an assessment of the impact and consequences of the reforms will follow this. Finally, we shall discuss how electoral systems interact with the party systems and together shape voting behaviour and the political structure. Moreover, all the former communist countries have adopted an absolute majority system with block vote in multimember districts (MMDs), usually with limited or no competitiveness.

Political liberalization and democratic transition in the 1980s and 1990s in many Pacific Asian countries was accompanied by reforms in the electoral system to a parallel system:

- First-past-the-post (FPTP) in single-member districts (SMDs) for a majority of the seats; with
- Proportional representation (PR) from party lists in one multi-member national district or several regional districts for a small portion of the seats.

For presidential elections, the same pattern is also clear (see Table 7.2). In the former communist states, the National People's Congress or National Assembly indirectly elects the president who is often a single candidate that has been nominated by the ruling party. This candidate requires, and will normally receive, an absolute majority. In non-communist, but non-pluralist states during the Cold War, presidents were also mainly elected indirectly.

A key element of political liberalization and democratic transition since the 1980s has been the change in the electoral system for presidential elections. Most pluralist states have now adopted the direct, popular vote model for presidential elections.

Case Study Lab 7.4

How political dynamics shape electoral systems in Pacific Asia

One particular way of understanding the electoral system, its structure and evolution is to look at the historical conditions and see how historical political background influenced both the structure and evolution of electoral systems in Pacific Asian countries:

- Colonial influence: Malaysia, Singapore and Indonesia have retained their inherited electoral systems since independence almost without major modifications;
- Communist influence: North Korea, Vietnam and Mongolia used the Soviet type absolute majority system for their non-competitive parliamentary elections;
- Influence of the plurality model: have either applied the plurality system in SMCs for a long time (Thailand, South Korea, Philippines) or used a special type of plurality system in MMCs, the single non-transferable vote (Japan, Taiwan). Laos and Cambodia, both with a French colonial background, introduced the plurality system in the 1940s under the monarchy and stuck to this institutional choice when election re-established under communist rule.

Nohlen, Crotz and Hartmann, 2001: 17–19

The **single non-transferable vote**, or SNTV, is a method of election from multimember districts in which each voter has only one vote to cast.

Grofman et al., 1999: xii

Let us now look at some of the unique features of the electoral systems in Pacific Asia that have had a significant impact on the shaping of political order in these countries.

The model for LDP dominance

First, we shall look at the role of districting and voting methods on election results, voting behaviour, the party system and political structure. One classic issue in this respect is how different electoral systems affect voting behaviour and party politics. As Hrebenar observes, 'Japan's electoral laws have had a significant impact on the nation's post-war political party system. Characterized by multimember parliamentary districts, chronic malapportionment, and straitjacket campaign activity restriction, Japan's electoral laws have operated to keep Japan a one-party dominant nation' (Hrebenar, 1992: 32).

Between 1947 and the 1993 electoral reform, Japan had a unique electoral system of medium-sized, multi-member districts with SNTV. Under this model, the 511 seats were allocated to 129 districts with each district having a number of seats in a range from one to six. In a four-seat district, for example, the LDP and its primary challenger, the Japanese Socialist Party (JSP), would all field four candidates for maximum possible vote gains. The SNTV voting method, however, allows each voter only one vote for one candidate even though there is more than one seat in the district. Consequently, the chances for candidates of the dominant political party to be elected, in this case the LDP, is much higher than for the other parties. From the candidates' point of view, voters already have an established view about the parties, so what matters, therefore, are the differences among candidates of the same party.

Because of this, candidates' election campaigns were aimed more against their fellow party candidate than those of other parties. Moreover, because of the intra-party competition, issues and debates in election campaigns were less about party platforms and national issues, and more about the personal style of the individual candidates and their service to voters and constituencies.

The **medium sized, multi-member district model** refers to the electoral system practiced in Japan between 1947 and 1993. It is the use of the SNTV method in multi-member districts that defines the precise nature of the Japanese electoral model.

Furthermore, because of this intra-party competition, the party's support for individual candidates is only general, while the support of the faction to which the candidate belongs is crucial. Factions were therefore more important than the party itself.

Finally, as the individual connection between the candidate and his/her constituency is important, the candidates devoted much of their resources, energy and time to building a close relationship with local voters. Once the candidate was elected to public office, (s)he would use public funds to set up 'pork barrel' projects (see Chapter 8) aimed at their local constituency, to sustain the close relationship. This electoral model therefore favours the party in power. All these things working together meant that this model led to the dominance of factions in the LDP, and the system favoured the dominant party and its incumbent candidates.

In 1993, political parties in Japan finally agreed on a package of electoral reform. The new electoral system provides a parallel model: FPTP for single-member districts plus proportional representation for multi-member regions. The reform was aimed at reducing the influence of factions, enhancing the role of parties in the political system and in elections, curbing the problem of money politics, and allowing more proportional representation in the Diet.

Views about whether the reform has achieved its goals are mixed. Some are more certain about what the reforms can and have achieved (Thies, 2002; Cox et al., 1999). They argue that factionalism has changed greatly since then, and that party centralization occurred as expected. Others, such as Krauss and Pekkanen, were less certain more than ten years on. Factions lost their pivotal role, but remain important. The LDP lost its dominance in the initial shock of the new system, but has come back in recent years. The reform of 1993 also led to more changes. As Krauss and Pekkanen have pointed out, 'the disillusioned and frustrated are wrong to think that no change has occurred; the theorists are wrong to think change would occur necessarily in the forms they predicted' (2004: 33).

The Japanese case demonstrates that democracies require the support of various institutions to work. Conversely, electoral rules shape political structure, party systems and electoral outcomes. So the fact that elections take place does not tell us much about what the political system is and how it works.

More pointedly, the SNTV was the dominant voting method in many Pacific Asian countries. For example, Japan, Korea and Taiwan all used the SNTV system. However, as Grofman et al. (1999) demonstrate, a similar electoral rule can have different consequences depending on the context in which it operates. In theory, for example, SNTV encourages intra-party competition. This was the case in Japan, but because of 'the DRP's abundance of resources, effective organization, and the strong leadership position of the president' in Korea during the Cold War, and the Responsibility Zone System by the KMT in Taiwan, the evidence of intra-party competition was weak in both Korea and Taiwan (Grofman et al., 1999: 380).

Same-number candidacy is a nomination method whereby the ruling party nominates the same number of candidates as the seats to be filled. The method was widely used in the former communist states and other single-party states during the Cold War, and at the time of writing is still used in North Korea, and countries such as China with indirect election of their president.

As a further example, SNTV provides strong incentives for party factionalism because of the incentives for intra-party competition at the district level and the localistic and particularistic orientation of candidates. While this was the case in Japan, the fact that the DRP put up only one candidate in most SNTV two-member constituencies reduced the incentive for factionalism in Korea. Factionalism in Taiwan was strong, but it was more a response to the national identity issue than an effect of the electoral rule (Grofman et al., 1999: 388).

Electoral rules in non-pluralist states

The above point also applies to non-pluralist political systems. Electoral rules can also be designed to ensure a particular political order. In non-pluralist states (both at present and in the past), there is a clear pattern of electoral system has been adopted. First, there is political control of the nomination process. Candidates have to undergo a political screening process by the ruling party. This was the case, for example, in Indonesia under Suharto's New Order, and almost all the communist states used this procedure.

Second, there is limited or no competition in the election, particularly for the communist parties. For this, the method of same-number candidacy has been widely used. For these countries, elections are 'referenda on the ruling party's administration, not decisions as to which party should govern' (Hsieh and Newman, 2002: 14).

Third, the national assembly elects the head of state indirectly, often with a single candidate fielded by the ruling party rather than through direct popular vote. In some countries, the national assembly is also elected indirectly. In China, for example, the President and the National People's Congress are both elected indirectly. Indirect election provides a level of control by the ruling party over the election outcomes.

Finally, non-pluralist states generally prefer absolute majority as the voting method. Partly because the same-number candidacy can easily allow this to happen, and partly because the elections in the non-pluralist states are seen as a showcase for the party's political support, absolute majority therefore is favoured by the ruling party.

In recent years, electoral reforms have also been seen in non-pluralist states. Vietnam seems to be one step ahead of China. Unlike China, Vietnam's national assembly is directly elected. Open and competitive elections have been introduced at all levels of public office. The numbers of non-VCP members and independent candidates have increased. As Reilly argues, in 'single-party autocracies like Vietnam, elections may not change governments but do provide important signals to the ruling regime about public attitudes' (Reilly, 2014: 225). Even for China, open, competitive elections have been introduced from the village level up. The new law stipulates that the number of candidates should be 30 per cent higher than the number of seats. Like the reform of political parties, there are clear signs of controlled and phased political liberalization without drastic structural change to the overall political system.

Elections and mass integration and mobilization

In countries such as China and Singapore, and Indonesia under Suharto, there are also some unique electoral mechanisms that serve the corporatist function of the national legislature. One of the mechanisms is representation by functional groups in the national legislature. In national congress-type states such as China, Indonesia and Vietnam, the political consultative body parallel to or above the national legislature is usually organized through functional groups: representatives are selected to represent various societal groups and professions, ranging from religious groups to the media.

Functional groups are special categories of the members of national legislative and consultative bodies in some Pacific Asian countries. It is an electoral method that allocates and organizes representation on the basis of societal groups.

There are several countries where functional group representation is or used to be significant. In China, for example, the members of the National People's Congress are selected and organized in provincial delegations. In addition to this, there is one particular group represented at the NPC by itself: the People's Liberation Army and Armed Police. Moreover, there is an ambiguous clause that requires each minority group to be represented at the NPC. In the 11th NPC of 2008, of the 2,937 NPC deputies, 265 were allocated to the army in a special category. By law, 14 per cent (411) are deputies from ethnic groups, with at least one deputy from each of the fifty ethnic groups nation-wide. There is also a 20 per cent quota for women (637). Representation at the Chinese People's Political Consultative Conference (CPPCC) is assigned completely by functional groups. In the 11th CPPCC of 2008, the 2,237 members are from thirty-four 'functional areas.'

A tactic like this was also used during Suharto's New Order in Indonesia. Out of 500 seats in the DPR, for example, 400 were elected through a popular vote and 100 (the number changed over time) were appointed military officers. In the post-Suharto transitional period until 2004, thirty-eight seats in the DPR were retained for appointed military personnel. The ruling party under Suharto, GOLKAR, was itself a 'party of the functional groups'.

Group Representation Constituencies (GRCs) in Singapore are essentially multi-member districts where voters block vote on group lists. One of the candidates in each group (of 4–6) must come from an ethnic community: Indian, Malay or other.

Non-Constituency Members of Parliament (NCMPs) is a special method of parliamentary representation in Singapore. A maximum of three NCMPs with restricted voting rights can be allocated to defeated opposition candidates who received the highest numbers of votes.

> **Nominated Members of Parliament (NMPs)** is another special method of parliamentary representation in Singapore. Up to 9 NMPs with restricted voting rights are nominated by functional groups and the general public and appointed to parliament by the president.

Such special electoral procedures are important for these countries. As discussed earlier, elections in these types of state have both showcase and corporatist functions. By imposing a quota of minimum representation of certain societal groups, which are either under-represented under normal circumstances, or important for the state's governing values and political concerns, the ruling party hopes to demonstrate its constitutional values and intention of mass integration.

Given the dominance of the ethnic Chinese in single-member districts with FPTP, a similar concern for representation of minority groups evolved in Singapore. In 1988, the parliament passed a law to create multi-member districts, Group Representation Constituencies (GRCs), with closed and blocked group lists. In the 2006 general election, there were fourteen GRCs, each with five or six seats (and nine single-member districts). Each group list is required to have at least one member from a minority community: Indian, Malay or other. As discussed in the Japanese case, multi-member constituencies favour the dominant party over opposition parties. While the GRCs may benefit minority ethnic groups, they can also support the continuing reign of the ruling party. In fact, opposition parties have never won seats in the GRCs.

Given the absence of representation of the opposition in parliament, Singapore also introduced provisions for Non-Constituency Members of Parliament (NCMPs) to Parliament in 1984 and Nominated Members of Parliament (NMPs) in 1990. NCMPs (up to three) are appointed from defeated opposition candidates with the highest number of votes in their constituency, to bring the number of opposition members in Parliament to a minimum of three. NMPs (up to nine) are nominated by functional groups and the general public and appointed by the president. The intention and effect of these unique electoral rules are a matter of debate. Many suggest that while the government's declared purpose of the unique electoral rules is one thing, its real intention is to make it difficult for the opposition to forge a challenge (Rieger, 2001: 243). Others recognize that while there is 'a rather widespread perception that the PAP purposely handicaps, and indeed hamstrings, the opposition ... there remains little demand for procedural change' (Mauzy, 2002: 241). One thing is clear, these electoral rules serve the corporatist nature of the political system.

Electoral culture

In 1990, Seymour Martin Lipset attempted to explain differences in similar political institutions in different regions by pointing to what he described as 'the centrality of political culture' (Lipset, 1990: 80). Lipset sought to change the focus of the debate over the variations in the development of democracy and functioning of democracy around the world and argued for analysis of economic and cultural factors even though 'Cultural factors deriving from varying histories are extraordinarily difficult to manipulate. Political institutions—including electoral systems and constitutional arrangements—are more easily changed. Hence, those concerned with enhancing the possibilities for stable democratic government focus on them' (Lipset, 1990: 83).

The question of how 'cultural factors deriving from varying histories impacts the functioning of elections in Pacific Asia is, as Lipset noted, not an easy topic to study. Chapter 2 explored this debate with reference to the Asian values debate, illiberal democracy and the resilience of one-party states in the region. With the republishing of Lucian W. Pye and Sidney Verba's 1965 classic, *Political Culture and Political Development*, the debate will surely continue (Pye and Verba, 2015). Studies looking for overall patterns of political behaviour and institutional development, such as Gilley's (2014) *The Nature of Asian Politics*, or Slater's (2010) *Ordering power: Contentious politics and authoritarian leviathans in Southeast Asia*, point to a coherent political culture across the region.

Moreover, as Chua (2007) argues in *Elections as Popular Culture in Asia*, elections are cultural 'events' embedded in everyday life and 'electoral processes must be viewed as embedded in the cultural milieu in which they are conducted' (2007: xii).

Box 7.14

Elections as popular culture

Conventional political science depicts legitimate elections as rational affairs in which informed voters select candidates for office according to how their coherently presented aims, ideologies and policies appeal to the self-interest of the electorate.

In reality, elections can more realistically be seen as cultural events in which campaigns by candidates are shaped, consciously or unconsciously, to appeal to the cultural understanding and practices of the electorate. The election campaign period is one in which the masses are mobilized to participate in a range of cultural activities, from flying the party colours in noisy motorcycle parades to attending political rallies for or against, or simply to be entertained by the performances on the political stage, and to gambling on the outcome of the contest.

If a candidate is to appeal to the electorate for votes, his/her campaign activities must draw on elements of the 'popular' culture, the cultural practices of the masses, in order to draw emotional and rational resonances from the electorate. So conceived, instead of being framed and delegated to procedural irregularities and social–moral deviances, differences in electoral practices would be foregrounded.

Chua, 2007: i, xii.

Box 7.15

The festive machine

Commenting on Taiwan's elections as popular culture, Yu-fen Ko observes:

> Elections in Taiwan are closer to Chatterjee's definition of the 'political' which refers not to autonomy, rationality and liberty but to confrontation, negotiations and calculations of power relations. Elections depend on the traditional or regional networks such as fraternities, the committees governing the temples, the system of domicile, family clans, village councils, military housing compounds, and other community alliances. These establishments are not the widely celebrated modern civil organizations but represent more traditional, deep-rooted connections, or *guanxi*, interpersonal relations based on kinship, neighbourhood and acquaintance. These consist of interest exchange, power networking and face. The modernizing goal of democracy is practiced through these alliances in a festive manner that combines traditional forces with commercial formats.

Witnessing Taiwan's spectacular mass gatherings of all kinds, one might wonder how the street movements and grass-root rallies of the 1980s have been transformed into the carnival-like, pop concert-like, Baptist sermon-style of the Empowerment Convention.

Ko, 2007: 24, 36

Using this frame, we can view elections in Asia in a number of ways, from electoral 'festivals' in Taiwan to electoral 'performances' in Indonesia. The rich fabric and diversity of Asian cultures ensures that, as Reilly (2007: 1369) argues, there is an 'identifiable Asian approach to the design of democratic institutions'. The act of electioneering and functioning of electoral politics will continue to be shaped by the diverse cultural contexts these institutions operate within.

Political funding and money politics

Our final section discussing electoral systems in Pacific Asia focuses on political funding and money politics. As the section illustrates, money has played an important role in the functioning of electoral politics in the region. Particularly during the early development of democratic systems, money politics presented a clear challenge to the clean functioning of elections and party politics.

At an extreme level, there are cases of corruption on the part of elected officials (see Chapter 5 for a general discussion of government corruption). An example of this is Prime Minister Tanaka being accused in 1976 of accepting bribes from the US aerospace company Lockheed to secure sales of aircraft to a Japanese company. Prime Minister Tanaka was found guilty in the lower courts and sentenced to jail time but appealed the ruling. In an unprecedented turn, Tanaka was re-elected to the Diet twice following the original allegations (but not as Prime Minister), the second time with a wide margin of popular support. Ironically, while Tanaka is clearly an example of what Johnson described as 'structural corruption', due to Tanaka's reigning in the power of the bureaucracy and breaking the old leadership structure, Japan also owes its 'belated democratization of the political system primarily to Tanaka Kakuei' (Johnson, 1986: 28).

At a less extreme level, party funding has been a source of money politics in Pacific Asian politics. Indeed, key aspects of political party systems in the region are closely related to one another, particularly in the catch-all parties: the funding systems led to the rise of factionalism, and both in turn encourage money politics.

There are generally four models of funding for political parties (see Box 7.16). Parties in the first model, mainly corporatist parties, are funded primarily through state funding as well as membership dues. There are no exact figures showing how much funding the state provides to cover the CPC's expenses. But, given the large bureaucracy, extensive functions and activities, the ever-growing population of the party cadre, and the extent to which state funds are used in corruption or simply wasted, the actual figure must be high.

The funding model for Japanese political parties is becoming increasingly the norm for party funding: public matching funds against the number of votes a party wins in a general election and political donations from corporations and individuals. Political donations can be legal and within the limits, but can also be undeclared, beyond the limits and therefore illegal. This is where the problem of money politics arises. Diet members are provided with funds for a limited number of staff for their offices. But most MPs have a much larger number of staff for their Diet office and their regional and local offices. They also have to spend money on liaison services with their constituency. Current and future MPs also need an increasingly large amount of funds for their election campaigns. These additional funds have to come from the party and personal donations.

Before the recent reforms in the 1990s, the party would have to rely on donations from corporations and individuals to support its activities. Moreover, the party's funds are distributed through factions, and individual MPs and candidates received party funds through their faction. This has made factions pivotal in Japanese party politics. Anyone aiming at advancing a political career with the LDP would have to connect him/herself to a faction, a strong and powerful faction that controls the distribution of party funding and career opportunities.

The funding model also cemented the party's close connection with corporations. Without large amounts of political donations by corporations, the party would not be financially viable. This is the institutional basis of the iron triangle (see Chapter 6).

A third funding model is the party funded primarily by a leader's personal wealth. One of the most interesting examples is Thaksin's TRT in Thailand. Thaksin Shinawatra became Thailand's 'billionaire prime minister' with a partially self-funded campaign and a platform of populism (Pye and Schaffar, 2008) before the 'anti-Thaksin movement' (Phongpaichit and Baker, 2008) led to yet another military coup and royal intervention in Thailand democratic politics. Neither Thaksin's personal wealth or his immense populism could prevent this coup.

Box 7.16

Four models of political party funding

Mainstream model:	State matching funds and political donations	Japan, Taiwan, Korea
Corporatist model:	State funding and membership dues	Corporatist parties such as China's CPC
Personal wealth model:	Party is funded primarily	Thaksin and his TRT of Thailand by leader's personal wealth
Party enterprise model:	Party funds itself with its own enterprise assets	Taiwan's KMT

Box 7.17

How political parties are financed in South Korea

Theoretically, South Korean parties' political funds can be classified as 'formal' and 'informal'. 'Formal' political funds are those which parties receive and spend following the rules of the Political Fund Act. They include membership dues, state subsidies, contributions through supporters' associations and donations directly and indirectly made through the Election Management Committee. In contrast, 'informal' political funds are those which are collected and spent illegally by the parties and politicians. One serious problem is that informal political funds, often related to political corruption, have been much higher than formal funds.

Kim, 1998: 153

Money politics refers to a pattern of party activities centred around securing political funds for the party, factions and individual politicians and election activities that use money to secure votes. Money politics is typically seen in catch-all parties.

The final model is the party enterprise model of Taiwan's KMT. This is unique to the KMT. The KMT arose in Mainland China as a political party that controlled the state, military and national economy. Key national industries were controlled by the party-state. During the rule of the Chiangs in Taiwan, the party and the state were not separate.

Much of the economy was owned by the state, and therefore by the party as well. Even since democratic transition after the late 1980s, the KMT still managed to maintain ownership of many large business enterprises. These enterprises are the economic arm of the party, and provide funding for party functions and activities. Party funding from public and private enterprises the party controls is also seen in Malaysia and Indonesia (Sachsenroder, 1998; Gomez, 2004).

Candidate buying is 'a situation where former members of Parliament and other prospective candidates with good electoral prospects are offered financial incentives to join or switch political parties. A "transfer fee.' ... might be offered.'

Surin, 2001: 191

The funding models have a great impact on how political parties operate, and the role of money in politics. On the one hand, costs associated with election campaigns and electoral services greatly exceed the party and candidates' own financial resources. Financial dependency by political parties and candidates on large corporations becomes an important source of money politics. On the other hand, given the weakening of the ideological and organizational basis of the party in countries with catch-all parties, the parties and candidates have to use money to secure electoral advantage. 'Candidate-buying, canvasser recruitment, vote buying' (Surin, 2002: 191) become an important part of the catch-all parties' functions and activities.

Making the institutions work better

Party system reforms

Factionalism, money politics, regionalism and the problem of intra-party democracy are characteristic of political parties in Pacific Asia. But the challenge has been different for the corporatist parties and catch-all parties. For the corporatist parties, the challenge is to increase transparency and intra-party democracy while resisting the multiparty solution.

The Chinese Communist Party, for example, has issued a series of written regulations on party organization and decision-making procedures. The party has begun to involve more input from the rank and file of the party as well as the general public, and to introduce competitive procedures for electing, rather than simply appointing, party officials. China under the Xi Jinping administration has at the same time strengthened party discipline and appears to have a strong collective leadership at the top level of the party.

Intra-party democracy is a concept describing efforts, particularly in those corporatist parties, to increase transparency, participation and accountability in party affairs and transform the system of appointing party officials from selection by party committee to election by party members.

Moreover, corporatist parties are actively engaged in adjusting themselves to the changing social, economic and political conditions brought by economic reform and the rise of the market economy. In particular, careful discussion and debate took place to rethink the ideological foundation of the party, membership criteria, and party organization. One of the most significant developments was a change to the Chinese Communist Party constitution at its national congress in 2002. It was declared that the CPC represents all advanced social forces, not just the working class.

This is significant because, if it amounts to membership for 'capitalist' classes, the end of communism as an ideology and organizational principle has finally been recognized in its constitution. Moreover, if this is opening up the party to competitive societal interests, it would provide a constituency basis for the formation of legitimate factions within the party in the future.

Political reforms in catch-all parties deal with a different set of political problems. Unlike political reforms in corporatist parties, where the party itself controls reform agendas, political party reforms in catch-all parties are a national issue that involves public debate, government programmes and changes in the law. Moreover, political party reform is not an isolated effort; rather, it is often part of a broader programme that involves reform of electoral law, political party law, political ethnic law and political funding law. South Korea, for example, passed a series of laws in the first year of the elected civilian government of Kim Yong Sam in 1993. These included the Public Officials' Ethics Law, the Real Name Financial Transaction System, the Integrated Election Act, and the Political Fund Act – all aimed at curbing the money problem in party politics.

Also in 1994, led by Prime Minister Morihiro Hosokawa, Japan's Diet passed a broad political reform bill centred on electoral reform. Scholars have debated the impact of the reform (Krauss and Pekkanen, 2004) and the general view is that the reform efforts recognized the problems within the political party system and did affect the organization of political parties, political funding, and the role of factions.

Political party reforms in the third category are much broader in scope: the transformation of mass bureaucratic parties into catch-all parties. Both the KMT of Taiwan and the GOLKAR of Indonesia, for example, survived political liberalization and democratic transition. But the survival and further development under the new political environment forced both parties to reform themselves significantly. In the case of the KMT, losing control of government in 2000 made the reform of the KMT a more urgent matter. These reforms were carried out on three fronts. The first was to shrink its bureaucracy, to cut down its decision-making power, organizational complexity and operational and staff costs. The extended bureaucracy was part of the mass-bureaucratic party the KMT used to be. Its reduction was important for the transformation. The second aspect of the reform was to de-emphasize the ideological undertone of the party. This was achieved through a series of ideological battles between leading factions in the 1990s, and pushed further with the leadership's centrist campaign

Case Study Lab 7.5

Transformation of dominant party systems in Pacific Asia

Edward Friedman and Joseph Wong, with their research team, employ a broader framework of dominant party systems to explain transformations of former dominant political parties:

- Political party system change is more than democratic transition from authoritarianism. The mainstream authoritarian-democracy binary framework is not enough to explain other forms of political transformation.
- Focus on adaptive choice and strategy of dominant parties shows they reinvent, re-programme and reorganize as well as other factors that shape the politics of adaptive choice.
- Explaining different outcomes of dominant party transition shows some collapse and disappear, others survive, and regain power; still others retain power.

Friedman and Wong, 2011: 2–4

Box 7.18

Political party system reforms

Aims	*Scope*	*Examples*	*Time period*
Transparency and intra-party democracy ideology, organization and membership curbing corruption	Internal	CPC (China) VCP (Vietnam)	ongoing ongoing
Transition from mass-bureaucratic party to catch-all party	Internal/KMT system-wide	(KMT, Taiwan) GOLKAR (Indonesia)	2000s 2000s
Correcting factionalism, money politics, regionalism	System wide Korea	Japan 1990s	1990s

platform in the 2008 presidential election. Finally, the KMT put all its party enterprises into a public trust as a gesture of separating the party from its businesses. At the core of the transformation of the KMT has been the recasting of itself as a political party separated from state institutions rather than as a political party in the control of the state institutions.

Electoral system reforms

Electoral systems in Pacific Asia are less stable than in Western democracies. Specific rules are often designed to support the dominant party's interests and accommodate political circumstances. During the era of non-pluralist politics in Indonesia, South Korea, the Philippines and Thailand, electoral rules such as the term of the presidency, forms of government, qualifications for candidates, campaign rules and so on, were often subject to change by the ruling party. In some countries, such as Korea and Indonesia, changes in electoral rules were incremental and occurred more often than in other counties, such as Japan and Taiwan.

But amid the diversity, there have been two clearly dominant trends in the development of electoral reform in Pacific Asian countries since the 1980s. First, there has been a movement towards parallel systems with a larger number of seats in SMDs with FPTP, and a smaller number of seats in MMDs with proportional representation (Japan, Taiwan and the Philippines). Accompanying the change there has also been a shift in the rules for presidential elections, from indirect election to direct popular vote (Taiwan, South Korea and Indonesia).

Second, many states insist on MMDs with a range of different voting methods. A significant example is provided by the changes in the electoral system in Singapore over the years. With the creation of the GRCs, 'Singapore's electoral system went from entirely single-member constituencies to a preponderance of multi-member constituencies' within a decade (Mauzy, 2002: 243). This runs against the first trend of moving towards a system of SMDs plus proportional representation.

Given the importance of the electoral reforms that reshaped the political structures in these countries, such reforms caused much debate there. Debates focus on the choice of electoral system, the problems electoral reform aims to deal with, and the effects of these electoral reforms on both the party system and the overall political system.

For many countries, electoral reforms have been driven by pluralist demands unleashed from their recent political liberalization and democratic transition. The old electoral systems are seen as supporting single-party dominance, and the new parallel systems are supposed to be more proportional, more accurate, and less distortional, allowing fairer representation and greater participation. Anticipating the reduction of power of the dominant parties, resistance to the reforms came mainly from these parties. Electoral reforms took place only when a dominant party was in trouble (in Japan, when the LDP was already forced to share power with other parties to form a coalition government in 1993, and in Taiwan when the KMT lost its power in 2000) or democratic movements overthrew the ruling dominant party (in the Philippines and South Korea).

In others, electoral reforms have been carefully designed to reinforce the corporatist functions of state institutions and allow single-party dominance to continue to be viable in the new political environment.

While it is easy to agree on the first two, the choice of an electoral system and the problems that the new system is expected to solve, the debate is still ongoing regarding the effects of the electoral reforms: have the electoral reforms in Japan, Korea, Indonesia and the Philippines led to better parliamentary representation or to instability? Are the electoral reforms in countries such as Vietnam and China leading to genuine political liberalization and eventually to democratic transition? Have the electoral changes in Singapore resulted in fairer representation or enhanced single party dominance?

Electoral rules, party politics and political order

Finally, let us put political party systems and electoral systems together and explain why these two sets of systems are important in determining how the political system works as well as in shaping political order, and discuss the significance of the electoral and party system in Pacific Asia in the broad context of comparative politics. The development of party and electoral systems in Pacific Asia has shown that in states where elections are genuine, electoral rules have a greater impact on how political parties are organized and operate, on how relationships among political parties develop and on how the overall political order is structured (Nohlen et al., 2001: 29). Japan is clearly a case in point. Most catch-all parties at the time of writing are also in this category. But on the question of whether there is a causal link between a specific electoral model and a particular party system, the evidence from Pacific Asia is mixed. For example, according to the so-called Duverger's Law, plurality in SMDs will lead to a two-party system. Duverger's hypothesis is that proportional representation is likely to lead to a multiparty system (Hsieh and Newman, 1982: 8; Riker, 1982; Nohlen et al., 2001: 29). But until recently, Malaysia, the Philippines and Singapore have long practiced FPTP in SMDs, and there has been little evidence of a two-party system there.

Moreover, proportional representation has been the principal electoral system in Indonesia and Cambodia. A multiparty system appeared in Indonesia only after the fall of Suharto in 1998. In countries that have adopted the MMP system, such as Japan, where the LDP has returned to dominance, it

Case Study Lab 7.6

How electoral rules and party politics shape political order: Japan in the 1990s

Japan experienced significant change in the overall political structure and influence of political forces in government and policy.

- The dominance of the LDP in the 1955 system was built on some key institutional elements in the party and electoral system: factionalism, Public Affairs Research Council system, policy elite groups, veto players of the LDP that connects LDP elites, bureaucracy and parliament policy deliberation.
- The 1994 electoral reform and the political reforms in the 1990s in general turn intra-party competition to interparty competition and force political leaders to take control of policy process from factional/veto players.
- The post-1955 system in Japan sees the weakening of the dominance of the LDP and factional and bureaucratic elites and a more influential role of political parties under a more effective political leader in the political and policy process, which is more open, populous and competitive.

Shintoda, 2008: 6–7

is not certain whether a two-party system is emerging. In Taiwan, where the KMT returned for two terms before being convincingly defeated by the DPP in the 2016 presidential and national legislature elections, the case for a genuine maturing of a two-party system is stronger. Finally, it is argued that a multi-seat district with SNTV favours the ruling party (Japan before 1993), but evidence also suggest that FPTP in SMDs also allows the ruling party to be 'overrepresented in Parliament at the expense of the opposition', as in the case of Malaysia (Chin, 2001: 214).

Scholars debate what type of state Japan is; many consider Japan during LDP dominance (and Singapore under Lee Kuan Yew) to be a state of 'soft authoritarianism' (Roy, 1994; Means, 1996). Such a view tends to start with a presumption of the nature of the political system and from there try to explain everything else. Alternatively, one can argue that those elements of soft authoritarianism – same-party dominance, the iron triangle between the state bureaucracy, the LDP and business elites, 'Japan, Inc.', types of political structure (see Chapter 6) and state-dominated state–business and state–society relations (see Chapters 6 and 8) – are consequences of the long development of state institutions among which the electoral system was essential.

In states where elections and political parties are controlled or managed – such as China (and most former communist states), Indonesia under Suharto and Singapore – the ruling political party, and indeed the overall ruling party-centred political structure, shaped which electoral system is chosen, how it is allowed to operate and the role it is expected to play in support of the overall political order.

Box 7.19

Partisanship and citizen behaviour in Pacific Asian democracies

Partisanship is the propensity of individual citizens to identify with and attach themselves to a particular political party. The linkage between citizens and parties is 'an essential aspect of democratic politics', as through this connection parties connect citizens to the democratic process (Dalton et al., 2007: 177).

There are two unique factors as to whether this is also the case for Pacific Asian countries.

- First, party politics was very much marginalized during the Cold War non-pluralist politics in most Pacific Asian countries. Political liberalization and democratic transition since the 1980s has seen the revival of political parties. It would be interesting to see whether this has led to an increase in partisanship and the impact of such partisanship on citizens' political behaviour.
- Second, as Dalton et al. (2007: 177–9) indicate, given the shallow bases of most parties, low levels of programmatic electoral competition, weak institutionalization in party systems, the short span of parties' existence and the global trend of the 'decline of parties', there is a general expectation that the linkage between parties and citizens in Pacific Asian countries can be weak, and the usefulness of partisanship in structuring citizens' political orientations 'can be attenuated'.

Research on the question provides conflicting findings.

- In the same project organized by Dalton et al., Russell Dalton and Aiji Tanaka find that lower-party polarization in Pacific Asia's new democracies and the newly-reformed electoral structure (to increase party cohesion and competition) has a weak impact on voters' electoral choice (Dalton and Tanaka, 2007).
- Examining the extent of partisanship, Emile Sheng finds that partisanship is relatively weaker in Pacific Asian countries and the level of partisanship varies with social status and age (Sheng, 2007).
- In assessing the effect of partisanship on citizen behaviour, Yun-han Chu and Min-hua Huang found that partisanship in East Asia exerts just as much influence on citizens' engagement in politics as in established democracies and the 'emerging competitive party system' has 'powerful socializing effects … on East Asian citizens' behaviour, preference, or even identity'.

Chu and Huang, 2007: 315

In Singapore, as Mauzy shows, the FPTP system reduces the number of parties that compete and tends to penalize the opposition by not translating votes into seats proportionately. The multi-member GRCs further disadvantage small parties that have difficulty in fielding competent teams; and they discourage the formation of new parties. Also, the large size of the GRCs tends to eliminate ethnic concentrations or socioeconomic blocs, which could perhaps be targeted by the opposition. Finally, the absence of elections below the national parliamentary level deprives the opposition of the opportunity to use local elections as a stepping-stone to power (Mauzy, 2002: 248–9).

A further argument is that the overall political order in the region is converging on a distinctive pattern of electoral reform, or as Reilly (2007) argues, to an 'Asian model of electoral democracy':

Convergent patterns of political reform across the region have seen the development of what appears to be an identifiable Asian approach to the design of democratic institutions, making the outcomes of democratization in the Asia-Pacific region quite distinctive by world standards. The increasing shift towards distinctively majoritarian mixed-member electoral systems and embryonic two-party systems in what were previously either one-party autocracies or unstable multiparty democracies is perhaps the most compelling evidence for this emerging Asian model of electoral democracy (Reilly, 2007: 1369).

In both catch-all parties and corporatist parties, the type of party and electoral system, and the type of reform experienced, are closely related to a country's larger political environment. The decades of non-pluralist politics during the Cold War saw same-party dominance in most countries and limited competitiveness in elections. Electoral reforms in the 1990s and 2000s in many countries were either a part or consequence of the movement of political liberalization and democratic transition. This is the case in Indonesia, South Korea, the Philippines and Taiwan, as well as for the 'regime shift' in Japan in the 1990s. The former communist states started to introduce limited and controlled reform of party and electoral systems but. But their overall party-state structure very much determined the pace and content of their reforms.

This, however, is also a focus of scholarly debate. On one side of the debate, many argue that economic and social changes require fundamental adjustments to the political system. But unless there are such changes in the overall party-state system, reforms in party and electoral systems can only reinforce this system. On the other hand, scholars argue that if we understand the critical role of electoral systems in shaping party politics and the overall political structure, there is reason to believe the incremental reforms in these corporatist party states can lead to change in the fundamental political structure.

The interactive and intertwined relations among electoral systems, party politics and the overall political order is not especially new or unique to Pacific Asia – though scholars do believe that, given the changes in electoral rules, party politics and the overall political order across the region over a long historical period, Pacific Asia does provide a set of rich empirical cases to investigate the close relationship among these three key aspects.

The historical experiences of Pacific Asian countries in these areas can add rich empirical evidence to the ongoing debates in political science on the original determinants of political behaviour, order and institutions.

Three major schools of thought dominate this debate. The institutionalists argue that institutions matter: electoral rules affect party politics and eventually the overall political order.

Structuralists argue that it is the fundamental political structure, the party-state, for example, under which the party politics and elections take place that matters. This fundamental political order sets the boundaries for party politics and electoral activities and makes sure they serve the overall interests of the political order.

Finally, culturalists see the role of established political habits and practices and their associated social forces and interests as crucial for shaping how the institutions work, and forming the substance of the political structure.

It is hoped that this chapter has given you enough material to understand these approaches in explaining the dynamics of electoral systems, party politics and the overall political order in Pacific Asian countries and some confidence to come up with your own views.

Chapter summary

- Traditionally, political parties were underdeveloped in Pacific Asia. This was further complicated by the spread of the Communist Party system as well as other forms of non-pluralist politics across Pacific Asia during the Cold War. Since the 1980s, political parties in various forms have converged into two main types: catch-all parties in pluralist polities; and corporatist parties in non-pluralist states.
- Differences between these two types of political party are reflected in the organization of political parties at national and grassroots levels, the procedures for candidate selection and the political support basis of the parties. Catch-all parties are more elitist and election focused; while corporatist parties are more mass-bureaucratic and mass integration orientated.
- Factionalism, regionalism and money politics are three unique features of the political party systems in Pacific Asia, particularly in the catch-all parties. Corporatist parties, on the other hand, tend to lack transparency and intra-party democracy, be over-bureaucratized, and function primarily as the organizational tool of the ruling elites to integrate the masses to accept their governing values and vision.
- Recent political reforms are designed to deal with factionalism, money politics, regionalism and same-party dominance in catch-all parties. Scholars debate the effect of party reforms. For corporatist parties, reforms are intended to allow a level of intra-party democracy, standardization and rationalization of party rules and procedures, and to make adjustments in response to changing conditions. Views vary as to whether these reforms are just a refinement of the existing political structure and party and state institutions or if they are part of a profound change.
- Electoral systems in Pacific Asian countries have experienced changes of various kinds. There has been, on the one hand, a shift from models of multi-member districts with various voting methods, to some form of single-member districts combined with proportional representation. On the other hand, multi-member districts are still in use in many states.
- The electoral systems in Japan and Singapore and those of the pluralist and non-pluralist states in general demonstrate that in pluralist states, the electoral system is instrumental in the shaping of the political party system and the overall political structure and, in non-pluralist states, the overall political structure and party-state institutions limit how the party and electoral system work, as well as what role they play in the country's overall corporatist organization of society and polity.
- The central theme of this chapter is that electoral rules, party politics and political order are interactive and closely intertwined. To what extent each can affect the others in individual cases depends on the overall political environment and the organization of the polity.

Further reading

For a survey of political party systems in Pacific Asia, see Sachsenroder and Frings (1998) and Hicken and Kuhonta (2014). For an overview of the electoral systems and their historical evolution in each country, see Hsieh and Newman (2002) and Nohlen et al. (2001). Nohlen et al. discuss major issues in elections across Pacific Asian countries with systematic data. As with Hsieh and Newman, much has changed since they were published, so you will need to access the latest information from other sources. Reilly (2007 and 2014) provides a more up-to-date and systemic view of electoral reform in Pacific Asia. Grofman et al. (1999) is an excellent volume on SNTV in Japan, Korea and Taiwan; and more generally, on how a particular electoral system shaped the party system, electoral politics and political structure. As a case study, Hrebenar (1992) is an excellent volume on the Japanese party system.

Study questions

1 Discuss the factors that shaped the development of modern political parties in Pacific Asia.

2 How does the catch-all party differ from the corporatist party in party organization? Why are they different?

3 Why did factions emerge as a primary form of party organization and decision-making in Japan's LDP?

4 How does regionalism in party politics affect the quality of democratic institutions?

5 What impact does Pacific Asia's 'electoral culture' have on the functioning of democracy in the region?

6 Using examples, highlight the key features of money politics in the region. Are these unique to the region or especially 'Asian'?

Key terms

Leninist party (176); Communist one-party system (178); Catch-all party (180); Corporatist party (181); Dominant party (179); One-party dominant system (181); Party-oriented model and Legislator-oriented model (183); Vote chiefs (187); Factions and Factionalism (188); Regionalism (190); Cadre system (188); LDP dominance (194); Single non-transferable vote (194); Medium sized, multi-member district model (192); Same-number candidacy (195); Functional groups (196); Group Representation Constituencies (196); Non-Constituency Members of Parliament (196); Electoral culture (197); Nominated Members of Parliament (197); Money politics (198); Candidate buying (200); Intra-party democracy (200).

Chapter 8
Political society: power, participation and advocacy

Access and participation are important for members of a political community. This chapter begins with a survey of scholarly views on the structure of political society in Pacific Asian countries. Given the dominance of state institutions, the way that political society is structured and how different sectors of society participate in the political process are of particular importance.

The chapter goes on to look at how individual citizens participate in the political process. Important here are the ways and means by which individuals can influence politics and policy within and beyond formal institutions and procedures. There are various ways in which an individual can exercise such influence: building relationships with key policymakers; demonstrating on the streets, and openly challenging government policies or even the government itself; offering bribes regarding a particular issue; organizing an action group; working in the government; or becoming a politician. The chapter surveys these means; and discusses why some are preferred over others and what they mean for the overall role of formal institutions and procedures.

> **Political society** is an arena in which political actors compete for the legitimate right to exercise control over public power and the state apparatus.
>
> Linz and Stepan, 1996: 16

Not all individuals are equal in their political influence. This is particularly true in Pacific Asian countries. Of particular importance is the unique influence of the elites. There is a recognized pattern of elite governance, where select individuals or groups have greater access and influence. A section of the chapter therefore looks at key elite groups and explains how they shape politics and governance.

While there is a consensus on the role of elites in Pacific Asian politics and society, views vary on the role and political attitude of other societal groups. Here we discuss gender and social inequality and ask how the position of women in society and government has changed from the traditionally men-dominant form in Pacific Asian social structure.

This is followed by a discussion of the debate on the concept of civil society, its relations with other political institutions, and its role in the overall political order. The chapter then moves on to a focused discussion on three key examples of politically significant societal groups: the middle classes, labour and environmental movements.

The final section overviews the role of the media, Internet and social media in the region. It presents the debate about who controls the media and what role it plays in state-society relations. It asks how international media and new media technologies have shaped state-society relations in the region.

The chapter highlights the point that, while citizens have equal constitutional rights to participate in the political process, the patterns of their actual participation, the ways in which they participate and the level of effectiveness of their participation are very much affected by the overall structure of the political society, the prevalent social norms and behavioural values, and individuals' ascriptive role and position in society. Moreover, given the varied degrees of effectiveness and feasibility for individual citizens, some methods of political participation are favoured over others.

State and society in Pacific Asia

In previous chapters, we have discussed various state institutions, branches and functions of government, as well as the formation and change in government and state institutions. We began this text with discussions on state institutions and structures. For many, however, the state is central in shaping politics, generating policy and structuring society. This state-centric view of state–society relations has led scholars to be inclined to understand the forces and structure of society from the perspective of the vision and functions, as well as the political and institutional dynamics, of the state. From this perspective, we cannot understand societal forces such as citizens, the middle class, the business community, labour, student activities or elites, without referring back to the state and its purposes and activities.

The state-centric view is part of the long intellectual tradition in the debate over state–society relations that goes back to the times of Karl Marx, Emile Durkheim, Max Weber and Talcott Parsons. Indeed, these earlier thinkers pioneered two diverging perspectives on state–society relations in modern and modernizing societies. Max Weber, given his emphasis on 'the rise of the modern state, the patterns of authority and legitimacy, the role of leadership, and the nature of bureaucracy, was led naturally to focus on the problems of carving out cohesive and centralized states, and on the critical roles of political leaders' (Kohli and Shue, 1994: 297). Much of contemporary state-centric thinking, one can argue, has been influenced or inspired by Weber's work.

On the other hand, for Karl Marx and Emile Durkheim, the state and politics were 'peripheral to the major processes of change under way ... They each considered a state's actions and a society's politics to be primarily a reflection of more fundamental dynamics of socioeconomic shift and variation' (Kohli and Shue. 1994: 296). This society-centric approach influenced the rise of modernization and dependency theory after the Second World War, which focused similarly on the effects of fundamental social and economic change on state structure and government institutions.

Post-Second World War Pacific Asia has been a fertile ground for the state-centric approach. As discussed in Chapters 1 and 2, the region is known for its long history of a strong state and penetrating government institutions, state-domination over society and centripetal society, though more so in Confucianism-influenced Northeast than Southeast Asia (Wittfogel, 1957; Pye, 1985). In Chapter 6, we have also seen the state-led drive for economic development and government-centred relations with

> **Box 8.1**
>
> ### State–society relations: the state-centric approach and its challengers
>
> ***State-centric***: The state is the defining force in state–society relations. See developmental state theory and the Weberian bureaucratic state.
>
> ***Society-centric***: The state is the product of the interplay of various forces in society. See democracy and modernization theory, social classes via Marxism, social structure via Durkheim, civil society theory and revolutions and social movements.
>
> ***State-in-society***: The state's capacity and effectiveness depends on the way it relates to social forces and institutions. See embedded autonomy theory and negotiated state theory.

industrial capital and other societal forces in support of economic growth campaigns. The developmental state model (see Chapter 6) and the public policy explanations (World Bank, 1993) focus clearly on the paramount role the state played in the national movement for economic development.

One significant exception to state centrism and the strong state tradition in Pacific Asia is the Philippines. As Patricio N. Abinales and Donna J. Amoroso show, there is a

> recurring dilemma of state–society relations in the Philippines. One horn of the dilemma is the persistent inability of the state to provide basic services, guarantee peace and order, and foster economic development ... Society regularly calls for better governance, business leaders for consistent policy implementation, urbanites for clean and affordable water, the middle class for professionalism and honesty, and the poor majority for a government that represents them. (Abinales and Amoroso, 2005: 1–2)

It is no surprise that the 'Bringing the State Back In' (Evans et al., 1985) movement, or what Skocpol called the 'revival of a continental European perspective' (Skocpol, 1985: 7), in the 1980s had much of its empirical support from Pacific Asian countries (Johnson, 1982; Haggard, 1990; Wade, 1990; Weiss and Hobson, 1995). It was the significant differences the state made in politics and economic development in Pacific Asian countries that motivated scholars to pay particular attention to the decisive role of the state in the shaping of state–society relations. States here are seen as 'promoters of economic development, and social redistribution', as well as shapers of transnational relations and the patterns of social conflict (Evans et al., 1985).

The state-centric approach to state–society relations in Pacific Asia is not without criticism. As Kohli and Shue comment, 'it often happens in the social sciences ... that new gains made on one analytical front may only give rise to newer and yet more challenging problems of analysis on the other fronts' (Kohli and Shue, 1994: 293). Scholars using the state-centric approach to analyse China, for example,

> find themselves struggling to re-conceptualize the workings of a Party-state that no longer directly dominates society and of an economy that no longer can be classified as 'Leninist command'. Observers of China find themselves faced with a system in free-fall transition to some system as yet unknown, to the point that it often becomes difficult to analytically frame what is occurring at present, let alone attempt analyses of China's probable future. (Unger and Chan, 1995: 29)

Making a similar argument, Moon and Prasad charge that the state-centric approach 'fails to uncover the complex and dynamic internal workings of the state structure by depicting the state as an internally cohesive, unitary actor' and suffers from its rigid dichotomy of 'state–society relations through the "dominance/insulation" hypothesis' (Moon and Prasad, 1994: 364, 370).

Alternative perspectives to state–society relations in Pacific Asia emerged to challenge the state-centric and society-centric approaches. Some argue that the role and capacity of the state depends very much on the close relations with social forces and organizations. Unger and Chan's concept of state corporatism in China (see Box 8.2), for example, explains the change in China

> from a Party command system that dominated directly (for which that frightening word 'totalitarian' was arguably accurate) to one that dominates partly through surrogates (authoritarian corporatist) ... What is being witnessed is a gradual devolution of power from the centre that widens the operational space of some of the existing bureaucracies and so-called mass organizations, rather than the rise of independent associations. (Unger and Chan, 1995: 39)

Peter Evans, investigating why state involvement works in some cases and produces disasters in others, argues that the success or failure of state action depends, among other things, on the way they are organized and tied to society. Predatory states extract at the expense of society, undercutting development even in the narrow sense of capital accumulation. Developmental states have not only presided over industrial transformation, but can be argued plausibly to have played a role in making it happen. In these developmental states, the state's autonomy for effective action is 'embedded in a concrete set of

Box 8.2

State corporatism

State corporatism is a form of state-led organization and management of society. Under state corporatism, the state integrates social groups into the state system, and engages social forces for overall state coherence and governance.

Jonathan Unger and Anita Chan observe 'the state recognizes one and only one organization (say, a national labour union, a business association, a farmers' association) as the sole representative of the sectoral interests of the individuals, enterprises, or institutions that comprise that organization's assigned constituency. The state determines which organizations will be recognized as legitimate, and forms an unequal partnership with such organizations. The organizations sometimes even get channelled into the policy-making processes and often help implement state policy on the government's behalf ... Under state corporatism, the government may even take charge of creating and maintaining all of the corporatist organizations and may grant itself the power to assign and remove their leaders as well. Often such "representative organizations" serve a function of pre-empting the emergence of autonomous organizations'. (Unger and Chan, 1996: 95–7)

social ties that binds the state to society and provides institutionalized channels for the continual negotiation and renegotiation of goals and policies' (Evans, 1995: 12).

In another study, Gary D. Allinson found that, instead of being the developmental state where the bureaucratic elites dominated as Johnson depicted, Japan since the 1970s has become a more contentious and competitive polity, or what Allinson calls a 'negotiated polity' (Allinson, 1993: 5), where there is 'an increase in the scope, frequency, and intensity of political bargains negotiated through organized and institutionalized groups ... [D]isorganized or unorganized groups in Japanese society have increased their ability to realize political ends that in some measure meet their needs' (Allinson, 1993: 8). The widening of political spaces sees a more contentious and competitive relationship among various participants in the political process.

Even in the Philippines, state weakness is blamed in part on the 'history of state capture by sectorial interests. The rural poor demand land reform – indeed, improving the country's productivity capacity depends upon it – but powerful landed elites oppose it, and it happens only very slowly. Such elites, along with political clans and opportunistic politicians who use government office as a source of booty, constitute a small but powerful minority' (Abinales and Amoroso, 2005: 2).

Embedded autonomy is the underlying structural basis for the developmental type of states. It is a contradictory combination of corporate coherence that gives state apparatuses a certain kind of 'autonomy, and connectedness to social forces that supply the state with both sources of intelligence and the ability to rely on decentralized private implementation'.

Evans, 1995: 12

All these new analytical frameworks see close intertwined, interactive and dynamic relations, blurred boundaries and a mutual impact between state and society. This new trend in the conceptualization of state–society relations in Pacific Asian countries clearly comes under the umbrella of the state-in-society movement in the social sciences.

Joel S. Migdal, a principal advocate of the state-in-society approach, argues in his contribution to a volume summarizing the key arguments of the movement that 'states are parts of societies ... There is no getting around the mutuality of state–society interactions: societies affect states as much as, or possibly more than, states affect societies' (Migdal, 1994: 2; see Box 8.3). As Kohli and Shue argue, state-in-society research is

> neither 'state-centered' nor 'society-centered.' It approaches the formations and transformations of states and societies as a reciprocal, rather than an autonomous process. It accepts that states in part constitute their societies and societies in part constitute their states. It dwells deliberately at the intersections of state and society, and focuses on the mutually conditioning interactions that occur between segments of state and of society. (Kohli and Shue, 1994: 321)

Case Study Lab 8.1

Contentious politics as an analytical framework

Increasingly there are diverse forms of political actions and activities in Pacific Asian societies. Conventional frameworks, focusing on state types, elite dynamics, social classes, the military, gender and religion, seem to be insufficient to provide an explanation. Dan Slater, exploring the role of social forces and conflicts in the shaping of political institutions and order in the rise of authoritarian rule in postcolonial Southeast Asia, uses contentious politics as an analytical framework that brings elite politics, authoritarian state powers and diverse forms of internal conflicts together in explaining the shaping of political order and institutions:

- Contentious politics encompasses a wide range of transgressive, collective mass actions – from labour strikes to ethnic riots, from rural rebellions to student protests, from urban terrorism to street barricades and from social revolutions to separatist insurgencies. While such plasticity in a concept can often be an analytical weakness, contentious politics proves quite useful as an umbrella term capturing the diverse types of internal conflict that have characterized and shaped the postcolonial world.
- Research on contentious politics has almost universally treated it as an outcome to be explained – as a product instead of a producer of political institutions. This approach argues contentious politics is an explanation in its own right.
- When a wide range of elites perceive danger to their property, privilege, and persons from contentious politics to be endemic and unmanageable under relatively pluralistic potential arrangements, they become prone to coalesce in protection pacts – broad elite coalitions unified by shared support for heightened state power and tightened authoritarian controls as institutional bulwarks against continued or renewed mass unrest.
- Protection pacts provide the strongest coalitional basis for authoritarian regimes to provide extra resources from elites and to organize their most power allies, as well as to facilitate the formation of powerful states, well-organized parties, a cohesive military and durable authoritarian regimes.

Slater 2010: 4–6

Box 8.3

State–society relations: the state-in-society view

Joel S. Migdal, Atul Kohli and Vivienne Shue summarize the key claims of the state-in-society framework as follows:

> States vary in their effectiveness based on their ties to society. A state's relative effectiveness is a function of the varied forms in which state–society relations are interwoven.
>
> States must be disaggregated. The state is not a coherent and unitary actor. The overall role of the state in society hinges on the numerous junctures between its diffuse parts and other social organizations.
>
> The boundaries between state and society are generally blurred. A deliberate analytical sensitivity to both the ubiquity and the variety of state–society lineage is required if we are to advance our understanding of states' simultaneous embeddedness in and relative autonomy from other operational social forces.
>
> States and other social forces may be mutually empowering and their interactions can be mutually transforming. This mutuality of influence suggests that a research focus on state capacities needs to be complemented with considerations of a given state's social setting.

Migdal et al., 1994: 2–4, 293–5

It is with the aid of this intellectual mapping of the contentious views about state–society relations that we now discuss various social forces and associations, how they relate to state institutions, in what forms they participate in the political processes, and what role they play in the function of the whole political system in Pacific Asian countries. We start at the very basic level: the individual citizen.

Being a politically active citizen

Citizenship is a modern concept. It is an important institution that defines the relationship between the state and an individual in modern societies, and provides the institutional basis for the interaction between the state and its citizens. Being politically active and participating in the political process is an exercise of such citizenship. There are two dimensions to this:

- Whether citizens are given equal rights and opportunities for political participation;
- Through which forms or methods citizens choose political participation and how effective these are.

On the first dimension, the right to vote is one of the key indicators. The development of the concept and practices of citizenship in Pacific Asian countries was influenced strongly by the universal suffrage movement in the late nineteenth and early twentieth centuries in Europe. In particular, the introduction of suffrage and universal suffrage in Pacific Asia has been closely related to the emergence of independent states out of largely European colonial rule. As can be seen from Table 8.1, most Pacific Asian countries introduced universal suffrage in the 1940s and 1950s at the same time the new state was established after the Second World War. Therefore, in contrast to the suffrage movement in Europe, the introduction of universal suffrage took place over a relatively short period of time in Pacific Asia.

A second feature of the universal suffrage movement in Pacific Asia is that, in contrast to the gradual, piecemeal and progressive removal of restrictions on the right to vote in Europe and North America, most Pacific Asian countries took just one step in introducing universal suffrage. The Philippines was an exception, where property ownership, gender, religion and literacy restrictions were lifted only across a period of several decades. In Malaysia and Indonesia, the idea of citizenship based on race or religion was attempted in the early years of state formation at the time of independence, but the principle of universal suffrage eventually prevailed (see Table 8.1).

Case Study Lab 8.2

Citizenship as an analytical tool for explaining Pacific Asian politics and government

Citizenship is a set of practices (juridical, political, economic and cultural) that define a person as a competent member of society, and as a consequence shape the flow of resources to people and social groups. Citizenship can be utilized as a powerful sociological tool for probing the socio-political character of ordinary East Asians' everyday lives in conjunction with the macro state-society relationship in each country and their regional political economic and sociocultural interdependence. Citizenship is therefore:

- A substantive concern for neglected individuals in society in relation to the state, their rights and status. East Asia is much less progressively liberal than Western societies, much less sensitive to the fundamental components of a liberal order.
- A theoretical perspective, leading to debunking of innumerable scholarly as well as practical issues in East Asian politics, society and economy.
- An analytical strategy that provides detailed and systematic accounts of state-society relations and citizen situations within the national society and polity.

Chang and Turner, 2012: 3–4

COUNTRY PROFILE

TAIWAN

		Regional Comparison	World Rank
GDP	1079 (ppp/bil)	3.29% of PA-18	20th (of 189)
HDI	0.882 (0 to 1)	PA-18: 5th	21st (of 186)
WGI	1.07 (–2.5 to 2.5)	PA-18: 4th	81 (%)

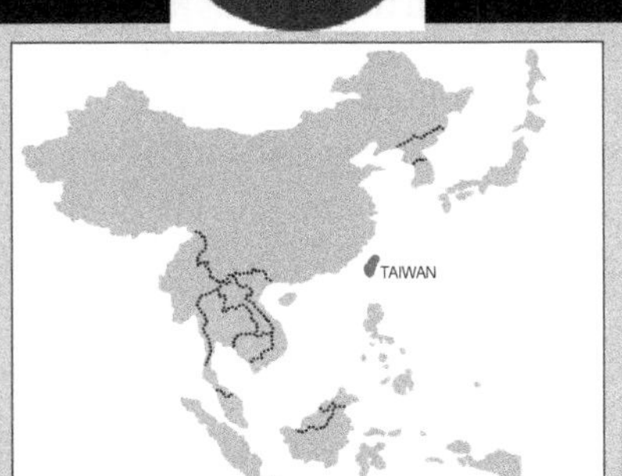

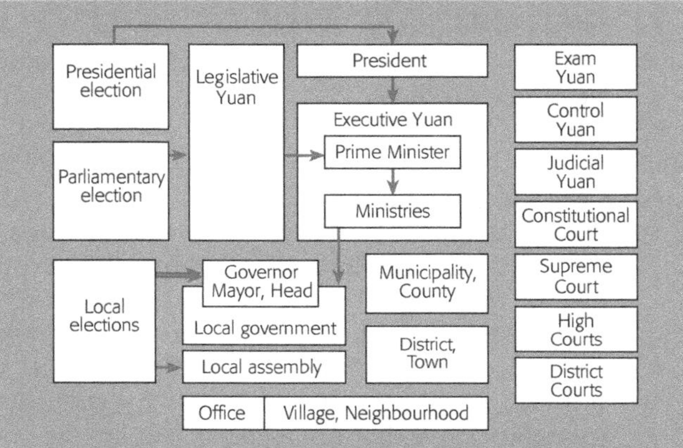

Key political facts

Electoral system for national legislature
Single-member district and mixed member proportional representation.

Political cycles
Presidential elections every 4 years.
Legislative Yuan elections every 4 years.
Annual government budget to be enacted by Legislative Yuan in November.

Further reading

Copper, 2012; Fell, 2012.

Timeline of modern political development

1945	Japan surrenders and the ROC regains control.
1947	Constitution of ROC with a National Assembly system and a five-branch form of government.
1947	The 228 Incident, the KMT government's brutal suppression of rebels and opposition.
1948	Temporary Provisions suspends the Constitution.
1949	Chiang Kai-shek moves the ROC central government to Taiwan. Martial law is declared.
1975	Chiang Kai-shek dies and his son, Chiang Ching Kuo takes over.
1979	The Kaohsiung Incident, the KMT government cracks down on democratic activists.
1987	Martial law is lifted. The Democratic Progressive Party is formed.
1991	Temporary Provisions abolished and constitution restored.
1991–2005	Constitutional amendments to fit the 1947 constitution to political reality in Taiwan.
1991	First Taiwan-based national assembly and parliamentary elections.
1994	Local autonomy laws to enhance local autonomy.
1996	First direct popular election of president.
2000	The DPP wins presidential election. The KMT's 55-year rule ends.
2003	Referendum Law passed. 2005 National assembly abolished.
2005	New electoral law, moving to SMDs and MMP.
2006	Government scraps the National Unification Council.
2008	President Ma apologies for the White Terror in the 1950s and 1960s.
2009	Former President Chen Shiu-bien goes on trial on corruption charges.
2010	Taiwan signs ECFA, a free trade agreement, with China.
2014	Taiwan's first government-to-government talks with China since 1949.
2015	Taiwan's President Ma Ying-jeou and China's President Xi Jinping hold first formal meeting since Chinese civil war ended in 1949 and the KMT set up government in Taiwan.
2016	Tsai Ing-wen led DPP wins both presidency and a majority in the Legislature Yuan.

Table 8.1 Introduction of suffrage in Pacific Asia

Country	*Male*	*Female*
Cambodia	1946	1956
China	1947	1947
Indonesia	1953	1953
Japan	1926	1946
N. Korea	1946	1946
S. Korea	1948	1948
Laos	1947	1957
Malaysia	1955	1955
Singapore	1959	1959
Taiwan	1947	1947
Thailand	1932	1932
Philippines	1907	1937
Vietnam	1946	1946

Nohlen et al., 2001, various chapters.

Third, while most new states instituted universal suffrage and other mechanisms of political participation in their constitution, in reality the exercise of political rights has not been without complications. In Chapter 2, we discussed the shift in the early Cold War years to non-pluralist politics in most Pacific Asian countries. The rights of citizens were severely curbed. In the communist countries – and in many non-communist countries too – citizens' rights were granted constitutionally in principle, but in reality the exercise of these rights became very difficult and an entirely different political show.

In countries run by a military or other authoritarian government, political rights were suspended completely. In yet other countries, elections were still regularly held, but the specific design or even manipulation of the electoral system and party system (see Chapter 7) rendered these elections almost meaningless.

In addition to the constraints of the overall political structure and environment on citizens' rights at times, there is also the issue of how political culture, or political habits, shape the function of political institutions, and indeed the pattern of political participation – a problem that Gabriel A. Almond and Sidney Verba identified in the 1960s in their theory of 'civil culture' (Almond and Verba, 1963). This theory highlights the second dimension in the problem of political participation. The right to vote is essential, but that is only part of the various different forms and methods of political participation. Not all forms are equal in terms of effectiveness, attractiveness or legitimacy. It has partly to do with the history of post-Second World War politics and government in these countries that were dominated by authoritarianism, elitism, one-party or a single-dominant party, and closed-door politics.

Formal institutions, such as elections, parliament, political parties and city councils, are organizations, relationships and processes governed by rules and procedures that are sanctioned and enforced by the state, and apply to every citizen.

The question is why certain methods are preferred over others in a given political society, and how effective they are in influencing politics and policy. There is, for example, plenty of evidence that No. 2 on the list of the methods (see Box 8.5) is widely practiced in Pacific Asian countries.

Table 8.3, with data provided by three primary surveys on political attitudes and values, shows the preferences of the populations in Pacific Asian countries in methods of political participation, and the patterns of their actual political participation. The first set of questions on attitudes towards elections suggests that people in Pacific Asian countries have a generally high opinion of the value of elections. Indeed, election turnouts are generally high in Pacific Asia (see Table 8.2). However, they are ambiguous about how much impact their participation can have on the government. Indicators of citizens' actual experiences of political participation in various other forms, on the other hand, show that participation rates are generally low.

Moreover, it is also clear from Table 8.3 that some methods are more popular in some countries than others. Signing a petition is more popular in Japan and South Korea, while contacting government officials happens more often in China, South Korea and Thailand.

Box 8.4

Three types of citizenship

Bryan S. Turner and Chang Kyung-sup use a framework of three types of citizenship to explain the evolutionary advance of citizenship and its role in modern political development in Pacific Asian countries, approaching the problem of citizenship as more than just legalistic membership, but also from the viewpoint of the political economy of the modern state and nation building.

- Development of citizenship is seen as a progressive process from one type to another:
  - Civil citizenship that concerns political rights;
  - Social citizenship that concerns social rights related to the welfare state and rights to education, healthcare and social security;
  - National citizenship as a political identity associated with state building and the forging of a nation.
- Key forces have helped shape the development of citizenship in Pacific Asia:
  - The political status of ordinary East Asian citizens has been compromised by developmentalist politics prevalent in the region;
  - Neoliberal globalization has critically destabilized the developmental foundation of East Asian citizenship;
  - Structural interdependencies among the countries have been strengthened, leading to the struggle between national unity and sociopolitical division.

Chang and Turner, 2012: 4–5

Table 8.2 Voter turnout (all elections since 1945)

Country	*%*	*World ranking*
Cambodia	90.5	3
Indonesia	88.3	6
Japan	69.1	75
S. Korea	74.8	56
Malaysia	59.0	116
Philippines	69.6	71
Singapore	62.0	102
Taiwan	70.1	70
Thailand	47.4	145
Philippines	69.6	71

IDEA, 2008.

Methods of political participation and action

Given the discussion above, is there a pattern of preferences in methods of political participation in Pacific Asian countries? And what factors influence these preferences? On the first question, given the research on Asian political culture showing the prevalence of social networks and corruption, one can argue that people in Pacific Asian countries may prefer political participation through informal institutions. Moreover, individuals in Pacific Asian countries are more passive than active participants. Given the hierarchical nature of Pacific Asian societies and the state-centric political structure, elites and masses tend to have different sets of preferred forms of political participation. Elites, because of their status and influence in society, find informal institutions more effective, while the masses, with limited access to informal institutions, have to go through formal institutions, and, if this fails, become more rebellious against those formal institutions.

The second question concerns theories of political action. Why do people participate in politics in the ways that they do? What are the most effective ways to influence politics and government? You have probably learnt about various theories in your

Box 8.5

Forms of political participation

- Voting in elections.
- Political networking, elite influences, donations and bribery.
- Demonstrations, strikes, boycotts.
- Revolutions.
- NGOs and organized in group action.
- Petitions and submissions through parties, MPs, the media, etc.
- Becoming a politician, seeking public office, working in government.

Table 8.3 Preferences in methods of political participation

	China	Indonesia	Japan	S. Korea	Malaysia	Philippines	Singapore	Taiwan	Thailand	Vietnam
Strongly agree or *agree* with the following (%)										
Citizens have a duty to vote in elections		97.1	87.3	94.7	96.1	94.6	95.9		99.3	97.2
Generally speaking, people like me don't have the power to influence government policy or actions		42.1	45.2	76.3	65.7	56.3	55.7		58.7	48.7
Politics and government are so complicated that sometimes I don't understand what's happening		62.0	56.7	81.7	68.6	66.9	48.0		71.7	36.6
Since so many people vote in elections, it really doesn't matter whether I vote or not		29.0	13.8	24.3	13.1	28.1	20.2		7.3	14.8
Did *once* or *more than once* the following (%)										
Contacted any government official to express your opinions?	33.8		7.2	30.5		17.8		8.9	35.6	
Contacted officials to express your opinions at higher level?	N/A		0.7	N/A		7.3		7.9	12.7	
Contacted elected legislative representatives at any level?	3.3		5.2	5.1		2.8		10.2	8.3	
Contacted political parties or other political organizations?	2.5		1.2	2.9		5.3		2.3	5.4	
Contacted non-government/civil society organizations?	N/A		2.6	5.9		6.3		3.6	7.2	
Contacted media to comment on something?	1.1		1.3	4.3		2.2		2.7	5.4	
Demonstrated, went on strike, or sat-in for something?	0.4		0.4	4.2		1.9		2.3	5.3	
Contacted other people?	0.5		0.4	N/A		N/A		0.6	3.0	
Have you done the following? (%)										
Signed a petition		4.8	56.8	47.2		9.2	7.2	10.4		5.3
Joined in boycotts		2.7	6.6	7.3		4.4	1.3	2.8		0.5
Attended lawful demonstrations		10.9	9.6	18.7		5.8	1.2	2.3		1.8
Joined unofficial strikes		1.9	2.0	7.6		2.2		0.3		0.3
Occupied buildings or factories		3.7	0.1	0		0.6		0		1.0

Hu and Chu, 2004; Inoguchi et al. 2004; European Values Study Group and World Values Survey Association, 2006 introductory courses on comparative politics. What we shall discuss at some length in this chapter are some of the issues in political participation in Pacific Asian countries, and through this discussion, try to discern some general patterns.

A primary factor affecting preferences in methods of political participation is the credibility of formal institutions. As Table 8.3 indicates, a significant proportion of Pacific Asian populations agree or strongly agree that 'politics and government are so complicated that sometimes I don't understand what's happening' and 'generally speaking, people like me don't have the power to influence government policy or actions'. The reasons for the lack of credibility of formal institutions are many. It has partly to do with the history of post-war politics and government in these countries that were dominated by authoritarianism, elitism, one-party or a single-dominant party, and closed-door politics.

Second, the history of modern institutions in most Pacific Asian countries is short. Many countries installed modern political institutions in haste after the arrival of independence. The first decade of experiences of pluralist politics turned out to be problematic in a large number of Pacific Asian countries (see Chapter 2). Newly installed modern institutions were given little time to establish themselves, and adjust to local conditions.

Third, modern political institutions originated mainly outside Pacific Asia. There has been a perennial problem of tension between modern institutions and traditional political structures and culture (see Chapter 2). Methods of politics and government in traditional Pacific Asia often became informal institutions in the process of modernization, competing with modern formal institutions.

Consequently, when individuals have a choice of methods for political participation – for example, between voting in elections, signing a petition or joining a political party on the one hand and developing personal relations with politicians, bureaucrats or party elites, or resorting to bribery on the other – the latter can be more attractive to those who have access to informal institutions that can be more effective and expeditious.

The lack of respect for formal institutions not only leads to their avoidance in the real political process but also more violent challenges to them by those who have limited (or no) access to informal institutions and therefore no alternatives to formal institutions. Boycotts, sit-ins and street demonstrations become useful methods for them.

Table 8.3 also shows that the true extent of political participation is significantly limited apart from voting in the formal election process. People are not very active in the various other forms of political participation – they are mainly 'passive participants'. Passive participation is not a unique problem to Pacific Asia, however. Low turnouts have long been recognized as an issue in Western democracies. More importantly, scholars have developed various theories explaining this passivity. Anthony Downs, for example, sees it as a collective action problem where the question of whether an individual votes or not depends on the rational calculation of the costs and benefits of not voting and can be a rational option under certain circumstances (Downs, 1957: 260–76).

In Pacific Asia, as seen in Table 8.2, the majority of the population disagrees with that reasoning. People do participate in voting. The collective action problem in Pacific Asian countries seems to be rather different and appears to lie mainly in other forms of political participation. For example, because of the generally much harsher political and social consequences for individuals participating in 'unlawful' political actions, such as occupying buildings or factories, or taking part in a street demonstration, and the fact a successful outcome from political action will benefit everyone regardless of whether they participate or not, an individual may well choose not to participate.

A consequence of this is the under-development of political society in many Pacific Asian countries except in the formal institution of voting, which the function of pluralist politics requires. As Table 8.1 shows, women gained the right to vote only after the Second World War – even in countries such as Japan, where modern political institutions have been in place since the Meiji Restoration (Ike, 1950).

We shall discuss this further when we consider civil society and the political orientation of the middle class later in this chapter.

Having laid out the general institutional setting for political participation, and how it affects the preferences of individuals and the extent of their participation, we now turn to specific forms of political participation that will help to illustrate the point further.

'People power' revolutions

People power revolutions were a dominant mode of political participation in Pacific Asian countries in the 1980s and 1990s. Table 8.4 includes seven countries where there was a significant major event that drew mass participation in street demonstrations, protests and violent confrontations against the government. For many of these countries, the major event that crystalized widespread uprising was not an isolated one. It was part of, and even a culmination of, a decade-long authoritarian, suppressive and even brutal rule by the governing regime. In Taiwan, Thailand and South Korea, people power movements of various sizes led to the most dramatic form of political participation.

Moreover, unlike other forms of political participation that are aimed primarily at government policy and programmes, people power revolutions are aimed at the governing system itself. With the exception of the people power revolution in the Philippines in 2001, all were seeking a democratic, representative political system. Apart from the cases of China and Myanmar, and the Philippines in 2001, all these revolutions led to the collapse or decline of the existing system, and the establishment and rise of democratic institutions. People power revolutions, therefore, are generally not a conventional form of political participation within the existing political system but rather a form of political action against it.

This constitutes an important part of the pattern of political participation and action in Pacific Asia: people generally participate in voting as well as people power revolutions as a collective action, but are less active in other forms of political participation that require individual effort.

Women in politics and government

Pacific Asian societies are known, both historically and culturally, for women's low status and power in social, political and economic life. There are three areas of issues in terms of the status and role of women as a group in politics and government in Pacific Asia. The first is formal institutions regarding women's rights.

As Table 8.5 shows, with the exception of Thailand and the Philippines, women were prevented from standing for election until after the Second World War – even in countries such as Japan, where modern political institutions have been in place since the Meiji Restoration (Ike, 1950). Moreover, many countries, given the historical and cultural reality of the position of women in society, needed to provide legal requirements for quotas of seats for women in the national legislature and government institutions. The number of women in ministerial positions remains extremely low.

Table 8.4 People power revolutions

	Movement		*Outcome*	
Taiwan	Formosa Movement	1979	Democratic transition	1987
Philippines	People Power Revolution	1986	Collapse of Marcos government and democratic transition	
	People Power Revolution II	2001	Collapse of Estrada presidency	
S. Korea	Kwangju Uprisings	1980	Armed suppression	1980
	People's March	1987	Democratic transition	1987
Myanmar	8888 Uprisings	1988	Collapse of Ne Win government, military rule, 1990 free elections	1990
China	Tiananmen Movement	1989	Armed suppression	
Thailand	May Uprising	1992	Democratic constitution and civilian rule	1997

Table 8.5 Women's political participation

	Stand for election	*First elected to parliament*	*Women in government at ministerial level (%)*
Cambodia	1955	1958	7.1
China	1949	1954	6.3
Indonesia	1945	1950	10.0
Japan	1946	1946	12.5
S. Korea	1948	1948	5.6
Laos	1958	1958	0.0
Singapore	1947	1963	0.0
Thailand	1932	1948	7.7
Philippines	1937	1941	25.0
Vietnam	1946	1976	11.0

UNDP, 2007: 341–5

Second, the social and economic development of women in Pacific Asian societies has been relatively strong. Pacific Asian countries rank well in social and economic development after decades of industrialization and economic development. Their scores on development are mainly above the world average, with Japan close to perfect equality.

Third, women's political empowerment includes not only the formal institutional right to vote but their positions in government, parliament and professional organizations and income level. Here, Pacific Asian countries are mainly below the world average – with Singapore the exception.

There is significant difference between empowerment and development over the region. Even this level of political empowerment reflects the substantial progress that has been achieved in these countries in the past decades. For example, on one of the indicators for women's political empowerment – seats held in parliament by women (see Table 8.6) – many countries have had a double-digit increase in women's share of parliamentary seats since 1990. Women's seats in parliament in China and Vietnam have always been around 20 per cent.

Becoming a politician

Voting, demonstration and boycotting are not the only means of political participation. In many Pacific Asian countries where government officials are traditionally of a privileged class, political systems are hierarchical and policy processes tend to be top-down. To become a politician is perhaps the most effective way of participating in political and policy processes and of influencing government and politics.

The greater diversity of political systems in Pacific Asia allows a wider range of possibilities for an individual to become a politician. Box 8.6 summarizes five typical paths through which a person may become a politician in Pacific Asian countries. Unlike the situation in the United States, for example, where a large number of politicians enter politics from a background as a successful lawyer, lawyers

Case Study Lab 8.3

Explaining the lack of gender equality in higher leadership positions in Thailand

There is a continual lack of gender equality in higher leadership positions. Both women's empowerment and political representation and participation are very weak in Thailand, even in comparison with fellow Pacific Asian countries. Investigating women and politics in Thailand, Kazuki Iwanmaga argues that obstacles to women's empowerment are structural and institutional, socioeconomic and cultural-religious:

- Institutional: the electoral system has a significant impact on women's representation in the Legislature.
- Socioeconomic: education levels, female labour participation rates, levels of socioeconomic development, and the strength of the women's movement.
- Cultural: stereotypes of women in politics; influence of the patriarchal culture and Thai Buddhism.

Iwanaga, 2008: 8–19

Case Study Lab 8.4

Gender relations, gender regimes and gender order under the New Order in Indonesia

There are various ways of explaining gender inequality in Pacific Asian countries, with perspectives ranging from the cultural tradition to social structure and to development theory. Kathryn Robinson takes the case of the particular gender regime and order under the New Order in Indonesia, looks at the political economy of the shaping of gender relations and order and explains how gender relations have been affected by the specifically gendered identities proffered by the state.

- Gender relations are an aspect of the exercise of power in society, a perspective for us to enquire into the generalized social and political effects of the unitary 'gender regime' which was a construct of New Order ideology.
- The New Order has been characterized as a repressive-developmentalist regime. The New Order promoted a normative vision of women's primary role as wife and mother, taking her place in a family in which the husband wielded patriarchal authority.
- The ideological project of the New Order to inculcate a unitary national model of domesticated femininity based on women's kodrat (biologically ordered role) and associated with the presumed natural patriarchy of the family … the presumed natural sexual hierarchy of the family with a core of patriarchal authority provided the ideological rationale for the Suharto regime and normalized the authoritarian power of the state.
- The gender order and regime influenced the forms of political mobilization in challenging the New Order: demand for women's rights, both in domestic and in public life, fed into the democratic process.

Robinson, 2009: 4–5

Table 8.6 Seats in parliament held by women (percentages)

	1990	*2007*
Cambodia	—	9.8
China	21.3	20.3
Indonesia	12.4	11.3
Japan	1.4	9.7
S. Korea	2.1	13.4
Malaysia	5.1	9.1
Singapore	4.9	24.5
Thailand	2.8	8.7
Philippines	9.1	22.5
Vietnam	17.7	25.8

UNDP, 2007: 34–35

are traditionally not as socially prestigious or politically influential in Pacific Asian countries.

Only recently have there been signs of lawyers turning into politicians in Korea and Taiwan, where the new political institutions, particularly those of South Korea, approximate those of the United States, and there has been a growing influence from the generation of lawyers that defended political activists of the democratic and civil rights movements in the 1970s against the authoritarian regime. President Roh Moo-hyun of South Korea and President Chen Shui-bian of Taiwan are typical examples. Both had legal backgrounds: Roh was a union lawyer and Chen a member of the defence team for the opposition activists charged under the KMT rule in the 1980s. Chen entered politics in the early 1980s, while Roh entered in the late 1980s. Similarly, Tsai Ing-wen, who was elected president in 2016, has a background as a law professor in Taiwan.

Business-people turned politicians are dominant in Pacific Asian politics and government. Japan has a long history of this, and a similar trend is found increasingly in new pluralist polities such as South Korea.

One classical example is Japan's Kakuei Tanaka, who was prime minister for only two years in the early 1970s. His political influence, especially the way he organized political support, has had a lasting impact on Japan's government and politics. Tanaka

Box 8.6

Five paths to becoming a politician

• Lawyer turned politician	Roh Moo-hyun (President, S. Korea, 2003–8); Chen Shui-bian (President, Taiwan, 2000–8)
• Business person turned politician	Kakuei Tanaka (Prime minister, Japan, 1972–4); Thaksin Shinawatra (Prime minister, Thailand, 2001–6); Lee Myung-bak (President, S. Korea, 2008–13)
• General turned politician	Susilo Bambang Yudhoyono (President, Indonesia, 2004–14); Roh Tae-woo (President, S. Korea, 1988–93); Fidel V. Ramos (President, Philippines, 1992–8) Thein Sein (President, Myanmar, 2011–16)
• Hereditary politician	Shinzu Abe (Prime minister, Japan, 2006–7, 2012–); Yasuo Fukuda (Prime minister, Japan, 2007–8); Lee Hsien Loong (Prime minister, Singapore, 2004–); Park Geun-hye (President, South Korea, 2013–) Xi Jinping (President, China, 2013–)
• Career politician	Hu Jintao (President, China, 2002–12); Junichiro Koizumi (Prime minister, Japan, 2001–6)

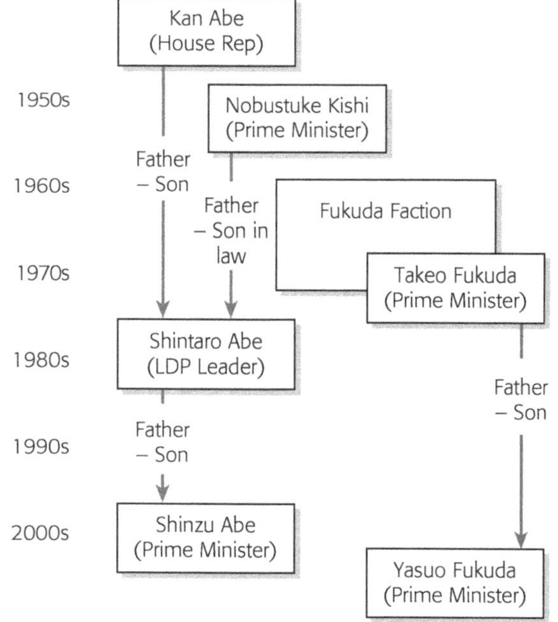

Figure 8.1 Hereditary politicians – Japan

entered politics after his success in the construction business. His business both financed and benefited from his political career. He built his political empire through his local political support group, Etsuzankai. At the peak of his political empire, his faction in the LDP was the largest in history, with 110 Diet members (out of a total of 491) under his faction's wing. He even managed to keep his Diet seat long after he was convicted in various bribery scandals, including the notorious Lockheed scandal (see Chapter 7).

Similarly, the recent case of Thaksin Shinawatra in Thailand indicates a pattern of a mixture of business and politics in a politician's career. Thaksin built the largest mobile phone company in Thailand and was said to be the richest person in Thailand when he entered politics in the mid-1990s. While a politician, he won a landslide victory in the 2005 election, representing a sea change in the overall political structure and mode of government in Thailand. Like his fellow business-people-turned politicians, his tenure as prime minister was also accompanied by controversies, and he was finally ousted by the military on corruption grounds.

Military generals becoming politicians is another tradition with a long history in Pacific Asian countries (see Chapter 2 for a discussion of the broader issue of the role of the military in politics). During the Cold War, it was not rare that after a military coup, the coup leaders would transform themselves into civilian politicians. This was the case with Park

Chung-hee and Chun Doo Hwan of South Korea; Suharto of Indonesia; and Prem Tinsulanonda and others of Thailand.

Hereditary politicians are those who become politicians because their parents are politicians. The fact that their parents are politicians serves as a role model for their children's career choice, provides them with personal experience of politics and gives them access to social networks and resources.

However, even after pluralist politics was restored, generals-turned-politicians can still be seen. The post-authoritarian South Korea elected a former general, Roh Tae-woo, as its first president under the new 1987 Constitution. Similarly, the post-Marcos Philippines elected the former army chief under the Marcos regime as its second president under the new 1987 Constitution, and post-Suharto Indonesia elected a former army chief as its fourth president after the fall of Suharto. All three held senior military positions before entering politics.

The fourth model is perhaps of more Pacific Asian 'character': becoming a politician because a parent is, or was an influential politician (see Figure 8.1 as an illustration of the case of Japan).

They are known as 'hereditary politicians' (Ishibashi and Reed, 1992). Michihiro Ishibashi, and Steven R. Reed observed 'the rise of second-generation Diet members and the increasing number of hereditary seats' in the 1980s and 1990s. In the 1990 general election, for example, 60 of the 133 candidates elected to the Japanese Diet 'were related to current or previous Diet members. In many of these cases, the 'new' candidate ran for a seat vacated by his father or other relative' (Ishibashi and Reed, 1992: 366).

Well-known examples of hereditary politicians include Chiang Ching-kuo, who succeeded his father Chiang Kai-shek as president in Taiwan in 1975; and Kim Jong-un of North Korea who succeeded his father Kim Jung-il in 2011 who had also succeeded his father Kim Il-sung in 1994. Lee Hsien Loong took over the post of prime minister of Singapore (after a fourteen-year interval of incumbency by Goh Chok Tong) following the thirty-year reign as prime minister of Lee's father Lee Kuan Yew. Shinzhu Abe of Japan also finally reached the post of prime minister, which his grandfather, Kan Abe, and father, Shintaro Abe, both influential politicians of their time, had failed to achieve. In China, children of the first-generation political leaders have clearly moved up the hierarchy of the political structure and taken up important positions in the party and government. The most notable example is Xi Jinping, who became president in 2012. His father, Xi Zhongxun, was deputy prime minister in the early 1960s.

Finally, there is a category of 'career politicians', who started a career in politics often as a worker in the party, election campaign organizer or an assistant to an MP, and worked upwards through the party apparatus. There are two slightly different types of career politician. In countries such as China, there is a system of training of young party cadres. The Communist Youth League of China (CYLC) is the principal platform for this. Since the 1970s, elite cadres rising from the CYLC have become a primary source of candidates for senior party and government positions in China.

Notable among them are Hu Yaobang, the secretary general of the Communist Party in the 1980s; Hu Qili, senior Politburo member in the 1980s; and Hu Jintao, president of the state, secretary general of the Party and chairman of the Central Military Commission during the first decade of the new century.

In another category, Junichiro Koizumi of Japan began his political career as a secretary to the then-prime minister, Takeo Fukuda, in the 1970s and worked his way up the LDP apparatus.

The appeal of becoming a politician as a form of political participation reflects the traditional political culture in Pacific Asian countries, which gives more respect to those working in government. Given the power and influence of government in Pacific Asian societies, and the general underdevelopment of political society, becoming a politician seems to be a more effective way of having an impact on government and politics than other modes. In the range of possible ways in which one can become a politician, there is a pattern indicating that some of the ways are more popular and effective than others. For example, there are more politicians with a previous background in business and the military than those practicing law. Moreover, family background and cadre credentials are also important factors shaping the pool of politicians.

How a politician generates and sustains political support

To be an effective politician is not simply a product of career planning. It requires the continual support of his or her political basis. Given the different ways in which one can become a politician and the nature of the political system in Pacific Asian countries, there are different platforms and mechanisms that a politician can use to generate and sustain political support. There are two different categories: those in a pluralist polity and those in a non-pluralist polity. In a pluralist polity, a politician usefully relies on following platforms and mechanisms to generate and sustain political support:

- Local personal support groups;
- Patron–client relations within the party;
- Alliances with political donors;
- Profile and publicity.

Local personal support groups, or *koenkai* in Japan and *houyuanhui* in Taiwan, are the primary basis from which a politician rises in the party apparatus. Essentially these local personal support groups are potential voters or vote chiefs (see Chapter 7) who can help to bring more voters. The party needs as large a political constituency as possible for the party, and therefore favours politicians with large contingents of political support.

A primary source, and indeed a measure of a politician's power and influence within a political party, is the size of his local personal support groups; that is, how many voters ,the politicians are able to generate for the party. Local personal support groups provide their politician with 'hard' votes, votes that go 'consistently and repeatedly to a particular person as a consequence of personal ties' or 'a sense of traditional obligation' (Curtis, 1971: 39).

This personal support can also be expected at the organization level, where members of organizations 'vote together for certain parties or candidates. Patterns of social-based voting can be detected in the support patterns of many Japanese organizations', such as labour confederations and religious associations (Hrebenar, 1992: 16). The local personal support groups are therefore a system of voter mobilization using vertical personal relations built around the politician.

There are two different types of local personal support group. For district-based MPs, local personal support groups are concentrated in his/her electoral district. These groups provide votes, volunteer work and at times financial support for the politician. Once the politician is elected into public office, (s)he will use their power and privilege to provide constituency services and channel 'pork-barrel' public-funded projects to the district.

For those who run for national office, or are on the party list, their personal support groups can be spread around the country. Usually when an election comes round, a personal support group will be set up for the candidate in each major city.

Patron–client relations are a special relationship between senior and junior politicians within a political party and beyond. Generally, a junior politician would need someone higher on the party apparatus

> **Box 8.7**
>
> ## 'Pork-barrel politics'
>
> Pork-barrel politics occurs when there is a clear pattern of legislators tending to be more interested in local issues and constituency matters than in national policies. Efforts to gain re-election often lead to much of their work in the legislature being devoted to seeking budget allocation of funds for community projects in their constituencies.
>
> Case I: The Philippines: For congressmen, the most important piece of legislation was the Public Works Act. Within that act, attention focused on 'community projects, better known as pork barrels. Within this portion of the act, members of congress had almost complete discretion over where and how money was to be spent ... These allocations were designed as a public show of interest in the constituency, usually fulfilling a promise to build a school or a road and calculated to employ as many men as possible in its construction ... About 20 percent of public work releases went to pork barrels' (Wurfel, 1988: 86).
>
> Case II Japan: Because of the personal nature of a legislator's basis of political support, 'Members of Parliament were snowed under with constituency business, but much less pressured by the electorate on matters of national or international importance. This in turn meant that parliamentary interventions into policymaking tended to take on a local 'pork barrel' character, and with certain regular and important exceptions, parliament did not much interfere in the affairs of the state (Stockwin, 1999: 98).

to provide an apprenticeship for him/her, to open up opportunities, resources and access within the party and to defend and protect him/her when facing political challenges. In return, the junior politician would often become a front-line supporter for the senior politician, extend the base of political support for the senior, form an alliance in internal party politics and play roles that the senior politician finds inconvenient.

Patron–client relations may be formal or informal. Formal patron–client relations exist naturally and legitimately among members of a faction where factions are an important organizational feature of a political party. This is the case with Japan's LDP and Taiwan's DPP. In a party where factions are less of a feature, patron–client relations are usually informal and private.

Politicians need money to campaign for public office, to provide projects and services for local constituencies and to do other things that require financial backing.

Funding from the party is a source, but either the party funding is very limited or the party has its own priorities. Relations with political donors are therefore very important. Such a relationship tends to be mutual: political donors give money to politicians and in return, politicians are expected to defend the donor's interests on particular issues or legislation and to help appoint the donor's personnel to government positions.

Finally, a high profile and publicity is critical for politicians to survive in the very competitive new party and electoral systems. In the past, party endorsement was essential for a politician's political career. Increasingly, however, both the party nomination system (based partly on public opinion surveys) as in the case of Taiwan, and the dominant new system of single-member district with proportional representation (both require high recognition and popularity among voters; see Chapter 7) force politicians to take publicity seriously. Social media, TV and other publicity are an effective way of attracting the attention of voters. Politicians are also more willing to take an extreme position on a single controversial issue. Physical boycotts and fighting in parliament are not uncommon in many Pacific Asian countries.

In non-pluralist polities such as China and Singapore, the overall logic of political support for politicians is different because of the way the political system is structured and the imperatives for political action. Consequently, there is a limited number of means that a politician can use to generate and sustain political support. Moreover, political support for politicians comes mainly from above rather than from below. Generating and sustaining political support is therefore a matter of seeking approval by the party of the politician's political loyalty, performance and image – all effects of the logic of upward accountability. As a general pattern, there are several methods that are effective in such a polity:

- Political correctness and loyalty;
- Patron–client relations;
- Image projects;
- Mass relations.

Political correctness and loyalty are primary requirements for anyone to be a successful politician in a non-pluralist polity. This is a two-way process. For the politician, (s)he needs to use all possible platforms and occasions to demonstrate such political correctness and loyalty: at party study sessions, mass gatherings and through regular reports, as well as statements to the leadership of the party branch. Certainly, the politician is expected to be on the correct side of politics on every occasion of political significance – this is critical when there is any uncertainty in the direction of party politics or there is a conflict within the party leadership over party lines. On the other hand, the party will use every opportunity to contest the extent of the politician's political loyalty, at each step of his/her advance in his/her political career, through panel reviews, self-reports, colleagues' comments and personal interviews.

Beyond this more formal institutionalized mechanism, there are also more informal ways for a politician to secure political support. As in a pluralist polity, patron–client relations are also important. Political support built on personal trust and mutual interests is much more reliable than that gained through formal institutionalized mechanisms, as discussed above.

Without genuine elections as a way of filtering politicians, as in a pluralist polity, an assessment of a politician's ability and performance is a matter of judgement by the senior party leadership. As such, 'image projects' are overtaken – where the public policy projects the politician undertakes are aimed at demonstrating the politician's ability and contribute positively to the party's image.

Finally, even in a non-pluralist polity public opinion matters. A popular politician can gain the party's attention and is more likely to be recruited. Because of the lack of a popular mandate via genuine elections, popular politicians are one of the ways the party uses to connect with the public.

It is clear from the above discussion that beyond the ways individuals participate in politics as a citizen, there are many alternative ways in which an individual can have an impact on politics and government. Becoming a politician is appealing to many, and a politician can participate and have an impact on politics on very different platforms and through different processes and mechanisms.

How elites influence politics and policy

To have an impact on politics and government, however, does not always require 'formal participation'. Indeed, there are individuals in society who exert an influence on agenda setting, public opinion and on government decision-making and policy processes because of who they are, the resources and social networks they control and the various connections they command with those who practice politics.

Let us first explore who the elites are in Pacific Asian societies before identifying ways in which they influence politics and government. This is followed by a discussion of state co-option of elites as a form of marginalizing and reducing their influence on politics and as a means of strengthening the ruling party's hold on political power.

Who are the elites?

There are two different approaches to the concept of elites. One set of definitions focuses narrowly on the state elites, or those occupying positions of power in government. Eva Etzioni-Halevy, for example, defines elites as those holding key positions in the government structure (Etzioni-Halevy, 1979: 2). Consequently, the discussion of the role of elites focuses on how the state controls and manages social forces and maintains its dominance. Duncan McCargo's 'elite governance', for example, is more a discussion of how the developmental state controls and manages society through 'exclusionary and inclusionary mechanisms' to strengthen its developmental dominance (McCargo, 1998). Here we are interested in a different, but arguably more revealing, issue of how elites in society participate in and influence government and politics.

Taking the role of elites from a different perspective, a broadly based concept of elites includes both state and social elites, but with more emphasis on the role of social, economic and civic elites on government and politics. In G. William Domhoff and Thomas R. Dye's discussion of power structure in society, for example, a 'power structure' is defined as 'a network of organizations and roles within a city or society that is responsible for maintaining the general social structure and shaping new policy initiates. A "power elite" is the set of people who are the individual actors within the power structure' (Domhoff and Dye, 1987: 9). 'Power structure research does not begin with the theoretical assumption that the state always is part of the power structure, but with the idea that the key policy initiating and decision-making groups and organizations in a society must be identified' (ibid.: 14).

> What is an '**elite**'? The dictionary defines it as 'a group of people considered to be the best in a particular society or category, especially because of their power, talent or wealth'. I shall be talking about the elite in a society or a country, meaning the core group of people who occupy key positions of power and influence, and set the direction for the whole society and country.
>
> Lee Hsien Loong, 2005

This broad definition allows us to see the unique participatory role of social, economic and civic elites penetrating into state institutions (thus becoming state elites) or affecting 'national political outcomes individually, regularly and seriously... by virtue of their positions in powerful organizations' (Field and Higley, 1985: 6).

This broad definition of elites is particularly useful in countries such as the Philippines, where a very small but powerful group of landed elites and others dominate society (Abinales and Amoroso, 2005). Instead of exerting their influence through a strong state, their very dominance has made the state weak, and incapable of effective national functions or policymaking and implementation.

Regarding Thailand, James Ockey identifies four types of individual that 'are particularly prominent' (Ockey, 2004: 150):

- Financiers, many of them holding lucrative concessions from the state;
- Provincial nobles, again with many of them holding concessions in their regions;
- Retired government officials (including technocrats), and retired army and police officers;
- Professional politicians.

In Ockey's view, the prominent role of elites creates a far more complex model of state–society relations than Riggs' bureaucratic polity model (Riggs, 1966, see Chapter 5) depicts, where the state elites dominate society.

Ockey's categorization is clearly an acute observation of Thai society. Across Pacific Asian countries, the component of national elites varies (Case, 1996: 16). In Malaysia and Singapore, for example, ethnic elites play a more prominent role than do retired military officers. In Indonesia, Thailand and Malaysia, religious elites are unique. In China and Singapore, party cadres are of an influential political and social class. In the Philippines, the landowner class and civil group leaders can overpower state institutions.

William Case uses three large categories to define elites in Malaysia (Case, 1996: 16):

- State elites: the ruling party, bureaucratic and military elites;
- Economic elites: industrial, commercial, financial and landed elites;
- Civic elites: opposition parties, trade unions, professional associations and ethnic, cultural, religious and civic group elites.

Case's categorization covers a broader range of prominent elites in Pacific Asian countries and clearly outlines the basis for their influence. We need to understand the nature of state elites in the framework of elite participation and influence on government and politics. When we examine the issue of how elites influence politics and government as a problem of political participation and action, one can separate state elites from social, economic and civic elites. On the one hand, they are themselves elites and there is therefore an issue of how, for example, bureaucratic and military elites relate to the state. On the other hand, there can be agents of social, economic and civic elites in state institutions. It is this latter influence on government and politics through government policy-makers, state bureaucrats and practicing politicians that underlies the pattern of elite governance.

How elites influence politics and government

Each elite group has its own ways of influencing government and politics. We discussed earlier how the state and business elites interact in close state-business (Chapter 6); how the bureaucratic elites dominate the state (Chapter 5); and how political elites shape government and politics (Chapter 7). We have discussed (in Chapter 2) how the military influence government and politics; and in this chapter how the media and opinion leaders influence government and politics. Here we summarize briefly the most-practiced methods.

Case Study Lab 8.5

Explaining the chronic political conflict in Thailand

There has been a decade of political tension and conflict in Thailand from the mid-2000s to mid-2010s involving the return of constitutionalism, the political rise of Thaksin and his new political party, mass street protests and confrontations between two key political forces, and the intervention of the monarch and the military. There are different ways to explain this chronic political conflict:

- An elite-mass framework;
- A monarch-military-politician framework;
- A modern-tradition framework.

Marshall, 2014

Build personal relations with potential and current policymakers

Elites have their own exclusive networks, clubs, institutions and occasions to socialize, where social investment can be made and social capital developed. Going to the same elite school in childhood can, for example, be an important source of such social networks.

Being part of the process of shaping public opinion and elite attitudes

Elites usually dominate the national media and broadcasting. Even if they do not own a media business, their views would be highly respected among the public. They can be influential in national agenda setting and swing public opinion.

Political donations

This is the most popular way through which elites can influence government and politics. The fact that they possess tremendous financial and material resources gives them access and influence.

Being in opposition

Elites usually have much at stake in the existing order and institutions and tend not to allow themselves to be in opposition. But there are times and conditions where opposition becomes the only viable option to advance the elites' interests and influence.

Leading social movements

Elites are usually influential individuals in particular social sectors. Because of their national influence and resources, and the unique interests they have in a particular social sector, they can be natural candidates to lead social movements and campaign on national issues.

Forging political alliances

Elites can be more effective when they join forces. Arend Lijphart's concept of elite coalescence identified a pattern of 'consensual unity' among elites in pursuit of their political interests. Elites choose to cooperate among themselves because of the fear of the 'dangers inherent in segmental cleavages and a desire to avert them' and 'the prior existence of a tradition of elite accommodation' (Lijphart, 1977: 100). Elites can form alliances among themselves or with state elites. Malaysia's ethnic bargaining and Japan's iron triangle (see Chapter 6) are good examples. More importantly, a swift alliance of elites can often have a decisive impact. Fidel Ramos's withdrawal of his support from Ferdinand Marcos dealt the final blow to the Marcos regime in 1986.

Linking with international forces

This was particularly significant in Pacific Asian countries before the deep involvement of international politics and global economy in domestic politics. Scholars observe that, in Indonesia, for example, it was not the state, nor the civil society, but the dominance of international capital in alliance with national elites that shaped much of the pattern of politics and economic development there (Robinson, 1986; Macintyre, 1990; Winters, 1996).

State co-option and accommodation of elites

The state is not just a target for elite penetration and manipulation. In Pacific Asian countries, where the state tends to be more assertive, a key factor determining the success of the developmental state is how the state incorporates the interests and capacities of the elites, and if that fails, neutralizes and marginalizes their influence. It is here that the distinction between state elites on the one hand, and non-state elites (economic, social and civic) on the other, becomes useful.

Methods the state uses to manage elite influences generally fall into two categories: more co-optation and accommodation on the one hand and more suppressive and exclusionary on the other. As the more suppressive and exclusionary approach is discussed in Chapter 2, we shall focus here on inclusionary politics. The idea of inclusion is to incorporate the interests of social elites into state functions and programmes, to broaden the social basis of governance, reduce possible challenges and competition from elites, and enhance the state's operational capability. In previous chapters, we have discussed various mechanisms of state corporatism in Pacific Asia. Briefly, methods of co-option and accommodation politics include the following.

Functional groups

This system organizes representation into functional groups (see Chapter 7), which usually correspond to the structure of elite groups. Through this system, elites of different social sectors can feel that their interests are catered for specifically. Such representation, as it is mainly found in non-pluralist polities, is more of an exercise in elite management than a genuine representation of social interests.

Consultation

Even when elites are not included in a formal system of representation, they are consulted regularly by the state on critical issues. China in more recent years has put into practice regular consultation with elite groups on important personnel and policy issues. These types of consultation, within the context of a non-pluralist polity, are voluntary on the part of the state, and the state in no way places itself in a position of being bound by the outcomes of such consultations. Following the consultation, it is at the state's discretion whether action is taken or not.

Political appointment

Elites can be appointed directly into government positions. In fact, many non-essential government positions are used to incorporate and accommodate social, economic and civic elites.

Informal networks

The state also incorporates elites through informal networks. Chalmers Johnson (1982) discussed MITI as a pilot organization that built the state's informal networks with industrial, commercial and business elites. Across Pacific Asian countries, there is a widespread practice that the state entrusts the elites in individual industrial and social sectors to manage matters for the sector, and serve as a bridge between the state and these individual sectors.

Overall, there is a clear pattern of elite participation in politics in Pacific Asian countries that favours informal institutions over the formal institutions of government.

Civil and civic society

Civil society groups have been growing rapidly in Pacific Asian countries (see Table 8.7). This has created major scholarly interest in analysing the place of such groups in the overall political order in these countries and led to major debates in the field. For example: Is the concept of civil society applicable to Pacific Asian countries? Can civil society develop in a Confucian state? Does democratic transition require civil society? What role does civil society play in political change?

The rapid growth of civil society has been shaped by several factors. The role civil society played in the collapse of the communist regimes in Eastern Europe and the Soviet Union had a significant impact on Pacific Asian countries, particularly on the communist states. It was no coincidence that democratic movements arose in China, South Korea, Taiwan, the Philippines, Thailand and Burma in the 1980s and early 1990s, around the same time when revolution was spreading in Eastern Europe and the Soviet Union.

At the same time, along with mass participation in social movements, there has been a rapid expansion of civil society organizations in Pacific Asian counties. Yun Fan, for example, reports that there was an almost 466 per cent increase in number of civil society groups in Taiwan during the twenty years between 1980 and 2001 (Fan, 2004: 177; see Table 8.7).

Table 8.7 Growth of civil society groups in Taiwan, 1980–2001

	Number of Group	
Type of Group	*1980*	*2001*
Education and culture	541	2801
Medicine and public health	48	526
Religious	64	725
Sports	50	2098
Social welfare and charity	2471	5794
International	51	2055
Business	–	1943
Others	735	2523
Total	3960	18465

Adapted from Fan 2004: 177.

Not all civil society groups are social movements. Indeed, certain types of civil society groups have long existed in Pacific Asian countries. Neighbourhood Associations in Japan, for example, have a long history that goes back to Japan's feudal period (Pekkanen 2004: 234). Robert Pekkanen lists activities that a typical Japanese Neighbourhood Association does (see Table 8.8). It has been one of the most successful local civil society groups, and has almost become an extension of government at the community level, as it is now promoted and subsidized by the government. Similar neighbourhood associations are found in Singapore and China.

Clearly, there are different types of civil society groups in Pacific Asian countries, and their

Table 8.8 What Japanese Neighbourhood Associations do

Activity	*NHAs that do this (%)*	*NHAs that consider this a priority (%)*
Festivals	85.5	32.3
Athletics meetings, sports events	79.0	21.7
Construction, maintenance of parks	39.5	6.5
Publishing newsletters	26.6	5.6
Community centre building	83.9	13.7
Distribution of government notices	89.5	16.1
Cleaning of gutters, rivers, roads	91.1	45.2
Preventing illegal dumping	81.5	28.2
Crime, fire prevention	84.7	32.3
Traffic management and safety	69.4	12.9
Travel	31.5	1.6
Funerals and weddings	54.0	3.2
Club activities	75.8	24.2
Study groups	39.5	0.8
Support for children's groups	89.5	26.6
Support for elderly people's groups	83.1	11.3
Support for women's groups	51.6	0.0
Support for youth groups	24.2	3.2
Co-operation with government collections	87.1	10.5
Presenting petitions from residents to local government	84.7	31.5
Support of politicians	25.0	2.4

Adapted from Pekkanen, 2004: 233.

relationship to the state also varies. Before we discuss these different types and some of the issues associated with them, we shall look at the concept of civil society itself and how it is debated in the Pacific Asian context.

The civil society debate

The problem of civil society has been a major focus in the study of Pacific Asian politics. There are two main reasons for this being a popular topic. First, civil society played a critical role in the collapse of the communist states and democratic transition in Eastern Europe in the 1990s (Keane, 1988; Tismaneanu, 1990; Rau, 1991; Glenn, 2001). This led to an expectation that political liberalization and democratic transition in non-pluralist Pacific Asian countries, particularly the communist countries, would need the active involvement of civil society (see, for example, Miller, 1992).

A second reason is related to the dominant type of society in Pacific Asian countries – the Confucian society. The original 'civil society argument' is that 'the strength and stability of liberal democracy depends on a vibrant and healthy sphere of associational participation' (Chambers and Kymlicka, 2002: 2). Studies of Pacific Asian countries have found that such a space either does not exist or is very much dominated by the state. Given the European origins and social and cultural context of the concept (Keane, 1988), questions are raised as to whether there is a significant presence of civil society in Pacific Asian countries, and whether such an analytical tool is useful in understanding the political structure and dynamics of these countries.

An important focus in the debates is on the concept of civil society itself. As with many other major concepts in political science, there are various definitions of 'civil society'. Some prefer a broad definition that includes all non-state associational organizations and activities. As Frank Schwartz proposes, in assessing civil society in Japan, 'we gravitate around a conception of civil society as that sphere intermediate between family and state in which social actors pursue neither profit within the market nor power within the state' (Schwartz, 2003: 23). Others, however, insist that

> civil society, as a concept, must be preserved for specifying a particular form of political space. It cannot include all independent, voluntary social organizations. Instead, a distinction must be drawn between civic and civil society, the latter involving regular attempts to advance the interests of members through overt political action. (Rodan, 1996: 28)

Alagappa's concept (see definition Box) provides a more inclusive though multi-component definition. Such a definition suggests three sets of relationships that need to be clarified for a substantive understanding of the concept. The first is civil society's relationship with the state. This is a core element defining civil society. Civil society is a realm of organization by non-state groups in pursuit of their collective interests on the basis of the separation of private and public spheres of operation.

> **Civil society** is, first, a realm in the interstices of the state, political society, the market and the society at large for organization by non-state, non-market groups that take collective action in the pursuit of the public good.
>
> Second, it is a distinct sphere for discourse and construction of normative ideals through interaction among non-state groups on the basis of ideas and arguments.
>
> Third, it is an autonomous arena of self-governance by non-state actors in certain issues areas.
>
> Fourth, it is an instrument for collective action to protect the autonomy of the non-state public realm, affect regime type and influence the politics and policies of the state, political society and the market.

> While **civil society** involves 'regular attempts to advance the interests of members through overt political action' (Rodan, 1996: 28), civic society is 'an arena of governance in its own right, not just an adjunct or a means to influence the state'.
>
> Alagapa, 2004: 32–33

This is one area where the concept has caused much debate. In countries such as China and Singapore, many civil society organizations, such as Neighbourhood Committees in China and People's Associations in Singapore, are part of the state corporatist arrangements and funded and administered within the state administrative system. Even in countries such as Japan, there is a question over how independent of the state and market civil society groups actually are. Table 8.9 shows that state bureaucracy has a substantial influence on the operation of civil society groups in Japan.

Second, the concept of civil society is also distinct from as well as overlapping with that of political society. Political society, according to Juan J. Linz and Alfred Stepan, is 'an arena in which political actors compete for the legitimate right to exercise control over public power and the state apparatus' (Linz and Stepan, 1996: 16). The aim of political society is the 'acquisition and exercise of state power' (Alagappa, 2004: 37). Therefore political parties are an important part of political society, while civil society organizations are not, as 'they do not organize themselves on a partisan basis to aggregate interests and formally compete for state office' (ibid.: 378).

However, as Alagappa points out, the relationship between civil society and political society is often blurred: they either affiliate with political parties on 'ideological or ascriptive grounds', or 'wield state power through the political party in office' (ibid.: 38).

Third, there is a difference between civil society and civic society (Rodan, 1996; Koh and Ling, 2000: 27–49; Lee, 2002). While civil society differs from political society in that it does not seek the acquisition and exercise of state power, it does intend to influence the policies of the state, as Alagappa's fourth component of the definition indicates. On the other hand, his third component suggests something else: the governance of non-state organizations – an arena that is sometimes referred to as civic society. While civil society involves 'regular attempts to advance the interests of members through overt political action' (Rodan, 1996: 28), civic society is 'an arena of governance in its own right, not just an adjunct or a means to influence the state' (Alagappa, 2004: 32).

The distinction between civil society and civic society is an important one, particularly in corporatist states. In these states, while the state is intolerant of civil society as a platform for challenging state authority, it is more accepting of or even encourages and promotes the idea of a civic society where civic activities and organizations are confined to effective and efficient management and governance of communal matters. Singapore's government, for example, has long promoted the idea of civic society, and taken its 'Civic Society Project' as the core of its efforts in defining Singaporean citizenship (Lee, 2002; Kadir, 2004).

Now the concept has been clarified, we can go on to look at the question of whether civil society exists in Pacific Asian countries, and whether the concept is applicable to them. One clear difficulty in identifying the presence of civil society in Pacific Asia lies in the fact that many tend to use a one-dimensional concept, drawn mainly from the experiences of the civil society movement in eighteenth-century Europe and late-1990s Eastern Europe. Such a culturally and historical specific concept excludes many of the civil society activities in Pacific Asia and leads to an inability to understand the diversity and variety of civil society organizations and activities in that area.

Of particular significance here is the question of whether the concept of civil society applies to Pacific Asian societies in general, and to Confucian societies in particular (Chamberlain, 1993; Huang, 1993; Ding, 1994; Ma, 1994; Chan, 1997; Metzger, 1997; Callahan, 1998; Gu, 1998; Yang, 2004). One of the key problems in applying the concept to Pacific Asian countries is, according to its critics, that 'it treats state–society relations as dichotomous, confrontational, and zero-sum' (Gu, 1998: 272; see also Ding, 1994; Yang, 2004). As many would point out, state–society relations in Pacific Asian countries are more sophisticated than the dichotomous state–civil society framework can explain.

Table 8.9 State influence in civil society groups: Japan

Administrative guidance (%)	45.8
Seconding of staff (%)	13.3
Post-retirement employment (%)	8.6
Exchange of opinions (%)	35.9

Pekkanen, 2004: 229.

Second, many argue that the whole concept of civil society is incompatible with the teachings and practice of Confucianism in Pacific Asian countries (see Chapters 1 and 2). Confucianism emphasizes social hierarchy and authority, mutual dependence between state and society, collective interests and social order. Civil society, on the other hand, at least in its European conception, seeks autonomy and self-governing.

Finally, all these suggest, according to the critics, that the theoretical discourse of the concept is far from the political reality in Pacific Asian countries. Shu-Yun Ma, for example, compares the discourse of civil society in China by domestic theorists in China and exiled intellectuals outside China and finds that there is a significant difference in their assessments of civil society in China.

Domestic theorists 'have focused on the making of a modern citizenry, consisting of law-abiding and civil members of society. Existence of this entity presupposes the active involvement of the state. The relation between civil society and the state was thus seen as an intimate and harmonious one'. Exiled intellectuals, on the other hand, are concerned primarily with 'the creation of a private realm that is independent of the state. There has been no mention of law, order, and civility' (Ma, 1994: 192). In examining the discourse of civil society in Korea and China, William Callahan argues that the concept and its discourses 'often impose a political and epistemic stability that does not adequately account for the varied and ambiguous practices that civil society seeks to describe' (Callahan, 1998: 277).

From democratization to advocacy

Based on the broad discussion above, we can identify a variety of types of civil society and the different roles each plays in the overall political order. This provides four general categories, or models, of civil society activities and organizations in the region (see Box 8.8).

Civic society

This includes activities and organizations in the 'nonstate public sphere' (Alagappa, 2004: 456). This

Case Study Lab 8.6

Analysing power relations and political contestation: taking social forces and actors seriously

There are popular approaches to explaining political change. Abriel Heryanto and Sumit K. Mandal, explaining challenges to authoritarianism in Indonesia and Malaysia, focus on the role of social forces and aspects of political dynamics beyond formal political institutions and expressions of authoritarianism.

- **Authoritarian-democratic polarity mode** measures how far different societies in this region have been able to move away from authoritarianism towards democracy; to identify what the impeding and facilitating factors are, and to predict or explain how soon these societies can overcome their impediments and advance towards attaining full democracy.
- **Conventional political economy** analyses power relations on the political elite and formal institutions, focuses on some key constructs by which progress is observed.
- **Cultural analysis.** When culture is inserted as a formal category such as economics or politics, into such a political analysis, it is conceived to be static, essentialist, form or substance that belongs exclusively to one definable community. This approach in turn becomes too easy a target for those more inclined towards positivism. Meanwhile, culture and power as developed in cultural studies appear to have minimal dialogue.
- **Social approach**, on the belief that social as a terrain where the political, cultural and economic relate to each other, focusing on the complex and often contradictory features of non-statist agencies, structures, practices and histories. The agencies in focus include urban-based professionals, non-government organizations (NGOs) and labour activities, religious communities and leadership, and women's group, as well as socially engaged artists. The central questions concern the constitution and history of these agencies, the dynamics of their assets and liabilities, and their structural relationships outside their immediate circles. The conditions of possibility for and observable practices of changing the prevailing power structure.

Heryanto and Mandal, 2003: 1–18

is a space the state has yielded to organizations, usually at the local level, to organize society in the interests of the public good. Civil society activities in this model concentrate on the management and governance of communal affairs and grassroots activities. A typical example of this is the neighbourhood committee in Singapore, Japan and China. Activities and organizations in this category are clearly separated from political society.

Political movements

Civil society activities in this category are found mainly, but not exclusively, in authoritarian regimes. The primary purpose of the organizations and activities in this category is regime change. In this sense, the organizations are usually not working within a space established by the government for organizing, advocating or protesting against government actions. Instead, as in the democratization movements in many countries in the 1980s and 1990s, groups agitate and protest often at great personal risk in order to effect regime change. Political movements have played a significant role in bringing political liberalization and democratic change to many countries in Pacific Asia. A good example of this type of civil society is the People Power Revolutions in the Philippines. This category is closest to political society.

NGOs

Organizations and activities in this category meet the criteria of the narrow definition of civil society: non-state actors, working in association for their collective interests, and autonomous from the state but seeking influence on government and politics. NGOs work independently of the state but seek influence over it.

This type of civil society activity will be familiar to most readers. It includes well-known international groups like Greenpeace that has branches in East Asia (Hong Kong, Macau, Taiwan, China and Korea), Japan and Southeast Asia as well as local

Box 8.8

Four categories of civil society activities and organization in Pacific Asia

Civic society	Non-state organizations and activities for community management and governance.
Political movements	Non-state organizations and activities aimed at regime change.
NGOs	Non-state organizations and activities aimed at changing law, policy and regulations.
Corporatist associations	Non-state organizations and activities sponsored, funded and directed by the state for grassroots mass integration, community management and governance.

NGOs like A Chance for the Poor Foundation in the Philippines or PC4peace in Kyoto. NGOs fall within the liberal model of civil society.

Even within this NGO model, however, as Robert P. Weller and his colleagues find, the 'split' between state and NGOs in Pacific Asian countries is very weak. They argue this is because 'the NGOs themselves give autonomy a fairly low priority' and 'the relationship between NGOs and states looks more symbiotic than antagonistic' (Weller, 2005: 7).

Corporatist associations

Civil society organizations in this category are sponsored, funded and directed by the state. The trade unions, women's leagues, youth leagues and people's associations in China and Singapore are typical examples. Organizations and activities in this category are part of extended state institutions, and work in collaboration with the state. The close relationship and codependency between the state and civil society organizations has created a lot of debate about the role of civil society in Pacific Asian countries.

Because of these different types of civil society organizations and activities and their varied relationship to the state, their role in the political system also varies – in particular in bringing about political change. It changes 'with the legitimacy of the nation-state and political system, the type of political system, and the stage of political development' (Alagappa, 2004: 50). Some types of civil society organizations and activities, particularly those in the social movement category (as we have seen in South Korea, Taiwan, the Philippines, Thailand and Indonesia), have been instrumental in advancing political liberalization and democratic transition.

Following democratization civil society organizations have shifted to advocating political reform and regulatory change. This shift has clearly occurred in conjunction with democratization and liberalization. In Japan, Singapore and China, civil society organizations and activities are less politically active and focus more on advocating specific issues. In China, civil society groups often play a supplementary role to the state through the governance of special functional groups and local communities. Most operate within a clearly defined and managed space that supports the overall political order. Overall, in Pacific Asia, as Alagappa claims, the relationship between civil society and political change, and democratic change in particular, is 'indeterminate', and contingent on 'propitious conditions' (Alagappa, 2004: 481–482).

Middle class politics

Liberal theories have long advocated a necessary link between a politically active middle class, and a genuine civil society, and ultimately democratic transition. While the early discourse on the development–democracy link in the 1950s and 1960s focused primarily on the democratic institutions as necessary conditions for development, it has shifted in recent decades to democracy as a necessary outcome of economic development because of the critical role of the middle class.

An underlying assumption of the middle-class theory is that democracy results from the increasing demands of the middle class expanding along with economic and social development. With economic development, the rise of living standards, more education and an increasing stake in state politics and policy, the middle class seek more involvement in

Case Study Lab 8.7

Understanding the social foundation of political movements: the role of public intellectuals in Indonesia

How do we actually understand the role of middle classes in political change? Conventional studies focus on the macro-level structure where civil society is discussed in its broad relations with the state. Abriel Heyanto, in examining the role of the middle class in democratization in Indonesia, focuses on the structure and agencies at the micro level in middle-class politics.

- Middle-class public intellectuals in post-colonies can take the most active role in the process of democratization.
- A democratic transition in post-colonies is effective when democratization friendly consciousness, ideas, practices and institutions have already found fertile ground in various forms, including in offices, schools, families or social organization, not from grand design or clear policy from an enlightened political elite.
- Democratic depositions that growth in everyday consciousness and discourses in small and local scales will provide a crucial foundation for the larger movement.

Heryanto, 2003: 24–25

national politics, more participation in policymaking, demand accountability of government and seek protection for their rights.

Civil society is clearly a platform for the middle class to exert such influence. There are interests of individual citizens that are distinct from those of the state and the market. Civil society is organization by individual citizens to protect and promote their interests through their collective action. Distinct interests of the middle class, and their willingness to act on them, therefore leads to a politically active civil society, quite possibly in the form of social movements.

Counterarguments challenging the middle-class theory point to the problematic claim in the theory on the causal link between the middle class and their liberal attitudes. David Brown and David Martin Jones (Brown and Jones, 1995), for example, argue that political liberalization and democratic transition does not necessarily mean the weakening of the state. There is a shared understanding of power that centres on securing access to power.

The middle class, because of the particular institutional setting under which they accumulated their wealth, and the fact they have benefited from the existing arrangements, tend to have a more conservative view about politics, a phenomenon Brown and Jones call the 'illiberal middle class'.

This illiberal middle class underlies the larger problem of 'illiberal democracy' (Bell et al., 1995; Zakari, 1997), and 'Asian democracy' (Neher and Marlay, 1995; see also Chapter 29) where, while democratic institutions may be established and are up and running, the political attitude of the society is overwhelmingly dominated by political values and practices defiant of competitive politics, civil liberty, rule of law or individualism.

The growth of the middle class in Pacific Asia presents a significant societal change in these countries. This was evident as early as the 1950s through Vogel's classic account of Japan's new middle class and the advent of the 'salaryman' (Vogel, 2013). The long-term impact of the middle class on political order in the region remains highly debated.

Cheng Li, in his study of the Chinese middle class, asks 'What impacts, current and future, might China's emerging middle class have on the country's social and political system?' Some studies have found China's middle class to be 'conservative' (see Unger, 2006) while another study using survey-data finds the middle-class support individual rights but distance themselves from political mobilization and score higher than other groups on measures of support for the current regime (Chen, 2013). In his review of the literature on the emerging Chinese middle class, Li illustrates how studies of middle class attitudes and preferences have too often mistaken support for political stability as a rejection of democratization:

> some scholars have challenged the conventional, dichotomous treatment of political stability and democracy. The middle class's current

preference for sociopolitical stability does not necessarily mean that it will oppose democracy in the future. In China, if democracy will lead to instability, political chaos, or even the dissolution of the country, there is no incentive for the Chinese people, including its emerging middle class, to pursue it. In a fundamental way, sociopolitical stability and democracy should be seen as complementary, rather than contradictory, phenomena. A democratic system enhances sociopolitical stability in a given country because it is based on the rule of law and civil liberties, and it provides for the peaceful and institutionalized transfer of power through elections'. (Cheng Li, 2010: 11, 21)

Just as Heryanto's study of Indonesian middle-class opposition in the 1990s illustrated how 'oppositions encounter obstacles that constrain them as movements for far-reaching social change' (Heryanto, 1996: 241), history has shown how the middle-class can become a key variable in the consolidation of stable democracy. While the middle-class certainly met obstacles in Indonesia in the 1990s, the decade ended with the fall of Suharto, democratic elections and a new constitution that many organizing for social and political change had the chance to take part in designing (Donald and Horowitz, 2013). In short, Pacific Asian politics is a rich empirical area for studying the role of the middle-class in democratization and the overall political order.

Labour activism

Social and economic gaps in Pacific Asian countries were a hotbed of radical political and social movements in the region for much of the twentieth century. Even at the start of the twenty-first century, social inequality is still a serious problem. While one can find countries in Pacific Asia with both small and large income gaps, the majority of the countries in Table 8.10 have a Gini index above the world average. Overall income gaps remain a significant challenge for the region.

Like the middle class, labour unions are also considered to be a key collective force for a genuine civil society, and an important indicator for the extent of political participation in a country. While in some countries, notably South Korea, labour unions are very active, they are generally less well organized

Table 8.10 The income gap

Cambodia	36.0	Malaysia	46.2
China	42.1	Singapore (2007)	42.5
Indonesia	38.1	Thailand	39.4
Japan (2007)	24.9	Philippines	43.0
S. Korea (2007)	31.6		

Notes: Gini index. 0 represents absolute equality, and 100 absolute inequality. World average in 2007 was 40.8.

UNDP, 2015 and 2007: 281–4.

and less active in Pacific Asian countries. There are important historical and institutional reasons for this. First, there is a pattern that unions were active in the early stage of economic development: Japan in the 1950s and 1960s; Singapore in the 1960s and 1970s; Korea in the 1980s and 1990s; and China in the 2000s.

After an initial period of intense labour–management confrontation, the government usually took steps to deal with labour movements – a process that Frederic Deyo described as 'labour subordination' (Deyo, 1989). On the one hand, strict laws were put into place to restrict union organization and activities. In Japan, unions were confined strictly to individual companies. In Singapore, the government-supported union, the National Trade Union Congress (NTUC), quickly marginalized the left-wing Singapore Association of Trade Unions (SATU), and some pro-communist unions were banned. In Taiwan, strikes are not permitted for those working in government, hospitals, schools and the military. In China, independent labour unions are not allowed. The government-sponsored unions are mainly agents of government corporatist efforts.

On the other hand, some forms of compromise arrangement have been worked out between labour and management, and mediated by the government. In Singapore, such a tripartite management of industrial relations has been institutionalized – for example, through the establishment of the National Wages Council, with representation from the employers' federations, trade unions and the government, to set annual wage guidelines for the country. In Japan, after the major Miike Strike (1961) the government negotiated with employers to offer job security for their employees with so-called lifelong employment

> **Box 8.9**
>
> ## Women, labour activism and civil society
>
> In many Pacific Asian countries, these issues uniquely come together, relate to each other and form an important part of the political society.
>
> - Export-oriented industrialization strategies favoured throughout East and Southeast Asian and more recently in parts of the subcontinent, brought with them a feminization first of factory labour and then of the diverse agglomeration of contract and home workers that now produce consumer goods for the world.
> - Female labour activities have been employed within and outside the organized labour movement.
> - Unions differ from Western unions. They are part of the state apparatus rather than independent vehicle for worker's interests.
> - Female labour activities have shaped the particular character of labour movements and the particular pattern of labour activism and organization in Pacific Asian countries.
>
> Broadbent and Ford, 2008: 1–8

and other improvements to labour rights and conditions. China is also experiencing this stage of development, where increasing labour unrest and protests have led the government to seek legislation to define labour rights and force employers to adopt, and comply with, labour standards.

An accommodationist approach, therefore, is found at both ends of the labour–management relationship. In a study of the rise of labour accommodation in Japan in the coal and steel industries in the 1960s and 1970s, Ikuo Kume demonstrates that under the government-structured market environment, labour found cooperation with management served their interests better than confrontation. Workers therefore 'eschewed labor activism, joined a crusade for productivity, retained jobs, and won a stable livelihood' (Kume, 1993: 156).

As well as the fact that political and legal settings in Pacific Asian countries are unfavourable to organized labour movements, a study by Deyo (Deyo, 1989: 211) found that economic structural factors were also responsible for the weak labour movement. The disproportionate expansion in industrial sectors led to conditions of employment to 'undercut independent unionization and effective collective action'. Moreover, such forms of industrialization are supported by communal, paternalistic 'labor systems wherein unionization, strikes, and other forms of collective action yield to more individualist, less overt conflict in nonpublic areas'. Finally, 'community organization generally fails to support autonomous worker action'.

With both restriction and accommodation, as well as the impact of structural factors, space for labour unions as a platform for civil society and political participation remains limited in Pacific Asian countries.

Environmental movements

The environment, pollution and climate change have emerged as key areas of concern for groups organizing civil society activities in Pacific Asia. This movement is interesting as a case study of civil society in action. While the movement is clearly linked to global concerns about environmental degradation and efforts to introduce policy to mitigate runaway climate change, the environmental movement in Pacific Asia has some unique features worth noting.

First, as Kalland and Persoon (1998) argue, environmental movements in Asia tend to have a local focus:

> Whereas many of the most successful Western campaigns (in terms of fundraising at least) focus on perceived problems in distant parts of the world (e.g., the campaigns against whaling, sealing, ivory trade and felling of rainforests), Asian campaigns are usually responses to very concrete problems in people's immediate neighborhoods. Hence, most of them are run by citizen action groups: people become involved in a cause for very practical reasons and not out of some sort of idealism. (Kalland and Persoon, 1998:2)

The lack of 'environmental interest groups' and a focus on local issues is, as Kalland and Persoon argue, most prevalent in those societies heavily influenced by Confucianism but it is also prevalent in other parts of Asia.

Second, Kalland and Persoon argue the environmental movement in Asia cannot be understood in isolation. It is intimately linked to political movements, such as the democratization movements and to opposition to pro-growth policies. Kim's comparative study of environmental groups in East Asia found:

> in terms of the relationship between the environmental movement and the state, South Korea represents a pattern of "congruent engagement" whereas Taiwan stands for a "conflictual engagement." These differences in the development of environmentalism are closely related to the different modes of democratic transition in the two countries. In South Korea, the intensive "politics of protest" by civil society groups resulted in drastic changes in the ruling bloc. In Taiwan, elite-led and paced transition largely enabled the ruling regime to maintain its control of society at large. As a result, in South Korea environmentalism emerged as a "new social movement" after the transition, whereas in Taiwan, it served as an essential component of the pro-democracy movement against the KMT government. (Kim, 2000: 287)

Moreover, Tang (2003) argues, the environmental movement has played a key role 'transforming the public sphere' and transitioning countries like Taiwan from 'electoral democracy' to 'liberal democracy'. Environmental advocacy, organizing for environmental protection and lobbying government played an important part in the development of the institutions of liberal democracy that provide a regulated space for civil society participation and checks and balances on traditional state and non-state elites.

Yok-shiu and So (1999) found that environmental movements have grown as a response to industrial policies that have led to environmental degradation in most Pacific Asian countries. By the 1970s there was a growing but limited public concern. By the late 1970s a number of NGOs had emerged as 'a vehicle for grassroots communities to express their political dissent and socioeconomic grievances. Since the 1980s, the increasing deterioration of the living and natural environment all over Asia has led to a gradual emergence of environmental consciousness among the citizenry and the evolution of various types of environmental movements' (Lee and So, 1999:5).

Finally, the pressing issue of climate change is helping shift the localized concern of environmental movements to a broader interest-based civil movement that deals with larger issues of public policy at the national and even global level. Pacific Asian countries, with their large industrial economies and large populations, are now some of the largest emitters of carbon dioxide. There is a growing realization that Asia cannot industrialize by following the same path as early developers and environmental NGOs and interest groups are beginning to advocate for low-carbon economies and for Asian leadership in global climate change negotiations.

The linkages between international environmental movements and domestic movements and capacity building in Pacific Asia, is important here. Katherine Morton, for example, argues:

> it is clear that China is moving away, albeit slowly, from its traditional state-centric focus on environmental management and towards a more comprehensive paradigm that embraces both market solutions and to a lesser extent participatory practices. Despite political and structural constraints, [international] environmental donors have had a small but significant part to play in facilitating this shift. (Morton, 2005: 10–11)

International linkages are an important part of the development of environmental movements in Pacific Asia that are part of broader epistemic communities. As Hasmath and Hsu note, for example, consortiums of NGOs like the Climate Change Action Network in China, suggest the slow evolution of the environmental movement into a network of professionals with an authoritative claim to policy-relevant knowledge, shared normative beliefs, notions of validity and common policy objectives (Hasmath and Hsu, 2015: 117).

Overall, environmental movements in Pacific Asia provide an important case study for how civil society functions within the overall political order. While we can identify major differences across Pacific Asian states that relate to the differing political orders in the region, overall, the growth of civil society organizations around issues of environmental protection and mitigation shows the region-wide growth of environmental ideals in society and increasing civil participation in policymaking.

The debate over civil society in Pacific Asian countries and the three examples we have discussed above are designed to provide a general idea of the issue, and illustrate how it fits into the overall pattern of government and politics in the region. It provides a starting point from which to further explore the concept, theories and related debates about civil society and the larger issue of patterns of political participation and political action in Pacific Asian countries.

The media, the Internet and new social media

The media, Internet and new social media are key mediums in state-society relations. The idea of democracy, for example, could not generate mass movements in South Korea and the Philippines without the elites and masses understanding and seeing its fundamental value. The market economy in China could not succeed without state-sponsored political persuasion. While conventional methods of political communication are still used such as pamphlets, mass rallies or education, increasingly, the media, particularly the electronic media, have become a primary platform for political communication and persuasion. Consequently, the media, Internet and new social media exert great influence on government and politics in Pacific Asian countries.

The assumption that the media plays a great role in politics and government, however, needs to be placed in the context of Pacific Asian countries. Scholars disagree over the precise role of the media, and particularly the nature of its relationship with the state.

In his work on media and politics in Pacific Asia, Duncan McCargo challenges the narrow interests of political scientists in the role of media, and the limited relevance of studies in the West of media–politics relations in Pacific Asia (McCargo, 2003: 1). The charge that political scientists are interested mainly in 'political communication' issues such as election coverage and campaigning is an interesting one. It calls attention to the role of the media uniquely associated with the patterns and dynamics of politics in Pacific Asian countries.

McCargo identities 'three possible functions for the media as a political institution' (McCargo, 2003: 3–5):

- As an agent of stability, charged with the task of helping preserve social and political order;
- As an agent of restraint with the function of day-to-day monitoring of the political order in the interests of more representative government, and to provide checks and balances;
- As an agent of change helping to shape political changes during times of crisis.

McCargo further associates each of these roles with a specific political regime type: the agent of stability in an authoritarian regime; the agent of restraint in a liberal democracy; and the agent of change in a transitional regime.

McCargo's framework is useful for us to understand the general political orientation of the media in a given society. It is particularly useful for us to understand the media's relationship to the state: whether to preserve it, restrain it, or challenge it. The framework, however, does not help us to understand exactly how the media relates to particular political institutions and forces in a given society, and thus the various different functions the media chooses to, or are used to, perform. It is possible that these three roles can all be seen in one country – at different times and in different issue areas. In their case studies of the media under 'authoritarian, transitional and newly post-authoritarian regimes' in Pacific Asia, Krishna Sen, Terence Lee and their associates (Sen and Lee, 2008) challenge the regime-based interpretation of the role of the media. More specifically, they question 'three common narratives underlying popular and academic writing on the mass media in authoritarian and transitional regimes' and find that (Sen, 2008: 1):

- Not even the most repressive regime, such as that in Burma, can completely control the production and consumption of media messages within their national borders.
- Privatization of media does not necessarily lead to the weakening of the state's political control over the operations of the media, nor indeed is

there any necessary correlation between diversified media ownership and democratization of media content in terms of whose images and voices are represented and how.
- Anti-authoritarian movements in Pacific Asia cannot necessarily depend on the support of Western 'democracies' or their 'free' media.

It is possible, therefore, to understand the role of the media in Pacific Asian countries in politics (see Box 8.10) not so much 'as a political institution' in relation to the state, but as an instrument or platform that can be utilized by various political forces and organizations, including the state, for political communication in the broadest sense.

Angela Romano, for example, seeks to understand the role of journalism and the mass media within a framework based on the original idea of development journalism and its theories of the role of the media. According to Romano, development journalism, which originated in the 1960s,

> initially envisaged that journalists would refine their reporting and writing skills so that they could help poorly educated audiences to better understand complex development processes. The aim was that journalists would focus less on 'spot' or 'sensationalist' news. They would instead identify and cover socio-economic and political processes so that communities could recognize, comprehend, and influence such processes. (Romano, 2005: 1)

Beyond this 'simple focus on clear, issues-based reporting', journalists were increasingly called upon to serve the prevalent national agenda of the state. Under such developmental journalism, there are two primary roles for the media: journalists as nation builders and journalists as government partners. In the former, 'the mass media was seen as a mobilizing agent for nation-building. The mass media were designated an important role in promoting this modernization of culture and ways of life'. In the latter, the role of journalists 'was usually fundamentally similar to the modernization approach above, except that there was a strong accompanying philosophy that press freedom should be restricted according to the nation's economic priorities and development needs' (Romano, 2005: 2, 4).

Box 8.10

Roles of the media in Pacific Asian politics

Regime type based interpretation (McCargo, 2003). The media plays different roles in different political regimes: agent of stability in a corporatist regime, agent of restraint in a democratic regime and agent of change in a transitional regime.

Developmental journalism (Romano, 2005). Journalism in developing countries is charged with the responsibility of helping the public to better understand the developmental process and support the developmental agenda. Journalists in this way are government partners and nation builders.

The closed shop (Freeman, 2000). The media is neither a watchdog nor a lapdog of the state, but rather a party to the closed, privileged and mutually benefiting relationship between government and the media.

More sensitive to the institutional cultural setting in the country under which the media operates, Laurie A. Freeman proposes a mutually dependent relationship between the media and the state. In her study of the media–state relationship in Japan, Freeman finds that, under what she calls the relational setting in Japan,

> the Japanese state, its political leaders, and its bureaucracies are protected from intensive scrutiny. Mechanisms such as Japan's press clubs provide political (as well as economic and intellectual) elites with a convenient means of filtering news and information and socially constructing the worldview held by the public. At the same time, this influence is at least partially reciprocated, as the media provide an important prism through which elites obtain news and information. (Freeman, 2000: 5)

From these different views about the role of the media in Pacific Asian politics, we can summarize the various different roles into two general categories, depending on the way they affect politics and government. First and foremost is the media as a platform for political mobilization in major political campaigns and movements. This can be for voter mobilization in pluralist polities; mobilization of mass political movements in transitional polities; and political campaigns by corporatist states. In voter mobilization, the media are very much the instruments through which political parties communicate with the electorate. The role of the media in elections and campaigns has largely been institutionalized and become an integral part of the electoral process.

The media's role in political change, particularly mass political movements, is well recognized. More significantly, the media can have a more dramatic and profound impact on political processes, particularly in those polities in the 'transition phase' (Randall, 1993: 646). In each and every mass political movement in recent decades, from the People Power Revolutions of 1986 and 2001 in the Philippines to the Tiananmen Movements in China in 1989, from the democratic movements of the 1980s in South Korea, to the movements in Thailand and Indonesia in the 1990s, the media was critical in shaping the direction and scope as well as the overall agenda of the political movement.

The media can also be an integral part of the political institutions in the corporatist polities. The Chinese Communist Party sees the media as the 'mouthpiece' of the party, with the primary function being to defend the party line and present that party line to the public. A similar approach to the media was also seen in most Cold War regimes in Pacific Asian countries. As former Indonesian president Suharto stated,

> as an integral part of our developing society, nation and state, the press has an important role to assist in managing this nation in all its complexity through the dissemination of news, opinions, ideas, grievances and hopes to the masses. It is in this respect that the press has a role to play in helping build and preserve our unity and cohesion as a nation. (cited in McCargo, 2003: 3)

The media here is a political institution performing functions for the state.

To ensure state dominance over the media, the media are largely incorporated into the party-state systems and, to varying degrees, into other Cold War regimes, as well. In China, at the time of writing, the media are largely still under the direct control and management of the Communist Party. The Party issues central guidelines on what to report and how to report it, and the media are generally expected to follow. On primary political issues, the Party will issue standard news texts through the official Xinhua News Agency for the media to adopt. Since the media are the employees of both the Party and the state, the Party's instructions normally prevail. For those going beyond the Party's instructions or guidelines, the Party has the power to remove them from their positions and ban publication or broadcasting schedules. The market economy has led to changes in direct state control of the media in China in recent years, however, either in terms of ownership and management, or coverage and editorship (Zhao, 1998). But the party line is still a real line, and a level of self-censorship prevails even in the market-orientated media.

Information cartel In Japan, the information-gathering process takes place within a 'closed shop' made up of journalists having proprietary access to information and sources. Contact with official sources is limited to a select group of individuals or organizations that have established a clearly defined, if not codified, set of rules and practices. The perpetuation of the closed shop is guaranteed by the enforcement of sanctions or the threat of their enforcement.

Freeman, 2000: 67–68

In the second category, the media is important in politics for its role in the everyday shaping of public opinion. Public opinion can exert a great influence on government policymaking, on national political processes and on state–society interactions. This role can be found in both pluralist and corporatist societies, though the context for the media's role in these two types of polities is different.

In pluralist polities, the media plays the role of mover and shaper of public opinion as well as being a government watchdog. In many Pacific Asian countries, however, there are various institutional, cultural and political constraints on the media's role as a genuine institution that can limit their capacity to check government. Studies of the media in Japan, particularly during the era of LDP dominance, show the media are indeed in an ambiguous position between the government and the public and are

Box 8.11

How public opinion influences decision-making and political change in China

There are at least three ways in which public opinion can influence decision-making and political change in China. First, public opinion gives useful indicators of the political mood and preferences of the population to which the state and political and social forces are compelled to respond. Second, public opinion can influence decision-making through mass political participation. As there are no direct elections of government officials, mechanisms and channels of various degrees of effectiveness that link public opinion and government decision-making have been growing rapidly in recent years. Third, public opinion can influence decision-making and political change through open protest.

Tang, 2005: 196–8

neither a watchdog nor a lapdog (Feldman, 1993; Freeman, 2000: 161–163; McCargo, 2001: 50–76).

One such institutional and cultural constraint is the persistent practice of press clubs and the cartelization of the press in Japan (Freeman, 2000). In Japan, these press clubs are associations of journalists attached to 'major governmental, political, and business organizations' (Freeman, 2000: 68). These clubs operate under strict rules and regulations. Journalists belonging to the club have privileged access to news and information provided by the government ministry. By limiting news privileges to a select few, the government is able to control how the news is reported and by whom, and thus put itself in a strong position to control national issue agendas and public debates.

Media as watchdog: the media works on behalf of the public to bring to light inconsistencies and irregularities in the activities and behaviour of politicians, civil servants, business people, and other political actors.

Media as lapdog: the media operates as a docile and obedient servant of the state, something akin to what one might expect to find in the 'party journalism' of the former USSR or in China today.

Freeman, 2000: 161–2

In countries such as China, while conventional methods of media control and management are still in place, the growth of public opinion (see Box 8.11) has presented the state with the challenge of relearning how to use the media (Tang, 2005). With China's overall controlled political environment, the mechanisms of political manipulation of the media are unique. For example, controlled media exposure can be an effective tool for the central government to discipline local governments. The media is also an effective platform for promoting the 'party line' – much more effective than the conventional circulations of official documents or channels of political implementation. But studies have also shown how ideological campaigns and propaganda in the media are not as effective as once thought. Chan (2007) argues, therefore, that since the 1990s 'guidance of public opinion' has become a major buzzword in the state's media policy:

> The party states shift of attention to the new idea of guiding public opinion after the Tiananmen Square Incident highlights the crisis of the propaganda model. It also suggests that the party state is moving further away from Mao's orthodoxy, which emphasized the prominence of ideology. At least in the realm of the mass media, the party state focuses on influencing the social agenda rather than promoting political ideology. (Chan, 2007: 558)

In corporatist states, the media remains overly controlled and access to free and impartial journalism is lacking. However, there has been a subtle shift from ideological control and use of the media for propaganda-style campaigns to educate the public to a system of agenda-setting that has provided limited space for non-state media and commentators to discuss politics and influence public opinion. As in the pluralist states, the advent of new media platforms has quickened the shift towards new and less state-controlled spaces for political communication.

Adding to the complexity of media–politics relations are two issues in Pacific Asian countries: the impact of the Internet and new social media, which is also a case of how technological developments affect politics and government; and, the role of the international media, which is largely a Pacific Asian phenomenon.

Internet and new social media

Internet use has grown rapidly in Pacific Asia, out of proportion to the levels of economic and social development in many countries. This is partly because much of the IT manufacturing takes place in the region, and its related technologies and products are easily accessible and partly because of high population density living in Pacific Asia's urban areas making for efficient rollout of internet technology.

There seems to be a consensus that the Internet changes how government and society interact. But views differ as to the precise nature of the change. Many believe the Internet empowers citizens and makes government and politics more transparent and more accountable. More pointedly, there have been high expectations that they can help to bring political liberalization and democratic transition to countries such as China. For many others, the state has access to the best technology and, as with what it did in the past with the conventional media, the government can and does dominate the Internet and finds ways to control and manage information flows over it. For this reason, the Chinese government's efforts in recent years to control Internet publications and access have received much scholarly attention.

More specifically, the Internet, especially new social media, allows the development of virtual political communities that make information access and sharing much easier, freer and instantaneous. They are also subject to few conventional barriers such as distance, venue, physical presence and so on. This poses a serious challenge to a state that relies on control of information to set the national political agenda and to control public opinion. Citizens and civil society on the Internet become part of the process of setting agendas of national issues and in creating public debate. Internet communities become effective pressure groups, exerting influence on government and forcing it to be more transparent and more accountable. The Internet, however, can also give the state more effective powers to control information and use it for political and policy purposes.

In a more balanced analysis of the impact of the Internet on state–society relations in China, Yongnian Zheng (2007) argues that the Internet empowers both state and society. The Internet provides a fundamentally different platform that gives both the state and citizens the power to engage with each other, and this interaction will reshape the relationship between them. More specifically, in Zheng's view, the Internet has an impact on Chinese politics in three ways (Zheng, 2007: 166):

The Internet has been an integral part of nation-state building on the part of the state and has empowered the state in developing a national economy and improving its governance.

The Internet has empowered society by providing new sources of information and channels for civic engagement. The Internet opens up a new arena, where both the state and society can empower themselves. It has enabled the state to deliver economic goods and services to the people more efficiently and has also enabled society to 'voice' its interests and to facilitate policy changes on the part of the state.

In this sense, the state and society can be mutually empowering over the Internet-mediated sphere. Furthermore, the Internet is also an arena in which the state and society compete for power and thus can confront each other.

With the rapid growth of new social media in Pacific Asian states, many scholars have explored the relationship of this media with regime-type. China, for example, has developed a wide-variety of platforms such as Weibo and WeChat but tightly controls access to foreign competitors such as Facebook and Twitter. China aside, most countries in Pacific Asia are well connected to these global platforms significantly enhancing their access to information and knowledge and developing a sense of global citizenry.

In a 2014 edited volume on the role of social media and politics in Pacific Asia, a group of authors provide an optimistic view of its role enhancing citizen participation in the region (see Willnat and Aw, 2014). Taken together, the studies show that 'posting comments, talking about politics on social media and belonging to political Facebook groups was found to be consistently predictive of increased political engagement'. The use of social media signals a shift in Pacific Asia, and other parts of the world, in 'the logic of citizen participation, which is increasingly moving away from organized, group-based engagement towards more personalized, identity-focused expressive acts of content co-production and sharing within networks of trusted relationships' (Skoric, 2016: 1–3).

The international media

Finally, the international media, mainly the Western media, play a unique role in Pacific Asian politics, for several reasons. As was shown earlier, dominant ideologies, values and political concepts are generally imported from Western countries. As such, international media, print, radio and TV broadcasting, movies, books and magazines naturally become the platforms for these ideologies, values and concepts. In this sense, the international media are an important shaper of ideologies, values and political discourses in Pacific Asian countries. Such a role of the international media can be more dramatic at times of political crisis and mass movements in these countries. They become an important facilitator of political movements and revolutions. In mass political movements in Pacific Asia in the recent past, from the Philippine's People Power Revolutions, to Thailand's May Events of 1992, to China's Tiananmen Movement of 1989, to Indonesia's Anti-Suharto Revolution of 1998, one can always discern the role of the international media.

Second, in day-to-day political reporting, the international media can easily be used by rival political forces for their own political purposes. McCargo documents the impact of the international media on domestic politics in Thailand (McCargo, 1999). Here, the international media is caught between opposing political parties and politicians. One side believes that international media coverage is part of a conspiracy by its opponents.

Third, in non-pluralist polities such as China, the international media are very much controlled. However, the international media can also be used by the ruling elites for domestic political purposes. In the days of Mao's reign, for example, there was a government-controlled internally circulated daily newspaper that carried selected news reports from the international media. The selection, however, generally reinforced the government line.

Fourth, the international media has an important role to play in the diffusion of international norms. For example, in a study of television in Japan, China and Hong Kong, White (2013) shows the importance of news flows from 'West to East' but a paucity of flows from 'East to West'. Such a one-sided flow of information shows societies in Pacific Asia are often far better informed and aware of global events, and knowledge and influenced by the norms and values promoted internationally.

In this chapter, we have discussed political society in Pacific Asia. We have explored the complex relations between state and society, overviewed methods of participating in politics and identified particular social groups with special access to the levers of power. The civil society debate was presented ultimately about the role of the state in civil society activities and the middle class, labour and environmental groups provided examples of the evolution and challenges of civil society in the region. Finally, we discussed the role of the media in political communication with a focus on the importance of the international media and the rapid growth of new social media as a platform for reshaping how state and non-state actors engage with politics in Pacific Asian countries.

Chapter summary

- Dichotomist theories, either state-centric or society-centric, cannot adequately explain the complexity of state–society relations in Pacific Asian countries. The state-in-society approach offers a useful analytical framework for understanding the intertwined, mutually dependent and dynamic state–society relations.
- There are different ways in which individuals are able to influence government and politics: through formal or informal institutions. There are many factors that affect decisions regarding political participation and preference for a specific method.

- Citizens in Pacific Asian countries are generally active in voting, but less active in other forms of political participation via formal institutions. Beyond formal institutions, there are other modes of political participation that are widely practiced in Pacific Asia.
- People power revolutions were a dominant form of political participation during the twentieth century, but particularly in the 1980s and 1990s. The popularity of people power revolutions reveals much of the nature of the political regimes at which these were aimed. It also provides an insight into people's attitudes towards formal institutions.
- Becoming a politician is another way of influencing government and politics. There are unique Pacific Asian mechanisms in the generation of continual political support for politicians.
- Elites are key movers and shapers of the national agenda, public opinion, government policy and politics. Their resources, wealth and social status, as well as their profile and political connections, shape their methods of political influence.
- Civil society is a prime source of activities of political participation. However, the concept has generated much scholarly debate. Civil society in Pacific Asia has raised many interesting questions regarding the concept, in particular, on the relationship between state and society. Three issues are examined (the middle class, labour and the environment), as examples of the nature and scope of civil society in Pacific Asian countries, and to help in understanding the nature of the debate and the diverse views of scholars.
- The media is an important platform of political communication. There is debate over how to determine the relationship between the media and the state in Pacific Asian countries. In recent years, the international media and new social media have revolutionized the media environment and changed how people in Pacific Asian countries engage information and the political process.

Further reading

For theories and debates on the problem of state–society relations, and in particular the state-in-society approach, see Migdal et al. (1994) and Migdal (2001). On citizenship in Pacific Asia, see Gilligan (1998). Political values and attitudes in Pacific Asian countries are tested systematically in three major multinational, multi-year surveys: Hu and Chu (2004), Inoguchi et al. (2004), European Values Study Group and World Values Survey Association (2006) and Wang (2008). Works on Pacific Asian countries based on these three surveys include Blondel and Inoguchi (2006), Dalton and Shin (2006) and Wang (2008). Alagappa (2004) provides a good analytical framework for understanding civil society in Pacific Asia. For analysis of development and functions of civil society in more concrete terms, see Heryanto and Mandal (2003). To examine how the concept of civil society is received in different secular and religious traditions, see Chambers and Kymlicka, 2002. For NGOs in Pacific Asian countries, see Shigetomi (2002) and Weller (2005). For the middle-class debate, see Bell et al. (1995), Brown and Jones (1995), Neher and Marlay (1995) and Zakari (1997). Deyo (1989) and Verma et al. (1995) give an overview of organized labour as a force for political participation. For environmental politics see Kalland and Persoon (1998) and individual countries, for example Morton (2005) for China.

For the media see McCargo (2003) and Ramono (2005). For politics and new social media see Willnat and Aw (2014).

Study questions

1 What are the state-centric views and society-centric views of state–society relations? Why do Joel S. Migdal and his associates believe a more sophisticated framework is needed for a fuller understanding of the state–society relationship?

2 Is there a pattern of preferences in methods of political participation in Pacific Asia? If so, what factors influence the preferences?

3 What are obstacles for women's empowerment in politics and society? Is this issue particularly relevant for politics and government in Pacific Asian countries?

4 Who are the elites and how do they influence politics and government?

5 Is the concept of civil society applicable to Pacific Asia? If so, why?

6 What are some of the key features and concerns of the environmental movement in Pacific Asia? Are their activities localized, or are environmental NGOs thinking globally and acting locally?

7 Does the media, particularly the Internet, new social media and the international media, fundamentally change the relationship between state and society?

Key terms

Political society (208); State-centric, society-centric, and state in society (209); State corporatism (211); Forms of political participation and influence (213); Embedded autonomy (211); People power revolution (219); Gender politics (220); Mass movements and elite politics (239); Formal institutions (215); Hereditary politicians (222); Patron–client relations (224); Contentious politics (212); Civil society (229); Labour activism (236); Middle-class-democracy thesis (234); Information cartel (241); Media as watchdog (242); Media as lapdog (242); Public opinion (242).

Chapter 9

Nation and state: ethnicity, religion and culture

The idea of the nation-state and the political movement to build the interstate system on a national basis is a core element of modern state building, particularly as seen in early modern state building in Europe (Tilly, 1975). In Pacific Asia, as in many other parts of the world, however, the boundaries and structural substance of nation and state are complicated and the forces that shaped their interaction and mutual constitution are highly complex. The various ways the tension between nation and state has been dealt with in contemporary Pacific Asia has led to the shaping of different models of how nation and state relate to each other. This issue continues to impact the constitutional character of the state, how state institutions relate to religion, and ethnic groups and the very existence of the state itself.

In this chapter we focus on the issue of identity and the nation-state in Pacific Asian government and politics. We will first look at the concept of the nation-state and nationalism as a political ideology and the political forces it represents that drove nations to seek independence as a state from the various colonial and imperial frameworks in much of the twentieth century. We will look at the various nation-state models that emerged from this process and how these different models, or state systems, affect the government and politics of the country. As the chapter shows, identity is a powerful variable in the formation and governance of nation-states in Pacific Asia, shaping the emergence or dissolution of states in the region. It will continue to shape the evolution of Pacific Asian states in the decades to come.

'Nation, religion and king': from trinity states to nation-states

The idea that nations in Pacific Asia are comparable to those in Europe, and should be able to run their own country with a strong and effective government, was essential for what is called nationalism today. Ernest Gellner best summarized the rationale for nations to be the substantive basis for the state in his well-received 'congruence' theory (Gellner, 1983). In this theory, Gellner sees the nation as a higher culture imposed on society where the modern economy brings significant change in its organization and underlying relations. The state is the most effective institution to enforce order in such a society.

> **Nationalism** is primarily a political principle, which holds that the political and the national unit should be congruent... It is a theory of political legitimacy.
>
> Gellner 1983: 1

Unlike how modern nation states emerged in Europe, there was generally a traditional model of state constitution and legitimacy in most political communities in Pacific Asia in the early twentieth century, with the nation, religion and king as three core-constituting forces. This reality is further complicated by the fact that most Pacific Asian countries were under some form of colonial governance where political boundaries cut across national boundaries.

Therefore, the movement to seek state boundaries to match with national boundaries not only brought independence movements across the Pacific Asian region, but also led to great efforts in nation building and state building to make the newly created nation states work. Efforts towards nation building involve enhancing national identity, religious pluralism, multiculturalism, political and economic and social integration of the population. Efforts towards state building aim at state institutions that reflect the national or ethnic configuration of the political community.

Nationalism in the early twentieth century

The nationalist movements in the early twentieth century for those few states still independent in Pacific Asia reflected the modern aspirations of the peoples and their longing for identity and boundaries in the age of imperialism and colonialism. Such nationalist movements carried both elements of nation-building and state building. The Meiji Restoration ended the feudal breaking up of Japan and restored national unity under the emperor.

In the Chinese case, the 1911 Revolution overthrew Manchu rule and restored the rule of China by Han Chinese. The Chulalongkorn reforms in Thailand stabilized the country, strengthened its ability to survive as a viable entity and ultimately allowed the country to avoid being colonized by the encroaching European powers. The nineteenth-century reforms in Korea were short-lived. The country was not able to survive as an independent state and became a colony of Japan in 1910.

Beyond the problem of national sovereignty, the nationalist movements in these countries focused primarily on state building. In both Japan and Thailand, some form of the trinity of 'nation, religion and king/emperor' emerged as the primary framework for political order, legitimacy and authority, as well as national unity and identity. In China, the monarchy was overthrown and the Republic was set up to replace the imperial system.

Under this new overall constitutional framework, efforts were made to build state institutions and national systems of military service, education, commerce and economy, transportation and communication, as well as political representation, citizenship and public policy deliberation (Zhao, 1996; Strauss, 1998). Zhao, for example, investigates the alternations between a cabinet system (1925–8, 1931–6)

Box 9.1

Japan's nation state: ethnicity, family and the emperor

Japan is considered a textbook example of the modern nation-state with less complications of ethnicity as seen in many other Pacific Asian countries. Notwithstanding, there are still some unique features that define the modern nation-state of Japan:

- There is no simple congruence with the discussions of nation and state in Western languages. *Kokumin-kokka* is the modern term used to describe the fusion of an ethnic national identity (*kokumin*) and an administrative apparatus (*kokka*).
- The Japanese nation-state was based on a particular modern concept of the family (*kazoku-kokka*), privileging a monogamous stem family based on patriarchy, patriliny and primogeniture. All individuals were registered in a stem family based on kinship ties.
- The Emperor acquired meaning as the core of modern Japan's national and cultural identity and was perceived to embody the historical as well as the transcendental aspects of the nation.

Germer, Mackie and Wöhr, 2014: 3

and a presidential system (1928–31, 1936–47) under the Nationalist government, and argues that this was indeed a product of constitutional efforts to build effective state institutions, however complicated they were by the balance of power among political elites at the time (Zhao, 1996: 1–19).

The nationalist movements, state-led reforms and modernization programmes produced different outcomes. For Japan and Thailand, these programmes and activities clearly strengthened the ability of these two countries to survive as independent nation-states and of their national system to undertake modern development. In China, political reforms failed to win the support of the ruling elites early on, and no effective central authority emerged following the overthrow of the ruling monarch. The whole country was on the brink of breaking up due to warlordism. It was apparent that the nationalist inspirations would have to be met by revolutions from below.

If nationalism in these countries was more about national sovereignty and modern transformation, nationalism in the rest of Pacific Asia was more of a classic case of seeking national independence from colonial rule. Nationalist movements led by charismatic leaders spread from Korea and Vietnam in the north, to Indonesia and the Philippines in the south. However, the first half of the twentieth century saw the continual consolidation of European colonial settlements in Southeast Asia, further integration of the local economies into the world system, and diverse forms of colonial governance in different countries. Nationalist sentiment grew in Indonesia in the 1920s and 1930s, and in the Philippines in the late nineteenth century before the Americans took over from Spain.

However, it was not until the Second World War that the grip of European powers on their colonies began to loosen. This was also the time when a new generation of local elites, often themselves educated in Western-style schools or in Europe itself (Ho Chi Minh of Vietnam went to France, and Sukarno of Indonesia went to a Dutch school), started to have an influence on national politics, representing nationalist sentiments as well as national economic and social interests against colonial rule.

The independence of Southeast Asian countries came through in several different ways, each leaving a different legacy on the politics and government of the post-independence state (see Box 9.3). R. E. Elson sees two models of independence: independence by violence and independence by negotiation (Elson, 1998: 82–4). Perhaps there is a third model – independence by plan. After defeating Spain in the American-Spanish war (1898) and reaching an agreement with the Filipinos on US colonial rule in 1901, the United States designed a schedule for the Philippines to become independent in 1935, but the country eventually gained independence in 1945, after the Americans drove out the occupying Japanese.

Given the circumstances, American colonial rule is seen as 'benign', under which new education and health systems were developed, using American money, and a new political system was established using the US model. Moreover, the path to independence was very much a joint project between the nationalist elites, often pro-American, and the US colonial administration. There was a weak sense of 'restoring the nation-hood' and replacing colonial rule, as could be seen in many other Southeast Asian nations.

The second model was one of negotiated settlement between nationalist movements and colonial powers. This was seen mainly in British colonies such as those in today's Malaysia, Singapore, Myanmar and Brunei (and for that matter, also Hong Kong). Indeed, the hostilities that required a political settlement after the Second World War were

Box 9.2

Monarchy and the modern state in Thailand

It is clear that the monarchy came to exercise increasingly important functions in the politics of Thailand following the Sarit coup of 1957. The institution plays the role of:

- Legitimizer of political power;
- Supporter/legitimizer of broad regime policies;
- Promoter and sanctioner of intra-elite solidarity;
- 'Broker' for transferring funds from the private sector to the state treasury;
- In addition to becoming the symbolic focus for national unity.

Chaloemtiaranba, 2007: 218

Box 9.3

Paths to independence

	New independent state	*Colonial rule*
Independence by plan	Philippines	United States
Negotiated settlement	Malaysia, Singapore, Burma	Great Britain
Armed campaign	Indonesia, Vietnam, Korea	Netherlands, France, Japan

more between different ethnic communities than between a unified nationalist movement and the colonial administration. Consequently, nationalism here was also of a twisted kind: not so much that of 'one nation, one state', but primarily a political compromise among the ethnic groups, and between their alliances on the one hand and the colonial authorities on the other.

In 1957, the Federation of Malaya became independent. In 1959, Singapore was allowed self-government, and in 1965 it became an independent state. In both Malaya and Singapore, colonial institutions, economic interests and culture were preserved in the political settlements brokered by the colonial power. The British parliamentary system, for example, was largely copied in these new states. English was chosen as the official language in Singapore. The negotiated political settlements, however, saw an 'incongruence' (Gellner, 1983) between the political and ethnic boundaries. Indeed, there was not so much a nation as a state. This became the root of the trouble for the new states, and dictated a particular model of nation-state building in the decades to come.

Finally, independence in Vietnam and Indonesia was hard won through armed campaigns. The French and Dutch had long cultivated their colonies in Southeast Asia. But the Second World War was a turning point. The first Indochina War (1946–54), between the French and the communist-led Vietnamese independence movement led to the end of French colonial rule and the partition of the country into the Democratic Republic of Vietnam in the north, under the Ho Chi Minh led communists, and the Republic of Vietnam in the south, under the wing of the USA. In Indonesia, Sukarno's national independence movement fought a war with the Dutch for two years and forced the Dutch to recognize its independence and sovereignty formally in 1949.

The ending of colonial rule in Vietnam and Indonesia through armed conflict cut their post-independence development from their colonial past. Both the French and the Dutch were absent from the post-independence states. Vietnam soon became a battleground between the United States and the Soviet Union for twenty years following the 1954 Geneva agreements. The country itself was divided between the communist north and the non-communist south, until 1975. Indonesia almost became a communist country, a process brutally stopped only by a military crackdown on the communists and their sympathizers in 1965.

The triumph of guerrilla warfare and revolutionary armed campaigns against colonial rule also brought a generation of charismatic leaders and their revolutionary political machinery to the helm of the newly independent states, such as Mao Zedong and his communist party in China, and Kim Il-sung and his Korean Workers' Party in North Korea.

World warfare and nationalist movements changed the political landscape of the region significantly. Unlike in eighteenth-century Europe, nationalism in twentieth-century Pacific Asia was a product of European influence and impact: European modern achievements, colonialism and, most importantly, European institutions, manners and power. All of these generated a strong and often radical sentiment against European colonial rule, and great expectations that the post-independence states could transform themselves rapidly into modern states under the new nationalist leadership.

Nationalism has, therefore, been effective at bringing the state together in Pacific Asia. A further challenge, however, has come managing the various national, ethnic and religious groups and identities within the state. This has posed a great challenge for twentieth century political development in the region and created a source of political tension, conflict and even war, at times threatening the very existence of the state. We will discuss the various approaches states have taken to managing identity politics in following sections. For now, however, we introduce the politics of identity and discuss the place of religion in the region.

The fact that people identify with and belong to certain groups can have significant implications for politics in the region. A Malay applicant for university entrance in Malaysia, for example, may get a different reception than a non-Malay. An urban resident in China may get special privileges that are not granted to a rural resident. The aboriginal population in Taiwan are able to get specially designated MPs in parliament. In the Group Representation Constituency system in Singapore, at least one candidate in each constituency must come from a minority ethnic group.

Just why these groups have secured special rights and privileges against the state is related to the role they played as traditional forms of public authority and their role in the process of state building as well as to the state's approach to managing ethnic, cultural and identity difference within its boundaries. The question of identity as a form of organizing politics is therefore important for understanding politics and government in the region.

Because of the significant implications of identity for politics and government, there is tremendous political interest and action by individuals, groups and the state over the challenge of managing identity within state boundaries.

Identity is a distinct quality in a group of individuals that sets them apart from others. Identity politics are political interests, activities and movements over the recognition of such qualities and consequent rights and privileges in existing political institutions.

Identity-driven politics can happen over various different kinds of identities: gender, ethnicity, religious, culture, nationality and so on. We focus our discussion here on politics over ethnic, religious, cultural, national identities as these are closely related to the tension between nation and state in the process of nation state building in Pacific Asia. We find that identity has been mobilized as a significant cause for political action in the development of state institutions and state society relations in Pacific Asian countries.

The role of religion in Pacific Asian politics

Before we discuss the role of religion in modern political development in Pacific Asia, let us start with a survey of the scope and character of the influence of religion in the region, particularly the different patterns in Northeast and Southeast Asia. First, unlike other areas in the world where a single religion dominates in a country and a region—Islam in the Middle East and Christianity in other parts of the world, for example—all the major world religions are present in the Pacific Asian region, and in some cases, there are many religions represented within a single country (see Figure 9.1).

Second, none of the major religions in Pacific Asian countries are 'home-grown': Buddhism came from South Asia, Islam from the Arabic world and Christianity from Europe. Third, there is generally an ambiguous attitude from the state towards

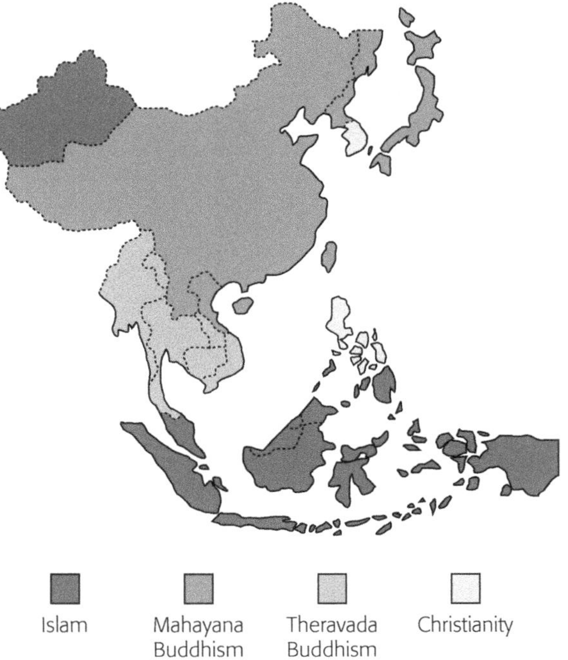

Figure 9.1 Mapping religions in Pacific Asia

COUNTRY PROFILE

PHILIPINES

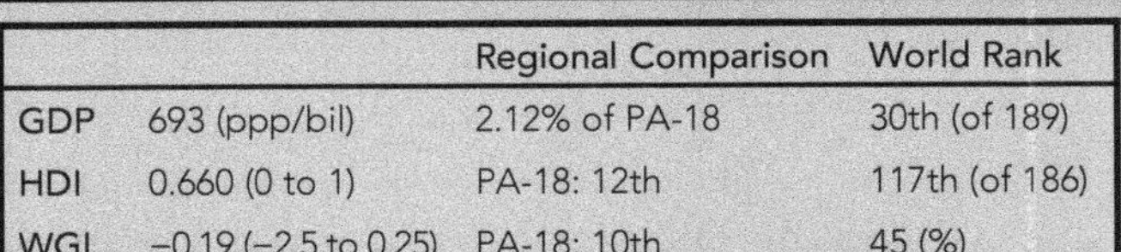

		Regional Comparison	World Rank
GDP	693 (ppp/bil)	2.12% of PA-18	30th (of 189)
HDI	0.660 (0 to 1)	PA-18: 12th	117th (of 186)
WGI	−0.19 (−2.5 to 0.25)	PA-18: 10th	45 (%)

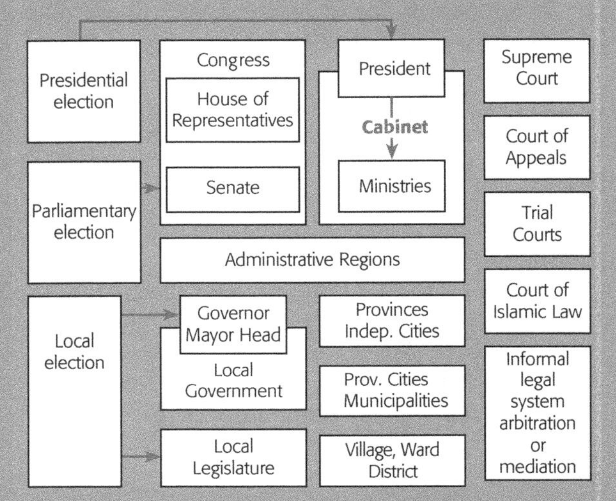

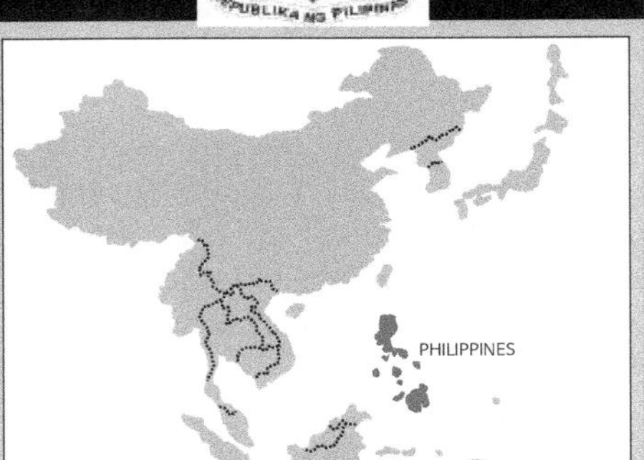

Key political facts

Electoral system for National Legislature

Mixed member proportional representation (MMP).

Political cycles

Presidential election, every 6 years;
Election of House Representatives and Senators (half), every 3 years;
Annual national budget bill to be passed by Congress in December.

Further reading

Morada and Tadem, 2006; White 2014

Timeline of modern political development

1946	Independence from the United States. Third Republic, adopted the 1935 Constitution with a bicameral Congress and a presidential 4-year term for a maximum of two terms.
1971	Constitutional amendment to remove term limits for president.
1972	Marcos declares martial law, rule by decree.
1973	New Society and Fourth Republic. New constitution with a parliamentary government and legislative powers vested in the national assembly.
1976	Constitutional amendment for a presidential system with the president allowed to hold the position of prime minister and exercise legislative powers.
1981	Martial law lifted. Constitutional amendments return the parliamentary system with a directly elected president and local autonomy.
1983	Opposition leader Benigno Aquino assassinated.
1986	People Power Revolution. EDSA I, Marcos flees the country.
1987	New constitution with an American model of government and a president elected for one 6-year term.
1991	Local Government Code, expanding local autonomy.
1996	Peace agreement with the Moro National Liberation Front (MNLF).
2000–1	People Power Revolution, EDSA II: Impeachment against President Estrada. Estrada steps down.
2003	Cease-fire with the MNLF and formal negotiation begins.
2006	Short-lived State of Emergency and failed people power revolution. Debate over return to a unicameral parliamentary system.
2007	Soldiers make failed coup attempt in Manila.
2012	Government signs a peace agreement with Muslim rebel Moro Islamic Liberation Front (MILF) ending 40 years of armed conflict and expanding the Muslim autonomous region in the south.
2013	Parliament vote for state-funded contraception over opposition from the influential Catholic Church.
2014	MILF rebel group signs a peace deal with the government that finally ends the conflict after more than 40 years.
2015	Muslim rebels in the southern Philippines register to vote in the 2016 elections under the peace deal.

religion. On the one hand, the state wishes to limit and confine the role of religion in politics and state matters, but on the other, it needs religion to provide legitimacy. As Charles F. Keyes and his colleagues found:

> state policies toward religion in Asia have been shaped not only by modernization goals, but also by the needs of states to legitimate their rule and unify their populace ... While commitment to modernization entails rejection of those aspects of a society's past deemed impediments to a rationalized bureaucratic order, nation building depends on the very opposite move ... The process of creating modern nation states has thus entailed two rather contradictory stances towards religion. (Keyes et al., 1994: 5)

The relationship between religion and modern state building is a complex one because these unique characteristics of the influence of religion. In one sense, the relationship is competitive and often negative. As Donald E. Smith pointed out, 'political modernization includes, as one of its basic processes, the secularization of polities, and the progressive exclusion of religion from the political system'. In this process, the relationship is 'negative' (Smith, 1974: 4). Indeed, this has clearly been a dominant process in Pacific Asia. In some countries, such as China and Korea, such 'negative' political relations existed long before modern times.

Polity **secularization** is a process by which a traditional system undergoes radical differentiation, resulting in separation of the polity from religious structure, substitution of secular modes of legitimation, and extension of the polity's jurisdiction into areas formerly regulated by religious authority.

Smith, 1974: 4

Political modernization led to marginalization of religion from state affairs and the removal of religion as a form of public authority. However, religion has resisted this process, with varying degrees of success. As Keyes et al. observe, 'the rulers of the various Asians states have sought to co-opt, reshape, marginalize, and in some cases, suppress religious communities within the territories under their control to ensure that these communities do not promote visions that are in tension or conflict with their own'. However, the modernization and nation-building projects of Pacific Asians states have 'failed to subordinate religious authority to state authority' (Keyes et al., 1994: 1).

Despite political modernization, religious activity has remained resilient and pervasive as a form of public authority. In the view of Keyes et al., the resurgence of religion in Pacific Asia at the time of writing is not an indicator of 'the incompleteness of modernizing and national building projects' but rather 'a crisis of authority created under the modern state' (Keyes et al., 1994: 15).

An **Islamic state** is a polity built on the principles of Islamic teachings and governed by Islamic law. In Pacific Asia, no country is, or is declared to be, an Islamic state.

The role of religion in modern state building can be seen in various ways. First, the rise of the modern state as the sole legitimate form of public authority directly challenges religion as a form of public authority. In Pacific Asia, particularly in Southeast Asia, the tension between religion and the state has been a major feature of politics in the region. Religion continues to seek to influence and dominate the state and the state seeks to marginalize and confine the political role of religion.

Second, this tension has significantly shaped the emergent government system and state institutions. Religious forces were closely related to independence movements, political party systems, legal systems and ethnic relations in Pacific Asian countries.

Third, religion can provide significant support for political change, primarily as a form of legitimacy. In Pacific Asia, we have seen, for example, that military regimes patronize religious elites for the regime's legitimacy. Religious forces were also important players in major democratic movements and social revolutions in Pacific Asia.

Because of the way religion spread and interacted with the prevalent political structure and social life, there are significant differences between Northeast and Southeast Asia in the impact of religion on government and politics, and the role of religion in modern political development. In Southeast Asian countries – particularly in Indonesia and Malaysia, for example, the role of religion has been more

Table 9.1 The official or dominant religion in Pacific Asian countries

	Religion	*Percentage of population*
Cambodia	*Buddhism (Theravada)*	95
Indonesia	*Islam (Sunni)*	88
Japan	*Shintoism and Buddhism (Mahayana)*	84
N. Korea	*Buddhism (Mahayana)*	62
S. Korea	*Christianity and Buddhism*	29 23
Laos	*Buddhism (Theravada)*	65
Malaysia	*Islam (Sunni)*	66
Myanmar	*Buddhism (Theravada)*	89
Singapore	*Buddhism (Mahayana)*	43
Taiwan	*Buddhism (Mahayana) and Taoism*	93
Thailand	*Buddhism (Theravada)*	95
Philippines	*Christianity (Catholicism)*	81
Vietnam	*Buddhism (Mahayana/ Theravada)*	85

prominent, for two reasons. First, Islam is the dominant religion in Malaysia and Indonesia and has been seeking a greater role in politics and state affairs since the countries achieved independence. Second, alongside the dominant religion, there are other significant religions, notably Buddhism and Hinduism, resulting in constant tension among these different religions over the precise religious character of the state.

Having identified the general patterns of political change in the early post-war years, we now turn to examine the principal forms of non-pluralist politics that emerged from this process. Islam was in a strong position at independence to shape the fundamental nature of the new post-independent states in Malaysia and Indonesia. The force for Indonesia to be an Islamic state, for example, was active in the years before Suharto's New Order. Suharto took a firm approach to separate Islam from the state and Islamic forces were largely subdued during his rule.

Politically speaking, the role of Islam in Indonesia is limited, given its prominent presence in Indonesian society. Indonesia is not an Islamic state. Islam, Catholicism, Protestantism, Buddhism, Hinduism and Confucianism are the official religions. National civic and criminal law apply to the whole country except in Aceh, where Sharia law applies and there

Box 9.4

Islamization, and state institutions and politics in Malaysia

- Islamization is the process by which Islamic laws, values and practices are accorded greater significance in state, society and culture. It is a contemporary phenomenon partly associated with the postcolonial era and partly seen as an assertion or reassertion of identity in response to modernization. Islamization is a quest for the Islam ideal. It is an attempt to restore a pristine Islam that is perceived to be lost or disrupted as a result of Western colonial domination.
- In Malaysia, Islamization policies were conscientiously undertaken by the state from the mid-1980s. Malaysia sought to combine ever more comprehensive and accelerated Islamization polices with a growing middle class, modern lifestyle and material or consumer culture.
- Islamization has been advanced by both the long-standing ruling coalition Barisan Nasional led by UMNO as well as the opposition Islamist party Parti Islam Se-Malaysia. Principal Islamization policies introduced by UMNO since the 1980s include: expansion of both civil and criminal sharia laws as well as the amendments to the Muslim family laws in the thirteen states and three federal territories that constitute the Federation of Malaysia.
- Islamization has great implications for constitutionalism, the maintenance of pluralism and social cohesion, the integration of the state and its national community of citizenship, as well as Malaysian politics in general.

Othman, 2003: 125–126

are parallel Sharia courts. Even though Islam has a limited impact on state institutions, as a political force it does shape the dynamics of Indonesian politics, and more so after the fall of Suharto.

In contrast, while Malaysia is constitutionally not an Islamic state, the Islamic nature of the Malaysian state is significantly stronger – so much so that a former prime minister declared on 29 September 2001 that Malaysia is an Islamic state. Indeed, Islam is the only official religion declared in the constitution. All Malays, who are given privileges in the constitution and under the New Economic Policy, must be Muslim. There are Sharia courts, parallel to the civil courts, that deal with religious and family matters. Islamic fundamentalist forces are active in politics. The Pan-Malaysian Islamic Party (PAS) has won state elections in the past, and won 10 per cent of seats in the national legislature in the 2008 general election.

Another pair of countries that share features of religious–political relations in Southeast Asia is Thailand and Myanmar. In both countries, Buddhism plays an active role in national politics. Unlike Mahayana Buddhism in Northeast Asia, Theravada Buddhism traditionally maintains a close two-way relationship with the state and is much more closely integrated with society at large. It has been a tradition that the state supports and protects Buddhism and gives Buddhists special benefits and privileges in society. In return, the government seeks legitimacy for its rule in its relations with the Buddhist *sangha*.

The relationship between religion and the state is more difficult in Northeast Asia. Historically, the state in Japan, China and Korea has tried to eradicate the military, economic and potentially political power of religious groups, and reduce them to a mere social and communal existence with no significant influence on state affairs.

Religious reforms in Japan, before the Meiji Restoration, significantly reduced the political and economic, as well as the military, power and influence of Buddhist temples. The control of religion by the state was also seen in Korea and China, where the state depoliticized all religions, and suppressed severely any religious forces and activities that were deemed to be politically motivated. In all three countries, the state–religion relationship had been settled long before modern times, and in their early modern reforms, this tradition has largely continued. In terms of the separation of state and religion, 'modernization' in these countries has been complete and thorough.

Religion, on the other hand, can also provide moral and spiritual support for the new state. In Japan, the Meiji founders promoted Shintoism to the level of state religion. In Korea and China, the function of religion was very much fulfilled by Confucianism. Today, religious freedom and the separation of religion from the state are constitutionally protected in Japan and Korea. In Korea, Christian organizations played an important role in the democratization movement in the 1980s. In China, religion remains controlled by the state that in different periods has cracked down hard on any form of organized opposition. Examples include a long-standing tension with Tibetan Buddhists and the banning of Falun Gong, a religious organization promoting qigong spiritualism, following a gathering of 10,000 Falun Gong practitioners in the political heart of Beijing in 1999.

As the above review shows, religion is an important part of the identity of the peoples living in Pacific Asia that does not always fit neatly into state boundaries. In some countries, particularly in Southeast Asia, religion has sustained political organization and played an important role in the development of state institutions. In Northeast Asia, there is a long tradition of marginalization of religion as a form of public authority and its role is mainly confined to private sphere, social organization and ethical guidance.

Nations in the state

Most countries in Pacific Asia gained independence at the end of World War II (see Chapters 1 and 2). However, many of them did not settle on an integral and distinctive national basis for the newly established or reinstated state. Many of them have multinational, ethnic or religious groups within the state structure, with perhaps one nationality, ethnicity or religion dominant (Singapore, Malaysia, Myanmar, China, Indonesia, Philippines). Others share one national, ethnic or religious group with other states. Others still were nation states that have been divided in two, such as South Korea and North Korea and China and Taiwan. Similarly, South Vietnam and

North Vietnam were divided but united in 1975. Likewise, China and Hong Kong became 'one country' under a 'two system' arrangement in 1997.

Pacific Asian countries are therefore very interesting cases for studying state approaches to multination states (see Box 9.5). These countries have developed significant experience in managing relations between nations and the state in a multinational or divided-nation state environment. In this process, there have been and continue to be great tensions between state and 'minority' ethnic groups, and between ethnic groups themselves for control of state institutions or to even break away from the state.

Ethnicity is a collective quality of shared history, ancestry, language, culture, religion and/or kinship among a group of people usually in a common territory and with some sense of collective consciousness about their unique collective quality.

There has been a great deal of vibrant and at times violent identity politics driven by ethnicity, race, religion, and culture in Pacific Asia. Ethnicity is a difficult concept to define, as ethnic groups vary in their precise combinations of relevant traits. Some ethnic groups may share a common religion while others do not. Some may have a common territory while others do not. The definition here serves only as a general framework.

There are two further points that require some discussion. First, ethnicity is also a subject matter. Max Weber was one of the first to recognize the importance of a 'subject belief' among members of an ethnic group in their 'common descent' (Weber, 1968: 389). Richard Schermerhorn argues that consciousness of some kind among members of a group is 'a necessary accompaniment' for the concept of ethnicity (Schermerhorn, 1996: 17). This collective consciousness is essential for generating political activities and movements over ethnic identity.

Second, there is a subtle but critical, and politically very significant, difference between ethnic identity and national identity. While the two concepts largely overlap, as Colin Mackerras points out, national identity 'is also a legally valid term denoting country of citizenship' (Mackerras, 2003: 9). Ethnic identity alone does not denote citizenship.

People with a shared ethnicity tended to form natural communities before the modern era. Indeed,

Box 9.5

Multination states and nation-state building in Pacific Asia

There are states in Pacific Asia that have more than one national group claiming nationhood and potentially statehood. This has been a major challenge for modern nation state building and a significant source of political instability and change in these countries.

- Multination states are states in which more than one group seeks equal status and recognition as a constitutive member, usually making claims to self-determination. The constitutive members are nations in that they seek a state, or representation within a state, that gives them powers of self-determination either in the form of autonomy or federalism or through power sharing arrangements based on equality with the other constitutive nations.
- Multination states face similar structures of conflict. Their existence poses a fundamental challenge to the idea of the homogenous nation state where each state represents a single, relatively cohesive nation. Where this was absent, such a nation needed to be built either on the basis of a common cultural heritage or on the basis of shared political principles.
- Nation building and state building are parallel processes. Whereas past emphasis on nation building was accompanied by policies designed to integrate and assimilate various groups into a common core, in recent decades, integration and assimilation have become much less common. Instead, accommodation of minorities and the establishment of alternative means of representation have become relatively widespread.

Bertrand and Laliberté, 2010: 2–5

ethnicity and natural communities were mutually supportive. The emergence of modern nation-states and the promotion of national identity caused tension between the nation-state institutions and ethnicity-based communities and structures. This is described by Ernest Gellner as an 'incongruence' (Gellner, 1983: 1) between the political boundaries of states and the traditional boundaries of ethnic groups.

Ethnic identity is a distinct quality of an ethnic population that separates it from other ethnic groups within state boundaries. National identity is a distinct quality of a population that separates it from others across state boundaries. These two identities, however, are not always mutually exclusive, nor are they static. One identity may simultaneously have both ethnic and national elements.

Identity politics informed by ethnicity can therefore fall into two different categories. Ethnic politics in the first category, like identity politics centred on gender or social class, concerns the problem of identity within the state boundaries. At the heart of this type of ethnic politics are the precise relationships between ethnic groups and the state (Gladney, 1998; Mackerras, 2003). This is a problem in particular for former colonial societies. The challenge for them is to develop a 'common will' and a 'common citizenship' (Furnivall, 1944: 447, 451), and indeed a common nation, over what S. J. Furnivall called a 'plural society', where two or more elements or social orders 'live side by side, yet without mingling, in one political unit' (Furnivall, 1944: 446).

In the second category, there are challenges to the state boundaries themselves on the basis of ethnicity, religion or even political economy. In the second category, the claims of ethnicity-based groups or populations are not about their rights and privileges within state boundaries but rather their sovereign rights as a political community separate from the state. The identity in question is national identity, the satisfaction of which requires a country of citizenship. Their ultimate aim is complete independence as a separate nation-state.

In reality, however, the line between ethnic politics within the existing state boundaries and ethnic

Case Study Lab 9.1

Ethnic politics and the 'character of the state': how ethnic politics influences the unity and stability of the nation-state

There are various forms of ethnic tensions and certainly different causes and circumstances in each country for variations in ethnic politics. More importantly, however, according to David Brown who systemically examined the problem of ethnic politics and the state in Southeast Asia, is how ethnic politics shapes political structure, political stability, unity and state institutions, or the 'character of the state'. Three approaches or perspectives have been put forward on this question:

Primordial perspective: Ethnicity as culturally embedded group loyalty. Ethnic identity is ascriptive, fixed and given as well as the place from which political action begins. The greater the tendency towards cultural pluralism the more societies with markedly different cultural communities will have problems managing their intergroup relations and the more likely it is that political instability can be avoided only by some form of authoritarian state.

Situationalist perspective: Ethnicity acts as a political resource that individuals employ in response to the environment. It promotes group coherence and facilitates the articulation of both group and individual interests. Politics, therefore, may result in either competitive pluralist bargaining or intergroup conflict.

State character perspective: Ethnicity is a form of ideological consciousness. Ethnicity is interpreted here as an ideology individuals employ to resolve insecurities arising from the power structures in which they operate. As the state has a decisive influence on such power structures and provides legitimacy for the structure, any analysis of ethnicity and its relationship to the unity and the stability of the nation-state must start with the character of the state.

Brown, 1994: xii–xix

politics in seeking national independence is not always clear. Ethnic groups tend to hold both ethnic and national claims. Political realities often lead to settlements, compromises or a status quo that stops short of complete independence. In the following sections, we shall look at cases of ethnic politics in the first category where different state strategies have shaped state–ethnic group relations in a modern society. This is evident in the two classic cases of Malaysia and Singapore. We then explore the impact of changing political boundaries on ethnic identity in the cases of Myanmar and China.

The Malaysian model: Ethnic bargaining

Three ethnic groups were politically significant for the new independent Malaya: Malay (50.4 per cent), Chinese (23.7 per cent) and Indian (7.1 per cent). When independence was granted in the 1950s, these ethnic groups were not geographically separate from each other. Therefore, they needed to learn to live with one another within a single 'political unit'.

The political reality, however, was that almost everything significant was divided along ethnic lines, including social and economic life and even political parties. The construction of the new state therefore started from this reality. As A. B. Shambul observes, 'the emergence of a nationalist discourse and movement in Malaysia inevitably has been shaped and given signification within an ethnic framework' (Shambul, 1998: 137). The reality that the Chinese and Indians were economically privileged while the Malays had the political power led to early failures in ethnic group–state relations. In the late 1940s, the British supported the Malay Union, which cut the power of the Malay rulers and gave citizenship to non-Malays. This, however, was only short-lived. Political relations among the three groups and their relations with the state were not settled even with the ethnic settlements after independence. Continuing tensions and conflicts led to the ethnic riots of 1969.

Positive discrimination: The New Economic Policy in Malaysia from the 1970s to the 1990s was designed to promote the interests, well-being and social status of Malays, in order to provide more balanced social and economic development among the different ethnic groups in Malaysia.

In Shambul's view, efforts to build Malay dominance started long before the 1969 riot. Shambul divided this process into two periods: the 'articulation of Malay dominance' during the pre-1969 period and the moving from 'dominance to hegemony' in the post-1969 period.

In particular, during the post-1969 period, the New Economic Policy introduced a series of initiatives to address the problem of the social and economic status of Malays (Shambul, 1998: 145–7), which included:

- Significant increases in public expenditure on social programmes for both rural and urban Malays, to create 'a community of Malay entrepreneurs';
- Special schemes to enhance educational opportunities for Malays;
- Poverty eradication programme for Malay poor;
- Legislation to ensure that Malay interests were non-negotiable and to outlaw 'politicking' on Malay-related issues;
- The Sedition Act of 1970 to declare seditious and punishable any public discussion on Malay rights and privileges, on Islam, on Malay rulers or the Malay language.

The views, however, are not unanimous on the ethnic nature of the Malaysian nation. Cheah Boon Kheng, for example, distinguishes Malay ethnonationalism and Malaysian nationalism in the making of the Malaysian nation, and argues that

> in spite of Malay dominance in Malaysia, the country has not become a 'Malay nation-state'. This process has been checked by the rival forces of multi-ethnic 'Malaysian nationalism' in peninsular Malaysia and the contesting nationalisms and communalism of the other indigenous communities, or bumpiptra, in the East Malaysian states of Sarawak and Sabah. (Cheah, 2002: back cover)

The construction of state–ethnic group relations in post-independent Malaysia clearly shows the power of ethnic identity in shaping politics and government, and the building of the modern state itself. Given that the core thrust of the development of state–ethnic group relations has been to enhance Malay's political as well as economic dominance through state programmes and initiatives, firm involvement by the state in the process is clearly apparent. Here, state dominance and ethnic dominance have supported each other.

The Singaporean model: Citizenship and multiculturalism

The makeup of founding ethnic groups in Singapore is similar to Malaysia's except that the percentages of Chinese and Malays were reversed: Chinese 76.8 per cent, Malay 13.9 per cent and Indian 7.9 per cent. The historical circumstances were also similar. Singapore was gaining independence from British rule and forming a new state with a designated territory that included distinct ethnic groups with different social and economic conditions and political agendas and influence. The dominant ethnic group, the Chinese, was also uneasy with the new state. What emerged in Singapore, however, was a very different model of state–ethnic group relations.

At the core of this was the fact the state in Singapore took a very different position towards the dominant ethnic group. Instead of privileging the dominant ethnic group over others, the state promoted the concept of citizenship over ethnic differences. Instead of fitting the state institutions to the ethnic reality, the Singapore state promoted 'Singaporean' as the new national identity over and above ethnic identities.

As discussed earlier, the Singapore state was imposed on a set of diverse ethnic populations. There was little substance in the notion of Singapore as a nation at the very beginning. 'On political independence, a "new nation" had to be formulated and produced' (Kuo, 1995: 106). Eddie Kuo lists the key aspects of 'formulating and producing' the new nation (Kuo, 1995: 106–16):

- The making of a new state that distances itself from specific ethnic groups and represents national interests in the campaign for national survival, and where possible ethnic claims are confined to the framework of multiculturalism;
- The making of a new economic order that requires a workforce, job training and resource and income distribution detached from one's racial background.
- The making of a new social order where housing, education, language and family planning policies enhance national identity.

The process of nation building can therefore also be a process of state building. A sense of national community, national identity and national interests reinforces the sense of statehood. The building of the nation also requires the use of state power, and thus strengthens the state's capacity and the development of state institutions. Michael Hill and Kwen Fee Lian argue the exercise of state power took three forms: economic, ideological and political (Hill and Lian, 1995: 22). Here, in particular, we see the role of ideology in the shaping of the nation and the national identity. The process of nation-state building in Singapore was simultaneously a process for the formation of the national ideology, what Beng Huat Chua called 'communitarian ideology' (Chua, 1995: 9–39).

Multiracialism: Singapore is promoted as a multiracial society through government initiatives and programmes, to ensure that 'racial tolerance is to be safeguarded in the law. In doing so, the government places itself in a neutral space that arguably compels it to act in ways that do not privilege any particular group; racial cultural practices are then relegated to the realm of private and voluntaristic, individual or collective, practices' (Chua and Kuo, 1995: 106).

The formation of state–ethnic group relations in Malaysia and Singapore saw two different strategies by the state to shape relationships with ethnic groups. As Hefner and his colleagues have observed, each country has developed a strikingly different response to the challenge of citizenship and diversity (Hefner, 2001). The Malaysian state, in preserving the Malay character of the state, promotes and protects the interests of the dominant ethnic group. One can argue that much of this politics and state building was driven by the ethnic reality of Malay dominance. In Singapore, the state separates the problem of ethnic groups from the state, and promotes and protects the interests of the state in relation to ethnic groups. In both cases, ethnic politics has been largely subdued and state power and capacity enhanced.

The Myanmar model

For many countries, including the Philippines, Indonesia, China, Thailand and Myanmar, different ethnic groups are included within the larger state. There are many historical reasons for their inclusion. However, in each case, relations between the state and these ethnic or religious groups are politically contested. Such tensions have led to armed conflict between the ethnic and religious groups and the state. Political and military solutions to these tensions have been used to attempt to fully integrate these groups into the state institutions.

In some cases, federalism and local autonomy for ethnic groups make a political solution possible. In other cases, ethnic groups are integrated into the state system through military force.

The case of Myanmar is instructive here. Ashley South (2008) provides a detailed overview of ethnic conflicts in Myanmar showing how a state of ethnic pluralism in the pre-colonial era was followed by intensive ethnic conflict for much of the post-World War II decades when the military government sought to integrate breakaway ethnic states into the nation-state through a military solution. Since the 1990s, however, as Smith (2007) argues:

> a greater understanding has developed among leading stakeholders about the fundamental need for change. A majority of ethnic nationality parties have modified their political stands from often separatist demands in their formative years to pro-federal positions today. (Smith, 2007: xi)

Faced with a military standoff, chronic underdevelopment and a long-term cycle of conflict, key actors representing sixteen ethnic groups and the military-controlled central government negotiated a ceasefire in 2015. The Myanmar model, therefore, shows how both political and military solutions have been sought to resolve long-standing ethnic conflicts where one or more ethnic group seeks secession from the state. However, most importantly, the case shows how political agreements and power sharing can create potential solutions to seemingly intractable ethnic conflicts and illustrates the ultimate futility of long-term military conflict.

The Chinese state and ethnic minorities

The strong state involvement in the formation of ethnic identity is demonstrated more clearly in the case of China. Unlike Singapore, Malaysia and Myanmar where state boundaries were drawn at the end of colonial rule, the constant shifting of the boundaries of imperial China has brought various ethnic populations within its political boundary.

An added complication has been the communist rule in China after the Second World War, which took an ideologically different approach towards the problem of state–ethnic group relations. A third factor in this state–ethnic group relationship is the fact that China deliberately chose a unitary state model rather than a federal state model at the establishment of the PRC (see Chapter 3). It is difficult to see the principles of unitary state and ethnic autonomy working well together.

China has a total of fifty-five 'ethnic/national minority' groups, with five of them granted the status of an autonomous region: Zhuang (Guangxi), Mongol (Inner Mongolia), Hui (Ningxia), Urgur (Xinjiang) and Tibetan (Tibet). Apart from Tibet and Xinjiang, which see activities and movements on both levels of ethnic and national identity, 'China's policy towards its minorities has been generally successful in integrating the various ethnic regions into China, at least in the sense that political control over these areas is generally firmer than at most periods in the past' (Mackerras, 2003: 42).

As Dru C. Gladney (1998b) argues, the problem of ethnic minorities is essentially related to modern nation-state building. The ultimate driving force behind the shaping and reshaping of ethnic boundaries/relations is the state and its persistence in control and domination. At the heart of ethnic politics is manipulation by the state, and its negotiation with ethnic groups, a process in which both the state and ethnic groups seek to strengthen their position over the other.

Ethnic/national minority is the term used in China for ethnic groups other than Han Chinese. While the concept 'is a useful one and is usually quite applicable' in conceptualizing the 'majority–minority relations' ... 'Some peoples do not accept the tag of "ethnic minority" and consider it demeaning and insulting' (Mackerras, 2003: 10).

Table 9.2 Top ten ethnic groups in China (millions)

Ethnic group	*Han*	*Zhuang*	*Manchu*	*Hui*	*Miao*	*Uygur*	*Yi*	*Tujia*	*Mongol*	*Tibetan*	*Buyi*
Population	1042	15.5	9.8	8.6	7.4	7.2	6.5	5.7	4.8	4.5	2.5
Status of Autonomous Region		Yes		Yes		Yes			Yes	Yes	

National Bureau of Statistics of China 1990.

The organizing principle of the unitary state compels the state to impose political, economic and cultural order, to enforce integration and assimilation and PRC citizenship over ethnic identities. Under such an overarching political order, the scope of autonomy is limited. As studies by Melissa J. Brown and Chih-yu Shih argue, ethnic identity in China is shaped through constant negotiation between the state and ethnic groups (Brown, 1996; Shih, 2002) in what Harrell describes as a 'civilizing project' (Harrell, 1995). Moreover, in a unified state like China there is always the potential for social justice issues to become conflated as ethnic conflict (Cheng, 2014).

States over religion, culture or nation

The situation is reversed in the case of states over divided nations, culture or religion. Major civic and geopolitical conflicts after World War II combined with shifting boundaries in the premodern, colonial and modern eras led to the rise of states over a divided nation. The Korean War from 1950 to 1953 led to the division of the Korean nation and the establishment of two Korean states. The Civil War in China culminated in the national government and Republic of China fleeing to Taiwan to maintain and build separate state institutions to the People's Republic of China. The Vietnam War resulted in North and South Vietnam for the three decades from the 1950s to 1975 at which time the North unified the country by force. Hong Kong was under British administration from 1841 to 1997 (excluding Japanese occupation from 1941 to 1945) following the cession of Hong Kong during the First Opium War (1839–42). Hong Kong was integrated into the PRC in 1997 under the 'one country, two systems' formula.

National identity and states

In the above sections, we discussed a critical difference between ethnic and national identities. Ethnic identity can be the basis for national identity (East Timor, for example), but national identity does not necessarily require ethnic identity (Singapore as a case in point). If ethnic identity is based on something we are born with (natural), then national identity can develop over time (nurtured). While ethnic identity can be accommodated within a large political unit, national identity, under the modern international system of nation-states, is a sense of exclusive membership in a sovereign political unit. For an ethnic group without such an exclusive political unit, national identity motivates them to seek one (such as in East Timor). It can also be the outcome of the process of identity formation for people in a political unit (for example, Singapore).

Table 9.3 shows claims and movements for a political unit of sovereignty or autonomy in Pacific Asia. Except in the unique case of Taiwan, which will be discussed in the following sections, all of them are ethnic groups within a state that have claims to independence and have sought separation from the state they have found themselves part of for a long period.

Of all the eight cases, only East Timor has gained independence, after twenty-five years of Indonesian rule and the collapse of the Suharto regime. All others either reached agreement with the state for various levels of political autonomy, or see no solution in sight for a political settlement.

The pattern of the claims and movements for independence in Pacific Asia reveals an important area of identity politics. Ethnic politics can be both a problem of state–ethnic group relations and a problem of international relations. Even though a majority of the cases settled for some form of political autonomy at the level of state–ethnic group relations, whether the existing ethnic tensions and conflicts will remain at the level of state–ethnic group relations or manifest as a problem of international relations is uncertain. It depends on the evolution of their relations with the state and the ever-changing international political environment.

Chinese civilization and the cultural identities of 'Confucian' societies

Identity politics is not only important within state boundaries. It is also a phenomenon across national boundaries. A unique case here is the legacy of Chinese civilization and Confucianism in societies, such as Japan, Korea, Taiwan, Vietnam and Singapore. These societies were once dominated (or are still dominated) by Chinese culture. This naturally raises the question of how people in these countries relate themselves to Chinese culture and Confucian values and to the question of cultural identity in Confucian societies.

The issue of the cultural identity of Confucian societies (Pye, 1985) is an important one, for several reasons. First, the ups and downs of Chinese culture and Confucianism over the past decades in Pacific Asia has led to some level of ambivalence among people in these societies over their cultural roots. The early wave of economic miracles in countries on the periphery of China raised challenging questions about the value of Confucianism and the relationship between China and Confucianism (Tu, 1991). Indeed, the question had been raised a hundred years earlier in Japan. The Meiji Restoration was a turning point, when Japan moved on from its intellectual and institutional tradition of Confucianism.

The question of the cultural identity of Confucian societies is also an issue in many of the political discourses and scholarly debates between East and West. The Asian values debate in the 1990s (see Chapter 2), for example, put the cultural identity of these Confucian societies to the test. While Singapore is a strong advocate of Asian values, Japan is more ambiguous on where it stands in the debate.

The issue also has real political economic implications. The rapprochement between China and South Korea since 1992 has aroused nostalgic feelings among South Koreans about their cultural roots and traditions. However, for many South Koreans, the real issue is not to reconnect to Confucianism or Chinese culture; it is a matter of rediscovering and redefining their own cultural identity that has long been under the shadow of Chinese culture. Popular views and perceptions in these two countries of their cultural heritage and identity led to a resentment on both sides over many historical and cultural issues. This has in turn impacted the political and diplomatic relations between the two countries. At the same time, shared historical memory between Korea and China, such as over Japanese representations of their wartime activities during the Imperial era (see Bukh, 2007 and Schneider, 2008), reinforces shared historical and cultural roots.

The political, social and economic implications of cultural identity in relation to China are more significant in Taiwan than in any other Confucian society. Identity politics in Taiwan have developed since the 1980s to a point where whether one claims to be Chinese, how schools teach Chinese history, whether companies should keep their Chinese names, and

Table 9.3 National identity claims and independence movements in Pacific Asia

	State involved	*Settlement*
East Timor	Indonesia	Independence in 2002
Aceh	Indonesia	Broad autonomy through the Peace Agreement of 2006
Malay Muslims in the south	Thailand	No
Taiwan	China	No
Tibet	China	Low-intensity tension
Muslims in Xinjiang	China	Low-intensity tension
Muslim Mindanao	Philippines	2014 peace agreement with broad autonomy
Ethnic groups in northern Myanmar	Myanmar	National ceasefire agreement October 2015

so on, have become major political issues. National identity and how one perceives Taiwan's relations with China have been a primary election issue and a rallying point for much of its national politics. Identity politics in Taiwan is clearly an example of where identity is a primary force shaping politics.

Korea and Taiwan: Nation and state

We have so far discussed two forms of ethnicity-centred politics: ethnicity and state–ethnic group relations; and national identity and independence claims and movements. There is another form of ethnic politics involved in the dynamics of identity formation and its interaction with contemporary political, economic and international processes. This is a form of identity politics where different national identities can develop among people of the same ethnicity. Inter-Korean relations and China–Taiwan relations are two such cases.

Korea has been an independent nation for thousands of years. However, as Samuel S. Kim observes, wars, conquests, colonialism and liberalization have clearly left their mark on the collective identity of the Korean people. The Korean War in particular 'initiated a decisive shift in identity politics from the competition of multiple identities to the dominance of the Cold War identity. As a consequence, the collective identity of Korea as a whole nation was weakened radically' (Kim, 2006: 3). For the Koreas, the Cold War identity means that while ethnically they may still be the same group, politically, economically and more importantly, ideologically, they are not. The Cold War structure in general and the Korean War in particular divided the nation in two.

Under this overall divisive international structure, separate systems of ideology, government, economy and social life developed inside North Korea and South Korea. The North Korean system features the *Juche* ideology, the communist party state, socialist economy, and controlled social life. In South Korea, there has been profound social and economic development and political change. At the time of writing,

Case Study Lab 9.2

Ethnic nationalism in Korea

There is a strong sense of ethnic national unity in Korea and a lot of research trying to explain the rise of Korean ethnic nationalism and its role in modern Korea. Gi-Wook Shin, for example, takes on some of the widely held conceptions and theories about nation, ethnicity and nationalism, explores and defines the powerful form of nationalism in Korea and discusses its role in the shaping of the modern Korean state.

- Explanations of ethnic nationalism in modern Korea inevitably centre around debate on nation, nationalism and ethnicity. Shin's analysis focuses on three areas of the debate and identifies the different ways of framing the problem:
  - Nationalism defines modernity or modernity defines nationalism? Modernity is defined by nationalism in the Korean case.
  - Nation as constructed, something new and modern, a product of nationalist mobilization of uniquely modern dimensions; or as primordial, the continuation of long-standing patterns of ethnicity, built on pre-existing geographic or cultural foundations. The prior existence of ethnicity explains much of modern nationality.
  - Traditional view that political nationalism is civil, integrative and constructive while ethnic nationalism is seen as dangerous, divisive and destructive. In Korea, ethnic nationalism has a positive role in nation-state building.
- There exists a substantial overlap between the levels of race, ethnicity and nation in Korea.
- The historical origins and politics of Korean national identity are based on a sense of ethnic homogeneity.
- Korean national identity based on ethnic homogeneity is a product of a particular historical process.
- Identity has crucial behavioural consequences. A sense of ethnic unity has served Koreans in a variety of ways from forming the foundation ideology for anti-colonialism to that of national unification.

Shin, 2006: 3–18

almost every aspect of the political, ideological and economic systems is fundamentally different from those of the North Korean system. This is perhaps the reason for Samuel S. Kim's observation that, decades after the Korean War, 'the end of the Cold War, as well as the collapse and transformation of the communist world, failed to turn inter-Korean identity politics around' (Kim, 2006: 3).

Today, both North Korea and South Korea are members of the United Nations. Inter-Korean (rather than intra-Korean) relations occur as relations between two states and are widely accepted and recognized by the two Koreas and by the international community.

The Korean case raises important questions for the nation-state debate. Mainstream theories from Max Weber onwards centre on the expectation that state and ethnic boundaries are 'congruent'. As the experiences elsewhere in Pacific Asia indicate, this can be achieved either by the domination of the state over a multiethnic society, or the domination of the state by a principal ethnic group. The Korean case suggests, first, that ethnic identity can be less relevant to the formation of a nation-state if other conditions are more important. The international structure and power politics and a sustainable development of political economy can be a vital part of the 'other conditions'. Moreover, national identity is often closely attached to an ethnic identity, but national identity can be based on other conditions despite existing ethnic identities.

The issue of ethnic identity, national identity and the nation-state is also seen in the case of Taiwan. There is a complicated and ambiguous relationship between ethnic and national identity in Taiwan, largely because of its difficult relations with China. Consequently, while many studies point to the trend of an increasing proportion of 'Taiwanese identifiers', others find that the people of Taiwan lack consensus on national identity issues (Huang, Chi, 2005: 66). One school of thought believes that there was a distinct Taiwanese identity and a Taiwanese collective consciousness, but this has been compromised by the rule of external and colonial powers. Efforts in recent years to promote a 'Taiwanese identity' are an attempt to restore the original Taiwanese roots (Makeham and Hsiau, 2005). June T. Dreyer holds a similar view, and argues that a sense of identity apart from that of China has existed in Taiwan for more than a century. The 228 Incident and the 1979 Kaohsiung Incident were important markers in the development of a modern Taiwanese identity (Dreyer, 2003).

Another school of thought seeks a political economic explanation for the emergence of a new Taiwanese identity. It places the formation of the new Taiwanese national identity within the large context of the post-war political and economic development in Taiwan (Gold, 2003; Chu, 2004). Undoubtedly, the emergence of Taiwanese consciousness and a collective identity is a consequence of the dynamics of the political economy on the island since the 1960s, which includes a separate domain of politics, economy, law and public administration, as well as membership of society and citizenship of the state. In particular, the separation of China and Taiwan in political and economic life for a century has cemented and perpetuated the distinct Taiwanese identity.

Moreover, intellectuals, politicians, civic movements and the mass media in Taiwan have actively promoted the idea of a distinct Taiwanese identity thereby supporting the rise of Taiwanese consciousness and collective identity. This is connected to what Shelley Rigger calls the policy preferences of various political forces over the political question of unification or independence (Rigger, 2003). It is an elite-led cultural and social movement, and a government-led political campaign, to reconstruct the collective identity, or what Christopher Hughes calls 'the post-nationalist identity' (Hughes, 1997: 155), and reform the institutional setting supporting the 'China-centered paradigm' of the past.

As Yun-han Chu observed, political and economic development in Taiwan, and internal politics in particular, have had a significant impact on the formation or reformation of national identity in Taiwan (Chu, 2004). For example, under Presidents Li Teng-hui and Chen Shui-bian, a strategy of Taiwanization was evident in education and government policy.

However, under President Ma Ying-jeou, as Hughes (2014) argues, there has been an administrative 'turn towards Chinese identity' which is as much 'a function of the international balance of power as it is the reflection of domestic actors' political views or leaders' personal preferences' (Hughes, 2014: 134).

This shift stabilized cross-strait relations but has not been universally popular. Disapproval culminated in 2014 in an unprecedented occupation of the Legislative Yuan and Executive Yuan by the Sunflower Student Movement in protest to ongoing economic deals opening cross-strait trade and services with China. With the 2016 election of Tsai Ing-wen and first ever DPP majority in the legislature, elite-led social and cultural movements may once again shift back to a focus on promoting Taiwanese, as opposed to Chinese, identity.

The relationship between Taiwanese politics, cross-strait relations and Taiwanese identity is therefore very fluid and contested. As Zhong (2016) argues, while Taiwan identity is complicated and multi-layered

> most Taiwanese people do not identify themselves with the mainland Chinese state even though they still associate themselves with the Chinese nation … [T]he Chinese government should … remain hopeful since an overwhelming majority of people in Taiwan still identity themselves as being part of the big Chinese nation … When people in Taiwan assume a new national ethno-cultural identity that is different from their current Chinese ethno-cultural identity, Taiwan will become a new nation-state. This shift is probably going to take a much longer time to occur. (Zhong, 2016: 16–17)

With such an intensified political nature of the issue of ethnic and national identity in Taiwan, it is clear that identity has played – and will continue to play – a central role in Taiwan's politics and government.

The problem of ethnic and national identity in Korea and Taiwan suggests that the relationship between the two identities is not simply a case of one leading to another. Under modern political, economic and social conditions, as well as the international structure and system, ethnicity is not always the primary factor in determining political boundaries, and does not necessarily always lead to a national identity. National identity can develop under various conditions in spite of existing ethnic identities. This is particularly true in times of war, international power politics, and subsequent political, economic and social change and development.

One country, two systems

In 1997, ninety-nine years after being leased to Great Britain, Hong Kong was returned to China. In the decades leading to the return, London and Beijing set up the Basic Law providing the constitutional basis for Hong Kong after return and defining Hong Kong's constitutional relations with China.

> Our policy is **'one country, two systems'**. More specifically, under the People's Republic of China, the mainland with its 1 billion population will have its socialism while Hong Kong, Taiwan will practice their capitalism. This policy will not change for 50 years.
>
> Deng Xiaoping, 1984: 58

The constitutional arrangement for Hong Kong to return to China and China-HK relations raised many important issues for politics and government, for the modern international system and for nation-state building in particular. First, under this agreement is the reference to 'one country' more a reference to one state or one country? In the Chinese wording (*yiguo*), there is no clear distinction between country and state. In practice, this gives some space for further political development. Second, is this formulation a question of merely 'two systems' (political, economic and perhaps social) or does this then extend to a question of 'two states'? Again, the Chinese wording (*liangzhi*) can be interpreted either way. The key marker for these questions will be the evolution of Hong Kong–Beijing relations in the coming decades.

Third, is this arrangement transitional, to be shaped by political forces and interests of parties involved, or will it stabilize as a permanent arrangement as time goes by? This is a significant question because the issue will provide a marker of how the current international nation-state system handles a complicated situation where nation and state emerged from a complex set of structural forces.

The heart of the challenge for Hong Kong and Beijing is how the political setup in Hong Kong works within the overall state system of China as well as how the overall constitutional order works. Hong Kong's position in the Chinese state system is complicated by its colonial experience, its distinct British-style legal and administrative systems, the

Hong Kong people's desire to achieve functioning representative democracy and China's own ongoing modern state building. The international system does not recognize political arrangements beyond the nation-state system. How a different 'system' functions within a singular constitutional order is therefore a serious challenge for nation and state building in China. A key variable in successful integration of 'two systems' into 'one country' will not only be how effective this integration is at a practical level, but how people in Hong Kong view the process vis-à-vis their own identity construction.

Taken together, these cases of identity politics show that ethnic and national identity is important for understanding politics and international relations in the region. Moreover, they show static and linear analysis of the role of identity politics cannot fully account for and explain the dynamic relations between identities and nation-state building in Pacific Asia.

Chapter summary

- Nationalism in the early twentieth century focused on nation building, sovereignty, struggles against colonial rule and state building. Nationalism has been effective at bringing the state together in Pacific Asia. A further challenge, however, has come from managing the various national, ethnic and religious groups and identities within the state.
- The influence of religion in Pacific Asian politics and government is moderate and generally confined by the state. Its effect on the modern state is much more significant in Southeast Asian than in Northeast Asian countries.
- Multination states are a significant issue in government and politics in Pacific Asia. They post a challenge to the broad trend of moving towards the unitary nation state. Ethnic politics generates significant pressures for both state and nation building. There have been different patterns in Pacific Asian countries of how ethnic tensions with the state are addressed and managed and how state-ethnic group relations are arranged.
- On the other side of the nation and state problem, many states have formed out of the same cultural and national basis either through postcolonial political settlements, the lingering effects of the breaking down of the traditional imperial and civilizational structure, and war and conflicts in the post-war years. There is a constant tension in the relations among these new states of the same historical, cultural civilization and even national background, their identity and institutions of interaction and their relations with the international system.

Further reading

For religion and the modern state, see Keyes et al. (1994), Smith (1971, 1974) and Haynes (2006). For religion and political change, particularly democratic change, see van der Veer and Lehmann (1999), Diamond et al. (2005), Cheng and Brown (2006) and Haynes (2006). For Islamization and nation-state in Pacific Asia, see Othman (2003). For the role of traditional institutions, such as the monarchy in the modern nation state, see Chaloemtiaranba (2007), Terwiel (2011) and Marshal (2014). For ethnicity, nation and nation state building see Bertrand and Laliberté (2010), Germar, Machie and Wohr (2014) and Shin (2006). On ethnic politics in Pacific Asia, particularly the problem of ethnic groups and their relations with the state, see Chua (1995), Hill and Lian (1995), Brown (1996), Gladney (1998), Hefner (2001), Shih (2002), Mackerras (2003) and Rossabi (2004).

Study questions

1 What are the differences between ethnic identity and national identity? How do the differences complicate ethnic politics in Pacific Asia?

2 How does Islamization in some Pacific Asian countries affect politics and government in these countries?

3 Are citizenship and multiculturalism an effective model of managing ethnic–state relations in multinational states?

4 The relationship between ethnic identity and national identity is a difficult one. Use examples from Pacific Asian countries to explain the differences between the two and the role of the state in the formation of ethnic and national identity.

5 Considering changes in Taiwanese identity, how could cross-strait relations evolve in the coming decades? Can ethnic nationalism in Korea provide the necessary foundation for a unitary Korean nation state in the future?

Key terms

Nationalism (248); Identity (248); Secularization (253); Islamic state and Islamization (254); Ethnicity (248); National, ethnic, cultural identity (248); Identity politics (251); Ethnic bargaining (258); Multiethnic society (264); National unification and national independence (264); Nation building and state building (256); Positive discrimination (258); Ethnic politics (257); Citizenship and multiracialism (259); Ethnic/national minority (260); Confucian societies (262); One country, two systems (265).

Chapter 10
Pacific Asia and the world

In earlier chapters, we found that one cannot fully understand politics and government in Pacific Asian countries without grasping the impact of the international system, regional structure, and transnational dynamics and movements. From colonialism to independence movements, from modernization to globalization, from Marxism and socialism to capitalism and democracy, all these major ideas, movements and institutional developments in Pacific Asian countries have their sources or roots outside these countries and outside this region. Conversely, politics and government in Pacific Asia have been sources of international tensions, confrontation, war, as well as development and world order.

This chapter explores two levels of interaction in the relations of Pacific Asian states, the regional structure and institutions and the world system and global dynamics. More specifically, we shall first have a brief discussion of how the traditional concepts and practices of the world system in Pacific Asia met with the global forces of imperialism, colonialism, nationalism, communism and capitalism. This will be followed by an examination of how regional institutions evolved in response to both national and global developments.

We shall examine the dynamics and general characteristics of regionalism in Pacific Asia, and the domestic sources of the regional behaviour of these countries. The chapter will then take up some key issues and demonstrate how global forces and movements shape the politics and governance of Pacific Asian countries. We shall also analyse motivations and constraints on Pacific Asian countries' responses to and the management of external influences. Finally, we shall discuss the growing influence of Pacific Asian countries in international relations and the implications for the international system. But first we shall begin with an analytical framework of linkage politics to help us to understand the dynamic interaction between domestic and international politics in Pacific Asia.

The nexus of global, regional and national politics

Since James N. Rosenau's study of linkage politics in the 1960s (Rosenau, 1969), it has been well established in the discipline that we cannot fully understand national politics and government without placing them in the context of the external forces and structure and dynamics with which they interact. The national–international linkage is 'any recurrent sequence of behaviour that originates in one system and is reacted to in another' (ibid.: 45).

In other words, patterns of domestic politics, such as political regimes, or political change, can be explained in part by movements, developments and structures at both global and regional levels. Two classic cases of this are the dominance of ideology in national politics in the 1950s and 1960s as a consequence of the Cold War and political liberalization and democratic transition in Pacific Asian countries in the 1980s and 1990s as part of the global wave of democratization.

Conversely, phenomena and activities at the international level can be partly explained by political dynamics, institutions and alliances of forces at the national level. The 'soft institutionalism' in building regional cooperation and integration in Pacific Asia, for example, is largely determined by the dominant concerns of the national elites in Pacific Asian countries over their national sovereignty and the political legitimacy of their governing regime.

As another example, for many, the wars in the post-Second World War Pacific Asia – the Korean War and the Vietnam War – and indeed the development of the Cold War were effects of the global Cold War structure. For many others, these wars had their roots deep in the internal civil and social conflicts of these countries. The linkages between national politics and international politics therefore are important for us to understand politics and government in Pacific Asian countries. We not only need to know that politics at these two levels are linked, but more importantly, also how they are linked.

Rosenau describes three basic types of 'linkage processes' (Rosenau, 1969: 46):

- Penetrative process: This occurs when members of one polity serve as participants in the political processes of another. They share with those in the penetrated polity the authority to allocate its values. Christian missionaries in the early modern period, foreign aid agents in the 1960s and 1970s, Greenpeace branches, and the operations of multinational corporations in contemporary times are all good examples of the penetrative process.
- Reactive process: This is brought into being by recurrent and similar boundary-crossing reactions rather than by the sharing of authority. Reactions in China to the West's criticism of Tiananmen in 1989; to the United States over its Belgrade bombings in 1999; and to Japan over historical issues in 2005 are all examples of a reactive process.
- Emulative process: This process corresponds to the so-called 'diffusion' or 'demonstration' effect, whereby political activities in one country are perceived and emulated in another. To a great extent, the democratic movements in the 1980s and 1990s can be seen as an example of such a process. Japan's imperialist expansion in the first half of the twentieth century is another. Reform of the electoral systems in Japan, Korea and Taiwan in the 1990s and 2000s are another example.

The discussion of the regional and global structures and dynamics in this chapter is therefore intended to help us to better understand the broader context of the patterns, dynamics and institutions in national politics, and the ways in which the political dynamics, structures and institutions at national and international levels affect one another.

The linkage between national and international politics, however, is not always as straightforward as described in Rosenau's model. Indeed, given the statist tradition in Pacific Asian countries, particularly their notion and practices of sovereignty, national–international linkages can be distorted, managed or interrupted. So before we move on to discuss the dynamics, structures and institutions at the regional and international levels, we shall first look at the factors that have impacted in the evolution principles and practices of the modern interstate system in Pacific Asia.

Modern interstate system in Pacific Asia

To understand the 'local–regional–global nexus' (Kim, 2004: 3) in Pacific Asia, we start with a survey of the changes in the political landscape since World War II (for early regional systems see Chapter 1). We argue the different types of states and their politico-economic development are the basis of the emergent interstate system in the region.

The section also covers the geopolitical and economic forces that shaped these developments and illustrates how they shaped interstate relations and efforts to build institutional frameworks for regional economic integration and cooperation. As the section illustrates, there is a complex relationship between the evolution of domestic political and economic structures, international forces and the evolution of the regional order.

The onset of the contemporary nation-state system is very much a post-war development for much of Pacific Asia. Before that, as we discussed in Chapter 1, the region was long dominated by the 'Chinese world order' (Fairbank, 1968) and by the Japanese empire in the first half of the twentieth century, while much of today's Southeast Asia was under colonial rule. The post-war years witnessed the transformation of the hegemonic and colonial-power dominated interstate system to the modern nation-state system in Pacific Asia. In this evolution, the challenge of developing guiding principles to manage and order the interstate system as well as managing competing expectations and visions of regional order has emerged. Moreover, a lack of 'common understanding' of the basis for regional order has had very serious consequences in the form of strategic and territorial tensions.

State authority and dominance reflects not only in the internal organization of government, but also in the way it relates to the international political system. Most Pacific Asian counties were 'born' into the established system of states, what is often referred to as the Westphalian system. Since the Westphalian settlements in the mid-seventeenth century, the interstate system has established itself as the primary framework for organizing the world. Underlying this system is the concept and practice of state sovereignty. This generally means the state holds the highest authority within the boundaries of its territories.

As with the problem of nationalism, the notion of sovereignty came to Pacific Asia with a unique appeal. The principle of national sovereignty has become one of the few cases where a core element of the international system serves as a key defence for the national interests of Pacific Asian countries, many of which remain suspicious of the international system following their experiences in the early stages of the modern era.

There are several reasons why the institution of national sovereignty is important for Pacific Asian countries. Many of these factors are related to state capacity, regime type and polity configuration in Pacific Asian countries. First, the principle of state sovereignty allows countries to argue against external intervention in their domestic affairs. Given the fact that many Pacific Asian countries are domestically and internationally weak, the principle of state sovereignty provides institutional protection for the state. This is particularly true for those states that are ethnically, economically, socially and politically divided.

Moreover, the regime types, political institutions, ideological orientations and government practices of many Pacific Asian countries are often at odds with those prevalent in the international system, making the idea of state sovereignty particularly useful. China, for example, is a staunch defender of the idea of state sovereignty, not only to protect China's own domestic politics and institutions but also as a general principle in the international system.

In broader terms, for historical and institutional reasons, Pacific Asian countries developed highly centralized forms of government (see Chapter 3). The tradition of oriental despotism, the challenges of early-stage modern state building, and Cold War ideological confrontations all added to the rise of a strong, centralized state across Pacific Asia for much of the early post-war period. The institution of state sovereignty tolerates, if not supports, such a domestic political structure.

Finally, the notion of state sovereignty is also an underlying ideology behind economic nationalism (Burnell, 1986; Huang, 2005: 17–18). This was instrumental in the rapid industrialization and economic development of Pacific Asia. New states in post-war Pacific Asia saw national control and management of resources and economic activities as an essential component of modern state building. The waves of rapid industrialization and economic growth arose from a model where the domestic market was separated from the international one, and domestic economic practices, ranging from trade and currency to corporate organization and banking practices, were distinct from the norms and standards of the international economic system (see Chapter 6).

COUNTRY PROFILE

VIETNAM

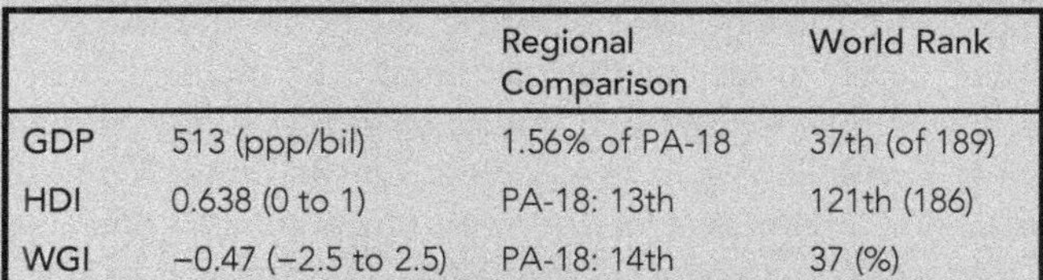

		Regional Comparison	World Rank
GDP	513 (ppp/bil)	1.56% of PA-18	37th (of 189)
HDI	0.638 (0 to 1)	PA-18: 13th	121th (186)
WGI	−0.47 (−2.5 to 2.5)	PA-18: 14th	37 (%)

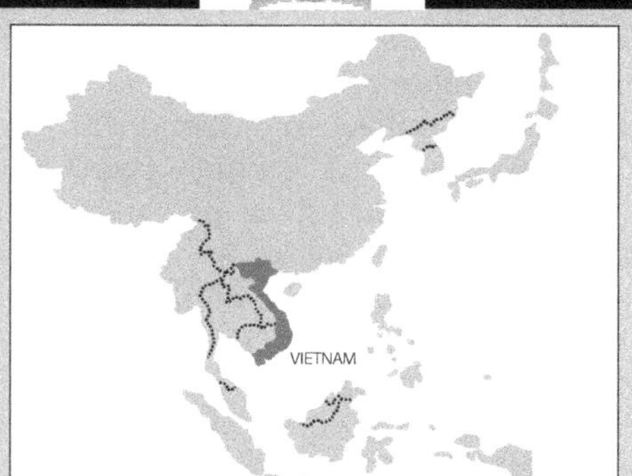

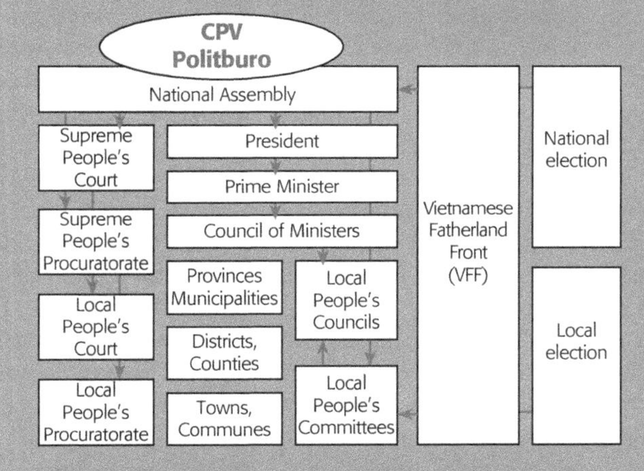

Key political facts

Electoral system for National Legislature

Electoral system for national legislature People's republic electoral system.

Political cycles

VCP holds national Congress every 5 years. Its Central Committee meets twice a year. National Assembly is constituted every 5 years and elects the president and prime minister. Its 30-day sessions meet twice a year, in May and October.

Further reading

London, 2014; McCargo, 2004

Timeline of modern political development

1945 Independence from French rule. Democratic Republic of Vietnam declared.

1946–54 First Indochina War between the Viet Minh and the French.

1954 French colonial administration ends and French Indochina dissolved. Vietnam divided into North and South through the Geneva Agreements.

1959–75 The Vietnam War.

1973 The Paris Peace Agreement

1975–6 Collapse of South Vietnamese government. Socialist Republic of Vietnam (SRV) established over a united Vietnam.

1980 Constitution with the new Council of State to replace the Standing Committee of the Assembly and to act as the collective chairman of the SRV.

1986 Party Congress introduces *Doi moi* (renovation) and institutions of pluralist politics begin to be introduced.

Late 1980s Economic reform package introduced.

1989 People's Council bill to create local governments with real authority. All plenary sessions of the National Assembly live on TV.

1992 Constitution restores the office of president.

1995 Public Administration Reform for government efficiency, effectiveness and accountability.

Late 1990s Law on grassroots democracy, decentralization and devolution.

Early 2000s More open and competitive process of selecting VCP central committee members and senior state officials introduced. Public debate on party and government policy and programmes.

2012 Parliament introduces annual confidence votes for the Prime Minister and President.

2016 12th Vietnamese Communist Party Congress confirms Vietnam is to strengthen socialist democracy, build a strong and pure party and turn the country into a modern industrialized country.

Countries in Pacific Asia were able to promote, protect and defend their particular models of political economy partly because of the existing international system, in particular due to the underlying ideology of state sovereignty. The strong state and the concentration of state authority within these countries reinforced the sovereignty-based international system in this part of the world.

However, the centralization of power in the hands of the state, particularly in the hands of the central government, is no longer always a viable option, nor a necessary one. This has occurred due to the significant economic and social development and progress building modern institutions and participatory democracy. As such, the strong emphasis on sovereignty in Pacific Asian countries has been moderated to some degree by their own political evolution and opening to the global economy.

In terms of political evolution, the problems of constitutionality, legitimacy and political representation have posed a major challenge for Pacific Asian countries since the 1980s. As previous chapters have shown, accountability, transparency, structural soundness, and institutional efficiency, effectiveness and fairness have been a major focus of reform. The importance of modern values has been high on the reform agenda in efforts to advance the overall quality of politics and government.

Seen from this historical perspective, there has been a region-wide process of reduction or weakening of state authority and power. In many Pacific Asian countries today, state power is much more balanced among the state institutions themselves and in relation to other sectors of society. The highly centralized model has been corrected to various degrees.

New developments from Pacific Asia show the state remains the key actor in the interstate system but the rationale and mechanisms for its functions and activities have changed in response to changing domestic and international circumstances. Domestic reforms have weakened state dominance. The campaign for industrialization, modernization and modern state building has strengthened these states' position in the international system and changed the rationale for their engagement. The global and regional system has created both opportunities and challenges in the form of economic globalization and participation in regional and international organizations.

Moreover, the states that emerged in post-war Pacific Asia had an ambiguous identity and orientation towards the advanced economies of the Western world. On the one hand, nationalism and the desire for self-determination drove a rejection and rebellion against the West. On the other hand, the ultimate goal of the modernization projects these states introduced was the Western model of development. Adding further to their complex relations with international society was the fact that many countries in Pacific Asia relied heavily on Western countries if not as a prime source of material support then as a major market and source of investment and technological transfer. Historical conditions and structures, such as the Cold War bipolar structure, further obscured a sense of position for Pacific Asian states in international society.

Southeast Asian countries, in particular, have arguably been searching constantly for an identity in the regional and global order (Steinberg, 1971; Acharya, 2000). Russell H. Fifield described the formative years of interstate relations in Southeast Asia as being driven by forces of nationalism, imperialism, Westernization, communism, neutralism, pacifism, racialism, regionalism and internationalism (Fifield, 1958). Today, with the evolution of regional institutions like the Association of Southeast Asian Nations (ASEAN) states in Pacific Asia are arguably finding their place and identity in Pacific Asia.

All of the above has combined to create an ambiguous regional order in Pacific Asia. Elements of the nation-state system, such as sovereignty, are well replicated in the foreign policy of Pacific Asian states while at the same time this principle has been applied to maintain many of the local features of the regime that have caused controversy with Western states. Sovereignty has been strengthened by the early prevalence for highly centralized domestic regimes. In recent decades, however, states have opened to the international economy and increasingly absorbed many of the norms and values of international society, such as democracy and the market economy. At the same time, the state has remained the key actor in the interstate system.

Evolution of the regional order

Extensive colonial rule in Pacific Asia and the two world wars in the twentieth century had a major impact on the regional order. It displaced the existing Chinese world order (see Chapter 1), established a transitional order based on the interests and activities of colonial authorities and paved the way for the integration of Pacific Asia into the international system. In much of the second half of the twentieth century, a bipolar structure dominated the region before partially breaking down through the flying geese pattern. However, even with the removal of the bipolar structure, the region has not taken on similar regional structure as we have seen in Europe, partly due to domestic concerns over development and sovereignty and partly due to competing visions of regional order. The section concludes with a discussion of the large multilateral trade initiatives in the region, including the TPP, RCEP and a potential FTAAP.

Pacific Asia and the new frontier of global colonialism, imperialism and wars

The Chinese interstate system and the China-centred, hierarchical and tributary order had been relatively stable until the nineteenth century when European powers began to encroach. The interstate system that subsequently developed was what W. G. Beasley has called the 'treaty port system' (Beasley, 1987: 14), an interstate system devised and imposed by Western powers in Northeast Asia around the mid-nineteenth century, led by Britain, 'to regulate their access to the trade of China on advantageous terms' (ibid.: 6).

The treaty port system developed in a series of treaty settlements between Britain and China at the end of wars between the two in the mid-nineteenth century and subsequent similar treaties between China, Japan and many other Asian countries and dozens of other European and American powers. All the key elements of the treaty port system were included in the original Sino-British treaties, as Beasley summarizes (Beasley, 1987: 14–20):

- Access to major Chinese ports without 'molestation or restraint'.
- Control of import and export duties by European powers.
- Extraterritoriality where foreign residents live.
- Protected foreign settlements are subject only to their own country's law, administered through consular courts.
- A most-favoured nation clause whereby any privileges given to one European power by China would accrue similarly to other powers.

In contrast to the 'informal' empires centred on the treaty port system imposed by the Western powers in East Asia, the interstate system that developed in Southeast Asia under European colonial rule was a mixture of formal European empires, the traditional mandala system, and the Chinese tribute system. The mandala system (discussed as a model of state structure earlier) may also be seen as a form of interstate system approximating to the Chinese tribute system, though much more unstable, and more fluid at the boundaries. This interstate system is described in Donald G. McCloud's study (McCloud, 1995: 93–4) as incorporating the following features:

- Universal sovereignty: the king's authority is divine and universal.
- The overlord–vassal system: similar to the Chinese tribute system, but the close proximity of many Southeast Asian states and the lack of ideological underpinnings made the tributary relations more unstable than in the Chinese case.
- Fluidity: Frequent rises and declines of kingdoms. When sustained control was not possible, plunder and retreat were common.
- Inexact boundaries. The multilevel system contains different levels of political authority: the territory over which the kingdom exercised continuous authority; principalities, city-states and other centres of power that were subordinate participants and contributors in the tribute system; and power centres whose submission was maintained largely in the minds and poems of the court chroniclers.

Historically, this interstate system was overlapped by the expanding Chinese imperial presence and its tribute system, in particular since the Ming Dynasty (1368–1644) (Stuart-Fox, 2003: 75). As European colonization became entrenched in Southeast Asia, European colonial governing structures began to play a far more significant role lessening the power, authority and influence of the Chinese state. Moreover, the treaty-port system in Southeast Asia was inextricably linked via trade and naval authority of the colonies of the respective European empires. The boundaries of the European empires in Southeast Asia were therefore not always in line with the boundaries of the traditional Mandala states or interstate system.

Box 10.1

Interstate systems in Pacific Asia before the Second World War

- Chinese world order: this interstate system, dominant before the European expansion in the region in the early nineteenth century, consisted of three concentric zones with China at the centre: the surrounding countries related to China through tribute relations, with Inner Asia, and 'barbarians' on the periphery.
- Treaty port system: an interstate system that developed through treaties in the mid-nineteenth century between China and Japan on the one hand, and European and American powers on the other, to regulate trade and the legal privileges of European and American powers in selected ports in China and Japan.
- Multilevel system: an interstate system in Southeast Asia that consisted of the mandala system (see Chapter 1), Chinese tribute system and European colonial empires (and later the Japanese Empire).
- Greater East Asian Co-Prosperity Sphere: a short-lived imperial system in the early twentieth century with Japan at the centre, occupied lands and puppet states, as well as former European colonies under Japanese military control and imperial authority.

Colonial order in Pacific Asia experienced major disruption from the late nineteenth Century with the rise of Imperial Japan following the Meiji Restoration (1868–1889). With the European powers finding themselves occupied with wars and conflicts back in their homelands, the Japanese empire rapidly expanded in the region. Its first major war with China over Korea in 1895 ended with a victory for Japan and signified the shift of the power centre in Pacific Asia from China to Japan. Japan then defeated Russia in the Russo-Japanese war in 1904–5 over their interests in Manchuria, the first major victory of modernizing Asian power over an existing European power. This consolidated Japan's position as a new power centre in the region. After this, Japan further advanced in Manchuria and Northern China in the 1920s and 1930s, and moved to conquer Southeast Asia in the 1940s. By the early 1940s, the Japanese world order, in the name of the Greater East Asian Co-Prosperity Sphere (GEACS), was in place (see Figure 10.1).

The rise of the Japanese empire in the first half of the twentieth century was not wholly a direct consequence of the decline of the Chinese world order.

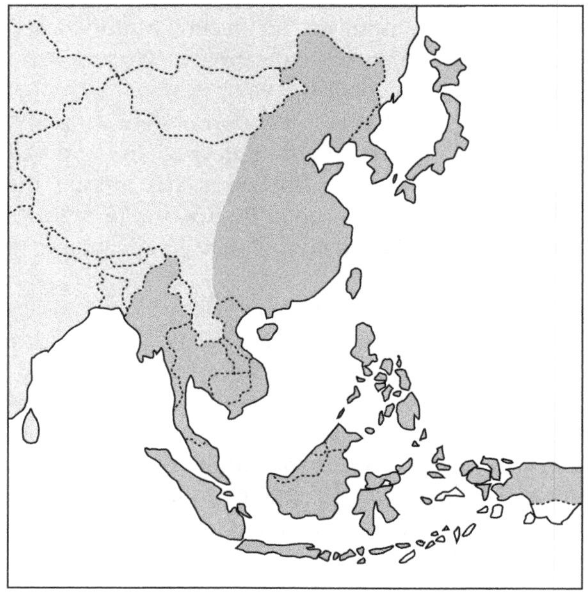

Figure 10.1 The Japanese empire, 1942

Some may argue that the Chinese world order and the Western treaty port system coexisted from the mid-nineteenth century to give 'a dualistic character' to the world order in the region up to the 1880s (Kim, 1980: 328). But, as W. G. Beasley (1987) has demonstrated, when Japan started to expand in Northeast Asia in the late nineteenth century, the treaty port system was already well established and had, particularly in Southeast Asia, supplanted the influence of the Chinese world order. Even Japan had found itself at the receiving end of the treaty port system that had through treaties opened Japan to trade, diplomacy and European interests and integrated Japan into the colonial order on largely European terms.

In Southeast Asia, European colonialism was 'a precondition' of Japan's advance there. 'In some respects', as Beasley claimed, 'the New Order and the Co-Prosperity Sphere were heirs to Western empire: partly because they incorporated those ingredients in it that survived, partly because the West's experience remained a factor in Japanese thinking' (Beasley, 1987: 252).

The establishment of colonial order in Pacific Asia therefore firstly undermined existing regional orders, namely the Chinese world order and the Mandala system. The English School of international relations, in particular, has taken a great interest in the process of Pacific Asian states integrating into international society by taking on the norms and values of the international system. China has been the object of much debate about when it entered international society and more recently how international society may be changing through China's increased participation (see Gong 1984; Zhang 1991a; and Zhang 2011).

Secondly, as European powers became occupied with events closer to home and as the pace of modernization progressed in Pacific Asia near the end of the colonial era, the indigenous power of Japan sought to replace European powers but maintain the colonial order. The rise of the Japanese Empire was the first example of Pacific Asian states successfully reforming and transitioning from the traditional political, economic and social systems to regain control of national development in the nineteenth century.

As the next section shows, this process was replicated in a number of different ways, particularly by states in Northeast Asia, while states in Southeast Asia that were more significantly entrenched in the colonial order established by European powers evolved within the colonial order until their independence was secured through the postcolonial movement following World War II.

Post-war bipolar structure and the 'flying geese' pattern

Post-war Pacific Asia saw two distinct processes of development in the regional structure. On the one hand, the onset of the Cold War in Pacific Asia separated the countries in the region into two ideological and geopolitical camps along a crescent line between continental Pacific Asia and maritime Pacific Asia (see Figure 10.2).

Most scholars believe that this bipolar structure in Pacific Asia was a product of the Cold War structure of the Soviet-led communist world on the one hand, and the US-led anti-communist world on the other. Some others, however, argue that the formation of the bipolar structure in Pacific Asia had its own dynamism and causes.

The Cold War started in Pacific Asia and it was the Korean War and Vietnam War that generated

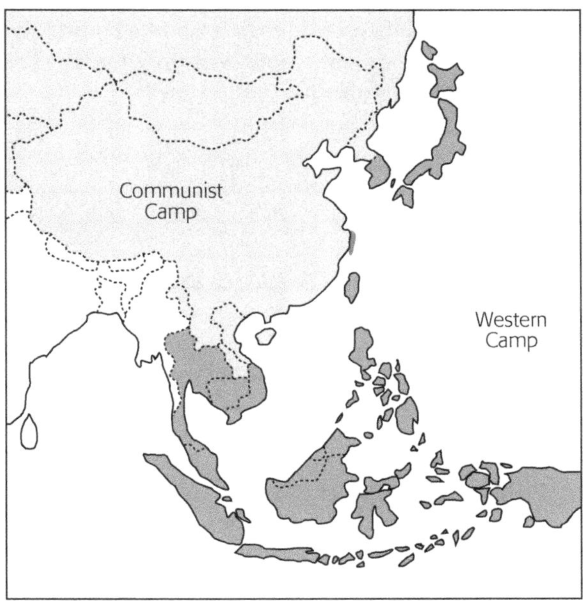

Figure 10.2 Cold War bipolar structure

substantial interest and dynamics for the bipolar structure at the global level (Cumings, 1981; Gallicchio, 1988; Chen, 2001). The transformation of the bipolar structure into a strategic triangle between the United States, China and the Soviet Union in the later Cold War period is a testimony to this (Dittmer, 1990; Chen 1992; Segal, 1992). The shaping of such global strategic relations was clearly also driven by domestic politics and the national interests of these countries (see Case Study Lab 10.1).

Within the bipolar structure were successive waves of take-offs by countries in the region in their post-war industrialization and rapid economic growth. As shown in Box 10.2, these successive take-offs, led by Japan in the 1950s and with a growing number of countries in the subsequent wave, cut across the ideological divide as seen in the bipolar structure. They formed a pattern of regional economic development that is often figuratively referred to as 'flying geese' (Korhonen, 1994; Huang, 2004).

The bipolar structure and flying geese pattern brought new dynamics into the shaping of the models of international relations in the region. If the bipolar structure was more divisive, the economic dynamics of the flying geese have been homogenizing. Moreover, while China was a strong player in the bipolar structure, and Japan a leading country in economic development, there was no country that dominated the region.

The patterns of post-Cold War international relations in the region have been less clear to date, and views vary as to the underlying pattern and future directions (see Box 10. 3). However, several factors are crucial in the shaping of the post-Cold War regional order. First is the dominance of the United States. The second is the re-emergence of China as a major power, this time, on a much larger global scale.

Third, multilateralism has gained greater acceptance among Pacific Asian countries. Regional institutions and frameworks have expanded their influence and relevance in the working of international relations in Pacific Asia. Given these general conditions, many see the emergence of a multipolar Asia, where the 'accelerating dynamics of multipolarity ... could increase chances of conflict' while the 'growth of mitigating factors ... should tend to dampen them and to improve the prospects for a continuing peace' (Friedberg, 1993: 27–8).

Others argue that the current interstate system is very much a hegemonic order dominated by the United States. The system in Pacific Asia, according to Peter van Ness, is not an isolated one. Pacific Asian regional order is merely a 'subsystem' of a globalized US hegemonic system (van Ness, 2002: 131). The role of China and Japan in the region can only be understood properly within this US hegemonic system.

Between them, scholars are convinced that what is unfolding in Pacific Asia is essentially bipolarity. Robert S. Ross insists, for example, that

Case Study Lab 10.1

Explaining domestic political sources of security policy in SEA

- State-centric approach: a top down view of security policy as being determined by anarchy and international structure that focuses on abstract national interests or interstate norms.
- Domestic politics approach: a bottom up view of how security policies are shaped by the particular constellations of power and interests that underpin states. There are other socio-political forces at play, such as classes, class fractions, business groups, ethnic and religious groups and other parts of the state apparatus. What actually emerges in practice reflects conflicts among these different forces as they struggle to impose their interests and reasoning.
- An approach that favours the idea that the roots of security policy in SEA are best sought not in the realm of abstract norms and national interests but rather in the domestic social conflicts that shape state power and policy. States and their policies are contingent outcomes of struggles for power and control. Domestic social conflict is therefore a vital explanatory factor for the forms taken in regional conflict and cooperation.

Jones, 2012: 346–347

Box 10.2

The flying geese

The sequence of take-offs of post-war industrialization and rapid economic growth in Pacific Asia:

1950s	Japan
1960s	S. Korea, Taiwan, Singapore
1970s	Malaysia, Indonesia, Thailand
1980s	China
1990s	Vietnam

Box 10.3

The faces of regional order: post-Cold War Pacific Asia

Scholars have different views on the structural nature of the post-Cold War regional order in Pacific Asia:

- A multipolar Asia, where multiple forces and players shape the region's international relations;
- A hegemonic order dominated by the United States;
- A bipolar structure, either between China and the United States or between China and Japan.

contemporary Pacific Asia is 'bipolar, divided into continental and maritime regions'. According to Ross, the bipolarity is stable because 'the lesser great powers – Russia and Japan – lack the geopolitical prerequisites to the poles' and the bipolarity is largely a 'US–China bipolarity'. Ross argues, they are the only two that have the geographical assets to be 'great power competitors' (Ross, 1999: 81).

Finally, the rise of China and the resurrection of Japan could also mean a return to the regional structure of the late nineteenth and early twentieth centuries that we discussed in Chapter 1.

The above discussion indicates that the pattern and structure of regional politics are very much determined by two sets of relations: those between Japan and China and those between the East and West. The evolution of the modern interstate system in the region closely follows the history of the rise and fall of Chinese and Japanese powers, and the encounters of Western powers in Pacific Asia. These two sets of relationships have had a great impact on the shaping of the interstate system in the region because these forces represented different ideas and principles on the internal organization of the polity and society, as well as the ideal organization of the interstate system.

Case Study Lab 10.2

Trade liberalization and trade protectionism: explaining the ambiguity in trade policy in Southeast Asia

The patterns of regional economic integration in Pacific Asia and the trade policies of Pacific Asian countries are, as Helen Nesadurai argues, highly ambiguous. Nesadurai argues this is because of the impact of domestic interest groups on trade policy that create the need for a high degree of balancing between openness and protectionism. This has resulted in the coexistence of liberal or internationalist trade policies on the one hand and protectionist and interventionist trade policies on the other.

- Protectionist demands from domestic business interest, sometimes acting through their respective business associations.
- Corporate players closely linked to ruling elites through patronage networks or coalitions.
- Politicians seek to favour these interests in order to maintain these mutually beneficial relations. Nationalist concerns to safeguard domestic industries and firms.

Trade policy in Southeast Asian countries has displayed a high degree of ambivalence, incorporating elements of trade liberalization and trade protectionism in some form of dynamic, accommodative equilibrium. Such accommodations are evident in their preferential trade arrangements, including liberalization agreements. What often seems like policy-makers and rulers lacking the political will to initiate and sustain liberal trade policies that will help place the economy on a sound footing is in fact the outcome of rational political calculations that go beyond purely economic imperatives.

Nesadurai, 2012: 326

Why is there no Asian Union?

Amid the rise and fall of the Cold War geopolitical structures and the dynamics of rapid economic growth and development, there has been a steady process of the formation of regional institutions (see Table 10.1 and Figure 10.3). There is no lack of enthusiasm for regional cooperation and integration. This is evident in the establishment of the Association of Southeast Asian Nations (ASEAN) in 1967, to the expansion of Asia-Pacific Economic Cooperation (APEC) to include all major Pacific Asian countries in 1998, the establishment of the ASEAN Regional Forum (ARF) in 1994 and the first East Asian Summit (EAS) in 2005.

However, in comparison with the significant development in regional integration and regional organization achieved in Europe, particularly the emergence and rapid expansion of the European Union in recent decades, the development of regional institutions in Pacific Asia is considered problematic. One thing is clear: there are no comparable regional institutions in Pacific Asia. This has prompted many to search for answers to such questions as 'Why is there no NATO in Asia?' (Duffield, 2001; Hemmer and Katzenstein, 2002), and ultimately 'why is there no Asian Union in Pacific Asia?'

For many, efforts to build regional institutions for cooperation and integration have simply ended in failure (Stubbs, 1995; Leifer, 1999; Webber, 2001; Ravenhill, 2002; Bowles, 2002; Narine, 2005). Regional cooperation and integration are seen as having low levels of institutionalization, competing visions for a regional community, and confusing, voluntary, rather than enforceable obligation and commitment systems.

John Ravenhill, for example, attributed APEC's failure to 'a voluntary, unilateral, and flexible approach to integration', which in his view, 'has provided governments with an excellent excuse for inaction'. For many, the role of the United States and its neoliberal agenda has been the cause for many of the problems with institutions such as APEC (Berger, 1999; Bowles, 2002). The lack of formal institutions in Bowles' view had a lot to do with the vision of the leadership who believe regional integration can be advanced primarily on the basis of private business.

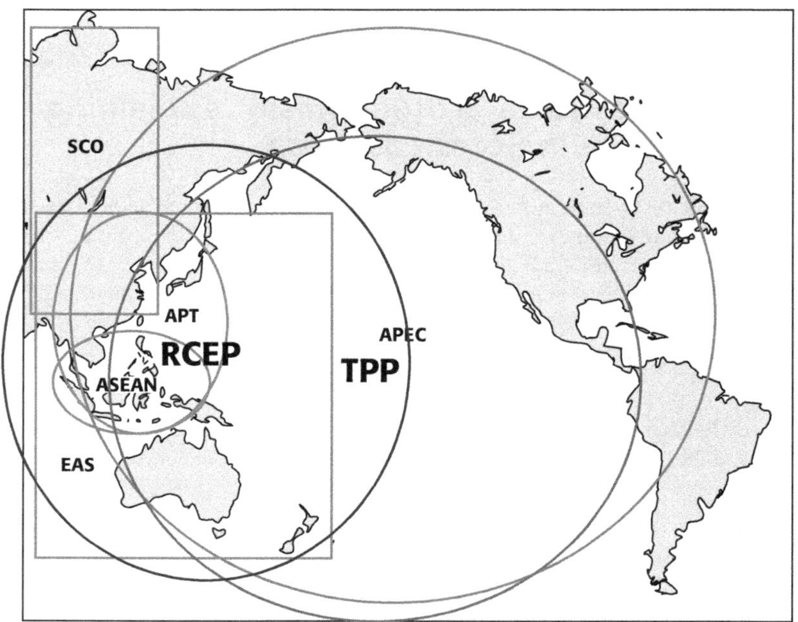

Figure 10.3 Scope of regional institutions

Table 10.1 Key regional institutions in Pacific Asia

Name	*Year established*	*Membership*	*Main purpose*
ASEAN (Association of Southeast Asian Nations)	1967	10 Southeast Asian states	Regional development and stability
APEC (Asia-Pacific Economic Cooperation)	1986	21 economies around the Pacific Rim	Trade and investment liberalization
ARF (ASEAN Regional Forum)	1994	24 countries relevant to security issues in Pacific Asia	Confidence building, preventive diplomacy and conflict resolution
APT (ASEAN Plus Three)	1999	ASEAN 10 and China, Japan and S. Korea	East Asian cooperation
CSCAP (Council for Security Cooperation in Asia-Pacific)	1999	21 countries relevant to security issues in Pacific Asia	Track II dialogue on security issues in Pacific Asia
EAS (East Asian Summit)	2005	ASEAN Plus Three plus India, Australia and New Zealand (16); The United States and Russia joined in 2011 (18)	Regional development and cooperation
SCO (Shanghai Cooperation Organization)	2001	China, Russia and 4 Central Asian states	Regional development, security and good neighbourhood relations
TPP (Trans-Pacific Partnership)	2016 (signed)	New Zealand, Australia, Brunei Darussalam, Canada, Chile, Japan, Malaysia, Mexico, Peru, Singapore, the United States and Vietnam	Liberalize trade and investment
RCEP (Regional Comprehensive Economic Partnership)	Negotiations began in 2013	10 members of ASEAN and Australia, China, India, Japan, Korea and New Zealand	Achieve a modern, comprehensive, high-quality and mutually beneficial economic partnership
FTAAP (Free Trade Area of the Asia Pacific)	Roadmap adopted 2014	APEC membership	Liberalize trade and investment across the entire APEC membership

Finally, the lack of progress in regional institution building is also seen as a consequence of the rift between two competing visions for Pacific Asian regionalism, the Pacific and East Asian visions (see Box 10.5). Baogang He, for example, argues that 'East Asia lacks a convincing and acceptable normative framework' for its efforts in regional cooperation and integration. The 'two competing orders (Asia-Pacific regionalism versus pan-Asianism) create different expectations and visions of how the East Asia region should evolve and they are in tension and lead to different directions' (He, 2004: 105).

These two visions indicate the geopolitical and ideological, as well as economic, tensions among Pacific Asian countries over the nature and scope of an institutional framework for regional cooperation and integration.

Box 10.4

FTAAP Roadmap

At the 2014 APEC Summit in Beijing, China, APEC members set the target for the realization of the Free Trade Area of the Asia Pacific (FTAAP). Members agreed to pursue the conclusion of initiatives considered as potential building blocks of the FTAAP, including to:

- Launch a collective strategic study on issues related to the realization of the FTAAP.
- Increase transparency of existing and recently concluded RTAs/FTAs by advancing work under the APEC Information Sharing Mechanism on RTAs/FTAs.
- Continue the capacity building activities in pursuit of the FTAAP under the Action Plan Framework of the 2nd Capacity Building Needs Initiative (CBNI).
- Accelerate 'at the border' trade liberalization and facilitation efforts, improve the business environment 'behind the border' and enhance regional connectivity 'across the border'.
- Strengthen engagement with the business sector via the APEC Business Advisory Council (ABAC) and other direct routes.

Box 10.5

The 'Pacific' and 'East Asian' visions for regional cooperation and integration

The **Pacific vision** envisages a regional community with a broad membership across the Pacific Rim, including American states in the East and Oceanic countries in the south. The idea has underlain Japan's efforts in building a regional community since the 1960s, with its initial project, the Pacific Basin Economic Council (PBEC) since the 1960s, its key role in setting the APEC agenda in the 1980s, and its efforts in broadening the East Asian Summit to include India, Australia and New Zealand in more recent years.

The **East Asian vision,** most notably championed by former Malaysian prime minister Mahathir bin Mohamad, intends to develop a regional organization with a narrower membership that excludes American and Oceanic states. This idea is reflected in his proposal in 1990 for a regional free trade zone, the East Asia Economic Group (EAEG), the formation of the ASEAN Plus Three in 1999, and the launch of the East Asian Summit in 2005.

While for some these issues are causes for its failures, for many others they are precisely the unique features of regionalism that have adapted the institutional requirements of regionalism to the conditions and circumstances in Pacific Asia. It is not a failure in institution building, but rather a product of a unique type of institution building. Scholars have attempted to define this unique type of institution building as 'soft institutionalism' or 'the ASEAN/Asian way', Asian regionalism, and so on. Amitav Acharya, for example, points out that

> institution-building in this region is more of a "process-orientated" phenomenon, rather than simply being an outcome of structural changes in the international system. The process combines universal principles of multilateralism with some of the relatively distinct modes of socialization prevailing in the region. (Acharya, 1997: 319)

In Acharya's view, the development of regionalism has been enhanced by the 'avoidance of institutional grand designs and the adoption of a consensual and cautious approach' (Acharya, 1997: 319). More specifically, Acharya sees the adaptation of four ideas as being 'crucial' to the process (ibid.: 319). He believes they constitute what he calls the 'Asia-Pacific way' or the 'ASEAN way':

- Cooperative security: the principle of inclusiveness. Security dialogue must take place among all parties involved, rather than among the like-minded against 'enemies'. It is confidence-building rather than deference-building.
- Open regionalism: the principles of non-discrimination and transparency. The outcome of trade and investment liberalization in the region will be the actual reduction of barriers, not only among APEC economies but also between APEC and non-APEC economies.

Box 10.6

Should Korea join the TPP?

With the conclusion of negotiations and the signing of the Trans-Pacific Partnership in early 2016, debate has shifted to the question of whether Pacific Asia economies not part of the first round of signatories, such as Korea, Taiwan and ASEAN economies, as well as China, should enter into negotiations to join the agreement.

On the pro-membership side, Schott and Cimino argue 'In weighing the advantages and challenges of participating in the TPP, we find a strong case for Korea to act promptly'. They believe joining the TPP would: 'deepen existing FTAs with countries in the Asia-Pacific region and secure new arrangements with others'; create 'important new export opportunities, encourage inflows of foreign direct investment, and spur improvements in the quality of economic institutions and economic governance' due to the domestic reforms required by TPP obligations; deepen 'US engagement in the Asia-Pacific region at a time of political and strategic challenges in Northeast Asia and the region at large' (2014: 14, 21–3).

Roh and Kwun are less convinced. They argue Korean membership should depend on the future membership of the TPP from a purely economic cost-benefit analysis. Their study finds 'the overall welfare impact from joining the TPP is critically dependent on China's presence in the TPP. To be specific, when Korea joins the TPP without China, overall welfare impact is slightly negative; however, when China subsequently joins the TPP, Korea experiences a net welfare gain' (Roh and Kwon, 2015: 23).

Manhee Lee places the membership decision in a broader geopolitical context and argues 'Korea should reconsider Japan's and ASEAN's reoriented behaviors in their relations with China. Under growing asymmetrical interdependence, they resort to the alliance with the United States while maximizing economic benefits in trade with China. Korea can also take a balanced posture by increasing economic benefits in its economic relations with China and by consolidating its ties with the United States' through the TPP (Lee, 2015: 320).

- Soft regionalism: preference for informality and avoidance of excessive institutionalization. Asian regional institutions are not formal structures of regional community but consultative mechanisms and dialogue forums.
- Flexible consensus: multilateral consultations and negotiations in a non-hostile setting with a necessary comfort level for all, decision-making with broad support and sensitive handling of intramural differences.

The shaping of regionalism in Pacific Asia is closely related to national politics in member states. Studies found that an important reason for the lack of commitment to formal institutions is the concept and practices of sovereignty in many Pacific Asian countries, and their concern with how independent international organizations in the region would affect their political legitimacy (Acharya, 2003; Beeson, 2004; Narine, 2005). Shaun Narine argues, for example, that,

> a significant majority of the states of East Asia see themselves as actively engaged in the process of creating coherent nations out of the disparate ethnic, religious, and political groups within the state. As a result, these states are reluctant to compromise their sovereignty to any outside actors. Indeed, the regional attitude towards multilateral institutions is that they should assist in the state-building process by enhancing the sovereignty of their members. (Narine, 2005: 423)

The statist tradition in Pacific Asia (see Chapter 3) and the very successful model of industrialization and rapid economic growth (see Chapter 6) make it difficult for states to surrender their authority to regional organizations. However, with domestic and regional changes, namely political liberalization and economic globalization, Pacific Asian states are transforming their approach to regional integration.

Acharya, for example, examined how the elite-led, politically illiberal regionalism in the past has undergone transformation as a result of rapid changes in domestic political structures. Political liberalization and democratic transition in domestic politics has led to a demand for more openness in regionalism

> **Box 10.7**
>
> ### Development of regional institutions in Pacific Asia: a failure, a success or a process?
>
> The development of regional institutions in Pacific Asia has been a failure because of:
>
> - Low levels of institutionalization;
> - Voluntary rather than enforceable obligations and commitments;
> - Competing visions for a regional community.
>
> The development of regional institutions in Pacific Asia has been a success as it has developed an effective and sensible way of regional cooperation and integration and a unique model of institutional building that include the principles of:
>
> - Cooperative security;
> - Open regionalism;
> - Soft regionalism;
> - Flexible consensus.

and 'advances in conflict management, transparency, and rule-based interactions' (Acharya, 2003: 375).

Associated with the growth of regional institutions and the development of regional cooperation is the emergence of a regional collective identity across countries that used to be divided by ideological, cultural, religious or ethnic differences. Indeed, as Amitav Acharya discovered, formation of a regional identity has been an essential part of the development of regional institutions (Acharya, 2004). However, as discussed above, there remain competing visions about the goal of regional organization and, indeed, how the identity of the region will evolve.

In summary, there is no 'Asian union' in Pacific Asia for a number of reasons. At one level, regionalism has evolved under a different context to that of the European Union and has been hampered by the bipolar structure of the Cold War. Clearly, regional organizations are evolving, but these have focused primarily on economic integration and settled for consensus decision-making and non-binding political and security agreements in diplomatic forums. Finally, competing visions, and indeed competition for influence in the establishment of regional institutions, means that for now, there is no Asian Union in Pacific Asia.

TPP, RCEP and FTAAP

Out of the great uncertainty over the direction of the scope, membership and purposes (integration or cooperation) of future regional institutions in the mid-2000s, great efforts were made to work towards a new free trade area in the form of a Trans-Pacific Partnership (TPP). This included twelve maritime Asia-Pacific countries. A movement to develop another free trade area quickly followed this. The Regional Comprehensive Economic Partnership (RCEP) was to include most East Asian countries, India, Australia and New Zealand. In some ways, these two regional groupings reflect the effective structure of the region's political economy that has been shaping up since World War II.

TPP and RCEP have raised more questions than provided answers to the problem of institution building in the region. First, interest in the proposed agreements initially focused on whether these were geopolitical strategies by major powers, the United States and China in particular, to shape regional political economic order.

As such, the TPP was viewed by some as a strategic branch of the American pivot to Asia (see Lieberthal, 2011). Others have viewed it as an attempt by each power to 'create a preferred regional framework in which it can exercise exclusive influence' before potentially socializing the other power into an agreement they designed and constructed (Hamanaka, 2014: 163). China is not a member of TPP and the United States is not a member of RCEP. Between them, there is a long list of countries torn between these two blocks and many that are members of both TPP and RCEP.

Scholars have pointed to comments from President Xi that 'it is for the people of Asia to run the affairs of Asia, solve the problems of Asia and uphold the security of Asia' (Xi, 2014) as well as to comments from President Obama that 'we can't let countries like China write the rules of the global economy. We should write those rules' (Obama, 2015). Such comments suggest a degree of strategic competition for influence over the creation of the institutions of regional economic integration in Pacific Asia.

Second, scholars question the ultimate goal of these agreements. Are these FTAs for a free trade area as originally declared, or due to the high quality, high standards, comprehensive 'twenty-first century' nature, are they more a form of regional economic integration and the basis for a more extensive regional institution?

Third, are these agreements stable arrangements or are they transitional pathways to a Pacific Asian free trade area and economic community? The 2014 Beijing APEC Summit adopted a roadmap for a free trade area in the Asia-Pacific (FTAAP), which brought this issue of expanding economic integration, either through expansion of either agreement or expansion of both, to attention (see Box 10.4).

TPP, RCEP and FTAAP, therefore, raise interesting questions about how the regional order in Pacific Asia is evolving. Perhaps only future developments in this area will provide some real answers to the questions raised above.

The rise of China and US pivot to Asia

The rise of China and US pivot to Asia are two major post-Cold War developments in the shaping of the geopolitical and political economic structure in Pacific Asia. These two sets of developments reflect the underlying logic of change and stability of the structure of international relations in Pacific Asia since the nineteenth century.

The rise of China has significant political economic as well as geopolitical implications for the region (Buzan, 2014, Goldstein 2007 Schweller and Pu, 2011). Driven by its profound economic growth and rapidly expanded international relations and interests, China will seek more substantive economic relations with countries in the region; advance new forms of international division of labour and production; expand markets, capital investment opportunities, industrial capacity diffusion, and production networks and supply chains. Efforts in advancing these have increasingly taken institutional forms, whether through existing multilateral arrangements, such as APEC, ASEAN-centred processes and platforms, or new initiatives of its own, such as Asian Infrastructure Investment Bank and One Bel One Road (OBOR) initiatives.

The geopolitical impact of this is inevitably felt in the region, as much of the international outreach of Chinese political economy in the region will look for adjustment and innovation in how international relations in the region are organized, and, in particular, how the existing institutions and platforms define, advance and legitimatize international relations and interests.

US pivot to Asia can be seen partly as a rebalancing in its global interests, relations and arrangements. It can also be seen as part of the reaction of the existing regional order towards the rise of China. More profoundly, though, it also suggests a reading or perhaps a conviction of the underlying structure of international relations in Pacific Asia and how the United States wants to organize international relations in the region around that structure (Cha 2009, Goh 2007).

The US pivot to Asia involves a significant strategic programme of global redistribution of its capability towards Pacific Asia and aims to restore, enhance and expand its network of allies, partners and friends in the region. This pivot to Asia is also political economic, including a major project for trade grouping, TPP. The focuses of these two are strikingly converging in Southeast Asia, or the maritime Pacific Asia, fitting well with the strategic thinking of US policy planners since the end of World War II as where the US interests are in Pacific Asia and what are the best ways to organize US relations with the region to advance these interests.

US–China strategic interaction in Pacific Asia (Friedberg 2011, Liff and Ikenberry 2014, Glaser 2015) is therefore structural, driven by the historical logic of the region's interstate system. It is also institutional, with competing relations and interests involved and different ways of organizing the relations and advancing the interests. It is furthermore global, reflecting the global nature of the interests, relations, capabilities of both China and the United States. How US-China relations will evolve in the years to come will have a greatest impact on the shaping of the structure of the interstate system, and international security and political economic order in Pacific Asia.

Pacific Asian states and the international system

Pacific Asia is a prime example of how dynamics, structures and institutions at the global level affect politics at regional and national levels. For example, we have already discussed in earlier chapters how the world wave of democratization in the 1990s affected movements for political liberalization and democratic transition in Pacific Asia countries (see Chapter 2). In this section we shall focus on how international political and economic structures shape politics at regional and state levels. 'International structure', as Kenneth Waltz defines it, is a system of interstate relations operating on a characteristic principle influenced largely by the distribution of capacity of the states (Waltz, 1979). As such, international structure can be anarchic, hierarchic or hegemonic, bipolar, unipolar or multipolar; and is influenced by major powers, superpowers and even small powers. International structure can affect politics at the regional and national levels because it produces constraining effects on states.

Development in government and politics in Pacific Asian countries is therefore not only closely related to the shaping of the regional geopolitical structure and the dynamics of political economic interactions and regional institutions, but also closely related to the working of the international system.

The relations of Pacific Asia and the international system have been more intensive in several key areas. First, international structure and geopolitics significantly influenced the evolution of geopolitical structure in the region, particularly during the Cold War decades. This had a large impact on the development of regional and national politics and government. A simple comparison of the types of states, forms of government, economic policy and state-society relations of countries in the communist bloc with countries in the anti-communist bloc illustrates this.

Second, globalization and international economic dynamics have been important forces supporting economic growth and development in the region and influencing the way economic growth is organized at the national and regional levels in Pacific Asia. The 'economic miracles' of all Pacific Asian states are deeply related to their opening and integration with the global economy, whether in trade, capital flows or the transfer of technology and intellectual property via multinational companies.

Third, since the Meiji Restoration in Japan, international society has evolved out of Europe and incorporated states, including Pacific Asian states, into the international community. An important part of this process has been the transformation of these countries and societies as they integrate with international society. Japan's early role in the League of Nations following industrialization, modernization and constitutional reform is an early example of this. China reforming its economic policy and institutions before joining the WTO in 2001 provides a more contemporary example.

Fourth, with the economic rise of Pacific Asia on a global scale, there is a growing impact of Pacific Asian countries on the international system. This can be seen in the governance of world political and economic affairs, such as in responses to the Global Financial Crisis and in the effects of Pacific Asian economies on the global economy and domestic economies from Greenland to New Zealand. This section will look at some of these issues in some depth.

How international structure shapes political development in Pacific Asia

The post-war international structure can be observed in two different categories: the international political structure and the international economic structure. The dominant international political structure during the Cold War was the bipolar structure from the 1950s to the 1980s, with each pole consisting of a superpower and its followers: the Soviet Union, Eastern European satellite states and communist countries around the world on the one hand; and, the United States, Western European allies and anti-communist states across the world on the other. The effect of the global bipolar structure on Pacific Asia was direct. Competition between the Soviet Union and the United States extended all the way to Pacific Asia, which became a primary theatre for the unfolding of the global Cold War structure. A bipolar structure mirroring the global bipolar structure developed in Pacific Asia between continental communist states and maritime anti-communist states.

At the national level, the global Cold War structure also encouraged the dominance of ideology in national politics across Pacific Asian countries. Pluralism was restricted. Constitutional order was compromised. Party politics were subdued and civil liberty suppressed.

The global bipolar structure also shaped the policy options of states. China's decision to 'lean to one side' (that is, to form an alliance with the Soviet Union in the 1950s) was a choice it had to make between the Soviet Union and the United States under the Cold War structure. Japan's Yoshida Doctrine (that is, to focus on economic development and rely on the United States for its international security), on the other hand, was a strategic choice for Japan to survive in the post-Second World War international and regional environment. While a

Case Study Lab 10.3

Imagining Pacific Asia in the world

In laying out the forces and dynamics that have structured modern Pacific Asia, Mark Borthwick (2014: 5–12) identifies three dominant perspectives to the problem of Pacific Asia in the world and the forces and structure that drive these approaches:

- Eurocentric perspectives emphasize modern development, the colonial Far East, the global expansion of the modern world economy and Europe's path to the Far East from the West through West Asia, the Middle East and South Asia. This perspective problematizes Pacific Asia through a range of analytical frameworks, including centre-peripheral, developed and underdeveloped and the Westphalia interstate system.
- Pacific Basin perspectives focus on geopolitical structure, economic integration and institutions, regime types, globalization and North America's engagement with East Asia from the New World through the North Pacific. This perspective problematizes East Asia in a range of analytical frameworks, including, communism, East Asia versus Asia-Pacific, globalization versus nation-states and open regionalism.
- There is a third cluster of views that look at the origins and evolution of the international system in East Asia, focus on China as the historical centre and view the rise and fall of the East Asian system as part of the historical cycle of regional history. These views problematize Pacific Asia in an arrangement of analytical frameworks including the Chinese Imperial system and modern international system, the Chinese world order, European colonial impact, and American political and economic dominance of Northeast and Southeast Asia.

large number of Southeast Asian countries chose to side with the United States, countries between the two camps were torn apart: Korea became North Korea and South Korea; Vietnam became North Vietnam and South Vietnam; and there were two Chinas: one on the mainland and one on Taiwan.

Similarly, the international economic structure was also significant in shaping the process of economic development of Pacific Asian states, and the nature and scope of their economic relations with the world. The international financial, monetary and trade regimes, particularly the Bretton Woods system and the overall free trade environment in the 1950s and 1960s, for example, facilitated the rise of Pacific Asian countries, heavily shaping their model of economic growth and creating opportunities for them in global markets (see Chapter 6).

However, from the 1980s onwards, the international financial, monetary and trade systems underwent significant changes. The Plaza Accord of 1985 devaluated the United States dollar against the Japanese yen by 50 per cent in two years, and changed the international environment for Japanese economic growth significantly. At the same time, the international financial architecture was increasingly dominated by what is called the Washington consensus, which demanded institutional reform and the opening up of the financial and monetary institutions in Pacific Asian countries when the growth of the new economy, generated by accelerating global capital inflows, was picking up momentum. The 1997–8 Asian Financial Crisis indicates, among other things, the close link between the global economic structure and the patterns and dynamics of the national economies in Pacific Asia.

East Asia: Becoming part of international society

This shift in the nature of interstate relations in the region was often taken up as part of the process in which the modern international system that developed in Europe expanded its legitimacy and influence in the world, and a process in which countries such as China and Japan transformed themselves to accept the standards and norms of international society (Bull and Watson, 1984; Gong, 1984). Hedley Bull and Adam Watson's study makes the case that international society initially emerged in Europe out of anarchy, and then expanded outside Europe. The expansion was resisted by non-Western civilizations but international society, which was built upon European historical experience, institutions, habits, codes of conduct and values, became established as a global system. Finally, non-Western civilizations were accepted and integrated into international society.

Box 10.8

The standard of civilization

The standard of civilization evolved to include the following requirements:

1. A 'civilized' state guarantees basic rights, that is, life, dignity and property; freedom of travel, commerce and religion, especially the rights of foreign nationals.
2. A 'civilized' state exists as an organized bureaucracy with some efficiency in running the state machinery, and with some capacity to organize for self-defence.
3. A 'civilized' state adheres to generally accepted international law, including the laws of war. It also maintains a domestic system of courts, codes and published laws which guarantee legal justice for all within its jurisdiction, foreigners and native citizens alike.
4. A 'civilized state' fulfils the obligations of the international system by maintaining adequate and permanent avenues for diplomatic interchange and communication.
5. A 'civilized state' largely conforms to the accepted norms and practices of 'civilised' international society, e.g. suttee, polygamy and slavery were considered 'uncivilized' and therefore unacceptable.

Gong, 1984: 14–15

In Gerrit Gong's study, all this comes down to what he calls the 'standard of civilization' – the specific code of international law and international relations. The imposition of the 'treaty port system' on China, in Gong's view, ushered in the clash of two different 'standards of civilization', or two different models of interstate relations. Furthermore, the abrogation of the 'unequal treaties' between European powers on the one hand, and Japan, China and Thailand on the other, indicated the prevalence of the European standard of civilization and its acceptance by Japan, China and Thailand.

Gong's work traced the emergence of the standard of civilization 'as an explicit legal principle', and argued that Japan's 'unequal treaties' were abrogated by 1899 and its 'great power' status assured by 1905, if not by 1895. Japan then became the first non-European country to gain full international status and full recognition as a 'civilized' power (Gong, 1984: 240). This, however, did not happen until the 1930s for Thailand, and 1943 for China, according to Gong. The acceptance of the standard of civilization and recognition by the world powers as a civilized state meant a transformation of the traditional Chinese world order into the European Westphalia system.

The idea that Japan, China and Thailand entered international society by adopting the rules and norms of the European-style international system has important implications for national politics in these countries, as well as regional interstate relations and Pacific Asian countries' relations with the world in general. Domestically, Japan, China and Thailand began to develop a sense of territorial boundaries for their own polity. Government agencies were established to deal with diplomacy and foreign policy. In Japan and Thailand, the internal change was swifter, adapting to the standards of civilization, and there was 'essentially voluntary accommodation' (Gong, 1984: 217) to the rules and norms of the international system.

However, Japan's 'voluntary accommodation' and behaviour as 'a keen student of Western diplomacy' (Suganami, 1984: 191) was found mainly in the early stages of its modern rise. There was enthusiasm on the part of young Meiji Japan to being part of international society – a national campaign driven by the idea of 'Becoming European out of Asia' championed by the modern Japanese thinker of the late nineteenth century, Yukichi Fukuzawa. Along with the whole package of modern reforms of government and society (see Chapters 1 and 2) was a more collaborative approach towards Western powers, and a more positive attitude towards their system of interstate relations. However, the failure of the League of Nations in the 1920s led to Japan's growing suspicion and defiance of European powers, and growing disillusion with 'Western models' (Hunsberger, 1997: 19). It was not until after the Second World War that Japan's entrance to international society was complete.

China's experience with international society was a real test of the notion of the norms and standards of international society, primarily because China had provided an interstate system that operated on a set of different, if not opposing, principles. Internal tensions and conflicts, and the encroachment of Western powers on China in the nineteenth century, led to the dismemberment of the empire, and consequently the collapse of the Chinese world order. But whether China entered international society, and when and how remains the focus of scholarly debate. Gong and Immanuel C. Y. Hsu believe China started to accept standards and norms of international society in the late nineteenth century; though, as Gong pointed out, this process was very slow until the 1940s.

Yongjin Zhang argues that China entered international society in the 1920s. Moreover, China 'entered international society, not by meticulously fulfilling that "standard" but by a revolt against the regime Europe introduced to regulate its relations with the non-European world' (Zhang, 1991: 196). In a follow-up study, Zhang found that the whole relationship between China and international society had to be restarted after the PRC came to power in 1949, and has gone from 'isolation and alienation to socialization and integration' since the 1950s. After all that, China's relationship with international society is still characterized by 'reciprocated ambivalence' (Zhang, 1998: 251). Even at the time of writing, nearly four decades after China's opening and reform, whether China is a status quo power – meaning it is part of international society – or a revisionist power – meaning it is against international society – is still very much a topic of debate among scholars (Johnston, 2003; Goldstein, 2003; Hempson-Jones, 2005; Qin, 2010).

The problem of Pacific Asian states' relations with international society is not confined to Japan and China. Many other Pacific Asian countries, particularly those in Southeast Asia, faced a great challenge in their relations with international society, the rules and norms of which were very much dominated by their former colonial rulers. The problem for these countries has been exacerbated by the tension between their two fundamental values in building a post-independent state: a break away from their past experience of being the victims of colonialism and imperialism, as well as industrialization, modernization and modern state-building. The former forced the new states to take a generally confrontational approach to their past colonial powers. In Vietnam and Indonesia, as in China and Korea, it took several decades to reconcile relations with the West in general, and their former colonial ruler in particular.

Globalization and Asian politics

In Chapter 2 we discussed globalization as part of the global expansion of the market economy and capitalism. Here we shall focus on the impact of global dynamics on Pacific Asian countries, and in particular on the politics and government in these countries. The regional–national interaction clearly indicates a close relationship between politics and government at the national level, and external dynamics and institutions at the regional and global levels. This can be seen more clearly in the relationship between global dynamics, international structure and the world system on the one hand, and politics and governance at the national level on the other. The structure of government and state authority in Pacific Asian countries has undergone significant change since the 1980s as a consequence of the process known as 'globalization'.

For different people, globalization can mean very different things. It means different things for a farmer in Busan, a banker in Bangkok, a shopper in Singapore or a Communist Party Secretary in Beijing. Even among Pacific Asian countries, every country seems to have its own view of what globalization is, and what it means for them (Kim, 2000). For academics, the list of definitions of globalization can compete with that of freedom or democracy. Generally, globalization is approached and analysed in three different areas:

- Trade, finance and technology;
- Politics and government;
- Institutions, culture and identity.

At the most basic level, globalization is the movement of products, people and ideas on a global scale. This in fact was not terribly new for Pacific Asian countries. Robert Robertson, for example, dated the first experience of globalization to more than 500 years ago, when China as 'the most advanced society' fuelled 'continental interconnectedness' (Robertson, 2003). But the more conventional views are to see the European worldwide colonial expansion in the late nineteenth and early twentieth centuries as the 'first wave of globalization', on the basis of significant changes in world industrial levels, global income gaps, degrees of capital markets, and financial integration and capital mobility; and macro trends in trade, investment, migration and factor prices, as well as economic ideas, policy and institutions (Baldwin and Martin, 1999; Chase-Dunn, et al., 2000; O'Rourke and Williamson, 2000).

The global expansion of European powers, particularly in the nineteenth and twentieth centuries in Pacific Asia, has changed the world significantly. However, given the levels of technology, and consequently the way political economy was organized at the time, the impact of early globalization was primarily on the surface and felt mainly in colonial centres.

The new wave of globalization from the late twentieth century has been qualitatively different. New technologies, and consequently new ways of organization, communication and transportation, have allowed the movement of people, products and ideas on a scale and intensity never previously seen. Moreover, unlike the early waves of globalization, Pacific Asian countries are not simply recipients of global movements this time, but have themselves become generators, with high proportions of world trade, capital flows, financial transactions and movements of people originating from Pacific Asia.

More importantly, along with these movements has been the increasing predominance of the institutions facilitating such movements – institutions that are associated mainly with the successful modern capitalist economy and related political ideas and values. With the collapse of world communism in the 1990s, there is no major collectively organized challenge to these institutions and values. Apart from societies of Islamic inclination, these institutions and values are no longer 'foreign' and imposed on local societies, but have become mainstream institutions and values around the world.

The impact of globalization on Pacific Asian countries is mixed. This has much to do with the particular development models and dominant political structures of these countries:

- First, the Asian model of economic growth in the past relied heavily on the nation-state as a barrier between the national economy and the international economic system.
- Second, for most Pacific Asian countries with their economies dependent on manufacturing exports to global markets, globalization is generally supportive of their fight against protection and trade barriers.

Table 10.2 Perceptions of the effects of globalization on life in Pacific Asia

For the following, globalization is	*Good*	*Bad*	*Neutral*
What you can buy in the shops	36.2	11.1	32.0
The kind of food available in the restaurants	32.3	11.1	31.6
The kind of people who live in your neighbourhood	27.0	10.0	35.9
Job security	30.5	16.6	27.7
More use of English among people	45.3	9.2	25.0
Your standard of living	37.7	10.3	32.1
Films and entertainment programmes on TV	33.6	14.7	34.1
The kind of things reported in the news on TV	44.6	9.9	30.1

Asia-Europe Survey; adapted from Ahn and Jang, 2006: 193.

- Third, globalization also goes in the other direction for Pacific Asian countries. Some key economic sectors, such as agriculture, infrastructure, energy, services and the media, have long been protected from international capital. Opening up these sectors forced many Pacific Asian countries to face global competition.
- Fourth, and more profoundly, globalization demands adaptation of local cultures, institutions and values to international norms and standards.

As to how globalization affects politics and government in Pacific Asian countries (see Box 10.9), there is a general view that globalization tends to reduce the power of the state (Brown, 1998; Compton, 2000; Beeson, 2003). There has been a cry of the 'state under siege'. For example, Beeson argues 'not only is globalization threatening to unravel existing governmental practices in Southeast Asia, but as a consequence we also need to re-think the way we understand core theoretical principles like sovereignty' (Beeson, 2003: 357). For Beeson, the notion of state sovereignty in Southeast Asia has become irrelevant, because authority and power no longer rests with nation-states, but with transnational powers. For a region where the notion of state sovereignty has been a critical institutional basis for state power and authority, globalization directly challenges the state.

More specifically, globalization weakens the ability of the state to exercise control over economic activities within the country. When the national economy is integrated with the world economic system, the national economy is shaped to a greater extent by conditions outside the country. The 1997–8 Asian financial crisis and the Global Financial Crisis (2007-8) are good examples. More importantly, to be able to participate actively in the world economic system, countries are subject increasingly to the rules and norms of prevailing economic regimes. International organizations compete with the state in shaping the behaviour of national economic organizations.

On the political front, globalization is linked to political change in Pacific Asian countries in a significant way, though the exact nature of such a link has been an issue of debate. For some, globalization, particularly the global process of democratization, is responsible for political liberalization and democratic transition in Pacific Asia. Global democratic and civil movements directly challenge non-democratic regimes. In this sense, globalization is indeed 'liberalizing' Pacific Asia (Nolt, 1999). For others, the wave of political liberalization and democratic transition was driven primarily by the internal and historical dynamics within these countries. Even if it plays a role, globalization may not necessarily lead to the liberal democracy one would expect. Between these two views, there is a subtler and more sophisticated argument (Kinnvall and Jonsson, 2002). The nature of 'the global–local nexus' is contingent on 'how global events, values, ideas are localized in interpretation and outcome' and how democracy and civil society are indigenized, interpreted, embraced or rejected (ibid.: 249).

While it is conventional to see how globalization affects the state, it can also strengthen the power of the state. States can and indeed have played with global dynamics to their own advantage. Particularly in those transitional societies where the state is not as effective on its own as before, it can use international forces as leverage against domestic resistance to its programmes and policies. China's entry into the WTO is a good example. While it appears that China is subjecting itself to international rules and norms, the government also relied on the great hopes and fears over the forces of globalization to sell its reform programmes to key domestic constituencies: state-owned enterprises, the government bureaucracy and party ideologues that would be mostly affected by China's entry into the WTO framework. Many commentators have discussed the potential for the TPP to present a similar opportunity for Chinese officials to rationalize further economic reform.

Furthermore, most states in Pacific Asia have benefited from economic globalization, with the state accumulating more resources and capacities. Facing the unpredictable impact of global economic forces, local industries, businesses and investors tend to look to the state to protect and promote their interests. That the governments in Singapore, Hong Kong, Taiwan and China played a huge role in protecting domestic markets, national currency and national wealth during the 1997–8 Asian financial crisis is good testimony to the continual relevance of the state in the age of globalization.

In many ways, therefore, globalization is like 'a double edged sword' (Kim, 2000: 25) for the nation-states in Pacific Asia. States can benefit from it but can also be affected negatively by it. It forces state institutions to adjust, adapt and reform. It fundamentally challenges the conventional notion of state sovereignty, particularly its practices in Pacific Asia.

Box 10.9

How globalization affects Pacific Asian politics

State under siege: globalization reduces the power of the state, and weakens the institution of national sovereignty.

Liberalizing effects: globalization promotes global norms and standards, and facilitates political and economic liberalization and the expansion of global civil society.

A double-edged sword: while globalization weakens the ability of the state, it also strengthens the hand of the state as the protector of domestic interests against global disruption. It can also be used by the state for domestic political purposes.

> **Box 10.10**
>
> ## Impact of globalization: Walmart in China
>
> In July 2006, Walmart issued a statement regarding a Chinese government request through its All China Federation of Unions that unions be allowed in Walmarts in China: The letter read: 'Should associates request formation of a union, Walmart China would respect their wishes.' No doubt, you know very well how to read a political statement by now. In plain language, it says Walmart will allow unions to be set up in its branches in China. In the meantime, Walmart insists that Walmart worldwide is still 'union free'. Indeed, Walmart is known for its corporate policy of being union free. This is a twisted case of how globalization affects government power and authority. In this case, the demand for unions came from a direction unexpected or anticipated by the theory that multinational corporations help to promote modern institutions and values in hosting countries.

But it has not diminished the role of the state. Global dynamics can create periodical instabilities in the international system, enlarge gaps between peoples, and impose uncertainty and insecurity on local communities. All of these would point to a significant role for the state continuing into the foreseeable future.

The economic rise of Pacific Asia and the international system

The relationship of Pacific Asian states to international society has been rocky during the twentieth century and beyond (see discussions earlier in this chapter), and the end of the Second World War left most countries in Pacific Asia, new and old, in a state of poverty, torn by civil and international conflicts. Some sixty years later, the position of Pacific Asian countries in the international system has improved significantly.

The change can be seen most obviously in the substantial rise in economic and social life in Pacific Asian countries. In the 1950s, Pacific Asia was one of the poorest regions in the world, but many Pacific Asian counties at the time of writing are among the richest in the world. More importantly, Pacific Asian countries are now some of the principal generators of world economic activity.

Japan and China, along with the United States, Germany and India, are the top five largest economies of the world. In Figure 10.4 we show Pacific Asia's regional share of world trade. As the figure illustrates, Pacific Asia accounted for a third (30.4%) of international exports in 2013, comparable to Europe and Central Asia (24.6%). Major exporting, and increasingly importing, countries like China and Japan, as well as Korea and Taiwan, make up a large proportion of this total. Moreover, as Figure 10.5 shows, in 2013 Pacific Asia accounted for nearly the largest regional share of world GDP

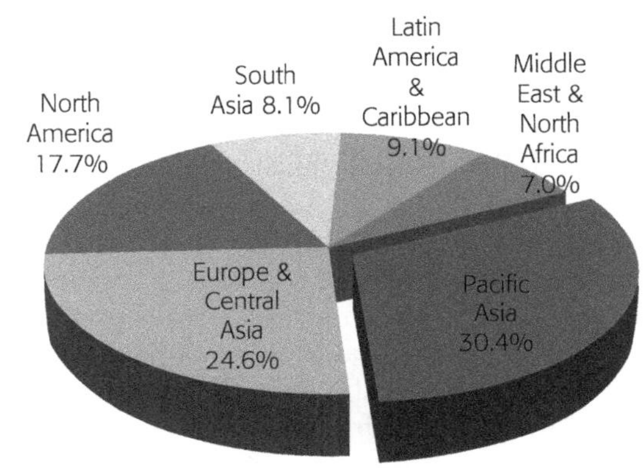

Figure 10.4 Share of Pacific Asian countries in world total exports, (2013, PPP base)
Source: World Bank 2015

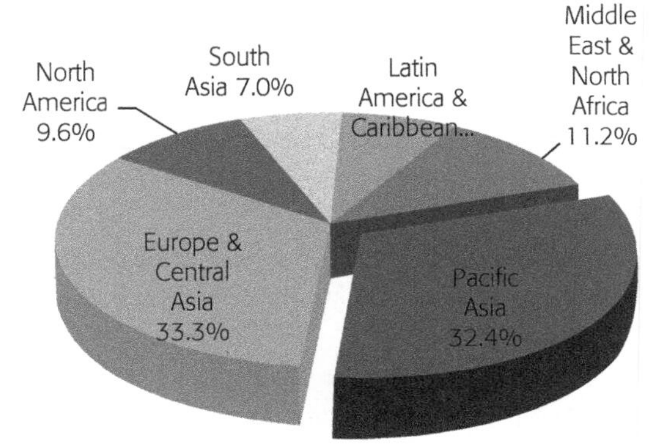

Figure 10.5 Share of Pacific Asia in world GDP (2013, PPP base)
Source: World Bank 2015

Pacific Asia in Context 10.1

International comparison on key indicators

Groups	Countries	Share in world GDP (PPP, %) 2014	Share in world trade (%) 2013	HDI (0–1) 2013	GCI (1–7) 2014–15	WGI (1–100) 2014	GNI per capita (PPP, $) 2014
Group A	Brazil	3.01	1.34	0.744	4.34	50.48	15,590
	China	16.62	12.28	0.791	4.89	39.41	13,130
Group B	India	6.82	6.11	0.586	4.21	41.29	5,640
	Germany	3.40	4.88	0.911	5.49	92.02	46,840
	Japan	4.27	2.52	0.890	5.47	87.95	37,920
	USA	16.06	8.11	0.914	5.54	84.08	55,860
Group C	Indonesia	2.47	2.02	0.684	4.57	44.01	10,190
	Mexico	1.96	2.12	0.756	4.27	43.49	16,500
	S. Africa	0.65	0.70	0.658	4.35	59.88	12,700
Group D	Singapore	0.42	2.53	0.901	5.65	88.31	80,270
	S. Korea	1.60	2.76	0.891	4.96	73.92	34,620
	UK	2.33	2.44	0.892	5.41	88.29	38,370

World Development Indictors, 2015. HDI (Human Development Index): UNDP, 2015; GCI (Global Competitiveness Index): World Economic Forum, 2015; GNI (Gross National Income), GDP (Gross Domestic Product), Trade (Merchandise and Service Export and Import), WGI (Worldwide Governance Indicators): World Bank Institute, 2015.

based on international dollars (PPPs). China will soon be, if it is not already, the largest national economy in the world using international dollar measures.

With the unprecedented growth in the economic power of the Pacific Asian region, many have expected to see a corresponding change in the amount of say these countries have in international organizations that manage the global economy. A major adjustment at the IMF in 2006 of its distribution of quotas among member states provided some evidence that this was beginning to occur. The distribution of the quotas, according to the IMF, reflects 'the relative weight and role of its members in the global economy'. In the new formula determining the quota distribution adopted in 2006, four of the ten top countries whose share in the total quotas increased were Pacific Asian countries, with China, Korea and Japan leading. Further reform in 2010 reflected the major changes in the share of Pacific Asian economies in the global economy. With the adoption of legislation in the United States in early 2016 it appears these reforms will progress meaning more than 6 per cent of quota shares will shift to emerging markets and China will join Japan as one of the top ten largest members of the IMF. As Table 10.3 shows, excluding Japan, the top economies in Pacific Asia in 2014, namely China, South Korea and Indonesia, had a share of global GDP higher than their share of voting rights in the IMF. China in particular, was disproportionate with 16.7% share of global GDP and only a 3.81% share of IMF voting rights.

The position of Pacific Asian countries in the international system is not even, however. Some countries, such as Japan, are among the world's richest in GDP per capita terms and size of economy. Others, such as Korea, Taiwan and Singapore, are wealthy on a per capita basis but not the world's largest economies. China alone is the world's largest economy but only upper middle income on a per capita basis. Many countries, such as Cambodia,

Myanmar or Laos remain poor and developing. Pacific Asia in Context 10.1 sets these differences out in comparison with other parts of the world.

Moreover, there is debate about whether Pacific Asia's political power has matched its rising economic power. For example, only one Pacific Asian country, Japan, is a member of G8, the group of the world's advanced industrial countries. Only one Pacific Asian country, China, has a permanent seat at the United Nations Security Council. In the governing international organizations such as the World Bank and the IMF, the voting power of the member states in their decision-making body is distributed in a hierarchical fashion and arguably remains disproportional to Pacific Asian countries' share of the global economy.

Finally, the political position of Pacific Asian states is slowly shifting. While Japan may be the only Pacific Asian country in the G8, China, Japan, Indonesia and South Korea are all members of the G20. Moreover, in recent decades, Pacific Asian states have taken the initiative to develop regional and international organizations to manage economic matters in the region and beyond. The Asian Development Bank was established as early as 1966 with Japan playing a leading role. The Asia Infrastructure Investment Bank opened for business in early 2016. This is a Chinese-led initiative to fund infrastructure development in the region and has thirty founding members from all around the world. Such changes have created a debate over how to interpret the 'rise of Asia' with some scholars asserting this century will be an 'Asian century'.

The myth of an Asian century

The Russo-Japanese War (1904–5) marked the first time a European power was defeated in Pacific Asia in the modern era. Japan went on to colonize much of Pacific Asia only to be defeated in the Pacific Theatre of World War II. Since that early victory, however, scholars have periodically put forward the idea that the world is heading towards an 'Asian century'. For example, more than 100 years after the Japanese navy attacked the Russian fleet at Port Arthur in Manchuria, retired British Army major general Jonathan Bailey tried to make sense of the dynamics of power relations in Pacific Asia during the twentieth century. Bailey asked whether the Asian century had arrived at last in the twenty-first century. This time, however, he argued, it was to be a century that is to be dominated not by Japan but by China (Bailey, 2007: 213).

Talk of an Asian century or a Pacific century is not new. Japan's early triumph over the Western powers in Pacific Asia led scholars to contemplate the rise of Asia as a logical consequence of the decline of the West (Spengler, 1926; Storry, 1979). The rise of Asia was tied to the decline of the West from the beginning, and much of what happened in Pacific Asia was framed in this perceived West–Asia zero-sum relationship.

This analytical framework has largely dominated post-Second World War thinking about the dynamics of Pacific Asian politics and modern development, though in three different and separate streams. The first stream was related to the threat of communism taking over Asia in the 1950s and 1960s. The rise of Asia through revolutions, independence movements and communist state power was again understood in relation to the West (see Chapter 2). This time, it was a real threat driven by communist ideology, values and political economic systems. 'Containment policy' and the two major wars in Pacific Asia in the 1950s and 1960s were intended to contain the communist threat in Pacific Asia.

A second school of thought was largely a response to the emergence of the economic power of Pacific Asian countries and the model of state-led industrialization and economic development (see Chapter 6). The successive waves of rapid economic development occurred across historical, geopolitical and cultural divides in Pacific Asia, and for the first time a largely shared model of economic development, social management and political governance developed in Pacific Asian countries (see Chapters 2 and 6). This, combined with the rapid expansion of these countries' global economic power and influence, led many to put forward the rise of Asia thesis again. In this perspective, Pacific Asia was not the threat it had been when communism was spreading. But it was seen as posing a challenge, even though people had different views as to the precise nature of this challenge in relation to the existing international system and the prevalent institutions and values of the twenty-first century.

Finally, there is a view predicting the rise of Asia not so much on the dynamics of development in

Box 10.11

What does 'the rise of Asia' mean to you?

- Does the rise of Asia indicate the decline of the West?
- Does the rise of Asia mean an economic threat?
- Does the rise of Asia represent a cultural and ideological challenge?
- Is the rise of Asia part of the historical pattern of the rise and fall of nations?
- Is the rise of Asia a natural step in its modern development?
- Is Asia really rising?
- The rise of China in the early years of the twenty-first century fits well into the Asian century discourse in many ways. Historically, there has been rivalry between China and Japan for dominance over Pacific Asia. This represents a different model of response to the challenge of modernization and that of Western-dominated international society. It provided a prime subject in the early debates on the challenge of Asia: communist Asia in the 1950s and 1960s; and developmental Asia in the 1980s and 1990s.
- Economies have some way to go to catch up to the world's leading industrial and technological powers. Moreover, in terms of economic influence, Asian economies may be the largest traders but are clearly not the largest global investors.

Pacific Asian countries themselves, nor on the decline of the West, but on the long-cycle patterns of the rise and fall of major powers. Paul Kennedy's thesis (Kennedy, 1987) argues that the rise and fall of great powers are essentially changes in the relative power position of great powers compared to others. These changes, according to Kennedy, are determined very much by the way economic resources are mobilized, and how this relates to the efforts by the great powers to maintain their prominent great-power position in the international system. Based on this, Kennedy predicted the decline of the Soviet Union and the United States in the twentieth century and the rise of China and Japan in the twenty-first century.

However, the idea of an Asian century is problematic. It is not clear what an Asian century entails. If it is more about economy and wealth, Pacific Asia is certainly much better placed than a century ago. Though, even on this score, Pacific Asian countries as a whole do not score that well in terms of per capita wealth; there is clearly a large discrepancy between countries such as Japan and, for example, Cambodia.

If it is about the challenge of the 'Asian way', the practices in Pacific Asia in economic development, social management and political governance, then this only raises questions about the prevalent systems of politics, government, economy and society. Pacific Asia is far from posing any serious, credible challenge here. As discussed in Chapter 2, does Asia present a 'credible systemic alternative' to the system of liberal democracy and market economy? If it is about the governing power in the international system, then Pacific Asian countries are making progress in getting themselves recognized in the international system, but are still as yet very much on the margins of the core governing structures of the international system.

Moreover, the differences among Pacific Asian countries are significant in terms of levels of economic development, ideological and cultural orientations of the societies, and roles and influence in the international system. Seeing Asia as a collective entity in the Asian century discourse is more a product of the analytical frameworks that define Asia from an outsider's perspective than a reflection of the reality of regional politics.

A good example of this is the variety of relationships the United States has in the region. As previous sections showed, the United States, and previously the former Soviet Union, plays a significant role shaping the geopolitical structure of Pacific Asia. It has enduring security ties with Japan, Korea and the Philippines and US primacy has provided the ultimate security guarantee that has allowed a relatively benign regional and international environment for Pacific Asian states. Détente between China and the US in the early 1970s ushered in an unprecedented period of development and global interaction. In recent years, however, some scholars argue competition for regional influence and different views of regional order have led to tension and a shifting geopolitical order. Differences in Chinese and US views are evident globally in multilateral institutions such as the United Nations as well as regionally in territorial disputes such as those in the South China Sea and between China and Japan.

Table 10.3 Voting rights of Pacific Asian countries at the IMF Board of Governors, 2015

Country	Share in IMF total voting rights (%)	Share in world total GDP (%, PPP, 2014)	In comparison	Share in IMF total voting rights (%)	Share in world total GDP (%, PPP, 2014)
Japan	6.23	4.4	USA	16.74	16.0
China	3.81	16.7	Germany	5.81	3.5
S. Korea	1.36	1.6	UK	4.29	2.4
Indonesia	0.85	2.5	France	4.29	2.4
Malaysia	0.73	0.7	Italy	3.16	2.0
Thailand	0.60	1.0	Saudi Arabia	2.80	1.5
Singapore	0.59	0.4	Russia	2.39	3.3
Philippines	0.43	0.6	Canada	2.56	1.5
Vietnam	0.21	0.5	Netherlands	2.08	0.7
Myanmar	0.13	0.2	Belgium	1.86	0.4
Brunei	0.11	0.03	Switzerland	1.40	0.4
Cambodia	0.06	0.05	Australia	1.31	1.0
Laos	0.05	0.03	Spain	1.63	1.4

IMF, 2008a; World Bank, 2015.

The greater presence and influence of Pacific Asian countries in the international system, implied in the Asian century thesis, does not have to come with the shrinking or decline of other countries or regions, and certainly not that of the West. The 'rise of Pacific Asia' can simply mean Pacific Asian countries have finally been able to catch up and become normal members of international society.

The zero-sum assumption in the rise of Asia/decline of the West discourse does not allow for the view that the world of the twenty-first century is so interdependent that the rise and predominance of one particular part is simply not healthy, nor likely to happen. In short, the Asian century discourse is misleading as an analytical framework. Instead, we suggest the significant progress Pacific Asian countries made last century and are making this century means they will play a significant and valuable role in the ongoing transformation of the international system in partnership and competition with other significant global players.

Chapter summary

- Politics and government in Pacific Asia cannot be fully understood without the international and regional context.
- There are different ways in which politics and government in Pacific Asia affect world political structures and the international system, and vice versa. But in Pacific Asia, the state, driven by its notion of sovereignty, is a critical factor intervening in domestic international interactions.

- Post-war Pacific Asia witnessed the powerful effects of the global bipolar structure and ideological confrontation, as well as a regional pattern of industrialization and rapid economic development. This, and other factors, has complicated the creation of regional institutions. Scholars debate whether the absence of an 'Asian Union' is a failure of regionalism or a unique pattern of institutional development.
- There is competition between East Asian and Pacific Asian visions of regional order with some scholars suggesting the TPP and RCEP initiatives reflect that competition.
- The integration of Pacific Asian states into the international system has been slow and difficult. Scholars argue this is related to the changes required in Pacific Asian countries for them to be considered as meeting the 'standards of civilization'.
- Pacific Asian countries are the recipients as well as generators of the effects of globalization and thus have an ambiguous attitude towards globalization.
- While Pacific Asian countries have significantly improved their positions in the international political and economic system, as a whole they are still on the margins of the global governing structure.
- Pacific Asian countries are more influential, confident and assertive than ever before, but talk of an Asian century is largely misleading. Pacific Asian states are playing an important role in the transformation of the international system.

Further reading

For works on general frameworks of domestic–international linkage, see Rosenau, 1969. For a discussion specifically on Pacific Asia, see Kim, 2004 and Jones, 2012. On theories and practices of sovereignty in Pacific Asia, see Alagappa, 1995; Beeson, 2003; and Narine, 2005. On transformation of the regional order see Kim, 1980; Gill, 1993; and Bailey, 2007. For a review of the three dominant perspectives on the problem of Pacific Asia in the world and the forces and structure that drive these approaches see Borthwick, 2014. For relations between Pacific Asian states and international society, see Bull and Watson, 1984; Gong, 1984; and Busan and Zhang, 2014. There is a large literature on regionalism in Pacific Asia. Start with Acharya, 1997; Berger, 1999; Webber, 2001; Hemmer and Katzenstein, 2002; and Kim, 2004. For globalization and Pacific Asia, see Kim, 2000. For perspectives on an Asian century, see Spengler, 1926; and Kennedy, 1987; and Berger Border, 1997.

Study questions

1 Discuss examples of linkage politics in Pacific Asian politics. What types of linkages do these examples demonstrate? Do you think Rosenau's model is useful for us to understand the connection between politics at international and national levels?

2 How do domestic politics influence patterns of regional politics?

3 Why is there no Asian Union? Should there be?

4 Do you take the view that TPP and RCEP are symptomatic of competing visions for regional order?

5 There are different frameworks explaining the changing relationship of China, Japan and Southeast Asian countries with international society: standards of civilization, colonialism and nationalism, and modernization. How well, in your view, does each of these explain why the relationship changed, and how it changed?

6 How did the post-war international structure shape the pattern of politics at the regional and national level in Pacific Asia?

7 Why is globalization a double-edged sword for Pacific Asian states?

8 What does the notion of an Asian century mean to you?

Key terms

Interstate system (269); Linkage politics (268); Colonialism (268); Imperialism (273); Empire (270); Regional structure and political order (273); Chinese world order (273); Treaty-port system (274); Japanese empire (274); Cold War bipolar structure (272); US dominant regional order (273); Flying geese (275); Multilateralism (276); 'Noodle bowl' of regional institutions (278); US pivot to Asia and the rise of China (283); Asia-Pacific and East Asian visions of regional community (279); International society, the standard of civilization (286); Globalization (287); 'State under siege' (288).

References

A

Abinales, Patricio N. and Donna J. Amoroso (2005) *State and Society in the Philippines* (Lanham, Md.: Rowman & Littlefield).

Abrahamsson, Bengt (1972) *Military Professionalization and Political Power* (Beverly Hills, CA: Sage).

Acharya, Amitav (1997) 'Ideas, Identity, and Institution-building: from the ASEAN Way to the Asia-Pacific Way?', *The Pacific Review*, 10(3), pp. 319–46.

Acharya, Amitav (2000) *The Quest for Identity: International Relations of Southeast Asia* (Singapore: Oxford University Press).

Acharya, Amitav (2003) 'Democratisation and the Prospects for Participatory Regionalism in Southeast Asia', *Third World Quarterly*, 24(2), pp 375–390.

Acharya, Amitav (2004) 'How Ideas Spread: Whose Norms Matter? Norm Localization and Institutional Change in Asian Regionalism', *International Organization*, 58(2), pp. 239–75.

Adams, Julia (2005) 'The Rule of the Father: Patriarchy and Patrimonialism in Early Modern Europe', pp. 237–66 in C. Camic, P. S. Gorski and D. M. Trubek, *Max Weber's Economy and Society: A Critical Companion* (Palo Alto, CA: Stanford University Press).

ADB (Asian Development Bank) (1999–2005) *Country Governance Assessment Report* (Manila: Asia Development Bank). (Thailand, 1999; Cambodia, 2000; China, 2004; Indonesia, 2004; Philippines, 2005).

ADB (Asian Development Bank) (2008) 'Elements of Governance'. Available at: http://www.adb.org/Governance/elements.asp.

Agénor, Pierre-Richard, Marcus Miller, David Vines and Axel Weber (1999) *The Asian Financial Crisis: Causes, Contagion, and Consequences* (New York: Academic Press).

Ahn, Chung-Si and Jiho Jang (2006) 'Public Support for Market Reforms in Nine Asian Countries: Divergence of a Market Based Economy', pp. 181–200 in Russell J. Dalton and Doh Chull Shin, *Citizens, Democracy, and Markets around the Pacific Rim* (Oxford: Oxford University Press).

Alagappa, Muthiah (1995) *Political Legitimacy in Southeast Asia: The Quest for Moral Authority* (Palo Alto, CA: Stanford University Press).

Alagappa, Muthiah (2001) *Coercion and Governance: the Declining Political Role of the Military in Asia* (Palo Alto, CA: Stanford University Press).

Alagappa, Muthiah (2004) *Civil Society and Political Change in Asia: Expanding and Contracting Democratic Space* (Palo Alto, CA: Stanford University Press).

Allinson, Gary D. (1993) 'Analyzing Political Change: Topic, Findings, and Implications', pp. 1–16 in Gary D. Allinson and Yasunori Sone, *Political Dynamics in Contemporary Japan* (Ithaca, NY: Cornell University Press).

Almond, Gabriel A. and Sidney Verba (1963) *The Civic Culture: Political Attitudes and Democracy in Five Nations* (Princeton, NJ: Princeton University Press).

Amsden, Alice H. (1989) *Asia's Next Giant: South Korea and Late Industrialization* (Oxford: Oxford University Press).

Amsden, Alice H. (2001) *The Rise of 'the Rest': Challenges to the West* (New York: Oxford University Press).

Amyx, Jennifer and Peter Drysdale (2003) *Japanese Governance beyond Japan Inc.* (London: Routledge).

Ananta, Aris, Evi Nurvidya Arifin and Leo Suryadinata (2005) *Emerging Democracy in Indonesia* (Singapore: Institute of Southeast Asian Studies).

Anderson, Benedict R. (1983) 'Old State, New Society: Indonesia's New Order in Comparative Historical Perspective', *Journal of Asian Studies*, XLII(3).

Anderson, Benedict R. O'G. (1990) *Language and Power: Exploring Political Culture in Indonesia* (Ithaca, NY: Cornell University Press).

Anderson, Benedict and Audrey Kahin (1982) *Interpreting Indonesian Politics* (Ithaca: Cornell University Southeast Asia Program Publications).

Arnason, Johann P. (2002) *The Peripheral Centre: Essays on Japanese History and Civilization* (Melbourne: TransPacific).

Arrighi, Giovanni (2007) *Adam Smith in Beijing: Lineages of the Twenty-First Century* (London: Verso).

Aspinall, Edward and Greg Fealy (2003) *Local Power and Politics in Indonesia: Decentralization and Democratization* (Singapore: Institute of Southeast Asian Studies).

B

Baerwald, Hans H. (1974) *Japan's Parliament: An Introduction* (London/New York: Cambridge University Press).

Bailey, Jonathan (2007) *Great Power Strategy in Asia: Empire, Culture and Trade, 1905–2005* (London/New York: Routledge).

Baldwin, Richard and Philippe Martin (1999) Two Waves of Globalization: Superficial Similarities and Fundamental Differences, NBER Working Paper 6904.

Bardhan, Pranab and Dilip Mookherjee (2006) *Decentralization and Local Governance in Developing Countries* (Cambridge, MA: MIT Press).

Barlow, Tani E. (1997) *Formations of Colonial Modernity in East Asia* (Durham, NC: Duke University Press).

Barr, Michael (2014) *The Ruling Elite of Singapore: Networks of Power and Influence* (New York: I B Tauris).

Barr, Michael and D. Ziatko Skrbis 2008. *Constructing Singapore: Elitism, Ethnicity and the Nation-Building Project* (Copenhagen: NIASK.

Beasley, W. G. (1963) *The Modern History of Japan* (London: Weidenfeld & Nicolson).

Beasley, W. G. (1987) *Japanese Imperialism, 1894–1945* (Oxford: Clarendon Press).

Beasley, W. G. (1990) *The Rise of Modern Japan* (New York: St. Martin's Press).

Bedeski, Robert E. (2001) 'East Asia as Conservative Civilization: Restoration and Preservation as Political Processes', *Korea Observer*, 32(1), pp. 83–110.

Beeson, Mark (2003) 'Sovereignty under Siege: Globalization and the State in Southeast Asia', *Third World Quarterly*, 24(2), pp. 357–74.

Beeson, Mark (2004) 'Sovereignty under Siege: Globalization and the State in Southeast Asia', pp. 159–76 in Kanishka Jayasuriya, *Governing the Asia Pacific: Beyond the 'New Regionalism'* (New York: Palgrave).

Bekke, Hans A. G., James L. Perry and Theo A. J. Toonen (1996) *Civil Service Systems in Comparative Perspective* (Bloomington: Indiana University Press).

Bell, Daniel (1960) *The End of Ideology: On the Exhaustion of Political Ideas in the Fifties* (Glencoe, Ill.: Free Press).

Bell, Daniel A. and Chaibong Hahm (2003) *Confucianism for the Modern World* (Cambridge: Cambridge University Press).

Bell, Daniel (2008) *China's New Confucianism: Politics and Everyday Life in a Changing Society* (Princeton: Princeton University Press).

Bell, Daniel A. (2015) *The China Model: Political Meritocracy and the Limits of Democracy* (Princeton University Press).

Bell, Daniel and Kanishka Jayasuriya (1995) 'Understanding Illiberal Democracy: A Framework', pp. 1–16 in Daniel Bell, David Brown, Kanishka Jayasuriya and David Martin Jones, *Towards Illiberal Democracy in Pacific Asia* (Oxford: Macmillan/St. Antony's).

Bell, Daniel, David Brown, Kanishka Jayasuriya and David Martin Jones (1995) *Towards Illiberal Democracy in Pacific Asia* (Oxford: Macmillan/St. Antony's).

Bello, Walden and Stephanie Rosenfeld (1992) *Dragons in Distress: Asia's Miracle Economies in Crisis* (London: Penguin).

Berger, Mark T. (1999) 'APEC and Its Enemies: The Failure of the New Regionalism in the Asia-Pacific', *Third World Quarterly*, 20(5), pp. 1013–30.

Berger, Mark T. and Douglas A. Borer (1997) *The Rise of East Asia: Critical Visions of the Pacific Century* (London/New York: Routledge).

Bertrand, Jacques, André Laliberté (2010) *Multination State in Asia* (Cambridge University Press).

Bickford, Thomas J. (2001) 'A Retrospective on the Study of Chinese Civil–Military Relations since 1979', pp. 1–37 in James C. Mulvenon and Andrew N. D. Yang, *Seeking Truth from Facts: A Retrospective on Chinese Military Studies in the Post-Mao Era* (Santa Monica, CA: Rand).

Blecher, Marc (2003) *China against the Tides: Restructuring through Revolution, Radicalism, and Reform* (London/New York: Continuum).

Blondel, Jean and Takashi Inoguchi (2006) *Political Cultures in Asia and Europe: Citizens, States, and Societal Values* (New York/London: Routledge).

Booth, Anne (1992) *The Oil Boom and After: Indonesian Economic Policy and Performance in the Suharto Era* (Oxford: Oxford University Press).

Borthwick, Mark (2014) *Pacific Century: The Emergence of Modern Pacific Asia* (Boulder: Westview Press).

Bowie, Alasdair (1991) *Crossing the Industrial Divide: State, Society, and the Politics of Economic Transformation in Malaysia* (New York: Columbia University Press).

Bow ornwathana, Bidhya, and Clay Wescott (2008) *Comparative Governance Reform in Asia: Democracy, Corruption and Government Trust* (London: Emerald)

Bowles, Paul (2002) 'Asia's Post-Crisis Regionalism: Bringing the State Back In, Keeping the (United) States Out', *Review of International Political Economy*, 9(2), pp. 244–70.

Boyd, Richard and Tak-wing Ngo (2005) *Asian States: Beyond the Developmental Perspective* (London: Routledge).

Boyd, Richard and Tak-wing Ngo (2006) *State Making in Asia* (London: Routledge).

Brecher, Michael (1963) 'International Relations and Asian Studies: The Subordinate State System of Southern Asia', *World Politics*, 15(2), pp. 213–35.

Brillantes, Alex B. (1988) 'The Executive', pp.113–31 in Raul P. de Guzman and Mila A. Reforma, *Government and Politics of the Philippines* (New York: Oxford University Press).

Broadbent, Kaye, and Michele Ford (2008) *Women and Labor Organizing in Asia* (London: Routledge).

Brown, David (1994) *The State and Ethnic Politics in Southeast Asia* (London: Routledge).

Brown, David (1998) 'Globalization, Ethnicity and the Nation-state: The Case of Singapore', *Australian Journal of International Affairs*, 52(1), pp. 35–46.

Brown, David and David Martin Jones (1995) 'Democratization and the Myth of the Liberalizing Middle Classes', pp. 78–106 in Daniel Bell, David Brown, Kanishka Jayasuriya and David Martin Jones, *Towards Illiberal Democracy in Pacific Asia* (Oxford: Macmillan).

Brown, Melissa J. (1996) *Negotiating Ethnicities in China and Taiwan* (Berkeley, CA: Center for Chinese Studies).

Bukh, Alexander (2007) 'Japan's History Textbooks Debate: National Identity in Narratives of Victimhood and Victimization', *Asian Survey*, 47(5), pp. 683–704.

Bull, Hedley and Adam Watson (1984) *The Expansion of International Society* (Oxford: Clarendon Press).

Burnell, Peter J. (1986) Economic Nationalism in the Third World (Brighton: Wheatsheaf).

Burns, John P. (1983) 'Reforming China's Bureaucracy, (1979–82)', *Asian Survey*, 23(6), pp. 692–722.

Burns, John P. (1987) 'China's Nomenklatura System', *Problems of Communism*, 36(5), pp. 36–51.

Burns, John P. (2015) 'Explaining Civil Service Reform in Asia', pp. 77–94 in *Comparative Civil Service Systems in the 21st Century* (New York and London: Palgrave Macmillan).

Burns, John P. and Bidhya Bowornwathana (2001a) *Civil Service Systems in Asia* (Cheltenham: Elgar).

Burns, John P. and Bidhya Bowornwathana (2001b) 'Asian Civil Service Systems in Comparative Perspective', pp. 1–23 in John P. Burns and Bidhya Bowornwathana, *Civil Service Systems in Asia* (Cheltenham: Elgar).

Burton, Michael G. and John Higley (1987) 'Invitation to Elite Theory: The Basic Contentions Reconsidered', pp. 219–38 in William G. Domhoff and Thomas R. Dye, *Power Elites and Organizations* (Newbury Park, CA: Sage).

Buzan, Barry (2014) 'The Logic and Contradictions of 'Peaceful Rise/Development' as China's Grand Strategy', *Chinese Journal of International Politics*, 7(4): 381–420.

Busan, Barry, Yongjin Zhang (2014) *Contesting International Society in East Asia* (Cambridge: Cambridge University Press).

C

Callahan, Mary P. (2005) *Making Enemies: War and State Building in Burma* (Ithaca, NY: Cornell University Press).

Callahan, William (1998) 'Comparing the Discourse of Popular Politics in Korea and China: From Civil Society to Social Movements', *Korea Journal*, 38(1), pp. 277–322.

Case, William (1996) *Elites and Regimes in Malaysia: Revisiting a Consociational Democracy* (Clayton, Victoria, Australia: Monash Asia Institute, Monash University).

Casper, Gretchen (1995) *Fragile Democracies: The Legacies of Authoritarian Rule* (Pittsburgh, PA: University of Pittsburgh Press).

Castells, Manuel (1992) 'Four Asian Tigers with a Dragon's Head', pp. 33–70 in Richard P. Appelbaum and Jeffrey Henderson, *States and Development in the Asian Pacific Rim* (Newbury Park: P Sage).

Cha, Victor D. (2009) 'Powerplay: Origins of the U.S. Alliance System in Asia', *International Security*, 34(3): pp. 158–196.

Chaloemtiarana, Thak (2007) *Thailand: The Politics of Despotic Paternalism* (Ithaca: Southeast Asia Program Publications, Southeast Asia Program, Cornell University).

Chamberlain, Heath B. (1993) 'On the Search for Civil Society in China', *Modern China*, 19(2): pp. 199–215.

Chambers, Simone and Will Kymlicka (2002) *Alternative Conceptions of Civil Society* (Princeton, NJ: Princeton University Press).

Chan, Adrian (1997) 'In Search of a Civil Society in China', *Journal of Contemporary Asia*, 27(2), pp. 242–50.

Chan, Alex (2007) 'Guiding Public Opinion through Social Agenda-setting: China's Media Policy since the 1990s', *Journal of Contemporary China*, 16(53), pp. 547–559.

Chan, Heng Chee (1976) *The Dynamics of One-Party Dominance: The PAP at the Grass-roots* (Singapore: Singapore University Press).

Chan, Joseph (1998) 'Asian Values and Human Rights: An Alternative View', pp. 28–41 in Larry Diamond and Marc F. Plattner, *Democracy in East Asia* (Baltimore, Md.: Johns Hopkins University Press).

Chang, Kyung-sup, and Bryan S. Turner (2012) *Contested Citizenship in East Asia: Developmental Politics, National University and Globalization* (London: Routledge).

Chang, Ha-Joon (2003) 'Kicking Away the Ladder: Infant Industry Promotion in Historical Perspective', *Oxford Development Studies*, 31(1), pp. 21–32.

Chao, Linda and Ramon H. Myers (1998) *The First Chinese Democracy: Political Life in the Republic of China on Taiwan* (Baltimore, Md.: Johns Hopkins University Press).

Chase-Dunn, Christopher, Yukio Kawano and Benjamin D. Brewer (2000) 'Trade Globalization Since 1795: Waves of Integration in the World-system', *American Sociological Review*, 65(1), pp. 77–95.

Cheah, Boon Kheng. (2002) *Malaysia: The Making of a Nation* (Singapore: Institute of Southeast Asian Studies).

Chen, Duxiu, (1919) 'Benzhi Zuiyuanzhi Dabian (defence of Benzhi)" *Xin Qinnian* 6(1).

Chen, Edward (1979) *Hyper-growth in Asian Economies: A Comparative Study of Hong Kong, Japan, Korea, Singapore, and Taiwan* (London: Macmillan).

Chen, Feng (1995) *Economic Transition and Political Legitimacy in Post-Mao China: Ideology and Reform* (Albany, NY: State University of New York Press).

Cheng, Grace. (2014) 'Interpreting the Ethnicization of Social Conflict in China: Ethnonationalism, Identity, and Social Justice', pp. 127–144 in Zhidong Hao and Sheying Chen, *Social Issues in China* (New York: Springer).

Chen, Jian (2001) *Mao's China and the Cold War* (Chapel Hill, NC: University of North Carolina Press).

Chen, Jie. (2013) *A Middle Class without Democracy: Economic Growth and the Prospects for Democratization in China* (Oxford University Press).

Chen, Jie, and Chunlong Lu (2011) 'Democratization and the Middle Class in China: The Middle Class's Attitudes toward Democracy', *Political Research Quarterly*, 64(3), pp. 705–719.

Chen, Min (1992) *The Strategic Triangle and Regional Conflicts: Lessons from the Indochina Wars* (Boulder, Col.: Lynne Rienner).

Cheng, Tun-jen (1989) 'Democratizing the Quasi-Leninist Regime in Taiwan', *World Politics*, (41), pp. 471–99.

Cheng, Tun-jen and Deborah A. Brown (2006) *Religious Organizations and Democratization: Case Studies from Contemporary Asia* (Armonk, NY: M. E. Sharpe).

Cheng, Tun-jen, Stephan Haggard and David Kang (1998) 'Institutions and Growth in Korea and Taiwan: The Bureaucracy', *Journal of Development Studies*, 34(6), pp. 87–111.

Cheung, Anthony B. L. and Ian Scott (2003) 'Governance and Public Sector Reforms in Asia: Paradigms, Paradoxes and Dilemmas', pp. 1–24 in Anthony B. L. Cheung and Ian Scott, *Governance and Public Sector Reform in Asia: Paradigm Shifts or Business as Usual?* (London: RoutledgeCurzon).

Cheung, Anthony B. L. and Ian Scott (2003) *Governance and Public Sector Reform in Asia: Paradigm Shifts or Business as Usual?* (London: RoutledgeCurzon).

Chin, James (2001) 'Unequal Contest: Federal–State Relations under Mahathir', pp. 28–61 in Khai Leong Ho and James Chin, *Mahathir's Administration: Performance and Crisis in Governance* (Singapore: Times Books International).

Chin, James Ung-ho (2002) 'Malaysia: The Barisan National Supremacy', pp. 210–33 in John Fuh-sheng Hsieh and David Newman, *How Asia Votes* (New York: Chatham House Publishers and Seven Bridges Press).

Ching, Julian (1993) *Chinese Religions* (Westport, CT: Praeger).

Chow, Peter C. Y. (2002) *Taiwan's Modernization in Global Perspective* (New York: Praeger).

Chow, Peter C. Y. and Mitchell H. Kellman (1993) *Trade: The Engine of Growth in East Asia* (New York: Oxford University Press).

Christie, Kenneth and Denny Roy (2001) *Politics of Human Rights in East Asia* (London: Pluto Press).

Chu, Yun-han (2004) 'Taiwan's National Identity Politics and the Prospect of Cross-Strait Relations', *Asian Survey*, 44(4), pp. 484–512.

Chu, Yun-han and Min-hua Huang (2007) 'Partisanship and Citizen Politics in East Asia', *Journal of East Asian Studies*, 7, pp. 295–321.

Chu, Yun-han, Larry Diamond, Andrew J. Nathan, Doh Chull Shin (2008) *How East Asians View Democracy* (Columbia University Press).

Chu, Yin-wah; Siu-lun Wong (2010) *East Asia's New Democracies: Deepening, Reversal, Non-liberal Alternatives* (London: Routledge).

Chua, Beng Huat (1995) *Communitarian Ideology and Democracy in Singapore* (London: Routledge).

Chua, Beng Huat (2004) *Communitarian politics in Asia* (London: Routledge).

Chua, Beng Huat (2007) *Elections as Popular Culture in Asia* (London: Routledge).

Chua, Beng Huat and Eddie C. Y. Kuo (1995) 'The Making of a New Nation: Cultural Construction and National Identity,' pp. 101–123 in Beng Huat Chua, *Communitarian Ideology and Democracy in Singapore* (London: Routledge).

Church, Peter (1995) *Focus on Southeast Asia* (New York: Allen & Unwin).

Clague, Christopher (1997) *Institutions and Economic Development* (Washington, DC: Johns Hopkins University Press).

Clifford, Mark (1994) *Troubled Tiger: Business, Bureaucrats and Generals in South Korea* (Armonk, NY: M. E. Sharpe).

Clifford, Mark L. and Pete Engardio (1999) *Meltdown: Asia's Boom, Bust, and Beyond* (Paramus, NJ: Prentice-Hall).

Cohen, Warren I. (2007) 'China's Rise in Historical Perspective', *The Journal of Strategic Studies*, 30(4–5), pp. 683–704.

Compton, Robert (2000) 'Reconstructing Political Legitimacy in Asia', *International Journal on World Peace*, XVII(4), pp. 19–39.

Conroy, Peter V. Jr. (1979) 'Rousseau's Organic State', *South Atlantic Bulletin*, 44(2), pp. 1–13.

Copper, John F. 2012. *Taiwan: Nation-State or Province?* (Denver: Westview Press).

Costopoulos, Philip J. (2005) 'Introduction', pp. ix–xxvi in Larry Diamond, Marc F. Plattner and Philip J. Costopoulos. *World Religions and Democracy* (Baltimore, MD/London: Johns Hopkins University Press).

Cox, Gary, Frances McCall Rosenbluth and Michael F. Thies (1999) 'Electoral Reform and the Fate of Factions: The Case of Japan's Liberal Democratic Party', *British Journal of Political Science*, 29, pp. 33–56.

Cribb, Robert (1999) 'Nation: Making Indonesia', pp. 3–38 in Donald K. Emmerson, *Indonesia Beyond Suharto: Polity, Economy, Society, Transition* (Armonk, NY: M. E. Sharpe).

Crouch, Harold A. (1996) *Government and Society in Malaysia* (Ithaca, NY: Cornell University Press).

Crouch, Harold and James Morley (1993) 'The Dynamics of Political Change', pp. 277–310 in James W. Morley, *Driven by Growth: Political Change in the Asia-Pacific Region* (Armonk, NY: M. E. Sharpe).

Cudworth, Erika, Timothy Hall and John McGovern (2007) *The Modern State: Theories and Ideologies* (Edinburgh: Edinburgh University Press).

Cumings, Bruce (1981) *The Origins of the Korean War* (Princeton, NJ: Princeton University Press).

Curtis, Gerald L. (1971) *Election Campaigning Japanese Style* (New York: Columbia University Press).

Curtis, Gerald L. (1999) *The Logic of Japanese Politics: Leaders, Institutions, and the Limits of Change* (New York: Columbia University Press).

D

Dalton, Russell J. and Doh Chull Shin (2006) *Citizens, Democracy, and Markets around the Pacific Rim* (Oxford: Oxford University Press).

Dalton, Russell J. and Aiji Tanaka (2007) 'The Patterns of Party Polarization in East Asia', *Journal of East Asian Studies*, 7(2), pp. 203–24.

Dalton, Russell J., Yun-han Chu and Doh Chull Shin (2007) 'Parties, Party Choice, and Partisanship in East Asia', *Journal of East Asian Studies*, 7(2), pp. 177–84.

Dalton, Russell J., Doh Chull Shin, Yun-han Chu (2008) *Party Politics in East Asia: Citizens, Elections, and Democratic development* (Bolder: Lynne Riener).

Davis, Deborah and Stevan Harrell (1993) *Chinese Families in the Post Mao Era* (Berkeley, CA: University of California Press).

de Bary, William Theodore (1988) *East Asian Civilizations: A Dialogue in Five Stages* (Cambridge, MA: Harvard University Press).

de Bary, W. Theodore (1991) *The Trouble with Confucianism* (Cambridge, MA: Harvard University Press).

de Bary, W. Theodore (1998a) *Asian Values and Human Rights: A Confucian Communitarian Perspective* (Cambridge, MA: Harvard University Press).

de Bary, W. Theodore (1998b) *Confucianism and Human Rights* (New York: Columbia University Press).

de Bary, W. Theodore (1998c) 'Confucianism and Human Rights', pp. 41–56 in Larry Diamond and Marc F. Plattner, *Democracy in East Asia* (Baltimore, MD: Johns Hopkins University Press).

de Bary, W. Theodore (2004) *Nobility and Civility: Asian Ideals of Leadership and the Common Good* (Cambridge, MA: Harvard University Press).

de Guzman, Raul P., Mila A. Reforma and Elena M. Panganiban (1988) 'Local Government', pp. 207–40 in Raul P. de Guzman and Mila A. Reforma, *Government and Politics of the Philippines* (New York: Oxford University Press).

Deng, Xiaoping (1984) 'June 22 1984 Speech', p. 58 in *Deng Xiaoping Collection*, III (Beijing: Renmin Chubenshe).

Deyo, Frederic C. (1987) *The Political Economy of the New Asian Industrialism* (Ithaca, NY: Cornell University Press).

Deyo, Frederic C. (1989) *Beneath the Miracle: Labor Subordination in the New Asian Industrialism* (Berkeley, CA: University of California Press).

Diamant, Neil J. (2000) *Revolutionizing the Family: Politics, Love and Divorce in Urban and Rural China 1949–1968* (Berkeley, CA: University of California Press).

Diamond, Larry (1992) 'Economic Development and Democracy Reconsidered', pp. 93–140 in Gary Marks and Larry Diamond, *Reexamining Democracy* (Newbury Park, CA: Sage).

Diamond, Larry and Marc F. Plattner (1998) *Democracy in East Asia* (Baltimore, MD: Johns Hopkins University Press).

Diamond, Larry, Marc F. Plattner and Philip J. Costopoulos. (2005) *World Religions and Democracy* (Baltimore, MD/London: Johns Hopkins University Press).

Dickson, Bruce J. (1997) *Democratization in China and Taiwan: The Adaptability of Leninist Parties* (Oxford: Clarendon Press).

Ding, X. L. (1994) 'Institutional Amphibiousness and the Transition from Communism: The Case of China', *British Journal of Political Science*, 24(3), pp. 293–318.

Dittmer, Lowell. (1990) *Sino-Soviet Normalization and Its International Implications, 1945-1990* (Seattle: Washington University Press).

Dittmer, Lowell, Haruhiro Fukui and Peter N. S. Lee (2000) *Informal Politics in East Asia* (Cambridge: Cambridge University Press).

Dixon, Chris (2004) 'State, Party and Political Change in Vietnam', pp. 15–26 in Duncan McCargo, *Rethinking Vietnam* (New York: RoutledgeCurzon).

Dixon, Rosalind, and Tim Ginsburg (2014) *Comparative Constitutional Law in Asia* (New York: Edward Elgar Publishing).

Djilas, Milovan. (1957) *The New Class* (Orlando, FL: Harcourt Brace).

Domhoff, G. William and Thomas R. Dye (1987) *Power Elites and Organizations* (Newbury Park, CA: Sage).

Downs, Anthony (1957) *An Economic Theory of Democracy* (New York: Harper).

Dreyer, June T. (2003) 'Taiwan's Evolving Identity', pp. 4–10 in Gang Lin, *The Evolution of a Taiwanese National Identity* (Washington, DC: The Wilson International Center for Scholars).

Dreyer, June Teufel (2005) *China's Political System: Modernization and Tradition* (New York: Longman).

Drucker, Peter F. (1998) 'In Defense of Japanese Bureaucracy', *Foreign Affairs*, 77(5), pp. 68–80.

Duffield, John S. (2001) 'Why Is There No APTO? Why Is There No OSCAP: Asia Pacific Security Institutions in Comparative Perspective', *Contemporary Security Policy*, 22(2), pp. 69–95.

Dupont, Alan (1996) 'Is There an "Asian Way"?', *Survival*, 38(2), pp. 13–33.

Duverger, Maurice (1954) *Political Parties: Their Organization and Activity in the Modern State* (London: Methuen).

E

Easton, David (1953) *The Political System: An Inquiry into the State of Political Science* (New York: Knopf).

Edwards, Louise and Mina Roces (2004) *Women's Suffrage in Asia: Gender, Nationalism and Democracy* (London/New York: RoutledgeCurzon).

Eisenstadt, S. N. (1996) *Japanese Civilization: A Comparative View* (Chicago: University of Chicago Press).

Eisenstadt, S. N. (2000) 'Multiple Modernities', *Daedalus*, 129, pp. 1–29.

Eklöf, Stefan (2004) *Power and Political Culture in Suharto's Indonesia: The Indonesian Democratic Party (PDI) and Decline of the New Order (1986–98)* (Copenhagen: NIAS).

Eldrige, Philip J. (2002) *Politics of Human Rights in Southeast Asia* (London/New York: Routledge).

Elson, R. E. (1998) 'Independence: State Building in South-East Asia', pp. 79–98 in Richard Maidment, David Goldblatt and Jeremy Mitchell, *Governance in the Asia-Pacific* (London: Routledge).

Emmerson, Donald (1995) 'Region and Recalcitrance: Rethinking Democracy through Southeast Asia', *Pacific Review*, 8(2), pp. 223–48.

Epstein, Leond (1967) *Political Parties in Western Democracies* (New York: Praeger).

Etzioni-Halevy, Eva (1979) *Political Manipulation and Administrative Power: A Comparative Study* (London/Boston, Mass.: Routledge & Kegan Paul).

Etzioni-Halevy, Eva (1993) *The Elite Connection: Problems and Potential of Western Democracy* (Cambridge: Polity Press).

European Values Study Group and World Values Survey Association, (2006) European and World Values Survey Four-Wave Integrated Data File, 1981–2004, v.20060423. http://www.icpsr.umich.edu/cocoon/ICPSR/STUDY/04531.xml Accessed April 2008. WVS, EVS and Zentral Archive are the data archives and distributors of the WVS/EVS data.

Evans, Peter B. (1995) *Embedded Autonomy: States and Industrial Transformation.* (Princeton: Princeton University Press).

Evans, Peter. B., Dietrich Rueschmeyer and Theda Skocpol (1985) *Bringing the State Back In* (Cambridge: Cambridge University Press).

F

Fairbank, John King (1968) *The Chinese World Order: Traditional China's Foreign Relations* (Cambridge, MA: Harvard University Press).

Fan, Yun (2004) 'Taiwan: No Civil Society, No Democracy', pp. 164–109 in Muthiah Alagappa, *Civil Society and Political Change in Asia: Expanding and Contracting Democratic Space* (Stanford, CA: Stanford University Press).

Fell, Dafydd (2012) *Government and Politics in Taiwan* (New York : Routledge).

Ferrara, Federico (2015) *The Political Development of Modern Thailand* (Cambridge: Cambridge University Press).

Feith, Herbert and Lance Castles (1970) *Indonesian Political Thinking,1945–1965* (Ithaca, NY: Cornell University Press).

Feldman, Ofer (1993) *Politics and the News Media in Japan* (Ann Arbor: University of Michigan Press).

Fewsmith, Joseph (2013) *The Logic and Limits of Political Reform in China* (Cambridge University Press).

Fields, Karl J. (1995) *Enterprise and the State in Korea and Taiwan* (Ithaca: Cornell University Press).

Field, Lowell G., and John Higley (1985) 'National Elites and Political Stability', pp. 1–11 in Gwen Moore, *Research in Politics and Society: Studies of the Structure of National Elites Groups, Vol. 1* (Greenwich, CT: JAI Press).

Fifield, Russell H. (1958) *The Diplomacy of Southeast Asia: 1945–1958* (New York: Harper).

Frederickson, H. George (2002) 'Confucius and the Moral Basis of Bureaucracy', *Administration & Society*, 33(4), pp. 610–28.

Freeman, Laurie Anne (2000) *Closing the Shop: Information Cartels and Japan's Mass Media* (Princeton, NJ: Princeton University Press).

Friedberg, Aaron (1993) 'Ripe for Rivalry: Prospects for Peace in a Multipolar Asia', *International Security*, 18(3), pp. 5–33.

Friedberg, Aaron L. (2011) *A Contest for Supremacy: China, America, and the Struggle for Mastery in Asia* (New York: Norton).

Friedman, Edward (1994) *The Politics of Democratization: Generalizing East Asian Experiences* (Boulder, CO: Westview Press).

Friedman, Edward and Joseph Wong (2008) *Political Transitions in Dominant Party Systems: Learning to Lose* (London: Routledge).

Fukui, Haruhiro (1985) *Political Parties of Asia and the Pacific* (Westport, CT: Greenwood Press).

Fukuyama, Francis (1989) 'The End of history?', *The National Interest*, 16, pp. 3–18.

Fukuyama, Francis (1992a) 'Asia's Soft-Authoritarian Alternative', *New Perspectives Quarterly*, 9(2), pp. 60–4.

Fukuyama, Francis (1992b) *The End of History and the Last Man* (London: Penguin).

Fukuyama, Francis (1995) 'Confucianism and Democracy', *Journal of Democracy*, 6(2), pp. 20–33.

Fukuyama, Francis (2001) 'Social Capital, Civil Society, and Development', *Third World Quarterly*, 22(1), pp. 7–20.

Fukuyama, Francis (2004) *State Building: Governance and World Order in the 21st Century* (Ithaca, NY: Cornell University Press).

Fukuyama, Francis (2011) *The Origins of Political Order: From Prehuman Times to the French Revolution* (Profile Books).

Fukuzawa, Yukichi (1885) 'Civilization and Modernization, Mirror of China and Korea, Western International System', *Current Affairs Shimbun*, March 16.

Funston, John (2001) *Government and Politics in Southeast Asia* (Singapore: Institute of Southeast Asian Studies).

Furnivall, John S. (1944) *Netherlands India: A Study of Plural Economy* (Cambridge: University Press).

G

Gallicchio, Marc S. (1988) *The Cold War Begins in Asia: American East Asian Policy and the Fall of the Japanese Empire* (New York: Columbia University Press).

Geertz, Clifford (1980) *Negara: The Theatre State in Nineteenth-century Bali* (Princeton, NJ: Princeton University Press).

Gellner, Ernest (1983) *Nations and Nationalism* (Oxford: Basil Blackwell).

Germer, Andre, Vera C. Mackie Ulrike Wöhr (2014) *Gender, Nation and State in Modern Japan* (London: Routledge).

Gesick, Lorraine (1983) *Centers, Symbols and Hierarchies: Essays on the Classical States of Southeast Asia*, Southeast Asian Studies Monograph Series No. 26 (New Haven, CT: Yale University).

Gill, Stephen (1993) 'The Hegemonic Transition in East Asia: A Historical Perspective', pp. 186–212 in Stephen Gill, Gramsci, *Historical Materialism and International Relations* (Cambridge: Cambridge University Press).

Gilligan, Beth (1998) *Voices & Values: Citizenship in Asia* (Carlton, Victoria, Australia: Curriculum Corporation).

Ginsburg, Tom (2000) 'Does Law Matter for Economic Development? Evidence from East Asia', *Law & Society Review*, 34(3), pp. 829–56.

Ginsburg, Tom, and Alberto Simpser (2014) 'Introduction: Constitutions in Authoritarian in Regimes', pp. 1–17 in Ginsburg and Simpser, *Constitutions in Authoritarian Regimes* (Cambridge: Cambridge University Press).

Gladney Dru C. (1998a) *Making Majorities: Constituting the Nation in Japan, Korea, China, Malaysia, Fiji, Turkey, and the United States* (Stanford, CA: Stanford University Press).

Gladney. Dru C. (1998b) 'Muslim and Chinese Identities in the PRC', pp. 106–131 in Dru C. Gladney, *Making Majorities: Constituting the Nation in Japan, Korea, China, Malaysia, Fiji, Turkey, and the United States* (Stanford, CA: Stanford University Press).

Glaser, Charles L. (2015) 'A U.S.-China Grand Bargain? The Hard Choice between Military Competition and Accommodation', *International Security*, 39(4), pp. 49–90.

Glenn, John K. III (2001) *Framing Democracy: Civil Society and Civic Movements in Eastern Europe* (Stanford, CA: Stanford University Press).

Glosser, Susan L. (2003) *Chinese Visions of Family and State, 1915–1953* (Berkeley, CA: University of California Press).

Godwin, Paul H. B. (1978) 'Professionalism and Politics in the Chinese Armed Forces', pp. 219–240 in Dale R. Herspring and Ivan Volgyes, *Civil-Military Relations in Communist Systems* (Boulder: Westview Press).

Goggans, Phillip (2004) 'Political Freedom and Organic Theories of States', *The Journal of Value Inquiry*, 38, pp. 531–43.

Goh, Evelyn (2007) 'Hegemony, Hierarchy and Order', pp. 101–121 in William Tow, *Security Politics in the Asia-Pacific: A Regional-Global Nexus?* (Cambridge University Press).

Gold, Thomas (2003) 'Identity and Symbolic Power in Taiwan', pp. 11–16 in Gang Lin, *The Evolution of a Taiwanese National Identity* (Washington, DC: The Wilson International Center for Scholars).

Goldstein, Avery (2003) 'An Emerging China's Emerging Grand Strategy: A Neo-Bismarckian Turn?', pp. 57–105 G. John Ikenberry and Michael Mastanduno, *International Relations Theory and the Asia-Pacific* (New York: Columbia University Press).

Goldstein, Avery (2007) 'Power Transitions, Institutions, and China's Rise in East Asia: Theoretical Expectations and Evidence' *Journal of Strategic Studies*, 30(4–5), pp. 629–682.

Gomez, Edmund (2004) *The State of Malaysia: Ethnicity, Equity, and Reform* (London: RoutledgeCurzon).

Gourvitch, Peter (2008) 'Containing the Oligarchs: The Politics of Corporate Governance System in East Asia', pp. 70–92 in Andrew MacIntyre, T. J. Pempel, John Ravenhill, *Crisis as Catalyst: Asian's Dynamic Political Economy* (Ithaca: Cornell University Press).

Gong, Gerrit W. (1984) *The Standard of 'Civilization' in International Society* (Oxford: Clarendon Press).

Grofman, Bernard, Sung-Chull Lee, Edwin A. Winckler and Brian Woodall (1999) *Elections in Japan, Korea, and Taiwan under the Single Non-Transferable Vote: The Comparative Study of an Embedded Institution* (Ann Arbor, Mich.: University of Michigan Press).

Gu, Xin (1998) 'Plural Institutionalism and the Emergence of Intellectual Public Spaces in Contemporary China: Four Relational Patterns and Four Organizational Forms', *Journal of Contemporary China*, 7(18), pp. 271–301.

Gaunder, Alisa (2011) *The Routledge Handbook of Japanese Politics* (London: Routledge).

Gwartney, James D. and Robert A. Lawson (2006) *Economic Freedom of the World: 2006 Annual Report* (Vancouver: Fraser Institute).

Gwartney, James, Robert Lawson, and Joshua Hall (2014) *2014 Economic Freedom Dataset, published in Economic Freedom of the World: 2014 Annual Report* (Fraser Institute).

H

Haas, Michael, Clark D. Neher, Christopher Lingle, Kurt Wickman, Derek Davies, Francis T. Seow, Richard A. Deck. (2014) *The Singapore Puzzle* (Los Angeles: Publishinghouse for Scholars).

Hadiz, Vedi R. (2012) 'Democracy and Money Politics', pp. 71–82 in Robinson, Richard, *Routledge Handbook of Southeast Asian Politics* (London: Routledge).

Haggard, Stephan (1990) *Pathways from the Periphery: The Politics of Growth in the Newly Industrializing Countries* (Ithaca, NY: Cornell University Press).

Hahm, Chaibong. (2004) 'The Ironies of Confucianism', *Journal of Democracy*, 15(3), pp. 93–108.

Hall, Peter A. and David Soskice (2001) *Varieties of Capitalism: The Institutional Foundations of Comparative Advantage* (New York: Oxford University Press).

Halligan, John (1996) 'The Diffusion of Civil Service Reform', pp. 288–318 in Hans A. G. Bekke, James L. Perry and Theo A. J. Tooen, *Civil Service Systems in Comparative Perspective* (Bloomington, Ind.: Indiana University Press).

Hamanaka, Shintaro. (2014) 'TPP versus RCEP: Control of Membership and Agenda Setting', *Journal of East Asian Economic Integration*, 18(2), pp. 163–186.

Hamilton, Gary G. and Cheng-shu Gao (1990) 'The Institutional Foundations of Chinese Business: The Family Firm in Taiwan', *Comparative Social Research*, 12, pp. 135–51.

Hane, Mikiso (1992) *Modern Japan: A Historical Survey* (Boulder, CO: Westview Press).

Haque, M Shamsul (1998) 'New Directions in Bureaucratic Change in Southeast Asia: Selected Experiences', *Journal of Political and Military Sociology*, 26(1), pp. 96–114.

Harding, Harry (1981) *Organizing China: The Problem of Bureaucracy 1949–1976* (Stanford, CA: Stanford University Press).

Harrell, Stevan (1995) *Cultural Encounters on China's Ethnic Frontiers* (University of Washington Press).

Harrison, Lawrence E. and Samuel P. Huntington (2000) *Culture Matters: How Values Shape Human Progress* (New York: Basic Books).

Hashimoto, Hidetoshi (2004) *The Prospects for Regional Human Rights Mechanism in East Asia* (New York/London: Routledge).

Hasmath, Reza, and Jennifer YJ Hsu (2005) *NGO Governance and Management in China* (Routledge).

Hassall, Graham and Cheryl Saunders (2002) *Asia-Pacific Constitutional Systems* (Cambridge: Cambridge University Press).

Hayao, Kenji (1993) *The Japanese Prime Minister and Public Policy* (Pittsburgh, PA: University of Pittsburgh Press).

Hayashi, Fumio, and Edward C. Prescott (2002) 'The 1990s in Japan: A Lost decade', *Review of Economic Dynamics*, 5(1): 206–235.

Hayes, Louis D. (2009) *Introduction to Japanese Politics* (London: Routledge).

Haynes, Jeffrey (2006) *The Politics of Religion: A Survey* (London/New York: Routledge).

He, Baogang (2004) 'East Asian Ideas of Regionalism: A Normative Critique', *Australian Journal of International Affairs*, 58(1), pp. 105–25.

Heady, F. (1996) 'Configurations of Civil Service Systems', pp. 207–26 in Hans A. G. Bekke, James L. Perry, and Theo A. J. Toonen, *Civil Service Systems in Comparative Perspective* (Bloomington, IN: Indiana University Press).

Hefner, Robert W. (2001) *The Politics of Multiculturalism: Pluralism and Citizenship in Malaysia, Singapore, and Indonesia* (Honolulu: University of Hawaii Press).

Held, David (1989) *Political Theory and the Modern State* (Stanford, CT: Stanford University Press).

Held, David (1992) 'The Development of the Modern State', pp. 71–126 in Stuart Hall and Bram Gieben, *Formations of Modernity* (Cambridge: Polity Press).

Hemmer, Christopher and Peter J. Katzenstein (2002) 'Why Is There No NATO in Asia? Collective Identity, Regionalism, and the Origins of Multilateralism', *International Organization*, 56(3), pp. 575–607.

Hempson-Jones, Justin S. (2005) 'The Evolution of China's Engagement with International Governmental Organizations: Toward a Liberal Foreign Policy?', *Asian Survey*, 45(5), pp. 702–21.

Henley, David and Jamie S. Davidson (2007) 'Introduction Radical Conservatism the Protean Politics of Adat', pp. 1–49 in Jamie S. Davidson and David Henley, *The Revival of Tradition in Indonesian Politics; The Development of Adat from Colonialism to indigenism* (London: Routledge).

Herson, Lawrence J. R. (1957) 'China's Imperial Bureaucracy: Its Direction and Control', *Public Administration Review*, 17(1), pp. 44–53.

Heryanto, Ariel (1996) 'Indonesian Middle-class Opposition in the 1990s', pp. 241–271 in Garry Rodan, *Political Oppositions in Industrializing Asia* (Routledge).

Heryanto, Ariel (2003) 'Public Intellectuals, Media and Democratization: Cultural Politics of the Middle Classes in Indonesia', pp. 24–59 in Ariel Heryanto and Sumit K. Manda (2003) *Challenges to Authoritarianism in Indonesia and Malaysia* (London: Routledge).

Heryanto, Ariel and Sumit K. Manda (2003) *Challenges to Authoritarianism in Indonesia and Malaysia* (London: Routledge).

Heston, Alan, Robert Summers and Bettina Aten (2006) Penn World Table Version 6.2, Center for International Comparisons of Production, Income and Prices at the University of Pennsylvania.

Hewison, Kevin (1997) *Political Change in Thailand: Democracy and Participation* (London: Routledge).

Hewison, Kevin, Richard Robison and Garry Rodan (1993) *Southeast Asia in the 1990s: Authoritarianism, Democracy and Capitalism* (North Sydney: Allen & Unwin).

Hewison, Kevin and Garry Rodan (2012) 'Southeast Asia: The Left and the Rise of Bourgeois Opposition', pp. 25-39 in Richard Robinson, *Routledge Handbook of Southeast Asian Politics* (London: Routledge).

Hill, Hal (1996) *The Indonesian Economy since 1966: Southeast Asia's Emerging Giant* (Cambridge: Cambridge University Press).

Hill, Hal (1997) *Indonesia's Industrial Transformation* (Singapore: Institute of Southeast Asian Studies).

Hill, Hal (2013) 'The Political Economy of Policy Reform: Insights from Southeast Asia', *Asian Development Review*, 30(1), pp. 108–130.

Hill, Michael and Kwen Fee Lian. (1995) *The Politics of Nation Building and Citizenship in Singapore* (London: Routledge).

Hilsdon, Anne-Marie, Martha Macintyre, Vera Mackie and Maila Stivens (2000) *Human Rights and Gender Politics: Asia-Pacific Perspectives* (New York: Routledge).

Hirschmeier, Johannes (1964) *The Origins of Entrepreneurship in Meiji Japan* (Cambridge, MA: Harvard University Press).

Ho, Wing Meng. (1977) 'Asian Values and Modernization', pp. 1–20 in Chee-Meow Seah, *Asian Values and Modernization* (Singapore: Singapore University Press).

Hobson, John M. (2004) *The Eastern Origins of Western Civilization* (Cambridge: Cambridge University Press).

Hoffmann, Stanley (1977) 'An American Social Science: International Relations', *Daedalus*, 106, pp. 41–60.

Holsti, Kalevi J. (1985) *The Dividing Discipline* (Boston: Allen & Unwin).

Hood, Christopher (1991) 'A Public Administration for All Seasons', *Public Administration*, 69(1), pp. 3–19.

Horowitz, Donald L. (2013) *Constitutional Change and Democracy in Indonesia* (Cambridge University Press).

House of Representatives, Japan (2007) *Guide to the House*. Available at: http://www.shugiin.go.jp/index.nsf/html/index_e_guide.htm.

Hrebenar, Ronald J. (1992a) 'Rules of the Game: The Impact of the Electoral System on Political Parties', pp. 32–53 in Ronald J. Hrebenar, *The Japanese Party System* (Boulder, CO: Westview Press).

Hrebenar, Ronald J. (1992b) 'The Changing Postwar Party System', pp. 3–31 in Ronald J. Hrebenar, *The Japanese Party System* (Boulder, CO: Westview Press).

Hsieh, John Fuh-sheng and David Newman (2002) 'Elections in the Asia-Pacific: A Decade of Change', pp. 1–17 in John Fuh-sheng Hsieh and David Newman, *How Asia Votes* (New York: Chatham House Publishers and Seven Bridges Press).

Hsiung, James C. (1985) *Human Rights in East Asia: A Cultural Perspective* (New York, Paragon House).

Hu, Fu and Yun-han Chu (2004) *East Asia Barometer Survey* (2001–2004), Department of Political Science. National Taiwan University. East Asia Barometer Survey project – available at: http://www.asianbarometer.org (Accessed April 2008).

Huang, Chi (2005) 'Dimensions of Taiwanese/Chinese Identity and National Identity in Taiwan: A Latent Class Analysis', *Journal of Asian and African Studies*, 40(1/2), pp. 51–70.

Huang, Jing. (2000) *Factionalism in Chinese Communist Politics* (Cambridge: Cambridge University Press).

Huang, Philip C. (1993) '"Public Sphere" and "Civil Society" in China', *Modern China*, 19(2), pp. 216–17.

Huang, Xiaoming (2002) 'Culture, Institutions and Globalization: What Is "Chinese" about Chinese Civilization?', pp. 218–41 in Mehdi Mozaffari, *Globalization and Civilizations* (London/New York: Routledge).

Huang, Xiaoming (2004) 'The Pattern of Rapid Economic Growth in East Asia: The Flying Geese Theory Revisited', *Review of Asia-Pacific Studies*, 27(2), pp. 1–22.

Huang, Xiaoming (2005) *The Rise and Fall of the East Asian Growth System, 1951-2000: Institutional Competitiveness and Rapid Economic Growth* (London: RoutledgeCurzon).

Huff, W. G. (1995) 'The Developmental State, Government, and Singapore's Economic Development since 1960', *World Development*, 23(8), pp. 1421–38.

Hughes, Christopher (1997) *Taiwan and Chinese Nationalism: National Identity and Status in International Society* (London, New York: Routledge).

Hughes, Christopher R. (2014) *Revisiting Identity Politics under Ma Ying-jeou* (London: Routledge).

Hunsberger, Warren S. (1997) *Japan's Quest: The Search for International Relations, Recognition and Respect* (Armonk, NY/London: M. E. Sharpe).

Hunsberger, Warren and Richard B. Finn (1997) 'Japan's Historical Record', pp. 15–32 in Warren S. Hunsberger, *Japan's Quest: The Search for International Relations, Recognition and Respect* (Armonk, NY/London: M. E. Sharpe).

Hunter, William C., George G. Kaufman and Thomas H. Krueger (1999) *The Asian Financial Crisis: Origins, Implications, and Solutions* (Boston, MA: Kluwer).

Huntington, Samuel P. (1957) *The Soldier and the State* (Cambridge, MA: The Belknap Press of Harvard University Press).

Huntington, Samuel P. (1962) *Changing Patterns of Military Politics* (New York: Free Press).

Huntington, Samuel P. (1968) *Political Order in Changing Societies* (New Haven, CT: Yale University Press).

Huntington, Samuel P. (1991a) 'Democracy's Third Wave', *Journal of Democracy*, 2(2), pp. 12–34.

Huntington, Samuel P. (1991b) *The Third Wave: Democratization in the Late Twentieth Century* (Norman, OK: University of Oklahoma Press).

Huntington, Samuel P. (1993) 'The Clash of Civilizations?', *Foreign Affairs*, 72(3), pp. 22–49.

Huntington, Samuel P. (1996) 'The West, Unique, Not Universal', *Foreign Affairs*, 75(6), pp. 28–46.

Huntington, Samuel P. and Clement H. Moore (1970) *Authoritarian Politics in Modern Society; The Dynamics of Established One-Party Systems* (New York: Basic Books).

Hutchcroft, Paul (1991) 'Oligarchs and Cronies in the Philippine State: The Politics of Patrimonial Plunder', *World Politics*, 43(2), pp. 414–50.

Hyden, Goran, Julius Court and Kenneth Mease (2003) 'The Bureaucracy and Governance in 16 Developing Countries', *World Governance Survey Discussion Paper 7* (London: Overseas Development Institute).

I

Ike, Nobutaka (1950) *The Beginnings of Political Democracy in Japan* (New York: Greenwood Press).

Inoguchi, Takashi (2005) *Japanese Politics: An Introduction* (Melbourne: TransPacific Press).

Inoguchi, Takashi et al. (2004) AsiaBarometer Survey Data (2004 AsiaBarometer2004.sav. AsiaBarometer Project (http://www.asiabarometer.org/) Accessed April 2008. AsiaBarometer is a registered trademark of Professor Takashi Inoguchi, Chuo University, Japan, Director of the AsiaBarometer Project.

IDEA (International Institute for Democracy and Electoral Assistance) (2008) *Turnout in the World - Country By Country Performance*. Available at: http://www.idea.int/vt/survey/voter_turnout_pop2.cfm (accessed April 2008).

IMF (International Monetary Fund) (1999) 'Conference on Second Generation Reforms', (Washington, DC: IMF Headquarters). Available at: http://www.imf.org/External/Pubs/FT/seminar/1999/reforms/index.htm#agenda.

IMF (International Monetary Fund) (2008a) 'Reform of IMF Quotas and Voice: Responding to Changes in the Global Economy'. Available at: http://www.imf.org/external/np/exr/ib/2008/040108.htm.

IMF (International Monetary Fund) (2008b) 'IMF Members' Quotas and Voting Power, and IMF Board of Governors May 22, (2008)'. Available at: http://www.imf.org/external/np/sec/memdir/members.htm.

Inoguchi, Takashi (2005) *Japanese Politics* (Melbourne: Trans Pacific Press).

Ishibashi, Michihiro and Steven R. Reed (1992) 'Second-generation Diet Members and Democracy in Japan: Hereditary Seats', *Asian Survey*, 32(4), pp. 366–79.

Itoh, Hiroshi (1989) *The Supreme Court: Constitutional Practices* (New York: Wiener).

Iwanaga, Kazuki (2008) *Women and Politics in Thailand* (Copenhagen: NIAS Press).

J

Janowitz, Morris (1964) *The Military in the Political Development of New Nations* (Chicago: University of Chicago Press).

Jayasuriya, Kanishka (1999) *Law, Capitalism and Power in Asia* (London: Routledge).

Jervis, Robert (1980) 'The Impact of the Korean War on the Cold War', *The Journal of Conflict Resolution*, 24(4), pp. 563–92.

Johnston, Alastair Iain (2003) 'Is China a Status Quo Power?', *International Security*, 27(4), pp. 5–56.

Johnson, Chalmers (1982) *MITI and the Japanese Miracle* (Stanford, CA: Stanford University Press).

Johnson, Chalmers (1999) 'The Developmental State: Odyssey of a Concept', pp. 32–60 in Meredith Woo-Cumings, *The Developmental State* (Ithaca: Cornell University Press).

Johnson, Chalmers. (1986) 'Tanaka Kakuei, Structural Corruption, and the Advent of Machine Politics in Japan'. *Journal of Japanese Studies*, 12(1), pp. 1–28.

Johnson, Chalmers A. (1995) *Japan, Who Governs? The Rise of the Developmental State* (Norton & Company).

Jones, David Martin (1997) *Political development in Pacific Asia* (Malden: Polity Press).

Jones, David Martin (2001) *The Image of China in Western Social and Political Thought* (London: Palgrave).

Jones, David Martin, Daniel Bell, Kanishka Jayasuriya and David Brown (1995) 'Towards a Model of Illiberal Democracy', pp. 163–7 in Daniel Bell, David Brown, Kanishka Jayasuriya and David Martin Jones, *Towards Illiberal Democracy in Pacific Asia* (New York: St. Martin's Press).

Jones, Eric (1994) 'Asia's Fate: A Response to the Singapore School', *National Interest*, 35(1), pp. 18–28.

Jones, Francis Clifford (1954) *Japan's New Order in East Asia: Its Rise and Fall, 37–45* (London/New York: Oxford University Press).

Jones, Nicola Anne (2006) *Gender and the Political Opportunities of Democratization in South Korea* (Basingstoke: Palgrave).

Jones, Lee (2012) 'Sate Power, Social Conflict and Security Policy in SEA', pp. 346-361 in Richard Robinson, Routledge *Handbook of Southeast Asian Politics* (London: Routledge).

K

Kadir, Suzaina (2004) 'Singapore: Engagement and Autonomy within the Political Status Quo', pp. 324–56 in Muthiah Alagappa, *Civil Society and Political Change in Asia: Expanding and Contracting Democratic Space* (Stanford, Calif.: Stanford University Press).

Kalland, Arne, and Gerard Persoon (1998) 'An Anthropological Perspective on Environmental Movements'. pp 1–43 in *Environmental Movements in Asia* (Richmond: Curzon Press).

Kang, David (2002) *Crony Capitalism: Corruption and Development in South Korea and the Philippines* (Cambridge: Cambridge University Press).

Kang, David (2003) 'Transaction Costs and Crony Capitalism in East Asia', *Comparative Politics*, 35(4), pp. 439–59.

Kang, David (2010) *East Asia Before the West: Five Centuries of Trade and Tribute* (New York: Columbia University Press)

Kaplan, Eugene J. (1972) *Japan: The Government–Business Relationship* (Washington, DC: US Bureau of International Commerce).

Kato, Toshiyasu, Jeffrey A. Kaplan, Chan Sophal and Real Sopheap (2000) *Cambodia: Enhancing Governance for Sustainable Development* (Manila: Asian Development Bank).

Kaufmann Daniel, Aart Kraay and Massimo Mastruzzi (2015) *Governance Matters VII: Governance Indicators for 1996–2014*, World Bank Policy Research Working Paper No. 4654 (Washington, DC: World Bank Institute).

Kausikan, Bilahari (1998) 'The "Asian Value" Debate: A View from Singapore', pp. 17–28 in Larry Diamond and Marc F. Plattner, *Democracy in East Asia* (Baltimore, MD: Johns Hopkins University Press).

Keane, John (1988) *Civil Society and the State: New European Perspectives* (London: Verso).

Kennedy, Paul (1987) *The Rise and Fall of the Great Powers: Economic Change and Military Conflict from 1500 to 2000* (New York: Random House).

Kershaw, Roger (2001) 'Brunei: Malay, Monarchical, Micro-state', pp. 1–35 in John Funston, *Government and Politics in Southeast Asia* (Singapore: Institute of Southeast Asian Studies/New York: Palgrave).

Keyes, Charles F. (1987) *Thailand, Buddhist Kingdom as Modern Nation-state* (Boulder, CO: Westview Press).

Keyes, Charles F., Laurel Kendall and Helen Hardacre (1994) *Asian Visions of Authority: Religion and the Modern States of East and Southeast Asia* (Honolulu: University of Hawaii Press).

Kidd, John B. and Frank Jurgen Richter (2003) *Corruption and Governance in Asia* (Basingstoke: Palgrave Macmillan).

Kihl, Young Whan (2005) *Transforming Korean Politics: Democracy, Reform, and Culture* (New York: Sharpe).

Kim, Dae Jung (1994) 'Is Culture Destiny? The Myth of Asia's Anti-Democratic Values', *Foreign Affairs*, 73, pp. 189–94.

Kim, HeeMin (2011) *Korean Democracy in Transition a Rational Blueprint for Developing Societies* (Lexington: University Press of Kentucky)

Kim, Key-Hiuk (1980) *The Last Phase of the East Asian World Order Korea, Japan, and the Chinese Empire, 1860–1882* (Berkeley, CA: University of California Press).

Kim, Kyong Ju (2006) *The Development of Modern South Korea: State Formation, Capitalist Development and National Identity* (London: Routledge).

Kim, Samuel S. (2000) *East Asia and Globalization* (Lanham, MD: Rowman & Littlefield).

Kim, Samuel S. (2003) *Korea's Democratization* (Cambridge: Cambridge University Press).

Kim, Samuel S. (2004) 'Northeast Asia in the Local–Regional–Global Nexus', pp. 3–61 in Samuel S. Kim, *The International Relations of Northeast Asia* (Lanham, MD: Rowman & Littlefield).

Kim, Samuel S. (2006) *The Two Koreas and the Great Powers* (Cambridge: Cambridge University Press).

Kim, Sunhyuk. (2000) 'Democratization and Environmentalism: South Korea and Taiwan in Comparative Perspective', *Journal of Asian and African studies*, 35(3) pp. 287–302.

Kim, Won Bae (1998) 'Family, Social Relations, and Asian capitalism', *Journal of International and Area Studies*, 5(1), pp. 65–79.

Kim, Yong-Ho (1998) 'Korea', pp. 132–78 in Wolfgang Sachsenroder and Ulrike E. Frings, *Political Party Systems and Democratic Development in East and Southeast Asia Volume II East Asia* (Aldershot: Ashgate).

Kim, Yun Tae (1999) 'Neoliberalism and the Decline of the Developmental State', *Journal of Contemporary Asia*, 29(4), pp. 441–61.

Kingsbury, Damien (2005a) *South-east Asia: A Political Profile* (Oxford: Oxford University Press).

Kingsbury, Damien (2005b) *The Politics of Indonesia* (South Melbourne: Oxford University Press).

Kinnvall, Catarina and Kristina Jonsson (2002) *Globalization and Democratization in Asia: The Construction of Identity* (London: Routledge).

Kirchheimer, Otto (1966) 'The Transformation of Western European Party Systems', pp. 177–200 in Joseph LaPalombara and Myron Weiner, *Political Parties and Political Development* (Princeton, NJ: Princeton University Press).

Koh, B. C. (1985) 'The Recruitment of Higher Civil Servants in Japan: A Comparative Perspective', *Asian Survey*, 25(3), pp. 292–309.

Koh, Gillian and Ooi Giok Ling (2000) *State-Society Relations in Singapore* (Singapore: Oxford University Press).

Kohli, Atul and Vivienne Shue (1994) 'State Power and Social Forces: On Political Contention and Accommodation in the Third World', pp. 293–326 in Joel Migdal, Atul Kohli and Vivienne Shue, *State Power and Social Forces: Domination and Transformation in the Third World* (Cambridge: Cambridge University Press).

Korhonen, Pekka (1994) 'The Theory of Flying Geese Pattern of Development and its Interpretations', *Journal of Peace Research*, 31(1), pp. 93–108.

Krauss, Ellis S. and Robert Pekkanen (2004) 'Explaining Party Adaptation to Electoral Reform: The Discreet Charm of the LDP?' *Journal of Japanese Studies*, 30(1).

Krauss, Ellis S., and Robert J. Pekkanen (2010) 'The rise and fall of Japan's Liberal Democratic Party', *The Journal of Asian Studies*, 69(1): 5–15.

Krugman, Paul (1994) 'The Myth of Asia's Miracle', *Foreign Affairs*, 73, pp. 62–62.

Kume, Ikuo. (1993) 'A Tale of Twin Industries: Labor Accommodation in the Private Sector', pp. 156–80 in Gary D. Allinson and Yasunori Sone, *Political Dynamics in Contemporary Japan* (Ithaca, NY: Cornell University Press).

Kuo, Eddie C. Y. (1995 'The Making of a New Nation: Cultural Construction and National Identity', pp. 101–23 in Chua Beng-Huat, *Communitarian Ideology and Democracy in Singapore* (London: Routledge).

Kuznets, Paul W. (1988) 'An East Asian Model of Economic Development: Japan, Taiwan, and South Korea', *Economic Development and Cultural Change*, 36(3), pp. S11–S43.

L

Lam, Peng Er (2011) 'The End of One-party Dominance and Japan's Emergence as a "Common Democracy" pp. 133-156 in Liang Foo Lye, and Wilhelm Hofmeister, *Political Parties Party Systems and Democratization in East Asia* (Singapore: World Scientific).

Lange, Matthe(2009) *Lineages of Despotism and Development: British Colonialism and State Power* (London: The University of Chicago Press).

Langlois, Anthony J. (2001) *The Politics of Justice and Human Rights: Southeast Asia and Universalist Theory* (Cambridge: Cambridge University Press).

Laothamatas, Anek (1997) 'Development and Democratization', pp. 1–20 in Anek Laothamatas, *Democratization in Southeast and East Asia* (New York: St. Martin's Press).

Larus, Elizabeth F. (2005) *Economic Reform in China, 79–2003: The Marketization of Labor and State Enterprises* (Lewiston, NY/ Lampeter, Wales: Edwin Mellen Press).

Lee, Byeong-cheon (2005) *Developmental Dictatorship and the Park Chung-hee Era: The Shaping of Modernity in the Republic of Korea* (Paramus, NJ: Homa & Sekey Books).

Lee, Chung H. and David H. Bohm (2002) *Financial Liberalization and the Economic Crisis in Asia* (London, Curzon Press).

Lee, Kuan Yew (1994) 'Culture Is Destiny: An Interview with Fareed Zakaria', *Foreign Affairs*, 73, pp. 109–26.

Lee, Namhee, (2007) *The Making of Minjung: Democracy and the Politics of Representation in South Korea* (Ithaca: Cornell University Press).

Lee, Hong Yung. (1991) From Revolutionary Cadres to Party Technocrats in Socialist China. Vol. 31 (University of California Press).

Lee, Manhee. (2015) 'Reconsidering Korea's FTA with China in Its Economic Security', *Pacific Focus*, 30(3), pp. 320–343.

Lee, Terence (2002) 'The Politics of Civil Society in Singapore', *Asian Studies Review*, 26(1), pp. 97–117.

Lee, Yok-shiu, F., and Alvin Y. So. (1999) *Asia's Environmental Movements: Comparative Perspectives* (ME Sharpe).

Leftwich, Adrian (1996) *Democracy and Development: Theory and Practice* (Cambridge: Polity Press).

Leib, Ethan J. and Baogang, He (2006) *The Search for Deliberative Democracy in China* (New York: Palgrave Macmillan).

Leifer, Michael (1999) 'The ASEAN Process: A Category Mistake', *The Pacific Review*, 12(1), pp. 25–38.

Leifer, Michael (2000) *Asian Nationalism* (London: Routledge).

Li, Cheng (2010) *China's Emerging Middle Class: Beyond Economic Transformation* (Brookings Institution Press).

Li, Cheng (2012) 'Leadership Transition in the CPC: Promising Progress and Potential Problems', *China: An International Journal*, 10(2), pp. 23–33.

Liang, Fook Lye; Wilhelm Hofmeister (2011) *Political Parties, Party Systems, and Democratization in East Asia* (London: World Scientific).

Lieberman, Victor (2003) *Strange Parallels: Southeast Asia in Global Context, c. 800–1830, Vol. 1: Integration on the Mainland* (Cambridge: Cambridge University Press).

Lieberthal, Kenneth (2004) *Governing China: From Revolution through Reform* (New York: W. W. Norton).

Lieberthal, Kenneth. (2011) 'The American Pivot to Asia', *Foreign Policy*, Dec 21.

Liff, Adam P., and G. John Ikenberry (2014) 'Racing toward Tragedy? China's Rise, Military Competition in the Asia Pacific, and the Security Dilemma', *International Security*, 39(2), pp. 52–91.

Lijphart, Arend (1977) *Democracy in Plural Societies: A Comparative Exploration* (New Haven, CT: Yale University Press).

Lijphart, Arend (1984) *Democracies: Patterns of Majoritarian and Consensus Government in Twenty-One Countries* (New Haven, CT: Yale University Press).

Lijphart, Arend (1994) *Electoral Systems and Party Systems: A Study of Twenty-Seven Democracies, 45–1990* (Oxford: Oxford University Press).

Lim, L. (1983) 'Singapore's Success: The Myth of the Free Market Economy', *Asian Survey*, 23(6), pp. 752–64.

Lim, Sunghack (2011) 'Political Parties and Party System in Korea after Democratization: Cartelized Party System and Oscillations between Two Models', pp. 211–242 in Lye, Liang Foo, and Wilhelm Hofmeister, *Political Parties Party Systems and Democratization in East Asia* (Singapore: World Scientific).

Limmanee, Anusorn (1998) 'Thailand', pp. 403–48 in Wolfgang Sachsenroder and Ulrike E, *Frings, Political Party Systems and Democratic Development in East and Southeast Asia Volume I Southeast Asia* (Aldershot: Ashgate).

Lin, Chun. (2006) *The Transformation of Chinese Socialism* (Durham, NC: Duke University Press).

Lindsey, Tim, (2002) 'History Always Repeats: Corruption, Culture, and "Asian Values"', pp. 1–23 in Tim Lindsey and Howard Dick, *Corruption in Asia: Rethinking the Governance Paradigm* (Sydney: The Federation Press).

Lingle, Christopher (1998) *The Rise and Decline of the Asian Century: False Starts on the Path to the Global Millennium* (Hong Kong: Asia 2000).

Linz, Juan (1978) *The Breakdown of Democratic Regimes* (Baltimore, MD: Johns Hopkins University Press).

Linz, Juan J. and Alfred Stepan (1996) 'Toward Consolidated Democracies', *Journal of Democracy*, 7(2), pp. 14–33.

Lipset, Seymour M. (1959) 'Some Social Requisites of Democracy: Economic Development and Political Legitimacy', *American Political Science Review*, 53(1), pp. 69–105.

Lipset, Seymour M. (1990) 'The Centrality of Political Culture', *Journal of Democracy*, 1(4), pp. 80–83.

Litvack, Jennie I. and Dennis A. Rondinelli (1999) 'Economic Reform, Social Progress and Institutional Development: A Framework for Assessing Vietnam's Transition', pp. 1–30 in Jennie I. Litvack and Dennis A. Rondinelli, *Market Reform in Vietnam: Building Institutions for Development* (Westport, Conn.: Quorum).

London, Jonathan D. (2014) *Politics in Contemporary Vietnam: Party, State, and Authority Relations* (London: Palgrave)

Low Donald, Sudhir Thomas Vadaketh (2014) *Hard Choices: Challenging the Singapore Consensus* (Singapore: NUS Press).

Luong, Hy V. (2003) *Dynamics of a Transforming Society* (Lanham, MD: Rowan & Littlefield).

Lye, Liang Foo, and Wilhelm Hofmeister (2011) *Political Parties Party Systems and Democratization in East Asia* (Singapore: World Scientific).

M

Ma, Shu-Yun (1994) 'The Chinese Discourse on Civil Society', *The China Quarterly*, 137, pp. 180–93.

MacIntyre, Andrew (1990) *Business and Politics in Indonesia* (North Sydney: Allen & Unwin).

MacIntyre, Pempel, Ravenhill Crisis (2008) 'East Asia in the Wake of the Financial Crisis,' pp. 1–25 in Andrew MacIntyre, T. J. Pempel, John Ravenhill, *Crisis as Catalyst: Asia's Dynamic Political Economy* (Ithaca: Cornell University Press).

MacKay, Joseph (2015) 'Rethinking the IR Theory of Empire in Late Imperial China', *International Relation of the Asia Pacific*, 15(1), pp. 53–79.

Mackerras, Colin (2003a) 'Ethnic Minorities in China', pp. 15–47 in Colin Mackerras, *Ethnicity in Asia* (New York: RoutledgeCurzon).

Mackerras, Colin (2003b) 'Introduction', pp. 1–15 in Colin Mackerras, *Ethnicity in Asia* (New York: RoutledgeCurzon).

Macmahon Ball, W. (1956) *Nationalism and Communism in East Asia* (Melbourne: Melbourne University Press).

Mahbubani, Kishore (1995) 'The Pacific Way', *Foreign Affairs*, 74, pp. 100–111.

Makeham, John and A-Chin Hsiau (2005) *Cultural, Ethnic, and Political Nationalisms in Contemporary Taiwan* (New York: Palgrave).

Malley, Michael (1999) 'Regions: Centralization and Resistance', pp. 71–105 in Donald K. Emmerson, *Indonesia Beyond Suharto: Polity, Economy, Society, Transition* (Armon, NY: M. E. Sharpe).

Mancall, Mark. (1984) *China at the Center: 300 Years of Foreign Policy* (New York: Free Press).

Marx, Karl, Frederick Engels (2002) *The Communist Manifesto* (London: Penguin).

Mauro, Paolo (1997) 'Why Worry About Corruption?', *IMF Economic Issues*, No. 6.

Mauzy, Diane K. (2002a) 'Electoral Innovation and One-Party Dominance in Singapore', pp. 234–54 in John Fuh-sheng Hsieh and David Newman, *How Asia Votes* (New York: Chatham House Publishers/Seven Bridges Press).

Mauzy, Diane K. and R.S. Milne (2002) *Singapore Politics: Under the People's Action Party* (London: Routledge).

McCargo, Duncan (1998) 'Elite Governance: Business, Bureaucrats and the Military', pp. 126–49 in David Goldblatt, Richard Maidment and Jeremy Mitchell, *Governance in the Asia-Pacific* (London/New York: Routledge/Open University).

McCargo, Duncan (1999) 'The International Media and the Domestic Political Coverage of the Thai Press', *Modern Asian Studies*, 33(3), pp. 551–79.

McCargo, Duncan (2003) *Media and Politics in Pacific Asia* (New York/London: Routledge).

McCargo, Duncan (2004) *Rethinking Vietnam* (New York: RoutledgeCurzon).

McCloud, Donald G. (1995) *Southeast Asia: Tradition and Modernity in the Contemporary World* (Boulder, CO: Westview Press).

McNally, David (1998) 'Globalization on Trial: Crisis and Class Struggle in East Asia', *Monthly Review*, 54(4), pp. 1–15.

McNamee, Stephen J. and Robert K. Miller, Jr. (2004) *The Meritocracy Myth* (Lanham. Md.: Rowman & Littlefield).

Means, Gordon P. (1996) 'Soft Authoritarianism in Malaysia and Singapore', *Journal of Democracy*, 7(4), pp. 103–17.

Menton, Linda K., Noren W. Lush, Eileen H. Tamura and Chance I. Gusukuma (2002) *The Rise of Modern Japan* (Honolulu: University of Hawaii Press).

Merryman, John Henry (1977) 'Comparative Law and Social Change: On the Origins, Style, Decline & Revival of the Law and Development Movement', *The American Journal of Comparative Law*, 25(3), pp. 457–91.

Metzger, Thomas (1997) 'The Western Concept of the Civil Society in the Context of Chinese History', *Hoover Monographs* (Stanford: Hoover Institute).

Migdal, Joel S. (2001) *State in Society: Studying How States and Societies Transform and Constitute One Another* (Cambridge: Cambridge University Press).

Migdal, Joel (1994) 'Introduction: Developing a State-in-Society Perspective', pp. 1–6 in Migdal, Joel, Atul Kohli, and Vivienne Shue, *State Power and Social Forces: Domination and Transformation in the Third World* (Cambridge: Cambridge University Press).

Migdal, Joel, Atul Kohli and Vivienne Shue (1994) *State Power and Social Forces: Domination and Transformation in the Third World* (Cambridge: Cambridge University Press).

Miller, Robert (1992) *The Developments of Civil Society in Communist Systems* (North Sydney: Allen & Unwin).

Milner, Anthony (2000) 'What Happened to "Asian Values"?', pp. 56–68 in Gerald Segal and David S. G. Goodman, *Towards Recovery in Pacific Asia* (London: Routledge).

Misra, Kalpana (1998) *From Post-Maoism to Post-Marxism: The Erosion of Official Ideology in Deng's China* (New York: Routledge).

Mitter, Rana (2004) *A Bitter Revolution: China's Struggle with the Modern World* (Oxford University Press).

Mohamad, Mahathir and Shintaro Ishihara (1995) *The Voice of Asia: Two Leaders Discuss the Coming Century* (New York: Kodansha International).

Moon, Chung-in and Rashemi Prasad (1994) 'Beyond the Developmental State: Networks, Politics and Institutions', *Governance*, 7(4), pp. 360–86.

Morada, Noel M. and Teresa S. E. Tadem (2006) *Philippines Politics and Governance: An Introduction* (Diliman: Department of Political Science, University of the Philippines Diliman).

Morgan, E. P. (1996) 'Analysing Fields of Change: Civil Service System in Developing Countries', pp. 227–246 in A. J. G. M. Bekke, J. J. Perry, and Th. A. J. Toonen, *Civil Service Systems in Comparative Perspective* (Bloomington: Indiana University Press).

Morley, James W. (1993) *Driven by Growth: Political Change in the Asia-Pacific Region* (Armonk, NY: M. E. Sharpe).

Morton, Katherine. (2005) *International Aid and China's Environment: Taming the Yellow Dragon* (London: Routledge).

Mulgan, Aurelia George (2003) 'The Dynamics of Coalition Politics in Japan," pp. 36–54 in Jennifer Amyx, and Peter Drysdale, *Japanese Governance beyond Japan Inc.* (London: Routledge).

Muramatsu, Michio (1997) *Local Power in the Japanese State* (Berkeley, CA: University of California Press).

Muscat, Robert J. (1994) *The Fifth Tiger: A Study of Thai Development Policy* (Armonk, NY: M. E. Sharpe).

N

National Bureau of Statistics of China, 1990 Fourth National Census Results, Report No 3. 14 Nov 1990. http://www.stats.gov.cn/tjgb/rkpcgb/qgrkpcgb/t20020404_16773.htm (accessed August 2008).

Narine, Shaun (2005) 'State Sovereignty, Political Legitimacy and Regional Institutionalism in the Asia-Pacific', *The Pacific Review*, 17(3), pp. 423–450.

Naughton, Barry (1995) *Growing Out of the Plan: Chinese Economic Reform, 1978–1993* (New York: Cambridge University Press).

Nee, Victor and David Stark (1989) *Remaking the Economic Institutions of Socialism: China and Eastern Europe* (Stanford, CA: Stanford University Press).

Needham, Joseph (1959) 'Review of Oriental Despotism', *Science and Society*, XXIII, pp. 58–65.

Neher, Clark D. (1994) 'Asian Style Democracy', *Asian Survey*, 34(11), pp. 946–61.

Neher, Clark D., and Ross Marlay (1995) *Democracy and Development in Southeast Asia: The Winds of Change* (Boulder, CO: Westview Press).

Nesadurai, Helen E. S. (2012) 'Trade Policy in SEA: Politics, Domestic Interests and the Forging of New Accommodations in the Regional and Global Economy', pp. 315–330 in Richard Robinson, *Routledge Handbook of Southeast Asian Politics* (London: Routledge).

Ng, Margaret (1998) 'Why Asia Needs Democracy: A View from Hong Kong', pp. 3–16 in Larry Diamond and Marc F. Plattner, *Democracy in East Asia* (Baltimore, MD: Johns Hopkins University Press).

Ngo, Tak-wing (2005) 'The Political Bases of Episodic Agency in the Taiwan State', pp. 83–109 in Richard Boyd and Tak-wing Ngo, *Asian States: Beyond the Developmental Perspective* (London: Routledge).

Nitobé, Inanzo (1905) *Bushido, the Soul of Japan* (New York: GP Putnamś sons).

Noble, Gregory W. (2003) 'Refom and Continuity in Japan's Shingikai Deliberation Councils', pp. 113–129 in Jennifer Amyx, and Peter Drysdale, *Japanese Governance beyond Japan Inc.* (London: Routledge).

Noble, Gregory W. and John Ravenhill (2000) *The Asian Financial Crisis and the Architecture of Global Finance* (Cambridge, Cambridge University Press).

Nohlen, Dieter, Florian Grotz and Christof Hartmann (2001a) 'Elections and Electoral Systems in Asia and the Pacific', pp. 1–44 in Dieter Nohlen, Florian Grotz and Christof Hartmann, *Elections in Asia and the Pacific* (Oxford: Oxford University Press).

Nohlen, Dieter, Florian Grotz and Christof Hartmann (2001a) *Elections in Asia and the Pacific* (Oxford: Oxford University Press).

Nolt, James H. (1999) 'Liberalizing Asia', *World Policy Journal*, 16(2), pp. 94–110.

Nordholt, Henke Schulte (2012) 'Decentralization and Democracy in Indonesia: Strengthening Citizenship or Regional Elite', pp. 229–241 in Richard Robinson, *Routledge Handbook of Southeast Asian Politics* (London: Routledge).

North, Douglass C. (1990) *Institutions, Institutional Change and Economic Performance* (Cambridge: Cambridge University Press).

North, Douglass C. and Robert Paul Thomas (1968) *The Growth of the American Economy to 1860* (Columbia: University of South Carolina Press).

North, Douglass C. and Robert Paul Thomas (1973) *The Rise of the Western World: A New Economic History* (Cambridge: Cambridge University Press).

NPC (Chinese National People's Congress) (2007) 'Decision on Issues Regarding the Allocation and Election of Delegates to the 11th NPC', available at: http://news.xinhuanet.com/misc/2007-03/16/content_5857677.htm.

O

Obama, Barrack, (2015) 'Statement by the President on the Trans-Pacific Partnership', *The White House*, 5 October, 2015, available at https://www.whitehouse.gov/the-press-office/2015/10/05/statement-president-trans-pacific-partnership.

Ockey, James (2001) 'Thailand: The Struggle to Redefine Civil–Military Relations', pp. 187–208 in Muthiah Alagappa, *Coercion and Governance: The Declining Political Role of the Military in Asia* (Stanford, CA: Stanford University Press).

Ockey, James (2004a) 'State, Bureaucracy and Polity in Modern Thai Politics', *Journal of Contemporary Asia*, 34(2), pp. 143–62.

Ockey, James (2004b) *Making Democracy: Leadership, Class, Gender, and Political Participation* (Honolulu: University of Hawaii Press).

O'Donnell, Guillermo (1973) *Modernization and Bureaucratic Authoritarianism* (Berkeley, CA: UC Institute for International Studies).

Oh, John Kie-Chiang (1999) *Korean Politics* (Ithaca, NY: Cornell University Press).

Oishi, Shinzaburo (1990) 'The Bakuhan System', pp. 11–36 in Shinzaburo Oishi and Chie Nakane, *Tokugawa Japan: The Social and Economic Antecedents of Modern Japan* (Tokyo: University of Tokyo Press).

Okimoto, Daniel I. (1989) *Between MITI and the Market: Japanese Industrial Policy for High Technology* (Stanford, CA: Stanford University Press).

Okochi, Akio and Shigeaki Yasuoka (1984) *Family Business in the Era of Industrial Growth: Its Ownership and Management* (Tokyo: University of Tokyo Press).

Olson, Mancur (1993) 'Dictatorship, Democracy, and Development', *American Political Science Review*, 87(3), pp. 567–77.

Öniş, Ziya (1991) 'The Logic of the Developmental State', *Comparative Politics*, 24(1), pp. 109–26.

Ooi, Can Seng. (1998) 'Singapore', pp. 343–402 in Wolfgang Sachsenroder and Ulrike E, Frings, *Political Party Systems and Democratic Development in East and Southeast Asia Volume I Southeast Asia* (Aldershot: Ashgate).

O'Rourke, Kevin H. and Jeffrey G. Williamson (2000) *Globalization and History: The Evolution of a 19th Century Atlantic Economy* (Cambridge, MA: MIT Press).

P

Painter, Martin (2004) 'The Politics of Administrative Reform in East and Southeast Asia: From Gridlock to Continuous Self-Improvement?' *Governance*, 17(3), pp. 361–86.

Painter, Martin (2006) 'Thaksinisation or Managerialism? Reforming the Thai Bureaucracy', *Journal of Contemporary Asia*, 36(1), pp. 26–47.

Palais, James B. (1996) *Confucian Statecraft and Korean Institutions Yu Hyongwon and the Late Choson Dynasty* (Seattle, WA: University of Washington Press).

Palais, James B. (1991) *Harvard University Asia Center Politics and Policy in Traditional Korea* (Cambridge: Harvard University Asia Center).

Panebianco, Angelo (1988) *Political Parties: Organization and Power* (Cambridge/New York: Cambridge University Press).

Parsons, Talcott (1951) *The Social System* (Glencoe, IL: Free Press).

Patapan, Haig, John Wanna and Patrick Weller (2005) *Westminster Legacies: Democracy and Responsible Government in Asia and the Pacific* (Sydney: University of New South Wales Press).

Patnaik, Prabhat (1999) 'Capitalism in Asia at the End of the Millennium', *Monthly Review*, 51(3), pp. 53–70.

Patrick, Hugh (1977) 'The Future of the Japanese Economy: Output and Labor Productivity', *Journal of Japanese Studies*, 3(2), pp. 219–49.

Patten, Chris (1996) 'Asian Values and Asian Successes', *Survival*, 38(2), pp. 5–12.

Peerenboom, Randall (2004) *Asian Discourses of Rule of Law* (London: Routledge).

Pei, Minxin (1994) *From Reform to Revolution: The Demise of Communism in China and the Soviet Union* (Cambridge, MA: Harvard University Press).

Pei, Minxin (1998a) 'The Fall and Rise of Democracy in East Asia', pp. 57–78 in Larry Diamond and Marc F. Plattner, *Democracy in East Asia* (Baltimore, MD: Johns Hopkins University Press).

Pei, Minxin (1998b) 'Constructing the Political Foundations of an Economic Miracle', pp. 39–59 in Henry S. Rowen, *Behind East Asian Growth: The Political and Social Foundations of Prosperity* (London: Routledge).

Pei, Minxin (2006) *China's Trapped Transition: The Limits of Developmental Autocracy* (Cambridge, MA: Harvard University Press).

Pekkanen, Robert (2004) 'Japan: Social Capital Without Advocacy', pp. 223–55 in Muthiah Alagappa, *Civil Society, and Political Change in Asia: Expanding and Contracting Democratic Space* (Stanford, CA: Stanford University Press).

Pempel, T. J. (1990) *Uncommon Democracies: The One-Party Dominant Regimes* (Ithaca, NY: Cornell University Press).

Pempel, T. J. (1992) 'Bureaucracy in Japan', *PS: Political Science and Politics*, 25(1), pp. 19–24.

Pempel, T. J. (1998) *Regime Shift: Comparative Dynamics of the Japanese Political Economy* (Ithaca. NY: Cornell University Press).

Pempel, T. J. (2008) 'Learning to Lose Is for Losers: The Japanese LDP's Reform Struggle', pp. 109–126 in Friedman, Edward and Joseph Wong, *Political Transitions in Dominant Party Systems: Learning to Lose* (London: Routledge).

Peou, Sorpong (2001) 'Cambodia: After the Killing Fields', pp. 36–73 in John Funston, *Government and Politics in Southeast Asia* (Singapore: Institute of Southeast Asian Studies/ New York: Palgrave).

Perlmutter, Amos (1977a) *The Military and Politics in Modern Times: On Professionals, Praetorians, and Revolutionary Soldiers* (New Haven, CT: Yale University Press).

Perlmutter, Amos (1977b) *The Military and Politics in Modern Times* (New Haven, CT: Yale University Press).

Perry, Elizabeth J. and Merle Goldman (2007) *Grassroots Political Reform in Contemporary China* (Cambridge, MA: Harvard University Press).

Phongpaichit, Pasuk and Chris Baker (2004) *Thaksin: The Business of Politics in Thailand* (Copenhagen: NIAS/Chiang Mai, Thailand: Silkworm).

Phongpaichit, Pasuk, and Chris Baker (2008) 'Thaksin's Populism', *Journal of Contemporary Asia*, 38(1), pp. 62–83.

Pierson, Christopher (2004) *The Modern State* (London and New York: Routledge).

Pistor, Katharina and Philip A. Wellons (1999) *The Role of Law and Legal Institutions in Asian Economic Development, 1960–1995* (Oxford: Oxford University Press).

Polidano Charles (2001) 'Don't Discard State Autonomy: Revisiting the East Asian Experience of Development', *Political Studies*, 49(3), pp. 513–27.

Popper, Karl (1963) *The Open Society and Its Enemies* (Princeton, NJ: Princeton University Press).

Porter, Gareth (1993) *Vietnam: The Politics of Bureaucratic Socialism* (Ithaca, NY: Cornell University Press).

Przeworski, Adam, Michael Alvarez, Jose Antonia Cheibub and Fernando Limongi (1996) 'What Makes Democracies Endure?', *Journal of Democracy*, 7(1), pp. 39–55.

Przeworski, Adam, Michael E. Alvarez, Jose A. Cheibub and Fernando Limongi (2000) *Democracy and Development: Political Institutions and Well-being in the World, 1950–1990* (Cambridge: Cambridge University Press).

Pye, Lucian W. (1962) 'Armies in the Process of Political Modernization', pp. 69–89 in John J. Johnson, *The Role of the Military in Underdeveloped Countries* (Princeton, NJ: Princeton University Press).

Pye, Lucian W. (1966a) 'Party Systems and National Development in Asia', pp. 177–200 in Joseph LaPalombara and Myron Weiner, *Political Parties and Political Development* (Princeton, NJ: Princeton University Press).

Pye, Lucian W., and Sidney Verba (2015) *Political Culture and Political Development* (Princeton University Press) [1965].

Pye, Lucian W. (1966b) *Aspects of Political Development* (Boston, MA: Little, Brown).

Pye, Lucian W. (1985) *Asian Power and Politics: The Cultural Dimensions of Authority* (Cambridge: Belknap Press).

Pye, Lucian W. (1999) 'Civility, Social Capital, and Civil Society: Three Powerful Concepts for Explaining Asia', *The Journal of Interdisciplinary History*, 29(4), pp. 763–82.

Pye, Oliver, and Wolfram Schaffar (2008) 'The 2006 Anti-Thaksin Movement in Thailand: An Analysis', *Journal of Contemporary Asia*, 38(1), pp. 38–61.

Q

Qin, Yaqing (2010) 'International Society as a Process: Institutions, Identities, and China's Peaceful Rise', *The Chinese Journal of International Politics*, 3(2), pp. 129–153.

Quah, Jon S. T. (2001) 'Singapore: Meritocratic City-state', pp. 291–327 in John Funston, *Government and Politics in Southeast Asia* (Singapore: Institute of Southeast Asian Studies/New York: Palgrave).

Quah, Jon S. T., Chan Heng Chee and Seah Chee Meow. (1987) *Government and Politics of Singapore* (Oxford: Oxford University Press).

R

Raadschelders, Jos C. N. and Mark R. Rutgers (1996) 'The Evolution of Civil Service Systems', pp. 67–99 in Hans A. G. Bekke, James L. Perry and Theo A. J. Toonen, *Civil Service Systems in Comparative Perspective* (Bloomington, IN: Indiana University Press).

Rajah, Ananda (1998) 'Ethnicity and Civil War', pp. 135–52 in Robert I. Rotberg, *Burma: Prospects for a Democratic Future*, (Washington, DC: World Peace Foundation).

Reilly, Benjamin (2007) 'Democratization and Electoral Reform in the Asia-Pacific Region Is There an "Asian Model" of Democracy?', *Comparative Political Studies*, 40(11), pp. 1350–1371.

Reilly, Benjamin (2014) 'Electoral Systems in Southeast Asia', pp. 225–236 in William Case, *Routledge Handbook of Southeast Asian Democratization* (London: Routledge).

Ramsdell, Daniel B. (1992) *The Japanese Diet: Stability and Change in the Japanese House of Representatives 1890–1990* (Lanham, MD: University Press of America).

Ramseyer, J. Mark and Frances McCall Rosenbluth (1993) *Japan's Political Marketplace* (Cambridge, MA: Harvard University Press).

Randall, Vicky (1993) 'The Media and Democratization in the Third World', *Third World Quarterly*, 14(3), pp. 625–46.

Rau, Zbigniew (1991) *The Reemergence of Civil Society in Eastern Europe and the Soviet Union* (Boulder, CO: Westview Press).

Ravenhill, John (2001) *APEC and the Construction of Pacific Rim Regionalism* (New York: Cambridge University Press).

Rebullida, Ma Lourdes G. Genato (2006) 'Martial Law, Constitutional Authoritarianism, and the Marcos Administration," pp. 153–176 in Noel M. Morada and Teresa S. E. Tadem, *Philippines Politics and Governance: An Introduction* (Diliman: Department of Political Science, University of the Philippines Diliman).

Richter, Frank-Jürgen (2000) *The East Asian Development Model: Economic Growth, Institutional Failure, and the Aftermath of the Crisis* (Basingstoke: Palgrave).

Rieger, Hans Christoph (2001) 'Singapore', pp. 239–60 in Dieter Nohlen, Florian Grotz and Christof Hartman, *Elections in Asia and the Pacific* (Oxford: Oxford University Press).

Rigger, Shelley (1999) *Politics in Taiwan: Voting for Democracy* (London: Routledge).

Rigger, Shelley (2003) 'Disaggregating the Concept of National Identity', pp. 17–21 in Gang Lin, *The Evolution of a Taiwanese National Identity* (Washington, DC: The Wilson International Center for Scholars).

Riggs, Fred W. (1966) *Thailand: The Modernization of a Bureaucratic Polity* (Honolulu: East-West Center Press).

Riker, William H. (1982) 'The Two-Party System and Duverger's Law', *American Political Science Review*, 76(4), pp. 753–66.

Robertson, Robert T. (2003) *The Three Waves of Globalization: A History of a Developing Global Consciousness* (London: Zed Books).

Robinson, Richard (2012) *Routledge Handbook of Southeast Asian Politics* (London: Routledge).

Robinson, Kathryn (2009) *Gender, Islam and democracy in Indonesia* (London: Routledge).

Robinson, Richard (1986) *Indonesia: the Rise of Capital* (Sydney: Allen & Unwin).

Robinson, Richard (2012) 'Interpreting the Politics of Southeast Asia: Debates in Parallel Universes', pp. 5–22 in Richard Robinson, *Routledge Handbook of Southeast Asian Politics* (London: Routledge).

Rodan, Garry (1996) 'Theorizing Political Opposition in East and Southeast Asia', pp. 1–39 in Garry Rodan, *Political Opposition in Industrializing Asia* (London: Routledge).

Roh, Jae-whak, and O-hyun Kwon (2015) 'Korea's Accession to the TPP', *Journal of Korea Trade,* 19(1), pp. 23–40.

Romano, Angela (2005) 'Asian Journalism: News, Development and the Tides of Liberalization and Technology', in Angela Romano and Michael Bromley *Journalism and Democracy in Asia* (London and New York: RoutledgeCurzon).

Romano, Angela and Michael Bromley (2005) *Journalism and Democracy in Asia* (London and New York: RoutledgeCurzon).

Rosenau, James N. (1969) *Linkage Politics: Essays on the Convergence of National and International Systems* (New York: Free Press).

Ross, Robert S. (1999) 'The Geography of the Peace: East Asia in the Twenty-First Century', *International Security* 23(4), pp. 81–118.

Rosett, Arthur, Lucie Cheng and Margaret Y. K. Woo (2002) *East Asian Law: Universal Norms and Local Cultures* (London: RoutledgeCurzon).

Rossabi, Morris (2004) *Governing China's Multiethnic Frontiers* (Seattle, WA: University of Washington Press).

Rostow, W. W. (1960) *The Stages of Economic Growth: A Non-Communist Manifesto* (Cambridge: Cambridge University Press).

Rowen, Henry S. (1998) *Behind East Asian Growth: The Political and Social Foundations of Prosperity* (London: Routledge).

Roy, Denny (1994) 'Singapore, China, and the "Soft Authoritarian" Challenge', *Asian Survey*, 34(3), pp. 231–42.

Roy, Denny (2003) *Taiwan: A Political History* (Ithaca, NY: Cornell University Press).

Rüland, Jürgen (2001) 'Indonesia', pp. 83–129 in Dieter Nohlen, Florian Grotz and Christof Hartmann, *Elections in Asia and the Pacific* (Oxford: Oxford University Press).

Rüland, Jurgen Meyer, Ziegenhain Nelson (2005) *Parliaments and Political Change in Asia* (Singapore: IDEAS).

S

Sachsenroder, Wolfgang (1998) 'Party Politics and Democratic Development in East and Southeast Asia – A Comparative View', pp. 1–35 in Wolfgang Sachsenroder and Ulrike E, Frings, *Political Party Systems and Democratic Development in East and Southeast Asia Volume II East Asia.* (Andover: Ashgate).

Sachsenroder, Wolfgang and Ulrike E, Frings (1998) *Political Party Systems and Democratic Development in East and Southeast Asia* (Andover: Ashgate).

Saha, Santosh C. (2007) 'Introduction', pp 1–6 in *The Politics of Ethnicity and National Identity* (New York: Peter Lang).

Saich, Tony (2015) *Governance and Politics of China* (Basingstoke: Palgrave/Macmillan).

Said, Edward W. (2003) *Orientalism* (London: Penguin).

Sano, Chiye (1973) *Changing Values of the Japanese Family* (Westport, CT: Greenwood Press).

Saw, Swee-Hock and K. Kesavapany (2006) *Malaysia: Recent Trends and Challenges* (Singapore: Institute of Southeast Asian Studies).

Scalapino, Robert A. (1989) *The Politics of Development: Perspectives on Twentieth-Century Asia* (Cambridge, MA: Harvard University Press).

SCAP (Supreme Commander for the Allied Powers) (1949) *Political Reorientation of Japan, September 1945 to September 1948: Report* (Washington, DC: US Government Printing Office).

Scheiner, Ethan (2005) *Democracy without Competition in Japan: Opposition Failure in a One-Party Dominant State* (New York: Cambridge University Press).

Schermerhorn, Richard (1996) 'Ethnicity and Minority Groups', in John Hutchinson and Anthony D. Smith, *Ethnicity* (Oxford: Oxford University Press).

Schneider, Claudia (2008) 'The Japanese History Textbook Controversy in East Asian perspective', *The ANNALS of the American Academy of Political and Social Science*, 617(1), pp. 107–122.

Schwarz, Adam (2000) *A Nation in Waiting: Indonesia's Search for Stability* (Boulder, CO: Westview Press).

Schwartz, Benjamin I. (1968) *Communism and China: Ideology in Flux* (Cambridge, MA: Harvard University Press).

Schwartz, Frank (2003) 'What Is Civil Society', pp. 23–41 in Frank J. Schwartz and Susan J. Pharr, *The State of Civil Society in Japan* (Cambridge: Cambridge University Press).

Schweller, Randall L. and Xiaoyu Pu (2011) 'After Unipolarity: China's Visions of International Order in an Era of U.S. Decline', *International Security*, 36(1): 41–72.

Schott, Jeffrey J., and Cathleen Cimino (2014) 'Should Korea Join the trans-Pacific Partnership?' *Policy Brief*, 14(22).

Seah, Chee-Meow (1977) *Asian Values and Modernization* (Singapore: Singapore University Press).

Segal, Gerald (1992) *The Great Power Triangle* (London: Macmillan).

Selznick, Philip (1952) *The Organizational Weapon* (New York: McGraw-Hill).

Sen, Krishna (2008) 'Mediating Political Transition in Asia', pp. 1–10 in Krishna Sen and Terence Lee, *Political Regimes and the Media in Asia* (London: Routledge).

Sen, Krishna and Terence Lee (2008) *Political Regimes and the Media in Asia* (London: Routledge).

Shafruddin, B. H. (1987) *The Federal Factor in the Government and Politics of Peninsular Malaysia* (New York: Oxford University Press).

Shambaugh, David (1991) 'The Soldier and the State in China: The Political Work System in the People's Republic of China', *The China Quarterly*, 127, pp. 527–68.

Shambul, A. B. (1998) 'Bureaucratic Management of Identity in a Modern State: "Malayness" in postwar Malaysia', pp. 135–50 in Dru C. Gladney, *Making Majorities: Constituting the Nation in Japan, Korea, China, Malaysia, Fiji, Turkey, and the United States* (Stanford, CA: Stanford University Press).

Sharma, Shalendra (2003) *The Asian Financial Crisis: New International Financial Architecture: Crisis, Reform and Recovery* (New York: Manchester University Press).

Sheng, Emile C. J. (2007) 'Partisanship in East Asia', *Journal of East Asian Studies*, 7(2), pp. 275–94.

Shigetomi, Shinichi (2002) *The State and NGOs: Perspective from Asia* (Singapore: ISEAS).

Shih, Chih-yu (2002) *Negotiating Ethnicity in China: Citizenship as a Response to the State* (London/New York: Routledge).

Shin, Doh C. (1999) *Mass Politics and Culture in Democratizing Korea* (Cambridge: Cambridge University Press).

Shin, Gi-Wook and Michael Robinson (1999) *Colonial Modernity in Korea* (Cambridge, MA: Harvard University Asia Center).

Shin, Gi-Wook (2006) *Ethnic Nationalism in Korea* (Stanford: Stanford University Press).

Shinoda, Tomohito (2013) *Contemporary Japanese Politics: Institutional Changes and Power Shifts* (New York: Columbia University Press).

Shirk, Susan L. (1993)*The Political Logic of Economic Reform in China* (Berkeley, CA: University of California Press).

Skocpol, Theda, (1985) 'Bringing the State Back In: Strategies of Analysis in Current Research', pp. 3–43 in Peter. B. Evans, Dietrich Rueschmeyer and Theda Skocpol, *Bringing the State Back In* (Cambridge: Cambridge University Press).

Slater, Dan (2010) Ordering Power: Contentious Politics and Authoritarian Leviathans in Southeast Asia (Cambridge: Cambridge University Press).

Smith, Donald Eugene (1971) Religion, Politics and Social Change in the Third World (New York, Free Press).

Smith, Donald Eugene (1974) *Religion and Political Modernization* (New Haven, CT: Yale University Press).

Smith, Martin (2007) 'State of Strife: The Dynamics of Ethnic Conflict in Burma', *Policy Studies 36* (Washington DC East-West Center).

Smoke, Paul (2005) 'The Rules of the Intergovernmental Game in East Asia: Decentralization Frameworks and Processes', pp. 25–52 in World Bank, *East Asia Decentralizes: Making Local Government Work in East Asia* (Washington, DC: World Bank).

South, Ashley (2008) Ethnic Politics in Burma: States of Conflict (London: Routledge).

Spengler, Oswald (1926) *The Decline of the West* (New York: Knopf).

Spruyt, Hendrik (1994) *The Sovereign State and Its Competitors* (Princeton, NJ: Princeton University Press).

Steinberg, David Joel (1971) *In Search of Southeast Asia* (New York: Praeger).

Steinberg, David I. (2001) *Burma: The State of Myanmar* (Washington, DC: Georgetown University Press).

Stephenson, Matthew (2008) 'Economic Development and the Quality of Legal Institutions', *in Rule of Law and Development, World Bank*, available at: http://siteresources.worldbank.org/INTLAWJUSTINST/Resources/LegalInstitutionsTopicBrief.pdf.

Stiglitz, Joseph E. and Shahid Yusuf (2001) *Rethinking the East Asian Miracle* (Washington, DC: World Bank).

Stockton, Hans (2006) *The Future of Development in Vietnam and the Challenges of Globalization* (Lewiston, NY: Edwin Mellen Press).

Stockwin, J. A. A. (1999) *Governing Japan* (Oxford: Blackwell).

Stokes, Geoffrey (2006) 'Critical Theories of Deliberative Democracy and the Problem of Citizenship', pp. 53–73 in Ethan J. Leib and Baogang He, *The Search for Deliberative Democracy in China* (New York: Palgrave Macmillan).

Storry, Richard (1979) *Japan and the Decline of the West in Asia, 1894–1943* (London: Macmillan).

Strauss, Julia C. (1998) *Strong Institutions in Weak Polities: State Building in Republican China, 1927–1940* (New York: Oxford University Press).

Streeck, Wolfgang, and Kathleen A. Thelen (2005) 'Institutional Change in Advanced Political Economies', pp. 1–39 in Streeck and Thelen, *Beyond Continuity: Institutional Change in Advanced Political Economies* (Oxford University Press).

Stuart-Fox, Martin (2003) *A Short History of China and Southeast Asia: Tribute, Trade and Influence* (Sydney, Australia: Allen & Unwin).

Suganami, Hidemi (1984) 'Japan's Entry into International Society', pp. 185–199 in Hedley Bull and Adam Watson, *The Expansion of International Society* (Oxford: Clarendon Press).

Surin, Maisrikrod (1992) *Thailand's Two General Elections in 1992: Democracy Sustained* (Singapore: Institute of Southeast Asian Studies).

Surin, Maisrikrod (2002) 'Political Reform and the New Thai Electoral System', pp. 187–209 in John Fuh-sheng Hsieh and David Newman, *How Asia Votes* (New York: Chatham House Publishers and Seven Bridges Press).

T

Tai, Hung-chao (1989) *Confucianism and Economic Development: An Oriental Alternative* (Washington, DC: Washington Institute Press).

Tambiah, Stanley J. (1976) *World Conqueror and World Renouncer: A Study of Buddhism and Polity in Thailand against a Historical Background* (Cambridge: Cambridge University Press).

Tamney, Joseph B. and Linda Hsueh-Ling Chiang (2002) *Modernization, Globalization, and Confucianism in Chinese Societies* (Westport, CT: Praeger).

Tan, Qingshan (2000) 'Democratization and Bureaucratic Restructuring in Taiwan', *Studies in Comparative International Development*, 35(2), pp. 48–64.

Tang, Ching-Ping (2003) 'Democratizing Urban Politics and Civic Environmentalism in Taiwan', *The China Quarterly*, 176, pp. 1029–1051.

Tang, James T. H. (1994) *Human Rights and International Relations in the Asia-Pacific Region* (London: Pinter).

Tang, Wenfang (2005) *Public Opinion and Political Change in China* (Stanford: Stanford University Press).

Tanzi, Vito and Hamid Davoodi (1998) 'Roads to Nowhere: How Corruption in Public Investment Hurts Growth', *IMF Economic Issues*, No. 12.

Terwiel, B. J. (2011) *Thailand's Political History: From the 13th Century to Recent Times* (Bangkok: River Books).

Than, Tin Maung (2001) 'Myanmar: Military in Charge', pp. 203–51 in John Funston, *Government and Politics in Southeast Asia* (Singapore: Institute of Southeast Asian Studies/New York: Palgrave).

Thies, Michael (2002) 'Changing How the Japanese Vote: The Promise and Pitfalls of the 1994 Electoral Reform', pp. 92–117 in John Fuh-sheng Hsieh and David Newman, *How Asia Votes* (New York: Chatham House Publishers and Seven Bridges Press).

Thompson, Mark R. (2004) *Democratic Revolutions: Asia and Eastern Europe* (London: Routledge).

Thornton, Patricia M. (2007) *Disciplining the State: Virtue, Violence, and State Making in Modern China* (Cambridge, MA: Harvard University Asia Center).

Tien, Hung-mao (1989) *The Great Transition: Political and Social Change in the Republic of China* (Stanford: Hoover Institution Press).

Tilly, Charles (1985) 'War Making and State Making as Organized Crime', pp. 169–91 in Peter B. Evans, Dietrich Rueschmeyer and Theda Skocpol, *Bringing the State Back In* (Cambridge: Cambridge University Press).

Tilly, Charles (1990) *Coercion, Capital, and European States, AD 990–1992* (Oxford: Blackwell).

Tilly, Charles, and Gabriel Ardant (1975) *The formation of national states in Western Europe. Vol. 8.* (Princeton, NJ: Princeton University Press).

Tismaneanu, Vladimir (1990) *In Search of Civil Society: Independence Peace Movements in the Soviet Bloc* (New York: Routledge).

Transparency International (2015) *CPI 2015*, https://www.transparency.org/cpi2015#map-container

Tsang, Steve (1993) *In the Shadow of China: Political Developments in Taiwan since 1949* (Honolulu: University of Hawaii Press).

Tu, Weiming (1991) 'Cultural China: the Periphery as Center', *Daedalus*, 120(2), pp. 1–32.

Tu, Weiming (2000) 'Implications of the Rise of "Confucian"' East Asia', *Daedalus*, 129(1), pp. 195–219.

Turner, Karen G. (2015) *The Limits of the Rule of Law in China* (Seattle, WA: University of Washington Press).

U

U, Eddy (2007) *Disorganizing China: Counter-Bureaucracy and the Decline of Socialism* (Stanford: Stanford University Press).

UNDP (United Nations Development Programme) (2015) *Human Development Report 2015* (New York: UNDP).

Unger, Jonathan (2006) 'China's Conservative Middle Class', *Far Eastern Economic Review*, 169(3).

Unger, Jonathan and Anita Chan (1995) 'China, Corporatism, and the East Asian Model', *The Australian Journal of Chinese Affairs*, 33(1), pp. 29–53.

Unger, Jonathan and Anita Chan (1996) 'Corporatism in China: A Developmental State in an East Asian Context?', pp. 95–129 in Barret McCormick and Jonathan Unger, *China after Socialism: In the Footsteps of East Europe or East Asia?* (Armonk, NY: M. E. Sharpe).

United Nations (2004–7) Public Administration Country Profile. Division for Public Administration and Development Management (DPADM) Department of Economic and Social Affairs (DESA) United Nations (Cambodia, 2004; Thailand, 2004; Vietnam, 2004; Philippines, 2005; East Timor, 2005; Singapore, 2005; Malaysia, 2005; Indonesia, 2005; Laos, 2005; China, 2006; Japan, 2006; North Korea, 2006; South Korea, 2007).

V

Van der Veer, Peter, and Hartmut Lehmann (1999) *Nation and Religion: Perspectives on Europe and Asia* (Princeton, NJ: Princeton University Press).

Van Ness, Peter (2002) 'Hegemony, Not Anarchy: Why China and Japan Are Not Balancing US Unipolar Power', *International Relations of the Asia Pacific*, 2, pp.131–150.

Vasil, Raj (2000) *Governing Singapore* (St. Leonards, Australia: Allen & Unwin).

Vatikiotis, Michael R. J. (1998) *Indonesian Politics under Suharto: The Rise and Fall of the New Order* (London: Routledge).

Veblen, Thorstein (1915) *Imperial Germany and the Industrial Revolution* (Transaction Publishers) [1990].

Verma, Vidhu (2002) 'Debating rights in Malaysia: Contradictions and Challenges in Democratization', *Journal of Contemporary Asia*, 32(1), pp. 108–30.

Verma, Anil, Thomas A. Kochan and Russell D. Landsbury (1995) *Employment Relations in the Growing Asian Economics* (London: Routledge).

Vogel, Ezra F. (2013) *Japan's New Middle Class* (Lanham, MD: Rowman & Littlefield Publishers).

Vu, Tuong (2014) 'The Making and Unmaking of the Communist Party and Single-Party System of Vietnam', pp. 136–161 in Edited by Allen Hicken and Erik M. Kuhonta, *Party System Institutionalization in Asia: Democracies, Autocracies, and the Shadows of the Past* (Cambridge University Press).

W

Wade, Robert (1990) *Governing the Market: Economic Theory and the Role of Government in East Asian Industrialization* (Princeton, NJ: Princeton University Press).

Wade, Robert H. (2003) 'What Strategies Are Viable for Developing Countries Today? The World Trade Organization and the Shrinking of "Development Space"', *Review of International Political Economy*, 10 (4), pp. 621–44.

Walder, Andrew G. (1995) *The Waning of the Communist State: Economic Origins of Political Decline in China and Hungary* (Berkeley, CA: University of California Press).

Wallerstein, Immanuel (1974) *The Modern World-System* (New York: Academic Press).

Willnat, Lars, Annette Aw (2014) *Social Media, Culture and Politics in Asia* (New York: Peter Lang).

Wang, Fei-Ling (2005) *Organizing Through Division and Exclusion: China's Hukou System* (Stanford University Press).

Waltz, Kenneth N. (1979) *Theory of International Politics* (Reading, MA: Addison-Wesley).

Wang, James C. F. (1994) *Comparative Asian Politics: Power, Policy, and Change* (Englewood Cliffs, NJ: Prentice Hall).

Wang, Zhengxu (2008) *Democratization in Confucian East Asia: Citizen Politics in China, Japan, Singapore, South Korea, Taiwan, and Vietnam* (Youngstown, NY: Cambria Press).

Weatherbee, Donald E. (2002) 'Indonesia: Electoral Politics in a Newly Emerging Democracy', pp. 255–81 in John Fuh-sheng Hsieh and David Newman, *How Asia Votes* (New York: Chatham House Publishers and Seven Bridges Press).

Webber, Douglas (2001) 'Two Funerals and a Wedding? The Ups And Downs of Regionalism in East Asia and Asia-Pacific after the Asian Crisis', *The Pacific Review*, 14(3), pp. 339–72.

Weber, Max (1947) *The Theory of Social and Economic Organization* (Glencoe: Free Press).

Weber, Max (1965) *Politics as a Vocation* (Philadelphia, PA: Fortress Press).

Weber, Max (1968) *Economy and Society* (New York: Bedminster Press).

Weigle, Marcia A. and Jim Butterfield (1992) 'Civil Society in Reforming Communist Regimes: The Logic of Emergence', *Comparative Politics*, 25(1), pp. 1–24.

Weiss, Linda (1998) *The Myth of the Powerless State* (Ithaca: Cornell University Press).

Weiss, Linda and John M. Hobson (1995) *States and Economic Development: A Comparative Historical Analysis* (Cambridge: Polity Press).

Weller, Robert P. (2005) *Civil Life, Globalization, and Political Change in Asia: Organizing between Family and State* (New York/London: Routledge).

Wescott, Clay G. (2001) *Key Governance Issues in Cambodia, Lao PDR, Thailand, and Viet Nam* (Manila, Philippines: Asia Development Bank).

White, James D. (2013) *Global Media: the Television Revolution in Asia* (London: Routledge).

White III, Lynn T. (2014) *Philippine Politics: Possibilities and Problems in a Localist Democracy* (London: Routledge).

White, Roland and Paul Smoke. (2005) 'East Asia Decentralizes', pp. 1–26 in World Bank, *East Asia Decentralizes: Making Local Government Work in East Asia* (Washington, DC: World Bank).

Wiarda, Howard J. (1997) *Corporatism and Comparative Politics: The Other Great 'ism'* (Armonk. NY: M. E. Sharpe).

William S. Turley and Mark Selden (1993) *Reinventing Vietnamese Socialism: Doi Moi in Comparative Perspective* (Boulder, CO: Westview Press).

Winkler, Edwin A. (1984) 'Institutionalization and Participation on Taiwan: From Hard to Soft Authoritarianism?', *China Quarterly*, 99, pp. 481–99.

Winters, Jeffrey. A. (1996) *Power in Motion: Capital Mobility and the Indonesian State* (Ithaca: Cornell. University Press).

Wittfogel, Karl A. (1957) *Oriental Despotism: A Comparative Study of Total Power* (New Haven, CT: Yale University Press).

Wolf, Charles, Jr. (1962) 'Economic Planning in Korea', *Asian Survey*, 2(10), pp. 22–8.

Wolters, O. W. (1982) *History, Culture, and Region in Southeast Asian Perspectives* (Singapore: Institute of Southeast Asian Studies).

Wong, Joseph (2004) 'The Adaptive Developmental State in East Asia', *Journal of East Asian Studies*, 4: 345–62.

Woo, Wing Thye, Jeffrey D. Sachs and Klaus Schwab (2000) *The Asian Financial Crisis: Lessons for a Resilient Asia* (Cambridge, MA: MIT Press).

Woo-Cumings, Meredith (1999) *The Developmental State* (Ithaca, NY: Cornell University Press).

World Bank (1993) *The East Asian Miracle: Economic Growth and Public Policy* (New York: Oxford University Press).

World Bank (2000) *East Asia: Recovery and Beyond* (Washington, DC: World Bank).

World Bank (2005) *East Asia Decentralizes: Making Local Government Work in East Asia* (Washington, DC: World Bank).

World Bank (2015) *World Development Indicators*. http://data.worldbank.org/data-catalog/world-development-indicators.

World Bank (2008a) 'Law and Development Movement' (Washington, DC: World Bank). http://siteresources.worldbank.org/INTLAWJUSTINST/Resources/LawandDevelopmentMovement.pdf. (Accessed May 2008).

World Bank (2015) World Governance Indicators http://info.worldbank.org/governance/wgi/index.aspx#reports (Washington, DC: World Bank).

World Economic Forum (2008) *The Global Competitiveness Report 2007/8*. (Geneva: World Economic Forum).

Wurfel, David (1988) *Filipino Politics: Development and Decay* (Ithaca, NY: Cornell University Press).

X

Xi Jinping (2014) 'New Asian Security Concept For New Progress in Security Cooperation' Remarks at the Fourth Summit of the Conference on Interaction and Confidence Building Measures in Asia, Shanghai Expo Center, 21 May 2014, available at http://id.china-embassy.org/eng/gdxw/t1160962.htm.

Xu, Dixin and Wu Chengming (1998) *Chinese Capitalism, 1522–1840* (New York: St. Martin's Press).

Y

Yagi, Kinnosuke (2004) 'Decentralization in Japan: Policy and Governance', *Working Paper Series No. 30*, Tokyo: Graduate School of Media and Governance, Keio University.

Yang, Dali L. (2004) *Remaking the Chinese Leviathan: Market Transition and the Politics of Governance in China* (Stanford, CA: Stanford University Press).

Yang, David Da-hua (2004) 'Civil Society as an Analytic Lens for Contemporary China', *China: An International Journal*, 2(1), pp. 1–27.

Yang, Sung Chul (1994) *The North and South Korean Political Systems* (Boulder, CO: Westview Press).

Yap, Sonny, Richard Lim and Leong Weng Kam, (2009) *Men in White: The Untold Story of Singapore's Ruling Political Party*, (Singapore: Singapore Press Holdings).

Yeoh, Brenda S. A., Peggy Teo and Shirlena Huang (2002) *Gender Politics in the Asia-Pacific Region* (New York: Routledge).

Yoda, Yoshiie (1996) *The Foundations of Japan's Modernization: A Comparison with China's Path towards Modernization* (Leiden, the Netherlands: E. J. Brill).

Young, Jason (2013) *China's Hukou System: Markets, Migrants and Institutional Change* (Palgrave Macmillan).

Young, Michael (1958) *The Rise of the Meritocracy 1870–2033* (Harmondsworth: Penguin).

Yutada, Tsujinaka (2003) 'From Developmentalism to Maturity: Japan's Civil Society Organizations in Comparative Perspective', pp. 83–115 in Frank J. Schwartz and Susan J. Pharr, *The State of Civil Society in Japan* (Cambridge: Cambridge University Press).

Z

Zakaria, Fareed (1997) 'The Rise of Illiberal Democracy', *Foreign Affairs*, 76(6), pp. 28–45.

Zhao, Dingxin (2009) 'The Mandate of Heaven and Performance Legitimation in Historical and Contemporary China', *American Behavioral Scientist*, 53(3): 416–433.

Zariski, Raphael (1960) 'Party Factions and Comparative Politics: Some Preliminary Observations', *Midwest Journal of Political Science*, 4: 26–51.

Zeng, Jinghan (2016) *The Chinese Communist Party's Capacity to Rule* (Palgrave Macmillan).

Zhang, Yongjin (1991) *China in the International System 1918–20: The Middle Kingdom at the Periphery* (New York: St Martin's Press).

Zhang, Yongjin (1991a) 'China's Entry into International Society: Beyond the Standard of "Civilization"', *Review of International Studies*, 17(1), pp. 3–16.

Zhang, Yongjin (1998) *China in International Society since 1949: Alienation and Beyond* (New York: Palgrave Macmillan).

Zhang, Yongjin (2001) 'System, Empire and State in Chinese International Relations', *Review of International Studies*, 27, pp. 43–63.

Zhao, Suisheng (1996) *Power by Design: Constitution-making in Nationalist China* (Honolulu: University of Hawaii Press).

Zhang, Xiaoming, (2011) 'China in the Conception of International Society: The English School's engagements with China', *Review of International Studies*, 37(2), pp. 763–786.

Zhao, Yuezhi (1998) *Media, Market, and Democracy in China: Between the Party Line and the Bottom Line* (Chicago: University of Illinois Press).

Zheng, Yongnian (2007) *Technological Empowerment: The Internet, State, and Society in China* (Stanford, CT: Stanford University Press).

Zheng, Yongnian (2014) 'The Institutionalization of the Communist Party and the Party System in China'. pp. 162–189 in Allen Hicken and Erik M. Kuhonta, *Party System Institutionalization in Asia: Democracies, Autocracies, and the Shadows of the Past* (Cambridge University Press.).

Zhong, Yang (2016) 'Explaining National Identity Shift in Taiwan', *Journal of Contemporary China*, 26(98), pp. 1–17.

Index